THE CHOMSKYAN TURN

𝕀𝔹

THE CHOMSKYAN TURN

edited by

ASA KASHER

BLACKWELL
Oxford UK & Cambridge USA

First published 1991
First published in paperback 1993

Blackwell Publishers
238 Main Street, Suite 501
Cambridge, Massachusetts 02142, USA

108 Cowley Road, Oxford, OX4 1JF, UK

Library of Congress Cataloging in Publication Data
The Chomskyan turn/edited by Asa Kasher.
   p.   cm.
   Papers presented at the international workshop on "the Chomskyan
Turn: Generative Linguistics, Philosophy, Mathematics, and
Psychology," held Apr. 11–14, 1988 at Tel-Aviv University; organized
under the auspices of the Institute for the History and Philosophy
of Science and Ideas and of the Van Leer Jerusalem Institute.
   Includes bibliographical references.
   ISBN 0–631–17336–6   ISBN 0–631–18734–0 (pbk.)
   1. Linguistics—Congresses. 2. Chomsky, Noam—Congresses.
I. Kasher, Asa.   II. Universitat Tel-Aviv. Institue for the
History and Philosophy of Science and Ideas.   III. Mekhon Van Leer bi-
Yerushalayim.
P23.C46   1991
410–dc20
                                             90–34846
                                                 CIP

British Library Cataloguing in Publication Data
A CIP catalogue record for this book is available from the British Library.

Typeset in 10 on 11pt Times
by Wearside Tradespools, Fulwell, Sunderland
Printed in Great Britain by
T.J. Press Ltd., Padstow, Cornwall.

Contents

List of Contributors

Sylvain Bromberger: Linguistics and Philosophy, Massachusetts Institute of Technology, Cambridge, Mass.

Noam Chomsky: Linguistics and Philosophy, Massachusetts Institute of Technology, Cambridge, Mass.

Victoria A. Fromkin: Linguistics, University of California, Los Angeles.

Morris Halle: Linguistics and Philosophy, Massachusetts Institute of Technology, Cambridge, Mass.

Norbert Hornstein: Linguistics, University of Maryland, College Park, MD.

Asa Kasher: Philosophy, Tel-Aviv University, Israel.

Shalom Lappin: IBM, Yorktown Heights, NY.

Justin Leiber: Philosophy, University of Houston, Houston, Tex.

Robert J. Matthews: Philosophy, Rutgers, New Brunswick, NJ.

Robert May: Cognitive Sciences, University of California, Irvine, Cal.

Frederick Newmeyer: Linguistics, University of Washington, Seattle, WA.

Zenon W. Pylyshyn: Cognitive Science, University of Western Ontario London, Ont., Canada.

Tanya Reinhart: Linguistics and Poetics, Tel-Aviv University, Israel

Luigi Rizzi: Linguistics, University of Geneva, Switzerland.

Susan D. Rothstein: Linguistics, Bar-Ilan University, Ramat-Gan, Israel.

Ken Wexler: Brain and Cognitive Sciences, Massachusetts Institute of Technology, Cambridge, Mass.

Preface

Linguistics, says Chomsky in a 1977 interview[1], "has yet to undergo something like a Copernican or Galilean revolution in very crucial respects . . . This shift of intellectual attitude from concern for coverage of data to concern for insight and depth of explanation, and the related willingness to deal with highly idealized systems in order to obtain depth of explanation – this shift of point of view has taken place very rarely, I think, in the history of thought. In linguistics I don't think it has taken place, really."

In other words:–

> "How would you assess your own contributions to linguistics?"
> Chomsky: "They seem sort of pre-Galilean."
> "Like physics before the scientific revolution in the seventeenth century?"
> Chomsky: "Yes. In the pre-Galilean period, people were beginning to formulate problems in physics in the right way. The answers weren't there, but the problems were finally being framed in a way that in retrospect we can see was right. . . . [M]y feeling is that someday someone is going to come along and say, 'Look, you guys, you're on the right track, but you went wrong here. It should have been done this way.' Well, that will be it. Suddenly things will fall into place."[2]

If it has not taken a revolution to put us on the right track, if it has not been a major intellectual shift which has put us on it, then it sure has been a sharp turn that central parts of the study of language have taken. This has been what we call the "Chomskyan Turn."

An international workshop on "The Chomskyan Turn: Generative Linguistics, Philosophy, Mathematics and Psychology" took place at Tel-Aviv University and the Van Leer Jerusalem Institute, from April 11 to 14, 1988. All the papers in this collection were presented at this conference, though some of them have been meanwhile thoroughly revised.

Noam Chomsky read both the opening and the closing papers of the conference. Since these two papers can be naturally viewed as forming parts of a unified presentation, they are published here together, as the first two chapters of this collection, its Part One.

Part Two of this book consists of papers, written by linguists, philosophers and cognitive scientists, whose contributions are directly related to major aspects of Chomsky's contributions to linguistics or to the adjacent fields of philosophy and psychology. Some of these papers discuss certain branches of language study: Phonology is the topic of *Bromberger and Halle*'s contribution, *Hornstein*'s paper is related to aspects of Semantics and *Kasher*'s to Pragmatics. Several papers address the "Chomskyan Turn" from certain psychological perspectives: *Matthews* discusses the "psychological reality" of grammars and *Pylyshyn* representational realism; *Wexler* focuses on language maturation. *Fromkin*'s and *Newmeyer*'s contributions are devoted to major developments in the history of Generative Linguistics, while *Leiber* considers facets of Cartesian Linguistics.

Part Three includes papers on syntax. *Rizzi*'s paper is on referential indices, in current theories as well as in earlier stages of Generative Syntax. The other four papers in this part of the book form a symposium on Logical Form. *May*'s paper discusses Syntax, Semantics and LF. *Lappin* and *Reinhart* present alternatives to May's views on LF. *Rothstein*'s comments on these different views.

The international workshop on the Chomskyan Turn was organized under the auspices of the Institute for the History and Philosophy of Science and Ideas and of the Van Leer Jerusalem Institute. We are very grateful to Yehuda Elkana, director of both, for his support, as well as to the administrative staff of these institutes, especially Yael Avner and Gabriela Williams, for their invaluable assistance.

Our meeting took place during the Intifada, the Palestinian uprising in the West Bank and the Gaza Strip. Much of everyone's attention was drawn to it in various ways. I assume I reflect an attitude shared by all the contributors to this volume, by dedicating it to the memory of all the innocent victims, in particular, the children, Arabs and Jews, Israelis and Palestinians alike, who were killed during the uprising. We share a hope: that no human being ever dies as a result of acts of injustice or war, oppression or terrorism. We have a dream: to see eradicted all such forms of human folly and wickedness. We have a goal: to see justice, peace and freedom soon reign through our part of the world.

Asa Kasher

NOTES

1 Conducted by Sol Saporta at the University of Washington; published in *Linguistic Analysis*, 4: 4 (1978), pp. 301–19, and republished, under the title "Language Theory and the Theory of Justice," in Noam Chomsky, *Language and Politics*, edited by C. P. Otero (Black Rose Books, Montreal and New York, 1988), pp. 232–50.

2 Conducted by John Gliedman; published in *Omni*, 6: 11 (1983), and republished, under the title "Things No Amount of Learning Can Teach," in Chomsky, *Language and Politics*, pp. 407–19.

Part I

Part I

1
Linguistics and Adjacent Fields: A Personal View

Noam Chomsky

I feel that I should begin, perhaps a bit ungraciously, by registering certain qualms about the general structure suggested for the conference, which I expressed to Asa Kasher when it was announced. Though the point is obvious enough, it may nevertheless be worth saying that to the extent that a subject is significant and worth pursuing, it is not personalized; and I think that the questions we are addressing are significant and worth pursuing. The topic "X's biology" – or economics, or psychology, or whatever – select X as one likes, could only have a useful sense in a primitive stage of some inquiry, a stage that one would hope would be quickly surpassed as the subject becomes a cooperative enterprise, with "X's linguistics," in our case, changing every time a journal appears, or a graduate student enters the office with some ideas to be thrashed out, or a classroom discussion leads to new understanding and fresh problems. All of this has been the norm for many years, fortunately, so that such phrases as "X's linguistics" are very much out of place, unless X is perhaps Panini or Wilhelm von Humboldt or Ferdinand de Saussure, with the understanding that even this is a substantial abstraction from a much more complex reality.

Similar comments apply to the proliferation of "theories" associated with one or another individual or group, again the sign of an immature discipline or a mistaken perception of the field as it actually evolves. To take a case that is close to home for me, such terms as "government-binding theory" should be abandoned, in fact should never have been used in the first place. Insofar as the concept of government enters into the structure of human language, every approach will have a theory of government, and the common task will be to determine just what this concept is and what exactly are the principles that it observes. Similarly, no approach to language will fail to incorporate some version of binding theory, insofar as referential dependence is a real phenomenon to be captured in the study of language, this being a common enterprise. There are real questions about government and binding, but no tentative set of hypotheses about language has any proprietary claim to these topics. The same is true far more broadly, with no need here to provide examples. If some approach to the study of language really does have doctrines or privileged notations that are not subject to challenge on pain of "abandoning the theory," some kind of perceived disaster, then we can be fairly confident that this approach is a byway to be avoided in the search for serious answers to serious questions.

Since I have been accorded the privilege of both opening and closing the conference, I will address the questions with which many of us are concerned in a fairly general way. I will try to outline how the study of language looks today, at least to me; how it reached its present stage, concentrating on the less familiar earlier period of contemporary generative grammar when leading issues began to be formulated in a way that sets a framework for much that has happened since; what kinds of problems are, realistically speaking, on the current research agenda; and what more distant ones remain out of reach although they may animate and in some ways guide current inquiry. I also want to consider how all of this relates to broader questions about mind and knowledge and behavior that have deep roots in our cultural and intellectual history. There is hardly a phrase in what I will say that is not controversial, and naturally I will not attempt here to resolve doubts that justly arise at every point; rather to sketch a path through a maze of obscurity that seems to me a plausible one, and one that has certainly been productive even if it will ultimately be shown to be misdirected.

Beginning with the broadest context, the study of generative grammar developed within what some have called "the cognitive revolution" of the 1950s, and was a significant factor in initiating this change of perspective with regard to human nature and action. To a certain extent it has remained so, though interests and assumptions, which were rather disparate from the start, have often diverged.

Notice to begin with that the terminology is inflated. Though it was not known at the time, and remains little understood today, the so-called "cognitive revolution" was in large measure a return to earlier concerns and reconstructed earlier understanding, long forgotten, sometimes in new ways. I include here such matters as representational-computational theories of mind, the Turing test for human intelligence, the question of innate conditions for the growth of knowledge and understanding, certain basic insights of Gestalt psychology, and much else. These ideas were developed and explored in a fairly lucid and thoughtful way in what we might call "the first cognitive revolution" of the seventeenth and eighteenth century.

If intellectual history were linear, continuous and cumulative, in place of the actual record of erratic leaps, false starts, and all-too-frequent regression, we could say, in retrospect, that the cognitive revolution of the 1950s, including the development of generative grammar, represents a kind of confluence of ideas and insights of the first cognitive revolution with new technical understanding about the nature of computation and formal systems that developed largely in this century, and that made it possible to formulate some old and somewhat vague questions in a much clearer way, so that they could be subjected to productive inquiry in a few domains at least, language being one.

The cognitive revolution is concerned with states of the mind/brain and how they enter into behavior, in particular, cognitive states: states of knowledge, understanding, interpretation, belief, and so on. An approach to human thought and action in these terms takes psychology, and its subfield of linguistics, to be part of the natural sciences, concerned with human nature and its manifestations and particularly with the brain. Accordingly, it is avowedly mentalistic in a specific sense of this term, this being the other side of the same coin.

The brain, like any other system of the natural world, can be studied at various levels of abstraction from mechanisms: for example, in terms of neural nets or computational systems of rules and representations. At each such level of inquiry, we construct certain abstract objects and seek to determine their properties and the principles they satisfy. We try to show how, in these terms, we can provide explanations for puzzling phenomena. We also hope to discover how these abstract entities are realized in physical mechanisms of a more "fundamental" nature and how the principles can be grounded in this way. Neural nets, for example, are highly abstract objects; they remain unchanged if molecules are replaced or some chemical transmission or reorientation of components takes place. The same is true of computational systems of rules and representations. We may refer to the study of these systems as part of the study of mind, but merely as a matter of terminology that respects certain historical antecedents without raising any novel metaphysical quandaries; we may refer to the mind, or the mind/brain, in the context of this abstract inquiry into physical properties of the brain. We take the abstract objects we construct to be real insofar as they enter into explanatory theories that provide insight and understanding.

All of this would be proper and appropriate procedure even if it had no models elsewhere. But in fact, it follows a familiar course. Though analogies should not be pressed too far, much the same has been true in the better-established natural sciences. For example, nineteenth-century chemistry and early twentieth-century genetics were concerned with such theoretical abstract notions as chemical elements, organic molecules, valence, the Periodic Table, genes and alleles, and so on. Discoveries about their nature led to attempts to discover more fundamental mechanisms to account for their properties and the principles that govern them. This proved to be no simple task. In the case of nineteenth-century chemistry, the concepts of fundamental physics were quite radically modified to achieve this goal, with the development of quantum theory, which explained "most of physics and all of chemistry" (Dirac) so that "physics and chemistry have been fused into complete oneness..."

(Heisenberg).[1] The discoveries of early genetics, in contrast, were essentially accommodated by mid-century within known biochemistry. In the case of the study of mind, we cannot now know which of these possibilities reflects the physical reality. It would come as no great surprise if the physical sciences, as currently understood, were to prove incapable of incorporating and accounting for the properties and principles of mind, just as Cartesian mechanics could not account for the motion of bodies, as Newton showed, and just as nineteenth-century physics could not account for properties of chemical elements and compounds.

Putting such speculations aside, we turn to the questions that we can realistically formulate and address within the theory of mind, now understood as an integral part of the natural sciences; in particular, in the study of language. The basic concept, which identifies the subject of inquiry, is the concept of "having" or "knowing" a language. We take this to be a cognitive state, a certain state of the mind/brain. Concerning this concept, three fundamental questions at once arise:

1   What constitutes knowledge of language?
2   How is such knowledge acquired?
3   How is such knowledge put to use?

There is also a further question: how can we integrate answers to these questions within the existing natural sciences, perhaps by modifying them? This question remains beyond reach, or rather, is premature. Just as nineteenth-century science provided essential guidelines for the physics of the subsequent period, so the study of mind should serve as a guide for the brain sciences of the future, exhibiting the properties and conditions that must be satisfied by the mechanisms of the brain, whatever they turn out to be.

At least in a rudimentary form, these questions were beginning to be the topic of lively discussion in the early 1950s, primarily among a few graduate students. In Cambridge, I would mention particularly Eric Lenneberg and Morris Halle, and also Yehoshua Bar-Hillel, whose role as a perceptive and sympathetic critic and constructive participant has been much undervalued. While we approached the issues from different starting points and backgrounds, there was a shared skepticism about the prevailing climate of opinion and increasingly, a shared perspective and a growing sense that the lines of thought we were pursuing, which related in complex ways to other developments of the period, were on the right track. I will not try to sort out these interactions here. Within a few years, a relatively coherent point of view had developed, which still seems to me essentially correct.

Each of the three basic questions that frame this inquiry has a classical flavor and earlier antecedents, as did the "cognitive revolution" generally. None of this was evident or more than vaguely sensed at the time, a fact that is not without interest. It reflects significant features of the social and cultural history of the period and the reigning political climate, important topics that I will not pursue here.

We might plausibly refer to the first and central question – what constitutes knowledge of language? – as *Humboldt's problem*, referring, in the first place, to his insight that language is a system that provides for infinite use of finite means. We may take these finite means to constitute a particular language; to know the language is to have these finite means represented in the mind/brain. Crucially, Humboldt regarded language not as a set of constructed objects, say, utterances or speech acts, but rather as a process of generation; language is *eine Erzeugung*, not *ein todtes Erzeugtes*. With a bit of interpretive license, we could understand him to be saying that a language is a generative procedure that enables articulated, structured expressions of thought to be freely produced and understood.

Notice that there is interpretive license in this account. In Humboldt's day, one could not clearly distinguish between, on the one hand, an abstract generative procedure that assigns structural descriptions to all expressions, and on the other, the actual *Arbeit des Geistes* that brings thought to expression in linguistic performance. There are passages in Humboldt's writings that suggest one or the other interpretation, some-times with fair explicitness, but to attempt to determine which notion he had in mind is an error, since the two concepts were not clearly disting-uished, and could hardly have been, the relevant concepts being lacking.[2] The conception of generative grammar that developed in the 1950s crucially, and properly, distinguishes these conceptions, distinguishing diachronic from synchronic in the manner clarified in modern linguistics, distinguishing performance from competence (in the sense of possession of knowledge), and construing knowledge of language as incorporation in the mind/brain of a generative procedure taken in the abstract sense.

From this point of view, the language faculty is regarded as a particular component of the human mind/brain. It has an initial state, an element of the human biological endowment that appears to be subject to little variation apart from severe pathology, and is also apparently unique to the species in essentials. Under normal conditions of social interaction, the language faculty comes to assume a steady state at a fixed maturational stage, a state that does not subsequently undergo fundamental change. This steady state – and, indeed, earlier transitional states – is characterized in terms of a generative procedure taken abstractly; this constitutes the acquired language understood as a psychological particular, now abstract-ing from the complexity of the actual social world in accord with familiar idealizations that are appropriate and indeed quite indispensable. Insofar as some group of individuals are not too different in the individual languages acquired, we may speak loosely of language as a community property, recognizing that there is little to say about the matter of any generality or significance, so it appears. I will return briefly to alternative conceptions.

In Humboldt's day, means were lacking to express these ideas clearly, and the insights were dismissed and largely forgotten. But by the mid-twentieth century such technical understanding was readily available, and the questions could be formulated, squarely faced, and very productively studied.

At an intuitive level, a language is a particular way of expressing thought and understanding the thought expressed (see note 4). To know a language is to have mastered this way of speaking and understanding. Rephrasing this intuition within a theory of mind understood in the terms of the "second cognitive revolution," a language is a particular generative procedure that assigns to every possible expression a representation of its form and its meaning, insofar as these are determined by the language faculty. The language, so construed, "strongly generates" a set of structural descriptions; we may take this set to be the structure of the language. This is essentially the point of view developed in my unpublished manuscript *Logical Structure of Linguistic Theory* of 1955 (*LSLT*),[3] differing only in terminology.

Since the terminology that was adopted has led to some confusion, which impeded subsequent research and led to much pointless controversy and still does, let me say a word about it. The standard practice of the time was to use the term "language" to refer to what Humboldt called "ein todtes Erzeugtes," "the totality of utterances that can be made in a speech community" in Leonard Bloomfield's phrase, or the set of well-formed expressions, in the usage of the study of formal systems such as formalized arithmetic. The influential American linguist William Dwight Whitney, contemptuously dismissing what remained of the rationalist and Humboldtian traditions at the origins of modern linguistics, defined language "in the concrete sense" as "the sum of words and phrases by which any man expresses his thought," with little of any generality to be said about this "vast number of items, each of which has its own time, occasion, and effect." "The infinite diversity of human speech," he said, "ought alone to be a sufficient bar to the assertion that an understanding of the powers of the soul involves the explanation of speech," a view repeated by Edward Sapir, who insisted that "speech is a human activity that varies without assignable limit," "a purely historical heritage of the group, the product of long-continued social usage" with no "instinctive base."[4] Such conceptions were reiterated for a long period, removing essential topics from the study of language in the mainstream professional discipline, because they could not possibly be studied in these terms. These practices were no doubt encouraged by the empiricist and behaviorist assumptions that prevailed in later years, which engendered the misconception that the set of expressions that constitute language "in the concrete sense" is somehow "given" or "closer to the data" than the "grammars" that characterize it. Again, a serious misconception, one that remains common in the literature.[5] The array of expressions made available for use by the means provided by a language is plainly not "given." Rather, what is given is some finite collection of data, which can be interpreted as evidence for a theory that might – or might not – assign some privileged status to a particular set of expressions. In the case of natural language, I think it probably does not, but whatever the facts may be in this regard, the "totality of expressions" or set of well-formed sentences is a high-level abstraction, further removed from mechanisms than the generative procedure that is held to specify it within a theory based on the available data.

The practice of using the term "language" to refer to an infinite set of expressions was taken over in early generative grammar. A different term was therefore required for the generative procedure internally represented in the mind/brain. The terminological decision, unfortunate in retrospect, was to use the term "grammar" with systematic ambiguity to refer both to the generative procedure and the linguist's theory of this cognitive system. Similarly, the term "linguistic theory" (later, "universal grammar" (UG)) was used to refer both to the initial state of the language faculty and to the linguist's theory of this innate component of the mind/brain. Although the systematic ambiguity of the terminology was repeatedly emphasized, it did lead to confusion and misunderstanding. To clarify the issues, I have suggested elsewhere that we refer to the generative procedure, the abstract version of Humboldt's "process of generation," as an *I-language*, where "I" is to suggest "internalized" (in the mind/brain) and "intensional" (a specific characterization, in intension, of a certain function that enumerates (generates) structural descriptions). The term "grammar," then, is restricted to the linguist's theory of the I-language, in the spirit of more traditional usage. Similarly, we may restrict the terms "linguistic theory" or "UG" to the linguist's theory of the initial state of the language faculty, the latter a component of the mind/brain, part of the fixed biological endowment. I-language in this sense is distinguished from what we may call "E-language," where "E" is to suggest "externalized" and "extensional"; the E-language is a set of expressions given a privileged status in some manner that has always been obscure.

Notice that the concept of I-language is rather similar to the concept of language of ordinary discourse, abstracting from the sociopolitical and other elements that enter into this usage, while the concept of E-language is very remote from ordinary usage. To say that a person knows a language is not to say that the person knows a particular set of expressions, or a set of sentence-meaning pairs taken in extension; rather, it is to say that the person knows what associates sound and meaning in a particular way, what makes them "hang together." But similarity to ordinary usage is a secondary matter. The more important point is that the notion of I-language is far less obscure than E-language, less abstract and remote from mechanisms, and not really controversial. There can be little doubt that knowing a language involves internal representation of a generative procedure that specifies the structure of the language in something like the sense just indicated. One may choose to ignore the basic questions raised earlier, but if they are to be faced, then we are quickly led to this conclusion. And the questions are surely proper ones, belonging in principle to the natural sciences, and central to the human sciences.

The notion E-language, in contrast, appears to play no role in the theory of language; it is doubtful that there is such an entity. Furthermore, though the notion is commonly used, I am not familiar with any attempt to characterize it within a theory of language that addresses itself to the questions proposed earlier. A particular version of this notion does figure in *LSLT*, but only derivatively, and in later work of mine, it appears only marginally or not at all. In *LSLT* a definition for what might be called "E-language" is suggested in the context of the theory of assignment of derived constituent structure by transformations; it was a derivative notion defined in terms of a specific theory of degrees of grammaticalness. In *LSLT*, it was assumed that every possible expression is given a structural description and placed somewhere in a hierarchy of grammaticalness, but it was soon apparent that the "dimensions of deviance" are far more varied than was there assumed and the theory of derived constituent structure was no longer pursued in these terms. The notion therefore lost whatever limited significance it had in *LSLT*.

As far as I can see, the concept of E-language has no clear status in the study of language, and is best abandoned. The concept of E-language, and the associated concepts of weak generation, extensional equivalence (in Quine's sense) and the like, derive in part from analogies to formal languages such as arithmetic, which are completely irrelevant and highly misleading; in part they derive from equally misleading analogies to constructs developed in automata theory and mathematical linguistics; in part from work in structural and earlier linguistics that did at times construe language in such terms; and perhaps from prevailing empiricist-behaviorist currents as just mentioned. Also contributing to these mis-understandings were expository passages in generative grammar that should, in retrospect, have adopted a different and less misleading terminology. Apart from such expository passages and the derivative and soon abandoned sense just noted, I have never used this concept in work within linguistics proper and see no way to do so. Even if it can be given a coherent formulation, I know of no reason to suppose that the properties of E-language, however construed, are of any empirical significance; in particular, no reason to believe that they have anything to do with problems of parsability or learnability. I also think one must reject the common assumption, deriving in large part from W. V. Quine, that the notion of "well-formedness" or "having meaning" is relatively unprob-lematic, in contrast to the notion of "sameness of meaning" or "semantic connection," which is held to be far more obscure; exactly the opposite is the case. There is a substantial literature in several fields taking a different position on these matters, and assumptions about the significance of E-language have had a notable impact on developments in the study of language in recent years. But I think that all of this is based on misunderstanding, and that it would be proper to return to the original conception of generative grammar in which I-language is a central notion, but E-language, if it exists at all, is derivative, remote from mechanisms, and of no particular empirical significance, perhaps none at all.

The shift of focus from the dubious concept of E-language to the significant notion of I-language was a crucial step in early generative grammar, and in the second cognitive revolution generally. The structural linguistics of the period, in both its European and American variants, took linguistics to be in effect a taxonomic procedure for analyzing utterances, language "in the concrete sense" in Whitney's phrase. The classic work of American structuralism, Zellig Harris's *Methods of Structural Linguistics*, was quite explicit in this regard. It outlined a series of procedures to be applied to a corpus of utterances to determine the segments of which these utterances are constituted, the categories to which these segments belong, the significant sequences of these categories, the classes of these sequences, and so on. Other analytic procedures selected different properties of these utterances and led to statements about their distributions in the corpus (e.g., long components). It was widely assumed in the early 1950s that these methods were essentially complete, apart from possible refinements. They were also commonly regarded as essentially arbitrary, carrying no truth-claim; Quine's repeated insistence that "there is no truth to the matter" in the description of these aspects of language would not have seemed surprising, in this framework. Thus one could develop taxonomic methods in various ways, depending on purpose and interest.

Harris's theory of transformations, at least in the version developed from the late 1940s through the following decade, presupposed that the linguistic analysis of the language of which a corpus of utterances was taken to be an adequate sample was essentially complete. Transformations were proposed as a device for extending to the analysis of discourse the "distributional methods" employed to provide a complete structural description of the expressions of the language. The segmentation-substitution methods of structural linguistics were inapplicable to actual texts because their sentences were too disparate and diverse. The basic idea, therefore, was to "normalize" the texts, reducing them to a form to which these taxonomic procedures could apply. A grammatical transformation, in these terms, is a relation among sentence forms, where these forms are determined by the prior application of the methods of structural linguistics to the language. These relations were to meet the condition that they preserved acceptability. Thus the passive transformation related the sentence forms N_1-V-N_2 and N_2-is-V-ed-by-N_1 in the sense that for any choice of phrases N_1, N_2 and V, the substitution instances of the two related forms have the same degree of acceptability. But crucially. analysis of the language, by the taxonomic procedures of structural linguistics, was taken to be complete, in principle; transformational analysis was an ancillary procedure, extending the methods of linguistics to a broader domain.

European structuralism of the Jakobson-Trubetzkoy variety was different in many respects, but shared the essential conception of taxonomic analysis. An utterance was taken to consist of an actual sequence of feature sets (phonemes), the features having a physical and perceptual realization. Larger units are composed of sequences of these elements arrayed in various patterns. As Jakobson often stressed, the two basic concepts of language are simultaneity and sequence, and the associated analytic operations are substitution in a fixed frame with the determination of a pattern of oppositions, and construction of significant sequences of the units so derived. In both varieties of structuralism, the units of language are segments of utterances, classes and features of such segments, sequences of these elements, and so on. The elements of language were taken to be constructed out of physical elements. Language was understood very much in terms of Whitney's "concrete sense."

Generative grammar adopted a very different standpoint. From this point of view, expressions and their properties are just data, standing alongside of other data, to be interpreted as evidence for determining the I-language, the real object of inquiry. The structural descriptions generated by the I-language are abstract representations of expressions, made available by the resources of the mind for thought and its expression. The elements of a phonological representation, for example, are not sets of physical segments or features, or sequences of such sets, etc., but are related to phonetic representation of physical segments and features by a rule system that may not preserve linear order or invariance of feature composition; and the relation of representations to utterances will typically be still more abstract at other levels of the structural description. The relation of these representations to utterances and situations depends on the interplay of rules of the I-language and involves the mediation of other faculties of the mind/brain: the motor and perceptual systems, conceptual systems, and possibly others. There is a definite truth claim in any account of I-language and the system of representations it strongly generates. While this is held to be controversial in the familiar Quinean paradigm, the arguments seem to me completely unconvincing for reasons I have discussed elsewhere, except as an expression of a form of skepticism that holds of empirical inquiry generally, was understood to be uninteresting by the seventeenth century, and hardly merits the enormous attention it has received in the philosophical literature of the past several decades.

The structuralist framework represented a considerable advance over traditional grammar in its insights into particular areas of language, but with a severe impoverishment of scope. In itself, this is no criticism. Such a combination is common as research progresses. Thus Galileo's theory of motion was impoverished as compared with the Aristotelian theory, which included growth of organisms and perception alongside of the motion of bodies to which Galileo restricted attention. But the narrowing of scope in structural linguistics proved to be a distortion rather than a sharpening of understanding, eliminating crucial factors essential for understanding the very phenomena with which it was concerned. A representational-computational theory of mind was able to face a far wider range of questions and also to overcome a variety of problems that appeared irresoluble in structuralist terms. To recall some simple examples, we plainly want to say that question-answer pairs are related by a transformation, if the notion has any significance at all. But there is no relation of sentence forms that includes the pairs ("John is here," "is John here") and ("John likes books," "does John like books"). At the phonological level, virtually everyone agreed that in such pairs as "writer"-"rider" the phonemic contrast must lie in the medial consonant, not the vowels two segments away; but the actual phonetic difference, in certain dialects, happens to lie in the vowels. Such problems as these, which abound, quickly dissolve in the framework of generative grammar and a representational-computational theory of language and mind.

The move towards an abstract theory of this sort is a step towards incorporating the study of language within the natural sciences, since the I-language is a component of the mind/brain, realized somehow in physical mechanisms. Evidence of any sort, in principle, is relevant to determining its nature. These moves were also extremely productive, though not without serious problems to which I will return directly.

While the approach of generative grammar, in part a return to an earlier tradition, differs in many respects from the various forms of structural linguistics, there are some crucial similarities as well. Any approach to language must involve some method for assigning structural descriptions to linguistic expressions. It must involve something akin to strong generation of structural descriptions for arbitrary expressions, since this is at the core of one's knowledge of language.

The generative grammar approach takes one component of UG to be universal phonetics, which provides a class of possible expressions that are available for human languages; or more precisely, it provides a class of phonetic representations, related to utterances through the medium of the motor and perceptual systems in ways that are language-independent. A particular I-language strongly generates structural descriptions for each of these expressions. Given some variety of what we informally call "English," the I-language will assign a structural description to the sentences I am now producing, to such deviant sentences as "the child seems sleeping" or "the knife cut the meat with a sword," to *wh*-island violations, ECP violations, sentences of Japanese and Swahili, and so on; each of these is assigned a particular structural description, and these enter into the way a speaker-hearer of this I-language will understand, interpret and use such expressions. A speaker of Hungarian will interpret all of these expressions differently. For example, in the case of the sentence "the knife cut the meat," some property of the I-language "English" determines that the phrase "the knife" is interpreted as referring to an animate agent if an instrumental phrase ("with a sword") is added, but not necessarily otherwise. As to whether the sentence with the instrumental phrase belongs to the E-language, that seems to be a matter of stipulation, not fact, the concept of E-language having no clear sense or known significance.

The several varieties of structural linguistics also incorporate some procedure for assigning structural descriptions to expressions, in effect, some method of strong generation. These procedures may be Harris's methods of segmentation and classification, or Trubetzkoy's analytic techniques of phonemic analysis, or something else; but they cannot be lacking.

Generative grammar, in short, does not differ from the several varieties of structural linguistics with regard to the concept of strong generation; rather, with regard to how it is formulated. The question is whether it is to be construed in terms of analytic procedures that yield units constructed from the elements of the physical expressions that constitute a concrete fragment of some presumed E-language, or whether it is to be construed in terms of a representational-computational theory of the mind/brain. These are real questions, which can be formulated as meaningful empirical questions, and the underlying issues are serious and significant. There is, again, current commentary that takes a different position on these matters, regarding strong generation of structural descriptions as itself a controversial position that stands in contrast to alternatives, such as an algebra of transformations in something like Harris's sense, or some other conception. But without tarrying on the matter here, I think it is clear that the main point is being missed. A Harrisian algebra of transformations, or any other approach, is and must be based on some method of determining sentence forms that is, in effect, a technique for strong generation of the structure of a language.

Notice that the shift from the taxonomic study of expressions and their properties to the study of I-language was, in a sense, a return to the Cartesian representational theory of perception, developed in the first cognitive revolution. In terms of these classical ideas, the sense organs receive a series of stimulations and the resources of the mind produce the representation of some external object. Thus the eye scans a surface, or a blind man taps it with a stick, these being essentially parallel operations for Descartes. The mind then uses this sequence of impressions to construct the representation of a cube or a triangle or a person, employing its own resources. In the language case, the mind produces the representation of a presented expression, making use of the I-language and of course much else.

Observe that we are now making a sharp distinction between perception and acquisition, here departing from the classical Cartesian conception, or at least, from the ways it was typically formulated. We want to distinguish between the transition from the initial state of the language faculty (and other systems of the mind/brain) to various subsequent states, including, at a certain maturational stage, a steady state that undergoes only limited and marginal change. Particular stages, achieved through some combination of maturational processes and environmental influences, provide their own resources for interpretation and action. If the resources available remained constant through successive stages and there were no steady state, then there would be some merit in the Cartesian failure to distinguish perception from acquisition; but this seems not to be the case, in general.[6]

Returning now to the first and fundamental question that arises within the second cognitive revolution, in terms of the notion of I-language we can formulate Humboldt's problem in what seems a proper way, and the task is now clear: to discover the various generative procedures (I-languages) that are made available by the human language faculty, and the elements and the character of the structural descriptions that they strongly generate; that is, to discover the nature of human languages and the structures of the human languages.

Holding off consideration of how this fundamental question has been addressed, let us turn to the second and third questions.

Again citing classical antecedents, we can refer to question (2) – how is knowledge of language acquired? – as a special case of *Plato's Problem*, the problem of how we know so much with so little evidence, and how it can be that these rich systems of knowledge are shared. Plato's answer was that the knowledge is "remembered" from an earlier existence. The answer calls for a mechanism; perhaps the immortal soul. That may strike us as not very satisfactory, but it is worth bearing in mind that it is a more reasonable answer than those assumed as doctrine during the Dark Ages of Anglo-American empiricism and behavioral science – to put the matter tendentiously, but accurately.

If we are disinclined to accept the immortal soul as a mechanism, we may follow Leibniz, who regarded Plato's answer as essentially correct, though it must be "purged of the error of pre-existence." Pursuing this course, and rephrasing Plato's answer in terms more congenial to us today, we will say that the basic properties of cognitive systems are innate in the mind, part of human biological endowment, on a par with whatever determines the specific internally-directed course of embryological development, or of sexual maturation in later years. In these terms we can hope to capture the Cartesian conception of innate ideas as tendencies and dispositions, and to respond to the Malebranchean objection that dispositions require a structural base, a matter recently discussed by Nicholas Jolley[7] – though of course now departing from the Cartesian two-substance metaphysics that was undermined by Newton's discovery of the inadequacy of Cartesian mechanics.

Probably nothing in early generative grammar has been so controversial, in appearance at least, as these conclusions about innate structure. I say "in appearance" because I do not believe that any substantive issue has been joined in the extensive debate over these matters, which still continues in current literature in all the fields concerned with these topics. The debate has a curious character, in that only one side of the argument participates. Thus Hilary Putnam, again in forthcoming work, rejects what he calls "the innateness hypothesis," but those who allegedly espouse this doctrine – I am supposed to be the arch-criminal in this regard – never respond by defending "the innateness hypothesis." The reason is, very simply, that there is no such general hypothesis, therefore nothing to defend. There are specific hypotheses about what is innate, and these may be considered on empirical grounds: hypotheses of universal grammar, of the theory of vision, and so on.

Exactly the same is and must be true of any other approach to the problems of thought and action; as agreed on all sides, without innate structure, the organism is unaffected by the environment. Thus for Hume, innate endowment is constituted of certain stipulated methods for associating faded impressions, and an "animal instinct" of induction; these ideas are at once refuted by considerations adduced earlier by Descartes on perception of geometrical figures and the like. Similarly, every branch of associationist or behavioral psychology produces its own conception of what is innate in the mind/brain. For Popper, what would be innate, I presume, is some method for interpreting data as experience and for forming conjectures and seeking refutations, but these ideas are not clear enough to be put to an empirical test, and insofar as we can give one or another specific formulation, they simply appear to be on the wrong track. For Quine, what is innate is a quality space, a distance measure, and some inductive technique for forming "genuine hypotheses." Again, insofar as these ideas are clear, they are at once refuted in the domains for which they are offered, on empirical grounds.

Proposals of this nature are primarily interesting, in my view, for what they reveal about a deep-seated and pervasive irrationality that seems to be difficult to overcome in the study of organisms, particularly humans. Notice that no-one would presume to stipulate principles about what "must be true" of inorganic matter, or about the innate conditions of physical growth and maturation. But when we turn to human beings above the neck, such reserve disappears; certain doctrines are stipulated, and those who see no reason to accept them, or who present arguments to refute them, are regarded as being committed to some form of "innateness hypothesis" that allegedly raises all sorts of philosophical issues that do not arise in other domains, say, animal cognition or the study of growth of physical organs apart from the brain. Descartes, in contrast, approached these matters as a scientist, reaching conclusions about what is innate in the mind/brain on the basis of observation and experiment, sometimes thought experiment as in his proposals, surely accurate in essence, as to how a child in infancy would perceive a certain figure as a distorted triangle, not as an exact instance of whatever curious figure it is.

I think we see here a residue of traditional mind-body dualism, but now in a pernicious and entirely unacceptable form. Cartesian dualism was quite rational; certain properties were discovered that appeared to be beyond the limitations of mechanism, as "body" was conceived, and therefore it was necessary to invoke some new principle, apart from body, much as Newton was led to invoke the concept of action at a distance, given the limits of the Cartesian (and common sense) concept of body in terms of a form of contact mechanics. The Cartesian move to two-substance metaphysics is no longer tenable, with the disappearance of the notion of body, and we proceed in a different way, taking "body" to be whatever is more or less understood and to some degree integrated with the core natural sciences, with connections to be clarified as we proceed. What has replaced Cartesian metaphysical dualism, however, is a kind of "epistemological dualism," which dictates, in essence, that we must not approach the study of the mind/brain in the manner that is regarded as legitimate elsewhere in empirical inquiry, specifically, in the natural sciences. Therefore we proceed on the basis of the arbitrary stipulations of the empiricist tradition and the behavioral sciences, regarding whatever falls beyond their bounds as somehow problematic or unacceptable for reasons that do not apply within the study of inorganic matter or organisms apart from the human mind/brain. All of this should, in my view, be committed to Hume's flames, whatever the psychological or cultural origins may be.

In this connection, we may try to make a distinction between a range of phenomena that we study under the concept of growth and maturation, and others that allegedly fall within the domain of learning. Neither concept is very clear, but some of the general outlines and guiding intuitions can be expressed, at least loosely. In the former category, we have such phenomena as the development of arms and legs, binocular vision and depth perception, walking, sexual maturation, imprinting in non-human organisms, and so on. These processes take place in a manner that we assume to be inner-directed, at stages of development determined by our biological nature, with no theory of general "organ growth" or "organism growth" apart from general biology, though these processes are influenced, sometimes profoundly, by the external environment with its triggering and shaping effects. The category of learning, in contrast, is supposed to involve trial and error, hypothesis formation, conjecture and refutation, generalization, conditioning, generalized domain-independent mechanisms, and so on, and is held to include such matters as language acquisition, concept formation, and theory construction in the sciences, among others. But to the extent that anything is understood about these matters, they seem to have essentially the properties of growth and maturation, not of learning. It is, in fact, doubtful whether conditioning is any more than an artifact, an odd and not very efficient method of providing an organism with information, which it will use in accord with its biological nature and the current states of its cognitive faculties. Trial and error learning can be illustrated, artificially, by selecting tasks beyond an organism's normal capacities so that no alternative remains. Study of such tasks is thus designed to ensure that little if anything will be learned about the nature of the organism, apart from its receptive capacities. Similar questions arise, though here the matter is far more obscure, in the case of conjecture and refutation or confirmation even in the sciences.

One may ask, in fact, whether the category of learning even exists in the natural world, as it is generally understood. True, there are phenomena that we describe in these terms in ordinary discourse. But we also talk about the rising and the setting of the sun, now understanding just why these terms, however appropriate for ordinary life, are inappropriate for the study of what happens in nature. Possibly learning is destined to go the same way. In any event, in the case of language and conceptual development, it seems to have little if any place. At the very least, serious questions arise about the appropriateness of these ideas, and we must be careful not to fall into the pervasive error of epistemological dualism, manifest in much of the inquiry into these matters, in my view. I would like to return to some of these questions in the concluding session.

Let us turn now to the third of the central questions concerning knowledge of language: how it is put to use? Again, there are classical antecedents. We can, quite appropriately I think, refer to this as *Descartes's problem*. The problem has two aspects: the production problem and the perception problem. For Cartesian thought, the former played a critical role, but there seems to be little to say about it and I will therefore put it aside now, returning to the question later on. Consider, then, the perception problem, also central to Cartesian thought. Descartes's major scientific contribution, perhaps, was his rejection of the neo-scholastic conception of a mysterious transfer of form from objects to the mind/brain, in favor of a representational theory of perception that seems to be in essence correct.

In the language case, the perception problem is concerned with the process by which a person assigns a structural description to a presented expression in a particular situation. Following Donald Davidson, let us refer to our model of the person performing this act as an "interpreter."[8] As Davidson observes, in real world communication, virtually any information and strategy can be used to try to determine what some person is saying in a given situation, or more accurately, what the person has in mind. Furthermore, little knowledge need be shared by the speaker and the interpreter. Davidson then draws the rather paradoxical conclusion that there is no notion of language in the sense used generally by linguists, philosophers and psychologists. There is no use for "the concept of language," for "shared grammar or rules," for a "portable interpreting machine set to grind out the meaning of an arbitrary utterance," and we are led to "abandon . . . not only the ordinary notion of a language, but we have erased the boundary between knowing a language and knowing our way around in the world generally."

This is an odd conclusion. The right conclusion from these correct observations is one familiar in the sciences: there is no such topic as the study of everything. We might hope to move towards some understanding of elements that enter into successful communication, but study of this topic in its full richness is no more a subject than the study of the motion of a particle under the influence of everything in the universe, including possible human intervention that might falsify the predictions of any physical experiment. We see here another example of how an unwillingness to accept the common understanding of empirical inquiry has led to very strange conclusions and pointless injunctions in the study of language and mind.

In attempting to deal seriously with the perception aspect of Descartes's problem, we will seek to isolate elements of the problem that can be subjected to inquiry, under appropriate idealizations, their appropriateness determined, as always, by the explanatory success achieved by adopting them. Contrary to what Davidson asserts, there is a very good use for "the concept of language" as a "portable interpreting machine set to grind out the meaning of an arbitrary utterance"; in fact, it is indispensable for the serious study of communication or any other aspect of language and its use: in particular, for gaining any insight into what Davidson calls the "mysterious process by which a speaker or hearer uses what he knows in advance plus present data to produce a passing theory" that is "geared to the occasion." Whatever else is happening in real world communication, or other normal uses of language, there can be little doubt that it involves resort to the I-language, partially shared by others in the various communities with which people associate themselves in their normal lives.

Can we identify other elements that enter into the full interpreter? One standard assumption is that it makes sense to construct an idealization that eliminates all aspects of the situation apart from the linguistic expression itself, regarded as input to a "parser" that incorporates the I-language along with other elements – certain strategies and procedures, a certain organization of memory, and so on – and assigns to the expression a structural description. While there can be little doubt of the existence of the I-language, the system of knowledge of language represented in the mind/brain, the abstract conception of a parser is somewhat more problematic, and it is not clear what kinds of properties should be attributed to it. Nevertheless, let us assume this to be a valid idealization. Notice that what appears to be the correct conclusion about the status of the I-language and the parser is the opposite of the one that is standard in the literature, which generally takes I-language (or "grammar") to be more problematic than the notion of a parser.

The parser associates structural descriptions with expressions; the I-language generates structural descriptions for each expression. But the association provided by the parser and the I-language will not in general be the same, since the parser is assigned other structure, apart from the incorporated I-language. There are many familiar examples of such divergence: garden path sentences, multiple self-embedding, and so on. There has been much confusion about this matter. It is sometimes argued that the language (or "grammar") should be *identified* with the parser, taken as an input system in something like Jerry Fodor's sense. Or it is argued that since all evidence comes from performance, we have no grounds for interpreting evidence as being about anything *but* a parser, which would be much like the argument that since all evidence comes from experiment and observation, we have no grounds for interpreting it as bearing on the systems of the world under investigation. It has been proposed as a condition on grammar that it account for the fact that the sentences of natural language are readily parsable. But this is not a fact, so it cannot be a condition on grammar. Crucially, it is not a fact. Languages are not "designed for parsability," whatever that is supposed to mean. With only a slight air of paradox, we may say that languages, as such, are not usable. If some expressions are not parsable, as is often the case, they are simply not used, and the language is no worse for that. Furthermore, so-called "ungrammatical" or "deviant" sentences are often quite readily parsable and are even perfectly intelligible, and quite properly used in appropriate circumstances – for example, "the knife cut the meat with a sword," referring, perhaps, to Mack the Knife.

Considerations of this sort bear on the possibility of providing so-called "functional explanations" for properties of language. If we construct two systems at random, one a generative procedure G that strongly generates structural descriptions, the other a parsing (or production) system P, we are likely to find some respects in which the two are well adapted to one another, others in which they are not. If G is incorporated in P, which has access to it for performance, then P will be able to make use of the information provided by G to the extent that the two systems are mutually adapted. It would be a mistake to conclude that G was designed for use by P just on the basis of the fact that there is a domain of adaptation. One would have to show that this domain goes beyond what might be expected on other grounds, not an easy task. These questions arise whenever functional accounts are offered.

Notice that analogous questions arise in connection with learnability. It is sometimes proposed that the natural languages are the possible languages that are readily learnable under ordinary conditions, but this is not necessarily true; it is not a condition on linguistic theory that the languages it makes available be learnable. Suppose the resources of the language faculty permit the set L_1 of languages, where L_2 is the set of learnable systems (assuming notations fixed, etc.). Then only the intersection of L_1 and L_2 will be able to be acquired. There will be possible unlearnable natural human languages, and there might be all kinds of evidence showing this. In fact, recent work suggests that L_1 *is* included in L_2, a rather surprising empirical discovery, if true. But it is not a conceptual necessity, as sometimes asserted.

So far, I have laid out the central issues pretty much as they were beginning to be understood at the outset of the second cognitive revolution, though in a somewhat broader context than was grasped at the time. Focusing now on Humboldt's problem and Plato's problem – the problem of grammar and UG – how were they addressed?

The earliest work had something of the flavor of traditional grammar. A traditional grammar has what are called "rules," actually hints and examples that can somehow be understood by a reader who knows unconsciously what a language is and must be. These quasi-rules give the basic phrase structures of sentences and indicate how to form expressions of particular grammatical constructions: there is a chapter on the structure of phrases, on the formation of passives, relatives, interrogatives, complex clauses, etc. Correspondingly, an early generative grammar had phrase structure rules and grammatical transformations that generated the structural descriptions of complex sentences from those underlying simple ones. One early argument was that phrase structure rules could be dispensed with entirely for complex sentences, leaving only very simple phrase structure rules; the structural descriptions of the more complex structures are then determined by general properties of transformations. These conclusions thus reduce considerably the range of variation of structures possible for language and the variety of relations among structures.

The idea of looking at a language as a rule system of this type was reinforced by the practice of generative phonology, which had been developed – or more accurately, revived – a few years earlier, based on rule systems of a very similar sort. Here the motivation was, very simply, historical linguistics – specifically, historical Semitic linguistics – which offers a concept of "explanation" that was lacking in the structuralist tradition. My own work on this topic in the late 1940s was based explicitly on this model, with the concept of explanation and ordered rules reconstituted in a synchronic framework; a substantial improvement in this work was suggested by Yehoshua Bar-Hillel, who suggested – correctly as it turned out – that the theory could be considerably improved by taking the historically reconstructed forms essentially as base forms for the synchronic grammar. The resort to rule systems for syntax was also reinforced by mathematical studies of formal systems, particularly the approach to recursive function theory based on ideas of Emil Post, which provided a natural framework for rule systems for phrase structure.

In these terms, the answer to Humboldt's problem is that a language is a generative procedure constituted of rules of these types, interacting so as to strongly generate the structure of the language with a structural description for every expression.

As for Plato's problem, the idea was basically this. The initial state of the language faculty provides a format for permissible rule systems and an evaluation metric that assigns a value to each such system. Presented with data, the mind selects the highest-valued generative procedure consistent with it. The person then knows that language, with all of its rich array of consequences. In informal exposition, this approach was sometimes described in terms of a hypothesis testing model, a fact that has misled a number of commentators (Jerry Fodor and Hilary Putnam, among others). The actual technical proposals do not have this character, however.

This approach led to many successes. A great deal of new empirical material was quickly discovered, including many very simple but quite puzzling phenomena that had escaped notice in the intuitive linguistics of earlier years. It is surprising, in retrospect, to see what a vast range of simple problems of this nature were ignored in the many centuries of intuitive linguistics that essentially took for granted the linguistic capacities of the reader of a traditional or pedagogic grammar, not attempting to reveal what exactly these capacities were. I think the major contribution of this work may have been to bring about the realization that very simple properties of language that are taken for granted in ordinary life are in fact extremely puzzling, something that required a certain psychological wrench or act of the imagination, and is always the beginnings of science – as when we see that to explain the fall of an apple it is not enough to say that the ground is its natural place, or when we recognize that it cannot be seriously maintained that the form of an object is transmitted in some mystical way to the brain of the person who sees it. Furthermore, the discipline of attempting to construct explicit rule systems quickly led to many empirical discoveries, since it invariably became clear that the obvious rules just didn't work, and had to be modified. There was also some degree of success in achieving genuine explanations, that is, in showing how surprising phenomena follow from fairly natural rule systems that are perhaps optimal, in the technical theory-internal sense of an evaluation metric.

Alongside of such successes, there were dramatic failures, basically of a uniform type. Over and over again, it was shown that simple rules do not work, and that people actually use much more complex ones. Thus the obvious simple rule for forming *wh*-questions would be : Front-*wh*-. But as we know, it is very far from accurate, as becomes clear when we construct moderately complex expressions and determine how they are interpreted, with *wh*-island violations, ECP violations, and so on. This conclusion, found everywhere, is highly paradoxical, because such rules as Front-*wh*- are not only extremely simple, but would also be highly functional for parsability and quite adequate for the data that serve as the basis for language acquisition. It is as if the child perversely ignores simple rules that would be adequate for the data available and would satisfy the exigencies of communication and language use generally, and instead unerringly settles on far more complex rules that raise all sorts of computational problems and make it impossible to express simple thoughts in a simple way. Again, it seems that the language is not usable. Furthermore, all children seem to make these paradoxical moves in the same way, unerringly, without choice or awareness. These conclusions are plainly nonsensical, and indicate that something is severely wrong. Such problems have set the main research agenda in linguistic theory, at least within the tendencies I am considering here, since about 1960.

The most productive approach has been to try to "factor out" certain general principles that govern rule application and assign them to the initial state of the language faculty, then allowing the rules of the language to remain in the simplest form, with these invariant principles ensuring that the observed phenomenal complexity is derived. An extreme variant of this approach would be to eliminate rules of particular languages entirely, deducing the "apparent rules" from general principles in the sense that the interaction of these principles would yield the phenomena that the rules were constructed to describe. The rules postulated for particular languages – and the quasi-rules of traditional and pedagogic grammars – would then be shown to be epiphenomena, on a par with sentences, but without the reality of sentences; that is, eliminable, perhaps entirely.

As you know, work along these lines has converged in the past several years to yield a conception of the nature of language that is very different from anything previously contemplated. For a substantial core of natural language, it seems that phrase structure rules are completely dispensable, which is not too surprising, since, as has been understood for many years, in part they redundantly express ineliminable properties of lexical items. As far as transformational rules are concerned, they are not similarly redundant, but it seems that they too can be eliminated in favor of the general principle Move-alpha, or perhaps even Affect-alpha in the sense of Howard Lasnik and Mamoru Saito. Other general principles then interact to yield the complex array of linguistic phenomena. Exactly how this works is far from understood, but the general outlines are coming into view and in some areas a fair amount of genuine understanding has developed.

If there were only one human language, the story would essentially end there. But we know that this is false, a rather surprising fact. The general principles of the initial state evidently allow a range of variation. Associated with many principles there are parameters with a few – perhaps just two – values. Possibly, as proposed by Hagit Borer, the parameters are actually restricted to the lexicon, which would mean that the rest of the I-language is fixed and invariant, a far-reaching idea that has proven quite productive.

It has also been productive to assume that if some phenomenon is overt in some language – say, a rich array of cases, or overt *wh*-movement – then this is true for a reason determined by UG, so that the same will be found in every language. If the processes are not overt, reflected in phonetic form, then they take place in parts of the computational apparatus that are "decoupled" from the sound system and do not feed the rules of the phonological component. As for the latter, it still seems to me that they have something like the form originally assumed in early generative phonology, now understood in the familiar broad sense.

If this conception is correct, then there are a finite number of possible languages, apart from choice of lexical entries, also sharply constrained, with consequences to which I will return later. To acquire a language, the child must determine the values of the parameters, which must be such that they can be fixed on the basis of very simple data. Notice that it would follow that every natural language is learnable, a surprising empirical result, not a conceptual necessity.

This conceptual shift to a principles-and-parameters theory is a very radical departure from the long history of the study of language, much more so than early generative grammar, in the context of the second cognitive revolution, which in many ways revived and clarified ideas that were traditional, if long-forgotten. The current picture is sharply different, however, and in fact has much more of a truly rationalist cast than the general and rational grammar of the seventeenth and eighteenth century. Perhaps Descartes, even Plato, might have been pleased.

We can see more clearly what is at stake by considering two properties that descriptive statements about language might have. They may be language-particular or language-invariant – call this property [±1p]; and they may be construction-particular or construction-invariant – call this the property [±cp]. The quasi-rules of traditional grammar are typically [+1p], [+cp], and the same is true of the phrase structure rules of early generative grammar. Thus the rule VP→V-NP is particular to certain languages and a certain construction, namely verb phrases. With regard to transformational rules, the matter is more complex. Taken as an unanalyzed whole, the *LSLT* rule of question-formation or formation of negative expressions is [+1p], [+cp], but it is analyzed into components (structural descriptions and structural changes) that appear in many different transformations, and were thus [-cp] and arguably [-1p].[9] Some statements are [-1p], [-cp]; for example, the statement that phrase structure is hierarchic. And one might find examples of the other possible categories as well.

In a principles-and-parameters theory, in contrast, there are general principles of language that are [-1p] and [-cp], and there is the specification of parameters, which is [+1p] and [-cp]. There is nothing else. The only property of descriptive statements is [±1p]. Constructions, in the traditional sense, may be simply an artifact, perhaps useful for descriptive taxonomy, but nothing more. If this proves to be correct, traditional grammatical constructions are on a par with such notions as terrestrial animal or large molecule, but are not natural kinds. There is no passive construction, interrogative construction, etc. Rather, the properties of the relevant expressions follow from the interaction of language invariant principles, with parameters set. The property [±cp] disappears. Notice that the property [±1p] cannot disappear. If nothing is [-1p], then Plato's problem is unsolvable, and if nothing is [+1p], there would be only one language, which is not true, perhaps surprisingly. Evolution didn't do us a good turn in this respect, at least from a certain point of view.

I have said nothing yet about the lexicon. Here the problems that arise are somewhat similar, but other issues, involving questions that have been the topic of much philosophical speculation and debate, also arise. I would like to make a few comments about these matters later on, turning also then to other questions about how the problems of the study of language might be rethought if this conception of language is generally correct, and a number of other topics, including some speculations about language design.

NOTES

1 Cited by Max Jammer, "The Problem of the Unity of Physics," *International Journal on the Unity of the Sciences*, 1.1 (Spring 1988).
2 For extensive and very illuminating textual analysis of this topic, see Gerd Webelhuth, *Cartesian Philosophy and the Study of Language*, Masters Thesis, University of Mass., Amherst, 1986.
3 The bulk of a 1956 revision of this manuscript was published, under the original title, in 1975 (Plenum, University of Chicago).
4 Thus Sapir writes "Language is a purely human and noninstinctive method of communicating ideas, emotions, and desires by means of a system of voluntarily produced symbols," "a merely conventional system of sound symbols"; "the popular mind" has been illegitimately "seduced ... into attributing to it an instinctive basis that it does not really possess" (*Language* (New York: Harcourt, Brace, 1921)). His narrow point with regard to "the popular mind," referring to language versus involuntary expression of feeling, is sound, but not the general conclusion, surely.
5 For one typical recent example, see Philip Miller-Marco Haverkort, review of my *Knowledge of Language, Revue Internationale de Philisophie* (1987), pp. 449–57.
6 Work on bilingualism by Suzanne Flynn suggests a sense in which it might be true in part (*A Parameter-setting Model of L2 Acquisition*, (Reidel, Dordrecht, 1987)). Her work suggests that at least some principles of UG remain active in adult acquisition, while parameter-changing raises difficulties. If this is true of

UG in general, then the steady state would be the state where all parameters are fixed. The distinction between perception and acquisition might be a matter of some subtlety.

7   "Leibniz and Malebranche on Innate Ideas," *Philosophical Review*, 97.1, January 1988.
8   Davidson, "A Nice Derangement of Epitaphs," in E. LePore, ed., *Truth and Interpretation: Perspectives on the Philosophy of Donald Davidson* (Basil Blackwell, Oxford, New York, 1986).
9   A curious historical point is that this feature of the *LSLT* system was commonly understood to be a defect of it, in that the same structural description (SD), sometimes of moderate complexity, appeared in a variety of different transformations, as if some generalization were lacking expression. According to the evaluation measure developed in *LSLT*, however, this property of the system was regarded as signifying its success, in that a particular SD was "factored out" of a variety of operations, thus moving us towards a theory that analyzed constructions into more elementary [-cp] components.

2

Linguistics and Cognitive Science: Problems and Mysteries

Noam Chomsky

I will now assume that the principles-and-parameters approach to the study of language is essentially accurate. If so, the major task is to determine what are the principles and parameters that constitute the initial state of the language faculty and thus determine the set of possible human languages. Apart from lexicon, this is a finite set, surprisingly; in fact, a one-membered set if parameters are in fact reducible to lexical properties.[1] Notice that this conclusion, if true, would help explain the surprising fact that there is more than one possible human language; namely, it would follow that in an interesting sense, there is only one such language. Surely if some Martian creature, endowed with our capacities for scientific inquiry and theory construction but knowing nothing of humans, were to observe what happens to a child in a particular language community, its initial hypothesis would be that the language of that community is built-in, as a genetically-determined property, in essentials. How else could Plato's problem be resolved? That is, the initial hypothesis would be much like the hypothesis concerning physical growth adopted without controversy or even discussion, and in the absence of any direct evidence or understanding, apart from studies of the human brain. And it seems that this initial hypothesis may be very close to true, apart from the lexicon, still to be discussed. Let us turn to that.

By the early 1960s, it was clear that the lexicon must be separated as a component of the I-language. This was one major step towards eliminating the partially redundant category of phrase structure rules. What must appear in a lexical entry are the idiosyncratic features of the item, for example, the information that *hit* takes a syntactic complement and assigns it a particular semantic role (one or the other of these properties possibly redundant). What should be excluded from the lexicon are general properties of lexical items, for example, the information that the complement of *hit* follows the verb head and that the two form a constituent that ultimately takes a subject, these being properties of lexical items generally, to be expressed in terms of the head-government parameters and X-bar theory, not properties of the individual form in question. If such information is expressed in individual lexical entries, evidently significant principles are being missed.

More recent work assigns to the lexicon a central place in "projecting" essential properties of the various levels of structural description from features of lexical items (the Projection Principle). There is a lively and productive debate in progress concerning exactly how the lexicon relates to syntactic rules. At one extreme, it is argued by Di Sciullo and Williams[2] that words are syntactic atoms, determined by principles that are entirely dissociated from syntactic rules. A very different view has been developed by Mark Baker,[3] who argues that the structure of complex predicates is in large measure explicable in terms of the principles that govern syntactic constructions as well, primarily through the process of head-movement satisfying ECP. It would follow, then, that languages that appear to be of radically different typological categories in fact fall together under a common system of principles, with differences reduced to morphological properties, in effect; that is, to differences in lexical entries, once again. Still another view was outlined by Hagit Borer at this conference. These questions promise to be a topic of much important research in the coming years, with ramified consequences. My own speculation, for what it is worth, is that the principled distinction between inflectional and derivational morphology suggested in the earliest version of the "lexicalist hypothesis" is tenable, with the former reduced to syntactic operations and the latter internal to the lexicon. With regard to complex predicates (causatives, etc.), the questions seem to me open, with something like Baker's view the more attractive (though not, for that reason, necessarily correct) because of the prospects it offers to explain properties of complex words in terms of independently established principles of syntax and to unify typologically different languages under principles of UG.

There is some evidence suggesting that syntax and lexicon might be acquired in different ways, and perhaps have a fundamentally different character. Susan Curtiss, surveying several cases of language deficit, suggests that they indicate a dissociation of "morphological and syntactic abilities," on the one hand, and "lexical and relational semantic abilities," on the other.[4] Curtiss's work with Genie, who was isolated from 20 months to past age 13, led her to conclude that Genie never was able to pass beyond "primitive syntactic and morphological ability" though she rapidly gained a "relatively well-developed semantic ability," including "colors and numbers, shape and size terms, supraordinate, basic, and subordinate class terms," distinctions among objects in visual and functional terms, ready ability to speak about nonpresent people and objects, memories, events to come, and so on. Genie's speech was largely "the stringing together of content words, often with rich and clear meaning but with little grammatical structure." Genie evidently understood such notions as predication, conditionals, and so on, but apparently expressed them only through the device of linear sequence. Grammatical devices to express her thought were largely lacking (relativization, pronouns, demonstratives, connectives, auxiliaries, simple transformations, etc.). Curtiss suggests functional atrophy of the left hemisphere in this strongly right-handed child.

In contrast, several cases of children and adolescents with very low IQ and barely testable in other ways reveal a pattern of speech with rich and accurate use of grammatical devices but in ways that are "semantically inappropriate and confusing" or simply "meaningless." The latter cases, however, do not clearly indicate a dissociation between syntax and lexicon, since they might be interpreted in terms of some pragmatic deficit, with both syntax and lexicon intact, a phenomenon suggested also by work of Marion Blank.[5] Eric Lenneberg's classic work also brought out the apparent dissociation of language acquisition from other aspects of cognitive growth, and similar patterns have been observed in aphasiology. Notice that in principle, one might hope to gain some insight into the relation of syntax to word formation and the general status of morphology from evidence of this nature.

Lexical-conceptual development seems to exhibit striking regularities, as shown, for example, by the proper use of color words at a certain maturational stage and by many intriguing examples discussed by Susan Carey,[6] one interesting case being an apparent shift from understanding of natural kind terms as cluster terms to a reinterpretation of them as rigid designators, as suggested by experimental studies of Frank Keil's. Particularly dramatic is the work by Lila Gleitman and her colleagues on the use of terms for visual experience by the blind, including children, and studies on the blind-deaf who have acquired language by touching the faces of speakers, a highly limited source of information, but one that suffices for acquisition of rich knowledge of syntax as well as vocabulary, including again visual vocabulary, to a remarkable degree.[7] This work again extends the depth of Plato's problem, for both syntax and lexicon. Evidently, very restricted experience suffices for the acquisition of language. There is even a case on record of acquisition of first language (sign language, in this case) with no apparent language experience at all.[8]

The concepts assigned labels during acquisition of the lexicon do not simply constitute a list, but rather a structured system based on such properties as the locational thematic relations of goal, source, object moved, etc., sometimes interpreted in quite abstract ways; and such notions as agent, patient, instrument, as well as cause, intention, event, and so on. This lexical structure imposes semantic connections among lexical expressions and the sentences in which they appear, connections determined by the language faculty itself, deriving, presumably, from the invariant initial state of the language faculty. If so, then semantic connections induced by lexical structure would have something of the same status as phonetic connections reflecting feature structure. Other semantic connections are induced by syntactic properties that are also plausibly assignable to the language faculty itself.

Though placed in a structured system with an apparently fixed framework, individual lexical items do not seem to be exhausted in their content by such features, as we find at every turn, for example, in the case of such sets as *kill, murder, assassinate, massacre*, etc. All of these terms are, in a sense, causative forms based on intransitive *die*, but the semantic residues do not, presumably, constitute possible lexical items in themselves. Thus it is implausible that *assassinate* has the lexical entry "cause to X," where X is an abstract lexical construction expressing the fact that the person who dies is important, the killing was done with malicious intent and broader sociopolitical motives, etc. Similar problems arise throughout the study of lexical structure.

The empirical study of the lexicon bears on questions that have been at the center of much philosophical reflection and debate. In the study of the lexicon, Plato's problem arises in a very sharp form, and the conclusions have to be more or less the same as elsewhere: the growth of the lexicon must be inner-directed, to a substantial extent. Lexical items are acquired by children at an extraordinary rate, more than a dozen a day at peak periods of language growth. To describe the meaning of a word is extremely difficult. Dictionary definitions do not even come close; like traditional grammars, they only provide hints for the reader who already has tacit knowledge of most of the answer. Apart from more advanced realms of science, explicit definitions are rare. To determine what we tacitly know the meaning of simple words to be – words like "thing" or "person" or "persuade" or "chase" or "murder" – is a tricky matter, often requiring arcane thought experiments; an interesting philosophical literature is devoted to such questions, with regard to the concept of person, for example, which plays a central role in moral discourse and in human thought generally. But children acquire knowledge of lexical items on the basis of very few presentations, perhaps only one, and under quite ambiguous circumstances. Furthermore, this is shared knowledge; children proceed in essentially the same way, placing the lexical entries in the same fixed nexus of thematic and other relations and assigning them their apparently specific properties. Barring miracles, this means that the concepts must be essentially available prior to experience, in something like their full intricacy. Children must be basically acquiring labels for concepts they already have, a view advanced most strongly by Jerry Fodor, and are somehow endowed with the capacity to identify the use of these concepts in real life situations, no trivial matter in itself but one that I will put aside.

In the study of meaning over the past several centuries, there has been a transition from a focus on the nature of the things named, to the cognitive base for semantic content, to the social context, a matter discussed in an illuminating work by Murray Cohen.[9] In the early 1970s, these various factors were noted by Hilary Putnam in his influential critique of the idea that meanings are "in the head," and with regard to the nature of the items named, by Saul Kripke. Here some qualifications are necessary, in my view. Kripke's discussion of rigid designators relies crucially on judgements concerning the use of names of individuals and kinds ("Richard Nixon," "table," etc.). But his inference to a form of essentialism relies on the assumption that such items are names in the logician's sense, whereas in fact, it seems that natural languages do not have names in this sense: rather, person names, color names, artifact names, etc. The judgements on which Kripke relies, then, reduce to matters of *de dicto* necessity, involving relations among concepts that have a cognitive base, and they do not support any form of essentialism. Even if the concept of rigid designator is reduced to that of variables in some regimented form of language or in some conception of "logical form" for natural language, similar problems arise. For example, the judgement that a particular object has the "essential property" of being a table, having a certain physical constitution, structure, function, etc., but is only accidentally movable, tells us nothing more than that this is the way artifacts are conceived in the terms made available by our cognitive resources, hence in the structure of the lexicon; for a differently constituted intelligence, a table might appear to be "essentially movable" and only accidentally used for such-and-such a purpose. Our cognitive systems determine the "nature" of artifacts in quite complex and special ways, for example, in terms of such notions as human agency; whether some particular object is a table or a hard bed depends, in part, on the intentions of the designer. Julius Moravcsik has suggested plausibly that a version of the Aristotelian theory of "causes" may be appropriate for understanding the framework of human concept formation; the similarity to Kripke's choice of "essential properties" is, in fact, rather striking. It is doubtful that the conclusions drawn from the intuitive judgements described can be sustained.[10]

Further questions arise with regard to the social context of meaning assignment. Consider what Putnam calls "the division of linguistic labor," that is, the fact that elements of the lexicon may be "semantically indeterminate" with reference to be fixed by resort to "experts" within the "community." These considerations do not undermine an approach to lexical structure from the individual psychology perspective of generative grammar. Rather, lexical items can be assumed to be individually specified in the mind/brain in just these terms. Furthermore, no sensible notion of "linguistic community" or "language as social practice" can be derived from these considerations. Thus it might be that my particular lexical entry for the words *elm* and *beech* resembles the biblical dictionaries with the entry "kind of tree," but with a notation specifying that I am to check the reference with an Italian gardener, with whom I share only the technical Latin names for species; and to fix the reference of *mass* and *momentum* my cognitive state may direct me to a monolingual German physicist. But we could not conclude, on this basis, that Italian and German are part of English, or that all of us form some kind of meaningful community. In fact, communities are formed in all sorts of overlapping ways, and there seems to be little of any generality that can be said about the matter.

In this connection, we might take note of the various forms of "Platonistic linguistics" that have been developed in recent years, or similar ideas arising from the conception of language as a social practice "in which people engage," a practice that "is learned from others and is constituted by rules which it is part of social custom to follow," in Michael Dummett's phrase, expressing views common among philosophers influenced by Wittgenstein, among others. In Dummett's version, this conception of social practice provides the "fundamental sense" of language. Thus Dutch and German are particular social practices in this "fundamental sense"; they exist "independently of any particular speakers," and each speaker has only a "partial, and partially erroneous, grasp of the language."[11] What is individually represented in the mind/brain, from this point of view, is a derivative concept, raising further problems: "one cannot so much as explain what an idiolect is without invoking the notion of a language considered as a social phenomenon,"[12] Dummett maintains, a proposal that at once leads to all sorts of quandaries that he does not address and that appear irresoluble. Scott Soames has argued that the actual practice of linguists in pursuing the "Leading Questions" that define the discipline – the study of language change and typology, for example – relies on a "Platonistic" concept of language as an abstract object, a conclusion that cannot be sustained; and Kripke has resorted to community practice to resolve his "Wittgensteinian" paradox concerning rule-following, unconvincingly I think, for reasons I have discussed elsewhere.[13]

All of these conceptions are at best highly problematic. As is well-known, the "fundamental sense" of language in the terms suggested by Dummett and others involves complex and obscure sociopolitical, historical, cultural and normative-teleological elements, which may be of some interest for the sociology of identification within various social and political communities and the study of authority structure, but which lie far beyond any useful inquiry into the nature of language or the study of meaning or the psychology of users of language. All such conceptions bear a heavy burden of proof, and it is doubtful that it can be met. They cannot be lightly assumed to be "clear enough" or even meaningful, as is the common practice in the philosophical literature.

In contrast, the approach of "cognitive grammar," so-called, within the framework of individual psychology, should not really be controversial. There is something about my brain – specifically, the state attained by its language faculty – that is different from that of monolingual speakers of Japanese, and is sufficiently similar to that of many others so that we can communicate, more or less. Contrary to what Dummett and others allege, there is no fundamental problem in "explaining" what this system is or how it functions in expression of thought, though to study communication, naturally, one must bring in social context. I can place myself within one or another "community" in all sorts of ways, depending on fluctuating interests and concerns, and to the extent that I follow the "norms" of such communities, it is on the basis of the nature of my I-language taken as a psychological particular and the full range of strategies and techniques available to the full "interpreter" in Davidson's sense, not a topic of inquiry for reasons I have already discussed. I may also have a wide range of beliefs, right or wrong, about the practices of these various overlapping communities, and varied and shifting intentions about conforming to their alleged practices. Apart from these considerations, "norms" are matters of authority structures that are quite irrelevant here. All of this bears as well on the concept "misuse of language" that plays a substantial role in recent reflection on language and meaning. This concept is also commonly used as if it is clear enough, along with the concepts of community, norm, social practice, etc.; again, it is not clear enough, and it is doubtful that any sense can be given to these notions that will be useful for the purposes for which they are devised.

Discussing the concept of idiolect and "common language," and Dummett's belief concerning the "fundamental" nature of the latter, Alex George argues correctly[14] that though the notion of idiolect is unproblematic, there is one sense of "fundamental" according to which these psychological particulars "fail to be fundamental," namely, "in *order of normativity*." Here we have to take into account the individual's beliefs and intentions with regard to community norms and authority. But it does not follow that there is, as George concludes, something else that *is* prior in "order of normativity." That is, it does not follow that there exists any abstract entity that is "a reification of social facts and processes," anything that would count as a "common language" determined by some "complex pattern of social activity," anything that would be "an objective reality confronting speakers, determining which changes in their idiolects yield error and which do not." It appears that there is no such entity. Idiolects are not prior in regard to normativity, but nothing else is either. Rather, there is a wide variety of considerations which, in individual cases, bear on normativity, and there is probably little to say about them, in general. Such considerations, varying from person to person and situation to situation, do not present us with an object, however abstract, that will serve as a "community" or a "common language" – except by accident, in some peculiar social or historical circumstances. There is nothing here that serves to save the concept of "common language," and insofar as philosophical discourse relies on such a concept, any conclusions that might be reached are hardly well-founded.

Fodor's conclusion that lexical entries are essentially "given" in advance of experience – and, we may assume further, placed within a fixed nexus of semantic properties that induce semantic connections determined by the individual language faculty – has struck many as not only extreme but even absurd. Hilary Putnam writes that "to have given us an innate stock of notions which includes *carburetor*, *bureaucrat*, *quantum potential*, etc., as required by Fodor's version of the Innateness Hypothesis, evolution would have had to be able to anticipate all the contingencies of future physical and cultural environments. Obviously it didn't and couldn't do this."[15] His counterargument, however, has a number of weaknesses. For one thing, no alternative is suggested, even vaguely. For another, it is far from clear that such concepts as *quantum potential*, acquired internally to a specific theory, belong in the same category as terms that are acquired in ordinary experience, without anything remotely like definitions and internal to theories only in a loose and metaphoric sense of the term, so far as we know. Putnam does argue that "the language of daily life" exhibits the same features as do scientific terms with regard to "meaning holism," but his argument is unpersuasive. It is that in ordinary inference we make use of unstated auxiliary hypotheses and other items of general information. That is surely true of common sense inference, but the observation falls short of establishing anything like the assumptions of meaning holism.

The argument that evolution could not have anticipated the full range of future contingencies is also not compelling.[16] First, it need not be claimed that the structure of the organism, however it achieved its current state, anticipates "all contingencies"; only those required for concept formation in the real world. Furthermore, as discussed by Massimo Piattelli, a similar argument had long been offered in immunology: namely, that the number of antibodies is so immense, even including antibodies for artificially synthesized substances, that it would be absurd to suppose that nature had provided a stock of antibodies. But it appears that something of the sort might be true, and that an animal "cannot be stimulated to make specific antibodies, unless it has already made antibodies of this specificity before the antigen arrives," so that the antigen plays only a selective and amplifying role in antibody formation, as Niels Kaj Jerne proposed in work that won him the Nobel Prize. Whether he is right or not, he could be, and the same could be true in the case of word meanings. The standard poverty of stimulus argument, in fact, suggests that something of the sort is true.

Putnam offers a counter-argument to the one based on analogy to the immune system, but it also lacks force. He argues that concepts "often arise from theories" and the number of theories (even "short" theories) is so immense as to make "the idea that evolution exhausted all the possibilities in advance wildly implausible." The same difficulties arise, however. It is, in the first place, far from clear that the lexicon is determined from theories in anything like the sense that Putnam has in mind. Second, no cardinality argument will bear on the question of how specific concepts (*carburetor*, *bureaucrat*, etc.) are acquired. We might agree that evolution couldn't have done *everything*, even what is beyond human capacity, but such an argument would not be relevant, even if it could be given a coherent form.

To clarify the matter, we should distinguish two issues. Assuming the language faculty to be a distinct component of the mind, it has a genetically-determined initial state S_0^L, which will include the resources dedicated to attainment of concepts associable with lexical items in the course of normal human experience. But the mind has other resources as well, and thus a more general initial state S_0^M, with other capacities for formation of concepts – for example, in the course of theory construction in the advanced sciences. Concepts that do not fall within the range of S_0^L might be constructible by the mechanisms available to S_0^M. The relevant empirical questions here have to do with S_0^L and its limits. We might well be able to construct concepts that do not fall within these limits. Though the matter is not relevant here, there seems no contradiction in supposing that S_O^M as well has definite bounds, even that we might discover these; it does not follow, for example, that such a discovery should permit us to construct unconstructible concepts. An organism limited to integers and pairs would be able to construct rationals but not reals, and might even characterize what it can attain (say, algebraically). It would find that its mathematics has odd gaps and its physics always fails in mysterious ways, that it can only attain approximations and not formulate plausible laws, but would be unable to discover why.

Returning to the language faculty, as in the case of syntax, there is no point arguing for or against some unformulated "innateness hypothesis." The empirical conditions of the problem are clear in a general way. What is required is further evidence to sharpen them, and some theoretical understanding of what the innate resources of the mind actually are in this domain. The ongoing debate seems to me rather futile and misdirected.

In the same connection, Putnam argues that the thesis of "meaning holism," with the Quinean principle that "revision can strike anywhere," contributes to undermining certain conclusions concerning the innate structure of conceptual systems and language generally. The question is, however, whether this principle is true. It cannot be established for natural language by stipulation, or by reflection on the norms of rationality for scientific discourse, the context in which the issue arose. Rather, it is an empirical problem, to be settled by empirical inquiry. It might turn out that reference is fixed on holistic grounds, as Putnam alleges, and even that there are no "'psychologically real' entities which have enough of the properties we preanalytically assign to 'meanings' to warrant an identification." But if so, this would still leave open the question whether "revision can strike anywhere." It might be, for example, that certain structural properties and semantic connections are fixed as a matter of biological endowment, and remain stable as other considerations lead to various choices about fixing of reference. Such a conclusion is, in fact, rather strongly suggested by current understanding of the empirical facts.

To see more clearly what is at stake, take some particular cases. Judgements concerning connections of meaning determined by the language faculty itself – in particular, analytic connections – appear to be as clear and replicable as any, and could be sharpened by further experiment if this were warranted. Thus there is little disagreement over the fact that in the sentence "John likes him," the pronoun is not referentially dependent on *John*, whereas in "John's mother likes him," it may be; or with regard to the qualitative difference in status between the sentences "the man who lives upstairs lives upstairs" and "the man who lives upstairs lives in England." Similarly, it is a clear and replicable judgement that, whatever the facts may be, if Mary expects to feed herself, then Mary expects that she, Mary, will feed Mary herself; whereas if I wonder who Mary expects to feed herself, then I wonder which female person Mary expects will feed that very person, not Mary. I may also wonder whether Mary expects to feed Mary herself in this case, but that is a question of fact, not settled by the language independently of whatever the facts may be. Furthermore, a good deal is understood about the basis for these semantic connections, yielding sharp cases of the analytic-synthetic distinction. In the domain of lexicon proper, there are equally clear judgements: thus if John killed Bill, then Bill is dead, though John may or may not be, depending on the facts; and if John persuaded Bill to go to college, then Bill decided or intended to do so, and did so without duress, though whether John also did so is a question of fact. The same is true in a vast range of other cases; and again, at least something is understood about why this should be the case.

As is well-known, Quine and others influenced by his arguments about meaning holism have advanced alternative ideas to account for these distinctions, which are not in doubt as empirical phenomena. Thus it is claimed that the differences are ones of more or less deeply held belief, or of "semantic importance" and role in inference or importance for language acquisition and communication, as Paul Churchland has proposed. It is proper, of course, to offer alternative theories to deal with the facts, but it is an illusion to believe that this has been done in the present case. To see why this is so, consider again the specific examples mentioned. Suppose that two people, Jones and Smith, disagree as to why such expressions as "everyone who lives upstairs lives upstairs" or "John persuaded Bill to go to college, so Bill decided or intended to go to college" have the special status that we all agree they have. Suppose that Jones holds that this special status follows from the syntactic and lexical structure of the language, and ultimately, their innate determinants, while Smith responds that it is a matter of deeply held belief or semantic prominence. We are by no means at an impasse, and we know exactly how to proceed to resolve the issue. Jones has the task of developing the relevant principles of sentence structure, referential dependence, thematic roles, and so on, and must proceed to support these proposals by inquiry into other aspects of language, other languages, language acquisition, and so on. To a significant extent, this has been done, with substantive results, and further research addressing these questions is on the way. Smith faces the comparable task of constructing a theory of belief fixation, inference, or whatever, that will yield these results. This task, however, has never been undertaken even in the most rudimentary manner, and a consideration of the empirical conditions of the problem suggests that it never will be. The fact of the matter, then, is that there is only one proposal on the table that merits serious consideration, the one based on language-determined connections of meaning; no alternative has been proposed, apart from verbiage that remains empty.

It is intriguing that the only proposal that is substantive, and in fact reasonably well confirmed, is generally assumed to have been refuted in favor of the proposal that has never been given a coherent formulation, let alone put to empirical test. That fact requires explanation. The explanation, I think, lies in part in an illegitimate inference from consideration of the norms of rationality proposed for scientific discourse to empirical claims about natural language, that is, about the real world. And in part it may again reflect the unwillingness to subject the study of language and mind to the requirements of rational inquiry, so that what amounts to little more than stipulation buttressed with a few unconvincing examples[17] is misunderstood as substantive argument.

Quine has long alleged that the notions of semantic connection or sameness of meaning are inherently more obscure than others that he finds tolerable: having meaning, well-formedness, and so on. And this idea has been an influential one. As I discussed earlier, the notions that he finds acceptable appear to have no status in empirical inquiry into language, and are surely no better founded in observation and experiment than those he regards as dubious and objectionable.

Insofar as the arguments of Quine and others for meaning holism are based on rational norms for science, they are not to the point here unless it is shown that language in empirical fact develops in terms of such norms; while this is not inconceivable, the evidence hardly supports this view, to put it mildly. These arguments also turn on the alleged indeterminacy of attributions of meaning, or for Quine, at least in some of his writings, the indeterminacy of all attributions of structure to language beyond what can be derived by methods he stipulates from the behavior of the speaker of the language, stipulated to be the only legitimate source of evidence. In both respects, the stipulations are arbitrary, apart from irrelevant historical antecedents, and it is difficult to see why they should be taken seriously. In general, this approach is so remote from normal empirical practice in the sciences or in the study of language as ordinarily – and properly – pursued that we may dismiss it, unless some argument is advanced that has, so far, not been forthcoming.

With regard to indeterminacy, no coherent argument has been given, to my knowledge, to suggest that the problem arises for attribution of meaning or other aspects of language structure in any way that distinguishes these topics from other domains of empirical inquiry where they are held not to arise in the same lethal form. It now seems to be generally agreed that this "bifurcation thesis," as Donald Hockney called it, cannot be established on epistemological grounds. In one recent discussion, Quine endorses Roger Gibson's proposal that the distinction is founded on ontological grounds, adding that this has been his position throughout.[18] That is, taking the distribution of "states and relations over elementary particles" to be fixed, we will still find alternative "manuals of translation" and grammars consistent with this fixed distribution but inconsistent with one another, so that there is no fact of the matter. But we can say exactly the same thing about two theories of organic chemistry, or of the neurophysiology of vision, or of embryological development, and so on; therefore, there is no fact of the matter in these cases either, by this argument. And if it turns out that the world really consists of strings vibrating in ten-dimensional space, then there will be no fact of the matter about elementary particles, by the same argument. Furthermore, if we fix the psychology, we can prove by the same argument that there is no fact of the matter about elementary particles. Fixing one part of science, we will find "indeterminacy," in Quine's sense, in other related parts. Nor will it help to point to the weakness or complete absence of known relations among domains of empirical inquiry; this is commonly the case in empirical inquiry, which seeks to overcome these limits of understanding, and sometimes succeeds in doing so. To allay misunderstanding, I do not conclude from these observations, as Gibson assumes, that "neither physics nor linguistics has a fact of the matter"; rather, that the entire discussion is confused and pointless, and when clarified, merely reduces to familiar forms of skepticism, understood for centuries to be without essential interest.

I do not see how anything sensible or useful can be resurrected from the extensive discussion of these matters, which has dominated a substantial part of the philosophical literature for some years. With regard to natural language, at least, we are dealing with empirical issues, and the conclusions of philosophical reflection have to be submitted to the same empirical tests as any others. Conclusions regarding meaning, language and psychology generally that have been regarded as extremely important and well-founded simply fail this requirement. Notice that the conclusions have been regarded as both important and well-founded. Richard Rorty, for one, regards Quine's alleged demonstration that there are no semantic connections intrinsic to the language system itself as one of two basic discoveries that compel us to abandon a traditional world picture, and Donald Davidson has argued that Quine "saved philosophy of language as a serious subject" by overcoming the pernicious analytic-synthetic dualism. I stress again that insofar as we are dealing with proposed norms of scientific rationality, empirical considerations of the sort I have mentioned may not apply; but they definitely do apply when the argument is held to bear directly on the real world, language and psychology in particular. Note further that questions of metaphysical realism do not arise in this connection. Take whatever view one likes on these subjects, and it remains the case that no "bifurcation thesis" is tenable; and if one is interested in obtaining answers to these questions, rather than simply harassing the soft sciences, then the place to look is where answers are likely to be forthcoming, that is, in the advanced sciences, where the questions can be pursued on the basis of a wealth of understanding and established theory.

I think there is more than a little irony in the fact that these ideas arose within a conception of philosophy that insists that it must be "naturalized" and made continuous with science, that as Rorty puts it, "a theory of meaning for a language" – and a theory of any other aspect of language – "is what comes out of empirical research into linguistic behavior."[19] To be sure, Rorty here means research that is properly pursued, in accord with the doctrines of "holism and behaviorism." The latter doctrine, however, is completely irrational in any of its forms and foreign to the nature of scientific inquiry, and the former remains at best an unargued hypothesis, one that does not seem particularly plausible in its full extent, at least. What comes out of current empirical research seems to undermine the doctrines that have been widely held.

One might hope that these issues too will be resolved in the coming years. As noted, the issues at stake have been regarded as of critical importance within recent philosophy of language and mind. Frankly, I doubt that this is true, and my own expectation, again for what it is worth, is that all of this will be regarded, some day, as another example of the surprisingly strong grip of behaviorist ideology and epistemological dualism on the contemporary imagination.

In the same connection, I suspect that much of the very fruitful inquiry and debate over what is called "the semantics of natural language" will come to be understood as really about the properties of a certain level of syntactic representation – call it LF – which has properties developed in model-theoretic semantics, or the theory of LF-movement, or something else, but which belongs to syntax broadly understood – that is, to the study of mental representations and computations – and however suggestive it may be, still leaves untouched the relations of language to some external reality or to other systems of the mind.

Let us consider further the ontological variant of Quine's interdeterminacy argument, now in the form presented by Putnam, attributed to Quine, that "the 'underdetermination' in psychology *remains* even if we 'fix' the physics."[20] Evidently, this conclusion would hold only if psychology is not part of "the physics," taken here to refer to the natural sciences generally; that is, if the relation of psychology to the natural sciences is different in principle – not merely in present status – from the relation of chemistry or biology to the natural sciences. But for this conclusion, no argument has been advanced. One might argue that the relations of those parts of psychology and linguistics that we are discussing to the "core natural sciences" have yet to be established; that is true, but not very informative. The task is to establish these relations, perhaps by modifying the "core natural sciences." By a similar argument, one might allege that there is no fact of the matter with regard to the motion of bodies, since it is not reducible to Cartesian mechanics, or that chemistry and genetics were once subject to a lethal indeterminacy, though no longer, as the core natural sciences have evolved. But this is plainly a hopeless line of argument, throughout.

One might make sense of this view, though I do not attribute this position to Quine or Putnam, on the assumption that relevant parts of the study of mind form a domain that cannot in principle be related to the natural sciences, thus reconstituting a Cartesian-style mind-body dualism. To take this stand, one would have to have some conception of the intrinsic limits of the study of the physical world. It is not easy to see what this might mean. Since Newton's refutation of Cartesian mechanics, we have had no fixed notion of "body" or of "the physical world." These terms refer to whatever there is, all of which we try to understand as best we can and to integrate into a coherent theoretical system that we call the natural sciences. Cartesian two-substance metaphysics was undermined by Newton's discovery of the inadequacy of Cartesian mechanics, a discovery that left us without a coherent way to formulate the mind-body problem in the

Cartesian sense – or in any sense, I believe. If it were to be shown that the properties of the world fall into two disconnected domains, then we would, I suppose, say that that is the nature of the physical world, nothing more, just as if the world of matter and anti-matter were to prove unrelated.

Perhaps one might interpret Thomas Nagel as holding that there is an unbridgeable divide between the study of the natural world and the study of mind, when he argues that we have no idea at all how a theory that views humans from an *external* point of view, as objects, can possibly come to terms with our view of ourselves from within, as agents, as sentient beings, so that the mind-body problem remains formulable in something like the Cartesian terms, and remains intractable. His observation about the limits of our understanding is accurate enough, but it is difficult to see why anything follows from it about some mind-body problem. A century ago, it was impossible to imagine how a theory of matter and motion could account for the states of matter, or the color of a chemical compound, or the growth of a living organism, or the fact that water boils at 100° Centigrade. But from this we do not conclude that there was then a body-body problem, or a color-body problem, or a life-body problem, or a gas-body problem. Rather, there were just problems, arising from the limits of our understanding. Only if one can delimit the theory of body in a definite way could such proposals become tenable, or even meaningful. Descartes could do so; he had a fairly definite concept of body in terms of contact mechanics. But we have no such concept. If physics tells us that there are massless particles, or infinite strings, or events happening in parallel without communication, or whatever might be proposed tomorrow, then so be it; that is the natural world. Subjective experience can be excluded from this domain only by fiat. Nagel, for example, argues against "the prediction that mental phenomena will eventually come to be counted as physical, once we understand them systematically – even if they are not reduced to terms already admitted as physical," a prediction he attributes to me, inaccurately.[21] His argument is that the account of "objective reality" is already complete without "annexing" the mental, so it cannot be "amplified" to include mental phenomena, in the way other phenomena were "annexed" as the natural sciences progressed. This argument presupposes some fixed notion of the "objective world" which excludes subjective experience, but it is hard to see why we should pay any more attention to that notion, whatever it may be, than to one that excludes action at a distance or other exotic ideas that were regarded as unintelligible or ridiculous at earlier periods, even by outstanding scientists.

Would it make sense to "predict" that the natural sciences will someday "annex" mental phenomena? It is difficult to see why; surely I would not do so. It might, for example, turn out that some of the questions we can pose lie beyond the scope of human intelligence, or that we might not even be able to pose the right questions in some domain because of the intrinsic limits of our intelligence. That should not surprise us, if it is true, on the assumption that humans are part of the natural world, not angels or gods. In particular, it is important not to fall prey to illusions about evolution and its adaptive miracles. Karl Popper observed long ago that it "is clearly mistaken" to suppose that "our quest for knowledge must necessarily succeed," that it must be possible for us to explain the world.[22] This conclusion should not appear controversial. We evidently have capacities to construct theories that we regard as intelligible in certain problem situations, taking a problem situation to be determined by some state of understanding, some array of phenomena subjected to inquiry, and some questions formulated about them. Since these capacities have definite structure – otherwise they would achieve nothing in any problem situation – they will have scope and limits, and there is little reason a priori to expect that these limits will include all matters we might hope to subject to inquiry. Looking at a rat from our point of view, we can readily understand why it is incapable of solving a maze that requires turning right at every prime number option, or even far simpler mazes; it simply lacks the relevant concepts, in principle. Similarly, knowing something about UG, we can readily design "languages" that will be unattainable by the language faculty, which will always make the wrong guesses. A differently constituted intelligence might be able to draw similar conclusions about human science, observing our stumbling failures, and we might even be able to do so ourselves, without contradiction. For those willing to adopt realist assumptions, the attainable sciences should be regarded as a kind of chance convergence of properties of our intelligence and the world as it is; and, of course, we fortunately have many ways to come to understand aspects of the world apart from our science-forming faculties, whatever their character may be.

In this context, we may return to an aspect of Descartes's problem that I left undiscussed in reviewing the basic questions of "cognitive linguistics" in my earlier lecture: the production problem. The study of parsers, one aspect of the perception problem, seems a feasible subject of inquiry, and provides at least a start towards understanding of linguistic communication at a relatively high level of abstraction. The study of the full interpreter may not be a feasible topic of inquiry, but for other reasons: it is a too-many-factor problem. What about the production problem? How do we speak in the normal fashion? Here it seems much harder to carve out an area of substantive inquiry. Descartes observed that normal human speech is unbounded, free of stimulus control, coherent and appropriate, evoking thoughts that the listener might have expressed in the same way – what we might call "the creative aspect of language use." He argued that these capacities lie beyond the power of any automaton, and he may have been right, in his sense of automaton, or indeed ours, which does not seem different in relevant ways. This is a central part of a more general problem concerning human action. In Cartesian terms, if the parts of an automaton are arranged in a fixed manner and the environment is fixed, then the automaton is *compelled* to act in a certain way (random elements, here irrelevant, apart); but a human, under similar conditions, is only "incited and inclined," not "compelled." Humans may act in the ways they are incited and inclined to act, so prediction of behavior may be possible and even a theory of motivation, but it will always miss the point; humans could have chosen to act otherwise, within the limits of their capacities. Human action is coherent and appropriate, but appropriateness to situations must be sharply distinguished from the causal effect of situations and internal states. There is little reason to suppose that human behavior *is* caused, in any sense of the word we understand. For Descartes, these considerations were at the heart of his dualist metaphysics, though not for us, because his theory of body quickly collapsed. These topics remain mysteries, beyond the range of our understanding, at least for now, possibly in principle, as a consequence of our biological nature. Here, we seem to be reduced to rather empty speculation, though one can imagine possible progress, at least in determining why the problem seems beyond our grasp.

In a contribution to a volume in honor of Yehoshua Bar-Hillel some years ago I suggested that we might distinguish "problems" from "mysteries," the former being questions that we seem to be able to formulate in ways that allow us to proceed with serious inquiry and possibly to attain a degree of understanding, the latter including questions that seem to elude our grasp, perhaps because we are as ill-equipped to deal with them as a rat is with a prime number maze.[23] There are certain recurrent features of the questions that constitute problems, in this sense. Thus we are able to deal with notions of natural number, set, continuity, with notions of determinacy and randomness, and with questions that can be formulated in input-output terms. But when such notions as these seem inapplicable, we are often at a loss, facing mysteries. It is possible that the production problem is such a mystery, for us. If so, that would in part vindicate Descartes's belief that "we do not have intelligence enough" to come to terms with these matters, though there is "nothing that we comprehend more clearly and perfectly" than "the liberty and indifference that exists within us" and that creates the divide, unbridgeable he thought, between causation of behavior by situations and internal states, on the one hand, and appropriateness of behavior to situations, on the other; between machines which are compelled, and humans who are only incited and inclined, to act in specific ways.

Returning to more solid ground, if the principles-and-parameters conception is generally correct, as seems to me to be the case, then many questions concerning language take on new forms. The internalized I-language is simply a set of parameter settings; in effect, answers to questions on a finite questionnaire. Language variation would, then, reduce to variation in such settings. Notice that change in a few parameters, even one, may have dramatic phenomenal consequences as its effects filter through a fixed network of principles, so that historically related languages might look rather different in their surface properties, in ways that do not seem closely connected; correspondingly, unrelated languages might share structural properties over a substantial range, because parameters are set in the same way. New questions are therefore suggested for the study of typology and language change. As for language acquisition, we would want to know to what extent, if any, maturational changes are involved in bringing parameters to functioning, a topic now under fruitful investigation by Borer and Wexler among others; and what interactions there may be among the parameters. Similar questions arise about parsing. It has generally been assumed that the parser, unlike the I-language, is fixed and does not undergo growth and maturation, or learning if such exists. The reasons for assuming this, apparently, are just that nothing is known about the matter, so we might as well adopt the simplest hypothesis. If it is true, then we would expect the parser to be essentially fixed for all languages, with only the values of parameters for a particular I-language to be "plugged in," possibly at the lexical level. In general, the picture of language that emerges is sufficiently unfamiliar that many questions will have to be rethought, if it proves correct.

Within a principles-and-parameters approach, we assume that language acquisition involves the fixing of parameters, yielding what we may call the "core language," including the lexicon. But what actually develops in the mind/brain of a person living in a normal environment is very different. It contains a "periphery" of marked exceptions such as idioms, irregular verbs and the like, and involves a mixture of systems resulting from the diversity of languages ("dialects" or "idiolects") that coexist in any real human community. When the study of language is able to extricate itself from prejudice, dogma and misunderstanding, we will, I believe, dismiss all of this as tenth-order effects resulting from uninteresting accident, focusing our attention on the deeper properties and principles that lead to real explanation and understanding of essential properties of the human mind. At that point, we will no longer distinguish core and periphery. Rather, linguistics will be the study of core language, a state that would be attained by the language faculty under ideal conditions, unrealized in a complex world. But that day is still far away.

Still bearing in mind the irrationality of the prevailing intellectual culture, we might observe that a vast array of phenomena of language lie far beyond our current understanding. In these areas, we can do nothing but construct descriptive rules, generally language-particular and construction-particular. These inevitable contingencies of empirical inquiry are sure to be adduced as evidence that something is fundamentally wrong in an approach – any approach – that seeks understanding of basic principles and attempts to deal with what I have taken to be the central problems: Humboldt's problem, our special case of Plato's problem, and Descartes's problem, insofar as we can give it a formulation that is intelligible in the terms available to us. Exactly the same is true in the case of biology, chemistry, physics, and in fact every domain of empirical inquiry. The phenomena that surround us in the real world of ordinary experience are generally not understood in any clear manner; they are too complex, they involve too many interacting factors, and our understanding is too limited for principled theories to explain a great deal of what is happening before our eyes. Most data fail to help us to attain insight into underlying principles and structure and are therefore uninteresting for the purpose of attaining rational understanding, however valuable they may be for many other aspects of human life.

Notice that there is no question of "right or wrong" in this connection. If I am taking a walk in the meadow, a Wild Flower Guide that organizes flowers in terms of colors, number of petals, etc., is far more valuable for me than a textbook of molecular biology. If I am trying to understand the nature of life, the opposite is the case. It is perhaps surprising that such truisms seem to be problematic and controversial; they should not be.

Let me conclude, finally, on a somewhat more technical note, leading to some speculations about the design of language. In the course of recent work in what has become the principles-and-parameters framework, certain concepts have developed that seem to have a real unifying character in that they appear throughout the various components of a highly modular system: c-command in Tanya Reinhart's sense and government, for example. There are also some fairly general principles, such as ECP, within the theory of government, though its exact formulation remains quite controversial; perhaps it should be understood in terms of a rather abstract locality condition on chains. I think we can also perceive at least the outlines of certain more general principles, which we might think of for the time being simply as "guidelines," in the sense that they are too vaguely formulated to merit the term "principles."

Some of these guidelines have a kind of "least effort" flavor to them. For example, the notion of "Full Interpretation" (FI), which holds that representations should contain no superfluous elements, or the "last resort" theory of movement, which has the effect of reducing the length of derivations. The idea of minimizing the form of representations and the length of derivations was pursued in the earliest work in contemporary generative grammar forty years ago, in the context of the study of evaluation procedures for grammars. There are, currently, a number of domains where we may be able to tease out some empirical effects of such guidelines, with a view towards elevating them to actual principles of language. I will only briefly sketch some of these topics here, hoping to return elsewhere to a more detailed presentation of material that belongs, so far, only to the oral tradition. I'll actually have to assume here a good deal of work both in this tradition, and in print, merely alluding to some of its general features, also introducing some modifications as I proceed, without specific notice.

Let us begin with some ideas of Jean-Yves Pollock[24] extending work of Joseph Emonds on verbal inflection in English and French. Emonds argued that in French-type languages, V raises to the inflectional elements I, which we may take to head the propositional category IP, whereas in English-type languages, I lowers to V (the rule of "Affix-hop"). He shows that a number of striking differences among these languages follow from this assumption about parametric difference. Pollock observes that the English auxiliaries *have* and *be* behave like French verbs in these respects, offering an interpretation for the parameter in terms of the agreement element AGR, which can be "strong," as in French, or "weak," as in English. Weak AGR prevents theta-marking elements such as verbs from raising to AGR; we may assume it to be too weak to permit elements adjoined to it to head theta-chains, so that a theta criterion violation would result from V-raising to weak AGR, though raising of English auxiliaries or of any element to strong AGR is permissible.[25] Furthermore tensed I is strong and infinitival I is weak, with comparable effects. Pollock also suggests that the tense-infinitive element I should be dissociated from AGR, dominating it, and that negation phrases headed by a negation element (*not* in English, *pas* in French) may intervene. The fully articulated proposition, then, is IP, headed by tensed or infinitival I, followed by a neg-P complement with negation as head and AGR-P as complement, headed by AGR with a VP complement, the latter including adverbial elements. Let us assume all of this to be correct. I will speak of "syntax" now in a narrow sense, restricted to the relation of D- to S-structure, as distinct from the operations of the LF component that relate S-structure and LF representation.

Skipping many crucial details, let us focus on questions relating to "least effort" guidelines. We must ensure that raising is necessary if possible; thus we must block lowering in French, to yield, e.g., NP-Adverb-V-NP as in English "John often reads books," permitting only NP-V-Adverb-NP, with V raising to AGR, then to tensed-I. The reason could be a "least effort" principle. Thus if I and AGR lower to V in the syntax, the V that is formed by adjunction must raise ultimately to I in LF, to avoid an unacceptable trace-headed chain. We thus have syntactic lowering followed by LF-raising, a longer derivation than simple syntactic raising. Thus raising is necessary if possible.

In English, where syntactic raising is blocked for verbs, a dummy element must exist to bear the affixes if lowering does not take place, as in questions, negation, etc.: the empty element *do*. Why, then, do we not have the option "John did leave" (with stressless *do*) instead of "John left"? The former involves at most the rule of *do*-insertion, whereas the correct form, *John left*, requires lowering of I and AGR to V and then raising of the complex V to I at LF to provide a proper chain. The natural answer is a sharpening of the "least effort" principle: operations of UG are "cheaper" than those of particular grammar, and the lowering and raising operations are simply instances of the general principle Move-alpha, whereas the rules involving the dummy element *do* are language-particular, and will be used, therefore, only when no output will otherwise result. At an intuitive level, we might think of the principles of UG as "hard-wired," near-costless in operation, as compared with the special properties of particular languages, which carry a cost.

A further problem arises at once: why we do not have such forms as "John not reads books," avoiding *do*-insertion, with lowering of the affixes to V followed by LF raising, all by principles of UG? One natural answer (not Pollock's, in this case) is that the LF-movement would violate the Head Movement Constraint (HMC), since LF-movement of V from AGR to I would cross the negation element. Assuming HMC to be derived from ECP, we would have an ECP violation in this case. Therefore, *do*-insertion is necessary.

But now another question arises: why is *syntactic* movement from V to

AGR to I permissible, crossing the negation element and thus violating HMC, as in "John hasn't read books" or all cases in French? A natural answer follows from taking quite literally the formalism of adjunction. When AGR and I are lowered to V, they form a V; subsequent raising of this V will leave V-traces, and these will violate ECP if raising crosses negation. But raising of V to AGR forms AGR, not V, and further raising over the negation element leaves an AGR-trace, not a V-trace. Suppose now that V-traces, and substantive elements in general, are undeletable, whereas AGR-trace, having no function in the language, is deletable; I will place this suggestion in a more general context directly. Then raising of V-AGR to I over negation does not violate ECP at LF, because the "offending trace" will be deleted, in the spirit of Lasnik and Saito. We conclude, then, that the real principle involved is ECP; the Head Movement Constraint is a descriptive artifact, valid only insofar as it follows from ECP, not otherwise.

Summarizing, the real principle is ECP, not HMC. Second, the principle of "least effort" requires raising at S-structure where possible, and requires application of principles of UG instead of language-specific rules where possible. Furthermore, we refine the notion of deletion, requiring deletion of irrelevant elements and forbidding the deletion of those that play an LF role.

We conclude that deletion and insertion are "last resort" operations, to be applied when, and only when, they are necessary. They thus fall together with movement, also a "last resort" principle, to be applied whenever necessary, not otherwise, a principle that yields the essential properties of the "chain condition" that requires that an A-chain be headed by an element in a Case-marked position and terminate in a theta-marked position, each unique. In short, all operations are "last resort" principles. We now have a specific interpretation of the general "least effort" guideline: the general principle Affect-alpha applies where necessary, but nowhere else.

The intuititive meaning of these observations is that nothing superfluous can take place in a derivation; there can be no superfluous rule application, in a special sense, defined in terms of the difference between universal and language-particular rules. At no point will there be optional application of a rule, a conclusion that may well be too strong, though it should be borne in mind that it is susceptible to various qualifications. Thus there might be a well-defined category of "stylistic rules," with specific properties, that admit optionality. There might be alternative derivations from a particular representation, each "minimal." Or it might be that lexical items have optional properties, each determining certain rule applications. Or certain items might have various properties that can be selectively "attended to" in rule-application. Thus suppose that infinitival I-trace is like AGR-trace in lacking theta properties, but like V-trace in that its projection "matters." It might then either delete or not, depending on which of these properties is considered; if it deletes, I could lower to AGR without "recovery" at LF, and if it doesn't, V and AGR would raise to I; we thus have alternative forms, as Pollock observes possible. There are a variety of such questions, which I will leave open here.

Consider now the analogous principle for representations: the principle that no superfluous elements may appear, the principle FI. I assume here that there are three "fundamental" levels of representation: D-structure, PF, and LF. Each constitutes an "interface" of the syntax (broadly construed) with other systems: D-structure is a projection of the lexicon, via the mechanisms of X-bar theory; PF is associated with articulation and perception, and LF with semantic interpretation. S-structure, on this view, is simply a structure that satisfies conditions established at the three interface levels; it is the solution to a certain set of equations, in effect. There may also be certain additional conditions holding of S-structure, e.g., binding theory conditions, or Case-marking. It then becomes an empirical question whether the choice of structures at the interface levels, or perhaps just D-structure and LF alone, uniquely determine S-structure; it appears that they do, as a matter of fact.

Returning to FI, we take this principle to apply at the three interface levels. It is satisfied by definition at D-structure. At PF and LF, an element can appear only if it receives an interpretation. In the case of a PF element, the interpretation is in terms of language-independent principles of the articulatory and perceptual systems. In the case of an LF element, the interpretation is in terms of language-independent principles of the conceptual system that yield, ultimately, semantic interpretations of expressions.

As a condition on PF representation, the principle FI is invariably adopted without notice or discussion. If some proposed representation contains elements not given a physical interpretation by language-independent rules, we simply do not call this a phonetic representation; rather, it must still be subject to phonological rules that overcome this discrepancy between the representation and the physical interpretation. We now extend this principle to the level LF.

Certain consequences of doing so have been noted in recent literature.[26] Thus, it is an empirical property of natural languages that unlike familiar formal languages, they do not permit vacuous quantifiers. We cannot interpret the sentence "who John met Bill" as meaning "John met Bill," in a manner analogous to familiar formal languages, where the expression "$(x)(2+2=4)$" is understood to mean that $2+2=4$. Rather, the quasi-quantifier *who* must be associated with some element that can serve as a bound variable, either a trace or a resumptive pronoun. The same is true of other quantificational elements; thus "every some student is here" cannot mean "some student is here," with *every* taken as a vacuous quantifier. Notice that this is from certain standpoints a surprising property of natural language. Formal languages are typically devised to permit vacuous quantification so as to facilitate their description and use. But in these respects, natural languages are "counter-functional." Notice further that if some approach to language requires specific rules or notations to exclude such expressions as "who John met Bill," then we know it is on the wrong track; these expressions are already excluded by the far more general principle FI, so that specific mechanisms and notations are an unnecessary elaboration to prevent them, and cannot be justified, on these grounds at least.

Not only do natural languages not tolerate vacuous quanitification, but they also, in a certain language-specific sense, do not permit free variables, say, interpreted as arbitrary names as in the course of natural induction, or as universally bound in the manner of familiar formal systems. Thus movement of empty operators, as in "John is too stubborn to talk to," leaves a variable, but this variable must be understood as referring to John, not treated as a free variable, referring arbitrarily or universally quantified. A variable of natural language must be "strongly bound": either assigned a range by its operator, impossible in the case of an empty operator, or assigned a value by some antecedent.[27]

We may construe the strong binding requirement as another consequence of FI, which disallows an uninterpreted element at LF.

Further consequences of this general guideline are suggested by consideration of what counts as a proper element at the LF level. The question here is analogous to the question of what counts as a phonetic element at the PF level. It seems that the following elements are required at LF:[28]

1 Arguments, which are A-chains headed by and terminating with an element in an A-position, the latter theta-marked, the former Case-marked
2 Adjuncts, which are A-bar chains, headed and terminated by elements in A-bar positions
3 Lexical elements, which are chains headed and terminated by elements in X^0-positions
4 Predicates, possibly predicate chains if there is predicate raising, VP-movement in syntax, and so on
5 Operator-variable constructions, each a two membered chain (X_1, X_2), where the operator X_1 is in an A-bar position and the variable X_2 is in an A-position.

Suppose that these are the only possible elements at LF. Then the rule Affect-alpha may apply (and must apply) only to yield such an element, given an illegitimate object. We conclude, on earlier assumptions briefly indicated, that AGR-trace must be eliminated, and a V-trace may not be eliminated, as required for the proper functioning of ECP if the argument sketched earlier is correct.

More broadly, consider successive-cyclic A-bar movement from an argument position. This will yield a chain that is not a legitimate object, and that can become a legitimate object, namely an operator-variable construction, only by eliminating intermediate A-bar traces. We conclude, then, that these must be deleted by LF.[29] In contrast, intermediate A-bar traces formed by successive-cyclic movement from an A-bar position need not be deleted, since the chain formed is already a legitimate object, namely, an adjunct; since they need not be deleted, they may not be deleted, by the "least effort" principle for derivations. the same is true for A-chains (arguments) and X^0-chains (lexical elements). The result is that we derive, in effect, the basic principle for trace-deletion stipulated in the Lasnik-Saito theory of ECP, now a consequence of the general principle of Full Interpretation, except that we strengthen "may delete" to "must delete." There are further consequences, and interesting questions arise with regard to the Specifier of Noun Phrases, which shares some properties of A-positions and other properties of A-bar positions, but I will not pursue these matters here.

Consider now the status of expletive elements, such as English *there*. This is not a legitimate LF object, so it must be somehow removed. Let us assume that it is undeletable, since it has specific features (the same will be true of expletive *pro*). Then we must treat *there* as in effect an LF-affix; something must be adjoin to it. Other principles conspire to yield the conclusion that the only element that can adjoin to the expletive is the phrase associated with it in the interpretation, for example, *a man* in "there is a man in the room"; this must raise to adjoin to the expletive at LF, yielding the phrase "there-[$_{NP}$ a man]" as subject. Making the natural assumption that *there* has no agreement features, these features will "percolate" from *a man* to the full NP in the normal manner, yielding the conclusion that verbal agreement must already have been established properly at S-structure, relating the AGR element of the clause with the associate of the expletive, as required. Furthermore, no binding theory (Condition (C)) problem arises with regard to the expletive and its associate, since these may simply have different indices (or no linking, in Higginbotham's sense; note that we cannot assume the expletive to be unindexed – thus it might have raised, leaving an indexed trace). It also follows that the relation between *there* and its associate must satisfy all movement conditions: binding conditions, ECP, and others. As noted by Luigi Burzio, this is true as a descriptive fact, now reduced to FI. Adopting Adriana Belletti's theory of partitive case, we can also account naturally for the fact that such expressions as "there seems a man to be in the room" are illegitimate, though binding conditions and others are satisfied by the pair (*there, a man*). We also derive some of the scopal properties of *there* noted particularly by Edwin Williams, since the phrase *a man* will be deeply embedded at LF and thus cannot take clausal scope. There are other interesting consequences that I will not pursue, particularly, when we bring into account observations of Howard Lasnik that undermine the concept of case-transmission through expletive chains.

Reviewing this line of argument, here only indicated in a sketchy way, we have a "least effort" principle that applies to derivations and to representations: there can be no superfluous steps in derivations, and no superfluous elements in representations. As illustrated, the empirical consequences of this assumption are quite ramified. Notice that there is no a priori reason to assume that any of this is true. On the contrary, it seems counter-functional in certain respects. In fact, these respects go far beyond what I have already indicated. Least effort properties such as these induce extreme problems of computational intractability, since they imply that the structural description of an expression must satisfy highly "global" properties. Therefore, if language design really satisfies these conditions, then languages are unusable in a far-reaching sense. I have already noted that they are unusable in more limited respects, a fact that in no way impedes communication, but here the problem is deeper, almost paradoxical.

The paradox, however, is resolvable. In each of the specific cases where we have found empirical consequences for these global "least effort" guidelines, now raised closer to the level of principles of UG, there are computational tricks that will overcome the problem of intractability. Thus the "last resort" condition on movement reduces to the condition that Case-marked elements cannot be moved, and the similar condition on deletion reduces to the requirement that AGR-trace must be eliminated and the Lasnik-Saito stipulation on intermediate A-bar traces, now slightly modified. These consequences of the principles are readily checked. The same is true in the other cases. The conclusion is that although the general design of the system yields computationally intractable problems, specific features of language design often allow them to be overcome by computational tricks. Only when such specific computational devices are available can the expressions be actually used. But this, as we have already seen, is all that is required for the use of language; unusable parts of the language are simply not used, as in the case of multiple-embedding, evidently a deep feature of language design.

Notice that the "least effort" guidelines, now expressed in terms of eliminating superfluous steps in derivations and superfluous elements in representations, have a kind of generality that is lacking in specific principles of UG, such as the principles of binding theory, Case theory, or the theory of government, though some of these too can be related to considerations of locality and others of some apparent generality. Nevertheless, the actual formulation of the principles appears to be highly specific to the language faculty. The generality is, furthermore, more a matter of elegance than utility; it is the kind of property that one seeks in core areas of the natural sciences, for example, in searching for conservation principles, symmetry, and the like.

The general conclusion that seems to come to the fore, if these speculations are on the right track, is that language is designed as a system that is "beautiful," but in general unusable. It is designed for elegance, not for use, though with features that enable it to be used sufficiently for the purposes of normal life. These are properties of language that have been observed in other respects as well. Thus it has often proven to be a useful guiding intuition in research that if some property of language is "overdetermined" by proposed principles, then probably the principles are wrong, and some way should be found to reconstruct them so as to avoid this redundancy. Insofar as this is true, the system is elegant, but badly designed for use. Typically, biological systems are not like this at all. They are highly redundant, for reasons that have a plausible functional account.

Redundancy offers protection against damage, and might facilitate over-coming problems that are computational in nature. Why language should be so different from other biological systems is a problem, possibly even a mystery. We must, of course, take into account the possibility that all such conclusions might prove to be a kind of artifact, a result of our methods of investigation and theory construction, not properties of the real object of the real world that we are investigating. There is fairly good evidence, however, that this is not the case, at least over a considerable range.

We might suppose that these properties of language, if indeed they are real, are related to other features of language that are unusual, possibly unique, among biological organisms. Language is, at its core, a system that is both digital and infinite. To my knowledge, there is no other biological system with these properties, apart from the number system, also a unique human possession it appears, and quite probably, derivative from the language faculty. Note that existence of the "number faculty" in humans is something of a problem for the theory of evolution, since evidently having this capacity was not a factor in human evolution. It must therefore have developed as a by-product of some other system, and the natural proposal is that it is derived from the human language faculty. We might imagine that the language faculty yields the number faculty by simple abstraction from the specific properties of language, leaving only the capacity for recursive enumeration. We still are left with the problem of how this capacity developed in humans and how a messy system such as the brain could have developed an infinite digital system in the first place. In this regard, speculations about natural selection are no more plausible than many others; perhaps these are simply emergent physical properties of a brain that reaches a certain level of complexity under the specific condi-tions of human evolution. Here, we move to questions that are, at the moment, intractable, though they do not seem as intractable as those that may well be true mysteries for human intelligence.

Reviewing where we now stand, with regard to the language faculty, a reasonable position seems to me to be something like this. For unknown reasons, the human mind/brain developed the faculty of language, a computational-representational system based on digital computation with recursive enumeration and many other specific properties. The system appears to be surprisingly elegant, possibly observing conditions of nonre-dundancy, global "least effort" conditions, and so on. It also seems to have many properties, including some deeply rooted in its basic design, that make it dysfunctional, unusable, although adequate for actual use over a sufficient range because of other special properties, a fact that might or might not be relevant to its persistence and development in the human species. The properties of the language faculty seem to be unique to humans in interesting respects and distinct from other subsystems of the mind/brain. The mind, then, is not a system of general intelligence, as has been assumed over a very broad spectrum, including classical rationalism and empiricism and modern variants of empiricist thought including dominant tendencies in contemporary philosophy and cognitive science, in particular most of the AI literature, and in modern psychology, including a spectrum that ranges from Skinner to Piaget. Rather, the mind has distinct subsystems, such as the language faculty, a cognitive system, a system of knowledge, not an input or output system.

This faculty, furthermore, is internally highly modularized, with separate subsystems of principles governing sound, meaning, structure and interpretation of linguistic expressions. These can be used, to a sufficient degree, in thought and its expression, and in specific language functions such as communication; language is not intrinsically a system of communication, nor is it the only system used for communication. The language faculty is based on fixed principles with limited options of parametric variation as the system is "tuned" to a specific environment, yielding a finite number of core languages apart from lexicon, also sharply constrained; it may be that these principles yield only one core language, apart from properties of the lexicon. Some day, I presume, we will reach the point of understanding that the notion of "core language" is eliminable, and we will not distinguish I-language from core language. That is, the systems found in the world will not be regarded as languages in the strict sense, but as more complex systems, much less interesting for the study of human nature and human language, just as most of what we find around us in the world of ordinary experience is unhelpful for determining the real properties of the natural world.

A rich system of knowledge, including in particular knowledge-that and knowledge-how, develops over a broad, in fact infinite range. Contrary to what is often supposed, knowledge-that and knowledge-how, in particular, cannot be understood in terms of ability; rather, ability to use a system of knowledge must be clearly distinguished from possession of this knowledge. Furthermore, such knowledge does not satisfy the standard conditions of epistemology; it is not obtained by general principles, is not based on good reasons or justified, or anything of the sort. Rather, what we come to know and understand is determined by our biological nature in quite substantial ways, which we can sketch out with some degree of specificity in a range of interesting cases. We have knowledge of some aspect of the world only when the systems that develop in the mind/brain, and our modes of interpreting data as experience, conform to a sufficient degree with elements of the world around us.

I have spoken only of language, which happens to be one of the few domains of cognitive psychology where there are rather far-reaching results. But I think it would hardly be surprising if the truth of the matter were qualitatively similar in other domains, where far less is known. As far as I can see, only ancient prejudice makes this prospect appear to many to be unlikely.

NOTES

1 We presumably want to interpret "lexical property" broadly, not restricted to properties of individual lexical items but including also such properties as

canonical government, stated over items of the X^0 category, hence in this sense a property of the lexicon.

2 Anna-Maria di Sciullo and Edwin Williams, *On the Definition of Word* (MIT Press, Cambridge, Mass., 1987).

3 Mark Baker, *Incorporation: A Theory of Grammatical Function Changing* (University of Chicago Press, Chicago, 1988).

4 Susan Curtiss, "Dissociations between language and cognition: cases and implications," *Journal of Autism and Developmental Disorders*, II. 1 (1981).

5 Marion Blank, "Language without communication: a case study," *Journal of Child Language*, 6 (1979).

6 Susan Carey, *Conceptual Change in Childhood* (MIT Press, Cambridge, Mass., 1985).

7 Barbara Landau and Lila Gleitman, *Language and Experience: Evidence from the Blind Child* (Harvard University Press, Cambridge, Mass., 1985); Carol Chomsky, "Analytic study of the Tadoma method: language abilities of three deaf-blind subjects," *Journal of Speech and Hearing Research*, 29 (September 1986), pp. 332–47.

8 See Susan Goldin-Meadow, "The resilience of recursion: a study of a communication system developed without a conventional language model," in *Language Acquisition: The State of the Art*, ed. E. Wanner and L. Gleitman (Cambridge University Press, Cambridge, 1982). Expressing a standard view, Edward Sapir writes (in *Language*) that if we "eliminate society," then "there is every reason to believe" that a child "will learn to walk," but "it is just as certain that he will never learn to talk." Neither conclusion is well-founded empirically; what form of locomotion a "wolf-child" might adopt is debatable, and the study just cited questions the certainty of Sapir's statement about language, though it is technically true, tautologically, as Sapir formulates it, taking "to talk" to mean "to communicate ideas according to the traditional system of a particular society."

9 Murray Cohen, *Sensible Words* (Johns Hopkins University Press, Baltimore, 1977).

10 On these matters, see my *Reflections on Language* (Pantheon, New York, 1975).

11 Michael Dummett, in *Truth and Interpretation: Perspectives on the Philosophy of Donald Davidson*, ed. E. LePore (Basil Blackwell, Oxford and New York, 1986).

12 Michael Dummett, "The social character of meaning," in *Truth and Other Enigmas* (Harvard University Press, Cambridge, Mass., 1978); cited by Alex George, "Whose language is it anyway?," ms., Wolfson College, Oxford, rejecting Dummett's claim.

13 On these matters, see my *Knowledge of Language* (Praeger, New York, 1986); and on Dummett, see also *Reflections on Language*.

14 George, "Whose language is it anyway?"

15 Hilary Putnam, *Representation and Reality* (MIT Press, Cambridge, Mass., 1988).

16 For references and further discussion, here and below, see my paper "Language and interpretation: philosophical reflections and empirical inquiry," ms., 1988; to appear in the University of Pittsburgh Series on the Philosophy of Science.

17 The examples commonly adduced are typically drawn from domains where little is understood, and where evidence is quite ambiguous. That such domains exist is not surprising, and tells us little. But in other areas involving

lexical items with relational structure and principles of syntax including referential dependency and the like, the evidence is often much clearer, and there is a considerable range of understanding. It is here, then, that we should turn in trying to resolve the issues.

18 Gibson, and Quine's response, in *The Philosophy of W. V. Quine*, ed., Edward Hahn and Paul Arthur Schilpp (Open Court, La Salle, 1986).

19 Richard Rorty, in *Truth and Interpretation*, ed. LePore.

20 The John Locke lectures, in Putnam's *Meaning and the Moral Sciences* (Routledge and Kegan Paul, London, 1978). See my *Rules and Representations* (Columbia University Press, New York, 1980), on this variant of the argument.

21 Thomas Nagel, "Subjective and objective," in *Mortal Questions* (Cambridge University Press, Cambridge, 1979).

22 Karl Popper, *Conjectures and Refutations* (Routledge and Kegan Paul, London, 1963). There seems to be some ambiguity on this matter in some of the work in "evolutionary epistemology," but I will not pursue the matter here.

23 Noam Chomsky, "Problems and mysteries in the study of human language," in *Language in Focus: Foundations, Methods, and Systems*, ed. Asa Kasher (Reidel, Dordrecht, 1976); reprinted in my *Reflections on Language*.

24 Jean-Yves Pollock, "Verb movement, UG and the structure of IP," *Linguistic Inquiry* 20 (1989), pp. 365–424. Pollock develops his ideas somewhat differently and with much broader empirical scope than is indicated here.

25 Alternatively, as Howard Lasnik suggests, it might be that a morphological property is involved, with only "strong AGR" able to host a "strong element."

26 See *Knowledge of Language*.

27 In these terms, we would interpret the empty operator binding *pro* in the sense of James Huang's work on Chinese as "restricted," in that it is necessarily discourse related. There are also semi-free variables such as PRO and *one*, which, however, always appear to have special properties, specifically, human or animate (e.g., "it is common to roll down a hill" does not refer to a rock).

28 Note that chains can be minimal, with only a single position.

29 They might be present at earlier stages, where licensing conditions do not yet apply, serving, as Norbert Hornstein observes, to permit the application of the principles Andrew Barss suggests for the interpretation of anaphors in displaced phrases.

Part II

3

Why Phonology is Different

Sylvain Bromberger and Morris Halle

1 INTRODUCTION

Those who have followed the development of generative syntax are aware of the fact that until well into the 1970s research was based on the presumption that the syntactic component of a grammar should consist of ordered transformations that derive S-structures (and later L-forms) from D-structures (themselves generated by phrase structure rules) through intermediate structures. Though there were discussions on whether the order of transformations peculiar to each language was entirely the consequence of universal principles or was in part language-specific, and though questions were raised about the significance of intermediate structures, there was general consensus about the basic premises. Even a cursory perusal of the journals of the period or of such influential textbooks as those by Akmajian and Heny (1975), Baker (1978), or Perlmutter and Soames (1979) shows that problems concerning the right ordering of transformations and their applicability to intermediate structures were at the center of research and teaching. This earlier state contrasts dramatically with the situation in syntactic theory in more recent times, especially since the publication in 1981 of Chomsky's *Lectures on Government and Binding*. Questions about the ordering of transformations and about intermediate representations have all but disappeared from syntax – at least in the versions of the theory that have accepted the GB framework and its later developments.

This course of events obviously raises the question whether phonology should not undergo a similar development, i.e. whether phonological theory should not be restructured in such a way as to exclude rule ordering and representations that are neither underlying representations nor surface forms.[1] And there have been a number of attempts in recent years to reformulate phonology without recourse to extrinsic rule order, strict cyclicity, etc.; see, e.g., Kaye and Lowenstamm (1986) and Majdi and Michaels (1987).

We shall argue here that derivations based on ordered rules (i.e., external ordering)[2] and incorporating intermediate structures are essential to phonology, i.e. represent an uneliminable aspect of linguistic knowledge. Some – though not all – of our arguments will turn out to be updated versions of original arguments advanced in support of external ordering in phonology (see e.g. Halle 1962), for many of these appear to be no less sound now than they were a quarter of a century ago when they were first advanced. The crux of our position is that facts pertaining to the two domains – phonology, on the one hand, and syntax and semantics, on the other – are of a very different nature and that there is therefore no reason to assume a priori that they must be covered by formally similar theories. Whether the theories are or are not similar is a contingent matter to be settled in the light of the evidence, and the evidence, as far as we can tell, indicates that they are not formally similar and that the structure of phonology is best thought of as that of a deductive system.

Syntax/semantics as practiced in the 1980s is primarily concerned with the conditions that the deep structure, surface structure, and logical form of a sentence must satisfy.[3] These include conditions peculiar to each level as well as conditions across levels. But the representation of a sentence at each level encodes information about the sentence (e.g., thematic role assignments, binding relations, sequential order, relative scope of operators, meaning, etc.) that is distinct from what a speaker must know in order to articulate a token.

As now understood, each of these three representations is assembled from words and other items stored in the lexicon in a manner instructively similar to the assembling of pieces of a three-dimensional jigsaw puzzle. Just as in the case of the jigsaw puzzle, the overriding considerations are whether – and how – the pieces fit together, and that at the end there be no holes in the assembled shape nor any pieces left over. But the order in which the pieces are assembled does not matter. To extend the analogy we may think of the relationship among the three representations on the analogy of the relationship among the different faces of a tetrahedron. The three representations, like the separate faces of the tetrahedron, are distinct from each other and abstractable from the whole. Yet, like the separate faces of the tetrahedron, they share elements, and thereby impose limits on each other. One might even go so far as to say – though at the price of oversimplification – that the sharing of elements is expressed by the celebrated single transformation "move alpha", while the distinctness of the representations is expressed by the fact that "move alpha" must respect conditions peculiar to each level of representation, e.g. the theta criterion, the ECP, etc. If this picture of the interrelation among syntactic representations is correct then clearly there is no theoretically significant ordering among the principles that govern the interconnections among the three representations, and there is no interesting sense in which any of the representations is "derived" from any of the others through a sequential application of rules and intermediate representations, just as there is no significant ordering among the mutual constraints between the faces of a tetrahedron and no derivation with intermediate forms of one face from another.[4]

Phonology, on the other hand, is primarily concerned with the connections between surface forms that can serve as input to our articulatory machinery (and to our auditory system) and the abstract underlying forms in which words are stored in memory. Whereas syntax is concerned with the relations among representations that encode different types of information requiring different types of notation, phonology is concerned with the relationship between representations that encode the same type of information – phonetic information – but do so in ways that serve distinct functions: articulation and audition, on the one hand, memory, on the other. Since underlying phonological representations of words are stored in speakers' permanent memory, whereas phonetic surface representations are generated only when a word figures in an actual utterance, there is a clear and theoretically significant sense in which underlying representations are prior to surface representations, a sense which justifies thinking of the surface form as "derived" from the underlying form. This fact in turn brings up the question as to the manner in which surface representations are derived from underlying representations. The answer clearly is to be decided by looking at the actual contingent evidence rather than by reflecting on a priori logical or methodological necessities. In particular, there is no a priori reason to hold that the derivations must be subject to a theory formally similar to the theory appropriate for syntax/semantics. We therefore turn next to an examination of some of the relevant evidence.

2   THE SYNCHRONIC EVIDENCE

As noted above, the phonological surface representation must encode how a word is pronounced. It must serve as input to our articulatory machinery, and as a first approximation we shall assume, in conformity with a well-supported tradition in phonology, that the representation required for the articulation of different words is given in the form of stipulations of discrete sound segments concatenated in the order in which they must be produced.[5] Thus, the English word *bell* is represented by a sequence of three symbols, of which the first stands for the plosive [b], the second for the vowel [e], and the third for the lateral [1].

An important result of the research of the last fifty years has been to establish the proposition first advanced by Jakobson (1938) that speech sounds are composite entities constituted by complexes of binary phonetic features such as voicing, nasality, aspiration, etc. As a first approximation we may think of this as an interpretation of the alphabetic symbols of the phonetic alphabet. Thus instead of the sequence [bel] we write (1). (It should be noted that the feature system employed here is that developed in Sagey (1986) with further modifications due to Halle (1988) and differs quite markedly from feature systems utilized in earlier publications by the present authors.)

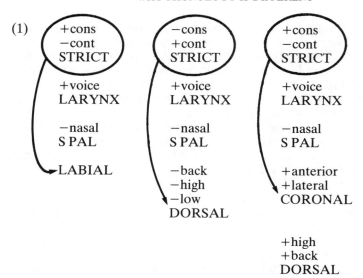

(1)

+cons
−cont
STRICT

−cons
+cont
STRICT

+cons
−cont
STRICT

+voice
LARYNX

+voice
LARYNX

+voice
LARYNX

−nasal
S PAL

−nasal
S PAL

−nasal
S PAL

LABIAL

−back
−high
−low
DORSAL

+anterior
+lateral
CORONAL

+high
+back
DORSAL

The representation in (1) encodes the information which enables a speaker to produce the sound sequence [bel]; i.e. (1) specifies the vocal tract gymnastics necessary for uttering the word *bell*. This gymnastics of the vocal tract is performed by a small number of (six) movable structures which we term *articulators* and which are represented in (1) with capital letters. Each articulator has a small repertoire of distinct (linguistic-phonetic) behaviors which we call *features* and represent by lower-case letters. These behaviors select between binary sets of options, and this fact is reflected by the utilization of coefficients whose value is either *plus* or *minus*. Thus, we can move the DORSAL (tongue body) articulator either backwards towards the rear wall of the pharynx (in response to the feature specification [+back]) or forward, away from the pharynx wall (in response to the feature specification [−back]). The absence of any other feature specification reflects the fact that in producing speech sounds no indication of degree of movement is linguistically significant.

Most features can be actualized only by a single articulator. Thus [nasal] is always implemented by the SOFT PALATE (S PAL), or [voicing] by the LARYNX. This fact is encoded graphically in (1) by grouping the different features and placing them above their articulators. These *articulator-bound* features contrast with *articulator-free* STRICTURE (STRICT) features such as [consonantal] and [continuant]; i.e. with features that can be executed by any one of the LABIAL, CORONAL, or DORSAL articulators. Since the choice of the appropriate articulator reflects a linguistically relevant distinction this choice must be encoded in the representation of the sound. We have indicated this graphically in (1) by means of the arrows connecting [consonantal, continuant] to the articulators appropriate to each sound. It is obvious that not every articulator is – or need be – actively involved in the production of every sound. For example, the tongue blade (CORONAL) and tongue body (DORSAL) articulators play no role in the production of the English consonant [b]. This is encoded in (1) by omitting mention of these articulators in the representation of [b]. In similar fashion a given articulator, though active in the production of a particular sound, may not execute in a linguistically significant way all features of which it is capable. For example, when producing consonants English speakers do not deliberately round the lips or spread them: the feature [round], a behavior of the LABIAL articulator, therefore does not figure in the representation of any English consonant, even of one like [b] which requires active involvement of the LABIAL articulator.

We have noted above that (1) is a surface representation of the English word *bell* in that in principle it provides the information needed by a speaker to produce this word correctly.[6] In addition to surface representations such as (1), words also have abstract underlying representations, i.e. representations that encode the form in which words are stored in memory; we must now elaborate on this. Utterances are, to a first approximation, sequences of word tokens produced one after another. But speakers can produce an utterance only if they know the words of which it is composed. But what does it mean for a speaker to know a word? At a minimum when a speaker knows a word she/he knows that a given sequence of speech sounds is a word in her/his language. E.g., speakers of English know the words [boy] and [bel] but not [naʕar] and [paʕamon], known by speakers of Hebrew. It is for this reason that under normal circumstances [boy] and [bel] may figure in their utterances, but not [naʕar] and [paʕamon].

However this sort of knowledge is not innate. It must be acquired and retained – as is obvious from the fact that children raised in different language communities acquire different lexicons. Thus learning a language involves – among other things – registering a long list of words in memory. There is good reason to assume that speakers represent words in their memory by means of a code that is directly related to ways of producing linguistic sounds and that words are stored in memory as sequences of items in such a code. Specifically, *boy* and *bell* are not represented in memory by a numerical code where some arbitrary numeral like 797 stands for the former and some other arbitrary numeral like 2593 for the latter. Rather the symbols in memory stand in a direct relation to the production of sounds, so that, for instance, *boy* and *bell* are both represented by three (complex) symbols, of which – in these two examples – the first are the same, and the other two different.

Not all of the information required for producing a word phonetically is needed by speakers for storing the word in memory and for retrieving it when the occasion arises, because a significant fraction of that information is predictable through general rules and principles that govern the pronunciation of English and that are also part of the speaker's knowledge of his/her language. For example, in English all vowels and the lateral [l] are invariably [+voiced] and [−nasal]. Moreover, the behavior of the tongue body (DORSAL) in the lateral is governed by special rules which depend on the phonetic context. Finally, in vowels the articulator-free features [consonant] and [continuant] are universally implemented by the DOR-SAL articulator. Moreover, vowels are always [+continuant]. When information recoverable through these rules is eliminated from (1) the word *bell* is represented as in (2).

(2)

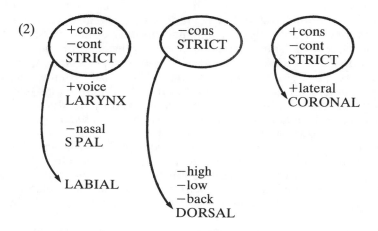

If, as implied above, memory storage and search time are at a premium in the case of language, then (2) will serve as an effective underlying representation of the word *bell*, since in (2) information which is retrieved through the general rules of the language is systematically omitted. It is important to notice that the omitted information is absolutely crucial for the correct phonetic realization of the word and that it must therefore be accessible to the speaker. Thus, both representations (1) and (2) play a significant role in accounting for our ability to speak.[7]

The rules supplying the information missing in the underlying representation must be applied in a definite order. As evidence consider the English rules of syllabification and of stress assignment. Both of these rules provide information essential for the production of English words, and account for the fact that this information is completely predictable and must therefore not appear in the underlying representations. In the overwhelming majority of English words stress is assigned to the (ante)penultimate syllable S* if the following syllable S** has a nonbranching core, otherwise stress is assigned to S**. (For details see Chomsky and Halle 1968 and Halle and Vergnaud 1987.) Since stress assignment is thus dependent on whether or not certain syllables have a branching core, stress cannot be assigned until the word has been syllabified. But syllable structure of an English word in turn is totally predictable from the sounds that compose the word. In short both syllable structure and stress are predictable, and therefore do not appear in the underlying representations, but are introduced into the surface representation as a result of the application of certain rules. But the rules assigning syllable structure and those assigning stress are distinct rules since they affect different aspects of the representation and do not always operate in tandem. Moreover, the stress rules must apply after the rule of syllable structure assignment since the stress rule requires information that is not present until syllable structure has been assigned.

The rules discussed so far are rules which add features omitted from underlying representations. But underlying representations can differ from surface representations not only in containing fewer specified features. They can also differ in assigning different values (coefficients) to features present in both. This difference between the two representations is ultimately a consequence of the fact that, like all physical systems, the individual articulators are subject to inertia and their movements are influenced by their earlier positions and movements and by simultaneous movements and positions of other articulators. Although these contextual effects are in their origin due to mechanical factors, they achieve certain articulatory optimizations which are brought about in different ways by different languages. They are thus not mere effects of the physics or physiology involved. They are brought about through the application of language-specific rules, i.e. rules that speakers acquire in the course of their linguistic maturation and that are part of their knowledge of their language.

A typical example of this sort is the process of English colloquial speech that turns intervocalic [t] and [d] into a voiced flapped stop. The main effect of flapping is to eliminate the distinction between /t/ and /d/ in certain contexts; as a result utterances (words) that differ in their underlying representations become phonetically indistinguishable as illustrated in (3).

(3)   plotting – plodding   wetting – wedding   butting – budding

In many dialects flapping takes place on some occasions and not on others. In some dialects, however, flapping is institutionalized so that it is applied consistently by speakers and failure to flap is perceived in such dialects as affectedness, "putting on an act", etc. We shall assume here that in such dialects flapping is in part due to a rule that somewhat informally is stated in (4).

$$(4) \begin{bmatrix} -\text{continuant} \\ \text{CORONAL} \end{bmatrix} \rightarrow [+\text{voiced}] \text{ in env.} \begin{bmatrix} -\text{consonantal} \\ \text{stressed} \end{bmatrix} \underline{\quad} \begin{bmatrix} -\text{consonantal} \\ \text{unstressed} \end{bmatrix}$$

As a result of (4), underlying voiceless /t/ in certain environments is phonetically implemented as voiced; or put differently, in certain contexts /t/ has a different specification for the feature [voice] in underlying representation to that for the surface representation.

A striking feature of many Canadian dialects of English is the implementation of the diphthongs [ay] and [aw] as [ʌy] and [ʌw] in position before voiceless consonants. We exemplify the contrasts in (5) and give an informal statement of the rule responsible for them in (6).

(5)   a   r[ay]z   r[ʌy]ce   r[aw]se   m[ʌw]se
             tr[ay]be   tr[ʌy]pe   cl[aw]d   cl[ʌw]t
      b   r[ayD]ing   wr[ʌyD]ing   cl[awD]ed   sh[ʌwD]ed

(6)   [−cons]→[−low] in env.   __   [−voiced]
                                 stressed

A fact of special interest is that in most Canadian dialects that are subject to both rules (4) and (6), rule (6) does not apply to words with underlying /d/ but only to words with underlying /t/. We have exemplified this in (5b).

We can predict this result if we assume that rule (6) is ordered before (4) and that application of a phonological rule is subject to Principle (7).

(7)   Phonological rules are ordered with respect to one another. A phonological rule R does not apply necessarily to the underlying representation; rather R applies to the derived representation that results from the application of each applicable rule preceding R in the order of the rules.

There are Canadian dialects where rule (6) does not apply in words of the type illustrated in (5b), but which do not differ from other dialects in the pronunciation of the words in (5a). As noted already in SPE these dialects differ from the latter in that rule (4) is ordered before (6) rather than after (6).

It is worth noting that Principle (7) was not needed to account for the order in which the rules of syllabification and stress assignment are applied in English. That ordering did not need to be explicitly stipulated. It could be achieved by the simple proviso that a rule applies whenever conditions for its application are satisfied. Principle (7) is needed if conditions for the application of more than one rule are satisfied simultaneously. The order of application then – as the Canadian example shows – becomes a language- specific matter. The validity of Principle (7) in phonology and its absence from syntax/semantics is one revealing manfestation of the fact that the representations treated by phonology differ in nature from those treated by syntax/semantics.

Rule ordering is one of the most powerful tools of phonological descriptions and there are numerous instances in the literature where the ordering of rules is used to account for phonetic effects of great complexity. Until and unless these accounts are refuted and are replaced by better confirmed ones we must presume that Principle (7) is correct. If we are right, Principle (7) is also one of the major features that distinguish syntax/semantics from phonology.

We have presented instances where the surface representation is derived from the underlying representation by the application of several ordered rules. It is, of course, possible to account for all of the empirically observed facts of phonology without rule ordering. Since the number of words stored in the memory of a fluent speaker is relatively small (hardly ever exceeding 100,000 items), it is in principle possible to account for the pronunciation of each word by a separate rule. Such an approach, however, would be grossly implausible since it would exclude rules like (4) and (6), which speakers clearly know, as shown, e.g., by the fact that when presented with written words they have not encountered before speakers pronounce these in conformity with rules (4) and (6). If every word were acquired with its own rule of pronunciation and if no phonological rules were known to speakers, then speakers would not know how to pronounce words not previously encountered and there would be no reason to expect speakers to pronounce them in a way that corresponds systematically to the way they pronounce other words.

Another logical possibility to be explored in which Principle (7) plays no role is that all rules apply to underlying representations, and hence that the relations between the underlying representations and the surface representations are never mediated by derivations made up of intervening forms. We believe that this possibility is rather implausible in the light of the following sort of evidence. Consider the second Canadian dialect mentioned above, in which the contrast between *riding* and *writing* is systematically eliminated; i.e. where, according to the account presented above, rule (4) is ordered before (6). If rules were applied to the underlying representation only, then instead of rule (4) we would need a rule such as (8) to account for the facts.

(8) $[-\text{cons}] \rightarrow [-\text{low}]$ in env. ___ $[-\text{voiced}]$
           stressed

   but not in env. ---- t V

This rule is more complex than rule (4) since it includes an exception stated in the "but not" clause. The inclusion of this clause is motivated solely by the theoretical decision to drop Principle (7). But note that Principle (7) purports to be a universal principle, i.e. a principle of universal phonology. It should thus be viewed as something that does not have to be acquired but is part of the innate endowment of potential speakers. Rules like (4) and (6) and (8) have to be learned separately. Complex rules with exception clauses are evidently more difficult to discover in a random corpus than are exceptionless rules.[8] Thus the hypothesis that rules like (8) are acquired, rather than rules like (6) under the guidance of (7), is much more difficult to reconcile with the known ease and rapidity with which children learn to speak their dialect, and that hypothesis is thus much less plausible.

It has been known, at least since Chomsky and Halle (1968) drew attention to this fact, that the strict linear order of rules implicit in (7) is not maintained everywhere. These deviant rule orderings are predictable in the sense that they occur only when specific conditions are met; they are therefore not violations of the principle of linear rule order but rather further characterizations of the principle.

The most important of these further characterizations are the following three. First, if A and B are two rules, and the conditions for the application of A include all the conditions for the application of B, but not vice versa (i.e. the application of A is subject to more conditions than the application of B) then A is ordered before B, and B cannot apply to any string to which A has applied. This type of *disjunctive* rule ordering has been studied by Kiparsky (1973); see also Myers (1985), Halle and Vergnaud (1987) and Mahajan (1988).

Second, the order of application of some rules is determined by the internal constituent structure of words. This is the famous cyclic order of rule application which has provoked some of the most ingenious work in modern phonology.[9]

Third, every phonological rule must be assigned to one of several blocks or *strata* and the strata to which it is assigned determine whether a rule applies cyclically to the immediate constituents of a word, or whether it applies only once to the entire word.[10]

When fully specified so as to incorporate these three extensions Principle (7) is exceptionless.

3   THE DIACHRONIC EVIDENCE

Further evidence for the psychological reality of ordered rules (and hence for derivations) in phonology is provided indirectly by the phenomenon of diachronic sound change. We recall that research on sound change began in the nineteenth century as an attempt to account for the observation that in Sanskrit, Greek, Latin and a number of other languages cognate lexical items exhibit widespread and systematic phonetic resemblances. As is well known it had been suggested by Sir William Jones, a high official in the British civil service in India, that the striking resemblances among cognate words in these languages, spoken in widely separate geographic locales, could not have arisen by accident and that the only plausible explanation for them is that these languages all descend from a common proto-language. Nineteenth-century linguistics adopted this proposition and devoted its major and best efforts to displaying in detail the regularities that link the different Indo-European languages to their proto-language. By the end of the nineteenth century the phonological system of the Indo-European proto- language had been reconstructed in a surprisingly convincing way. A crucial aspect in this reconstruction was the postulation of "sound laws" relating earlier stages of the language to later stages.

Consider for instance the first part of Grimm's Law, surely one of the most securely established of all "sound laws," which accounts for phonetic correspondences between the words of Germanic on the one hand and those of the other Indo-European languages, such as Greek, Sanskrit, Latin, and Baltic, on the other. The "law" consists of three distinct parts, of which the first part, which is of especial interest here, can be stated formally as in (9a).

(9)   a $\begin{bmatrix} -\text{cont} \\ -\text{voiced} \end{bmatrix}$ →[+cont] except after obstruent

The evidence for this "law" is found in correspondence such as those in (9b) below:

b	Germ	Greek	Latin	Sanskrit	Baltic	
	fot	pod	ped	pad	ped	"foot"
	θre	tri	trēs	tray	tri	"three"
	xund	kun	kan	svan	sun	"dog"
	naxt	nukt	nokt	naktis	nakt	"night"

Formally this "law" is indistinguishable from a phonological rule such as (10a) which accounts for the fact that English [p t k] must be aspirated in the words in (10b) but unaspirated in the words in (10c).

(10)   a $\begin{bmatrix} -\text{cont} \\ -\text{voiced} \end{bmatrix}$ →[+aspirated] at the beginning of a stressed
syllable

   b   pill till kill

   c   spill still skill   soapy naughty shaky

(9a) and (10a) have exactly the same format and differ only in the features indicated to the right of the arrow, i.e. the features affected and in the respective contexts in which the rules apply.

   This formal similarity could be viewed as a mere coincidence. However there is a much more plausible explanation of this similarity, and this is that the addition of phonological rules to a language is the main mechanism responsible for phonetic change. According to this explanation, lawlike phonetic change occurs when speakers add a new rule to their language. The character of the diachronic "sound law" then follows trivially from the character of the added rule, since it simply reflects the latter's operation. So, for instance, on this view, the first part of Grimm's Law given in (9a) describes a diachronic change of forms brought about by the fact that later speaker/hearers had (9a) in their phonology while earlier speaker/hearers did not.[11]

If we accept this explanation – and the arguments in its favor are very strong – information about diachronic linguistic change yields information about the rules in the synchronic phonology of certain speaker/hearers.

The question now arises whether such information can also tell us anything about rule ordering.

In order to answer this question it is necessary to recall that there is a second part to Grimm's Law, which can be formally stated as (11a) and which accounts for the correspondences between Germanic and the other Indo-European languages illustrated in (11b).

(11)   a $\begin{bmatrix} -\text{continuant} \\ -\text{aspirated} \end{bmatrix} \rightarrow [-\text{voiced}]$

	Germ	Greek	Latin	Sanskrit	Baltic	
b	two (Eng.)	duo	duo	duva	divi (Latv.)	"two"
	yoke (Eng.)	dzugon	yugum	yugan	yungas (Lith.)	"yoke"

Grimm's Law thus produced the two sets of changes illustrated in (12): those in (12a) are due to rule (9a), while those in (12b) are produced by rule (11a).

(12)   a   p→f   t→θ   k→x
        b   b→p   d→t   g→k

Is there any reason to believe that these two sets of changes were ordered so that the set in (12a) applied before the set in (12b)?

Bloomfield (1933: 368) thought that there was and his reasons are interesting: "it is clear that in pre-Germanic time, the Primitive Indo-European [b, d, g] can have reached the types of Primitive Germanic [p, t, k] only *after* Primitive Indo-European [p, t, k] had already been changed somewhat in the direction of the type of Primitive Germanic [f, θ, h] – for the actual Germanic forms show that these two series of phonemes did not coincide." Bloomfield assumed rightly that if a language had first undergone the change (12b) and then the change (12a) the effect would have been to turn both [p] and [b] into [f], [t] and [d] into [θ] and [k] and [g] into [x], contrary to known facts about Germanic. In the quoted passage Bloomfield was, of course, talking about diachronic ordering, not about ordering of rules in a synchronic Germanic phonology. However if we assume that the mechanism of rule addition is responsible for the diachronic facts, then Bloomfield's considerations can be turned into reasons for holding that (12a) was ordered before (12b) in the synchronic phonology of Germanic speakers, since, by the same reasoning, the reverse order would also have had the false consequences just described.

So it would seem that evidence from language change does show that the two parts of Grimm's Law must be ordered in the phonology of Germanic.

Unfortunately, the evidence, as it stands, is inconclusive. It does not rule out another possibility, and it is noteworthy that Bloomfield – or to our knowledge any other student of sound change – never entertained it. The other possibility is that both sound changes apply to underlying representations directly. Viewed synchronically this possibility comes down to a denial of Principle (7), at least for rules that bring about linguistic change. Under that hypotheses such rules would not be ordered at all. Since no rule would then have any effect on the input to any other, that would be compatible with the facts that led Bloomfield to order (12a) before (12b). In other words, these facts tell us how Grimm's Law/rules are ordered in the phonology of Germanic *if they are ordered*, but they don't tell us that they are ordered. We therefore also need evidence which shows that rules responsible for diachronic change abide by Principle (7), i.e. do not apply exclusively to underlying representations.

Such evidence is provided by Verner's Law, formally stated as (13):[12]

(13)   [+cont]→[+voiced] after unstressed vowel

Verner's Law is generally believed to have come into the language after Grimm's Law (9a). The evidence adduced for this ordering is that Verner's Law applies not only to the continuant /s/ (which Germanic inherited unchanged from proto Indo-European) but also to continuants that have appeared as a result of (9a). That evidence, conjoined now in the familiar way with the hypothesis that "sound laws" are the effect of the addition of phonological rules, unlike the earlier evidence, does constitute a conclusive argument for the view that in the phonology of Germanic, Verner's Law operated after (9a). This is so, because the new evidence shows that (13) must apply to some outputs of (9a), whereas the evidence used by Bloomfield showed that (12b) may not apply to outputs of (12a). It was evidence against one way of ordering rules, not for ordering them in a certain way.

However, it might be objected, as long as we restrict ourselves to diachronic evidence, (13) – i.e. Verner's Law as usually stated – is not the only way to describe the facts. The changes it describes can also be described with a different, more complicated rule that applies to underlying representations, viz. (14).

(14)   [+cont]→[+voiced]

$$\begin{bmatrix} -\text{cont} \\ -\text{voiced} \end{bmatrix} \rightarrow \begin{bmatrix} +\text{cont} \\ +\text{voiced} \end{bmatrix}$$ after unstressed vowel

$$\begin{bmatrix} -\text{cont} \\ -\text{voiced} \end{bmatrix} \rightarrow \quad [+\text{cont}]$$ except after obstruent or unstressed vowel

If we knew that the changes described by Verner's Law did in fact occur historically after the changes described by Grimm's Law, then we would have a reason to prefer (13) over (14), since we would have reason to believe that (13) describes a set of changes that actually occurred and affected the output of a law (Grimm's) that had already had its effects. But we don't know that. We have no records that bear on these facts.

We might of course appeal to the fact that (13) is simpler than (14). But simplicity by itself does not constitute evidence about what happened in history. Simplicity considerations become pertinent, however, if we remember that the central mechanism of phonological change is the addition of phonological rules. Diachronic laws are nothing but phonological rules that were added to the language at some point in its history. One of the things that distinguishes Germanic from other Indo-European languages is that speakers of Germanic added to their phonology rules that today we call Grimm's Law, Verner's Law, etc. These laws were at one point phonological rules that were actually acquired by individual human beings in the course of their linguistic maturation. As a rule of synchronic phonology (14) is much less plausible than (13), and this for the sort of reasons already cited in connection with the formulation of the rules of Canadian English, i.e., rules (4) and (6). We noted there that it is unlikely that children (learners) innately equipped with Principle (7) would acquire a rule containing a special *exception* clause (see rule (8)) when a functionally equivalent exceptionless rule (i.e. (6)) is available. By the same reasoning the *exception* clause makes it unlikely that children would be able to acquire (14) through exposure to ambient speech, whereas (13) would be relatively easy to acquire by children already equipped innately with Principle (7).[13]

In short then, there are known facts about diachronic changes that are best explained as resulting from the introduction of new phonological rules in the grammar of certain speaker/hearers. When we try to specify what these phonological rules might have been, we find that the more plausible answer assumes that Principle (7) holds of these rules too, and hence that these rules too are ordered in the phonology and operate through derivations.

4 A NOTE ON RECENT HISTORY

Extrinsically ordered rules obeying Principle (7), much like those illustrated above, were employed in a synchronic account of the phonology of a language by the great Sanskrit grammarian Pāṇini over twenty-five hundred years ago. They were assumed standardly – without much discussion – during the nineteenth century (and later) in accounts of different sound changes. Attempts to utilize extrinsically ordered rules in the description of synchronic rather than historical phenomena date back to the 1930s. One of the earliest is Bloomfield's (1939) paper "Menomini

Morphophonemics."[14] Bloomfield describes his approach in the following much quoted passage:

> The process of description leads us to set up each morphological element in a theoretical base form and then to state the deviations from this basic form which appear when the element is combined with other elements. If one starts with the basic forms and applies our statements . . . in the order in which we give them, one will arrive finally at the forms of words as they were actually spoken. Our basic forms are not ancient forms, say of the Proto-Algonquian parent language, and our statements of internal sandhi are not historical but descriptive, and appear in a purely *descriptive order*. However, our basic forms do bear some resemblance to those which would be set up for a description of Proto-Algonquian, some of our statements of alternation . . . resemble those which would appear in a description of Proto-Algonquian, and the rest . . . as to content and order, approximate the historical development from Proto-Algonquian to present-day Menomini. (pp. 105–6)

It is somewhat difficult to empathize today with the belief widely held among linguists in the 1930s that principles operative in languages conceived as synchronic systems functioning autonomously were totally different from the principles operative in the historical evolution of languages. In particular, Principle (7) and derivations of the sort illustrated above seemed to them appropriate only to historical descriptions not to synchronic accounts. In fact, in his book *Language* (1933) Bloomfield fully shared the views about the irrelevance of rule order in synchronic descriptions. He writes:

> The actual sequence of constituents, and their structural order . . . are a part of the language, but *the descriptive order of grammatical features is a fiction* and results simply from our method of describing the forms; it goes without saying, for instance, that the speaker who says *knives*, does not "first" replace [f] by [v] and "then" add [-z], but merely utters a form (*knives*) which in certain features resembles and in certain features differs from a certain other form (namely, *knife*). (p. 213 – our italics)

As we have seen, some six years later, by the time of composing "Menomini Morphophonemics," Bloomfield had changed positions. The fact that Bloomfield had changed his views on this matter, however, was totally ignored by the American linguistic community in the 1940s and 1950s. The article was omitted – "inadvertently" according to Hockett (1970: 494) – in Hockett's "Implications of Bloomfield's Algonquian Studies," which was published in the issue of *Language* (24. 1) dedicated to Bloomfield on the occasion of his sixtieth birthday in 1948. It is not referred to in Hockett's (1954) influential "Two Models of Grammatical Description" (which echoes the passage quoted above from Bloomfield (1933) almost verbatim);[15] nor was it reprinted in Joos's *Readings in Linguistics* of 1957. In fact, the article was so unknown in America that Chomsky tells us that he had not read "Menomini Morphophonemics" until his attention was drawn to it by Halle in the late 1950s. And thereby hangs a tale (with a moral perhaps) with which we conclude this paper.

In the years immediately after the Second World War graduate students in linguistics were taught that words and morphemes had a number of distinct representations each of which corresponded to a specific descriptive level. Three such levels were recognized: the morphophonemic, the phonemic and the phonetic, and at each level the representations were composed of entities that were specific to that level: morphophonemes, phonemes, and phones. The primary focus was on discovering *the correct* phonemic and morphophonemic representations; the correct phonetic representation did not have to be discovered as it was directly given in tokens. Implicit in this doctrine was the further assumption that at each level there was only a single representation, and it is this assumption of the standard theory of the 1950s that distinguished it fundamentally from Bloomfield's (1939) (and Pāṇini's) model. As noted, however, the fact that an alternative approach to phonological description had been tested successfully by Bloomfield was hardly known at the time, and the consensus in the 1940s was that derivations and ordered rules did not belong in synchronic accounts of the phonology of a language.

The prevailing wisdom was challenged in Chomsky's 1951 MA thesis *Hebrew Morphophonemics*. In this early study Chomsky explicitly dissents from the proposition that utterances have single representations at each of the descriptive levels. Rather he assumes that at least some levels are constituted by a set of representations generated by extrinsically ordered rules. Chomsky describes the morphophonemic level as follows: "Beginning with a sequence of morphemes . . . each statement of the . . . grammar specifies certain changes which must be undergone by any sequence of a certain shape. It will appear that an order is imposed on the statements relative to certain criteria of simplicity. Thus the statements are ordered so as to present a maximally simple grammar" (p. 4). In fact, the ordering of the statements is a central objective of Chomsky's investigation; he says "this investigation is limited in that only one 'dimension' of simplicity is considered, viz. ordering" (p. 5).

In the version of Chomsky's thesis published by the Garland Press there is no reference to the fact that, like the rules in Bloomfield's "Menomini Morphophonemics," some of the synchronic rules of Modern Hebrew are identical with well-known sound changes; e.g. MR 34 is identical with the rule of post-vocalic spirantization (see Brockelmann 1916: 84), whereas MR 28 (p. 42) is identical with Vowel Reduction (*ibid*.: 61). As a student of Semitic languages, Chomsky was of course fully aware of these parallels between synchronic and diachronic rules. Unlike most linguists of that period Chomsky (pc) was not concerned about confusing synchronic and diachronic descriptions, and viewed the parallels between the two types of rules as evidence in support of his proposed analysis. He assumed that sound changes are due to the addition of phonological rules, and as a consequence it did not seem to him at all strange that some sound changes should survive as synchronic rules for long periods of time.

Chomsky's treatment of the segholates offers another example in which the historical evolution of forms receives a synchronic interpretation and a form such as [melek] is derived from underlying [malk]. Chomsky reports that this replaces an earlier account where [melek] rather than [malk] was the basic underlying form from which the different surface variants were derived. Chomsky made the change at the suggestion of the late Yehoshua Bar-Hillel, who was one of the few people to study the rather forbidding text of *Hebrew Morphophonemics* in considerable detail. Bar-Hillel pointed out to Chomsky that the assumption that [malk] is the underlying form led to a simpler account than the alternative that had figured in the earlier version that Bar-Hillel was reading. He also noted that this account paralleled the known historical evolution of the language.

In 1951 Chomsky was thus independently led to the same conclusions that Bloomfield had reached twelve years earlier. It is a matter of some puzzlement that none of Chomsky's teachers at the University of Pennsylvania drew his attention to Bloomfield's paper and suggested that he take account of Bloomfield's paper at least by including it in his bibliography. It is idle at this distance in time to speculate as to the reasons for this oversight. In any event, as noted above, Chomsky learned of the existence of Bloomfield's paper only in the late 1950s, many years after submitting his MA thesis.[16]

In his opening paper at this symposium (this volume, chapter 1) Chomsky noted that his work on the phonology of modern Hebrew naturally led him to explore whether some of the devices he had used there might also have a use in syntax. Such a project was especially attractive at that time as phonology was then widely viewed not only as the most advanced branch of the field but also as a model for all other linguistic domains to follow. It took two decades of intensive research for Chomsky to conclude that a syntax of a language does in all likelihood not include a system of extrinsically ordered rules (ordered transformations). Since, as we have tried to suggest in the introductory section of this paper, the subject matter of phonology is intrinsically different from that of syntax, the consequences of this conclusion for phonology are far from self-evident: whether and how the principles-and-parameters approach of Chomsky (1981) should be extended is an empirical question. None of the arguments and facts that led Chomsky to this radical change in position with regard to syntax has any detectable bearing on the structure of phonological theory. By contrast there is much evidence, of the sort adduced above, in support of the view that in phonology extrinsically ordered rules play a major role. In the absence of evidence to the contrary, it would therefore be a mistake to try to eliminate such rules from phonology. To construct phonology so that it mimics syntax is to miss a major result of the work of the last twenty years, namely that syntax and phonology are essentially different.

NOTES

This is a modified version of the paper presented on April 14, 1988 in Jerusalem at the symposium *The Chomskyan Turn*. The authors gratefully acknowledge the support for work on this paper provided by the Van Leer Foundation, Jerusalem, the Center for Cognitive Science, MIT, and the Center for the Study of Language and Information, Stanford University. For critical discussion and advice we are indebted to J. Goldsmith, J. Harris, N. Hornstein, M. Kenstowicz, P. Kiparsky, J. McCarthy, K. P. Mohanan, D. Pesetsky, D. Pulleyblank and J.-R. Vergnaud.

1 We deliberately eschew in this discussion the use of "declarative rules" and "procedural rules" in characterizing the differences between syntax/semantics on the one hand and phonology on the other hand. That terminology, which carries a number of associations from the domain of computational linguistics, strikes us as unhelpful.

2 For the purpose of this paper we limit our use of "derivation" and of "ordering" to non-degenerate cases, i.e. derivations of more than one step and orderings of more than one rule.

3 We set aside here issues surrounding the need to assume logical form as an autonomous level of representation – see, e.g., Williams (1988). Nothing in what follows requires that we take a stand on that issue.

4 J.-R. Vergnaud has drawn our attention to the fact that in accounting for constructions with parenthetical phrases such as *John is not – what I'd call – a great lover* vs. **I would not call what John is a great lover* it may be necessary to assume that the surface structure representation is derived from the deep structure representation. Vergnaud notes, however, that to the best of his knowledge there do not exist outside of phonology derivations where the order of application of a pair of rules or principles must be extrinsically ordered, and it is the existence of this type of derivations and of intermediate representations that is at issue here. In short the issue is not whether representations themselves can be meaningfully ordered, but whether the rules or principles applicable to them are ordered prior to any application (and whether the rules generate intermediate representations).

5 For present purposes we restrict attention exclusively to the articulatory aspect of language and ignore the auditory interpretive system. The role of memory in the interpretation of utterances is obviously very different from its role in production, but we believe that here again words must be stored in maximally succinct form in order to expedite the search. See also note 8.

6 For expository reasons (1) has been simplified by omitting a number of features and other phonetic properties such as sonorant, stress, pitch, length, etc. which would have to be included in a full surface representation of the word.

7 John McCarthy has objected to our attributing the requirement of nonredundant underlying representations to memory limitations. He notes that whatever evidence we have on this matter argues that memory is freely available but that word recognition is hard. Phonology must therefore provide "lots of different ways to get from speech back to the lexical entry," and this retrieval process is most effectively accomplished if the lexical entry is stored in the least redundant form, so that there are numerous ways of getting back from phonetic surface to stored entry. We agree with McCarthy's points about the relevance of retrieval requirements. But we believe that memory limitations

probably also play a role. However, when talking about optimizing memory storage we must distinguish between what is required in order to maximize the number of words that can be stored and what is required in order to store a particular word. We believe that there is probably an upper (but very high) limit to the number of representations that can be memorized and in addition also an upper (relatively low) limit to the complexity of any representation that can be stored or is likely to be stored on the basis of a few exposures. There may be a trade-off between the two limits – i.e., the simpler the representations, the more of them can be stored. We know too little about this to say anything more. But the fact that matters for our purpose – and that is relatively uncontroversial – is that our ability both to store and retrieve representations is increased when what has to be stored is constituted of fewer elements.

8   Norbert Hornstein has rightly pointed out to us that this argument is based on an assumption which needs independent justification, viz. on the assumption that it is easier to learn rules (4) and (6) *and their relative ordering* than it is to learn rules (4) and (8) and nothing about their ordering. All other things being equal the learning of three things must be harder than learning two things, but all other things are not equal here. Note that (8) is a rule of great complexity when stated fully; i.e., when formalized in the full phonological notation. Moreover, the elimination of Principle (7) would not merely require the replacement of (6) by the more complicated rule (8), but would also require the replacement of a host of other relatively simple rules by rules of greater complexity. Consider also that our examples deal with the ordering of only pairs of rules, but that a real phonology involves ordering of triplets, quadruplets, quintuplets, etc. The added complexity in such cases renders the replacement rule totally untransparent, if not unstatable. Finally, there is no reason to believe that these added complexities share general properties which can be encoded in a principle that is available to a learner in the way in which rule ordering is available to a learner equipped with Principle (7). Without some such principle it is unlikely that a learner would discover the exception clauses. Thus the evidence available to us at this time suggests that the answer to Hornstein's question is that a theory based on rules ordering is more plausible than one based on complicated contextual restrictions. We are grateful to Hornstein for drawing our attention to this issue which we had previously overlooked.

9   We cannot discuss this in detail here but see Chomsky and Halle (1968) – e.g., the English stress rule. This cyclic rule order has played a major role in discussions of the theory of Lexical Phonology. See especially Pesetsky (1979), Kiparsky (1982), Halle and Mohanan (1985), Halle and Vergnaud (1987), and Halle (1987b). The concept of "strict cycle" in phonology that has resulted from these discussions is, in our opinion, one of the most intriguing and profound results of modern phonological investigations.

10   See Halle and Mohanan (1985) and Halle (1987b).

11   Although all but self-evident today, it took linguists almost three-quarters of a century to accept the fact that "sound laws" are nothing but phonological rules. The reason for this was that the status of phonological rules in a speaker's knowledge of her/his language was not properly understood until relatively recently. Thus, as Halle (1987a) has argued, Schuchardt's opposition to the "neo-grammarian" doctrine of the exceptionless functioning of the "sound laws" was founded on his belief that a speaker's knowledge of the phonology of his/her language consists exclusively of the knowledge of words and that phonological rules play no role in it.

12 Verner's own formulation reads: "IE *k*, *t*, *p* first became *h*, *θ*, *f* everywhere; the voiceless fricatives that arose in this fashion as well as the voiceless fricative *s* inherited from IE were subsequently voiced in voiced environment syllable-initially, but remained voiceless in position after stressed syllables" (Verner 1876: 114). See also Saussure 1949: 200–2 and Bloomfield 1933: 357–8.

13 Paul Kiparsky has observed that the above account assumes that at the stage where Verner's Law entered the language part 1 of Grimm's Law (i.e. rule (9a)) was still part of the phonology of the language. It is conceivable that this assumption is incorrect and that the effects of Grimm's law had become lexicalized by the time Verner's Law entered the language. Though far from conclusive, there is some evidence militating against the lexicalization of the effects of Grimm's Law. As indicated in (9a) this part of Grimm's Law was contextually restricted so as not to apply in position after obstruents. As a result part 1 of Grimm's Law did not eliminate voiceless stops from the language altogether but only restricted their distribution, and this fact would have to be reflected formally in the phonology, by means of a rule much like (9a). Moreover, (9a) predicts that voiceless obstruents at the beginning of Germanic suffixes should alternate between stop and continuant depending on whether or not these suffixes are attached to stems that end in an obstruent. That prediction is borne out by the behavior of the participial suffix /t/, which regularly alternated in the predicted way. In view of these facts it seems to us somewhat unlikely that the effects of Grimm's Law were lexicalized by the time Verner's Law went into effect.

14 Very similar in approach is Swadesh and Voegelin's (1939) paper on Tübatu-labal. It is difficult at this distance in time to establish whether Bloomfield influenced Swadesh and Voegelin, whether the latter influenced Bloomfield, or whether the ideas were developed independently.

15 According to Hockett a model with extrinsically ordered rules and derivations (which in Hockett's paper is referred to by the initials IP) had been rejected by some workers in favor of a model that expressly violates Principle (7) (the latter approach is labeled IA)

> because of a feeling of dissatisfaction with the "moving-part" or "historical" analogy implicit in IP. At the very least, these analogies seem to imply the necessity of making certain decisions in a possibly arbitrary way. Critics of IP would prefer to circumvent such decisions altogether. For example . . . if it be said that the English past-tense form *baked* is "formed" from *bake* by a "process" of "suffixation," then no matter what disclaimer of historicity is made it is impossible not to conclude that some kind of priority is being assigned to *bake*, as against either *baked* or the suffix. And if this priority is not historical, what is it? Supporters of IP have not answered that question satisfactorily. (p. 211)

16 Noam Chomsky has remarked that our presentation of the positions of structuralist phonology – both American and Praguean – fails to bring out their empiricist and anti-mentalistic foundations. For structuralists phonemes are defined as similarity classes of phones, and morphophonemes as similarity classes of phonemes: all phones of a given phoneme therefore had to share a specific set of phonetic properties that distinguished them from the phones of any other phoneme. In Bloomfield's "Menomini Morphophonemics" the relation between morphophonemes and phonemes and/or phones was conceived in a radically different way: morphophonemes were related to phonemes or to phones by means of rules that "translate" (or map) sequences

of morphophonemes into sequences of phonemes/phones. In effect then, in spite of his frequently professed anti-mentalism, here Bloomfield viewed the two kinds of sequences as equally real (mental) representations of the words, phrases, or sentences of a language. Moreover, on this view there is no longer an a priori (definitional) requirement that the set of phonemes/phones which correspond to a given morphophoneme share some distinguishing set of properties.

The proposition that phonology should deal with mental representations – i.e., with facts that go beyond physical and directly observable events (classified by the linguist) – was not one that linguists were ready to accept in the 1940s and early 1950s when naive forms of positivism were almost universally taken for granted. As a consequence, Bloomfield's paper was treated as a curious experiment – not to say, indiscretion – that did not merit extensive discussion.

REFERENCES

Akmajian, A. and Heny, F. 1975: *An Introduction to the Principles of Transformation Syntax*. Cambridge, Mass.: MIT Press.
Baker, C. L. 1978: *Introduction to Generative-Transformational Syntax*. Englewood Cliffs, New Jersey: Prentice Hall.
Bloomfield, L. 1933: *Language*. New York: Holt.
—— 1939: Menomini morphophonemics. *Etudes dédiées à la mémoire de M. le Prince N. S. Trubetzkoy: Travaux du Cercle linguistique de Prague*, 8, 105–15.
Brockelmann, C. 1916: *Semitische Sprachwissenschaft*. Berlin: G. J. Goschen'sche Verlagshandlung.
Chomsky, N. 1951: *Morphophonemics of Modern Hebrew*. MA Thesis, Department of Linguistics, University of Pennsylvania; published in 1979. New York: Garland Press.
—— 1981: *Lectures on Government and Binding*. Dordrecht: Foris.
Chomsky, N. and Halle, M. 1968: *The Sound Pattern of English*. New York: Harper and Row.
Halle, M. 1962: Phonology in a generative grammar. *Word*, 18, 54–72.
—— 1987a: Remarks on the scientific revolution in linguistics 1926–1929. In K. Pomorska et al., eds., *Language, Poetry and Poetics – The Generation of the 1890: Jakobson, Trubetzkoy, Majakovskij*. Berlin: Mouton de Gruyter, 95–111.
—— 1987b: On the phonology–morphology interface. Unpublished paper, Department of Linguistics, MIT.
—— 1988: Features. To appear in *Oxford Encyclopedia of Linguistics*, Oxford University Press, Oxford and New York.
Halle, M. and Mohanan, K. P. 1985: Segmental phonology and modern English. *Linguistic Inquiry* 16, 57–116.
Halle, M. and Vergnaud, J.-R. 1987: *An Essay on Stress*. Cambridge, Mass.: MIT Press.
Hockett, C. F. 1970: *A Leonard Bloomfield Anthology*. Bloomington: Indiana University Press.
Jakobson, R. 1938: Observations sur le classement phonologique des consonnes. *Proceedings of the 3rd International Congress of Phonetic Sciences*, Ghent. [Also in *Selected Writings* I, Mouton, The Hague and Berlin.]
Joos, M. 1957: *Readings in Linguistics*. Washington: American Council of Learned Societies.
Kaye, J. and Lowenstamm, J. 1986: Compensatory lengthening in Tiberian

Hebrew. In L. Wetzels and E. Sezer, *Studies in Compensatory Lengthening*. Dordrecht: Foris.

Kiparsky, P. 1973: "Elsewhere" in Phonology. In S. Anderson and P. Kiparsky, eds., *A Festschrift for Morris Halle*. New York: Holt, Rinehart, and Winston, Inc., 93–106.

—— 1982: Lexical morphology and phonology. *Linguistics in the Morning Calm*. Seoul: Hansin, 3–91.

Mahajan, A. 1988: Hindi stress. Unpublished paper, Department of Linguistics, MIT.

Majdi, B. and Michaels, D. 1987: Syllable structure, gemination and length in Iraqui. Unpublished paper presented at 62nd Annual Meeting of Linguistic Society of America.

Myers, S. 1985: The long and the short of it: a metrical theory of English vowel quantity. CLS (Chicago Linguistic Society) 21, 275–88.

Perlmutter, D. and Soames, S. 1979: *Syntactic Argumentation and the Structure of English*. Berkeley: University of California Press.

Pesetsky, D. 1979: Russian morphology and lexical theory. Unpublished paper, Department of Linguistics, MIT.

Sagey, E. C. 1986: *The Representation of Features and Relations in Non-Linear Phonology*. Doctoral Dissertation, Department of Linguistics, MIT.

Saussure, F. de 1949: *Cours de linguistique générale*. Paris: Payot.

Swadesh, M. and Voegelin, C. F. 1939: A problem in phonological alternation. *Language* 15, 1–10.

Verner, K. 1876: Eine Ausnahme der ersten Lautverschiebung. *Zeitschrift fuer vergleichende Sprachwissenschaft*, 23, 97–130.

Williams, E. 1988: Is LF distinct from S-structure? *Linguistic Inquiry*, 19, 135–46.

4

Language and Brain: Redefining the Goals and Methodology of Linguistics

Victoria A. Fromkin

1   INTRODUCTION: THE PRE-CHOMSKY PERIOD

Participants invited to *The Chomskyan Turn* workshop were asked to respond to a number of questions, among which were the following:

"To what extent does the methodology of research implicit in Chomskyan Linguistics influence other human sciences and social sciences? To what extent did the Chomskyan methodology come into conflict with prevailing naive methodologies and philosophical orthodoxies?"

My paper is concerned with both these questions and will start with the second, in the attempt to provide some historical context for Chomsky's dramatic influence on all studies of mind and language.

The field of linguistics, like all modern sciences, has undergone numerous paradigm shifts. The publication of *Syntactic Structures* (Chomsky 1957) radically changed the goals, the methodology, and the research questions of the field. Whether one agrees with Leiber's (1975) or Newmeyer's (1980) view that this book was a spark that ignited the flame of a scientific revolution or with Chomsky's view to the contrary (Rieber, 1983), its dramatic influence on the field can be seen by comparing any of the curricula of the seventy-nine programs now offering Ph.Ds in linguistics in the United States with the Ph.D requirements of the handful of doctoral programs which existed in the ante-*Syntactic Structures* era.

Prior to the mid-1960s, the typical MA student, at least at UCLA, was required to have a "theoretical" background based on Joos's (1958) *Readings in Linguistics*, including Bloomfield's (1939) *Linguistic Aspects of Science* and Bloch's (1948) *Postulates*. A major topic in seminars concerned "item and arrangement" vs. "item and process" analysis. Bloomfield's (1933) *Language* and Hockett's (1958) *A Course in Modern Linguistics* were the texts for the prerequisite courses for graduate study. Phonetics and phonemics comprised one course in 1962, the year Peter Ladefoged joined the UCLA faculty; students learned to distinguish the cardinal vowels, received an excellent training in traditional phonetics, learned to produce ejectives and implosives and at least eight contrasting clicks, and became acquainted with Firthian phonology and structural phonemics. UCLA students were somewhat unique in this regard since the British school of prosodic phonology was not on most US linguistics curricula. While Sapir's "Psychological Reality of Phonemes" (Mandelbaum 1949) was read, the only procedures permitted for phonemic analysis had to strictly obey the tabu against "mixing of levels." At UCLA, morphology and syntax, like phonetics and phonemics, were also combined into one course; this presented no problem since little, if any, syntax was taught. Even Harris's (1951) *Methods* was not required reading.

The *Field Methods* course provided excellent training on how to collect and analyze data "in the bush." There was something deeply satisfying about "doing" linguistics, which for us consisted of eliciting utterances from an informant (in my case a Tamil speaker), recording them in a narrow phonetic transcription on three-by-five cards which we filed in the traditional shoe boxes, organizing them into minimal pairs or near-minimal pairs, and analyzing them into a phonemic inventory, complete with all the allophones.

Yet, the early years following the publication of *Syntactic Structures* were exciting ones; the "revolution" had begun. The weekly linguistics seminars at the Rand Corporation in Santa Monica more resembled the storming of the Winter Palace than scholarly discussions. Passions rose, as did voices arguing more about "discovery procedures" and the philosophy of science than about the nature of language. Any semblance of "scientific objectivity" disappeared as the old guard took up arms against the views of the young upstart, Chomsky, and his followers, who, they maintained, were attempting to substitute the "unscientific" notion of intuition for solid empirical data and methodological precision. In our classrooms and in the literature we were required to read, we found ourselves engulfed in a mire of behaviourism, mechanism, empiricism, and inductivism, which still represented the linguistic scientific paradigm of the period.

The famous or infamous mechanistic conclusion of Laplace, formulated in the early part of the nineteenth century, and destined to live only a few scant years in physics, found a rebirth in the field of linguistics with the publication of *Language* (Bloomfield 1933), which was still, in 1962, called the "bible" of American linguistics. Recall Laplace's (1986) position: "Given for one instant an intelligence which could comprehend all the forces by which nature is animated and the respective positions of the beings which composed it, if, moreover, this intelligence were vast enough to submit these data to analysis, it would embrace in the same formula both the movements of the largest bodies in the universe and those of the lightest atom: to it, nothing would be uncertain, and the future as the past would be present to its eyes."

This fundamental error – the assumption that all necessary relationships are already known or derivable from existing relationships, and that all that is required is to supply data to the existing "machine" – was resurrected by Bloomfield a half-century later, as evidenced by the following quotation from *Language*, read and discussed in linguistics courses throughout the country:

> The materialistic (or, better, *mechanistic*) theory supposes that the variability of human conduct, including speech, is due only to the fact that the human body is a very complex system. Human actions . . . are part of cause-and-effect sequences exactly like those which we observe, say in the study of physics or chemistry . . . We could foretell a person's actions (for instance, whether a certain stimulus will lead him to speak, and, if so, the exact words he will utter) . . . if we knew the exact structure of his body at the moment, or . . . the exact make-up of his organism at some early stage – say at birth or before – and then had a record of every change in that organism, including every stimulus that had ever affected this organism. (p. 33)

Science, according to this Laplacean-Bloomfieldian view, consists of the accumulation of more and more data; when you have accumulated it all (and, in terms of mechanistic principles, this should be possible) you will know the "truths." In such a view, there is no theory, only description, and thus no explanation.

This view of science differs sharply from that of the Nobel laureate geneticist François Jacob (1982) who states:

> Whether mythic or scientific, the view of the world that man builds is always largely a product of his imagination. For, in contrast to what is frequently believed, the scientific process does not consist merely in observing, in collecting data and deducing a theory from them. One can watch an object for years without ever producing any observation of scientific interest. Before making a valuable observation, it is necessary to have some idea of what to observe, a preconception of what is possible. Scientific advances often come from uncovering some previously unseen aspect of things . . . by looking at objects from a new angle.

In the same vein, Einstein (1934) stated that "there is no logical path to (scientific) laws; only intuition, resting on sympathetic understanding of experience, can reach them," a position which, until Chomsky's entry into the field, was alien to the main stream of American twentieth-century linguistics.

In looking back at the "state of the art" in linguistics which existed in this earlier period, one is reminded of Poincaré's view of sociology, when he said that while physicists had a subject matter, sociologists were engaged almost entirely in considering their methods. Poincaré could have been referring to Trager and Smith's (1951) view of science, exemplified by their definition of language as "an orderly description of observable features of behavior" and their conception of "the grammar of a language [as] simply an orderly description of the way people in a given society talk – of the sounds that people utter in various situations, and of the acts which accompany or follow the sounds." Given this view, theory became equated with the procedures to be used in constructing an "orderly description."

Hockett (1942) explicitly defined the nature of linguistics to be a classificatory science, with the linguist's task that of classifying data. It is fortunate that the leading linguists of the pre-Chomskyan era did not practice what they preached, since they contributed theoretically insightful ideas as well as invaluable language descriptions. They did not produce the coherent classification and description of languages by simply classifying a collection of actual utterances. Such utterances are replete with false starts, filled and unfilled pauses, and ill-formed sentences such as the following produced by English speakers:

(1) a the last I knowed about it
      b he swimmed in the pool nude
      c I already tooken a bath
      d in one ear and gone tomorrow
      e give him an inch and he'll hang himself
      f does it hear different?
      g it would be interesting to see
      h she was waiting her husband for
      i I know where they're all – all are.
      j I (John) would be easy to prove that
      k the rule agrees those segments in voicing

Errors such as these would seem to provide unquestionable support for Chomsky's differentiation between linguistic competence and performance (Chomsky 1965). But Hockett, who was interested in such deviant utterances, rejected any such distinction as his (1967) article on speech errors reveals. His view was that "the structure of individual utterances . . . reflect[s], though perhaps only with great distortion, the abstract 'sets of habits', or 'system', or 'internalized grammar' . . . that constitutes the language." He argues that the notion of competence "is unmitigated nonsense, unsupported by any empirical evidence of any sort" and proposes instead that "All speech, smooth as well as blunderful, can be and must be accounted for essentially in terms of . . . analogy, blending, and editing. An individual's language, at a given moment, is a set of habits – that is, of analogies; where different analogies are in conflict, one may appear as a constraint on the working of another." He continues in the same vein: "Speech actualizes habits . . . Speech reflects awareness of norms; but norms are themselves entirely a matter of analogy (that is, of habit), not some different kind of thing."

Many of the errors cited above may indeed be the result of "analogy" and/or "blending." *Knowed* would, according to this analysis, have been produced "on the analogy" with regular past tense formation of verbs, such as *rowed* or *sewed*; and *In one ear and gone tomorrow* a blend of *In one ear and out the other* and *Here today and gone tomorrow*. But for words and phrases to be blended they must be stored, that is, they must be mentally representated in their "normal" form. Furthermore, the fact that one recognizes that errors have been produced implies a notion of knowledge (i.e. competence) of the correct forms from which the produced forms differ.

This notion of competence as "a certain system of knowledge, represented somehow in the mind, and ultimately, in the brain in some physical configuration" (Chomsky 1988) which has been "acquired by the learner, and used by the speaker-hearer" (Chomsky 1986) had no place in pre-Chomskyan American structuralism, in which language was defined as "a set of utterances," "[a]n utterance [as] . . . an act of speech" and an act of speech as "an item of human behavior with certain physiological and sociological characteristics" (Hockett 1942).

If "grammar of a language is simply an orderly description of the way people . . . talk" (Trager and Bloch, 1941) rather than "a system of rules that relate sound and meaning in a particular way," the logical conclusion is that there are no "errors" or "slips of the tongue" – since this is simply the way people talk. In fact, this is the position of Roy Harris, the former Professor of Linguistics at Oxford, which follows from his denial that there is a difference between knowledge and its use, or linguistic competence and performance (Harris, personal conversation). Yet, in order to know what an error is or even that one has occurred, there must be knowledge of why the utterance was an error, that is, of the "rules" or "principles" that have been violated.

Harris's position is more logical than Hockett's although certainly not more appealing; Harris's denial of a distinction between knowledge and processing leads to his denial of the existence of performance errors. Hockett, however, rightfully suggests that an error is a deviation from some "norm," however it is defined. The problem lies in trying to understand the meaning of "norm" without a concept of pre-existing knowledge which is accessed to produce the analogy, blend, or editing, that Hockett suggests accounts for errors.

Speech errors are performance errors; they reflect competence although they are not identical with nor a mirror of the mental grammar.

Since "knowledge" presupposes "mind," and the mind did not exist in the early behaviorist philosophy of language, "the universe of discourse" of linguistics had to be constrained to "a set of utterances" (Hockett 1942) and "noises" produced by speakers, a position specifically put forth in Bloomfield's (1926) criticism of non-linguists who, he says, "constantly forget that a speaker is making noise, and credit him, instead, with the possession of impalpable 'ideas.' It remains for linguists to show, in detail, that the speaker has no 'ideas' and that the noise is sufficient."

Contrary to Bloomfield's suggestion, it remained for a linguist to show instead that Descartes, rather than Bloomfield was correct in recognizing that "the normal use of language is constantly innovative, unbounded, apparently free from control by external stimuli or internal states, coherent and appropriate to situations" (Chomsky 1988). For whether or not the "speaker's words act with a trigger-effect upon the nervous systems of his speech fellows," as Bloomfield claimed, his speech fellows can respond appropriately or not, or remain silent. No matter how much information one has available about the prenatal, postnatal, physiological, biological, anatomical, or experiential past of a speaker, it would be impossible to predict the "exact words" he would utter or anything else about his behavior in response to the "noises" he was hearing.

2   THE MIND RESTORED

Once Chomsky put the mind back into the brain, exposed the fallacies of the simplistic mechanistic and empiricist view of science, and substituted theory for procedural methods, it was possible to ask the kinds of questions which would make it possible for linguistics to become a theoretical and explanatory science.

Lees (1957), in an eloquent *Language* review of *Syntactic Structures*, contrasted the "prescientific stage of collection and classification of interesting facts" with Chomsky's attempt to construct a scientific "comprehensive theory of language . . . [which] is not a mere reorganization of the data into a new kind of library catalogue, nor another speculative philosophy about the nature of Man and Language, but rather a rigorous explication of our intuitions about our language" (pp. 377–8).

The changes which took place in cognitive psychology and in the relatively new area of psycholinguistics as a result of Chomsky's influence were as dramatic as those in linguistics. Newmeyer (1980) shows this in his citation of the statement of George Miller (1962): "I now believe that mind is something more than a four letter, Anglo-Saxon word – human minds exist and it is our job as psychologists to study them" (p. 761).

The distinction between linguistic competence and performance made it possible to investigate both, with the recognition that "Performance provides data for the study of linguistic competence. Competence is one of many factors that interact to determine performance" (Chomsky 1972).

Chomsky, of course, was not the first to make this distinction. While Saussure's (1916) *langue* and *parole* are not identical to Chomsky's notions of competence and performance, they did provide the background for the insights of, for example, some of the Praguean linguists like Skalička (1948) who asked: "What is *parole* in fact? *Parole* consists of the individual utterances by which *langue* is made real." He suggests that "there are many words in a language which clearly form a theory of *parole*, cf., for example, *to speak, speech, to stammer, to stutter, to ask, to answer, to speak to the point, to speak at random, intelligible, comprehensible, ambiguous*, etc. All are expressions to which the scientific terms of linguists do not apply" (p. 377). While this view of *parole* differs from our view of performance, it seems more insightful than the view that equates language with the noises produced by speakers.

3   BRAIN AND LANGUAGE

Chomsky's new research objectives and philosophy of language brought changes in neuropsychology as well as psychology, and led to the development of a new "hyphenated" area – neurolinguistics – the study of the relationship between brain and language. The dramatic explosion of new journals and books in the field attest to this fact. A journal called *Brain and Language* whose editor received his Ph.D in linguistics would have been as impossible pre-Chomsky as would journals like *Mind and Language*, *Cognition*, *Cognitive Neuropsychology*, *Language and Cognitive Processes* with editorial boards that include many linguists and whose contents are filled with articles by linguists.

The entry into the brain/mind/cognition studies was a logical development of the Chomskyan intent to understand the nature and form of human linguistic knowledge, how it is acquired, "how . . . this system of knowledge arise[s] in the mind/brain?" and "how . . . this knowledge [is] put to use in speech?" (Chomsky 1988).

The research on the theory of grammar which has been conducted these last thirty years provides ample evidence in support of Chomsky's original proposal that the human animal is able to acquire language because it is genetically endowed with "a distinct 'language faculty' with specific structure and properties." The investigation of parametric variation across languages leads to an elucidation of the general principles of Universal Grammar, i.e. "the innate, biologically determined principles which constitute one component of the human mind – the language faculty," (Chomsky 1986). The search for the biological basis of this language faculty also underlies neurolinguistic research, spurred on by Lenneberg's (1967) seminal work on this question.

Interest in the biological basis of language and cognition, however, goes back about 2,000 years. Aristotle's view that the brain is a cold sponge whose primary action is to cool the blood was not shared by the Graeco-Roman physicians, who, writing in the fifth century BCE, recognized that the loss of speech and the loss of language could be distinguished and that speechlessness was often associated with paralysis of the right side of the body. The Hippocratic view was that the brain is "the messenger to the understanding" and the organ whereby "in an especial manner we acquire wisdom and knowledge" (Arbib, et al., 1982).

We even find a recognition of asymmetries of brain function and a relationship between the right hand and language in one of the Psalms (135: 5–6): "If I will forget thee, Jerusalem, let my right hand die – let my tongue stick to the roof of my mouth." And in the New Testament, St Luke reports that Zacharias could not speak but could write.

Maximus (circa 30 CE) provided an early illustration for Chomsky's (1975) notion of language as a special "organ" and Fodor's (1983) "modularity of mind" concept is illustrated by Maximum (circa 30 CE) in his report of a scholar in Athens who suffered "a loss of letters" after a head injury with no other behavioral or cognitive deficit (Benton 1981). It is not clear whether this referred to a speech or a reading deficit but either reflects distinct abilities.

In the early part of the nineteenth century Gall and Spurzheim put forth theories of "localization," holding that different human abilities and behaviors are traceable to specific brain structures. Gall's contributions to our understanding of the relationship between the brain and mind should not be judged by his espousal of phrenology. It is said that he believed the frontal lobes of the brain were the locations of language because, in his youth, he had noticed that the most articulate and intelligent of his fellow students had protruding eyes reflecting overdeveloped brain material. One should not, however, reject his insights concerning distinct cortical/cognitive modules, even if one is not "a practicing witch" as the writer of a recent book on phrenology describes herself (Marshall 1987).

4 THE LEFTIST NATURE OF LANGUAGE

It was not until 1861 that the scientific study of language and brain was begun. Paul Broca (1861) presented a paper in Paris during an anthropology conference discussion on brain localization of cognitive processes. In his (1865) paper, Broca specifically related language to the left side of the brain. He presented autopsy evidence showing that a localized (anterior) left hemisphere lesion resulted in a loss of ability to speak, whereas focal lesions in similar parts of the right brain did not. He managed to convince his Parisian audience (and most of neurology) that "On parle avec l'hémisphère gauche."

Wernicke (1874) pointed out that damage in the posterior portion of the left temporal lobe results in a different form of language breakdown to that occurring after damage to the frontal cortex (now called Broca's area). These different kinds of acquired language loss – aphasias – continue to be corroborated.

The speech output of Broca's aphasia patients is characterized by word-finding pauses, loss of grammatical morphemes, and quite often, disturbed word order. Auditory comprehension for colloquial conversation gives the impression of being generally good, although controlled testing reveals considerable impairments. The term *agrammatism* has been used as almost synonymous with Broca's aphasia, although some Broca's patients are not agrammatic and some agrammatics would not classify neurologically as Broca's. (And today there are those who question this kind of broad classification of aphasic symptoms; they are used below simply to show the kinds of post-brain-damage language deficits that result).

Patients clinically classified as Wernicke's aphasics produce fluent speech with good intonation and pronunciation, but with many word substitutions (both semantically similar and dissimilar), neologisms and phonological errors. They also show comprehension difficulties.

One Wernicke's aphasia patient, for example, replied to a question about his health with: "I felt worse because I can no longer keep in mind from the mind of the minds to keep me from mind and up to the ear which can be to find among ourselves." (Kriendler et al. 1971). Another patient, when asked about his poor vision said: "My wires don't hire right." And an aphasic physician, asked if he was a doctor, replied: "Me? Yes, sir, I'm a male demaploze on my own. I still know my tubaboys what for I have that's gone hell and some of them go." One aphasic described a fork as "a need for a schedule" and a spoon as "How many schemes on your throat."

These fluent but uninterpretable utterances are very different from the Broca's aphasic's answer when asked what brought him to the hospital: "Yes – ah – Monday – ah – Dad and P. H. (the patient's name) and Dad . . . hospital. Two . . . ah doctors . . . and ah . . . thirty minutes . . . and yes . . . ah . . . hospital. And, er Wednesday . . . nine o'clock and eh Thursday, ten o'clock . . . doctors. Two doctors . . . and ah . . . teeth. Yeah . . . fine" (Badecker and Caramazza 1985).

Early comparisons of Broca's and Wernicke's aphasia – poor production with intact comprehension and vice versa – can only be accounted for if one accepts the distinction between linguistic competence and performance, unless one accepts the view that our ability to speak is independent of our ability to comprehend speech, a possible but highly improbable and inelegant view of the linguistic system. Similarly, patients who can perform a linguistic task in one modality but not in another must have an intact competence which is neutral as to production and comprehension. This observation led Weigl and Bierwisch (1970) to suggest that "aphasia syndromes in general are to be understood as disturbances of complexes of components or subcomponents of the system of performance, while the underlying competence remains intact." They did, however, suggest an exception to this – agrammatism when it affects both speech and comprehension. They conclude that "competence and performance must be psychologically different aspects of the general phenomenon of speech behaviour . . . The distinction . . . is not merely a heuristic or methodological assumption but reflects a fact that can be established neuropsychologically."

Aphasia research by linguists has been motivated by the fact that focal damage to specific brain areas results in the disruption of distinct cognitive functions, as well as motor and perceptual abilities, and that the selectivity appears to be specific as to the parts of language which are affected, supporting a modular conception of the grammar itself, in which the components are interactive but independent of each other, since these components as well as the hierarchy of linguistic units posited by linguists appear to be just those parts which can be differently destroyed or damaged.

Jakobson (1940; 1955; 1964) was the first linguist to conduct aphasia research, following up on the insights of de Courtenay (1895) and Saussure (1916) who had expressed the belief that a study of language pathology could contribute to linguistics. Jakobson used aphasia data to support his notions of phonological markedness and then later his views of syntactic theory.

Except for Jakobson, few linguists followed up the early interest in linguistics by neurologists who drew on linguistics concepts in their investigations of aphasia. The Soviet neurologist, Luria (1947), in his now classic *Traumatic Aphasia* reveals both the influence of and his interest in linguistic concepts to explain different forms of language breakdown and the relationship between brain and language. A similar interest was shown by Goldstein (1948) (with different interpretations of the data). Even much earlier, the years which followed Broca's and Wernicke's discoveries stimulated neurologists throughout the world, such as Broadbent (1879) and Bastian (1887) in Britain, Pick (1913) and Salomon (1914) in Germany, and Moutier (1908) in France, to apply linguistic analyses to aphasia data.

It is not surprising that, working in the period when linguistic research was constrained by behaviorism, Jakobson's pioneering work in this area lay dormant for many years. Blumstein (1973), one of his students, followed his lead in her dissertation which, upon publication, further stimulated linguistic investigations of aphasia. She, and those that followed her, added a new dimension to aphasia research since they were interested in what aphasia data could contribute to our understanding of language, rather than with clinical concerns.

Linguists ask different questions than those that have been asked by the neurologists and neuropsychologists in their aphasia research, who, since the nineteenth century have been trying to discover direct centers where language capacities can be localized. Linguists who are interested in the biological basis of language will undoubtedly find interesting the discovery that specific lesion sites produce different aphasic symptoms. Such findings would be directly relevant to linguistic theory if they reveal that these differential deficits reflect different grammatical components or even units and rules. But no research on or discovery of anatomical brain localization of function, such as whether the anterior portion of the left temporal lobe is more directly responsible for syntactic processing than the posterior portion, can contribute to syntactic theory specifically or reveal the nature of the syntactic deficit, which can only be explained by the theory itself. Neurology can neither analyze nor explain agrammatic utterances of the patients who omit main verbs, such as the following:

(i)   The young . . . the girl . . . the little girl is . . . the flower. (In trying to describe the picture of a girl giving flowers to her teacher.)

or who use nominalizations instead of verbs:

(ii) The girl is flower the woman.

(iii) The man kodaks . . . and the girl . . . kodaks the girl. (Describing a picture of a man photographing a girl.) (Badecker and Caramazza 1985)

Without the input of linguists who on principled theoretical grounds distinguish between derivational and inflectional morphemes, aphasiologists were unable to explain why certain agrammatic patients have difficulty with inflectional affixes but not with derivational affixes (Badecker and Caramazza 1985; Kean 1977). In addition, a plausible account is provided by Grodzinsky (1984) for patients who omit grammatical formatives and patients who do not omit them but substitute incorrect grammatical morphemes and inflectional affixes. In his study of a number of Hebrew-speaking aphasics, he points out that vowels in Hebrew are predictable, according to inflectional and derivational morphological rules. For example, the vowel in the word for a single male child is "e" *yeled*, is "a" for a female child *yalda*; the plural for these two singular nouns is *yeladim* and *yeladot*, respectfully. Since the roots of Hebrew words consist only of consonants, e.g. /y-l-d/ in the examples given, agrammatic aphasic Hebrew speakers would be unable to talk at all if they omitted the inflectional and derivational morphemes which are realized vocalically. What these Hebrew speakers did instead was to substitute incorrect vowels in words such as those exemplified, and omit free-standing grammatical morphemes.

Hyams (1988) also discusses agrammatic aphasics who differ cross-linguistically in whether they tend to omit inflections or not. She points out that her analysis, based on Government-Binding syntactic theory which distinguishes core from peripheral inflectional systems, makes exactly the right predictions regarding the agrammatic output that occurs. When inflection is a core property of the grammar as in Italian, Russian, or Hebrew, agrammatic aphasics do not omit inflectional morphemes; when inflection is a peripheral property of the grammar as in English, they do.

Caplan (1987), using linguistic methods to analyze the utterances of agrammatic patients, concludes that these patients do not only have difficulty with grammatical morphemes, but "have an impairment in the construction of normal syntactic structures." Many of these patients also show that syntactic competence as well as syntactic processing mechanisms may be impaired. Contrary to the notion that agrammatism is solely a production deficit, linguistic investigations show a relationship between production and comprehension syntactic deficits (Heilman and Scholes 1976; Schwartz et al. 1980). For example, Caramazza and Zurif (1976) demonstrated that such patients were unable to understand sentences whose meanings depend on syntactic structure, which in some cases is due to difficulties with non-derivational grammatical formatives and inflectional morphemes.

5   NEUROLINGUISTICS AND THE LEXICON

More and more evidence is mounting that suggests that lexical and grammatical morphemes form separate and distinct classes in the lexicon, as exemplified by a patient of Newcombe and Marshall (1985) who, following brain damage, demonstrates severe reading problems. G. R. often substitutes semantically similar words for lexical items and has even greater difficulty in reading grammatical morphemes. The data given in (2) show that he makes derivational reading errors and substitutes one function word for another or is unable to read grammatical morphemes, even with errors.

(2)   Patient G. R. (Newcombe and Marshall 1985)

	Stimulus	Response
a	ARRIVE	"arrival"
	TRUTH	"true"
b	FOR	"and"
	HIS	"she"
	BE	"small words are the worst"
	SOME	"one of them horrid words again"

(3) further illustrates the distinction G. R. makes between lexical and grammatical homophones:

(3)   Patient G. R. (Newcome and Marshall 1985)

Stimulus	Response	Stimulus	Response
WITCH	"witch"	WHICH	"no!"
BEAN	"oh, I know . . . well . . . soup"	BEEN	"no!"
HOUR	"time"	OUR	"no!"
EYE	"eyes"	I	"no!"
HYMN	"bible"	HIM	"a boy? no!"
WOOD	"wood"	WOULD	"no!"
FOUR	"four"	FOR	"no!"
MOOR	"fog . . . mist?"	MORE	"no!"

In addition to interest in these distinct lexical classes, which are shown to be treated differently not only by language-impaired individuals but also in normal processing, psycholinguistic and aphasia research has become increasingly concerned with lexical representation and access. (See, for example, Morton 1969; Morton and Patterson 1980; Friederici 1983; Garrett 1975; Garrett 1980; Fodor 1983; Forster 1979; Forster 1981; Marslen-Wilson 1975.

Simultaneously, current linguistic research is being conducted on the lexicon and the morphological component of the grammar. (Halle 1973; Lieber 1980; Lieber 1983; Selkirk 1982; Borer 1984.) Given that "a large part of 'language learning' is a matter of determining from presented data the elements of the lexicon and their properties" (Chomsky 1982), it is not surprising that the power and structure of the lexicon have been greatly expanded in recent grammatical theory (Kiparsky 1982; Mohanan 1982; Kaplan and Bresnan 1982; Chomsky 1981; Gazdar 1982). Morphology is also included as a separate component of the grammar which interacts with the lexicon, the syntax, and the phonology in some theoretical models (Anderson 1982; Aronoff 1976).

In light of this interest, some linguists are looking at neurolinguistic data to see if impaired language can provide any insight into lexical representation and organization, based on the claim that if in the abnormal brain we find differential impairments to different parts of language or the components of the grammar, that shows that such independent parts must exist in the normal intact brain, or, at least, must be separately accessible.

There is much published literature reporting on reading and writing deficits following brain injury which seem relevant to the organization of the lexicon. (Coltheart et al. 1980; Patterson et al. 1985). Some patients are able to read words but not nonsense forms, and often substitute semantically similar words. This is illustrated in (4).

(4)   Patient G. R. (Newcombe and Marshall 1984)

Stimulus	Response
BUN	"cake"
GNOME	"pixie"
CRAFT	"sculpture"
LITTLE	"short"
KILL	"murder"
OZ	"pound"
XII	"BC"

(5) shows two responses to the same stimulus words given on different days. In some cases, the same error is produced, but in other cases, different words are substituted. In addition, at one reading the patient may produce the correct response whereas an error is made at another reading, supporting Weigle and Bierwisch's position that these are performance errors.

(5)   Patient G. R. (Newcome and Marshall 1984)

Stimulus	Response 1	Response 2
ACT	"play"	"play"
APPLAUD	"laugh"	"cheers"
EXAMPLE	"answer"	"sum"
HEAL	"pain"	"medicine"
SOUTH	"west"	"east"

Many of these patients can only read words (with or without errors) but are unable to read nonsense forms at all, even if they obey the orthographic and morphological rules of their language. Learning to read involves learning both consciously and unconsciously a set of grapheme-to-phoneme (and vice versa) rules which enables one to pronounce words encountered for the first time as well as non-words or nonsense forms. These patients seem to have had such rules erased or to have lost the access routes to these pronunciation rules. The fact that some words are read correctly implies that there must be a direct processing route from visual orthography to orthographic listing which leads in turn to a phonological representation. Since reading errors consist of semantically related word substitutions, semantic representation appears to be separate from the orthographic and phonological representation; after the orthographic listing is accessed, it must be first mapped onto a semantic listing which then connects to the phonology. If the wrong semantic listing is selected, the wrong phonological representation is also selected and produced.

Another category of acquired dyslexics also have difficulty with reading non-words, but do not produce semantic substitutions. They have no difficulty with any actual word – regularly or irregularly spelled – but often are unable to understand or provide a meaning for words read correctly. One woman, reported on by Schwartz et al. (1980), for example, could read *broad* as well as *road*, and *tortoise*, *leopard*, *climb*, *both*, *own*, and *flood* but could not say what the words meant. These patients also show an inability to access pronunciation rules, and illustrate the probability of separate but connected orthographic, phonological, and semantic listings; patients are able to access the phonological representation of the words through an orthographic mapping, but cannot go from there to their semantic representations.

A third category is exemplified by a patient with whom I have worked over the last number of years, referred to as Kram and MS in the literature. (Fromkin 1985; Newcombe and Marshall 1985.) Kram shows good language comprehension and fluent intelligible speech production, with greatly impaired reading and writing ability.

(6) presents examples of errors made by Kram reading aloud and writing to dictation.

(6)   Kram

Stimulus	Reading Pronunciation	Writing to Dictation
"fame"	[fæmi]	FAM
"cafe"	[sæfi]	KAFA
"cape"	[sepi]	KAP
"tone"	[toni]	TON
"fight"	[fɪg-hət]	FiT
"goes"	[goɛs]	GOZ
"thing"	[tahiŋ]	FiNG
"charm"	[s-ha:m]	. . . ARM
"wheel"	[w-hil]	WEL

Unlike the first two categories of dyslexics, in reading, Kram cannot access the phonological representation via the orthographic stimulus. Furthermore, he is unable to access (if they are still intact) the normal grapheme-phoneme rules; he neither reads nor writes according to these rules, but uses his own idiosyncratic rules which result in the errors illustrated above. The spelling and pronunciation errors are similar to those made by many children who are first learning to read and write, for example, the use of letter names, pronouncing the letter A as /e/, I as /aj/ etc. All of Kram's "rules" do not follow this pattern. It is also of interest that Kram did not make these kinds of errors pre-injury, as is revealed in a number of notebooks and letters written by him prior to the accident.

Kram cannot understand the meaning of a word by the orthography but only through its phonology; when he mispronounces a word in reading aloud he is unable to state what it means and he cannot use it correctly in a sentence. If he happens to produce a different though actual word via his pronunciation rules than the written stimulus, he can provide the meaning of the word produced. If he produces a non-word, a nonsense form, he cannot provide a meaning and, in fact, is not sure whether it is a word or not since he knows he is making mistakes in reading. The examples in (7) illustrate this fact.

(7) Kram

Stimulus	Pronunciation	Meaning
sum	[sʌm]	"I've got *some* money"
can	[sæn]	"I don't know. If it was 'm' it would be 'Sam'"
hymn	[haj-hi-hay-mən]	"hymen?"
for	[fɔ:]	"four – I have four fingers and a thumb"
rob	[rad]	"fishing"
rib	[rajd]	"I know – a motor bike"
pig	[pɪg]	"oink oink"
was	[wæs]	"don't know"
so	[so]	"so you can tell"

Due to visual confusion (resulting from the brain injury) Kram reads *rob* as "rod" and gives its meaning by reference to the word "fishing." This also accounts for why he talks of a motor bike in misreading "rib" as "ride."

Other similar cases reported in the literature (Patterson et al. 1985) also reveal that these patients can only access the semantic representation via the phonology, as is shown in 8.

(8)

Stimulus	Reading Pronunciation	Meaning Supplied
listen	"Liston"	"the famous boxer"
begin	"beggin"	"collecting money"
island	"iss-land"	"there's no such word"
bee	"bee/be"	"to be or not to be"
oar	"or/oar/ore"	"that's the ore of metal, raw materials"
billed	"build"	"to build up – buildings"
sighs	"size"	"size is measurement or bit of stuff they use in glue"
pair	"pear/pair"	"it's either two of a kind or fruit for eating"

Data such as those above have been considered by psycholinguists and neuropsychologists in constructing lexical processing models. For the most part these models attempt to account for the ability or inability of subjects (and patients) to read, write, or name single words, or for results of such subjects in psycholinguistic experiments. The latter may involve lexical decision tasks, priming experiments, phoneme monitoring or the like with monomorphemic words or polymorphemic words (derivationally or inflectionally complex).

In one such model, given in figure 1, the lexicon is composed of "sub-lexicons" as well as rule components (Fromkin 1985; Fromkin 1988). Each entry in each of the lexical components is connected to its parallel representation through an addressing system. Obviously this is just one way of representing the networking of the phonological, semantic, orthographic representations. The numerical addresses are metaphorical – to suggest that entries with numerically close addresses are "on the same street" or at least "in the same city". This is to account for normal or aphasic speech errors in which semantically related, or phonologically similar words are incorrectly selected.

It is obvious that this lexical model is not a model of the lexical component of the mental grammar, or even a model of the lexicon that is accessed in production and comprehension, although some of the required properties are included, e.g. the phonological form of each entry. The semantic properties, however, must include selectional properties of construction heads (s-selection), e.g. nouns, verbs, adjectives, and prepositions/postpositions (Chomsky 1986) and the categorical selection (c-selection) properties. Evidence is still needed for where and how such properties should be represented in the lexicon that is accessed in linguistic processing. But without such information, there could be no recognition that the examples in (9) are errors of speech.

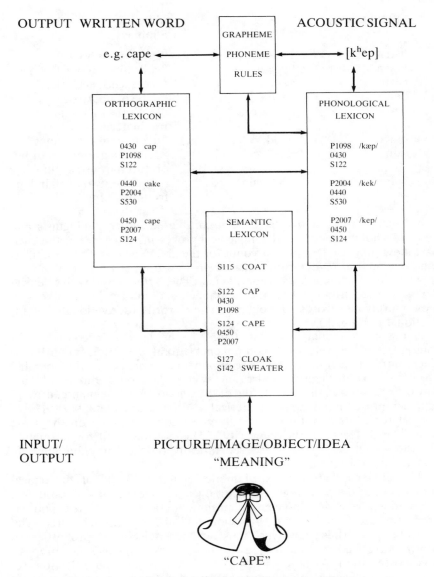

Fig. 1   Lexical Subcomponents for a Linguistic Processing Model

(9) a   I would be easy to prove that
     b   She made him to do the assignment over
     c   the rule agrees those segments in voicing

There are errors which violate s-selection and c-selection properties, and it is our knowledge of these properties as represented in the lexical entries of each word that permits us to recognize the deviation.

It is not clear whether the separation of the lexicon into sub-lexicons as presented in figure 1 creates any problems for a theory of grammar (except to determine where and how selectional properties, as well as morphological rules, etc. are to be represented). There is no a priori reason why the structure and organization of the lexicon in the grammar must be identical or even isomorphic with the lexicon assessed during processing. When isomorphism exists between parts of the grammar constructed on the basis of linguistic evidence and language deficits following brain damage, we have additional evidence for the linguistic hypotheses.

Suppose, however, that one finds that following brain damage, no patients display language deficits restricted to the syntactic aspects of the grammar; one cannot conclude that there is no syntactic component. Or, suppose one finds no patient who shows differential deficits in producing or comprehending derivational versus inflectional morphemes. How derivation and/or inflection is represented in the grammar will depend for the most part on solid linguistic evidence. (Cf. for example Anderson 1988).

This would seem obvious; yet, it is not a view accepted by all psycholinguists or even all linguists. Scientific revolutions, like political revolutions, may engender overt and covert counter revolutions. The realism inherent in Chomsky's approach, and the concern that grammars be "psychologically real" in the sense of Kiparsky (1968) gave rise to a resurgence of empiricism and reductionism in a new form. The data collected by experimental psycholinguists and phonologists as well as various kinds of "observable" or "hard core" performance data such as speech errors, aphasic speech, etc. began to be regarded as a more acceptable kind of evidence than traditional linguistic evidence such as speakers' intuitions, morphophonemic alternations, subcategorization constraints, etc.

The new behaviorists, however, do not provide any rationale to explain why response latencies in phoneme monitoring tasks or lexical decisions in priming experiments should be more real than the linguistic data analyzed by linguists.

As Grodzinsky (1984) points out, formal constructs in syntactic theory may account for a particular deficit in agrammatism, where non-linguistic concepts cannot. In addition, one theory may lead to an explanation of such data which cannot be provided by another.

In answer to the neo-empiricists Chomsky argues for the equal status of data as evidence:

> Suppose that someone were to discover a certain pattern of electrical activity
> in the brain that correlated in clear cases with the presence of *wh*-clauses,

relative clauses (finite and infinitival) and *wh*-questions (direct and indirect). Suppose that this pattern of electrical activity is observed when a person speaks or understands [a particular sentence]. Would we now have evidence for the psychological reality of the postulated mental representations?

We would now have a new kind of 'evidence' but I see no merit to the contention that this new evidence bears . . . reality whereas the old evidence only relates to hypothetical constructions. The new evidence might or might not be more persuasive than the old; that would depend on its character and reliability, the degree to which the principles dealing with this evidence are tenable, intelligible, compelling and so on. (Chomsky 1978)

But note that Chomsky does not dismiss any kind of evidence, since "evidence concerning the character of the I-language and initial state could come from many different sources apart from judgments concerning the form and meaning of expressions: perceptual experiments, the study of acquisition and deficit or of partially invented languages such as creole, or of literary usage or language change, neurology, biochemistry, and so on. As in the case of any inquiry into some aspect of the physical world, there is no way of delimiting the kinds of evidence that might in principle prove relevant" (Chomsky 1986).

Without a theory we do not know what constitutes data at all, and without a theory of normal function, it would be impossible to understand linguistic abnormalities. It is in this sense that linguistics has and is making a major contribution to the studies of brain, mind, and cognition.

6 THE LANGUAGE ORGAN

One contribution of neurolinguistic studies to an understanding of the nature of human language consists of the findings which show that localized brain damage affects different cognitive functions selectively, for example, language versus non-language, providing additional support for a modular conception of mind and a separate and distinct language "organ" (Fodor 1983; Chomsky 1980).

Whether one looks at the selective impairment or preservation of language abilities in child development or in the mature brain, one can find little to support the view of language as derivative of some general intellectual capacity, and yet this view continues to be held by both linguists and non-linguists.

There are numerous case studies of children who have few cognitive skills and virtually no ability to utilize language in sustained meaningful communication and yet have extensive mastery of linguistic structure. Yamada (1983) reports on one severely retarded young woman, Marta, with a nonverbal IQ of 41–44, lacking almost all number concepts including basic counting principles, drawing at a preschool level, and processing an auditory memory span limited to three units, who could nonetheless produce syntactically complex sentences like

"She does paintings, this really good friend of the kids who I went to school with last year and really loved."

or

"Last year at school when I first went there, three tickets were gave out by a police last year."

Marta cannot add $2 + 2$. She is not sure of when "last year" is or whether it is before or after "last week" or "an hour ago," nor does she know how many tickets were "gave out" nor whether 3 is larger or smaller than 2. But the structure of her sentences reveals sophisticated knowledge of complex syntactic rules. She embeds relative clauses, conjoins verb phrases, produces passives, inflects verbs for number and person to agree with the grammatical subject, and forms past tenses when the time adverbial structurally refers to a previous time. In a sentence imitation task she both detected and corrected surface syntactic and morphological errors. Yet she is unable to tie her shoes.

Marta is but one of many examples of children who display well-developed phonological, morphological and syntactic linguistic abilities, seemingly less developed lexical, semantic, or referential aspects of language, and deficits in non-linguistic cognitive development (Curtiss et al. 1981; Curtiss et al. 1979). Furthermore, as shown by Blank et al. (1979), grammatical knowledge can be acquired without parallel pragmatic knowledge or "communicative competence." And cases of schizophrenic and autistic children reveal similar dissociation between the ability to acquire the language system and the ability to learn the conventions for the use of the language in social settings (Kanner 1943; Elliott and Needleman 1981; Goodman 1972).

Such developmental asymmetries argue against the view that linguistic ability derives from more general cognitive "intelligence", since in these cases language develops against a background of deficits in general and non-linguistic intellectual abilities.

There are also cases of children with little grammar but with other verbal abilities, such as Genie (cf. Fromkin et al. 1974; Curtiss 1977). This "modern-day wild child" was physically and socially isolated from the world until almost 14 years old, with no language input during that period. Following her discovery and social emergence, she learned to use a sewing machine and scramble eggs; she remembered every face she saw, could go directly to a car parked in a crowded five-level parking structure after a five or six hour interim period, she did phenomenally well on the Mooney faces test, and after her social emergence she very rapidly acquired a large vocabulary. But she never went beyond the rudiments of syntax acquired by a two-year old child. Her utterances remained ungrammatical, devoid of morphological endings, or syntactic operations. This contrast between word lists and grammatical rules is indicative of different and distinct cognitive abilities, and supports the view of language as an autonomous system which, in itself, consists of separate components.

Perhaps the most telling and dramatic findings on the brain/language relationship which support the conception of the brain and mind as consisting of neurological and cognitive interactive but autonomous modules is revealed by the exciting research on sign language conducted by Bellugi and her colleagues (Bellugi et al. 1988). The linguistic study of sign language over the last 25 years has already revealed that these languages of the deaf have all the crucial properties common to all spoken languages, including highly abstract underlying grammatical and formal principles.

Since the same abstract linguistic principles underlie all human languages – spoken or signed – regardless of the motor and perceptual mechanisms which are used in their expression, it is not surprising that deaf patients show aphasia for sign language similar to the language breakdown in hearing aphasics following damage to the left hemisphere. Furthermore, while these patients show marked sign language deficits, they can correctly process non-language visual-spatial relationships. The left cerebral hemisphere is thus not dominant for speech, as had been suggested, but for language, the cognitive system underlying both speech and sign. Hearing and speech are not necessary for the development of left hemispheric specialization for language. This has been a crucial point in determining that the left hemisphere specialization in language acquisition is not due to its capacity for fine auditory analysis, but for language analysis *per se*. As long as linguists concerned themselves only with spoken languages, there was no way to separate what is essential to the linguistic cognitive system from the constraints imposed, productively and perceptually, by the auditory-vocal modality, that is, to discover what the genetically, biologically determined linguistic ability of the human brain is.

Other evidence for the uniqueness of language is provided by the many studies showing that linguistic prosody can be destroyed while the ability to comprehend non-linguistic or affective prosody can be retained and vice versa, depending on which part of the brain has suffered injury. For example, Emmorey (1988) has shown that patients with lesions in the left hemisphere have difficulty in distinguishing noun phrase-noun compound contrasts.

Patients with right hemisphere lesions, however, can process linguistic contrastic stress, but have difficulty with affective intonation reflecting non-linguistic emotional states. The processing of linguistic prosody, determined by the grammar, is thus a function of the left hemisphere, whereas affective prosody is processed by the right hemisphere.

Further evidence for the separation of cognitive modules is provided by the neurological and behavioral findings that auditory agnosia (inability to recognize sounds), color agnosia, prosopagnosia (loss of the ability to recognize familiar faces), can all be distinguished from visual object agnosia. (Warrington and Shallice 1984.) Even within the specific agnosia we find evidence of distinct categories. One agnosia patient at the Radcliffe

Infirmary in Oxford shows particular difficulty in recognizing animals, and less difficulty with non-animate objects. Lexical semantic categories thus are disassociable as well as syntactic categories.

While such studies are providing new information about the biological basis for cognition, including language, they have not to date contributed anything substantive to linguistic theory itself.

Linguistics raises questions for the neurologist, the brain researcher, and the neuropsychologist, questions that could not have been raised within the pre-Chomskyan behaviorist, anti-mentalist paradigm. As the Nobel laureate, Jerne (1984) said in his Nobel prize address:

> It seems a miracle that young children easily learn the language of any environment into which they are born. The generative approach to grammar, pioneered by Chomsky, argues that this is only explicable if certain deep, universal features of this competence are innate characteristics of the human brain. Biologically speaking, this hypothesis of an inheritable capability to learn any language means that it must somehow be encoded in the DNA of our chromosomes. Should this hypothesis one day be verified, then linguistics would become a branch of biology.

Chomsky has already stated his belief that linguistics "is a theoretical biology, (or), if you like, a theoretical psychology" (Sklar 1968). Whatever it is, because of him, "it has passed beyond the stage of stamp collecting" and has become a theoretical science.

NOTE

Sections of this paper appeared in an earlier form in Fromkin (1988).

REFERENCES

Anderson, Stephen 1982: Where's morphology? *Linguistic Inquiry*, 13, 571–612.
—— 1988: Morphology as a parsing problem. *Linguistics*, 26, 521–44.
Arbib, M. A., Caplan, D. and Marshall, J. C. 1982: Neurolinguistics in historical perspective. In *Neural Models of Language Processes*, ed. by M. A. Arbib, D. Caplan, and J. C. Marshall. New York: Academic Press.
Aronoff, Mark 1976: *Word Formation in Generative Grammar*. Cambridge, Mass.: MIT Press.
Badecker, B. and Caramazza, A. 1985: On considerations of method and theory governing the use of clinical categories in neurolinguistics and cognitive neuropsychology: the case against agrammatism. *Cognition*, 10, 17–24.
Bastian, C. 1887: On different kinds of aphasia with special reference to their classification and ultimate pathology. *British Medical Journal*, 2, 931–6.
Benton, Arthur 1981: Aphasia: historical perspectives. In *Acquired Aphasia*, ed. by M. T. Sarno. New York: Academic Press, 1–21.
Blank, M., Gessner, M. and Esposito, A. 1979: Language without communication: a case study. *Journal of Child Language*, 6, 329–52.
Bloch, Bernard 1948: A set of postulates for phonemic analysis. *Language*, 26, 86–125.

Bloomfield, Leonard 1926: A set of postulates for the study of language, *Language*, 2, 53–64.

—— 1933: *Language*, New York: Holt and Co.

—— 1939: *Linguistic Aspects of Science*. International Encyclopedia of Unified Science vol. 1, no. 4. Chicago: University of Chicago Press.

Blumstein, Sheila 1973: *A phonological investigation of phasic speech*. Mouton: The Hague.

Borer, Hagit 1984: The projection principle and the rules of morphology. *Nels*, 14, 16–33.

Broadbent, W. H. 1879: A case of peculiar affection of speech, with commentary. *Brain*, 1, 484–503.

Broca, Paul 1861: Nouvelle observation d'aphémie produite par une lésion de la moitié postérieure des deuxième et troisième circumvolutions frontales. *Bulletin de la Société Anatomique de Paris*, 3, 398–407.

—— 1865: Sur le siège de la faculté du langage articulé. *Bulletin d'Anthropologie*, 6, 377–93.

Caplan, David 1987: *Neurolinguistics and linguistic aphasiology*. Cambridge: Cambridge University Press.

Caramazza, A. and E. Zurif 1976: Dissociation of algorithmic and heuristic processes in language comprehension: evidence from aphasia, *Brain and Language*, 3, 572–82.

Chomsky, N. 1957: *Syntactic Structures*. The Hague: Mouton.

—— 1972: *Language and Mind*, 2nd edn. New York: Harcourt Brace Jovanovich.

—— 1975: *Reflections on Language*. New York: Pantheon Books.

—— 1976: *Aspects of the Theory of Syntax*. Cambridge, Mass.: MIT Press.

—— 1978: On the biological basis of language capacities. In G. A. Miller and E. Lenneberg, eds, *Psychology and biology of language and thought: Essays in honor of Eric Lenneberg*. New York: Academic Press. 208–9.

—— 1980: *Rules and Representations*. New York: Columbia University Press.

—— 1981: *Lectures on Government and Binding*. Dordrecht: Foris.

—— 1982: *On the generative enterprise: a discussion with Riny Huybregts and Hank van Riemskjik*. Dordrecht: Foris.

—— 1986: *Knowledge of Language: Its Nature, Origin, and Use*. New York: Praeger.

—— 1988: *Language and Problems of Knowledge: The Managua Lectures*. Cambridge, Mass.: MIT Press.

Coltheart, M., Patterson, K., and Marshall, J. C. (eds) 1980: *Deep Dyslexia*. London: Routledge & Kegan Paul.

Curtiss, Susan 1977: *Genie: A Psycholinguistic study of a modern-day "wild child."* New York: Academic Press.

Curtiss, S., Kempler, D., and Yamada, J. 1981: The relationship between language and cognition in development: theoretical framework and research design. *UCLA Working Papers in Cognitive Linguistics*, 3, 161–75.

Curtiss, S., Yamada, J., and Fromkin, V. 1979: How independent is language? On the question of formal parallels between grammar and action. *UCLA Working Papers in Cognitive Linguistics*, 1, 131–57.

de Courtenay, Baudouin 1895: *Versuche einer Theorie phonetischer Alternationen*. Strassburg: K. J. Trueb.

Einstein, Albert 1934: *Essays in Science*. New York: Philosophical Library.

Elliott, D., and Needleman, R. 1981: Language, cognition and pragmatics: The view from developmental disorders of language. *UCLA Working Papers in Cognitive Linguistics*, 3, 199–207.

Emmorey, Karen, E. 1987: Morphological Structure and Parsing in the Lexicon. Ph.D. Dissertation, UCLA.

Fodor, Jerry A. 1983: *The modularity of mind*. Cambridge, Mass.: MIT Press.

Forster, K. I. 1979: Levels of processing and the structure of the language processor. In W. Cooper and E. Walker (eds), *Sentence processing*. Hillsdale, NJ: Erlbaum.

Forster, K. I. 1981: Priming and the effects of sentence and lexical contests on naming time: evidence for autonomous lexical processing. *Quarterly Journal of Experimental Psychology*, 33a, 465–95.

Friederici, A. D. 1983: Perception of words in sentential contexts: Some real-time processing evidence. *Neuropsychologia*, 21, 351–8.

Fromkin, V. A. (ed.) 1985: *Phonetic Linguistics*. New York: Academic Press.

—— 1988: Grammatical aspects of speech errors. *Linguistics: The Cambridge Survey II*, edited by F. J. Newmeyer. Cambridge: Cambridge University Press, 117–38.

Fromkin, V. A., Krashen, S., Curtiss, S., Rigler, D. and Rigler, M. 1974: Lateralization in the case of Genie. In D. Walters (ed.), *Cerebral Dominance* (UCLA Brain Information Service Report, 34, 13–14).

Garrett, M. 1975: The analysis of sentence production. In G. Bower (ed.), *The Psychology of learning and motivation: advances in research and theory*, 9. New York: Academic Press.

—— 1980: Levels of processing in sentence production. In Brian Butterworth (ed.), *Language Production 1*. London: Academic Press, 177–220.

Gazdar, G. 1982: Phrase Structure Grammar. In P. Jacobson and G. Pullum (eds), *The Nature of Syntactic Representation*. Dordrecht: Reidel.

Goldstein, K. 1948: *Language and Language Disturbances*. New York: Grune and Stratton.

Goodman, J. 1972: A case study of an autistic savant: Mental function in the psychotic child with markedly discrepant abilities. *Journal of Child Psychology and Psychiatry*, 13, 267–78.

Grodzinsky, Y. 1984: The syntactic characterization of agrammatism. *Cognition*, 16, 99–120.

Halle, Morris 1973: Prolegomena to a theory of word formation. *Linguistic Inquiry*, 4, 3–16.

Harris, Zellig 1951: *Methods in Structural Linguistics*. Chicago: University of Chicago.

Heilman, K. M. and Scholes, R. J. 1976: The nature of comprehension errors in Broca's, conduction, and Wernicke's aphasics. *Cortex*, 12, 258–65.

Hockett, Charles 1942: A system of descriptive phonology. *Language*, 18, 3–21.

—— 1958: *A Course in Modern Linguistics*. New York: Macmillan.

—— 1967: Where the tongue slips, there slip 1. In *To Honor Roman Jakobson*. The Hague: Mouton.

Hyams, Nina 1988: The Core/Periphery Distinction in Language Acquisition. *Proceedings of the Eastern States Conference on Linguistics, IV*, 21.

Jacob, François 1982: *The Possible & the Actual*. New York: Pantheon Books.

Jakobson, Roman 1940: *Kindersprache, Aphasie and allgemeine Lautgesetze* Almqvist u. Wilsells, Uppsala. Reprinted as *Child Language, Aphasia, and Phonological Universals* (1968) The Hague: Mouton.

—— 1955: Aphasia as a linguistic problem. In H. Werner (ed.), *On Expressive Language*. Clark University Press, Worcester, Mass., 69–81.

—— 1964: Towards a linguistic typology of aphasic impairments. *Disorders of language*, ed. A. V. S. de Reuck and M. O'Connor. Boston: Little, Brown, 21–41.

Jerne, Niels 1984: The generative grammar of the immune system. *Science*, 229, 1057–9.

Joos, M. 1958: *Readings in Linguistics*. Washington, D.C.: ACLS.

Kanner, L. 1943: Autistic disturbances of affective contact. *Nerv. Child*, 2, 217–250.

Kaplan, Ronald and Joan Bresnan 1982: Lexical-Functional Grammar: A formal system for grammatical representation. In Joan Bresnan (ed.), *The mental representation of grammatical relations*. Cambridge, Mass.: MIT Press, 173–281.

Kean, Mary Louise 1977: The linguistic interpretation of aphasic syndromes: agrammatism in Broca's aphasia, an example *Cognition*, 5, 9–46.

Kiparsky, Paul 1968: How abstract is phonology? Reprinted in *Phonological representations* (1973), ed. Osamu Fujimura. Tokyo: TEC. 5–56.

—— 1982: Lexical morphology and phonology. *Linguistics in the Morning Calm*. Seoul: Linguistic Society of Korea. 3–92.

Kriendler, A., Calavuzo, C. and Mihailescu, L. 1971: Linguistic analysis of one case of jargon aphasia. *Revue Roumaine de Neurologie*, 8, 209–28.

Laplace, Pierre Simon 1886: *Théorie Analytique des Probabilités*. Introd. Oeuvres. Paris.

Lees, Robert B. 1957: Review of Noam Chomsky, *Syntactic Structures*. *Language*, 33, 357–408.

Leiber, J. 1975: *Noam Chomsky: A Philosophic Overview*. New York: St Martin's Press.

Lenneberg, E. 1967: *Biological Foundations of Language*. New York: Wiley.

Lieber, R. 1980: On the organization of the lexicon. Unpublished MIT Ph.D. dissertation.

—— 1983: Argument linking and compounds in English. *Linguistic Inquiry*, 14, 251–86.

Luria, A. R. 1947: *Traumatic Aphasia*. The Hague: Mouton (reprinted in translation 1970).

Mandelbaum, D. 1949: *Selected Writings of Edward Sapir*. Los Angeles: UC Press.

Marshall, John 1987: Phrenology revived. *Nature*, 306, Nov. 10, 137.

Marslen-Wilson, William D. 1975: Sentence perception as an interactive parallel process. *Science*, 189, 266–8.

Miller, G. 1962: Some psychological studies of grammar. *American Psychologist*, 17, 748–62.

Mohanan, K. P. 1982: Lexical phonology. MIT dissertation.

Morton, J. 1969: The interaction of information in word recognition. *Psychological Review*, 76, 165–78.

Morton, J. and Patterson, K. 1980: A new attempt at an interpretation. In M. Coltheart, K. Patterson, and J. C. Marshall (eds), *Deep Dyslexia*. London: Routledge & Kegan Paul, 91–118.

Moutier, F. 1908: *L'aphasie de Broca*. Paris: Steinheil.

Newcombe, F. and Marshall, J. C. 1984: Varieties of acquired dyslexia: a linguistic approach *Seminars in Neurology*, 4, 2. 181–95.

—— 1985: Sound-by-sound reading and writing. In *Surface Dyslexia*, edited by Coltheart, M., K. Patterson, and J. C. Marshall (eds), *Surface Dyslexia*, London: Routledge and Kegan Paul, 35–72.

Newmeyer, F. J. 1986: (second edition) *Linguistic Theory in America*. New York: Academic Press.

Patterson, K. E., Marshall, J. C. and Coltheart, M. 1985: *Surface Dyslexia*. London: Lawrence Erlbaum.

Pick, A. 1913: *Die Agrammatischen Sprachstorungen*. Springer: Berlin.

Rieber, R. W. (ed.) 1983: *Dialogues on the Psychology of Language and Thought: Conversations with Noam Chomsky, Charles Osgood, Jean Piaget, Ulric Neisser and Marcel Kinsbourne.* New York and London: Plenum Press.

Salomon, E. 1914: Motorische Aphasie mit Agrammatismus und Sensorischagrammatischen Storungen. *Monatschrift fur Psychiatrie und Neurologie*, 35, 181–208, 216–75.

Saussure, Ferdinand de 1916 [1959]: *Course in General Linguistics* (translation of *Cours de Linguistique Générale*). Paris: Payot.

Selkirk, Elizabeth 1982: *The syntax of words.* Cambridge, Mass.: MIT.

Skalicka, V. 1948: The need for a linguistics of *la parole.* Reprinted in J. Vachek (ed.), *A Prague School Reader in Linguistics,* Bloomington: University of Indiana Press, 1964: 375–90.

Sklar, R. 1968: Chomsky's revolution in linguistics. *The Nation,* September 9, 213–17.

Trager, G. L. and B. Bloch 1941: The syllabic phonemes of English. *Language*, 17, 223–46.

Trager, G. and Smith, H. L. 1951: *An Outline of English Structure.* Studies in Linguistics: Occasional Papers, no. 3. Norman, OK: Battenbergt Press.

Warrington, E. K. and Shallice, T. 1984: Category-specific semantic impairments. *Brain*, 107, 829–54.

Weigl, E. and Bierwisch, E. 1970: Neurospychology and Linguistics: Topics of common research. *Foundations of Language*, 6, 1–18.

Wernicke, C. 1874: The aphasic symptom complex: a psychological study on a neurological basis.

Kohn and Weigert, Breslau. Reprinted in R. S. Cohen and M. W. Wartofsky (eds) *Boston Studies in the Philosophy of Science, vol. 4.* Reidel: Boston.

Yamada, J. 1983: *The independence of language: a case study.* Ph.D. dissertation, UCLA.

5
Grammar, Meaning, and Indeterminacy

Norbert Hornstein

In contemporary thinking in the philosophy of language one pair of names stands out: Chomsky and Quine. Like Robin Hood and the Sheriff of Nottingham, Chomsky and Quine have staked out the poles on a variety of issues: language acquisition, mentalism, empiricism/rationalism, and the scientific status of grammatical theory. Within professional philosophy, Chomsky has appeared the brigand, leading raiding parties deep into enemy territory to reclaim portions of the intellectual inheritance for an unabashed mentalistic study of mind. Quine has appeared the defender of an orthodoxy which denies legitimacy to any such enterprise. With Skinner, Quine has played the role of unrepentant behaviorist, gleefully consigning all forms of mentalism to the first circle of pseudo-science.

This "debate" has gone on for over 20 years. In this time, sentiments have shifted away from Quine to a position more clearly sympathetic to Chomsky. It is a tribute to Chomsky, that, for the most part, contemporary philosophers of language take it for granted that mentalism is a legitimate position to adopt in studying the human mind. Indeed, except for parts of Cambridge, Mass., where philosophy of language has been replaced by history of philosophy – "all is confusion and we'll tell you who was muddled first" – and Southern California, where the very existence of mind is denied – neural connections everywhere but no mental life anywhere – almost everyone else under fifty now takes it for granted that Chomsky has successfully rebutted the most extreme forms of Quinean skepticism. Wherever professional sympathies might lie, the weight of consensus seems to favor Robin Hood and his merry band of grammarians.

In my opinion, this is as it should be. In the last 30 years, Chomsky has clearly demonstrated the viability and fecundity of unabashed mentalism. He has refashioned traditional rationalist commitments to a richly structured mind into powerful specific tools for the investigation of the language faculty. Chomsky has demonstrated that a favored rationalist argument-form – the argument from the poverty of the stimulus – can be used to illuminate the detailed fine structure of the language faculty. If Descartes were alive today he would be "schepping nachas."

This said, however, knowing Chomsky, I am sure that the last thing that he wants is this sort of consensus. Consequently, in this paper, I will try to stir Quine's pot once again and suggest that there is a version of Quine's complaint that is worth reconsidering. However, before taking this tack, a couple of caveats are in order. Quine's position is notoriously hard to discern. As such, I will no doubt be putting some unwanted words into his mouth. In this respect, what I will try to defend might not be a position that Quine himself might not be happy with, though, it is, in my opinion, the only defensible non-question-begging version of the indeterminacy thesis.

Second, my conclusions concerning the efficacy of Quine's concerns are considerably more anemic than he or partisans of his views have supposed. I believe that Chomsky's approach to the study of language raises virtually no methodological problems, at least in the core areas of research. Nonetheless, I believe that Quine's concerns point to serious difficulties for the study of meaning, at least in its most popular philosophical varieties. In what follows, I will try to suggest that Quine's arguments, though they leave grammatical theory virtually unscathed, do provide reasons for questioning the scientific status of semantic theory. It is because philosophers have construed an attack on semantics as an attack on linguistics as a whole that the conclusion has been erroneously drawn that indeterminacy implies that mentalist linguistics of the Chomsky variety is scientifically ill-conceived.

In what follows, I will review Quinean arguments on four related topics. The status of the analytic/synthetic distinction, the indeterminacy of translation, the inscrutability of reference and the museum myth of meaning. My conclusion will be that Quine's indeterminacy arguments are surprisingly successful when semantic theory is the intended target. Indeed, a careful rereading of Quine's arguments indicates that indeterminacy threatens when words must get correlated with extra mental entities. Quine is rather dubious that Chomsky's program can be fruitfully developed. However, Quine's reservations do *not* rely on considerations of indeterminacy except when his concerns turn to semantical concerns. In short, not surprisingly perhaps, it is the coordination of words with objects which gives rise to indeterminacy. On this reading, the inscrutability of reference is a simple corollary of the indeterminacy thesis.

As for the dissolution of the analytic/synthetic distinction and the unmasking of the museum myth, I will argue that neither obviously succumbs to Quine's arguments. There might well be a place for notions similar to those Quine criticizes, though they will not carry the epistemological implications that characterized the earlier set of distinctions that he criticized.

My conclusions concerning the success of Quine's indeterminacy thesis might appear bad for the viability of Chomsky's grammatical enterprise. The success of the indeterminacy of translation thesis has been taken to directly threaten the scientific legitimacy of linguistic theory. This conclusion, however, is relatively easy to resist when it is appreciated that what permits the thesis some plausibility are commitments to a style of semantic theorizing that Chomskyan linguistics has little sympathy with or need of.

These are the conclusions. – Let's begin and see whether it is possible to sail safely between Kendall Square and Harvard Square, the Scylla and Charybdis of the philosophy of language, without running aground.

1   THE ANALYTIC/SYNTHETIC DISTINCTION

Quine's celebrated attack on the analytic/synthetic distinction was first launched in "Two Dogmas." His arguments divided into two distinct parts. In the first four sections of the essay, Quine argued that standard definitions of analyticity in terms of substitution *salva veritate*, necessity, etc. are all viciously circular. In what does the vicious circularity consist? It resides in the fact that all the proposed definitions presuppose exactly the same epistemological issues as those concepts that are being defined. Thus, the complaint is not that it is in general illicit to have definitions that are circular – in some sense all systems of definitions are circular – but that the nature of the circle is such that it throws no light whatever on the alleged connections between issues in the theory of meaning and the theory of knowledge:

> [T]he philosophically important question about analyticity and the linguistic doctrine of logical truth is *not* how to explicate them; it is the question rather of their relevance to epistemology.[1]

In Quine's view, the relevance is zero. Consider an illustrative example.

In section 4 of "Two Dogmas," Quine considers one possible approach to defining analyticity. Defenders of the distinction blamed its inherent fuzziness on the inexact nature of natural languages. In exact formal languages, it was said, the fuzziness could be eliminated and exact characterizations of analyticity could be given. Quine challenges this view.

Consider the following definition of analyticity. A statement S is analytic if it follows exclusively from the semantical or syntactic rules of the language. In formal languages, these rules are explicitly provided and so it should be easy to define analyticity. Not so, says Quine. Though for any given formal language one can define analyticity, it is not the case that a definition of the notion exists in general. The problem is to define "S is analytic in L" for variable S and L. It is this more general notion which is of interest. Why?

Epistemology within Carnap's program consisted in logically reconstructing the true sentences of a theory into those that are true due to meaning and those true contingently. By so categorizing statements one laid bare their epistemological bases and so could account for a theory's knowledge claims. But for such a procedure to be epistemologically fruitful it is necessary to have criteria for dividing up the statements of a theory into those that pertain to empirical and those that pertain to framework considerations. The reconstruction is correct if all analytic statements are true due to the nature of the linguistic rules and none of the contingent statements are. But to know this one must have a notion of analyticity which holds for variable S and L. Otherwise, it will be impossible to tell if a given reconstruction is adequate or not.

To put this another way. The linguistic rules in a proper reconstruction encode a certain epistemological distinction for Carnap. But for precisely this reason they can't in turn define the distinction.

In the last sections of "Two Dogmas," Quine gives another way of grounding the analytic/synthetic distinction. He suggests that the distinction could be saved if verifications were true. Verificationist theories of meaning hold that the meaning of a sentence is the method of empirically confirming it. Analytic sentences are those sentences which are confirmed no matter what.

According to Quine resort to verificationism cannot save the analytic/synthetic distinction for it depends on an inadequate reductionist picture of meaning. As is well known, Quine denies that sentences in general have cognitive content taken singly. Rather, sentences meet experience as "a corporate body." This makes it impossible in general to distinguish those aspects of the meaning of a sentence due to its interanimation with other sentences from those due entirely to its confrontation with experience.

Two points are worthy of note in Quine's original argument. First, it is primarily aimed at the epistemological pretensions of the analytic/synthetic distinction. And second, it does not rely on any specific theories of learning or particular accounts of the activities of the field linguist.

It is important to recall that the analytic/synthetic distinction was of philosophical significance for its epistemological implications. Carnap, for example, exploited this distinction among statements in his reconstructions of scientific theories. In Quine's mind, Carnap's use of the distinction enforced "a double standard for ontological questions and scientific hypotheses" ("Two Dogmas," p. 45). The very demarcation of science from metaphysics rested on the distinction between analytic and synthetic statements. The point of Quine's attack was to undermine this dualism. The focus of the attack was a technical epistemological notion central to Carnap's philosophical attempt to demarcate the boundary between pragmatic questions of ontology and real questions of science. Quine's intent was to "repudiate such a boundary" and to "espouse a more thorough pragmatism."

The reason it is worth recalling the object of Quine's blast is that it is hard, if not impossible, to evaluate the success of his argument without doing so. In addition, it becomes quite difficult to assess the limits of the argument's efficacy. Let me explain.

Analyticity played a role in both Carnap's epistemological pronouncements and it still plays a role in the everyday practice of the linguist. It is entirely possible that Quine's argument successfully undermines the utility of Carnap's notion without affecting the linguistic notion. I believe that this is indeed the case.

I have argued at length elsewhere that there is a version of Quine's argument that does not rely illicitly on behaviorism and that successfully undermines Carnapian dualism.[2] However, it is equally clear that this argument does not call into question the legitimacy of an analogous technical distinction within the linguistic theory of meaning. As Chomsky has recently pointed out, no-one observing the methods of the field linguist could have been led to say that he eschews the analytic/synthetic distinction. Nor would a grammarian wish to deny that there are semantic connections attributable to the operations of the language faculty rather than other more general systems of belief. Examples abound. Consider a simple case of the passive.

(1)   a   John kissed Mary
      b   Mary was kissed by John

It is hard to see anyone denying that these sentences are equivalent in meaning. In both cases, John is the kisser and Mary the kissee. Further-more, virtually every generative linguist would attribute the synonymy of these sentences to the operations of linguistic rules. The passive, in cases such as (1), is meaning-preserving.

The same can be said for some cases of lexical meaning. So for example (2)b follows from (2)a because of the meaning of "assassinate."

(2)   a   John assassinated Bill
      b   Bill is dead
      c   Bill was cremated

This contrasts with (2)c for example. The truth of this latter sentence is independent of the truth of (2)a in ways that (2)b is not. Moreover, anyone queried about the relationship of these three sentences will report these connections.

A convenient way to model the distinctions among the sentences in (2) is to trace the relationships between (2)a and (2)b to the operations of the language faculty, or the structure of the lexicon, while attributing the relationship between (2)a and (2)c to some other mental faculty or system of belief. In this way, we reconstitute a version of the analytic/synthetic distinction. The relationship between (2)a and (2)b is a function of linguistic rules alone, while that between (2)a and (2)c would require some extra-linguistic input. Moreover, the legitimacy of the distinction in this domain can only be challenged on the basis of dubious behaviorist premises.

The challenge would go as follows. The relationship of (1)a and (1)b is forged through training on the basis of reinforcement by the speech community. This, after all, is how language training proceeds. Thus, the fact that native speakers treat these sentences as synonymous indicates not that they share the same meaning, or that their links are due to the operations of the language faculty, but because of the schedule of training and reinforcement which in turn reflects the linguistic experience of the native speaker. All links are rooted in experience and training by the speech community.

Needless to say, the premises of this argument are quite controversial. It is quite unlikely that anything like this obtains for the cases at hand. Training has not proven to be a useful notion in accounting for language acquisition, not even acquisition of lexical knowledge.[3] The standard reasons for rejecting behaviorism undermine this sort of response.

However, it is quite unlikely that the acceptability of a linguistic distinction between links forged through the operation of the language faculty and those derived from the operations of other cognitive components can be used to save Carnap's analytic/synthetic distinction. For Carnap, the fact that a sentence was analytic was intended to confer epistemological privileges on it. Such sentences were immune from revision. Choosing such sentences for scientific purposes involved pragmatic rather than empirical considerations. In short, being analytic had rich epistemological consequences. It is hard to see how the linguistic notion of analyticity could support these epistemological privileges. Just because the relationship of a set of sentences can be traced to the operation of the language faculty does not appear to confer any epistemological privileges on them. We can, after all, decide to ditch our innately-provided grammar and lexicon along with the relations it privileges if the emipirical need arises. Just because a relationship is made easily available by the language faculty does not endow it with epistemological advantages such as immunity from revision.

What's the upshot? I have argued that Quine's argument against the analytic/synthetic distinction should be seen in a specific light. Seen as an attack on Carnap's epistemology it is rather successful. However, this success does not undermine the utility of related notions in linguistics. On the other hand, the success of these notions in linguistics does not confer legitimacy on Carnap's epistemologically-oriented notions. There are many reasons for advocating an analytic/synthetic distinction. They need not be mutually supporting.

2   THE INDETERMINACY OF TRANSLATION

In section 1, I argued that Quine's disparaging comments concerning the analytic/synthetic distinction carried a reasonable amount of weight if aimed at Carnap's distinction but very little if directed towards the linguistic one. In this section, I will try a more wholesale defence of one of Quine's positions: the indeterminacy of translation thesis. I will argue for three points. First, Quine's arguments are quite successful when aimed at

semantic theory. Second, their success is to be expected given a commitment to a mentalist approach to linguistic knowledge. Third, the success of
this argument fails to have any broad ramifications concerning the scientific
legitimacy of Chomsky's brand of generative grammar. In short, the
indeterminacy thesis is more or less correct but it does not really matter
much for Chomskyan linguistics.

As is well known, the indeterminacy thesis is cast as a thesis about
language and one's ability to translate it. The scenario has a field linguist of
definite behaviorist tendencies go out into the bush to translate a language
of which he is entirely ignorant and which is entirely unrelated to any
languages he knows anything about. To effect the translation he has access
to the notion of stimulus meaning, which he uses to correlate sentences
from his language with sentences of the native language. A sentence S in
his language is translated into a sentence N of the native's language if they
similarly correlate with certain patterns of nonverbal environmental sti-
mulation. To give the linguist a fighting chance, Quine gives him access to
the native's version of "yes" and "no." He also defines two more refined
notions of stimulus meaning for the linguist – affirmative and negative
stimulus meaning. It is on the basis of these notions alone that the linguist
proceeds. What Quine investigates is how far the linguist gets sticking
exclusively to these procedures.

The types of sentences the linguist investigates are of three kinds. There
are occasion sentences, which are quite closely tied to environmental
conditions of verification, truth-functional sentences, and standing sentences which are more remote and not as closely tied to observation
conditions. Radical translation proceeds quite efficiently when confronted
with the first two kinds of sentences. But, when it comes to translating the
standing sentences, stimulus meaning becomes inadequate in accounting
for the cognitive meaning of these sentences. Why so?

To relate standing sentences to experience requires mediation. They
must first be related to other sentences. When this is required, when
sentences must be interanimated, stimulus meaning breaks down and
analytical hypotheses come into play. To relate sentences to one another,
one must break sentences into sub-sentential units – words – and relate
these words to their referents. The problem for Quine's linguist is that this
cannot be done within the confines of the previously defined notion of
stimulus meaning. Why not?

The problem comes not in breaking sentences down into words, but in
relating words to referents.

> He [the field linguist] is in a position . . . to translate the observation sentence
> into English, though only holophrastically; that is, *without imputing any*
> *relevance to the individual English words* beyond the observable situation
> that they combine to report . . . He cannot, without exceeding his evidence,
> impute to the native sentence, or to any segment of it, the distinctive
> significance of "rabbit" as against "rabbit stage" or "rabbit part."[4]

The reason for the difficulty is that ostensively, the exact same stimulus situation obtains when one points to an object, an undetached object part, an instance of objecthood, etc. Thus, on the basis of stimulus meaning alone the referential apparatus cannot be linked to behavior. At that point in translation where cognitive meaning crucially relies on relating sentences to one another, and hence parts of sentences to things, indeterminacy intrudes.

One philosopher's *modus ponens* can be another's *modus tollens*. The fact that indeterminacy arises at all might be seen less as a problem for linguistics and more a problem for the notion that all one should avail oneself of is stimulus meaning. Why restrict oneself to this alone? This, indeed, has been the line of attack taken by those wishing to avoid Quine's conclusions. Chomsky was the first to emphasize the behaviorist flavor of so restricting one's evidentiary base.[5] Many have followed his lead.

However, it is important for my purposes here that we be clear about the precise locus of indeterminacy. Where, *specifically*, does Quine claim it arises? It intrudes when we must gloss words *with their referents*. The problem, then, is not in segmenting the sentence into words, but into terms, i.e. parts that refer. Though Quine has occasionally asked for methodological criteria for choosing between extensionally equivalent grammars, for example in "Methodological Reflections on Current Linguistic Theory" (henceforth MR), he has *not* invoked indeterminacy to suggest that there are principled reasons for thinking that it cannot get done.[6] This is not to deny that Quine's behaviorist predilections dispose him to think that such criteria will not be forthcoming. But he appears to concede the possibility that there may be many behavioral, in the broad sense, criteria for doing this. This concession is sufficient to indicate that Quine is treating these sorts of difficulties, however serious he considers them, as different from cases of indeterminacy. Recall that, in matters of indeterminacy, there is no possible "fact of the matter."

Actually, in MR, Quine suggests ways of distinguishing extensionally equivalent systems: "It could be a question of dispositions to accept certain transformations and not others; or certain inferences and not others" (MR: 444). I am not endorsing these ways of choosing among competing grammars. I only wish to point out that even for Quine, choices such as these fall *within* the bounds of the empirical, in contrast to issues of indeterminacy.

Quine does not actually expend much effort in denying that at least some forms of grammar choice are empirical and possible in principle. Rather, the trouble arises when we must relate these sub-sentential elements to their semantic values. And the problem is that there are too many semantic values to choose from, all of which are compatible with getting the truth conditions of the occasion sentences right and the behavior of the speaker accounted for. As Quine put it elsewhere, observation does not suffice to determine what objects the speakers of a language believe in.[7] The problem is that stimulus meaning allows no non-arbitrary way of operationalizing the reference relation.

Why not? First, because ostension will not resolve the relevant issues.

Pointing only individuates objects against a given referential background. Pointing to a rabbit also counts as pointing to an instance of rabbithood. Disambiguation follows if we can translate the apparatus of individuation, e.g. the "is" of identity, quantifiers, etc. If "is" means "is the same object as," then we know that it is a standard ontology that is being presupposed. But how are we to determine this? Quine's point is that saddling someone with ontological commitments is all too *easy* to do. Behavior, even broadly construed, does not really fix the background ontology a speaker is presupposing. As semantics, for Quine, is ontologically pregnant – it is "real" semantics in Chomsky's phrase – issues of meaning and ontology are closely intertwined.

Let me repeat that it is ontology, and hence semantics, that is problematic, not syntax, at least when the details of Quine's criticism is considered.

Quine's many approving references to Dewey indicate that it is the theory of meaning that he is after. In "Philosophical Progress in Language Theory,"[8] he claims that Dewey's dictum that meaning is primarily a property of behavior and Wittgenstein's dictum that meaning is use constitute a Copernican "flip" of great significance. In addition, here Quine appears to adhere to a form of empiricism that accepts "innate dispositions." In context, it seems clear that innateness, no matter how robust, is not his target. Rather, it is philosophical referential meaning theories.

I stress this, for recent commentators have taken Quine's argument to start from the premise that all of linguistics is illicit if not behaviorist in the narrow sense. Ricketts has tried to show that this positions of Quine's is not arbitrary but has a reasonable philosophical basis within his overall position.[9] George has criticized Ricketts's defence of Quine and favors a position which sees Quine's critique as based on broadly empirical considerations.[10] In my view both explications of the controversy are inadequate, as they both presuppose that Quine and Chomsky are at loggerheads over the scientific status of contemporary linguistics in general. The problem with both interpretations is that it leaves Quine holding a very weak position. The fact is that Quine *never* really addresses the issues of contemporary linguistics in any detail. He never discusses an actual case of what Chomsky takes to be a successful explanation and explain why it fails.

Ricketts (p. 135) suggests that this is because Quine does not recognize as data what Chomsky seeks to explain. But why not? According to Ricketts, it is because

> though Quine's science explains each instance of speech behavior, putative regularities in linguistic behavior described in such mentalistic or cognitive terms as "assertion" go unsubsumed, unexplained by Quine's science. On the basis of this explanatory deficiency, Chomsky challenges the explanatory omnicompetence of Quine's science.

However, whether or not Chomsky would lodge a complaint on these bases, it is not what Chomsky actually does.[11] In case after case, Chomsky points out that speakers categorize sets of sentences differentially, based on acceptability. He proposes a theory to account for this. Chomsky's claim has always been that to explain these sorts of data, a rich mentalist theory is required. Now, *pace* Ricketts, acceptability judgements do not presuppose the notion of "assertion," any more than seeing an Escher drawing as "funny" does. Chomsky's objections to Quine's behaviorism are much simpler and much more potent.[12]

George argues against Ricketts that the disagreement between Chomsky and Quine is not over what counts as data. Rather it is a difference in research strategy. Quine is betting that physiology will ultimately explain everything and that there is no need for the kind of explanation Chomsky advances. However, if this is Quine's position he has done precious little to defend it. One defends a research strategy by showing how it can be put to work. One advances it by showing that it can explain most of what rival strategies can explain and then some. The fact of the matter is that neurophysiology has, at present, NOTHING to say about linguistic competence or "dispositions to linguistic behavior." We have no idea about how linguistic knowledge or behavior is realized in neural wet ware. If George's interpretation is correct then Quine's position is laughably weak and Chomsky is on strong methodological grounds when he dismisses Quine's concerns.

There is, however, another interpretation of the indeterminacy thesis which is more defensible and that makes Quine's views and Chomsky's rather similar. Indeterminacy is primarily aimed at discrediting semantic theory, not grammatical theory in general.

When it comes to issues of meaning, Quine and Chomsky often sound quite a bit alike. For example, consider cross reference. Quine does not deny that any language permits cross reference. He just denies that this implies any ontological commitments or implicates semantic mechanisms. Indeed, at times Quine seems to be saying that it is best to see ontology as simply following syntactic form.

> The positing of attributes is accompanied by no clue as to the circumstances under which attributes may be said to be the same or different ... We understand the forms as referential just because they are grammatically analogous to ones that we learned earlier, for physical objects, with full dependence on the identity aspect.[13]

This is not at all crazy for many natural language cases of cross reference. As Chomsky has emphasized in a different context, syntactic form rather than semantic value determines co-reference behavior. Take for example the locution "the average man" or "a flaw" in cases such as (3).

(3) a   The average man believes himself to be handsome.
     b   John discovered a flaw in the argument. It undermined the stated conclusion.

In these sorts of cases, Chomsky has urged, cross reference should not be seen as implying ontological commitment to flaws or average men. Rather the apparatus of cross reference is syntactically driven. As such no semantic conclusions and no ontological conclusions should be drawn.

To this point I have rephrased Quine's argument and have highlighted the fact that its central concern is with semantics. I have pointed out that indeterminacy arises when word/thing relationships have to be established. Quine identifies the target of his concerns quite explicitly in some places. He observes that "[the] behaviorizing of meaning . . . is simply a proposal to approach *semantical* matters in the empirical spirit of natural science. An aid to taking this proposal seriously is the *gedankenexperiment* of radical translation" (my emphasis).[14] Observe that it is semantics, not linguistics as a whole, which is here the target of the indeterminacy thesis.

In addition, I have noted Quine's contention that linguistic behavior, even broadly construed, underdetermines ontological commitment and hence semantic form. I have noted that Chomsky provides some cases in which seem to indicate sympathy for this sort of view in the case of cross reference.

Nonetheless, there is still a behaviorist shadow darkening Quine's conclusions. My claim is that Quine's behaviorism is benign in the case. Moreover, partisans of the Chomskyan viewpoint should by sympathetic with Quine's conclusions. The reason is that the indeterminacy thesis can be seen as just a trivial consequence of methodological solipsism or the syntactic theory of the mind.

As articulated by Fodor, for example, mental representations face two ways. They are syntactic objects and semantic vehicles. *Qua* semantic vehicles they are true or false: NPs refer to objects, predicates pick out properties. However, it is only as syntactic objects that representations have behavioral effects and are causally efficacious psychologically. Psychology simply does not require any semantic theory to explain competence or behavior: "truth, reference and the rest of the semantic notions aren't psychological categories."[15] The computational regularities psychological theories provide, and this holds for linguistics too, being a branch of cognitive psychology, treat the mind as a "syntax-driven machine."[16] Methodological solipsism is the theory that mental processes are computational, hence syntactic. What this means is that psychological states and laws are individuated without respect to their semantic evaluation (*Psychosemantics*, pp. 42–3). In a word psychology does not require quantification over semantically specified states: "If mental processes are formal . . . then they have no access to the semantic properties of . . . representations, including the property of being true, of having referents, or . . . the property of being representations *of the environment*" ("Methodological Solipsism," p. 231). As such, to account for linguistic behavior *broadly construed* requires taking no ontological or semantic hostages.

This syntactic picture of the mind is currently the accepted wisdom. If one sees the mind as a computing device of some sort, it is close to anxiomatic that its representations will interact as a function of their structure, not what they semantically stand for. Computers crunch form. As such, strictly speaking, semantic value is psychologically inert.[17]

This view is not idiosyncratic to Fodor. Aside from him, it has been championed by Stich, Schiffer, Soames, yours truly and even Chomsky.[18]

These authors have pointed out that if one's interests are psychological then real semantics is irrelevant, empirically superfluous. But this just means to say that psychology radically underdetermines ontological commitment. In other words, if we take semantics, as Quine does, as ontologically pregnant, then if the syntactic theory of mind is correct, the indeterminacy of translation thesis must be true. If, after all, only syntax is relevant, then behavior will be compatible with any semantics that can be welded onto the correct syntax. What functions in practice to hide this from us is the tacit assumption that the mapping from syntax to semantics must be relatively transparent. However, as the examples cited from Chomsky above indicate, we often resist the obvious mapping if it commits us to the existence of flaws or average men.

Where does this bring us? Most discussions of the indeterminacy thesis have seen Quine's critique as stemming from a general jaundiced view of mentalism as a result of a strong commitment to a radical behaviorism of the Skinnerian variety. I completely agree with Chomsky that this sort of stance is entirely untenable for *scientific* reasons. If Quine's position reduces to a taste for behaviorism, as Ricketts for example has suggested, then it is hardly credible. In addition, in contrast to George, it is currently clear that Quine's position has, at present, very little going on for it empirically.

However, there is another way of reading Quine which takes his argument not as aimed at linguistics in general but as directed against a particular *kind* of theorizing; semantics. Even partisans of mentalism should be able to agree that mentalism should not be taken for granted. There is no a priori reason for thinking that mentalism in semantics will be scientifically useful or fecund. Quine's argument can be taken as claiming that a mentalist referential semantics, the philosophical meaning theory of choice, will never make any empirical difference. As such, the presupposition that semantics so construed is a legitimate scientific pursuit should be dropped.

The distinction between syntactic theories and meaning and true semantic ones coming up in Quine's discussion of the relative indeterminacy of substitutional theories of quantification versus objectional accounts. For Quine, the former are rather benign, no worse off than fixing the interpretation of conjunction. As for the latter, Quine states:

> From the point of view of radical translation and indeterminacy, objectual quantification is worse off than substitutional quantification. For we cannot identify such quantification, in the native language, without also getting clear on what to count in the native language as names and what to count as singular terms and, to some extent, what to count them as referring to. And I have argued that this sort of thing cannot, in an objective sense, be known. (PP, p. 14).

The distinction between these two approaches to quantification is important for my purposes here, for it highlights the fact that it is linking words
to *objects* that Quine considers problematic. If we eschew real semantics,
indeterminacy is of no great significance. The contrast regarding indeterminacy that Quine draws between these two forms of quantification is
telling. Syntactically, these two forms of quantification are on a par. The
only difference is that objectual quantification requires the identification of
terms – expressions that refer to non-linguistic objects – while substitutional theories deal in nothing but expressions. Quine's discussion identifies the
precise locus of indeterminacy. It arises where objectual quantification
parts company with substitutional theories, viz. at that point where
expressions must be coordinated with real-world non-linguistic objects.

I have argued that the indeterminacy arises within Quine's scheme just at
the point where word/world semantic relations have to be forged. At this
point, Quine argues, stimulus meaning cannot get us to a unique ontological scheme and so semantics is radically underdetermined by linguistic
behavior. But this is not a conclusion that we should find surprising or
disturbing. Partisans of the syntactic theory of mind should feel comfort-
able with a position that argues that semantic relations, i.e. word/world
reference relations, play no role within psychology proper. Whatever
psychological fact we wish to explain can be explained without invoking
semantic relations. This is what a commitment to computationalism
entails. Another way of saying the same thing is that any given psychological fact can be accounted for using arbitrarily different semantic schemes. If
it is the syntax which is doing all the work, then *vis à vis* semantics linguistic
behavior is radically indeterminate.

Quine's reaction to the conclusion that indeterminacy exists is to urge us
to give up the museum myth of meaning. What this comes to, is the
suggestion that we simply abandon the view that "words and sentences
have their determinate meanings" even "in cases where behavioral criteria
are powerless to discover them for us." This has often sounded ominous,
with behaviorist overtones suggesting that we abandon the study of
meaning. However, a more benign reading suggests itself. It is referential
semantics that should be abandoned, the view that words have definite
ontological moorings in a speaker's mind even if it never manifests itself in
any observable way, even if the assumption that words refer to things is
theoretically idle within our best psychological theories. In other words,
referential semantics of the kind pursued by philosophers of language just
makes no behavioral sense. As such it should be dumped. As Quine has
observed, "if by these standards there are indeterminate cases, *so much the
worse for the terminology of meaning.*"[19]

This sentiment is echoed by Chomsky's *Knowledge of Language*. He too
points out that semantics realistically construed is of dubious scientific
value and does not appear to add anything of empirical significance to
linguistics. Like Quine he urges against treating this form of theorizing
with respect.

There seems no obvious sense in populating the extra-mental world with corresponding entities, nor any empirical consequence or gain in explanatory force in doing so. (p. 45)

Chomsky explicitly draws the connection between his brand of mentalism and the rejection of real semantics, the ontologically interesting variety Quine was discussing.

The scope of the shift to a mentalist or conceptualist interpretation . . . is broader than has been sometimes appreciated . . . I think that it . . . includes much of what is misleadingly called "the semantics of natural language" – I say "misleadingly" because I think that much of this work is not semantics at all, if by "semantics" we mean the study of the relation between language and the world – in particular the study of truth and reference. (*Knowledge of Language*, p. 44)

Please observe that the conclusion we have drawn does not require any behaviorist commitments. On the present view, the indeterminacy thesis is just a corollary of the computational view of the mind. If the mind is a syntactic engine, and semantics is irrelevant, then the behavioral/empirical equivalence of incompatible semantic schemes should come as no surprise. Observe as well that, read in this way, the indeterminacy thesis is an attack not on mentalism but on the scientific utility of ontological and semantic concerns. It is not mental constructs in general that are scientifically suspicious. Rather it is semantic primitives that are of dubious explanatory value.

This is not a conclusion that I am inclined to resist. However, what is of more importance is that it is not a conclusion that threatens the scientific legitimacy of grammatical theory. The main reason is that the semantic theorizing that Quine attacks and that the syntactic theory of mind renders ineffectual is not part and parcel of contemporary linguistics.

For Chomsky, for example, the proper tools of meaning theory are syntactic and deal with the interrelationship of entities in various domains of mental computation. Meaning theory so construed disregards the "real" referential properties of mental forms. Thus, as Chomsky has repeatedly emphasized, meaning theory is actually just another form of syntax.

One can speak of "reference" or "co-reference" with some intelligibility if one postulates a domain of mental objects associated with formal entities of language by a relation with many of the properties of reference, but all of this is internal to the theory of mental representations; it is a form of syntax. (*Knowledge of Language*, p. 45)

If this is correct, then Quine's arguments are of dubious relevance for Chomsky's project. Indeed, one might go further. It seems that both Chomsky and Quine see little that is scientifically worthy in traditional philosophical semantics. From the perspective outlined here, Quine's challenge is not to mentalism *per se* but mentalist semantic theory. And his conclusions are very similar to Chomsky's: Forget about it!

I have argued here that Quine's and Chomsky's views over the issue of indeterminacy are not that dissimilar. Indeed, they both question the value of semantic theory if one's aim is the explanation of human psychology. This does not mean to suggest that Chomsky and Quine agree on how the empirical work is to proceed. There are many passages in Quine that can only be read as endorsing behaviorist tendencies of dubious value. However, whatever his taste in psychological theory, it is not clear that the indeterminacy thesis is vitiated by these commitments. The thesis has a narrower focus than mentalism. Its aim is to discredit a peculiarly *philosophical* type of meaning theory; one that construes meaning as consisting in the relation of linguistic objects – words – to non-linguistic entities in the world. Quine points out that this sort of relationship is vastly undetermined by behavioral evidence. Chomsky points out that it is largely irrelevant for the study of human linguistic capacity or behavior. To my ear this is close to agreement. Who would have guessed it?

3   CONCLUSION

I have argued that translating between Quine's concerns and Chomsky's is fraught with indeterminacy. This is largely due to the fact that their targets were often quite different. Quine was interested in removing what he considered to be the baneful influence of Carnap's positivism from epistemology and replacing it with a thoroughgoing naturalism. Chomsky has been largely concerned in making the world of philosophy safe for mentalism. These differing interests have intersected over common vocabularies. However, when one gets behind the words to the larger programs, a surprising amount of agreement exists. To my mind, this is of some importance. When both Chomsky and Quine agree that there is something wrong with some particular enterprise, then there probably is. Semantics beware!

However, before dispensing with semantic theory, I would like to say one word in its defense. Let us assume for the sake of argument that semantic theorizing is superfluous in the sense that we can do everything syntactically. There might still be a sense in which "going semantic" would be an intelligent research tack to take. This would be methodologically wise if it turned out that our syntactic theories were more or less transparent with our semantic ones. In other words, it might turn out to be the case that natural languages were logically perfect in the sense that all of the relevant structure and categories of our syntactic theory mirrored what our intuitive semantic theories required. If this were to happen we could construe our syntax as tracking semantics and it would be very helpful to "look at the world" to determine our mental syntax.

This is not merely a hypothetical possibility. The strategy of building "real world" constraints into the mental syntax constitutes a good chunk of

Marr's research agenda in early vision. As Neil Stillings and Pat Kitcher have both recently emphasized, there is a good sense in which Marr's methodology eschews solipsism for wide content.[20] It searches for real world constraints that then get syntactified. Though strictly speaking still a syntactic theory, Marr's work gets considerable mileage from assuming that the world strongly constrains the formal properties of the syntax.

There is another possibility however. In contrast to this weak syntactic theory of mind, it might also turn out that the categories and structures of one's mental syntax are only loosely related to some natural scheme of interpretation. In this case, one's theory would be strongly syntactic. The regularities and laws of a strongly syntactic theory would run against the semantic grain.

My own view is that the language faculty is strongly syntactic. I have argued as much at length in other places.[21] However, whether it is or it isn't, I think that investigating the degree of transparency between syntax and interpretation turns out to provide a very fruitful research agenda. Do all semantic quantifiers also act like quantifiers syntactically, i.e. move to A' position in the syntax? Are all elements that act as syntactic operators also semantic operators? Are all semantic bound variables also syntactically bound? Is semantic scope a unitary syntactic phenomenon? Does syntactic structure faithfully mirror semantic predicate argument structure? These are empirical questions, answers to which will help illuminate the question whether or not the language faculty is strongly syntactic and where in particular transparency assumptions concerning the relationship of syntactic to semantic structure break down. I urge that we try climbing the semantic ladder before kicking it away. Both failure and success should prove to be illuminating.[22]

NOTES

I would like to thank Sidney Morgenbesser for extensive discussion of the topics covered in this paper and for his comments on an earlier draft.

1   From *The Philosophy of W. V. O. Quine*, ed. Lewis Edwin Hahn and Paul Arthur Schilpp (Open Court, La Salle, Ill., 1986), p. 207.
2   The relationship between Carnap and Quine on these issues is discussed at greater length in my "Foundationalism and Quine's indeterminacy of "translation thesis," *Social Research*, 49, 1 (1982).
3   For some recent extended discussion of these issues see Massimo Piattelli-Palmarini, "Evolution, selection and cognition: from 'learning' to parameter fixation in biology and the study of mind," Occasional Paper no. 35 (1988), MIT Center for Cognitive Science.
4   The emphasis is mine. The quote is from Quine, "Philosophical Progress in Language Theory," *Metaphilosophy*, 1, 1, 10. Henceforth (PP).
5   See Noam Chomsky, "Quine's empirical assumptions," in *Words and Objections*, ed. D. Davidson and J. Hintikka (Reidel, Dordrecht, 1969).
6   Quine's essay appears in *The Semantics of Natural Language*, ed. D. Davidson and G. Harman (Reidel, Dordrecht, 1972).

7   W. V. Quine, "Speaking of objects," in *Ontological Relativity* (Columbia University Press, New York, 1969), p. 11.
8   *Metaphilosophy*, 1.1 (Jan. 1970), pp. 6–7.
9   Thomas G. Ricketts, "Rationality, translation, and epistemology naturalized," *Journal of Philosophy*, LXXIX, 3 (March 1982).
10 Alexander George, "Whence and whither the debate between Quine and Chomsky," *Journal of Philosophy*, LXXXIII, 9 (Sept. 1986).
11 As George points out, Ricketts' reconstruction of Quine's position requires ignoring some rather specific comments Quine makes regarding mentalism. Quine points out that "the naturalist's primary objection . . . is not an objection to meanings on account of their being mental entities." From "Ontological Relativity," in *Ontological Relativity* (Columbia University Press, New York, 1969), p. 27.
    Note two points concerning this quote. First, *pace* Ricketts, Quine is not attacking mentalism *per se*. Second, it is *meaning* that is the object of concern, not other kinds of grammatical posits. This latter point is developed below.
12 In every book Chomsky writes he discusses grammatical examples that he takes to be problematic for any theory that eschews a rich mentalist set of assumptions. Surprisingly, Quine's defenders never deem it necessary to discuss these sorts of cases. They prefer the rarefied Olympian heights of philosophy. However, unless they stoop down to the level of detail and explain why the cases that Chomsky cites as paradigmatic explanations fail, their objections to Chomsky's mentalism will ring hollow.
13 Quine, "Speaking of objects," in *Ontological Relativity* (1969), p. 19.
14 Quine, "Philosophical Progress in Language Theory," p. 8.
15 See J. Fodor, "Methodological Solipsism as a Research Program," reprinted in *Representations* (MIT Press, Cambridge, Mass., 1981), p. 253.
16 See J. Fodor, *Psychosemantics* (MIT Press, Cambridge, Mass., 1987), ch. 1, p. 20.
17 Sidney Morgenbesser (personal communication) has pointed out two important caveats. First, this argument goes through without a general commitment to a syntactic theory of mind. It suffices if we assume such a theory for the domain of language.
    More importantly, Morgenbesser observes that it is unclear that "syntax" suffices to account for all aspects of intelligence. It will depend on the extension of "syntax" and "intelligence." To the degree that we construe intelligence as inferential capacity then syntax should suffice. However, whether this exhausts intelligence or creativity is far from clear. There are, at first blush, at least three distinct forms of creativity. First, is the understanding or production of new instances of familiar patterns. This is accounted for in terms of rules to which the novel instances conform. Grammars are meant to account for this form of creativity. The instances all conform to the same rules.
    The second kind of creativity resides in the novel application of old rules. Puns, jokes, etc. are common instances of this kind of linguistic creativity. They may stay within the "rules" of the language but they rely on having these rules used in novel ways. This is closer to what Chomsky has meant by the creative use of language; the *appropriate* use of language in circumstances never before encountered.
    The third kind of creativity is when new rules are introduced. This is less typical in the domain of language. However, great scientists and poets often change the rules of their disciplines by focusing on new questions, developing

new techniques and standards. They think up entirely new ways of doing something.

The distinction between these various kinds of creativity is not all that sharp. Philosophers often try to reduce these kinds to one another, most often to the first kind. However, they seem to be prima facie different. Once one considers the possibility that inference does not exhaust intelligence of thinking the possibility arises that these other forms of creativity might require extra syntactic resources. Whether this is so awaits a deeper understanding of these kinds of intelligence.

I am deeply indebted to Sidney Morgenbesser for bringing these observations to my attention.

18 See S. Stich, *From Folk Psychology to Cognitive Science* (MIT Press, Cambridge, Mass., 1983); Steven Schiffer, *Remnants of Meaning* (MIT Press, Cambridge, Mass., 1987), especially ch. 7 where Schiffer argues that all one requires to account for language understanding is a substitutional semantics; N. Hornstein, *Logic as Grammar* (MIT Press, Cambridge, Mass., 1984); S. Soames, "Semantics and Psychology," in J. J. Katz, ed., *The Philosophy of Linguistics* (Oxford University Press, Oxford, 1985); and N. Chomsky, *Knowledge of Language* (Praeger, New York, 1986).

19 Quine, *Ontological Relativity*, p. 29. There is another way of interpreting the museum myth so that it is not a myth. The idea of acquiring lexical items is essentially labelling of innate concepts might well be right. For some discussion of this point see Piatelli-Palmerini, "Evolution, selection and cognition."

20 See Neil Stillings, "Modularity and naturalism in theories of vision," in *Modularity in Knowledge Representation and Natural Language Understanding*, ed. J. L. Garfield (MIT Press, Cambridge, Mass., 1987); and P. Kitcher, "Marr's computational theory of vision," *Philosophy of Science*, 55, 1 (1988).

21 See N. Hornstein, *Logic as Grammar*, and "The Heartbreak of Semantics," *Mind and Language*, forthcoming.

22 This topic is pursued at greater length in my forthcoming "Folk Psychology as a Research Program."

6

Pragmatics and Chomsky's Research Program

Asa Kasher

1 INTRODUCTION

The growth of any science involves a process of maturation. While "immature science" consists of a mere uneven pattern of trial and error, a "mature science" consists of research programs, continuous series of theories.[1]

This continuity, which welds a succession of theories into a research program, is created by several threads: a conception of objectives, a sensible methodology, a philosophical "hard core," as well as an evolving conceptual framework of description and explanation.

Generative linguistics, as it has been depicted by Chomsky since its inception, is a research program. The continuity of its series of theories should be manifest to every careful reader of Chomsky's books about language. *The Logical Structure of Linguistic Theory* (1955) and *Aspects of the Theory of Syntax* (1965) share their basic conception of objectives and their sensible methodology with, say, *Reflections on Language* (1975) and *Knowledge of Language* (1986). Similarly, the philosophical hard core of *Language and Mind* (1968) is the same as that of *Rules and Representations* (1980) or *Language and Problems of Knowledge* (1988a).

The continuous series of theories that the research program of generative linguistics has comprised so far has had syntax in focus. However, the methodological and philosophical threads of this research program clearly transcend its succession of studies of "linguistic form."

Chomsky has recently expressed this transcendence in the preface to his *Knowledge of Language*:

If we can discover something about the principles that enter into the construction of this particular cognitive system . . . [w]e can then ask whether an approach that meets with a degree of explanatory success in the case of human language can at least serve as a suggestive model for similar inquiries in other cognitive domains. (p. xxvi)

Chomsky's belief "is that the principles do not generalize, that they are in crucial respects specific to the language faculty, but that the approach may indeed be suggestive elsewhere" (ibid.). A somewhat stronger position would be that, indeed, syntactic principles do not generalize, because they are specific to a certain faculty, that is to say, because they form aprt of the emerging content of the evolving parts of the research program of generative linguistics and as such are not supposed to be applicable outside the language faculty dedicated to linguistic form. However, "the approach," the general framework of the research program, including its basic conception of objectives, as well as its underlying methodology and philosophy, is applicable to related cognitive domains.

The purpose of the present paper is to show how this approach actually applies to the case of pragmatics.

2 PRAGMATICS IN CHOMSKY'S WRITINGS

A certain notion of pragmatics has been present in Chomsky's writings since the very beginning of generative linguistics. It makes its first published appearance in the paper "Explanatory Models in Linguistics" (Chomsky 1962).[2] Knowledge a speaker of a language has acquired constitutes "an implicit theory of the language that he has mastered, a theory that predicts the grammatical structure of each of an infinite class of potential physical events, and the conditions for the appropriate use of each of these items" (p. 528).[3]

Chomsky's 1973 introduction to *The Logical Structure of Linguistic Theory* portrays "the overarching semiotic theory in which the theory of linguistic form is embedded" in the same vein.[4]

Towards the end of the seventies this "thin" notion of pragmatics is replaced by a richer conception, that of "pragmatic competence." In "Language and Unconscious Knowledge" (Chomsky 1978)[5] a distinction is drawn between "grammatical competence," which involves knowledge of form and meaning, and "pragmatic competence," restricted "to knowledge of conditions and manner of appropriate use, in conformity with various purposes" (p. 224). The pragmatic competence "places language in the institutional setting of its use, relating intentions and purposes to the linguistic means at hand" (p. 225). The same conception appears in the main part of the book *Rules and Representations*.[6]

This move, from the notion of conditions for appropriate use to the notion of pragmatic competence, is most significant, because it clearly suggests the application to pragmatics of the general approach of the research program of generative linguistics. The introduction into pragmatics of the very idea of competence marks the adoption of the underlying methodology and philosophy of generative linguistics. Thus incorporated into the study of language use is a variety of abstractions, such as those brought forward by the distinction between competence and performance.[7]

The formative influence of this move has not been confined to the methodological and philosophical ingredients of the research program of generative linguistics. Once the suggestion is being made that a pragmatic competence exists and can be studied on a par with the grammatical competence, new research avenues come to the fore. For example, the notion of an innate "universal grammar," as used in the research program of generative linguistics, will play a similar, major role in the research program of pragmatics, viz. in the basic conception of the objectives of pragmatics. Each of these research programs is a pursuit of an explanatory specification of the initial state of a certain competence.[8]

Although appropriate use of language is, according to the present view, the subject matter of the knowledge embodied in the pragmatic competence, not every reference to language use in Chomsky's writings is an allusion to this competence. Hence, some clarification of the use of "use" seems in place.

In *Syntactic Structures* (1957), for example, it is pointed out that "[w]e can judge formal theories in terms of their ability to explain and clarify a variety of facts about the way in which sentences are used and understood" (p. 102). This reference to uses to which sentences are put has, however, nothing to do with conditions of appropriate use or the pragmatic competence. This becomes clear when one reads the next sentence: "In other words, we should like the syntactic framework of the language that is isolated and exhibited by the grammar to be able to support semantic description." Here, to use a sentence is to use a syntactic device.

Accordingly, semantics is characterized in the 1973 introduction to *The Logical Structure of Linguistic Theory* as "concerned with problems of meaning and reference, and with the systematic use of the syntactic devices available in the language" (p.18).

In Chomsky' recent books, *Knowledge of Language* (1986) and *Language and Problems of Knowledge* (1988a), certain issues of language are discussed in some detail, but there is no simple way of drawing from the discussions of use of language in these two books strong conclusions as to the nature of knowledge embodied in the pragmatic competence and our understanding of it. Three "basic questions" that arise in the study of generative grammar, are discussed in these books, viz. "(i) What constitutes knowledge of language? (ii) How is knowledge of language acquired? (iii) How is knowledge of language put to use?" (Chomsky 1986: 3; see also Chomsky 1988a: 3). The third basic question "breaks down into two parts: a "perception problem" and a "production problem." Let us have a closer look at each of these parts of the question.

"The perception problem would be dealt with by construction of a parser that incorporates the rules of the I-language along with other elements: a certain organization of memory and access . . . certain heuristics and so on" (Chomsky 1986: 25). Construction of such a parser could not be part of an inquiry into the pragmatic competence, because a solution of this "perception problem," which is a natural objective of a grammatical performance theory, as is clear from its incorporation of principles of organization of memory and access, heuristics and so on, could not be plausibly held to be part of the study of the conditions for appropriate use of sentences in contexts, which is what a theory of pragmatic competence is all about.[9] In other words, the "third question" in the study of the grammatical competence – how is grammatical knowledge put to use? – should not be confused with the "first question" in the study of the pragmatic competence – what constitutes knowledge of appropriate use of language in context?[10]

Indeed, in pursuing a broad inquiry into pragmatics, we are going to face "basic questions" on a par with those that have arisen in such an inquiry into grammar. In addition to that "first question" of the nature of pragmatic knowledge, we shall have the "second question" – how is pragmatic knowledge acquired? – as well as a "third question" – how is the pragmatic knowledge put to use? and a "fourth question" – "[w]hat are the physical mechanisms that serve as the material basis for this system of knowledge and for the use of this knowledge," to use Chomsky's wording in *Language and Problems of Knowledge* (p. 3).

The second part of the "third basic question" which arises in the study of generative grammar is the "production problem." This problem is of an utterly different nature. Actually, it is the problem of the nature of "the creative aspect of language use" (CALU), as discussed by Chomsky, for example, in the paper "Current Issues in Linguistic Theory" (1964), in the book *Cartesian Linguistics* (1966), then in his *Knowledge of Language*[11] and most recently, in much more detail, in *Language and Problems of Knowledge*,[12] where it is naturally dubbed "Descartes's problem."[13] This problem "has to do with what we say and why we say it" (Chomsky 1988a: 5). The question, then, arises of the relations between the creative aspect of language use and the pragmatic competence, and we would like to answer it by making three observations.

First, notice that the creativity under consideration is not some creative aspect of language, but rather the creative aspect of language use:

> The central fact to which any significant linguistic theory must address itself is this: a mature speaker can produce a new sentence of his language on the appropriate occasion, and other speakers can understand it immediately, though it is equally new to them . . . [I]t is clear that a theory of language that neglects this 'creative' aspect of language is of only marginal interest . . . Clearly the description of intrinsic competence provided by the grammar is not to be confused with an account of performance . . . Nor is it to be confused with an account of actual potential performance. The actual use of language obviously involves a complex interplay of many factors of the most disparate sort, of which the grammatical processes constitute only one. It seems natural to suppose that the study of actual linguistic performance can be seriously pursued only to the extent that we have a good understanding of the generative grammars that are acquired by the learner and put to use by the speaker or hearer. (Chomsky 1964: 50–2)

The creative use of language is attributed to grammatical performance. In response to Drach, 1981, Chomsky, 1982, makes this point explicitly, referring to the passage we have just quoted and to additional ones:

> In fact, the passages are perfectly explicit in attributing the CALU to performance, not competence; the CALU is an aspect of the "use of language" (i.e. performance), which is "not to be confused" with competence. (Note also that the passage stresses at once the relevance of "appropriateness" to the CALU . . .) The passage is explicit that it is language use that is being discussed, and stresses the importance of distinguishing the study of competence from the study of language use, which obviously involves "factors of the most disparate sort" apart from the mechanisms of grammar.

Strictly speaking, the present distinction is between grammatical competence and grammatical performance, that is to say, between the grammar itself, on the one hand, and all the human systems the operation of which involves the grammar as well as other factors of various sorts. Attributing the creative aspect of language use to grammatical performance is compatible with a general theory of language which specifies and explains a grammatical competence, a pragmatic competence, as well as several other components, including psychological mechanisms and neurological systems. According to this conception, the pragmatic competence is, actually, a component of grammatical performance.[14]

Secondly, "Descartes's problem" of the creative use of language is a problem which rests, in a sense, not only beyond the grammatical competence, but beyond the pragmatic competence too. To see that, recall what Chomsky describes as "[t]he central fact to which any significant linguistic theory must address itself," viz. "a mature speaker can produce a new sentence of his language on the appropriate occasion, and other speakers can understand it immediately, though it is equally new to them." Thus, the mature speaker's ability involves at least the following ingredients: (a) a grammar, according to the rules of which, what the (ideal) speaker utters are well-formed sentences; (b) a pragmatic system, according to the rules of which, what the (ideal) speaker utters at some context is appropriate; and (c) a third element, which enables the speaker to create speech events of new types, violating neither the grammatical rules nor the pragmatic ones. All creative uses of language are, therefore, performed within the limits set by the rules of these two competences. "Descartes's problem" of the nature of the creative use of language is the problem of understanding element (c), given an adequate understanding of (a) and (b).

Thirdly, Chomsky has recently argued, with respect to "Descartes's problem," that "despite much thought and often penetrating analysis . . . this problem still remains unsolved, much in the way Descartes formulated it" (1988a: 147), and suggested a Cartesian explanation of this puzzling failure, in terms of the nature and limitations of human intellectual grasp.

"Descartes's problem" of the creative aspects of "what we say and why we say it" is directly related to our pragmatic competence, because what we say is constrained by conditions for appropriate use of sentences in contexts, and why we say what we say is part of the context of language use and should, therefore, be expected to play a role in some rules which govern appropriate use of sentences in context. A fully-fledged pragmatic theory would specify our knowledge of rules which govern appropriate use of sentences in contexts which explain it in terms of the innate, initial state of the pragmatic competence and the specific conditions of its growth in a certain pragmatic environment.

However, there is no reason to assume that our research program of pragmatics is bound to lead us to a futile attempt at reaching beyond the limits of our understanding. Some progress has already been made within the present research program of pragmatics, as a result of which we have gained some understanding of the nature of the linguistic appropriateness of sentences to contexts.[15]

To be sure, pursuit of understanding the pragmatic competence does not depend on our ability to solve "Descartes's problem." Knowledge of the conditions which constrain "what we say" in a context is different from an understanding of the creative aspects of "what we say and why we say it."

To see that, consider, first, the simpler case of the relation between a move in a game of chess and its "context," the latter being determined, say, by all the previous moves of both players in the same game. Knowledge of the conditions which constrain "what we do" in the course of such a game would not provide us with an understanding of the creative aspects of chess playing, of "what we do and why we do it."

More generally, knowledge of the conditions an act or an object should satisfy for it to be a solution of a given problem does not amount to an understanding of any of the creative aspects of the situation. Knowledge of the rules which govern the pairing of a problem and a solution would explain neither the creative aspects of raising that problem, nor the creative aspects of suggesting that solution, no matter how highly rule-governed is the conceptual framework in terms of which both the problem and its solution are couched. Here too, the "pragmatic problem" of understanding appropriateness conditions is clearly different from "Descartes's problem" of understanding creativity where satisfaction of such appropriate conditions is being sought.[16]

3 LANGUAGE AND COMMUNICATION: A NEGATIVE HEURISTIC

Research programs, such as that of generative linguistics, include characteristic methodological rules. Some of these rules "tell us what paths of research to avoid," to quote Lakatos, who called such rules "negative heuristics" (1970: 132).

Methodological rules which tell us what paths of research to avoid fall under two heads. Lakatos himself was interested in negative heuristics which redirect research from the conceptual "hard core" to some "protective belt" of "auxiliary hypotheses" which "has to bear the brunts of tests and get adjusted and re-adjusted, or even completely replaced" to defend the core (ibid.: 133).

Negative heuristics of another type tell us to avoid certain paths of research for different reasons: do not be led astray by alternative research programs, friendly as these may seem in disguise.

Within the research program of generative linguistics, a prevailing negative heuristic of the latter type tells us to shun according communication linguistic prominence.

This methodological directive flies in the face of what used to be the wisdom of students of language. For many linguists, psychologists and philosophers it is still a truism to say that natural language is a system of communication.

Roman Jakobson, for example, in a 1970 paper entitled "Language in relation to other communication systems," considers the relation between natural language and communication so basic as to warrant a delimitation of linguistics:

> The science of language investigates the makeup of verbal messages and of their underlying code. The structural characteristics of language are interpreted in the light of the tasks which they fulfill in the various processes of communication, and thus linguistics may be briefly defined as an inquiry into the communication of verbal messages. (p. 3)

Similarly, a recent introduction to the philosophy of language has on the top of the list of "the most salient features of language" the observation that "[a] language is a system for communicating information between ourselves and others . . ." (Devitt and Sterelny 1987: 4).

These philosophers have not been guilty of disregarding the obvious: third on their list of "the most salient features of language" is what they call "private uses": "we talk to ourselves, we write for our own future benefit" (ibid.). These examples of "private use" of language involve two points of view, albeit of the same person. It would be reasonable to assume that according to the suggested depiction of language as "a system for communicating information," those "private uses" of language should also involve communication, even if it is of a peculiar type: in a "private use" of language, a person talks to oneself, as if one talked to another participant in a dialogue, who happened to be oneself.[17]

Subscription to the view that natural language is a system of communication is often nothing more than an expression of some crude intuition, hardly meant to be of any theoretical significance. However, sometimes this view has underlain subtle theoretical moves. A famous example is the Gricean theory of meaning, whether in his own version of it or in Strawson's or McDowell's.[18]

An interesting example of another nature is the case of a certain trend within developmental psychology. Consider, for instance, the following seemingly innocent definitions used by Elizabeth Bates and her associates, in a study of "intentionality prior to and at the onset of speech":

> [F]or present purposes the imperative is defined as the use of the adult as the means to a desired object. Conversely, the declarative is defined as the use of an object (through pointing, showing, giving, etc.) as the means to obtaining adult attention. (Bates, Camaioni and Volterra 1975: 115; cf. Ochs's remarks in Ochs and Schieffelin 1983: 189).

Those definitions paved the way to the discovery of what have been called "proto-imperatives" and "proto-declaratives," prior to the onset of speech. Such apparent discoveries would not have been possible, had it not been assumed that both natural language and pre-verbal gestures are related systems of communication.

Actually, this assumption played a major role in the study of language development, during "the fifth day" of its creation, to put it in terms of a parable used by R. M. Golinkoff and L. Gordon, in their 1983 paper "In the beginning was the word: a history of the study of language acquisition." During the fifth day, some notions of pragmatics were introduced into the field, by Jerome Bruner and others, causing

> language acquisition to be thought of as embedded in a social and cultural context . . . Increasingly, as researchers moved back earlier and earlier in the child's life in an attempt to bridge the transition from preverbal to verbal communication, the study of language merged into the study of communication. (ibid.: 7)

Consequently, the sixth day is being devoted by some to an attempt at reinstating a clear distinction between language and communication and then reshaping the study of language acquisition.[19]

Thus, the methodological shunning of according linguistic prominence to communication is neither self-evident nor insignificant. It would, therefore, be interesting to compare the research program of generative linguistics with competing ones on that score.

We turn, then, to some observations on the independence of language in some respects. However, before we do that in any detail we have to briefly clarify the notion of "independence" of language from communication. It is not our intention to defend a view which could be naturally interpreted as dissuading anybody from a proper inquiry into communication as done with words. Indeed, the objectives of some overarching theory of language will be to show and explain how several linguistic competences are exercised, for instance, in thought and in communication.[20] The objectives of another theory are to specify and explain talk-in-interaction, including communication in a strict sense as one form of talk-in-interaction.[21] However, the existence of neither of these theories would render language dependent on communication in the following sense of the term. A thesis of "dependence" of some competence upon communication is a positive answer to the question whether primitive notions of a theory of communication are indispensable to adequate description and explanation of that competence. A thesis of "independence" is a negative answer to the same question.

Such independence of grammatical competence from communication has been defended within the research program of generative linguistics in different ways. Chomsky's *Reflections on Language* defends "the thesis of autonomy of formal grammar" against claims made by John Searle and others, in the context of the philosophical tradition of analyzing meaning in terms of communication-intentions.[22] Frederick Newmeyer's *Grammatical Theory* includes a defense of the same thesis against attempts made by some linguists to show that grammar is grounded in communication- or discourse-based principles.[23]

An additional argument rests on two intriguing case studies.[24] John was three years old. His referral to a certain medical center

> was based upon his total failure to speak in the nursery school either to teachers or to other children. His manner, though, was pleasant, and he smiled readily and appropriately when something pleased him ... [H]e spontaneously displayed normal levels of skill in the non-verbal sphere. (Blank, Gessner and Esposito 1979: 330)

A careful analysis of John's behavior yielded the following results: First, John's verbal productions were "within the range of his peers" (ibid.: 338), but, secondly, most of John's (recorded) utterances

> offered inadequate responses ... He seemed to show no interest or ability in accommodating his comments to the other participant's utterance. Rather he simply used the verbalization as a stimulus to impose his own – generally unrelated – utterance. (Ibid.: 344)

Thirdly,

> John appeared to evidence little if any interest or skill in preverbal or a-verbal communication ... His troubles were graphically demonstrated with the pointing gesture. He himself never pointed when referring to an object, and he appeared totally bewildered if his parents pointed when trying to draw his attention to an object. (Ibid.: 347)

John's parents "could not recall his ever having responded to peek-a-boo or pat-a-cake, nor ever having pointed or waved bye-bye" (ibid.: 331).

The case of John is, indeed, a case of a child in whom syntax and communication "are markedly disparate" (ibid.: 330), to quote the authors who aptly entitle their report of this case study "Language without communication." Manifestation of a capacity for verbal communication is, then, not a necessary condition of the presence of grammatical competence. Is the presence of verbal communication a sufficient condition of the presence of grammatical competence?

A clear negative answer emerges from the famous case of Genie, as described by Susan Curtiss (in her 1977 and 1982). Genie started acquiring her first language as a teenager, undergoing extreme isolation and deprivation until she was 13.5 years old. Her ensuing language development resulted in a "markedly uneven [linguistic] profile" (Curtiss 1982: 290). Her grammar is very poor: "Sick people lady driving ambulance" would be the expression of the observation that a lady is driving sick people in the ambulance. Moreover, Genie is very limited in using certain linguistic forms as communicative devices. For example, she produces no vocatives or grammatically marked questions and has no topicalization or focusing devices save repetition (ibid.: 286). On the other hand, Genie is a powerful "nonlinguistic communicator. She has, for example, well-developed use of gesture, facial expression, eye gaze, attention-getting devices, and turn-taking knowledge" (ibid.: 286f). Thus, Genie is an example of a person in whom grammatical competence and communication are markedly disparate in another way.

The cases of John and Genie show us that the grammatical competence is dissociated from manifestation of a capacity for verbal communication. We have presented these cases in some detail, not only because of their contribution to the defense of the autonomy thesis of grammatical competence, but also because of their possible import in a related context, viz. in examining the extent to which the pragmatic competence is also independent from communication. We turn now to a discussion of this independence problem.

4   PRAGMATICS AND COMMUNICATION

We take it for granted that there is a pragmatic competence, which is a system of knowledge related to acts of sentence-use. It is assumed that by having acquired a pragmatic competence a speaker has mastered a family of sub-systems, each governing acts of a certain type, such as assertion, request or advice. We also assume that each of these sub-systems takes the form of rules which constitute conditions for appropriate use of certain sentences.[25] Different systems of rules govern "speech acts" of different types.[26]

Independence from communication of the pragmatic competence requires independence from communication of that family of sub-systems, each governing speech acts of a certain type. Since various types of speech act seem independent of each other, asking and advising, for example – it would be only natural to raise a separate problem of independence from communication with respect to each type of speech act.

It is not clear how to go about establishing dependence of some type of speech act upon communication. A constitutive requirement that an appropriate addressee should be present at the context of use seems a necessary condition of such dependence. Let us call this condition "the addressee condition."

Notice, first, that this necessary condition is clearly not a sufficient one. Thus, in a certain "semantical analysis of English illocutionary verbs,"[27] presence of an appropriate "hearer" is required by the rules which govern assuring, threatening, urging, congratulating and a few other acts. However, communication, in the pre-theoretical sense of passing on information, is hardly the point of any of these acts.

Secondly, since the addressee condition is a necessary condition of dependence of a speech act type upon communication, its denial is, of course, a sufficient condition of independence of that speech act type from communication. Hence, if we show that for a certain type of speech act the addressee condition does not hold, we thereby show that our notion of speech act in general is independent of communication, and consequently, that the pragmatic competence is independent of communication.

Assertion is our prime example of a speech act type which does not satisfy the addressee condition. Events of putting sentences in the indicative to an assertoric use do not have to involve an addressee. Right now, when I am trying to write this paper, I am trying to express my own defensible thoughts, to present my justifiable views, to put forward some of my supportable representations, and I am doing it by using various sentences. However, I am not addressing anybody else, nor do I address myself, in the sense of bearing to myself the relations I would bear to some interlocutor. There seems to be no reason to analyze "I put forward some of my (supportable) representations by using [sentence] S," "I present my (justifiable) views by using S" or "I express my (defensible) thoughts by using S" in terms of "I address S to person X" and "X = me." Many cases of the so-called "private uses" of language do, indeed, involve making assertions addressed to nobody.[28]

This observation seems fairly obvious, though it has been often disregarded. Among those who failed to notice it one finds Russell, who claimed in *An Inquiry into Meaning and Truth*, that

> [i]n adult life, all speech . . . is, in intention, in the imperative mood. When it seems to be a mere statement, it should be prefaced by the words 'know that'. We know many things, and assert only some of them; those that we assert are those that we desire our hearers to know." (1940; 1962: 24)

The most interesting counter train of thought was suggested by R. G. Collingwood. In his autobiography he mentions "a principle of logic" which he found it "necessary to state," viz.

> the principle that a body of knowledge consists not of "propositions," "statements," "judgments" . . . but of these together with the questions they are meant to answer; and that a logic in which the answers are attended to and the questions neglected is a false logic. (Collingwood 1939: 30)

Moreover, in order to find out what a person has meant, having "spoken or written with perfect command of language and perfectly truthful intention," says Collingwood, "you must also know what the question was (a question in his own mind, and presumed by him to be in yours) to which the thing he has said or written was meant as an answer" (ibid.: 31).[29]

According to this view, questions are, in a sense, more basic than assertions. An adequate analysis of an assertion renders it an answer to a certain question. If this is correct, it eliminates our prime example of a speech act which is governed by rules which make no allusion to an addressee: If every assertion rests on some question and every question constitutively requires the presence of an addressee, then every assertion involves the presence of an addressee.

Our present problem is, then, which are the more basic, questions or assertions?

Formal analyses of questions have not settled this problem. On the one hand, some logicians and linguists have analyzed questions in terms of assertions. For example, within the framework of Hamblin, 1973, an answer is, indeed, a proposition, and questions are defined as sets of possible answers, i.e. as sets of propositions. Similarly, in Karttunen, 1977, a question is a property of propositions, the property of those propositions which correspond to true answers.[30]

On the other hand, some completely different analyses have also been proposed. Peirce suggested that questions are requests for information, and requests are imperatives of a special kind.[31] More recently, Aqvist, since his 1965, and Hintikka, since his 1974, have tried to show how to capture this idea in an appropriate formal way.[32] From the present point of view, imperatives seem to be on a par with interrogatives, because they also seem to constitutively require the presence of an addressee. However, such formal analyses of questions in terms of imperatives could not settle the issue of whether questions are more basic than assertions or not.

To see why Collingwood's suggestion to consider questions as more basic than assertions should be rejected, compare it with the Aristotelian approach (in *Topics*), according to which what has been said has to be seen against the background of the question under discussion and the answers already given.[33] Whereas for Collingwood the question in the background determines the meaning of what has been said, according to the Aristotelian conception that question is related to the purpose which has been intended to be served by uttering what has been said. The distinction is significant: according to the former view a sentence has any meaning, only if it is considered against the background of a certain question; without such a question in the background it cannot be understood at all. According to the latter view a sentence has its meaning in the language to which it belongs and can be understood as such. It is, rather, an act of utterance that cannot be understood unless its purpose is reckoned. A question already asked and answers already given enable one to clarify the issue at hand, as well as the purpose for which the sentence has been used.

The Aristotelian view seems compelling. The alternative view rests on a confusion of understanding an act of using a sentence and understanding this sentence itself. Once this distinction is noted there seem to be no grounds for the suggestion that questions are more basic than assertions.

Notice, furthermore, that assertions can be felicitously performed against the background of no question at all. An unprompted utterance of a sentence, used in an appropriate assertoric way, can introduce into a conversation a new topic, thus serving a new purpose. And then, sometimes questions arise only against the background of some assertions. A process of argumentation, for example, is usually initiated by a challenge to some proposition. Such challenges often take the form of a question and they "may be motivated by a variety of propositional attitudes: puzzlement, doubt, skepticism, rejection, devil's advocacy . . .' (Blair and Johnson 1987: 45), all directly related to some background assertions.[34]

Having rejected Collingwood's view of assertation, there seems to be no reason to assume that the speech act type of assertion involves the addressee condition. It would, therefore, be reasonable to consider assertion as conceptually independent of communication. Consequently, the pragmatic competence, as such, could also be reasonably held to be independent of communication.

Is assertion the only type of speech act which does not involve the addressee condition? Somewhat surprisingly, perhaps, both questions and commands seem to be explainable in terms of systems of governing rules which also do not satisfy the addressee condition. In a nutshell, the idea is to analyze an act of posing a question as an act of raising a problem,[35] and to analyze an act of issuing a command as an act of invoking a norm.

An act of raising a problem does not require for its felicitousness the presence of another person. Raising problems in soliloquy is very common. To be sure, one's raising a problem in the presence of some other person may result in the latter's providing the former with a solution of the raised problem. Social prudence has encouraged cooperation under the circumstances of problem raising. Actually, cooperation under such circumstances has been entrenched, to the extent that most often it is being taken for granted that it is part of one's linguistic knowledge that questions have to be answered, if possible. This commonly held view about the linguistic nature of questions and answers is, however, wrong. Linguistic knowledge determines only the problem raised by an utterance of a question and the induced space of possible answers. Understanding a question amounts to figuring out the related problem and the induced space of possible answers. Answering a question is basically pointing out one of the solutions of the raised problem. Having to answer a question, in case one knows how, means having to point out a solution of a problem that has been raised in one's presence, in case one knows how. Since answering a question is also making an appropriate assertion, answering a question is pointing out what one takes to be a solution of the problem raised by posing the question. Having to answer a question, in case one knows how, means, therefore, having to solve the raised problem and to point out what is held to be a solution of it. However, having to solve problems that have been raised in one's presence is, clearly, not a matter of linguistic rules, but rather of social policy or social norms of cooperation in general.

Similarly, an act of invoking a norm does not require for its felicitousness the presence of another person. Invoking norms in soliloquy, for instance, when one is driving alone, when one is trying to solve a chess problem in the presence of nobody else or when one is praying, is not a rarity either. Of course, one's invoking a norm in the presence of some other person may, under appropriate circumstances, result in the latter's following of the norm the former invoked. Certain social institutions require that, under appropriate circumstances, norms invoked by a speaker be followed by the addressee. Again, obedience under such circumstances has been entrenched, to the extent that most often it is being taken for granted that it is part of one's linguistic knowledge that commands should be obeyed, if possible. And again, this commonly held view about the linguistic nature of commands is, however, wrong. Linguistic knowledge determines only the norm invoked by an utterance of a command. Understanding a command amounts to identifying the related norm. Now, obeying a command is following the norm invoked by it. Having to obey a command, in case one knows how, means having to follow a norm invoked in one's presence, in case one knows how. However, having to follow norms, as invoked under certain circumstances, is also not a matter of linguistic rules, but rather of some general social policy or certain institutional norms.[36]

Raising a problem with words and invoking a norm with words do not require the presence of another person. Do they require the presence of oneself as both a speaker and an addressee? As long as one carefully avoids begging the question of language and communication, it seems one has no reason to analyze "X raises a problem" as derived from "X addresses a problem to Y" and "Y = X." Such an analysis would conflate characterization of an act with characterization of common reasons for performing it. The reasons for raising a certain problem or invoking a certain norm, under some circumstances, may well involve an addressee, either someone else or oneself, but specifying those reasons goes beyond an adequate description of the act itself.

We have, then, argued that assertions, questions and commands involve, for their linguistically appropriate performance, neither the presence of another person nor oneself playing the role of an interlocutor. These observations lead us to the conclusion that the pragmatic competence, as such, is independent of communication.

Dummett has recently argued that "cases in which we employ language with no direct, and sometimes no remote, communicative purpose . . . prove nothing," because it is generally agreed that language is both a vehicle of thought and an instrument of communication (1989: 201). However, our arguments to the effect that assertions, questions and commands are not, as such, acts of communication involve more than examples of language used with no communicative purpose. The suggested general analyses of assertion, question and command, as not involving the addressee condition, explain why language is not primarily an instrument of communication, though it can be put to use both in thought and in communication.

On the grounds of our conclusion, that it is reasonable to hold the pragmatic competence, as such, independent of communication, it would be natural to predict the existence of a psychological or even a neuropsychological counterpart of this dissociation. In other words, it would be plausible to predict that a certain brain damage would result in a loss of the capacity to communicate, leaving intact, say, the capacity to assert, or vice versa. Actually, the above-mentioned cases of John, the child with "language without communication," and of Genie, the girl deprived of a linguistic environment until she was 13.5 years old, seem to provide us with the expected examples, but a thorough examination of the data is still required, on grounds of some articulated theories of the pragmatic competence and of communication, before that prediction could be deemed fully confirmed by the evidence.

This concludes our discussion of the "negative heuristics" of the research program of generative linguistics. In the next parts of this paper some "positive heuristics" will be considered.

5   MODULARITY OF PRAGMATICS

A research program tells us not only what paths of research to avoid, but of course also what paths to pursue. The research program of generative linguistics tells us to try to explain cognitive phenomena in terms of "modules," separate systems of knowledge, each with its own properties. The principles of a module specify its content as a system of knowledge, but they also enter into the processes of acquisition of this knowledge and of its use. This modular approach seems to be a distinguishing feature of the research program of generative linguistics (see Newmeyer 1983: 2–3), and it would, therefore, be interesting to see what happens when we pursue this modular path in our study of the pragmatic competence.

The question whether there is a pragmatic module seems a natural one to raise and answer on grounds of our present knowledge of language use, but the issue is actually far from being settled. The reason is simple: one should not hasten to accept a distinct answer to an indistinct question. We cannot set ourselves to look for a "pragmatic module" without having in mind some notion of "pragmatics" and some notion of a "module." Apparently conflicting answers that have been given to this question involve, as a matter of fact, different delimitations of pragmatics or different characterizations of modularity.

Leaving aside, for a moment, the question whether pragmatics is embodied in a separate module or not, consider, first, claims that have been made to the effect that pragmatics is embodied in the right hemisphere of the brain (of right-handed persons). Sheila Blumstein compares the role of the right hemisphere processing to that of the left one:

> While the left hemisphere appears to be specialized for processing the linguistic grammar per se ... the right hemisphere contributes to the "pragmatics" of language use, on the one hand, and the integration of the

linguistic grammar with cognitive (nonverbal) processes, on the other (1981: 250).

Although it has already been established that the right hemisphere has considerable linguistic ability (see, e.g., Eran Zaidel's survey "Language in the right hemisphere," 1985), the idea that the right hemisphere controls the pragmatic competence is somewhat puzzling, if according to one's general conception of language, ordinary uses of sentences involve both the grammatical and the pragmatic competences. Common use of sentences by subjects with complete cerebral comissurotomy would involve mysterious, minute coordination on the part of these two informationally disconnected hemispheres. How could the left hemisphere produce a genuine speech act, that involves an utterance of a sentence, in a context held to be appropriate, if the right hemisphere controls the pragmatic aspects of a speech act, while the left hemisphere controls the syntactic ones? In order for the left hemisphere to be in a position to produce a felicitous utterance of a sentence, it must be informed that the context of utterance is held to be appropriate. However, if pragmatics is controlled by the right hemisphere, then the information that the context is held appropriate is at the right hemisphere. Hence, in order for the left hemisphere to be in a position to produce a felicitous utterance of a sentence it needs information which is at the right hemisphere. Under normal conditions information can flow from one hemisphere to the other, but in subjects with complete cerebral commissurotomy this is impossible. How could they, then, produce felicitous speech acts? This is "the puzzle of pragmatics in the right hemisphere." The puzzle disappears when the evidence is carefully scrutinized.

What is the main evidence? Howard Gardner, Hiram Brownell and their associates found that right-brain damaged subjects have deficits in interpreting metaphors and idiomatic expressions, in understanding sarcastic and humorous texts as well as cartoons, and in retelling stories and getting their point.[37] Claus Heeschen, Nancy Foldi and others discovered that right-brain damaged subjects have severe deficits in understanding the so-called "indirect speech acts." For example, when such subjects encounter an interrogative sentence commonly understood as an "indirect request," they would consistently respond to the literal interpretation rather than fulfill the intended request.[38]

All these are highly interesting phenomena and many of the experimental results seem to be of significance not only within neuropsycholinguistics, but within linguistic and philosophical studies of pragmatics as well. However, with the view of defending the hypothesis that the pragmatic competence is embodied in the right hemisphere, perhaps in a right hemisphere module, the evidence seems rather weak in several respects.

First, if the hypothesis of pragmatics in the right hemisphere were the best explanation of all those deficits found in right-brain damaged subjects, one would have expected that in a case of complete cerebral commissurotomy the disconnected left hemisphere would manifest the same deficits and would perform on a chance level. This is not what happened, when the Right Hemisphere Communication Battery of Gardner and Brownell was administered to four split-brain subjects (Zaidel and Kasher 1988; Spence, Zaidel and Kasher 1989). This battery includes tests related to humor, prosody, indirect requests, metaphors, sarcasm and several other phenomena. Although these four subjects were performing significantly worse than controls, there was no test in which all the four performed on a chance level. This result suggests that none of the tests in the battery is related to an exclusively right hemisphere phenomenon.

Moreover, whereas right-brain damaged subjects show severe deficits in all the sub-tests, one of the split-brain subjects, LB, has shown severe deficit only in a few of them, viz. story retelling, interpretation of indirect requests and prosody. Only mild deficits have been found in LB's performance on other tests, including pictorial metaphors and understanding sarcasm.

These results show that even on an understanding of "pragmatics" as being related to humor, emotion, non-literal language and integrative processes, the pragmatics-in-the-right-hemisphere hypothesis should be significantly revised or perhaps even replaced by an utterly different one.

Secondly, notice that most if not all of these deficits involve phenomena which are hardly understood on any abstract explanatory level. In the absence of adequate theories of metaphor, sarcasm and humor, for example, it is not clear what actually is being tested when any of the related tests is given to a subject. Moreover, without better theoretical understanding of each of these phenomena there seems to be no good reason for combining them to form a separate competence. Again, an hypothesis that a pragmatic competence operates in the right hemisphere cannot be grounded on results pertaining to a heterogeneous cluster of such poorly understood phenomena.

Thirdly, even if we do cluster such phenomena under some notion of a pragmatic competence, the problem arises of the relation this competence bears to various families of phenomena which have often been investigated under the heading of "pragmatics," for instance, basic speech acts and performatives, conversational and conventional implicatures, politeness and the like.[39] Are these phenomena additional members of the same cluster, or are they rather related to another competence, and, in any case, why?

In other words, the suggested affirmative answer to the question whether a pragmatic competence exists seems to rest on some diffused, unwarrantable notion of pragmatics. The question whether there is a pragmatic module, in a different, more justifiable sense of "pragmatics," remains, therefore, in want of an appropriate answer. Notice that a sensible delimitation of what should be understood under "pragmatics" will bring us closer to such an answer mainly because it is going to render clearer the question itself. However, without some clarification of the notion of "module" as well, the question is going to remain hopelessly ambiguous.

Consider, for example, Fodor's notion of "module" in his *Modularity of Mind* (1983: 47–101). Input systems are modular, in Fodor's view, since they are domain-specific, mandatory, informationally encapsulated, "exhibit characteristic and specific breakdown patterns" (ibid.: 99) and have several other properties. It is a "main thesis of [Fodor's] work that the properties in virtue of which input systems are modular are ones which, in general, central cognitive processes do not share."[40]

If a module is an input system which has the nine properties Fodor enumerated, then there is no pragmatic module, in the sense of a module which embodies the knowledge which we commonly find under "pragmatics." Conditions of appropriate use of sentences involve much more than a syntactic analysis of an input sentence and a perceptual analysis of some contextual features. They also involve institutional analysis and thereby allude to beliefs entertained by the user at the context of use. Many of these beliefs belong to some central cognitive system rather than to any input device. Recall, for example, beliefs which are mentioned in the rules constitutive of promising, such as "S believes H would prefer his doing A to his not doing A" (Searle 1969: 58). Thus, conditions of appropriate use involve beliefs to which input systems do not have access, which shows that the pragmatic competence is not embodied in an input system.

If a module is a system which has the properties Fodor enumerated, whether it is an input system or not, there still is no pragmatic module, in the sense of a module which embodies the knowledge used in deriving conversational implicatures. I have argued elsewhere that Grice's maxims follow from some rationality "most effective, least effort" principle (Kasher 1976 and 1982), which applies to all intentional acts, including acts of language use as well as artistic acts. Accordingly, a cognitive system which derives conversational implicatures involves application of a general, most probably central principle to the output of some linguistic system. Hence, it would be implausible to assume that some domain-specific cognitive system produces conversational implicatures. Moreover, as Grice demonstrated, such implicatures can be cancelled ("John arrived and Bill left, but not necessarily in this order"), which makes it implausible to assume that some mandatory cognitive system produces them.

Similarly, understanding a so-called "indirect speech act" involves an attempt to understand a use of sentence as meant to attain more than one end. First, there is the "literal end," the one determined by the rules governing the literal use, but then this end is understood as an intermediate one, a sub-goal, and an attempt is made to find another end, the attainment of which would be served by attaining the former, literal one. Indeed, under quite ordinary circumstances, such an attempt requires access to one's general system of beliefs. Thus, no informationally encapsulated cognitive system could embody the knowledge required for understanding indirect speech acts.

Since the property of being informationally encapsulated seems to be one of the major ingredients of the idea of modularity, the so-called indirect speech acts are not understood by a pragmatic module, in any interesting sense of the term "pragmatic module."[41]

We conclude this discussion by making three general remarks about these observations.

First, the modular approach to the study of mind in general and language in particular has given rise to a new form of delineation problem. Individuation of a cognitive domain will often involve much more than finding the "right" category in some arbitrary or useless taxonomy. It will rather rest on an explanatory characterization of a related module, a cognitive system which has some required properties, including being domain-dedicated and informationally encapsulated.[42]

Secondly, as a result of applying this modular approach to the study of language use, a new conception of pragmatics seems to have emerged. There seems to be room for a division of whatever has been labelled "pragmatics" into the following parts.

1 What we would like to dub "core-pragmatics," which consists of the family of systems of rules which govern basic speech acts. Core-pragmatics is autonomous, though whether it should be described as a module or not, depends on the notion of "module" one would apply to it. It is reasonable to assume that core-pragmatics is domain-dedicated, given the special nature of the systems of rules which govern speech acts, namely their being constitutive systems of rules. Whether core-pragmatics is informationally encapsulated or not seems to depend on the delimitation of the class of speech acts. If it is confined to speech acts which are syntactically marked (in ways yet to be understood), core-pragmatics seems to be encapsulated. Being both dedicated and encapsulated it is, in some interesting sense, a pragmatic module. However, if core-pragmatics is taken to include, say, promises, then, as has been pointed out earlier, one's general system of beliefs turns out to be involved in understanding and production of speech acts of core-pragmatics. This would mean that core-pragmatics is not encapsulated.[43]

2 "Amplified core-pragmatics," which consists of all the systems of rules governing "things done with words" which are not basic speech acts. "Basic speech acts," such as assertion, questions and commands are distinguished from "things done with words," many of which, such as baptisms and acquittals, are not basic speech acts. Whereas knowledge of the former is part of knowledge of language, knowledge of the latter is social or institutional rather than linguistic in nature.[44] Clearly, amplified core-pragmatics is not informationally encapsulated. The "central" system of one's beliefs often "penetrates"[45] processes of understanding non-basic speech acts. For instance, whether production of a certain sentence in a certain context of utterance is understood as a speech act of acquittal or not depends on one's institutional knowledge, in a way one's understanding a similar event as a speech act of assertion does not.

3 Then, there is a "central pragmatic" system, which involves the application of some general rules and strategies, such as those governing rational intentional action in general, to cases of speech activity.[46] This is

how (and, in a sense, where) conversational implicatures are generated.[47] This is also where politeness considerations participate in speech activity.[48] Whether such a "central pragmatic" system is a module, in some interesting sense, is an interesting open question.[49]

4 There is reason to assume that alongside the "central pragmatic" system, which involves principles of intentional action in general, there is a special system of rules governing basic aspects of "talk-in-interaction," such as organization of turn-taking, organization of sequences and organization of repair.[50] Studies of these types of action seem to lend plausibility to the hypothesis that the processes involved constitute a separate module, even in a rich sense of this term.

5 In addition to these parts of pragmatics, there seems to exist an additional class of various "interface" features, to be dubbed "interface pragmatics." Understanding indexicals, for example, involves the integration of the output of a language module with the output of some perception module, both serving as input for some "central" unit which produces the integrated understanding of what has been said in the context of utterance.[51]

6 Finally, one may introduce "extended pragmatics" which would include, for instance, some of the areas tested by the above-mentioned Right Hemisphere Communication Battery.[52]

Thirdly, the idea of a "central pragmatic" system bears an interesting relation with "Descartes's problem," of "how language is used in the normal creative fashion" (Chomsky 1988a: 138), a problem which, to use Chomsky's arguments and terms, is unsolvable, a mystery.[53]

The more we explain pragmatic facts in terms of a general intentional action theory as applied to instances of language use, the closer we come to solving parts of "Descartes's problem." Creative use of language can be factored into (a) creative choice of ends and (b) rational pursuit of those ends. Factor (b), of the rational pursuit of given ends, seems to be amenable to explanations in terms of general rationality principles, which are parts of a general intentional action theory. However, factor (a), of the creative choice of ends, does perhaps constitute an unsolvable problem, a mystery.

NOTES

This is a revised version of the paper read at the "Chomskyan Turn" conference, April 1988. Comments made during the discussion by several participants – Noam Chomsky, Vicky Fromkin, Norbert Hornstein, Shalom Lappin and Zenon Pylyshyn – have been of much help in my attempts at improving the paper. On other occasions I have had the benefit of discussing the paper or certain aspects of it with Jonathan Berg, Tyler Burge, Julius Moravcsik, Marleen Rozemond, Manny Schegloff and Eran Zaidel, as a result of which many other revisions have been made. I am most indebted to all of them.

1 Here and in the sequel we use major ingredients of Lakatos's methodology of research programs, as discussed in Lakatos 1970, especially pp. 132–8 (47–52 in Lakatos 1978).

2   Chomsky 1962 is published in a volume which is the Proceedings of the 1960 International Congress of Logic, Methodology and Philosophy of Science.

3   These parts of the characterization of a mature speaker's knowledge are mentioned by Chomsky when he is discussing "the abilities" that such a speaker has developed using a traditional grammar of some language. However, as is clear from the rest of the paper, any mature speaker of any natural language has mastered the same kind of knowledge. Cf. Chomsky 1962: 530–2.

    In order to avoid possible confusion and misunderstanding, we replaced Chomsky's use of "abilities" a mature speaker has developed (e.g., pp. 528, 530, 531) by "knowledge." See also our note 6.

4   See Chomsky 1955: 5, 20 and 45.

5   This paper was written in 1976, first published in 1978 and then reprinted in *Rules and Representations* (Chomsky 1980). Page references will be to the latter edition.

6   See, for example, Chomsky 1980: 59–60 and 93. Notice the knowledge of conditions and manner of appropriate use should not be characterized as an ability to do something, a system of dispositions, or a "knowledge how," but "in terms of mental state and structure" (ibid.: 48). See also Chomsky 1988b. I thank Norbert Hornstein for a discussion of this point.

7   For an enumeration of conditions for specifying a competence, see Moravcsik, 1990.

8   Moreover, the description of the initial state of the pragmatic competence can perhaps be attempted in a framework of principles and parameters, on a par with the framework that has recently been used for the characterization of the initial state of the grammatical competence. We shall return to this suggestion elsewhere.

9   We will soon return to the problem of the relations between pragmatic competence and grammatical performance. Note that our argument here is not that the "perception problem" has nothing to do with pragmatic competence because it is a problem of grammatical performance. Our argument is that it is not part of the subject matter of a pragmatic competence theory because it is not a problem of conditions for appropriate use of sentences in contexts.

10   Strictly speaking, there is a whole family of appropriateness relations that one could study. According to one sense of "appropriateness," one's assertion of p is inappropriate if one believes that p is not the case. According to a second sense of "appropriateness," "[y]ou know somehow to talk to different people in different ways, and you know what to presuppose about what they are saying" (Chomsky 1984: 43). According to a still third sense of "appropriateness," making an impolite remark would be regarded as making an inappropriate speech act.

    We are interested in a "purely" linguistic notion of appropriateness. In the sequel we use this term in a non-technical sense, which, however, is meant to be purely linguistic in nature.

    Goffman (1983) thought study of properties of speech acts should be assigned to sociology, rather than to philosophy or to linguistics. However, there seems to be an obvious difference between saying what one holds not to be true, interrupting another person and hurting someone's feeling by making some blasphemous remarks. Assigning all of them to the study of social action involves obliterating an important distinction. See Schegloff, 1988, for additional objections to Goffman's suggestion.

11   Chomsky 1986: 222–3 and 234.

12   Chomsky 1988a: 5 and 138–52.

13 On the Cartesian roots of the problem, see Chomsky 1966. The "characteristics of being unbounded, free from stimulus control and evocative and/or appropriate," all to be found in Descartes's discussions, form "the creative aspect of language use" (Chomsky 1984: 6).

   For Descartes's discussion of appropriate use of words, including the case of replying "to the sense" of whatever has been said in one's presence, see Descartes 1637 (AT): 56 and 57. See also his November 23, 1646 letter to the Marquess of Newcastle, where he takes regular speech to involve words "that are relevant to particular topics" (Kenny 1981: 206). I thank Marleen Rozemond for her help here.

14 If the distinction between competence and performance were drawn in some absolute terms, rather than from the point of view of a certain system, such as grammar, then the notion of a pragmatic competence would have been incoherent, being a competence and an element of performance at one and the same time. However, there is nothing incoherent in an idea of a pragmatic competence being a component of grammatical performance.

15 Classical works by Wittgenstein, Austin, Grice, Strawson and Searle from a tradition in the philosophical study of language use. Our own work in pragmatics draws major ingredients from this philosophical tradition, but reshapes them, to fit the framework of a Chomskyan research program. See Kasher 1977 for a general discussion, and also Kasher 1976, 1978, 1981, 1982, 1984 and 1987.

16 A couple of times recently, we have heard the view that pragmatics is impossible being ascribed to Chomsky, on grounds of his attitudes towards "Descartes's Problem." It is clear from our discussion that this is a misguided ascription, resting on a confusion of "Descartes's problem" with the "pragmatic problem."

17 Jonathan Berg has convinced me that there is more in such a depiction of "private uses" of language than meets the eye. Nevertheless, analysis of "private uses" in terms of several parts of one's "self" still seems conceptually misguided in its attempt to portray certain thoughts as odd communication events. Some of the ingredients of this analysis are really odd, e.g. the depiction of some "private uses" of assertion as communication with a future, yet non-existent part (or stage) of one's "self", while being perfectly aware that this is the nature of the "other" party. Could one happily communicate with what one holds not to exist?

   Notice that we do not deny the claim that a speaker "does not merely frame propositions and acknowledge some of them as correct: he asks himself questions, draws conclusions, forms resolves, make plans, reproaches himself, exhorts himself, ridicules himself" (Dummett 1989: 210). What we deny is rather that all these acts are examples of things that some one does when one is addressing only oneself. We do not assume that every speech event has to be addressed to someone. Indeed, the content of one's utterance can include a reference to oneself, but this would not render it self-addressed.

   What we claim is similar, and perhaps not unrelated to a claim that David Kaplan has recently made in lectures and conversations, viz., that "a = a" is, in some sense, not simply a result of replacing "a" for "b" in "a = b".

18 Grice 1957 and 1982, republished in Grice 1989; Strawson 1971; McDowell 1980. See also Avramides 1989. For a discussion of this approach, see Chomsky 1975. The most recent discussion of the related philosophical issues is Dummett 1989.

19 See also Chomsky's remarks in Piattelli-Palmarini 1980: 264.

20 "[T]he more general theory of language . . . will be concerned with meaning and reference, the conditions of appropriate use of language, how sentences are understood, performance in concrete social situations, and in general, the exercise of linguistic competence in thought and communication." (Chomsky 1975: 45).

21 See Schegloff 1982, 1986 and 1987, for discussions of various aspects of talk-in-interaction. I thank Manny Schegloff for many helpful conversations.

22 Chomsky 1975: 53–77.

23 Newmeyer 1983: 96–129.

24 Both cases are briefly mentioned in Chomsky 1980: 265. See also Blank 1975, mentioned in Chomsky 1984: 43. For another type of language and communication dissociation, see D'Ambrosio 1970.

25 See Kasher 1977 for a general discussion of the framework.

26 The term "speech acts" is misleading, to the extent that it suggests overtness of these acts, but any attempt to replace it by a better one would presently seem futile.

27 Searle and Vanderveken 1985: 179–216.

28 Cf. Chomsky 1975: 56–7 and 60–2; and Chomsky 1980: 229–30. See also our note 17 above.

29 For related discussions, see also Collingwood 1940: 108ff. John Dewey made similar remarks, within the framework of his own philosophy. See his 1948 and also Thayer 1968: 137.

30 See Scha 1983 and Walton 1984 for discussions of these proposals.

31 See Peirce, *Collected Papers* 8.369.

32 For discussions of this approach, see also Harrah 1987, Hilpinen 1986 and Hintikka 1987: 312–18.

33 For a discussion of this conception, see Blair and Johnson 1987.

34 See also Kasher 1987.

35 I thank Julius Moravcsik for suggesting this example as well as for many additional insightful remarks on other parts of this paper. Peirce pointed out the relationships between question-answer pairs and doubt-belief ones. See his *Collected Papers* 7.313.

36 Our claim that commands do not satisfy the addressee condition should not be confused with the claim that norms do not need a social background. Whereas it is our view that commands, as such, do not satisfy the addressee condition, it seems to us plausible to assume that some norms do hinge on an appropriate social background and some do not.

37 See, e.g., Winner and Gardner 1977; Gardner, Brownell, Wapner and Michelow 1983; Foldi et al. 1983; Gardner 1987, and Weylman, Brownell and Gardner 1988.

38 See, e.g., Hirst, LeDoux and Stein 1984; Foldi 1987; Weylman, Brownell, Roman and Gardner 1989.

39 For a discussion of these topics, see Kasher 1971; 1976 and 1982; and 1986, respectively.

40 For a discussion of Fodor's (1983) concept of module and of modularity of some central systems and output systems, see Marshall 1984, especially pp. 234–8, and Shallice 1988: 269–306. See also Fodor 1987.

41 For an emphasis of the property of being informationally encapsulated, see Fodor 1989.

42 On the properties of being dedicated and encapsulated, see Fodor 1989.

43 Presently, we are inclined to prefer the former conception of core-pragmatics. See Kasher 1988a.

44 See Kasher 1978 and 1981.
45 See Pylyshyn 1984 as well as 1991, in this volume.
46 At this point, it would be interesting to reconsider Chomsky's remarks, in *Language and Mind*, on the possibility of there being a competence of intentional action:

> Are there any other areas of human competence where one might hope to develop a fruitful theory, ananlgous to generative grammar? Although this is a very important question, there is very little that can be said about it today. One might, for example, consider the problem of how a person comes to acquire a certain concept of three-dimensional space, or an implicit "theory of human action," in similar terms. Such a study would begin with the attempt to characterize the implicit theory that underlies actual performance and would then turn to the question of how this theory develops under the given conditions of time and access to data – that is, in what way the resulting system of beliefs is determined by the interplay of available data, "heuristic procedures," and the innate schematism that restricts and conditions the form of the acquired system. At the moment, this is nothing more than a sketch of a program of research." (Chomsky 1968: 64; 73–4 in the 1972, 2nd edn)

47 See Kasher 1976 and 1982 for detailed arguments to the effects that conversational implicatures, as derived by Gricean principles, can all be directly derived from general rationality principles.
48 See Kasher 1986 for a detailed explanation of this point.
49 On the possibility of a there being modules that "cross the boundaries" of competences, see Marshall 1984: 235–6.
50 See Schegloff's papers mentioned in our note 21, as well as Sacks, Schegloff and Jefferson 1974; and Schegloff, Jefferson and Sacks 1977.
51 See Kasher 1984 for an elaboration of this point.
52 Some of these areas are related to uses of language which are not fully literal, such as irony and metaphors. An explanation of such phenomena being related to the right hemisphere could perhaps be couched in terms of some monitoring of left hemisphere activity being done by the right hemisphere.
    For reasons to assume that those phenomena are not exclusively right hemisphere ones, see D. Zaidel and Kasher 1989; and Spence, Zaidel and Kasher 1989.
53 See Chomsky 1975: 137; and 1988a: 138–52.

REFERENCES

Aqvist, L. 1965: A new approach to the logical theory of interrogatives. Mimeographed. Uppsala: Filosofiske Foreningen i Uppsala.
Avramides, A. 1989: *Meaning and Mind, An Examination of a Gricean Account of Language*. Cambridge, Mass. and London: MIT Press.
Bates, E., Camaioni, L. and Volterra, V. 1975: The acquisition of performatives prior to speech. *Merrill-Palmer Quarterly* 21, 205–266; republished in and quoted from E. Ochs and B. B. Schieffelin (eds), *Developmental Pragmatics*. New York: Academic Press, 1979.
Blair, J. A. and Johnson, R. H. 1987: Argumentation as dialectical. *Argumentation*, 1, 41–56.
Blank, M. 1975: Mastering the intangible through language. *Annals of the New York Academy of Sciences* 263, 44–58.
Blank, M., Gessner, M. and Esposito, A. 1979: Language without communication: A case study. *Journal of Child Language* 6, 329–52.

Blumstein, S. 1981: Neurological disorders: Language-brain relationships. In S. Fiskov and T. Boll (eds), *Handbook of Clinical Neuropsychology*. New York: John Wiley.

Chomsky, N. 1955: *The Logical Structure of Linguistic Theory*. Manuscript, Harvard University. Republished, with an introduction by the author, New York and London: Plenum Press, 1973.

—— 1957: *Syntactic Structures*. The Hague: Mouton.

—— 1962: Explanatory models in linguistics. In E. Nagel, P. Suppes, A. Tarski (eds), *Logic, Methodology and Philosophy of Science*. Stanford: Stanford University Press, 528–50.

—— 1964: Current issues in linguistic theory. In J. A. Fodor and J. J. Katz (eds), *The Structure of Language*. Englewood Cliffs: Prentice-Hall, 50–118; also as a book, under the same title, The Hague: Mouton, 1964.

—— 1965: *Aspects of the Theory of Syntax*. Cambridge: MIT Press.

—— 1966: *Cartesian Linguistics*. New York and London: Harper and Row.

—— 1968: *Language and Mind*. 2nd enlarged edn, New York: Harcourt, Brace, Jovanovich, 1972.

—— 1975: *Reflections on Language*. New York: Pantheon.

—— 1978: Language and unconscious knowledge. In J. H. Smith (ed.), *Psychoanalysis and Language, Psychiatry and the Humanities*, vol. 3. New Haven: Yale University Press; republished in Chomsky 1980: 217–54 and 287–90.

—— 1980: *Rules and Representations*. Oxford: Basil Blackwell.

—— 1982: A note on the creative aspect of language use. *Philosophical Review*, XCI, 423–34.

—— 1984: *Modular Approaches to the Study of the Mind*. San Diego: San Diego State University Press.

—— 1986: *Knowledge of Language*. New York: Praeger.

—— 1988a: *Language and the Problems of Knowledge*. Cambridge, Mass. and London: MIT Press.

—— 1988b: Language and interpretation: Philosophical reflections and empirical inquiry. Manuscript, MIT; forthcoming in University of Pittsburgh Series on Philosophy of Science.

Collingwood, R. G. 1939: *An Autobiography*. London: Oxford University Press; reprinted, with a new introduction by S. Toulmin, Oxford: Oxford University Press, 1978.

—— 1940: *An Essay on Metaphysics*. Oxford: Clarendon Press.

Curtiss, S. 1977: *Genie: A Psycholinguistic Study of a "Modern-Day Wild Life,"* New York: Academic Press.

—— 1982: Developmental dissociations of language and cognition. In L. K. Obler and L. Menn (eds), *Exceptional Language and Linguistics*. New York: Academic Press, 285–312.

D'Ambrosio, R. 1970: *No Language But a Cry*. New York: Doubleday.

Descartes, R. 1637: *Discours de la Méthode [Discourse on Method]*. In C. Adam and P. Tannery (eds) Oeuvres de Descartes (= AT). Paris: Cerf, 1897–1913.

Devitt, M. and Sterelny, K. 1987: *Language and Reality*. Oxford: Basil Blackwell.

Dewey, J. 1948: *Reconstruction in Philosophy*, enlarged edition with a new introduction by the author. Boston: Beacon Press.

Drach, M. 1981: The creative aspect of Chomsky's use of the notion of creativity. *Philosophical Review*, XC, 44–65.

Dummett, M. 1989: Language and communication. In A. George (ed.) 1989: 193–212.

Fodor, J. A. 1983: *The Modularity of Mind*. Cambridge, Mass. and London: MIT Press.

—— 1987: Modules, frames, fridgeons, sleeping dogs, and the music of the spheres. In J. L. Garfield (ed.), *Modularity in Knowledge Representation and Natural-Language Understanding*. Cambridge, Mass. and London: MIT Press, 25–36.

—— 1989: Why should the mind be modular? In A. George (ed.) 1989: 1–22.

Foldi, N. 1987: Appreciation of pragmatic interpretation of indirect commands: Comparison of right and left hemisphere brain-damaged patients. *Brain and Language*, 31, 88–108.

Gardner, H., Brownell, H., Wapner, W. and Michelow, D. 1983: "Missing the point: The role of the right hemisphere in the processing of complex linguistic materials." In E. Perecman (ed.), *Cognitive Processing in the Right Hemisphere*. New York: Academic Press, 169–91.

—— 1987: Beyond modularity: Evidence from developmental psychology and neuropsychology. Manuscript, Harvard University.

George, A. 1989: *Reflections on Chomsky*. Oxford: Basil Blackwell.

Goffman, E. 1983: Felicity's condition. *American Journal of Sociology*, 89, 1–53.

Golinkoff, R. M. and Gordon, L. 1983: In the beginning was the word: A history of the study of language acquisition. In R. M. Golinkoff (ed.), *The Transition from Prelinguistic to Linguistic Communication*, Hillsdale, New Jersey and London: Lawrence Erlbaum Associates, 1–25.

Grice, H. P. 1957: Meaning. *Philosophical Review*, LXVI, 377–88; republished in Grice 1989: 213–23.

—— 1982: Meaning revisited. In N. V. Smith (ed.), *Mutual Knowledge*. London: Academic Press, 223–57; republished in Grice, 1989, 283–303.

—— 1989: *Studies in the Way of Words*. Cambridge, Mass. and London: Harvard University Press.

Hamblin, C. L. 1973: Questions in Montague English. *Foundations of Language* 10, 41–53.

Harrah, D. 1987: Hintikka's theory on questions. In R. J. Bodgan (ed.), *Jaakko Hintikka*. Dordrecht: Reidel, 199–213.

Hilpinen, R. 1986: The semantics of questions and the theory of inquiry. *Logique et Analyse*, 29, 523–39.

Hintikka, J. 1974: Questions about questions. In M. K. Munitz and P. K. Unger (eds), *Semantics and Philosophy*. New York: New York University Press, 103–58.

—— 1987: Replies and comments. In R. J. Bogdan (ed.), *Jaakko Hintikka*. Dordrecht: Reidel, 277–344.

Hirst, W., LeDoux, J. and Stein, S. 1984: Constraints on processing of indirect speech acts: Evidence from aphasiology, *Brain and Language*, 23, 26–33.

Jakobson, R. 1970: Language in relation to other communication systems. *Linguaggi*, Milano: Olivetti, 3–16.

Karttunen, L. 1977: Syntax and semantics of questions. *Linguistics and Philosophy*, 1, 3–44.

Kasher, A. 1976: Conversational maxims and rationality. In A. Kasher (ed.), *Language in Focus: Foundations, Methods and Systems*. Dordrecht: Reidel, 197–216.

—— 1977: What is a theory of use? *Journal of Pragmatics*, 1, 105–20; republished in A. Margalit (ed.), *Meaning and Use*. Dordrecht: Reidel, 1979, 37–55.

—— 1978: On pragmatic demarcation of language. *Theoretical Linguistics*, 5, 251–60.

—— 1981: Minimal speakers and necessary speech acts. In F. Coulmas (ed.), *Festschrift for Native Speaker*. The Hague: Mouton, 93–101.

—— 1982: Gricean inference reconsidered. *Philosophica* (Gent) 29, 25–44.

—— 1984: On the psychological reality of pragmatics. *Journal of Pragmatics*, 8, 539–57; an extensively revised version of this paper, under the title "Pragmatics and the modularity of mind," will appear in S. Davis (ed.), *Pragmatics*. Oxford: Oxford University Press, 1990.

—— 1986: Politeness and rationality. In *Pragmatics and Linguistics*, Festschrift for Jacob L. Mey. Odense: Odense University Press, 103–14.

—— 1987: Justification of speech, acts, and speech acts. In E. LePore (ed.), *New Directions in Semantics*. London: Academic Press, 281–303. Also in: G. di Bernardo (ed.), *Normative Structures of Social World*, Poznan Studies in the Philosophy of the Sciences and the Humanities, vol. 11. Amsterdam: Rodopi, 1988, 135–57.

—— 1988: The pragmatic modules. Manuscript, Tel-Aviv University.

Kenny, A. 1981: *Descartes: Philosophical Letters*, translated and edited by A. Kenny. 1st edn, Oxford: Oxford University Press, 1970; 2nd corrected edn, Minneapolis: University of Minnesota Press, 1981.

Lakatos, I. 1970: Falsification and the methodology of scientific research programmes. In I. Lakatos and A. Musgrave (eds), *Criticism and the Growth of Knowledge*. Cambridge: Cambridge University Press, 91–196; reprinted in Lakatos, 1978, 8–101.

—— 1978: *The Methodology of Scientific Research Programmes*, ed. J. Worrall and G. Currie. Cambridge: Cambridge University Press.

Marshall, J. C. 1984: Multiple perspectives on modularity. *Cognition*, 17, 209–42.

McDowell, J. 1980: Meaning, communication and knowledge. In Z. van Straaten (ed.), *Philosophical Subjects*. Oxford: Clarendon Press, 117–39.

Moravcsik, J. M. 1990: *Thought and Language*. London: Routledge & Kegan Paul.

Newmeyer, F. J. 1983: *Grammatical Theory*, Its Limits and its Possibilities. Chicago: University of Chicago Press.

Ochs, E. and Schieffelin, B. B. 1983: *Acquiring Conversational Competence*. London: Routledge & Kegan Paul.

Peirce, C. S. 1931–1960: *Collected Papers of Charles Sanders Peirce*, ed. C. Hartshorn, P. Weiss and A. W. Burks. Cambridge, Mass.: Harvard University Press.

Piattelli-Palmarini, M. (ed.) 1980: *Language and Learning: The Debate between Jean Piaget and Noam Chomsky*. Cambridge: Harvard University Press.

Pylyshyn, Z. 1984: *Computation and Cognition*. Cambridge, Mass. and London: MIT Press.

—— 1991: Rules and representations: Chomsky and representational realism. In this volume.

Russell, B. 1940: *An Inquiry into Meaning and Truth*. Quoted from the edition of London, Penguin, 1962.

Sacks, H., Schegloff, M. A. and Jefferson, G. 1974: A simplest systematics for the organization of turn-taking for conversation. *Language*, 50, 696–735.

Scha, R. J. H. 1983: Logical Foundations for Question Answering. Manuscript, Philips Research Labs, Eindhoven.

Schegloff, E. A., 1982: Discourse as an interactional achievement: Some uses of "uh huh" and other things that come between sentences. In D. Tannen (ed.), *Analyzing Discourse: Text and Talk*, Georgetown University Roundtable on Language and Linguistics. Washington: Georgetown University Press, 71–93.

—— 1986: The routine as achievement. *Human Studies*, 9, 111–51.

—— 1987: Between micro and macro: Contexts and other connections. In J. C. Alexander, B. Giesen, R. Muench and N. J. Smelser (eds), *The Micro-Macro Link*. Berkeley, Los Angeles and London: University of California Press, 207–34.

—— 1988: Goffman and the analysis of conversion. In P. Drew and A. Wootton (eds), *Erving Goffman, Exploring the Interaction Order*. Cambridge: Polity Press, 89–133.

Schegloff, E. A., Jefferson, G. and Sacks, H. 1977: The preference for self-correction in the organization of repair in conversation. *Language*, 53, 361–82.

Searle, J. 1969: *Speech Acts*. Cambridge: Cambridge University Press.

Searle, J. and Vanderveken, D. 1985: *Foundations of Illocutionary Logic*. Cambridge: Cambridge University Press.

Shallice, T. 1988: *From Neuropsychology to Mental Structure*. Cambridge: Cambridge University Press.

Spence, S. J., Zaidel, E. and Kasher, A. 1989: The right hemisphere communication battery: results from commissurotomy patients and normal subjects reveal only partial right hemisphere contribution. Manuscript, University of California, Los Angeles.

Strawson, P. 1971: *Logico-Linguistic papers*. London: Methuen.

Thayer, H. S. 1968: *Meaning and Action, A Critical History of Pragmatism*. Indianapolis: Bobbs-Merrill; quoted from the 1973 edition.

Walton, D. 1984: *Logical Dialogue-Games and Fallacies*. Lanham, MD: University Press of America.

Weylman, S. T., Brownell, H. H. and Gardner, H. 1988: "It's what you mean, not what you say": Pragmatic language use in brain-damaged patients. In F. Plum (ed.), *Language, Communication, and the Brain*. New York: Raven Press, 229–44.

Weylman, S. T., Brownell, H. H., Roman, M. and Gardner, H. 1989: Appreciation of indirect requests by left- and right-brain-damaged patients: The effects of verbal context and conventionality of wording. *Brain and Language*, 36, 580–91.

Winner, E. and Gardner, H. 1977: The comprehension of metaphor in brain-damaged patients, *Brain*, 100, 719–27.

Zaidel, D. and Kasher, A. 1989: Hemispheric memory of Surrealist versus realistic paintings. *Cortex*, 25, 617–41.

Zaidel, E. 1985: Language in the right hemisphere. In D. F. Benson and E. Zaidel (eds), *The Dual Brain*, Hemispheric Specialization in Humans. New York and London: Guilford Press, 205–31.

Zaidel, E. and Kasher, A. 1988: The right hemisphere communication battery: Performance of commissurotomy and hemispherectomy patients. Manuscript, University of California, Los Angeles.

7
"Cartesian" Linguistics?

Justin Leiber

Many commentators have felt that Professor Chomsky introduced unnecessary confusion by labeling the sort of linguistics he thought viable,
"*Cartesian* linguistics." John Lyons' popular little book about Chomsky,
for example, commends Chomsky's solid work in linguistics, and sniffs
skeptically both about any claimed connection between this work and
Chomsky's views about psychology and philosophy, and about these
psychological and philosophical views themselves. Similarly, many philosophers have been ready to accept (or ignore) much of what they would
call Chomsky's linguistic work but would deny any suggestion that this has
any real philosophical import, deny that this work provides any support for
Cartesian rationalism and nativism. Equally, psychologists have denied
any implications for psychology in Chomsky's work: the "psychological
reality," if any, of transformational-generative linguistics can only be
shown through proper laboratory experiments administered by psychologists. Similarly, some primatologists have robustly insisted that apes think
and can have language. Similarly, philosophers like John Searle, psychologists like Jerry Brunner, animal psychologists and animal rights advo-
cates, claim that Chomsky has blindly followed Descartes in exclusively
emphasizing the cognitive and formal aspects of language and thought. The
usually soberminded philosopher, Patricia Churchland, scornfully insists,
without explicit citation, evidence, or argument,

> [i]ndeed, as some ethologists are wont to point out, it is starkly evident that
> the higher animals at least, *are* conscious, and that these canny but dumb
> creatures manage to pull this off despite lacking membership in a human
> language community ... The uncompromising Cartesian view that animals
> are mere automata, incapable even of feeling pain, seeing red or hearing
> sounds, is nowadays regarded as impossible to defend without appearing
> downright ludicrous.[1]

So both by speaking of *Cartesian* linguistics, and indeed by reinforcing
this label through extended reference in *Language and Mind* and *Cartesian*

Linguistics to Descartes and subsequent work in his spirit, Chomsky is supposed to have introduced interdisciplinary confusion – the very label, "Cartesian," defiantly presupposing that linguistics can and should support the most sweeping philosophical, psychological, and biological claims, claims that are now even more preposterous than when originally presented by Descartes.[2] Thus Chomsky should, so this story goes, have avoided the label, "Cartesian linguistics," and the historical resurrection that the label suggests.

To the contrary, in my remarks I will champion the label and the historical comparison that it suggests. I think that there is something to be learned by a brief look at the portion of Descartes's views that justifies the label and at the historical reception of those views, particularly the Beast-Machine thesis, which may well have caused more heated debate in the decades after Descartes's death than any other view he held. There is also something to be learned by looking at contemporary characterizations of this debate. Indeed, pleasing mischaracterizations of historical disputes can often choke off a correct understanding of recent ones. I hasten to add that Chomsky, most obviously in *Cartesian Linguistics*, uses the term to take in Descartes *and* a number of philosophers and scientists who follow in, extend, and amend his thought, forming a coherent tradition stretching from the Port-Royal grammarians, who forged Descartes's general ideas into explicit linguistic theory and description, through to Humboldt, a tradition that has been renewed and given a more formal and precise realization, and further conceptual refinement, in the generative linguistics of the last four decades. Here, however, I confine myself, almost entirely, to Descartes's own views, though mostly those that stimulated the larger tradition of which Chomsky has written. (In particular, I will try to make sense, in contemporary terms, of some of the dualist claims of *Meditations* about consciousness, personal identity, and the emotions that the larger tradition has not emphasized).

As mention of the beast-machine debate may suggest, I will attend to the emotional and moral underpinnings of attacks on Cartesian linguistics. As Socrates suggests, in the *Apology*, the most emotional and important accusations may not be made explicitly, yet they must be dug out and confronted to reach a reasonable adjudication.

In brief, I take it that Cartesian linguistics is constituted by four views of Descartes, and that these views, particularly with emendations and extensions suggested by recent work, stand up fairly well, particularly after various historical and contemporary distortions are removed.

The views are these:

i   There is a distinction in kind between creatures with minds (= thinkers, e.g., humans) and animals (finite automata).
ii There is a test for this distinction, which is what we now call the Turing test though Descartes states it clearly enough, a test which suggests an intimate connection between language and thought, between having a language and having a mind.

iii   Consciousness (mind) has autonomy, freedom, unity, recoverability, indivisibility, transparency, and immortality.
iv   Animals do not think, are non-conscious, and do not feel pain as creatures with minds do, i.e., as conscious, linguistically-mediated *perceptions* of bodily states.

Thesis three, which I call "the Cogito," requires the most tinkering and correction. Still, I think a case can be made for much of it, particularly if we emphasize thesis two and drop the Cartesian claim that mind is a substance; that is, the Cogito should be required as an inward reading of the folk-psychological, intentional idiom. But I want to start, as I suggested, with the beast-machine debate, particularly with the characterizations now offered of Montaigne and Descartes, as opponents in the debate.

I

Mary Midgley, in *Animals and Why They Matter*, finds Descartes to be the seminal "hard-line dismissalist."

> The extreme form of this rationalist view was that of Descartes, who identified the human soul or consciousness so completely with reason as to conclude that animals could not be conscious at all, and were in fact just automata ... On this view, claims on the behalf of animals are not just excessive but downright nonsensical, as meaningless as claims on the behalf of stones or machines or plastic dolls.[3] [Midgley has it in for stones, machines, and plastic dolls, which appear again on page 14 as "dismissed kinds," and again on page 16 as evidence of the inconsistency of game hunters. "Sane people do not usually congratulate themselves if they have merely smashed a machine or a plastic toy, or even blown up an enlarged boulder. They choose a large animal because they can think of it, not just as an obstacle, but as an *opponent* – a being like themselves in having its own emotions and interest."]

Midgley gives not even a line in justifying the dismissal of stones, machines, and plastic dolls, though her list is carefully selected, for the reader would not find the flow so easy if she wrote of smashing a computer that passed the Turing test (as dramatized in the film *2001*) or, rather differently, of shredding the only manuscript of a lost play of Shakespeare, burning down an oak forest, or atomic-bombing the Grand Canyon. But Midgley complains, ignoring the Descartes/Turing test and Descartes's total silence on the issue of the treatment of animals,

> [s]uch drastic and convinced excluders are also those least interested in arguing for their position. They find it obvious. On the other side, Montaigne had argued at length, in "Apology for Raymond Sebond," strongly and quite carefully against ill-treatment of animals. Descartes, though he probably had Montaigne's remarks in mind, dismissed the subject briskly.[4]

Similarly, Peter Singer sees "the first genuine dissent" in Leonardo da Vinci's vegetarianism and Giordano Bruno's belief that "'man is no more than an ant in the presence of the infinite,'" and Montaigne, who rejects humanist self-exaltation, is

> [t]he first writer since Roman times to say that cruelty to animals is wrong in itself.
>
> Perhaps, then, from this point in the development of Western thought the status of nonhumans was bound to improve? The old concept of the universe, and man's central place in it, was slowly giving ground; modern science was about to set forth on its now-famous rise.
>
> But the absolute nadir was still to come. The last, most bizarre, and – for the animals – most painful outcome of Christian doctrines emerged in the first half of the seventeenth century, in the philosophy of René Descartes . . .
>
> In the philosophy of Descartes the Christian doctrine that animals do not have immortal souls has the extraordinary consequence that they do not have consciousness either. They are mere machines, automata. They experience neither pleasure nor pain, nor anything else. Although they may squeal when cut with a knife, or writhe in their efforts to escape contact with a hot iron, this does not, Descartes said, mean that they feel pain in these situations . . .
>
> For Descartes the scientist the doctrine had still another fortunate result. It was at this time that the practice of experimenting on live animals became widespread in Europe. Descartes's theory allowed the experimenter to dismiss any qualms he might feel. Descartes himself dissected living animals in order to advance his knowledge of anatomy, and many of the leading physiologists of the period declared themselves Cartesians and mechanists. The following eye-witness account of some of these experimenters, working at Port-Royal, makes clear the convenience of Descartes' theory.
>
> They administered beatings to dogs with perfect indifference, and made fun of those who pitied the creatures as if they felt pain. They said the animals were clocks . . . They nailed poor animals up on boards by their four paws to vivisect them and see the circulation of the blood which was a great subject of conversation.[5]

The only citation Singer gives us, as evidence for this account, is the source of the end-quote from N. Fontaine's *Mémoires pour servir a l'histoire de Port-Royal* (1738) in L. C. Rosenfield's *From Beast-Machine to Man-Machine*.[6] Stephen Clarke in *The Moral Status of Animals* makes exactly the same reference via Rosenfield, which makes one wonder whether too much is made to rest on a single source.[7] Clarke adds, "And it is perhaps worth remembering the story of St Eustace, who was converted to Christianity when the stag he was hunting turned at bay to reveal a crucifix between his antlers."[8] Clarke, surely more right historically, sees Descartes's views as a heartless scientistic departure from Christianity, rather than as a fulfillment of it; indeed, *pace* Singer, the Cartesians lost the debate with animal soul adherents because their opponents were able to argue that the beast-machine hypothesis threatened Christianity, and man's immortal soul in particular.[9]

Indeed, one must assume that Singer, though perhaps not Clarke, couldn't be bothered to look at the original source. In the paragraph following the one quoted, Fontaine's hero, M. de Saci, remarks that both Aristotle and Descartes have subverted Christianity but that Descartes, in attacking Scholasticism, is much worse, for he is like a thief who has killed another thief to take his booty. Further, Saci remarks,

> God made the world . . . to manifest his greatness and to depict the invisible in the visible. Descartes destroys both. "The sun is a beautiful thing," one says to him, to which he replies, "No, it's a mass of refuse." [un amas de rognures] Instead of recognizing invisible things in the visible, as in the sun, the God of nature, and to see Him in its effect on plants, he, on the other hand, tries to provide a reason for everything.[10]

Fontaine's Mémoires de Port-Royal were published, with various changes by his editors, some nearly thirty years after his death and were written, according to his editors, a long time after the events described and with many chronological mistakes – and all this by a man who held Cartesianism to be scientistic blasphemy and held that we should detest any fact, or concern with truth, that did not trumpet forth Christianity.[11] If N. Fontaine perhaps embellished the truth a trifle in the good cause of his anti-scientific master, this should not surprise us. During his life his publications consisted of several books about Old, New Testament, Roman, medieval, and more recent saints.[12]

It appears that, rather in the manner of Fontaine, Singer's basis for claiming that Descartes gaily dissected living animals is that he had a possible excuse and that, several decades after Descartes's death, some unnamed persons at Port-Royal did so in offensively good cheer, as reported many decades after that by someone who lived an edifying and miraculous story and hated modern science. It is also troubling in that Singer trusts Rosenfield enough to quote her with assurance and yet ignores what she writes about Descartes's treatment of animals. She writes,

> Descartes, himself, was evidently fond of dogs, and no accusation of personal cruelty to animals was ever leveled against him. Indeed, the leading exponent of the theory of animal automatism kept a pet dog called "Monsieur Grat." He apparently prized him, too, for as a gift to his friend in Paris, the Abbé Picot, he sent Monsieur Grat, via his faithful valet Macon, "with a little female, in order to give some of this breed to Abbé."[13] [The letter, which Rosenfield cites from M. Baillet's Vie de M. Descartes, II, 456, is also in Oeuvres de Descartes, ed. C. Adam and P. Tannery (Paris: Leopold Cerf, 1908); Rosenfield's summary is misleading in that the servant himself is going to work for the Abbé, who had complained to Descartes about bad service, and is only incidentally transporting the two dogs.]

Rosenfield adds, "What strange, potent magic these little machines can work!," which is to make the same point that Descartes has often made, that nature produces much more marvelous mechanisms than humans can construct (at present). But Descartes would have added that our wonder should increase as we attend to the ingenious way in which mechanism can achieve such effects. It is a wonder to be savored in knowledge, not in superstitious ignorance. There is simply not a line in Descartes to suggest that he thought we are free to smash animals at will or free to do so *because* their behavior can be explained mechanically.

Descartes, indeed, performed several dissections, his experiments being confined to the heart and circulatory system; from his letter to Plemp (15 February, 1638) it is evident that Descartes vivisected fish and, in one case, a hare.[14] There is nothing in Descartes's detailed account to suggest anything but a most serious and painstaking pursuit of truth. He frequently saw his physiological investigations as justified by the hope of practical medical applications.

Let us look at what Midgley calls Montaigne's "strong and quite careful" defense of animals, what Singer sees as a great leap in the rise of civilization. Then we may compare this with Descartes "brisk" and "bizarre" remarks.

Midgley refers us to Montaigne's "Apology for Raymond Sebond," a sprawling essay that amounts to 220 pages in the George B. Ives translation from which I will quote.[15] A good half of it is devoted to fabulations about animals and of this Ives writes, "He then enters on an argument (if it may be so called by courtesy)," (p.174), adding,

> in Montaigne's day of scientific ignorance there can have been no fixed limits to a thinker who, like Montaigne, had emancipated himself from dependence on the evidence of his senses, or on his personal experience.[16]

While in the extent and absurdity of his compendium Montaigne is an Herodotus of Herodotus, ransacking the entire household of Latin authors for frivolous confabulations, his central beliefs and inclinations respecting animals are not uncommon today. He regards it as (1) obvious that animals are conscious, have an inner life, think, and feel, all in much the same way as humans (any animated Disney film provides the relevant characterizations); (2) likely that some animals literally can or do have human speech, that in any case all or most animals have some equally powerful substitute for it, one as unknown or unknowable to us as our language, is to them, and that quite apart from that there is an infinitely expressive natural language of gestures and facial expressions that many animals understand just as we do; (3) for such reasons, and because of impatience and distaste for, and doubt about, actual empirical investigation, we may expect never to understand, and perhaps should not understand, what the inner conscious lives of various animals are like, though we may confidently fling in the face of the mechanist our infallible assurance that they have such inner experience.

Concluding an opening passage in which he rebukes the exaltation of human reason by pointing out that human lives are really determined by the influence of the stars, and that human reasoners have even reached such preposterous beliefs as that the moon is a sphere like earth, with mountains and valleys, Montaigne asks,

How does he know, by the strength of his understanding, the internal and secret stirrings of the animals? By what comparison between them and ourselves does he determine the dulness which he attributes to them?[17]

Montaigne, however, does not blanch at this challenge. After asking how, respecting the government of beehives, "can we imagine it to be carried on without reasoning and foresight?," Montaigne continues,

Can the birds, in the beautiful and wonderful construction of their buildings, make use of a round shape rather than a square one, of an obtuse angle rather than a right angle, without being aware of the condition and the consequences? Do they floor their palaces with moss or with down, without foreseeing that the tender members of their little ones will thus lie more softly and at ease . . . Why does the spider use now this kind of knot, now that, if she does not deliberate and reflect and decide?[18]

Tool use and medicine follow quickly,

The elephant sharpens the tusks he uses in war (for he has some special ones he reserves for this use alone). The mongoose, when he comes to grips with the crocodile, strengthens his body, and encrusts it all over with mud very tightly packed and well kneaded, as with a cuirass . . . The goats of Candia, if wounded by an arrow, select dittany to cure them; the tortoise, when she has eaten a snake, instantly seeks wild marjoram to purge herself; the dragon rubs and brightens his eyes with fennel – why should we not say this is learning and skill?[19]

Similarly, we learn that the oxen of Susa can count to a hundred, while we reach adolescence before doing so, and that there are many human nations with no knowledge of number.[20] There is the usual staff about hedgehogs as meteorologists, birds who use "intelligence and reasoning" in navigation, Androcles and his lion, all this hedged with reference to "some superior faculty in them, which is hidden from us; as are many others of their properties and powers of which no appearance can reach us."[21] Though Montaigne finds creatures, compared with clocks, as wondrous as Descartes, he lacks the same interest in understanding them.

We are conscious, in our own clumsier works, of the faculties that we employ in them, and that our minds make use in them of all our powers; why do we not think that animals do as much? Why do we attribute to I know not what innate and mechanical inclination the works which surpass all that we can produce by nature and by art?[22]

Montaigne has a remarkable proof that dogs, at least, can speak,

And since it is the case, as the cosmographers say, that there are nations which accept a dog for a king, it must be that they give a definite interpretation to his voice and his motions.[23]

However, the same paragraph begins with the more hedged and familiar view that animals have something equivalent to speech.

> This deficiency that prevents communication between them and us, why is it not in us as much as in them? It is a matter of conjecture whose fault it is that we do not understand one another; for we do not understand them any more than they us. By this same reasoning they may think us dullards as we think them. It is no great wonder if we do not understand them; neither do we understand the Basques and the Troglodytes.

In particular, beasts who lack voices may,

> even as our mutes, dispute and argue and tell stories by signs. I have seen some of them so agile and well fashioned for this, that in truth they fell in no wise short of perfection in ability to make themselves understood.[24]

And Montaigne adds much more about the ability to communicate fully with eyes, face, or hands.

Let us consider what Midgley calls Descartes's brisk dismissal of Montaigne (she may have in mind his November 23, 1646 letter to the Marquess of Newcastle, though she gives no reference); for this and a more prolix passage addressed to More on February 5, 1649 and one to Plempius of October 3, 1637, I quote from Anthony Kenny's translation, *Philosophical Letters*,

> I agree that some [animals] are stronger than us and there may also be some who have an instinctive cunning capable of deceiving the shrewdest human beings. But they only imitate or surpass us in those of our actions which are not guided by our thoughts. It often happens that we walk or eat without thinking; and similarly, without using our reason, we reject things which are harmful for us, and parry blows aimed at us. Indeed, even if we expressly willed not to put our hands in front of our head when we fall, we could not prevent ourselves.[25] [Pavlov remarks that, "Descartes evolved the idea of the reflex. Starting from the assumption that animals behaved simply as machines, he regarded every activity of the organism as a *necessary* reaction to some stimulus, the connection between the stimulus and response being made through a definite nervous path."[26]]
>
> In fact, [Descartes continues] none of our external actions can show anyone who examines them that our body is not just a self-moving machine but contains a soul with thoughts, with the exception of words, or other signs that are relevant to particular topics without expressing any passion. I say words or other signs because deaf-mutes use signs as we use spoken words.[27] [A more explicit version of the Descartes/Turing test is to "arrange speech in various ways, in order to reply appropriately to everything that may be said in its presence," from *Discourse on Method*.[28]]

Descartes notes that "Montaigne and Charron may have said that there is more difference between one human and another than between a human being and an animal," but he nonetheless insists that even madmen and the lowest types of humans all uniquely share language and hence thought.[29] Thus Descartes would also be bemused by such recent Montaignean comments as,

> for all we know, the differences between my conscious states and those of a gorilla may be no more differences in *kind*, and no more significant, than those obtaining between a medieval serf and a modern man steeped in biological and physical theory, or between a child with Down's syndrome and a professional musician, between Captain Fitzroy and the inhabitants of Tierra del Fuego, between oneself at five and at sixty-five.[30]

Equally, Descartes, quite unlike Montaigne, and much in keeping with recent linguistics, clearly distinguishes the fully-fledged language of deaf signers from animals' reflexive use of a few signs to express passions. Descartes concludes his letter to More by noting a related problem in the beast-soul hypothesis

> There is no reason to believe it of some animals without believing it of all, and many of them such as oysters and sponges are too imperfect for this to be credible.[31]

This, as Descartes presumably realized, is one of the gravest difficulties for one who champions the beast-soul, or animal consciousness. Montaigne is ecumenical in this respect, claiming consciousness for spiders and ants, and even writing of our duties to trees and plants.[32] Singer and Clarke agree in denying consciousness to sponges.[33] Singer locates the distinction somewhere between the shrimp and the oyster.[34] He, with rather considerable convenience for one who is thundering hard accusations at others, slides by the case of insects and spiders and bacteria; they, *pace* Montaigne, apparently and rather conveniently do not feel pain. The intrepid Midgley, on the other hand, seems willing to speculate about the subjective experience of tapeworms.[35] I shall soon examine the claims of a recent Montaignean, Thomas Nagel, for bat consciousness, but he appears to draw the line at flounders and wasps, though more recently he speaks of the inner life of cockroaches.[36] But all these writers, it seems to me, fumble for reasons to rationalize views that, as Descartes remarks, "we are all accustomed to from our earliest years," such as that it is, for example, obvious that dogs are conscious and are not to be eaten, while pigs are not conscious and are perfectly proper food, or the other way around, that it is appalling to club baby seals while meritorious to lay down poisons that subject rats to a slow death from internal bleeding, that bees in hives are paragons of happy workers, while ant-hills are totalitarian evil empires, that dolphins are happy, tender-minded sorts, while sharks are consumed by malevolent visions (consult Walt Disney for milder, the Brothers Grimm for crueler, variations).

Aristotle found that the postulation of final causes was necessary to biology. Things happen, not simply from efficient and formal causes, but for a purpose, designed for living. What Descartes found most objectionable in Aristotle's claim that, with "natural" objects, these forms of causation collapsed into each other, is the suggestion, which is not at all found in Aristotle, that animals must "know their purpose" and act out of this knowledge as rational, self-conscious beings. God, presumably, designed them so as cleverly life-preserving organisms, but we can understand them in such a way that we can know, on purely mechanical terms, why they have to behave as they do. Their self-knowledge is not necessary in explaining why they are as they are.

Let us examine, in some detail, a recent Montaignean, Thomas Nagel.

II

In "What is it like to be a bat?," Professor Thomas Nagel robustly and without argument asserts that there is something that it is like to be a bat.[37] He equally robustly asserts, with little more argument, that we do not, never will, and perhaps simply cannot ever, know or reasonably suspect *what* it is like to be a bat. Though we may well learn everything about bat neurophysiology, understanding of what it is like to be a bat is forever beyond us. Therefore, Nagel rather grandly concludes, physicalism is in trouble, for the recalcitrant subjective experience of being a bat is forever beyond us.

> Reflection on what it is like to be a bat seems to lead us, therefore, to the conclusion that there are facts that do not consist in the truth of propositions expressible in a human language.[38]

Nagel takes it for granted that (1) everything in, and everthing true about, the "physical universe" must be fully-describable in every human language, and, hence, be capable of being fully understood by human speakers of human language(s); Nagel tries to show (2) that there is a mysterious, luxuriant "subjective multiverse" that is partitioned into countless mutually-unintelligible subjective "world versions," perhaps one for each animal kind, and more generally for each "subjectivizing kind" including all the various hypothetical intelligent extraterrestrials – and as Nagel recently insists on even insects having such a rich, and to all others uknowable and unintelligible world view, one can hardly discount the humble cognitive strivings of electric eyes and thermostats, let alone the claims of Crays. But Nagel's assumption (1) appears bizarre, at least for a realist who believes that the universe exists apart from what we may say or can know about it. The universe is an enormously complicated affair, the organisms of earth, and those elsewhere, presenting one of its most stunning complexities. Even the mildest sort of realist should find it extraordinary to suppose a priori that every truth about this melange is expressible in human language and hence can be learned and understood by humans. And even the mildest sort of mathematical realist might point out that the various incompleteness and incomputability results establish formally that there are nonsubjective truths forever beyond our grasp. As I shall show, by way of a representative pragmatic example – a chess-playing computer – we *characteristically* have to understand much of the behavior and cognitive structure of even fairly simple organized beings in design or intentional modes, and thus we often find concrete and causal understanding beyond our grasp, pragmatically incomputable now and perhaps, in some fuller theory of human cognition, incomputable within the acquisitionally-available, or learnable, structures of human intelligence.[39]

Actually, while Nagel vastly (or idealistically) over-estimates the possibility of our understanding all possible truths about the "physical" universe, I shall soon show that Nagel displays a most careless and, like Fontaine, whimsical and contemptuous disdain for such matters (*un amas de rognures* as Saci would say). Perhaps this is because Nagel supposes himself in an infinite jungle of such truths, fearing more that he will buried in a truthful fruitfall than eager for such enlightenment. Empirical researchers should be so lucky. Respecting the "subjective multiverse" (2), on the other hand, Nagel is most respectfully and resolutely mystified, insisting both that it is endlessly rich in truths and that these truths are forever beyond us. Let us follow Nagel's particular exemplification of this claim in the case of bats.

Nagel is, as Montaigne was, in much the same position as the Wittgenstein of whom Ramsey remarked, "If you can't say it, you can't whistle it either." For he wishes both to make it out that bats have a lively subjectivity *and* that its character is also forever beyond our grasp. Indeed, he writes,

> Bats, although more closely related to us than wasps or flounders, nevertheless present a range of activity and a sensory apparatus so different from ours that the problem I want to pose is exceptionally vivid.[40]

Bats, Nagel writes,

> perceive the external world primarily by sonar, or echolocation, detecting the reflections, from objects within range, of their own rapid, high-frequency shrieks.[41]

Nagel indeed gives whistling a brief try. He imagines that,

> he has webbing on his arms . . . has very poor vision, and perceives the surrounding world by a system of reflected high-frequency sound signals . . . [but Nagel soon breaks off with the conclusion that this, quote,] tells me only what it would be like for *me* to behave as a bat behaves. But that is not the question. I want to know what it is like for a *bat* to be a bat.[42]

And that, Nagel is sure, he cannot know.

Here Nagel carries the carefree attitude respecting facts found among those who bemoan the arrogance of science into the slander of an entire mammalian order.

Just to get one point out of the way, it isn't so much the bat's arms that are webbed as its four enormously enlarged fingers. My use of the word "fingers" reminds us that bats, indeed, are mammals. Further, the bat order is the most closely related to primates. Indeed, some zooligists hold that bats *are* primates. (One offspring is normal, with a long period of maternal upbringing.)[43]

More significantly, all bats have good eyesight. Indeed, the large fruit bats, Megachioptera, one of the two bat suborders, don't employ echoloca-tion and rely entirely on eyesight to navigate. The largely nocturnal Microchioptera do employ echolocation to catch nearby insects and to avoid nearby objects. However, their eyesight assists echolocation for near *objects* and replaces it for distant ones. Blindfolded bats cannot find their way back to the nest, while bats without echolocation can. "Blind as a bat," is typical Montaignean fabulation.

But there's a further point about echolocation itself. In a revealing, almost self-contradictory footnote, Nagel writes,

> Blind people are able to detect objects near them by a form of sonar, using vocal clicks or taps of a cane. Perhaps if one knew what that was like, one could roughly imagine what it would be like to possess the much more refined sonar of a bat.[44]

Nagel here extends his lack of real interest in bats to blind humans. In fact, a lot of researchers, some blind themselves, have devoted consider-able time to answering Nagel's question. In several studies over as many decades, researchers have asked blind people how they manage their familiar ability to "sense" a nearby wall (without deliberate vocal clicks or cane taps).[45] They "just sense" the flatness in front of them, "feel pressure" on their faces, and so on. They deny that they make use of their hearing. However, they cannot manage to sense the wall if the sonic vibrations they make use of are interfered with. It is wrong to say that they hear the wall, for that is not their subjective experience. Rather, they visualize the wall, though this is managed, unconsciously, through their ears. After all, they need a spatial representation of the environment. Sounds aren't spatially flat; you don't bump into them.

What of Nagel's limp, "Perhaps if one knew what that was like"? Doesn't the research I've mentioned begin to give one an idea of what it is like? Assuming you are not blind, reflect on the experience of walking through a totally dark, but familiar, room. The walls, doors, chairs, etc., loom up spacially, not as memories in their brightly-colored daylight dress, but as vague, dark, spatial presences. In his *Optics*, Descartes writes,

> No doubt you have had the experience of walking at night over rough ground without a light, and finding it necessary to use a stick in order to guide yourself. You may then have been able to notice that by means of this stick you could feel the various objects situated around you, and that you could even tell whether they were trees or stones or sand or water or grass or mud or any other such thing . . . Consider it in those born blind, who have made use of it all their lives: with them, you will find, it is so perfect and so exact that one might also say that they see with their hands.[46]

Similarly, consider the familiar accounts come of blind people who experience visual/tactile transfer. An image of the forward visual array is converted into a spatially-isomorphic pattern of stimuli on the blind person's back. He feels uninterpretable pinpricks on his back; then he begins to make rudimentary guesses about what is in front of him from the pinpricks. After some time, the pinpricks are no longer experienced, and somewhat colorless, dimly-illuminated, objects appear in front of him, objects that he can reach and touch, move around, and so on.

So I may conclude that *insofar as it makes sense* to talk about what it is like to be a bat who's using echolocation to move through a complicated spatial array, it is reasonable to guess that the bat, like the blind person, employs a spatial array and not a lot of high-pitched shrieks. The bat needs to know what's in front of it and where. Shortly, I shall clarify the rather anemic sense – the design stance – in which it makes sense to talk this way.

Indeed, one wonders whether bats "subjectively-experience" sound at all, whether bats ever experience shrieks. For us it is a very familiar experience to hear subjectively, i.e. locationlessly. We say we hear a sound, or sounds. But we never, unless we are philosophers, psychologists or psychedelic drug-users, say we see a sight, or sights. Our visual faculty is persistently, even obdurately, objective. An organism that uses sound to sort out the world spatially, just as we use light, might be simply incapable of hearing subjectively. After some exotic operation that allows us to tap into his inner life, one imagines the much-abused little squeaker saying, in the manner of an Oxford philosopher.

> I never 'hear sounds,' to mouth your absurd jargon; I hear walls and stalactites, flies and moths, bats and owls, and so on, and I don't hear them all over the place – or in my ear drums or the inside of my brain – I hear them where they are, which is out there in front of me, in the spatial positions they occupy as objects in our common physical world. You chappies eyeballs 'em – I 'ears 'em . That's *my* experience, *that's what it's like to be me*."

Of course, my image of the little squeaker has now become patently absurd. But it is rewarding to consider where the absurdity comes in. The first point is that the term, "subjective experience," gets its sense from contrast with "objective experience," and it is a product of a sophisticated, perhaps necessarily linguistically-mediated, understanding. The following phrases capture the necessary interplay between objective and subjective experience:

> At first, as I listened, I was caught up totally in his account of the riot, but then his accent and breathing, and the static on the line, made my attention waver.
> I saw a rabbit but, latterly, I realized I could also see a duck.
> It seems hot but then I've just come in from the snow storm.

These are sophisticated perceptions, playing on the contrast between objectivity and subjectivity, and I doubt bats are much given to them. I think that one cannot have experience in the sense suggested by these sentences unless one is in possession of something like a language with the appropriate first person pronouns and other resources, such as other speakers and appropriate interchanges in which one can play off a grasp of one's and other's points of view. In short, unless one can tell and understand stories about oneself and others. (Since I am not myself a metaphysical dualist, I do suppose that these abilities are grounded in cognitive competencies that are physically realized in our brains.)

More simply: no subjective experience without a subject. And no subject without objects. And, finally, no subject and objects without an appropriate language.

Or, as Descartes in effect puts it, we, as conscious thinkers, are entities for whom it generally makes sense to ask, e.g., did she experience thus and so in this sort of way or that, or did she not *experience* thus and so at all but acted unconsciously or reflexively with respect to that stimulus? What place can such questions have with bats?

In my rendition of the little speaker the description became absurd when I introduced consciousness, i.e., fully-fledged subjectivity. I had claimed it made some sense to believe that microchioptera used a spatial array rather than experiencing a lot of shrieks from which it inferred what lay in front it, this supposition making sense from the point of view of someone thinking about the design of such an organism, someone thinking about the purpose of the parts. While I believe that bats have no experience, no point of view or inner life, in any sort of fully-fledged sense, I do think that it makes some sense to talk about the bat in the way that I have. I shall return to this after I borrow, extent, and rearrange Daniel Dennett's pragmatic transcendental argument.[47]

When we play chess with a microcomputer, one stance is to regard the computer as a deterministic machine and try causal analysis as a strategy. The computer is just an enormous number of off/on switch trees. Since one can in theory trace the most probable physical effect of one's move through the microchip forest, one can derive what move the computer will make in response. One can, in theory, continue this prospective causal analysis until one sees a forced win. Indeed one could in this way find a winning sequence without knowing anything about chess rules or strategy. Of course, as you know, the causal analysis required to predict one move would contain hundreds of thousands of on/off steps. The length of causal analysis required is numbing to calculate. (Chess has a mechanical solution. But since the number of possible sequences for the first 20 moves alone exceeds the number of atomic particles in the universe, we may have to wait for it. Our transcendental arguments are, as I said, pragmatic.)[48]

So the first, deterministic stance is insufficient in practice as a way to play chess against a computer. Physicalists should concede that this is equally true of playing against a human being. Your brain may consist of a network of millions of neurons, but I shall get nowhere trying to play chess with you if I think of you that way. Similarly, *this* sort of neurological account of the bat's brain will not *by itself* do the job of helping *us understand how* it coordinates sensory stimuli inputs and motor outputs.

The second stance that Dennett mentions he calls "the design stance." I may know or infer something about the computer's program (not necessarily about the specific lines). Perhaps the computer never "looks" more than three moves ahead, so I look for four move sacrificial combinations, which the computer accepts because it gains material to its analysis limit. Similarly, some early microprograms were "pawn grabbers," seeking minor gains in material, while ignoring more subtle considerations of space and development. One runs into human players with similar traits. Recent programs have fewer blatant design weaknesses. Speaking metaphorically but fruitfully, one can also think of plants and animals in this way. Whether one thinks of God or Darwin's nature as the molder for the life preservation contest, biological understanding often inevitably starts by asking how cellular, organ, and behavioral systems are designed to succeed.

This brings us to Dennett's third stance. I regard the computer as a conscious human chess player. I understand it with intentional predicates such as "attacking my king side," "planning to queen its queen's knight's pawn," "seeing the need to occupy the open file," and so on. Similarly, "it obviously believes my passed pawn isn't dangerous, for it moved its rook away"; "it believes that that exchange of pieces is bad for it, because it interposed the pawn"; "in general it values bishops more highly than knights"; "it has learned to avoid stalemate." When does this way of speaking become more than a helpful metaphor? More generally: when, imagining a computer-robot that simulated the round of human cognitive capacities, would we say we had genuine consciousness and thought? Even sticking with the chess example, which presumably might constitute one minor facet of the range of talents needed to pass the Descartes/Turing test, several points are in order.

1   The intentional stance (and the design stance for that matter) is not a causal analysis. I am often sure what move the computer will make in reply to a particular move of mine. But that is not because I understand how it was caused to make that particular move. Rather it will be because, e.g., that is the only legal response, or more commonly, because that move is obviously the best response. I may believe the computer is a deterministic machine, as I may equally when playing a human opponent. But this faith has in itself little practical application. I see my opponent as an able strategist, representing the possibilities to itself and choosing among them.

2   I use the pragmatically unavoidable intentional stance in the same way both to understand the opponent and myself. Except in the comparatively rare cases when I can make use of the design stance (or information about my human opponent's quirks), I understand my opponent's moves, and possible moves, in much the same way as I understand my own. "What would that move do?," or "Why might someone do that?," are questions I ask myself in the same logical tone of voice, whether it's a move I can make or one my opponent can.

3   Such intentional understandings are wholistic, non-explicit, and within a range indeterminate. When I reasonably ascribe to a program or a

human opponent a tendency to "pawn grabbing," there may be a vast number of different ways that this may be realized in the computer or human. There need not be any specific program lines or neurological tissues that constitute this proclivity. I make my ascription to the whole, which is thus taken as an indivisible point, a unity.

4 The grasp of one's own subjectivity in playing chess comes with difficulty in the chess player's career. One learns from other's failures to say "He is a pawn grabber," or "She sees too many virtues in cramped positions." It is difficult to turn such characterizations round on oneself. To see how one is seeing, or mis-seeing, the board is sophisticated self-assessment learned in the characterization of others. It's not the prising open of a secret inner door, through which you finally see the real thinking you've been doing all along.

5 There is not, in present-day programs, this sort of sophisticated and articulate grasp of subjective characterizations, either of other players or of the program itself. A "pawn-grabbing" program can't characterize itself or another as a pawn-grabber. Similarly, a program that is designed to exploit pawn-grabbing in others may have no explicit way of characterizing these others as pawn-grabbers or itself as a pawn-grabbing exploiter. Chess programs do not grasp themselves.

However, a few recent programs can, in an unsophisticated way, learn from their mistakes, which is to say that they can revise some explicit clause in their strategic instructions. But it is instructive that these very crude "learning programs" are much less successful in play than the non-learning programs. Such learning-programs require much much more memory and processing time than comparably strong micro programs. None of the top main frame programs is a learning program. The requirements for even the most limited sort of introspection are prohibitive. A bat is highly unlikely to be able to afford it.

We return to Nagel's artfully ambiguous question, "What is it like to be a bat?"

Firstly, one could interpret this to mean, "What is the causal analysis of a bat's navigating and insect-seeking behavior?" The answer to this question is that it is extraordinarily complicated to understand a bat in this way. A bat certainly doesn't.

Second, one could take the question to be, "What is a reasonable design characterization of a bat's near insect- and obstacle-detecting, capturing, and evading ability?" I think I have already given a rough bit of such an understanding. The claim that a bat needs a spatial characterization could be thought similar to the claim that a chess-playing program needs an evaluation metric for the value of the various chess pieces. In neither case do we suppose that the bat or the computer is aware of its mode of representation. Such a level of representation is an intolerably inefficient and cumbersome requirement. In this sense I can know more about what it is like to be a bat than the little squeaker can. (To put the point more generally, our ability to grasp our inner life seems to follow after and employ much the same means as our shared and interworked understand-

ing of the people and things around us, all this threaded through with the
development of our linguistic abilities. It is hard to imagine that the bat has
room for and can reasonably set aside the brain equipment to maintain this
sophisticated end product – consciousness – while neither having the help
of a shared language and education, nor the manifest benefits of a shared
language and intellectual culture.)

Third, one can take Nagel's question to be, "What is the bat's own
picture of its cognitive processes? – does it notice, e.g., a dimness of the
background when it uses echolocation, does it consciously hear the squeaks
or merely experience the visual array?" I think the answer to this question
simply has to be that it is extraordinarily unlikely (not, of course, logically
impossible, though perhaps biologically impossible) that the bat has any
picture at all of its own cognitive processes. To have cognitive processes is
not at all the same thing as to experience, or understand, oneself as having
such processes. Further, to understand various parts of one's cognitive
processes is not to open an inner door so that one can directly see them as
they have been working all along; it is the extraordinarily sophisticated
task of constructing a view of these processes.

For all I've said, a sophisticated Montaignean may still feel a temptation
to say something like this: "Surely the bat *must* have some kind of inner
subjective experience, given its complicated behavior, its swiftly coordinated sensory inputs and motor outputs. And, in any case, what earthly
basis can you have for arguing that the bat *doesn't* have an inner experience
of its immediate surroundings – of the moth it is about to capture, of the
fellow bat it must avoid, and so on. What chauvinist arrogance to speculate
negatively about such matters!"

I believe that bats have no such inner experiences and, indeed, lack the
cognitive wherewithal even in principle to know or tell me of this deficit.
Consequently, like Descartes, I appeal to accounts of human experiences,
where we find our only robust characterizations of what it is like to be
something.

Consider the phenomena Professor L. Weiskrantz describes as "blind
sight."[49] Humans with certain brain lesions report that they can't see half
or more of their normal visual field. Yet these individuals can, quite
accurately, reach out and grasp objects in this "blind" area. They "see" in
a functional sense but have no conscious access to this process. I think it
would be a mistake to say of such individuals that they have inaccessible
subjective visual experiences when they reach for objects in their blind
area. I don't see why bats can't be blind and deaf in at least this sort of way.

Of course, I *could* be factually mistaken about the blind-sighted human.
Some brain change might make such an individual suddenly say,
"Strangest thing – I suddenly somehow have a lot of new memories; in
addition to my familiar memories of *not-seeing* the left half of this room, I
have these new memories of seeing it (and of part of me wanting, but being
unable, to say what I had been seeing in those damned experiments)." I
think it unlikely that this, or the like, will happen. One neurophysiological
basis for this speculation is that the retina stimulates two distinct neurolo-

gical systems, one running through the superior colliculus, the denser and richer other running through the lateral geniculate nuclei; the latter supports experienced vision (damage to it is the cause of blind sight) while the former apparently serves blind sight. The bat lacks such a densely differentiated arrangement. In any case, the basic point remains: there is simply no necessity that complicated sensory/motor coordination be accompanied by inner experience; moreover, the bat does not affort the dense and differentiated system that underwrites experience in humans.

An artful incompleteness about Nagel's paper is that while he does say that we can understand what it is like to be a human, he never says in what this understanding is supposed to consist. But unless this understanding is supposed to be something unchallenging to the physicalist, or scientific, account of the universe, what can be the justification for leading us off on a wild bat chase? If accounts of what it is like to be a human impugn physicalism, then that's obviously where to make one's case, rather than appealing to a few fuzzy, and largely mistaken, beliefs about bats. If good accountings of what it is like to be, e.g., Tom Nagel, Winston Churchill, or Marcel Proust can show up physicalism, why bring up bats?

Perhaps an effective biography, autobiography, or *roman à clef* of an individual man may give us a sense of what it is like to be that man in a way no neurological characterization ever could. But if Nagel had begun his bat paper by saying just that, his argument would have been haunted by the need to whistle out something like the supposition that a bat grasps batelese narratives of itself and its fellow bats.

III

Toward the beginning of this paper I mentioned that the Descartes/Turing test has stood up well. Descartes, whose earliest notes speak of making mechanical men as well as animals, maintained that the human body is as much a mechanical automaton as any animal. He proposed that the one "sure test" by which we could distinguish a genuine – conscious and thinking – human from a mechanical fake was whether it could "arrange speech in various ways, in order to reply appropriately to everything that may be said in its presence." Alan Turing proposed the same test in his "Computing machinery and intelligence," though he of course thought that it was possible that a humanly-constructed computer might eventually pass the test.[50]

In a recent paper, Daniel Dennett has, I think successfully, defended the Descartes/Turing test against various objections, particularly against the objection that it is too easy, that a simulation that obviously does not really think can pass it.[51] He also in effect opts for what we might, perhaps wrongly, take as the explicitly more stringent Cartesian version of the test: that is, if we interpret Descartes's "reply appropriately to whatever is said in its presence" to require various motor, sensory, and narrative features such as, in Dennett's phrase, "eyes, ears, hands, and a history."[52]

We should recall that Descartes thought that the human body, just as animal bodies, was a mechanical device. Indeed, in his earliest writings he is as much concerned to make mechanical humans as mechanical animals. In *Cogitationes Privatae* 34–6 we find a description of a mechanical man who moves through the use of magnetism.[53] It is possible that Descartes underestimated the complexity of such accounts. His championing of the beast-machine theory can be understood not only as a denial of animal consciousness but also as a denial of what came to replace the beast-soul hypothesis, namely the notion of *élan vital*, the notion that living organisms are wholly different from inorganic things and require the postulation of wholly new emergent forces.

As I suggested above, for pragmatic and heuristic reasons, we may need to make use of design, or functional, characterizations in understanding complicated devices (whether human, animal, or mineral, hydrocarbon or silicon chip, or anything else). In this sense, as indeed and differently in physics, we have to weaken the strict Cartesian notion of mechanism. For similar and stronger reasons, we have to call into play full intentionality and consciousness in characterizing and explaining humans and other things that have the ability to pass the Descartes/Turing test (whatever their chemical constituents). Do we need to postulate that mind is a nonphysical substance? – one that has, to return to the Cogito list of the beginning of this paper, autonomy, freedom, unity, recoverability, indivisibility, transparency, and immortality? Is it the case, so to speak, that a mind with all these characteristics need only *coincidentally* have language, or indeed need not have language at all? Or is it perhaps, at least in our case, that possession of language brings intentionality and consciousness and many of these other characteristics in its wake? (I take this latter alternative to subsume the view that possession of language is *equivalent* to possession of consciousness and intentionality and something of the other characteristics. And, as I suggested above, I assume that linguistic abilities are grounded in cognitive competencies that are concretely realized in particular neurological structures, so that we could have cases of damage to peripheral mechanisms in which an individual might temporarily be unable to hear or answer the Turing test, while still possessing the cognitive competencies, as we might directly establish by showing that the relevant neurological structures are undamaged. Similarly, neurological science might, at some future date, show us that bats had a relevantly-equivalent architecture, fully functional, but with no input/output processes (transducers) as in humans. I think we are close to a proof that the information storing capacity of the neurons in a Microchioptera bat cannot hold sufficient information to realize such an architecture.)

Turing speaks to the relation between language and consciousness when he speaks to justify the imitation game as a test for consciousness. His remarks are so vigorous and compelling that I will quote some of them. Turing suggests that the Descartes/Turing test, which he modestly calls "the imitation game," is our only real basis for believing that other human beings think and are conscious. One might even suspect, as I shall soon suggest, that it may be, for each putative thinker, the only secure test that he/she might adopt for their own case.

Tackling what he calls "the argument from consciousness," Turing begins by quoting a rendition from Professor Jefferson's Lister Oration (1949),

"Not until a machine can write a sonnet or compose a concerto because of thoughts and emotions felt, and not by the chance fall of symbols, could we agree that machine equals brain – that is, not only write it but know that it had written it. No mechanism could feel (and not merely artificially signal, an easy contrivance) pleasure at its successes, grief when its valves fuse, be warmed by flattery, be made miserable by its mistakes be charmed by sex, be angry or depressed when it cannot get what it wants."

This argument [Turing comments] appears to be a denial of the validity of our test. According to the most extreme form of this view the only way by which one could be sure that a machine thinks is to *be* the machine and to feel oneself thinking. One could then describe these feelings to the world, but of course no-one would be justified in taking any notice. Likewise according to this view the only way to know that a *man* thinks is to be that particular man. It is in fact the solipsist point of view. It may be the most logical view to hold but it makes communication of ideas difficult. A is liable to believe "A thinks but B does not" while B believes "B thinks but A does not." Instead of arguing continually over this point it is usual to have the polite convention that everyone thinks.

I am sure [Turing continues] that Professor Jefferson does not wish to adopt the extreme and solipsist point of view. Probably he would be quite willing to accept the imitation game as a test. The game is frequently used in practice under the name of *viva voce* to discover whether someone really understands something or has "learned it parrot fashion." Let us listen in to a part of such a *viva voce*:

INTERROGATOR: In the first line of your sonnet which reads "Shall I compare thee to a summer's day," would not "a spring day" do as well or better?
WITNESS: It wouldn't scan.
INTERROGATOR: How about "a winter's day"? That would scan all right.
WITNESS: Yes, but nobody wants to be compared to a winter's day.
INTERROGATOR: Would you say that Mr Pickwick reminded you of Christmas?
WITNESS: In a way.
INTERROGATOR: Yet Christmas is a winter's day, and I do not think Mr. Pickwick would mind the comparison.
WITNESS: I don't think you're serious. By a winter's day one means a typical winter's day, rather than a special one like Christmas.

And so on. What would Professor Jefferson say if the sonnet-writing machine was able to asnwer like this in the *viva voce*? I do not know whether he would regard the machine as "merely artificially signaling" these answers, but if the answers were as satisfactory and sustained as in the above passage I do not think he would describe it as "an easy contrivance." . . .

In short, then, [Turing concludes] I think that most of those who support the argument from consciousness could be persuaded to abandon it rather than be forced into the solipsist position. They will then probably be willing to accept our test.[54]

Turing may be a trifle optimistic about Professor Jefferson and his ilk. Dennett, indeed, not only insists that the test, "as he conceived it, is (as he thought) plenty strong enough as a test of thinking. I defy [Dennet confidently insists] anyone to improve on it."[55] But the mistaken reception of the test as somehow trivial, which Dennett deplores, and indeed the epoch of skeptical and introspective, and ultimately solipsistic philosophizing that Descartes unwitting initiated in his *Meditations*, suggest that some may well prefer solipsism. (Solipsism, as Turing seems to take it, is the view that I have no convincing reason for thinking that others think.)

What I, like Turing and presumably Dennett, simply find no way round is the point that if one denies that passing the Descartes/Turing test establishes that a computer, or some visiting extraterrestrial anthropologist, thinks, then you must deny that passing some variation of the test establishes that other human beings think. You must in short embrace solipsism, as indeed David Hume did, embracing the logic of the Cogito without accepting the Descartes/Turing test.

But, as you know, Hume's skepticism progressed further. He denied that he had knowledge of himself, of the "I" of the Cogito. He could not confidently assert that he, himself, as opposed to other possible minds, existed. While Descartes found it inescapable that the "I" accompanied all inner experience, Hume found this, though tempting through the associations (secondary impressions) of experience, nonetheless without rational basis (note the role of skepticism about other minds – had Hume accepted the Descartes/Turing test his dilemma would not have been present). What, Hume asked rhetorically, could possibly mark some experiences as distinctively his, as requiring the subject, the "I," as opposed to others? In this century, Bertrand Russell vacilated between holding Hume's position, which William James titled "neutral monism," and that of holding, like Descartes, that the "I" necessarily accompanied all conscious mental representations. How could such gifted and intelligent men hold such different views about something supposedly so basic and so open to inner inspection? Surely, this is *not* likely if the mind, the inner self, has always existed quite independently of what language, what style of self-narration, what pronomial system, it might contingently use as a mode of expression.

Indeed, if I deny the efficacy of the Descartes/Turing test for validating the consciousness of others, with what, recalling how perplexing Hume found this task, can I validate my own consciousness? How can I claim an identity, an ongoing self-awareness that clearly distinguishes what belongs to me from what belongs to others and the outside? Given that one skeptically eschews a bodily test of continuing identity, one may well consider John Locke's vague *psychological* criterion, namely, an inner sense of continuity, of an ongoing, more or less unified, collections of feelings, beliefs, memories, all of which can reliably be recalled and reworked, and so on. But what does this really amount to? Is it possible that the root idea is, in effect, the application of the Descartes/Turing test to oneself?

As I pointed out, when one has an internal dialogue about chess moves that one, or one's opponent, might make, one speaks in the same logical tone of voice, and when one, self-aggrieved, says, "Why did I make that silly mistake?," one will have much the same basis as one's opponent for coming up with an answer. Similarly, one might write, "How shall I compare thee to a summer's day" as the beginning of a love poem and then, wondering whether this line that popped into one's head was coherent and artful, one could launch into exactly the kind of dialogue that Turing sketches, merely by changing pronouns and making a few related adjustments. Of course, we certainly don't want to say that one has to be able to play chess or write poetry to be conscious, to be a thinker. But, surely, it is the capacity to learn how to conduct these, and countless other, internal (and external) dialogues that we do want to ascribe to thinkers. What about the more central, or essential, monologues and dialogues?

What may seem central is the ability to carry on a monologue or dialogue about oneself and others in the intentional idiom, to be able to give life narratives about oneself and others. To be able to distinguish, at least to some degree, how one feels from how one appears to feel, to be able to distinguish the content of one's inner experience from the environmental medley and unconscious processing that give rise to this experience: in brief, to be able to say what's on one's mind, what one wants, and what one believes, and how all these have a certain degree of unity, justification, and coherence. If language is the foundation for this ability, the medium in which self-construction can take place, rather than a mere signaling system which allows us to communicate an antecedent, fully-fledged self-conscious self, then much of what is puzzling about the Cogito, about Descartes's and Hume's conflicting intuitions about inner experience, and about much recent work on cognitive development, and the evolution of consciousness, falls neatly into place.

Whatever the fate of the particular details of accounts by Piaget and others of the child's development, it surely seems right to say that the child, learning its first language, is in entirely different circumstances from someone who, as Wittgenstein put it, has already learned a human language and is just trying to learn a new one, perhaps simply in order to translate it back into the one already known. Equally, much evidence seems to suggest that from conception, through birth to some early age or another, infants are unconscious and lack a sense of self and certainly a sense of identity through time that Locke wrote about. Descartes himself comments that if it were not for what infants become, he would not regard them as thinkers. (As what about Montaigne's Basques or Troglodytes, or the wild children – is it not our secure sense of what they might become, or might have become, something that we could converse with, that fires our sense that they are like us? Much supports the view, brilliantly championed in Gombrich's *Art and Illusion*, that our schooled grasp of our narrative subjectivity and subjective visual perspective is substantially advanced by Homer, and the Greek painters and sculptors who followed his project.[56] Nagel, Churchill, and Proust did not have greater souls than Homer's great-grandfather; rather, their construction of their subjectivity called into play a rich panorama of creations and successful experiments in the development of self-consciousness.)

Of course, our intentional idiom continually intimates to us the message of the Cogito, that consciousness is instantaneous, locationless, indivisible, and transparent, like an interior room whose light bulb is either brilliantly on or pitch black – certainly the particular version of the intentional idiom Descartes employs continually beguiles us so in the *Meditations*, whose self-narrative is one of the most powerful, compelling, and convincing ever written. But, *as the lengthy dialogic character of the "one, sure" Descartes/ Turing test immediately shows us, a single flash, a single interior or exterior mouthing of words, shows us nothing*. Descartes says that it would be easy enough to make a simple automaton that responded with "I am in pain" whenever we touched it, and that, so Descartes asserted, does not show us in the least that the mechanism thinks or is conscious. But, if that's true, why should it make any difference if the automaton says (loudly or *sotto voce*) *"Cogito ergo sum"*? What makes the sentence significant is that the creature mouthing or minding it has the secure ability to go on, responding appropriately to questions we or the creature might ask itself ("secure ability" is a blank check for the cognitive competencies realized in concrete mechanisms that make the ability secure as opposed to miraculous or coincidental).

Someone may say, "Either the interior light is on, or it isn't – that's all there really is to it – and we can never know, respecting another, whether it is or isn't!" But this is hopelessly blatant and empty homunculizing. It says nothing and tells us nothing of the thing within who looks about the cozy, well-lit room – and why should not the thing within be a good navigator in the dark or blind, even an heroic Helen Keller of the inner room, managing to will and think in echoless darkness? *What makes the Cogito mean something is that Descartes has already embedded, and can go on to further embed, this sentence within a self-questioning dialogue and self-narrative that makes it powerfully clear that Descartes passes his own test.*

Is it possible that the issue between Descartes and Hume (or the one that Russell found himself bouncing from side to side on) is stylistic, a matter of what mode of self-narrative seems the most compelling and convincing?

I can only be sketchy and suggestive here, but there were changes in narrative mode taking place in French and English from the seventeenth through the eighteenth century, changes that lead into the perfection, first fully and substantially realized in English and Jane Austen's work toward the end of Hume's century, of the modern grammatically third person narrative in which unitary point-of-view allows the full simulation of the inner life of characters (not, I hasten to add, by writing anything like "She thought . . ."; rather, by describing the world through which the character flows like a TV camera always looking over his shoulder, so that his ego is a ghostly reflection – without an inescapable grammatical "I" – implied by the narrative). Familiarly, the first novels, or novel-like narratives, of Descartes's time were grammatically first person narratives, often put forward as the supposed autobiographical accounts of shipwrecked sailors or retired criminals (Defoe's *Robinson Crusoe* and *Moll Flanders*); similarly, in both English and French, we find supposed diaries or series of letters. What developed through Hume's century is a grammatically third person narrative that sketches the inner life and focus of an individual by limning the world as that individual receives it. Is it possible that Hume's "realization" that nothing in his experiences marks them as distinctively his, as constitutive of his I, is a realization that his self-narrative could be given in unitary point-of-view, grammatically third person narrative? (Certainly, if we had two different "eighth generation" computers, who had both gone much the distance with the Descartes/Turing test, but then one computer began to engage in Humean self-doubts while the other remained confidently first person, I doubt we would on this count decide that the one was a tinkling gong, while the other was a conscious thinker.)

Like Descartes and Hume, while we are engaged in familiar narrative modes, we are liable to forget the role of pronouns and narrative style: we are just, as it were, thinking, and these matters of pronouns and style are irrelevant surface niceties. But we may be caught up short, as I certainly was, when we venture more far afield. A few years ago I wrote a novel, *Beyond Rejection*, whose background was the familiar functionalist distinction between mind, as the abstract, software, characterization of the functioning realized in the hardware brain.[57] Dramatizing the distinction in a most blatant way, I imagined that it might, long in the future, be possible to offload a mind and implant it in another brain, as I may transfer the contents of the RAM from one computer to another. Not unnaturally, I upped the ante by having my protagonist wake, after the implant operation, as a female body that remembers having a male one. At that point in my narrative I found it necessary to switch from the third person narrative in which I described the operation to first person. The reason I had to shift, of course, is that had I remained in third person I would have had to sex the pronouns with which I described my protagonist – but that, of course, would have wrecked the story because an essential element in the story is the ambiguity my protagonist feels, and must resolve, about sexual identity. I was startled to discover, sometime later, that *Beyond Rejection* could not be translated well into Berber, along with some other North African languages. For in Berber it is obligatory to sex the first person pronoun, as well as second and third person. Of course, doubtless some sort of approximation of my narrative might appear in Berber (though a translator might be tempted to introduce a new word in Berber), but it is hard not to believe that the story would be very different. Similarly, in Old Japanese, there is only a distinction between "hereabouts or with us" and "somewhere/someone else." It would be hard to imagine the Cogito of *Meditations* seeming so compelling in such a language. (To say that these matters arise from contingent variations in natural languages is simply to say that, e.g., a Berber or Japanese infant would learn English as easily as my child, or the reverse.)

Now someone might object to this, perhaps accusing me of reviving a discredited Whorfianism. Surely, this someone might say, one's sense of the structure of one's consciousness, or, as you put it, self-narration, is quite independent of the particular linguistic resources of one's particular language, just as, so Eleanor Rosch showed against Whorf, people whose language afforded them but a contrast between light and dark nonetheless split up color chips into the same bunches as those who speak English. But the cases differ crucially, for I am maintaining that the only place in which identity and a sense of self can find a realization is in the possession of a language, while it is perfectly possible to be able to make systematic color discriminations without a language, as indeed some non-human animals clearly do.

The Cogito is, in general, the intentional theory of self that every human language underwrites, but some aspects of the Cogito are, more narrowly, a product of the kind of self-narrative Descartes found most familiar. This, I suppose, is what we would expect if it is language, in the context of the Descartes/Turing test, that underwrites consciousness and our sense of what it is like to be ourselves, rather than unitary, indivisible consciousnesses coincidentally happening to employ language as a mere signaling system with which to convey their antecedently complete thoughts. This conjecture is strengthened by the realization that the unitary characterization of consciousness that our intentional idiom so insists on is one that is enormously helpful to the whole business of maintaining a community, assigning responsibility and rights, assorting praise and blame, forging a common and individuated understanding of each other.

Someone may object that I have skirted a central feature of the Cartesian view of humans, namely, the autonomy and freedom of mind. This is the feature that the Cartesian tradition emphasized in speaking of the "lack of stimulus control" as typical and discriminative of human linguistic action and also in speaking of the originality and creativity that our linguistic faculty underwrites. My reply is that to say that the intentional idiom is forced upon us in our attempts to comprehend the actions of ourselves and other humans is to say that we have to take humans as "free of stiumulus control," as having an autonomous and free authorial consciousness. What the Descartes/Turing test tests, above all, is the command of the intentional idiom, in characterizing the test-taker and other agents. Something like this line of argument has been basic to the revival of Cartesian linguistics, which insists that a human language, with an infinite number of linguistic structures fully-describable by the universal and parametrical restrictions on transformational movement rules, is clearly unlearnable on any strict version of behaviorist theory, and that, hence, we tacitly understand, and as linguists must explicitly describe, linguistic competence, while a full causal theory of performance will be long in coming and may well be forever beyond our grasp.

IV

Please allow me to close with some brief remarks about the ape language experiments and about how we treat non-human animals and other things.

These remarks will be of a more personal character.

I was present in the Oxford University Science Museum in 1971 when Beatrice Gardner first presented, in England, films of the chimpanzee Washoe expressively making some hand gestures that approximated a number of individual signs in American Sign Language.[58] Invoking an American war-in-Vietnam metaphor, in her informal remarks she spoke passionately and contemptuously of someone she called, "the linguist." As soon, as she put it, as there seemed to be "light at the end of the tunnel," the linguist "will up the ante." In her rendition, they had shown that Washoe could do one thing and another that the linguist had held to be the essence of language, only to find as soon as the demonstration was complete, that the linguist had added some new requirement, which met, another would be added. The latest, according to her, was the requirement of the production of sentences with syntactic structure.

But, one would have thought, that was always the minimal requirement. Indeed, as the previous discussion may suggest, the requirement of sentence production would only be acceptable if such productions occur in the context of ongoing conversations in which it would be more or less clear that sentences were genuinely understood, used appropriately and not merely mouthed. Of course, one would be willing to accept all sorts of rough approximations. One was hardly looking for something like Turing's *viva voce* of "How shall I compare . . ." Rather, simply, some kind of rough but real conversational interchange.

Subsequently, I have spent some time with chimpanzees, both in the United States and in Japan; on one occasion, several hours daily for two weeks in intimate contact with an individual from whom the resident graduate students kept a fearful distance. While I felt love, awe, affection, and cheer, I cannot say that I was much impressed by the signing abilities of chimpanzees. The remark I most remember, in all of this, was a most confidential one from a brilliant and somewhat sorrowful primatologist who had spent several years as a graduate student in chimpanzee signing projects. That individual said, simply, "I know now that I am never going to have a conversation with a chimpanzee."

And that individual, and we, have a right to be sad, surely. Perhaps it was an improbable hope but the prospect of learning what a chimpanzee thought of jungle, or human trailer life, of learning *exactly* how scrambled eggs tasted to my hairy congener, of learning first sign, so to speak, what it was like to be a chimpanzee, held overwhelming excitement. But did this mean that the disappointed primatologist took to eating chimpanzee steaks for breakfast or to nailing chimpanzee limbs foursquare so that a gleeful eviceration might efficiently proceed? Not in the least. Nor did the primatologist give up the study of apes or cease to be fascinated and affectionate toward them, any more than an astronomer should lose interest in the sun because he ceases to see it as the face of God.

For something like a year of my life, I had daily physical interaction, instruction and play, with a large member of the cat family, *Felis concolor*, both inside and outside of her cage, which I, along with others, regularly mopped and scoured (more regularly, I might add, than any primate installation I have visited in the US and Japan). Though I did not believe she was conscious, I believe it would be fair to say that she was more important to my life at that time than any other thing, human, animal, or mineral. If you take it that that was true, I don't mind if you think I was then odd, but I deny and resent the claim that I was inconsistent, a hypocrite, a patronizing sentimentalist, or a selfish exploiter of a free spirit (an Auschwitz guard who enjoys playing with an inmate child).

In the introduction to his *Animal Liberation*, Peter Singer enjoys contempt for two middle-aged ladies who, having been told of his concern for animals, ask what animals he lives with. He sternly replies that, of course, he has no pets; his concern is with the rights of animals as free, independent beings, whom we have no right whatsoever to interfere with or to exploit for experiment or food.

The problem is that we live in a small and precious world, and, as Singer is forced to admit at every turn of his book, we humans are, at least for the present, the only ones who can reason together about how to make it better, happier, more beautiful and so on. Inevitably, non-human animals will live with us if they live at all. We have to decide for them, even as indeed we have to decide for our own bodies; neither they, nor our bodies, can reason. It is not, I insist, that humans (*qua* free, thinking, conscious beings) have a near infinite value *on the same scale* on which animals show up as pittances, plants as less, and "stones, machines, and plastic dolls," as off scale or pittances of pittances. Rather, it is simply the case that free, thinking, conscious beings are the only entities that can *reason* about what is best for all concerned and *choose* effectively among the available options. If, as is undoubtably too often the case, we often reason and choose in narrow, chaivinist, unimaginative, and philistine ways, that calls for better, fuller, and more careful discussion, not for Montaignean fabulations. If one is willing, as I would wish to think I am, to lay down one's life for the moon or for the last mating pair of cheetahs, one should do it for what these things are and not because one fabulates a man's face for the first or two silent singers of savanna epics for the second.

This is *not* to say that only humans, or only thinkers, have value. The reason I stressed Midgley's flip way with stones, machines, and plastic dolls is that she is apparently committed to the view that only animals, in their supposed capacity for inner experience, have "intrinsic value." Everything else is merely a means to animal ends. Literally, this would seem to require that if the preservation of a humble mouse necessitated the annihilation of the moon, or an animal-evacuated Grand Canyon, this must be done. To the contrary, I incline to the view that anything may have value and to the view that not only may the mouse be less valuable than the moon or Grand Canyon, so may a human being be, too. There is, surely, a kind of philistinism in the view that only living animals have "intrinsic value" (and only living animals insofar as they have subjective experience).

In the manner of G. E. Moore's *Principia Ethica*, my critic may reply that, of course, the moon has value, but it is only the "instrumental value" of affording humans pleasant vistas and dogs, a pretext for appreciative vocalizations. More tersely, things are just means for the use of sentients; even the bodies of animals, *as* chemical collections, *as* matter, are only the means for subjective experience, which is the only source of real value whatsoever.

There are two equally decisive objections to this Moorean line of thought.

One is that meanings aren't (just) in the head, wholly stipulated, and all value comprised within the circle of our inner psychological experience. As so many have argued so persuasively recently, our vocabulary, particularly the words in which we realize our intentional states, is endlessly and inevitably hooked into the actual vagaries of the physical and external social world, as opposed to the often mistaken and invariably sketchy specifications achieved within our "purely experiential" existence. To adapt Putnam's familiar example, Thales believed H_2O to be the basic stuff of the universe, though the term and modern chemical theory were not familiar to him. But much the same follows in the evaluative sphere. I love Barbara's *face* rather than the psychological state that it occasions, and if that face is also "Ruby's", I love Ruby's face, though I may not recognize the nickname. It is the Grand Canyon that is awesomely beautiful, not my reaction to it (and if a "subjectively-identical" reaction is produced in me while I stare at the wall under the influence of the powerful drug you slipped in my coffee, I have not again experienced the awesome beauty of the Grand Canyon).

Two, if it really were the case that only purely "inner experiences of sentients" have "intrinsic value," one could argue – for example, on utilitarian grounds – that we ought, for the maximization of happiness, to invent drugs and fantasy-and-life-support "cocoons" that will ensconce us all in endlessly-varied, vividly-happy "experienced inner worlds," while robots, whose only happiness is in the maintenance and expansion of this beatific system, carry on objectively (since I imagine that these cocoons will consume comparatively little energy and create little waste, I imagine the robots could stack the earth with them, eagerly test-tubing up more and more humans for cocooning, thus achieving both qualitive and quantitative maximization of "subjectively-experienced intrinsic value").

This dystopian nightmare is not intended as a reductio of utilitarianism, for one could argue for it as well on Kantian grounds. If nothing has intrinsic value but a good will, and such a will can be characterized and comprised in a purely psychological and subjective way, we can as well program our cocoons for subjectively-experienced saintliness as for endless pleasure. The point of my argument is to cast doubt on the view that only subjective experience can be genuinely good or intrinsically valuable, all else being but mere ends to conjure up such experience. Once we accept this, we can confidently believe that an animal is a beautiful, valuable, and dazzlingly ingenious masterwork of nature without feeling that we also have to believe that it is conscious.

NOTES

I presented a similar, earlier version of this paper at the international workshop on *The Chomskyan Turn: Generative Linguistics, Philosophy, Mathematics and Psychology* (April 11–14, 1988) at the University of Tel Aviv and the Van Leer Jerusalem Institute. My thanks for the generous support of the Institute, and the comradery, intelligence, and gracious humanity of Tanya Reinhart, Jonathan Berg, Bob Matthews, Morris Halle, Asa Kasher (the host) and other conferees (W. H. Auden's line, "ironic points of light flash out where the just exchange their messages," tempts one, if only because the line, "as the last hopes expire of a low, dishonest decade," consorts with it in his poem, "September 1st, 1939"). With a few regretted misprints this paper appeared in *Philosophia* 18 (1988). Noam Chomsky made extensive and helpful comments on an earlier draft of this paper; from my own Department, Bredo Johnsen made several useful editorial corrections and Greg Brown made an essential scholarly suggestion; Dora Pozzi (Classics, University of Houston) did the real work of the translation of footnote 51; my student, Valerie Walker, made several careful critical comments. Rom Harré and Roy Bhaskar had useful things to say about an unpublished paper titled "Consciousness and Narration," which included much of section II, along with other material on narrative, that I delivered to the Conference on Narratology (November, 1986) held at Linacre College, Oxford.

1   Patricia Churchland, *Pacific Philosophical Quarterly*, 64 (1983), pp. 86–7, 92.
2   Noam Chomsky, *Cartesian Linguistics* (New York: Harper & Row, 1966).
3   Mary Midgley, *Animals and Why They Matter* (London: Chapman & Hall, 1980), pp. 10–11.
4   Ibid., p. 45.
5   Peter Singer, *Animal Liberation* (London: Jonathan Cape, 1976), pp. 217–20.
6   L. C. Rosenfield, *From Beast-Machine to Man-Machine* (Oxford University Press, 1940), p. 54.
7   Stephen Clarke, *The Moral Status of Animals* (Oxford University Press, 1977), p. 197.
8   Ibid., p. 197.
9   Rosenfield, *From Beast-Machine to Man-Machine*, pp. 180–90.
10 Nicholas Fontaine, *Memoires Pour Servir A L'Histoire de Port-Royal* (Autrecht, 1736), vol. II, p. 54.
11 Fontaine, *Mémoires*, vol. I, p. V. "Comme ces Memoires n'ont ete ecrits ques long-tems apres la plupart des evenemens qui y font rapportes, & que M. Fontaine ne cherchoit qu'a fe rappeller sous les yeux de Dieu les merveilles que sa grace avoit operees, sans s'embarrasser de la suite des faites, il n'a pas toujours garde l'ordre des tems."
12 The Port-Royal in which Arnaud and other Cartesians studied grammar, physiology, and other scientific subjects was also the Port-Royal of Saci and Fontaine, who not only viewed the growth of modern science with amused disdain and dismay, but were much more deeply caught up in a world of miracles and faith, and of conflict between the call of God and the dictates of the French king. Indeed, the monarchy imprisoned Fontaine and others of Port-Royal for views that seemed to subvert the authority of the crown. Arnaud's daughter came to be claimed as the Saint of Port-Royal, a controversial, mystical, and cult-breeding saint.

13 Rosenfield, *From Beast-Machine to Man-Machine*, p. 70.
14 A. Lindeboom, *Descartes and Medicine* (Amsterdam: Rodopi, 1979), p. 41. The letter to Plemp appears in Appendix II, pp. 111–17. Lindeboom documents Descartes's lifelong concern with medicine. Respecting a professional concern of his ancestors Descartes often stated that the overriding aim of the bulk of his work was ultimately medical. In correspondence, he often discusses, and makes experimental proposals and claims about practical cures. He was not an idle experimenter.
15 *Essays of Montaigne, vol. II*, trans. George B. Ives (Harvard University Press, 1925).
16 Ibid., p. 174. A more recent translator into English prudently eliminates ninety percent of this part of the essay. M. Montaigne, *In Defense of Raymond Sebond*, trans. Arthur H. Beattie, New York: Frederick Ungar, 1959, viii–ix.
17 M. Montaigne, trans. George B. Ives, *Essays*, p. 201.
18 Ibid., p. 205.
19 Ibid., p. 211.
20 Ibid., p. 217.
21 Ibid., p. 223.
22 Ibid., p. 205.
23 Ibid., p. 202.
24 Ibid., p. 203.
25 René Descartes, *Philosophical Letters*, trans. Anthony Kenny, (Oxford University Press, 1970), p. 206.
26 *Conditioned Reflexes* (New York: Dover, 1960), p. 4.
27 Until recently, it was (at least barely) respectable to claim, along with Montaigne, that human sign language, as opposed to spoken language, is transparently iconic, finite and nonrecursive, and more or less natural (or naturally accessible) to some animals as well as to humans. See U. Bellugi and E. Klima, *The Signs of Language* (Harvard University Press, 1980) and Poizner, Bellugi, Klima et al., *What the Hands Reveal about the Brain* (Cambridge, Mass.: MIT Press, 1987) for a decisive refutation of such views. American Sign Language, for example, is highly inflected, processed through formal rather than semantic means, subject to the same underlying constraints as spoken languages, and is quite opaque to the previously unexposed interpreter. Human sign language is fully comparable to spoken natural language, and it is not at all like animal communication or the highly limited version of signing that has been taught to some apes. See also my "The Vindication of the Language Organ," *New Ideas in Psychology*, 1983, pp. 157–68, of which a slightly longer version may be found as "The Strange Creature," in *The Meaning of Primate Signals*, eds. Rom Harre and Vernon Reynolds, (Cambridge University Press, 1984), pp. 77–89.
28 "Discourse on Method," *The Philosophical Works of Descartes*, trans. E. S. Haldane and G. R. T. Ross (Cambridge University Press, 1979), p. 116.
29 Descartes, trans. Kenny, *Philosophical Letters*, p. 206.
30 Churchland, in *Pacific Philosophical Quarterly*, p. 92.
31 Descartes, trans. Kenny, *Philosophical Letters*, p. 208.
32 Montaigne, trans. Ives, *Essays*, p. 169.
33 Singer, *Animal Liberation*, p. 188.
34 Singer, *Animal Liberation*, p. 188.
35 Midgley, *Animals and Why They Matter*, p. 100.
36 Thomas Nagel, *The View From Nowhere* (Oxford University Press, 1986), p.

25. "We will not know exactly how scrambled eggs taste to a cockroach even if we develop a detailed objective phenomenology of the cockroach sense of taste."

37   *Philosophical Review* 83 (1974), pp. 435–50. I will quote from the more widely available reprint of the paper in *The Mind's I*, ed. Douglas R. Hofstadter and Daniel C. Dennett (New York: Basic Books, 1981), pp. 391–402.

38   Ibid., p. 396.

39   I owe much of this passage to comments of Professor Chomsky, both in personal communication and in the two papers, as he then delivered them, at *The Chomskyan Turn* workshop (April 11–14, 1988): "Linguistics and Adjacent Fields" and "Linguistics and Cognitive Science: Problems and Mysteries." In both papers Chomsky refers to "Descartes's problem," as the question of how knowledge of language is put to use or, more specifically, the problem of speech perception and the problem of speech production. Respecting the first aspect of Descartes's problem, and following Descartes's representational and realist theory of perception, we have made, Chomsky argues, some progress. Respecting the latter, we may, as realists, suspect we may never be to achieve a real understanding – along with, even more clearly, many other real features of the universe – though, again as scientific realists, we must deny any a priori "methodological dualist" argument that such knowledge is in principle impossible or "indeterminate"; speech production mostly clearly exemplifies the creative aspect of linguistic activity and the freedom from stimulus response, as Descartes makes clear in his version of the "Descartes/ Turing test" (see section III of this paper.)

40   Nagel in *The Mind's I*, p. 393.

41   Ibid., pp. 393–4.

42   Ibid., p. 394.

43   M. Brock Fenton, *Just Bats* (Toronto: University of Toronto Press, 1983).

44   Ibid., p. 397.

45   Donald Griffin, *Listening in the Dark*, 2nd edn (Dover: New York, 1974). Also J. J. Gibson, *The Senses Considered as Perceptual Systems* (Westport, Ct.: Greenwood Press, 1983).

46   *The Philosophical Writings of Descartes*, ed. John Cottingham et al. (Cambridge University Press, 1983), p. 153.

47   *Brainstorms* (Montgomery, Vt.: Bradford Books, 1978), pp. 4–9. See also Norton Nelkin, "What is it like to be a person," *Mind and Language*, 2 (1987), pp. 221–41.

48   Cf. Dennis H. Holding, *The Psychology of Chess Skill* (Hillsdale, New Jersey: Lawrence Erlbaum, 1985).

49   L. Weiskrantz, E. K. Warrington, and M. D. Saunders, "Visual capacity in the hemianopic field following a restricted occipital ablation," *Brain*, 97 (1974), pp. 709–28.

50   *Mind* LIX, no. 236 (1950). Again, I will quote from the more commonly available reprinting in Hofstadter and Dennett, eds, *The Mind's I* (New York: Basic Books, 1981).

51   "Can Machines Think?," in *How We Know*, Nobel Conference XX, ed. Michael Shafto (San Francisco, Cal.: Harper Row, 1985).

52   See also Asa Kasher, "Pragmatics and Chomsky's Research Program," this volume.

53   *Ponatur statua, aliquid ferri habens in capite & pedibus; ponatur super funem vel virgam ferream exiguam, sed vi magnetica tinctam; item supra caput ejus alia sit, vi etiam magnetica tincta, quae altior sit & quibsudam in locis majori vi*

distincta. Statua autem habeat in manibus baculum oblongum ad modum funambuli, qui sit excavatus & in eo nervo contentus, cui interea principium motus automati intus includsi: quo levissime tacto, statua omnis pedem promoveat, quoties tangitur & in locis majore vi magnetis in summo tactis, sponte, scilicet cum pulsabuntur instrumenta. "Let us place a statue that has some iron parts in its head and feet upon an iron rod which is short but magnetized; and let us put on the head of the statue another rod, equally magnetized, but longer and having in some areas greater magnetic power. Let the statue hold in its hands (just as a puppet would) a rather long stick, and let this stick be hollowed out and locked onto that part inside which is located the beginning of the automatic motion: when this [rod] is touched very lightly, the whole statue will advance its foot. It will do this as often as it is touched; and if the places with greater magnetic power are touched, it will move spontaneously, that is to say, the statue will move as the instruments are moved." *Oeuvres de Descartes*, ed. Charles Adam and Paul Tannery (Paris: Leopold Cerf, 1908), vol. X, p. 231. There is a shorter account in French on p. 232.

54 Hofstadter and Dennett, *The Mind's I*, pp. 60–1.
55 Dennett, "Can Machines Think?," in *How We Know*, p. 123.
56 E. H. Gombrich, *Art and Illusion* (Princeton University Press, 1984).
57 Justin Leiber, *Beyond Rejection* (New York: Ballantine Books, 1980).
58 Beatrice Gardner, University Museum, Oxford, Hilary Term, 1971. In introducing Professor Gardner, Rom Harré pointed out that we were in not only the building which held Huxley/Wilberforce debate on evolution but also, if one put a charitable interpretation on heir-lines under interior reconstruction, the very room.

8
Psychological Reality of Grammars

Robert J. Matthews

1   INTRODUCTION

It is a measure of the depth of the conceptual revolution wrought by Noam Chomsky in linguistics that few linguists would quarrel with his notion that theoretical linguistics is a subfield of psychology.[1] Specifically, theoretical linguistics is taken to be that part of psychology concerned with human linguistic competence, viz., "the system of rules and principles that we assume have, in some manner, been internally represented by the person who knows a language and that enable the speaker, in principle, to understand an arbitrary sentence and to produce a sentence expressing his thought" (1980: 201). So construed, linguistics is not directly concerned with linguistic performance; however, it is assumed that models of language use will incorporate these knowledge representations:

> A generative grammar is not a model for a speaker or a hearer. It attempts to characterize in the most neutral possible terms the knowledge of the language that provides the basis for actual use of language by a speaker-hearer. . . . No doubt, a reasonable model of language use will incorporate, as a basic component, the generative grammar that expresses the speaker-hearer's knowledge of the language; but this generative grammar does not, in itself, prescribe the character or functioning of a perceptual model or a model of speech production. (1965: 9)

Many philosophers, psychologists, and AI-researchers, and indeed more than a few linguists, remain deeply skeptical of Chomsky's linguistics-as-psychology program. These critics find his claim for the "psychological reality" of the grammars made available by linguistic theory empirically unsupported, if not simply unfounded, especially when one considers the empirical evidence upon which linguistic theory is apparently based.

In this paper I wish to defend Chomsky's claim. The argument that I sketch rests on considerations regarding the sort of relation of grammars to performance models that would justify the claim that grammars are psychologically real. Grammars true of a speaker/hearer, I argue, bear such a relation to performance models. I begin by considering Chomsky's own defense of his claim. I then turn to Bresnan and Kaplan's (1982) argument against the psychological reality of transformational grammars. My criticism of their notion of psychological reality provides a context in which I can sketch my own argument. I conclude with reasons for thinking this argument is *largely* consistent with Chomsky's. What differences there may be between our respective arguments focus on the psychological reality not of the grammars but of the constructs that figure in those grammars.

2   CHOMSKY'S ARGUMENT FOR THE PSYCHOLOGICAL REALITY OF GRAMMARS

Chomsky's response to his critics (1980: 106ff) has been to deny what seems to be presumed by their arguments, namely, that there is a principled epistemological distinction between evidence that counts towards the psychological reality of the constructs of linguistic theory and evidence that counts "merely" towards the truth of that theory. Chomsky argues that there cannot be any such epistemological distinction, since the existence of that distinction would entail that there is a principled distinction between a linguistic theory's constructs being psychologically real and the theory's being true, and this second distinction he also denies (1980: 107).

Chomsky (1980: 189ff) contends that it makes no more sense to question the psychological reality of the theoretical constructs of linguistic theories that we accept as true than it does to question the physical reality of the theoretical constructs of physical theories that we accept as true. But is this true? Questions of the latter sort would presumably arise only in the context of a metaphysical discussion of the existential commitments of a physical theory that we accept as true, since in all other contexts, *physical* reality is what true *physical* theories are taken to describe. Questions of the former sort, however, could very well arise in non-philosophical contexts in which we are concerned *not* with the question of whether we should accept the existential commitments of our best linguistic theories (clearly we should, but see pp. 26ff), but with the *psychological import*, if any, of those commitments.

This, I take it, is the point of questioning the psychological reality of grammars, rules, representations, etc.: it does not follow from the fact that our best linguistic theory commits us to the existence of such *linguistic* entities that they have any *psychological* import, i.e. have any significance for the explanatory concerns that define psychology. Claims for the psychological reality of linguistic constructs will therefore be justified only insofar as we are able to establish their psychological import.

3   BRESNAN AND KAPLAN ON THE PSYCHOLOGICAL REALITY
OF GRAMMARS

Bresnan and Kaplan's (1982) criticism of Chomsky's argument for the psychological reality of grammars rests on their assumption that generative-transformational grammars have not been successfully incorporated in "psychologically realistic" models of language use (1982: xvii). Bresnan and Kaplan, hereafter B&K, see Chomsky's argument as an attempt to preserve the claim that generative-transformational grammars represent a *psychological* hypothesis despite these grammars' failure to be incorporated in any realistic models of language use. Against Chomsky's claims for the psychological reality of transformational grammars, B&K's basic contention is this:

> Linguistically motivated descriptions of a language need not bear any resemblance to the speaker's internal description of the language. Therefore, one cannot justifiably claim "psychological reality" for a grammar (in any interesting sense) merely because the grammar has some linguistic motivation. (1982: xxi–xxii)

According to B&K, justifiable claims for the psychological reality of a grammar require more than evidence that the grammar provides us with a description of the linguistic knowledge domain; they require evidence that "the grammar corresponds to the speaker's *internal* description of that domain" (1982: xxiii). More precisely, B&K require that psychologically real grammars be able to play the appropriate role in models of language use that satisfy what they call the "strong competence hypothesis," which they define as follows:

> Suppose that we are given an information-processing model of language use that includes a processor and a component of stored linguistic knowledge K, [where] as a minimum . . . K prescribes certain operations that the processor is to perform on linguistic representations, such as manipulating phrases or assigning grammatical functions. . . . We call the subpart of K that prescribes representational operations the *representational basis* of the processing model. (The representational basis is the "internal grammar" of the model.) . . . A model satisfies the *strong competence hypothesis* if and only if its representational basis is isomorphic to the competence grammar. (1982: xxxi)

This construal of the notion of "psychological reality" provides the basis of B&K's argument against generative transformational theory. Schematically, their argument runs as follows:

1   it is an adequacy condition on linguistic theory that the grammars made available by a theory be psychologically real;
2   such grammars can be psychologically real only if they can satisfy the (strong) competence hypothesis; hence,

3 the grammars made available by an adequate linguistic theory must satisfy the competence hypothesis;
4 transformational grammars have not, and indeed cannot, satisfy the competence hypothesis (as is evidenced by the failure of the so-called Derivational Theory of Complexity); hence,
5 the grammars made available by transformational theories are not psychologically real, and those theories themselves fail a basic adequacy condition.

The crux of B&K's argument has to do with their claim that a grammar can be psychologically real only if it can satisfy their strong competence hypothesis. This is a strong claim indeed, for unlike Chomsky's notion of psychological reality which levies no specific performance-related requirements on psychologically real grammars, B&K's claim levies a very specific and hence restrictive requirement on the role that a psychologically real grammar must be able to play in a model of language use. In particular, to be psychologically real, a linguist's grammar must be isomorphic to the representational basis – the "internal grammar" – of a processing model of language use for that language.

B&K offer little by way of a justification of their strong competence hypothesis. They suggest (1982: xix) that to reject the hypothesis is "to adopt the theoretical alternative that a different body of knowledge of one's language is required for every type of verbal behavior," but why should this be so? Why couldn't there be a single body of linguistic knowledge that is recruited in the production of every type of verbal behavior, but that is not isomorphic to the grammar made available by the best linguistic theory? There would seem to be no reason whatever, unless B&K assume that an isomorph of this grammar will for other reasons have to be internally represented anyway, so that the issue here is simply one of parsimony of knowledge structures. This does indeed seem to be their assumption. They assume without argument that what is acquired in acquiring a language is an isomorph of the linguist's grammar. Given this assumption, it is not surprising that B&K would embrace their competence hypothesis, for they would certainly not wish to be driven to the view of Fodor, Bever, and Garrett (1974: 370ff) according to which language acquisition involves the internalization of a grammar of the sort made available by linguistic theory, yet that internalized grammar is never used in language processing. It would certainly be preferable to assume in the absence of contrary evidence that the same knowledge structure that is acquired in the course of learning a language is used in language processing.

4 MUST THE GRAMMARS OF LINGUISTICS BE INTERNALLY REPRESENTED?

B&K take it to be uncontroversial that "stored knowledge structures underlie all forms of verbal behavior" (1982: xix). Their assumption is *not* uncontroversial;[2] but even if it were, it would not suffice to establish the premise that their argument for the competence hypothesis apparently needs, namely, that isomorphs of the grammars of linguistic theory must be internally represented. In the absence of an argument for this premise, B&K effectively lack any argument for taking the grammars of linguistic theory to be isomorphic representations of the knowledge structures – the internal grammars – that are said to figure in these processes.

Others have attempted to establish the needed premise. Fodor, Bever, and Garrett (1974), for example, argue that the existence of linguistic universals requires that an explicit representation of the grammar made available to linguistic theory be part of the language processor:

> There are linguistic universals which serve precisely to constrain the form in which information is represented in grammars (i.e., the form of grammatical rules). The question is: If the universals do not also constrain the form in which linguistic information is represented in a sentence-processing system, how is their exercise to be explained? Surely, if universals are true of anything, it must be of some psychologically real representation of that language. But what could such a representation be if it is not part of a sentence encoding-decoding system? (1974: 369–70)

This line of argument suffers from an obvious defect: the conclusion depends on an equivocation between grammars as representations of linguistic knowledge (what the linguist constructs) and grammars as that knowledge itself (what's in the head). The argument fails to establish what is at issue, namely, that the speaker/hearer uses an explicit representation of his knowledge of language that is isomorphic to the linguist's grammar. In fact, the argument fails to establish that the speaker/hearer has as a component of his language processing mechanism *any* explicit representation of his grammatical knowledge. Consider a class of automata, each of which has been hardwired to recognize a particular member of a class of formal languages. A formal characterization of this class would mention certain linguistic universals true of each of the automata; yet none need contain an explicit representation of these universals or of the language they recognize, any more than a hand calculator must contain an explicit representation of the axioms of arithmetic.

A more subtle argument for the assumption that B&K need rests on a defense of what Jerry Fodor with characteristic impartiality calls the "Right View," which holds the following:

> (a) Linguistic theories are descriptions of grammars. (b) . . . learning one's native language involves learning its grammar, so a theory of how grammars are learned is *de facto* a (partial) theory of how languages are learned. (c) . . . the grammar of a language is internally represented by speaker/hearers of that language; up to dialectical variants, the grammar of a language is what its speakers have in common by virtue of which they are speaker/hearers of the *same* language. (d) . . . the intentional representation of the grammar (or, equivalently for these purposes, the internally represented grammar) is

causally implemented in communication exchanges between speakers and hearers insofar as these exchanges are mediated by their use of the language that they share; talking and understanding the language normally involve exploiting the internally represented grammar. (1981a: 199)

The Right View clearly entails B&K's assumption and indeed their competence hypothesis itself, for as Fodor points out, the view "construes learning a language as a process that eventuates in the internal representation of a grammar, and it construes the production/perception of speech as causally mediated by the grammar that the speaker/hearer learns" (1981: 201).

But appellation not withstanding, why should we believe the Right View to be the right view? In particular, why should one endorse the notion that the speaker/hearer's knowledge of language takes the form of an internally represented grammar of the sort made available by linguistic theory? Fodor's reply, if I understand him correctly, is that the assumption that grammars are internally represented is warranted by a Realist principle to the effect that one should accept the ontology that the best explanation presupposes. Specifically, the appropriate form of argument for the assumption that grammars are internally represented is to show that this assumption, when taken together with independently motivated theories of the character of other interacting variables (such as memory limitations and the like), yields the best explanation of the data about the organism's mental states and processes and/or the behaviors in which such processes eventuate.[3]

While I am inclined to endorse a Realist principle of the sort that Fodor invokes in defense of the Right View, I do not think that it can be used to support the claim that the language processor incorporates an internal representation of the grammar postulated by linguistic theory. We do, of course, have linguistic theories that correctly predict many of the linguistic intuitions of speaker/hearers. And certainly the best explanation of their predictive success is that these speaker/hearers have the linguistic *knowledge* that is represented by the grammars attributed to them. But nothing, so far as I can see, suggests that these grammars are internally represented by speaker/hearers, if by this one means explicitly represented or tokened. Given what little we know about the computational organization of the brain, we are simply not in a position to say how the linguistic knowledge represented by means of a grammar is realized and used computationally. Indeed, as Stabler (1983) has argued, given what we know about other, better understood computational systems, it seems reasonable to suspect that grammars are *not* explicitly represented at all: the limited plasticitiy (and lability) of acquired grammatical competence would seem to render explicit representation unnecessary, while the relatively greater efficiency of processors whose programs are "hardwired" rather than explicitly represented would seem to render it undesirable. But here again, these are speculations whose resolution must await further evidence regarding the computational organization of the brain. The present point is simply that

Realist scruples argue neither for the Right View nor for the competence hypothesis that this view entails. Of course, these scruples *do* dictate that we take the grammar postulated by an explanatorily adequate linguistic theory to have the speaker/hearer as a model, but this does not entail that this model incorporates an explicit representation of that grammar. The grammar could be realized in any way whatever, so long as the realization preserved the truth of the claim that the grammar represents the speaker/hearer's linguistic knowledge. The realization might be extremely abstract, by which I mean that there might be no answer to the question "What structures and/or processes of the language processor specifically represent the speaker/hearer's knowledge of language?"

To Representationalists, the suggestion that this question may have no answer seems tantamount to admitting that there may be nothing for the grammar made available by the true linguistic theory to be true of, except the behavior of the individual to whom the grammar is ascribed. Thus, for example, Fodor writes:

> If, then, the notion of internal representation is *not* coherent, the only thing left for a linguistic theory to be true of is the linguist's observations (*de facto*, the intentions of the speaker/hearer as extrapolated by the formally simplest grammar). Take the notion of internal representation away from linguistic metatheory and you get positivism by subtraction. (1981a: 201)

Yet the options here are not only representationalism or postivism (more specifically, behaviorism). There is the option mentioned above: the grammar ascribed to an individual can be true of an individual, though not in virtue of any explicit representation in the individual of that grammar. Rather than ascribing any particular computational structure to the individual, the ascription of a grammar would simply ascribe to the individual the property of being able to recover and use the grammatical information marked by the structural descriptions that the speaker/hearer's grammar associates with sentences of his language. The ascribed capability is clearly not behavioral, since there is no presumption that an individual to whom this sort of capability is ascribed is able to manifest it.

5   TRANSPARENCY AS THE MEASURE OF PSYCHOLOGICAL REALITY

There are many different ways in which a speaker/hearer might realize a grammar (or, equivalently, the grammar be true of that speaker/hearer), none of which would have to involve the individual's having an explicit representation of that grammar. Some of these ways might involve the individual's having no "internal grammar" whatever; others would involve his having such a grammar, but not one isomorphic to the linguist's grammar that the individual realizes.

The Marcus (1980) parser is an example of the latter sort. That parser, which implements a version of Chomsky's Extended Standard Theory (EST), incorporates a grammar, i.e. a rule system that governs the interpretive processes of the parser; however, it is *not* a grammar of the sort made available by EST (or any other linguistic theory, for that matter). The incorporated grammar, as Marcus explains, is a set of pattern-action rules similar to the rules of Newell and Simon's production systems: each rule is made up of a *pattern*, which is matched against some subset of contents of the input buffer and active node stack (the two data structures maintained by the interpreter), and an *action*, which is a sequence of operations on these contents. These pattern-action rules are quite different from the phrase-structure and transformational rules of EST. The most notable difference between the grammar incorporated in the Marcus parser and those made available by EST is that the former's pattern-action rules reflect in direct fashion assumptions about the design of the parser, namely, that it maintains two data structures, that only certain contents of these structures are accessible, and so on. The grammars of EST, by contrast, do not wear their algorithmic implementation on their sleeves – there is no commitment within the theory as to how the knowledge characterized by the grammar made available by this theory is implemented or used by speakers.

Although the Marcus parser does not incorporate (in any usual sense of the word) an EST grammar for English, EST does bear an *explanatorily transparent* relation to the parsing theory that would have this parser as one of its models. By this I mean that the syntactic generalizations that are captured by means of the theoretical constructs of EST (e.g. rules, principles, and structures) are *explained* in terms of the organization and operation of the mechanisms postulated by the parsing theory. These generalizations are explained in the straightforward sense that one can see, for example, that the generalizations stated in an EST grammar for English would be true of a speaker who incorporated a Marcus parser (or, to put it another way, EST is true of all models of the parsing theory); moreover, and more importantly, one can see *why* these generalizations would hold for such a speaker. Thus, for example, in the version of EST that Marcus's theory satisfies, passive constructions involve the application of a transformation rule ("Move NP") that moves a postverbal NP into subject position, leaving a phonetically unrealized trace in the postverbal position that is co-indexed with the moved NP. The Marcus parser builds the same EST-annotated surface structure, not by actually moving an NP from a postverbal position but rather by creating an appropriately co-indexed trace in the postverbal position after encountering a verb with passive morphology. If Marcus's theory of parsing were true of speaker/hearers, then that theory would provide a detailed explanation of why EST was true of them, too, since EST bears this explanatorily transparent relation to Marcus's theory.

B&K's (strong) competence hypothesis attempts to guarantee the psychological reality of grammars by requiring that the grammars made available by an adequate linguistic theory be such that the correct parsing theory will bear an explanatorily transparent relation of a very particular sort to that linguistic theory. Specifically, the hypothesis requires that a psychologically real grammar satisfy the following condition: a model of the parsing theory – i.e., a parser for a particular language – must include a knowledge structure isomorphic to the grammar for the language parsed that as a minimum prescribes the operations that the processor/interpreter is to perform on linguistic representations. It is unclear why B&K would suppose that psychological reality would require that the operations of the parser be isomorphic to the derivations of the grammar, much less that these operations be controlled by a data structure isomorphic to the grammar, i.e. by an explicit representation of the grammar. Why shouldn't an explanatory transparency of the sort exhibited by EST suffice? After all, the various constructs that appear in an EST grammar receive an *interpretation* in the Marcus parser, in the straightforward sense that by appeal to the organization and operation of the parser we can explain why the EST grammar is true of a speaker/hearer who realizes the Marcus parser. Certainly, the rationale that B&K actually offer for their competence hypothesis is not compelling: there is, we have seen, no reason to suppose that the unification of linguistic knowledge structures requires it. The true rationale, I suspect, has more to do with *constraints* on linguistic theory: B&K want a methodological principle that will guarantee the pertinence of psycholinguistic experimental results, notably those involving measures of reaction time, to the problem of choosing between competing linguistic theories. This goal, they realize, requires the isomorphism that they postulate.

B&K's idea is not new. Miller and Chomsky (1963) proposed a similar competence hypothesis, arguing that if the isomorphism held, then the psychological "plausibility" of proposed grammars would be strengthened, since "our performance on tasks requiring an appreciation of the structure of transformed sentences [would be] some function of the nature, number, and complexity of the grammatical transformations involved" (1963: 481). If B&K's competence hypothesis were taken as a methodological principle, then experimental evidence regarding our performance on such tasks could be brought to bear on proposed grammatical theories in a straightforward way. In fact, the task of bringing such psycholinguistic evidence to bear on grammatical theories is *not* straightforward, even if the hypothesized isomorphism holds. Real time, as measured in reaction time experiments, need not bear any simple relation to "algorithmic time," as measured by the number of steps executed in the course of a computation. In order to bring psycholinguistic evidence to bear on the evaluation of grammatical theories, B&K's competence hypothesis would have to be supplemented with a theory of human computational complexity that would relate real time with algorithmic time. (Such a theory would minimally specify the computational architecture, the time and resource costs for primitive machine operations, and the implementation of the algorithm on that machine.) A theory of the requisite sort is presently beyond reach: we know very little about the computational machinery involved in language processing. We are not therefore in a position to use experimental evidence regarding language processing, even if the isomorphism postulated by B&K's competence hypothesis obtains.

Berwick and Weinberg (1984) argue that it is unlikely that models of a plausible parsing theory of natural language will be isomorphic realizations of the grammars for the languages they parse. They do acknowledge that there is nothing known to date that would preclude a *type-homomorphic* realization of the sort once endorsed by Bresnan (1978: 3), where grammatical rules are mapped into parser operations in such a way that different rule types of the grammar are associated with different operation types of the parser.[4] Yet if the intent of B&K's competence hypothesis is to insure that psycholinguistic evidence can be brought to bear on grammatical theories, then a homomorphic realization will not suffice, since under such a realization the derivation complexity of the grammar need not reflect the algorithmic complexity of the parser. B&K's competence hypothesis thus fails as a methodological principle not simply for want of a theory of human computational complexity that would enable us to apply the principle, but also because it seems doubtful that theories within its domain of application are even in principle capable of satisfying it. (This raises the obvious question: Why have a methodological principle that no theory can satisfy?)

As a criterion of psychological reality, B&K's competence hypothesis fares little better: it is unreasonably stringent and fails to provide for the comparative assessment of the psychological reality of the different grammars. Consider a parser that incorporates heuristic procedures of the sort hypothesized by Fodor, Bever, and Garrett (1974). Such a device would, for the sentences that it parses, recover the structural descriptions that the grammar for the language parsed associates with those sentences, yet it would do so in a way that bears no relation to the way in which derivations are constructed using the grammar. The generalizations stated in the linguistic theory of the grammar would be *satisfied* by models of this heuristic theory; however, they would not be explained by these models. Suppose this heuristic theory provided a correct account of language processing. The relation of parser to grammar would be explanatorily opaque, yet the grammar might nevertheless be regarded as psychologically real, inasmuch as the grammar correctly specifies the descriptions under which linguistic utterances are processed and interpreted. Fodor, Bever, and Garrett (1974) envisage just such a possibility in their discussion of the psychological reality of then proposed grammars. They argue that although there is little evidence for "the computational processes specified by transformational grammars," the structural descriptions specified by these grammars are psychologically real, since "the parameters that these descriptions mark enter, in one way or another, into a variety of psychological processing concerning language" (1974: 273–4).

Fodor, Bever, and Garrett's remarks suggest the usefulness of being able to distinguish both degrees and kinds of psychological reality, something that B&K's competence hypothesis fails to do. For reasons that will become clear shortly, I propose to distinguish two kinds of psychological reality: that of grammars, and that of the linguistic constructs to which grammars advert. Truth, as Chomsky argues, is the relevant measure for the psychological reality of grammars. Explanatory transparency is a reasonably good measure for the psychological reality of the grammar's constructs, since the more explanatorily transparent the relation of parser to grammar, the more information (roughly speaking) the grammar carries regarding the structure of the parser.

6   CHOMSKY: GRAMMARS AS PSYCHOLOGICAL HYPOTHESES

Chomsky often writes as if he were a proponent of what Fodor calls the "Right View." He speaks of mental computations involving rules, of the mental representations that these computations provide, and of the role of these computations in the etiology of behavior. Thus, for example, in concluding an extended example in which our inability to form a particular question is explained in terms of the so-called *wh*-island constraint, Chomsky says the following:

> Tentatively accepting this explanation, we impute existence to certain mental representations and to the mental computations that apply in a specific way to these mental representations. In particular, we impute existence to a representation in which (12) [[$_s$ which for PRO to play Sonatas on t]] appears as part of the structure underlying (5) [What sonatas are violins easy to play on?] at a particular stage of derivation, and to the mental computation that produces this derivation, and ultimately produces (5), identified now as ungrammatical because the computation violates the *wh*-island constraint when the rule of *wh*-movement applies to *sonatas* in (12). We attribute psychological reality to the postulated representations and mental computations. In short, we propose . . . that our theory is true. (1980: 196–7)

These conclusions certainly sound like an endorsement of the Right View, until, reading further, we learn that unlike proponents of the Right View who take themselves to be describing certain computational mechanisms and processes, Chomsky takes the linguist to be describing "abstract conditions that unknown mechanisms must meet" (1980: 197). When we couple this characterization of the linguist's project with Chomsky's often repeated insistence that a generative grammar is not a model for a speaker/hearer, that it does not prescribe the character or functioning of such a model, then we should begin to suspect that the so-called Right View is not Chomsky's view. But what, then, is his view; and how is his talk of computations and representations to be to be understood?

   The mental computations to which Chomsky refers are, as he says in the above quotation, those that produce a particular syntactic *derivation*; the mental representations are the *structures* that appear in a derivation as a result of these computations. Chomsky ascribes psychological reality to these computations and representations, yet at the same time he insists that the derivations in which these computations and representations figure do not pretend to model the psychological processes of a speaker/hearer: "When we say that a sentence has a certain derivation with respect to a particular generative grammar, we say nothing about how the speaker or hearer might proceed, in some practical or efficient way, to construct such a derivation" (1965: 9). The psychological reality that he ascribes to these constructs is not that bland, uncontentious reality to which he sometimes appeals when answering his critics, namely, that of these constructs being *true* (or *true-of-an-individual*). Rather, as Chomsky's criticism of Dummett makes clear, it is a psychological reality that would justify claims to the effect that linguistic theory is a *psychological* hypothesis.

Dummett, it will be recalled, claimed that his theory of meaning is not a psychological hypothesis because "it is not concerned to describe any inner psychological mechanisms" (1976: 70). Chomsky rejects this line of reasoning, arguing that "Dummett's theory of meaning is a 'psychological hypothesis,' though one that abstracts away from many questions that can be raised about inner mechanisms" (1980: 111). Dummett's theory is a psychological hypothesis, Chomsky argues, because it specifies *conditions* that the "inner psychological mechanisms" are alleged to meet.

Grammars are psychological hypotheses in precisely the same sense: they specify conditions that inner psychological mechanisms of the spaker/hearer are alleged to meet. A grammar does this, Chomsky argues, by specifying *intensionally* the function that these inner mechanisms are alleged to compute:

> The grammar is a system of rules and principles that determines a pairing of sound and meaning (or better, a pairing of conditions on sound and meaning given by appropriate representations). The grammar is a function in intension, though this remark is misleading, since the grammar has many important properties beyond specifying a language in extension and in fact may not even specify such a language. (1980: 82)

The notion that a grammar is an intensional specification of a function is, as Chomsky says, misleading if we conclude from this that the grammar is merely a way of providing a finite specification of antecedently given language: "Since the language is infinite, it makes no sense to speak of it as 'given', except insofar as some finite characterization – a function in intension – is given" (1980: 84). The point here, I take it, is that what is given are speaker/hearers, not languages (construed as infinite sets), and grammars provide a characterization of these speaker/hearers by specifying the function (i.e. the pairing of sound and meaning) that they compute in the course of language use.

On what I take to be Chomsky's intended construal of grammars as intensional specifications of the function that speaker/hearers compute (hereafter, the "intended construal of grammars"), he is clearly justified in construing grammars as psychological hypotheses, despite his unwillingness to interpret these grammars as making any performance claims.

Specification of the function computed in the exercise of a cognitive capacity is, as many have emphasized, a crucial step in the development of a psychological theory of that capacity; indeed, if Marr (1982) is correct, specification of the function computed – what he called the "theory of the computation" – is *the* crucial step in the development of such a theory, since in the absence of such a specification, the inquiry into psychological mechanisms is in most domains hopelessly unconstrained. Chomsky endorses claims by Marr (e.g., 1982: 28) that linguistic theory is such a theory of computation, i.e., that it is concerned with the function computed by speaker/hearers and not with the algorithms or mechanisms by which that function is computed. Citing Marr, he says:

> We may consider the study of grammar and UG to be at the level of the theory of the computation. I don't see any useful distinction between "linguistics" and "psychology," unless we choose to use the former term for the study of the theory of the computation in language, and the latter for the theory of the algorithm. (1980b: 48–9)

On the intended construal of grammars, Chomsky is surely also justified in insisting on the "psychological reality" of grammars. To the extent that a grammar correctly specifies the function computed by a speaker/hearer, the grammar is true of that speaker/hearer. What point could there be in denying the psychological reality of such a grammar, except on the grounds that it is false of the speaker/hearer, i.e., that it provides an incorrect specification of the function computed by the speaker/hearer? It is not as if we have any other way of specifying the function. Certainly we cannot specify the function extensionally, since the set that defines the function is infinite. In principle we could specify the function intensionally by specifying the mechanisms that compute the function. But surely we are not now in a position to provide such a specification, and even if we were, that would not impugn the psychological reality of the grammar in question, since the grammar would still be true of the speaker/hearer; it would still provide a correct specification of the function computed by the speaker/hearer, albeit at a more abstract level of description.

Chomsky's construal of transformational grammars as specifications of the functions computed by a speaker/hearers has not gone unchallenged. Stabler (1984) argues that the construal is untenable. He points out that the domains of the grammars made available by current transformational theory are not coextensive with the domains of the parsing mechanisms that speaker/hearers embody; indeed, their domains fail to be coextensive even under idealizations of the parsing mechanisms that abstract away from various performance limitations (e.g. memory limitations). Thus, speaker/hearers both succeed in understanding certain ungrammatical sentences that fall outside the domain of the grammar attributed to them and at the same time fail to understand certain grammatical sentences that fall within the domain of that grammar. Moreover, ambiguous sentences get multiple representations within the grammar, while empirical evidence seems to indicate that speaker/hearers typically compute only a single representation.

By itself, the apparent disparity of domains does not impugn Chomsky's construal of transformational grammars, since it might simply be attributed to errors in current linguistic theory. Chomsky, after all, is not committed to the view that the grammars made available by a false linguistic theory specify the functions computed by speaker/hearers. Stabler attempts to buttress his argument against this line of response by arguing that the disparity manifests methodological commitments in transformational linguistics which are inconsistent with the computational-theoretic enterprise described by Marr. The methodological commitments that he discusses, most notably the emphasis upon the formal simplicity of proposed theories, may very well impugn the attempts of Berwick and Weinberg (1984) to offer a computational-theoretic interpretation of certain of the linguistic constructs to which transformational grammars advert (viz. subjacency); however, such commitments will serve to impugn Chomsky's construal of transformational grammars only if it can be demonstrated that they lead to the specification of functions that speaker/hearers are unable to compute efficiently over the range of sentences that these speaker/hearers can use and understand. In the absence of such a demonstration, Stabler would seem to have no grounds for impugning Chomsky's construal. Nor does it seem likely that such a demonstration will soon be forthcoming. Given our impoverished understanding of human computational architecture, we are not now in a position to provide a demonstration based upon empirical considerations regarding human computational powers. And for the reasons detailed by Berwick and Weinberg (1984), a compelling demonstration based upon mathematical parsability results seems extremely unlikely; the application of those results to human language processing is tenuous in the extreme.

7 PSYCHOLOGICAL REALITY OF LINGUISTIC CONSTRUCTS

While on their intended construal, grammars true of a speaker/hearer are psychologically real, it would seem an open question whether the linguistic constructs to which grammars advert, including rules, representations, and the computations that figure in syntactic derivations, are psychologically real. Chomsky (1980: 197) argues that we are justified in attributing psychological reality to the constructs postulated by a grammar true of speaker/hearer. In effect, the psychological reality of these constructs is assumed to be inherited from that of the grammar. But this assumption seems arguable. It might be objected that in the absence of specific evidence for their existence, these constructs must be assumed to be artifacts of the particular way in which the function computed by the speaker/hearer is specified, and as such cannot inherit the psychological reality of the grammar in which they figure.

Realist principles, which I endorse, dictate that we should accept the existential commitments of our best theories. Determining the existential commitments of our theories, however, is not the simple task that many assume. It is not just a matter of blindly Ramsifying our theories in the way that the slogan "to be is to be value of a bound variable" might *seem* to suggest. Suppose, for example, that the best "theory" of my present location on the Earth's surface includes a statement to the effect that I am presently located at 40 degrees 30.25 minutes North latitude, 74 degrees 26.04 minutes West longitude. Whatever the existential commitments of that theory, it is surely *not* committed to the existence of a certain quantity of something called "latitude" or "longitude." What the theory is presumably committed to is the existence of the physical location that is *specified* in terms of latitude and longitude. Latitude and longitude are *representational constructs* that figure in the system of representation that we employ in the theory to specify location. The point here is a very general one: in determining the existential commitments of a theory, we must distinguish the *theoretical magnitudes* to which the theory *is* existentially committed from the representational constructs to which the theory is *not* existentially committed and which serve only to specify the theoretical magnitudes. In most cases, the distinction between theoretical magnitudes and representational constructs is reasonably easy to draw: there is an intended interpretation of the theory, and that interpretation draws the required distinction. In practice, the distinction is often facilitated by the conventional nature of the system of representation in which the representational constructs figure: we recognize that the system could, in principle at least, be replaced by an alternative system of representation with different representational constructs without compromising the intended interpretation of the theory. (My present location, for example, could have been specified in polar coordinates or simply by street address.)

The distinction that the intended interpretation of a theory draws between theoretical magnitudes and representational constructs can be, and often is, redrawn by reinterpreting the status of certain terms in the theory. Typically this occurs as a consequence of new empirical and/or theoretical considerations that lead theorists to reconstrue the status of the theory's representational constructs. In the case of Balmer formula for the spectral lines of hydrogen, for example, the integers of that formula initially received no physical interpretation; however, when Bohr succeeded in deriving the generalized version of the Balmer formula from his theory of the atom, these integers were then interpreted as quantum numbers. Even more striking perhaps is the case of Maxwell's equations, in which the scalar and vector potentials were initially interpreted by virtually all physicists as representational constructs, but under the pressure of subsequent theoretical developments have come to be regarded as the essential existential commitments of the equations. Similar cases within the domain of linguistic theory are difficult to come by, for the simple reason that there are no theories or models of sentence-processing mechanisms that are sufficiently compelling to force an interpretation of the theoretical constructs that figure in linguistic theory.[5]

On their intended construal, therefore, grammars are not assumed to bear an explanatorily transparent relation to underlying performance mechanisms. As Chomsky himself puts it,

> Although we may describe the grammar G as a system of processes and rules that apply in a certain order to relate sound and meaning, we are not entitled to take this as a description of the successive acts of a performance model. (1968: 117)

Chomsky's point, I take it, is that it is not part of the intended interpretation of grammatical theories that the linguistic constructs that figure in a grammar are to be construed as descriptions of underlying mechanisms. The intended interpretation is to take the grammar as simply the intensional specification of the function – "the pairing of sound and meaning" – that the speaker/hearer computes.

The conclusion that I wish to draw here should be clear: on the intended construal, what is taken to be psychologically real is not the linguistic constructs that figure in the grammar, but the function that these constructs serve to specify. These constructs, which include rules, representations, and the computations that figure in syntactic derivations, constitute the representational constructs of grammatical theory, and as such are *not* among the existential commitments of that theory. The function specified in terms of these constructs, on the other hand, *is* among the theory's existential commitments, and hence presumed to be psychologically real. Of course, evidence might be forthcoming which would force a reconstrual of certain, perhaps all linguistic constructs in the grammar. Specifically, we might obtain evidence establishing the existence of an explanatorily transparent relation between the grammar, on the one hand, and the computational mechanisms by which a speaker/hearer computes the function specified by the grammar, on the other. In such event, we would surely acknowledge the psychological reality of the linguistic constructs that receive an interpretation under the transparency relation. But the point to be emphasized here is that acknowledging the psychological reality of these constructs would involve a *re*construal of the grammar; it is not now part of the intended construal of grammatical theories that these constructs are presumed to be psychologically real. Whether this presumption will be overturned remains an open empirical question.

NOTES

1 By "psychology" we understand that scientific inquiry concerned with human cognitive capacities, with the mental structures that underlie those capacities, and with their exercise.
2 See Dennett (1983), Matthews (1984), Matthews (1988), and Stabler (1983).
3 I am here paraphrasing Fodor's (1981b: 120) account of what would constitute evidence for the claim that the postulates of logic are internally represented.
4 Bresnan's adequacy condition for "realistic" grammars:

We should be able to define for [a grammar] explicit realization mappings to psychological models of language use. These realizations should map distinct grammatical rules and units into distinct processing operations and informational units in such a way that different rule types of the grammar are associated with different processing functions. If distinct grammatical rules were not distinguished in a psychological model under some realization mapping, . . . the grammar could not be said to represent the knowledge of a language user in any psychologically interesting sense. (1978: 3)

5   Marcus (1980) and Berwick and Weinberg (1983, 1984) have claimed that a deterministic model of sentence processing explains the existence of, and some of the properties of the subjacency constraint on natural languages imposed by current transformational theories; however, Fodor (1985) argues that the empirical arguments offered in support of this claim are flawed and the purported explanatory relationship between determinism and subjacency is weak.

REFERENCES

Berwick, R. and Weinberg, A. 1983: Syntactic constraints and efficient parsability. *Proceedings of the 21st Annual Meeting of the Association for Computational Linguistics*, 119–22.
—— 1984: *The Grammatical Basis of Linguistic Performance*. Cambridge, Mass.: MIT Press.
Bresnan, J. 1978: A realistic transformation grammar. In M. Halle, J. Bresnan, and G. Miller (eds), *Linguistic Theory and Psychological Reality*. Cambridge, Mass.: MIT Press, 1–59.
Bresnan, J. and Kaplan, R. 1982: Introduction: grammars as mental representations of language. In J. Bresnan (ed.), *The Mental Representation of Language*. Cambridge, Mass.: MIT Press, xvii–lii.
Chomsky, N. 1965: *Aspects of the Theory of Syntax*. Cambridge, Mass.: MIT Press.
—— 1968: *Language and Mind*. New York: Harcourt, Brace, Jovanovich.
—— 1980: *Rules and Representations*. New York: Columbia University Press.
Dennett, D. 1983: Styles of mental representation. *Proceedings of Aristotelian Society*, 213–26.
Dummett, M. 1976: What is a theory of meaning? (II) In G. Evans and J. McDowell (eds), *Truth and Meaning*. London: Oxford University Press, 67–137.
Fodor, J. 1981a: Some notes on what linguistics is about. In N. Block (ed.), *Readings in the Philosophy of Psychology*, Vol. II. Cambridge, Mass.: Harvard University Press, 197–207.
—— 1981b: Three cheers for propositional attitudes. In *Representations*. Cambridge, Mass.: MIT Press, 100–123.
Fodor, J., Bever, T. and Garrett, M. 1974: *The Psychology of Language*. New York: McGraw-Hill.
Fodor, J. D. 1985: Deterministic parsing and subjacency, *Language and Cognitive Processes,* 1: 3–42.
Marcus, M. 1980: *A Theory of Syntactic Recognition for Natural Language*. Cambridge, Mass.: MIT Press.
Marr, D. 1982: *Vision*. San Francisco: W. H. Freeman.
Matthews, R. 1984: Troubles with representationalism. *Social Research*, 51: 1065–97.

—— (1988): The alleged evidence for representationalism. In S. Silvers (ed.), *ReRepresentation*. Dordrecht: Reidel, 103–72.

Miller, G. and Chomsky, N. 1963: Finitary models of language users. R. Luce, R. Bush, and E. Galanter (eds.), *Handbook of Mathematical Psychology*, vol. II. New York: Wiley, 185–94.

Stabler, E. 1983: How Are Grammars Represented? *The Behavioral and Brain Sciences*, 6: 391–402.

9
Rules and Principles in the Historical Development of Generative Syntax

Frederick J. Newmeyer

1 INTRODUCTION

A recent characterization of the history of generative syntax is one of steady progress throughout a process of accretion. This view points to a succession of discoveries, each building on prior ones, that have steered the field on a straight course that has led inexorably to the government-binding (GB) theory of the present day. To be specific, this account characterizes the principal task of the syntactician of thirty years ago to have been to construct grammars of individual languages, each consisting of a list of language-particular rules. Between that time and the present, our ever deepening understanding of the principles of universal grammar (UG) has led to a steady reduction of the complexity and language-particularity of these rules. Today, our understanding of these principles is profound; in fact, we are close to the point where we can attribute virtually all observable differences among languages to the parameterization of these principles within highly circumscribed limits.

This interpretation is largely due to Chomsky and it receives its clearest exposition in his 1986 book *Knowledge of Language*. In a discussion spanning over one hundred pages, Chomsky reviews how progress in developing the principles that govern the general form of grammars has allowed, first simplification in the statement of individual rules, and then their literal elimination, to the point where now we have arrived at "a conception of UG as a virtually rule-free system" (93).

It is clear that Chomsky views progress toward this goal as having been achieved in a fairly gradual fashion. The results that he cites as having led to the current highly developed conception of UG seem fairly evenly distributed over the past quarter-century. From the 1960s, Chomsky cites the principle of recoverability of deletion and the A-over-A principle (Chomsky 1964), followed by Ross's (1967) "island constraints." The

1970s saw the principle of subjacency (Chomsky 1973), Emonds's (1970, 1976) structure-preserving constraint, and Freidin's (1978) first attempts to derive principles of rule application. From the 1980s, Chomsky makes reference to the current formulation of principles of government and binding and the projection principle. Each such development has contributed one step further toward the goal of "reduc[ing] the recourse to rule systems" (84).

This essentially linear progress-through-accumulation view of the history of generative syntax has become quite accepted, at least by those who feel that GB is on the right track. Indeed, I have endorsed it myself (Newmeyer 1986: 198). Even introductory texts contrast favorably today's elegant model of interacting principles with the clumsy rule-dominated work of the early days. As van Riemsdijk and Williams puts it in their overview of GB: "From today's perspective most research carried out before the late 1960s appears data-bound, construction-bound, and lacking in appreciation for the existence of highly general principles of linguistic organization" (1986: 175).

The purpose of this paper is to challenge the accretionist interpretation of the history of generative syntax. While as a statement of the evolution of *Chomsky's thinking*, it may well have merit, this interpretation does not characterize adequately the course of development of the field itself. One must be careful not to identify Chomsky's views at any point in time with those of the mainstream in generative syntax. At certain times the two have coincided, and at other times they have not. His current conceptions of the organization of grammar in fact do command the allegiance of the majority of generative syntacticians (as I will argue below), just as in the years following the publication of his seminal work *Syntactic Structures* in 1957 his ideas were predominant. But for at least half of the time between 1957 and the present, Chomsky has been in a minority among generative syntacticians on many major questions. And once we disregard Chomsky's minority positions and focus instead on the mainstream line of research at any given period, we will see that the accretionist interpretation has little to recommend it.

I will offer instead a more cyclical interpretation of the history of generative syntax. In place of a gradual progression from a rule-oriented conception of grammar to a principle-oriented one, I will suggest that there have been four successive stages in the development of the field, alternatingly rule-oriented and principle-oriented. Before defending this claim, however, it is essential to clarify what exactly is being implied by identifying a period as "rule-oriented" or "principle-oriented." Specifically, I will characterize a period as "rule-oriented" if the generally accepted central task is seen to be to propose, motivate, or argue against the existence of language-particular rules. The period will be identified as "principle-oriented" if mainstream research focuses on motivating principles of UG.

Whether a period is rule-oriented or principle-oriented is tangential to which particular *research topics* happen at the time to be engaging the

interest of a significant number of syntacticians. For example, in the past
three decades, topics such as the nature of the interface between syntax
and semantics, that between syntax and phonology, whether syntactic
processes are fundamentally distinct from morphological ones, the number
of syntactic levels, the form of syntactic rules, and so on have, at various
times, been at the top of the collective research agenda. Yet each can be
(and has been) approached from either a rule-oriented or principle-
oriented direction. Thus the nature of a period cannot be surmised simply
by examining the *questions* raised at a particular point in time; rather, it is
more a function of the *form of the solutions* to the problems that are put
forward.

It must be stressed that there is no sensible criterion, scientific or
otherwise, that would single out either a focus on motivating principles or
one of motivating rules as an inherently more desirable enterprise. Indeed,
both are indispensable tasks in linguistics, as are their analogues in other
sciences. And, as we shall see, each successive transition in the development of generative syntax, whether from a rule-oriented period to a
principle-oriented period, or in the opposite direction, has represented a
major step forward in our understanding of the nature of syntactic
processes.

Also, as a final qualification, motivating rules and motivating principles
are not wholly incompatible tasks. One can hardly imagine a paper that put
forward some new principle of UG that did not at least call attention to,
and perhaps reformulate, a language-particular rule, if only to show how
its application is constrained by the principle. Likewise, virtually all work
that has motivated a rule or rules has done so in the context of providing
support (implicit or explicit) for a particular model of grammar, that is, for
a theoretical principle. The best work in generative syntax, in fact, has
taken rule-motivation and principle-motivation to be entirely complementary tasks. Consider, for example, the work of Emonds, cited
above, which involves careful formulation of rules of English (and, to a
lesser extent, of French) in the context of showing how these rules and
their precise formulation bear on an important principle of UG, the
structure-preserving constraint. Much other work, as well, has taken
rule-motivation and principle-motivation in conjunction, in some cases to
the point where it is impossible to characterize it as a rule-oriented or a
principle-oriented piece of research.

Nevertheless, at different times in the history of generative syntax, there
has been a different sense of *priorities*, a shifting conception of where the
greatest progress can be made and thus where one should devote one's
energies. At certain times attention to particular rules has been seen as the
most rewarding enterprise, at other times attention to general principles.
Thus it is possible to divide the history of the field into four periods, which
are summarized in the following table:

Period	Nature	Years predominant	Principal Inspiration
Early transformational grammar	Rule-oriented	1957–1967	Chomsky, *Syntactic Structures* (1957)
Generative semantics	Principle-oriented	1967–1972	Katz and Postal, *An Integrated Theory of Linguistic Descriptions* (1964)
Lexicalism	Rule-oriented	1972–1980	Chomsky, "Remarks on Nominalization" (1970)
Government-binding	Principle-oriented	1980–	Chomsky, "Conditions on Transformations" (1973)

To summarize the evolution of the field, the publication of Chomsky's *Syntactic Structures* in 1957 ushered in the rule-oriented period of early transformational grammar that lasted until around 1967. It was replaced by a period in which the predominant framework was the principle-oriented generative semantics and which derived its main inspiration from Katz and Postal's 1964 book *An Integrated Theory of Linguistic Descriptions*. Generative semantics gave way around 1972 to the rule-oriented lexicalist period, whose course was charted by Chomsky's "Remarks on nominalization" paper from 1970, and which flourished until around 1980. Since then, we have been in the second principle-oriented period, dominated by the government-binding framework, and owing its inspiration to Chomsky's 1973 "Conditions on transformations" paper.

It should be noted that there can be a substantial time lag between the appearance in print of the work that would form the "principal inspiration" of a given period and that period's predominance – one of seven years, in fact, in the case of the current period.

In some cases, it is a trivial task to identify a "principal inspiration." The ritualistic invocation of *Syntactic Structures* in virtually all generative syntactic work published between 1957 and 1965 leaves no room for doubt as to its inspirational effects. However, in other cases, it may not be so clear that one work can be singled out as having played this role; and, to be sure, there is no logical reason why in all cases one even *should* exist. For example, can one point to a single principal inspiration for generative semantics? Even if the answer to this question is affirmative, it is by no means obvious that it should be identified as Katz and Postal's *Integrated Theory of Linguistic Descriptions*. Thus I will devote considerable space to arguing that it should be accorded this role, though I will conclude that generative semantics followed the path charted by that book more in an "atavistic" than in a conscious sense.

I shall further defend a claim that I assume to be more controversial – as well as more interesting – than that there have simply been four alternating periods in the development of the field. I will argue that the *internal structure* of each period has been roughly the same. The beginning of each period is marked by a major leap in our understanding of syntactic processes and brings with it impressive publications whose fundamental insights are not diminished by subsequent research. At the same time, the field sees a burst of enthusiasm accompanied by a level of activity unknown since the beginning of the previous period. After a time, however, a levelling-off begins to take place, followed by a period of stagnation. This is marked by a decline in the level of argumentation and, more seriously, by the beginnings of an entry into a phase in which mere descriptions of phenomena, divorced from serious discussion of how such descriptions might bear on the choice between competing theories, become the order of the day. When this takes place in a rule-oriented period, a rule become little more than a short-hand way of referring to the superficial properties of a construction in a particular language. In a principle-oriented period, a parallel shift takes place: while the rhetorical focus might remain on principles of UG, the actual practice becomes to focus on language-particular constructions without serious consideration of their relevance to these principles.

In this context, the next turn is taken: to a principle-oriented stage from a rule-oriented one, or to a rule-oriented stage from a principle-oriented one. A new upsurge takes place in the field, and the process begins anew.

2   THE FIRST RULE-ORIENTED PERIOD: EARLY TRANSFORMATIONAL GRAMMAR

It is hardly necessary to go into detail here on what the publication of *Syntactic Structures* meant for the field of linguistics. By breaking from structural linguistics, both in its rigidly empiricist American version and its less rigid, though equally taxonomic European version, the book put forward a new research program for linguistic analysis. *Syntactic Structures* itself can hardly be characterized either as rule-oriented or principle-oriented. Indeed, it is a masterpiece of the integration of general principles of grammar with compelling detailed analyses of particular phenomena in English. As Chomsky reminds the reader:

> . . . neither the general theory nor the particular grammars are fixed for all time, in this view. Progress and revision may come from the discovery of new facts about particular languages, or from purely theoretical insights about organization of linguistic data – that is, new models for linguistic structure. But there is also no circularity in this conception. At any given time we can attempt to formulate as precisely as possible both the general theory and the set of associated grammars that must meet the empirical, external conditions of adequacy. (1957: 50)

In *Syntactic Structures*, there is never any question of how the rules proposed bear on the conception of language introduced and defended in that book: there is a constant appeal to their abstractness and complex interaction, which Chomsky clearly regards to be of greater theoretical significance than the precise details of their formulation. Furthermore, it is clear that Chomsky does not regard the existence of a particular *construction* in English to be prima facie evidence that there is necessarily a single *rule* to characterize that construction. While it is in general the case that rules are construction-specific, there are several instances in which a single rule is involved in the generation of more than one construction and in which the derivation of a single construction involves the interaction of several rules. Both are illustrated by Chomsky's ingenious analysis of the English auxiliary. The failure of the Auxiliary Transformation (later called "Affix-Hopping") to apply predicts the environment for the occurrence of supportive *do* in both negatives and questions, while the generation of simple yes-no questions involves the application of two rules, the Auxiliary Transformation and a fronting rule ("Tq"), both of which are at work in the generation of other constructions.

Other early work in transformational syntax maintained a comparable degree of subtle interplay between general theory and particular rule-statement: Lees's *Grammar of English Nominalizations* (1960) and Bach's 1962 paper on the order of elements in a transformational grammar of German come to mind as particularly good illustrations of work that comes close to matching *Syntactic Structures* in this respect.

However, as the number of people working in transformational generative grammar increased in the first decade of its existence, the emphasis of the typical paper or thesis began gradually to shift. More and more over this period, we find the standard appeal to *Syntactic Structures* taking on little more than ritualistic value. Reading a random selection of this work gives one a very different feeling for the nature of the period than does a reading of Chomsky, Lees, Bach, and the other leading generativists of the early years. It is not just that the work is not as insightful or as intricate in its argumentation – one would hardly expect the average work at any point in time to exude brilliance. Rather, this work is different *conceptually*. In it, one finds very little in the way of interplay between rules and principles. On the contrary, this work is almost exclusively rule-oriented. The author identifies a construction, then writes a transformational rule which comes close to mimicking its surface characteristics. In other words, for many linguists, transformations had become little more than a new descriptive device to supplement those that had been provided in the past decades by structural linguistics.

In this typical work of the first decade, it is not simply a matter of questions of UG being de-emphasized; in many cases one feels that the author is not aware that such questions were even on the agenda. Only the occasional rule-ordering argument prevents this work from being in the same mold as that of Zellig Harris, in whose work transformational rules were explicitly regarded as a device for capturing surface co-occurrence relations. In other words, in mainstream generative grammar by the mid-1960s, transformations had become a vehicle for doing descriptive syntax.

One might object that since there were so few people engaged in generativist research in the first decade of its existence, generalizations such as the above are meaningless. But this is not the case. In fact, there were dozens of people working in transformational generative grammar by the early 1960s. A bibliography compiled by William Orr Dingwall in 1965 lists well over 100 contributions in this area, including theses, dissertations, and working papers, as well as published books and articles (many of which, to be sure, appeared in fairly obscure journals).[1]

Another objection that one might raise is that the work that I am referring to here was not central to the development of generativist theory; that at the time it was not considered mainstream research or even considered worthwhile by leading figures in the field. But even if that were true, it would be beside the point. My goal is to characterize the *typical* work of each period, what the "ordinary working grammarian" (to use Fillmore's phrase) was involved in doing. And in the first decade of transformational grammar, this work was overwhelmingly rule-oriented and became, as time went on, increasingly descriptivist.

Actually, the point can be made that even work by the most prominent generative grammarians in this period tended to emphasize rules over principles, for the most part. One is struck by the relative frequency with which principles of UG were proposed in one work, then ignored in work that followed it. For example, in *Syntactic Structures*, Chomsky proposed the following general condition on derived constituent structure, one effect of which would be to guarantee that the *by*-phrase created by the passive transformation would receive the label "PP":

If X is a Z in the phrase structure grammar, and a string Y formed by a transformation is of the same structural form as X, then Y is also a Z. (1957: 73)

This principle is not even mentioned in Lees (1960), though he could have made use of it. Likewise, so far as I have been able to determine, no reference is made to Chomsky's A-over-A principle, proposed at a 1962 conference and published in 1964, until Ross's 1967 dissertation.

The publication of Chomsky's *Aspects of the Theory of Syntax* in 1965 did little to change the increasingly rule-oriented and descriptivist direction that transformational generative grammar was taking in the mid 1960s. The most important and memorable part of that book is its first chapter, "Methodological preliminaries," in which the "rationalist" nature of linguistic theory is defended at length and the case is made that the problem of the validation of a theory of grammar and that of the construction of a theory of language acquisition are one and the same. This chapter sparked a debate among psychologists, philosophers, and anthropologists – not to mention linguists – that has continued unabated to the present time. However, this chapter did little to affect the actual *practice* of generative syntacticians.

There were, of course, important principles of UG proposed in *Aspects*, the three most far-reaching of which were base recursion, the principle of cyclic application of transformational rules, and the separation of category-introducing rules from those of subcategorization.[2] But interestingly, none of these had the contagious effect of leading syntacticians in a more principle-oriented direction. In fact, they had the opposite effect. Each had the effect of "cleaning up" the phrase-structure and transformational components of the grammar. By doing so, they made rule writing an easier and more immediately gratifying experience.

It is interesting to recall that the topic in *Aspects* that receives the longest single treatment is quite in keeping with the rule-oriented spirit of the early years of the theory: the extended and often tortuous discussion in chapter 2, where Chomsky puts forward and evaluates a variety of formats for lexical insertion, an issue that appeared even then to many linguists to have few interesting implications for UG, and which had little impact on subsequent work in the field.

The most important analytic work wholly within the *Aspects* framework is generally regarded to be Peter Rosenbaum's 1965 MIT dissertation *The Grammar of English Predicate Complement Constructions*, published in 1967, in which he provided an analysis of English subordination and associated phenomena. It was Rosenbaum's formulation of rules such as Equi-NP-Deletion (which he called the "Identity Erasure Transformation"), Extraposition, and Raising (essentially his "Pronoun Replacement"), which, after modification in G. Lakoff (1968a), would come to represent the "standard" analyses of these phenomena for over a decade, partly as a result of their being enshrined in Akmajian and Heny's 1975 syntax textbook.

It is interesting then, considering the longevity of Rosenbaum's proposals, to recollect what his stated goals were. Rather than to motivate or provide support for some principle of UG or to constrain the power of linguistic theory, they were far more modest. To be specific, he wrote that "[t]he aim of the present study is to develop an adequate framework for *describing* certain types of sentential complementation in English" (1967: 1) (emphasis added).

While Rosenbaum's work may have been the first empirical study of significance to incorporate base recursion and the cycle, it presents no *arguments* for either of these principles. Indeed, the rules would have required only the most minor revisions to work without either of them.

In short, the first decade of generative syntax was a higly rule-oriented one. More and more in this period, descriptive goals came to outweigh explanatory ones. In much work in this period – perhaps largely outside of the MIT mainstream, but nevertheless numerically significant – transformational grammar had become little more than descriptive linguistics with a transformational veneer.

It was in this context that an approach to grammar whose rhetorical emphasis valued explanatory principles over detailed formulation of language-particular rules was bound to fall on welcome ears, and to present a pole of attraction for those whose interest in current work was flagging. That model was generative semantics.

3   THE FIRST PRINCIPLE-ORIENTED PERIOD: GENERATIVE SEMANTICS

The shift from a rule-oriented to a principle-oriented approach to grammar had begun to be felt around 1966 and 1967, when works appeared that were devoted in their entirety to the motivation of a single principle of UG or a set of related principles. The two most important of these, which, while not full-blown generative semantics themselves, were to prepare for this framework through their successful demonstration that there were impressive pay-offs to be had in emphasizing principles over rules, are Ross's 1967 doctoral dissertation, *Constraints on Variables in Syntax*, and Postal's *Cross-Over Phenomena*, circulated in mimeographed form in 1968 and published as a book in 1971.[3] Ross's work was to underlie all subsequent studies of movement constraints, while Postal's, in addition to providing a wealth of interesting generalizations that would occupy syntacticians' attention for years, would turn out to provide some of the best evidence for movement rules leaving traces at the site of extraction (see Wasow 1972, Chomsky 1975).

This work by Ross and Postal is a perfect illustration of the above claim that the major contributions at the *beginning* of each period balance the postulation of principles of UG with solid motivations of language-particular rules. Both Ross's and Postal's essays are principle-oriented, to be sure, but they nevertheless contain dozens of formulations of transformational rules, many of which undergo modification as the principles argued for undergo refinement.

The impressive quality of these works helped to ensure that Ross and Postal, along with George Lakoff and James McCawley (among others), would have little difficulty weaning most syntacticians away from the kind of work that had characterized early transformational syntax and toward the new framework of generative semantics that they were in the process of developing.

There are many ways in which generative semantics can be compared with the earlier work that preceded it and with the lexicalist model that by the mid-1970s had supplanted it, but I feel that the most important way is typically overlooked or downplayed. Generative semantics was, first and foremost, a *principle-oriented* approach to grammar. Virtually every paper written in that framework put forth some novel principle governing UG or sought to provide evidence for some already proposed one. At the same time, language-particular rules were downplayed to the point that in most generative semantic work, not a single one was formalized.

The typical research strategy in the generative semantic period was to motivate some broad principle by showing that a number of already accepted lesser principles led to analyses that suggested its correctness. Consider a position that generative semanticists had come to in the late 1960s, namely that the inventory of syntactic categories is isomorphic to the categories of predicate logic (see especially McCawley 1967, 1968a). This principle is certainly an interesting one, although subsequent research has shown it to be untenable. How was it motivated? For the most part, by pointing to earlier analyses which *themselves* were motivated on the basis of an appeal to principles.

Let me offer a concrete example. The idea that syntactic categories are mirrored by logical categories presumably entails that there is no category "Auxiliary." Hence, McCawley (1967) appealed to Ross's (1969) conclusion that the auxiliary is a subclass of the category Verb, which itself can reasonably be regarded as isomorphic to the predicate of logic. Ross justified this conclusion by arguing that to deny it would fly in the face of other, independently motivated, principles. One such principle would be widely accepted today, namely that rules can refer only to constituents. This led Ross to reject the *Syntactic Structures* treatment of the auxiliary, in which the subcomponents of the category AUX represented in (1) are referred to in the rules forming yes-no questions and simple negatives, even though they do not form a constituent:

$$(1) \qquad \text{Tns} \left(\left\{ \begin{matrix} M \\ \text{have} \\ \text{be} \end{matrix} \right\} \right)$$

Ross advocated instead replacing the elements in (1) with the category V, which would have the features $[+V, +Aux]$.

Another principle that led Ross to his conclusion was never put in explicit form, though it guided a great deal of generative semantic research. It can be stated roughly as in (2):

(2)   If two lexical items occurring in similar environments appear to undergo the same rule, then they must belong to the same syntactic category.

In fact, before the introduction into the theory of features ranging over the major lexical categories (an idea that was hinted at, but not developed, in Chomsky 1970), there was little alternative to principle (2) if one wished to avoid disjunctive elements in the structural descriptions of transformational rules. On the basis of this principle, Ross concluded that copula *be* belongs to the category V since it seems to share with true verbs the property of undergoing the rule of Gapping (cf. (3)a–b; to complete the argument, since auxiliaries share with the copula (now established to be a

V), the property of allowing quantifiers to "hop" over them (cf. (4)a–b), they too must belong to the category V:

(3)a I ate fish, and Bill __ steak.
   b I am American, and Bill __ Canadian.
(4)a They all/both/each are handsome → They are all/both/each hand-some
   b They all/both/each have gone/must go → They have all/both/each gone / They must all/both/each go

Some of the principles put forward by generative semanticists were genuinely interesting and challenging, and provided an air of excitement to the enterprise of doing syntactic research that had been missing a few years earlier. One might be tempted to downplay the contributions of that framework or even to dismiss it out of hand, given that many of the principles that it put forward proved to be empirically deficient and that by the mid 1970s the body of practitioners of that framework had dissolved almost completely. But that would be a serious mistake. The fact that many of its ideas resurfaced in modified form in later work suggests that they contained more than a small kernel of correctness.

Let us consider three examples of generative semantic principles of UG that were adapted subsequently by later frameworks. The first is the conception that there exists a word-internal syntax that parallels in crucial respects phrase-internal syntax (Weinreich 1966; McCawley 1968b; Postal 1970), an idea which, in generative semantics, was manifested through the device of lexical decomposition. This conception promised to provide the first generative characterization of the notion "possible lexical item." While generative semanticists were unsuccessful in getting this idea to work, subsequent approaches to grammar have not fared any better in finding a syntactic or semantic basis for distinguishing possible from impossible words in a language. Furthermore, current research in a variety of frameworks has resurrected the idea of word/phrase syntactic parallels in various ways (see Dowty 1979, Selkirk 1982, Baker 1985), and even lexical decomposition itself has reappeared in semantic theories such as that presented in Jackendoff (1983).

A second generative semantic principle worth mentioning is the idea that syntactic rules (or at least a large subset of them) are stated in terms of semantic categories, rather than syntactic ones (see especially Green 1974, Newmeyer 1974). Again, this principle, could it be maintained, would have placed a strong constraint on syntactic operations. While, of course, it could not be maintained, the germ of the idea survives in theories of the lexicon that posit that the rules applying in that component are sensitive to – or are actually stated in terms of – the thematic roles of the elements involved (see Anderson 1977, Williams 1981).

Finally, the generative semantic principle that, at one syntactic level, sentences are disambiguated in terms of the scope of their logical elements

(McCawley 1968a; G. Lakoff 1970) has become a mainstay of the government-binding framework (May 1977 and much subsequent work).

It is perhaps inviting, given the spectacular rise of generative semantics in the late 1960s and its equally spectacular collapse less than a decade later, to dismiss it as little more than a phenomenon to be attributed to sociological or personal factors. While such factors were clearly involved (for discussion, see Newmeyer 1986: 101–3, 126–7, 137–8), there was an intellectually far more respectable reason for its success, however, short-lived. Generative semantics promised to ground syntax in a theory of universal principles in a way that its precursor of the first decade of generative syntax did not and that its emergent rival, the lexicalist model, was perceived not to.

Rules played an ever-decreasing role in generative semantics in the period that it flourished, and were almost never formulated precisely. Transformations such as Passive, Predicate Raising, Nominalization, Equi and others were often referred to, but rarely received any motivation beyond the observation that they seemed a necessary intermediary between two structural configurations whose correctness had already been decided upon for independent reasons. That is, whenever generative semanticists needed a transformation to collapse two clauses, they postulated Predicate Raising at work; to raise a noun phrase to a higher clause, Raising; to make an object a subject, Passive. Little independent motivation for the application of these rules was ever given, aside from the need to relate pre-determined structures (for further discussion, see Newmeyer 1986: 129).

In an early generative semantics paper, George Lakoff made explicit the marginality of rules and their motivations in this framework. After positing essentially identical deep structures for the sentences *Seymour sliced the salami with a knife* and *Seymour used a knife to slice the salami* on the basis of their shared semantic properties, Lakoff wrote:

> Due to the nature of the definition of deep structure, one can provide arguments for identity of deep structures without proposing what these deep structures are *and without proposing any transformational devirations*. This type of argument differs considerably from the type of argument that has been used in transformational research so far. To date, research in transformational grammar has been oriented toward proposing rules. Arguments concerning generalizations of deep structure selectional restrictions and co-occurrences have been brought up only in support of some given set of rules. What we have done here is to show that arguments of this sort can be used by themselves *without discussion of rules at all*. (G. Lakoff 1968b: 24, emphasis added)

By 1972, many generative semanticists had abaondoned even *in principle* the possibility of motivating and formalizing grammatical rules. In that year, Ann Borkin edited a manuscript that was devoted to criticizing the rule-formulations in Burt's 1971 textbook, but offered no alternatives to them. George Lakoff wrote in the foreword that "the old goal of actually writing a complete grammar for a language has become at best a hope for future centuries and at worst a joke" (1972a: i).[4] In an interview that year, Lakoff offered the opinion that "the time has come to return to the tradition of informal descriptions of exotic languages" (1974: 169).

Generative semantics owes its primary inspiration not so much to the work by Ross and Postal referred to above, but to a book that had been published several years earlier: Katz and Postal's *An Integrated Theory of Linguistic Descriptions* from 1964. This book must be considered the intellectual antecedent of generative semantics for three reasons.[5] First, it was fundamentally different in its general orientation from work in the first decade of generative syntax, yet it presaged the spirit of research that would come to characterize the generative semantic period. The primary goal of Katz and Postal was not to motivate a language-particular rule or set of rules. Rather, the book was devoted in its entirety to motivating a principle of UG, namely that transformational rules do not affect meaning, or, otherwise stated, that underlying syntactic representations contain all information necessary for semantic interpretation. (This principle has come to be known informally as the "Katz-Postal Hypothesis"). Some language-particular rules are discussed, to be sure, and a few of them are formalized, but, significantly, such work is undertaken only if they appear to be troublesome for the principle!

The second reason that Katz and Postal must be regarded as proto-generative semantics is that the *particular* principle proposed there, the Katz-Postal Hypothesis, would underlie all generative semantic theorizing. Indeed, it is argued in Newmeyer (1986) that if this principle is followed consistently, there is no way to avoid arriving at generative semantics.

Third, that book proposes a novel heuristic for "investigating syntactic structure" that would guarantee that work that followed it would downplay the importance of rules. Katz and Postal phrase their heuristic as follows:

> Given a sentence for which a syntactic derivation is needed; look for simple paraphrases by virtue of synonymous expressions; on finding them, construct grammatical rules that relate the original sentence and its paraphrases in such a way that each of these sentences has the same sequence of underlying P-markers. Of course, having constructed such rules, it is still necessary to find independent syntactic justification for them. (1964: 157)

This heuristic seemed to suggest that doing syntax involves four steps: first, formulating some seemingly reasonable principle of UG (in this case the principle of meaning-preservation); second, positing structures that support the principle; third, filling in the rules as needed; fourth, looking to see whatever other evidence might support these rules. In practice, however, the heuristic led to a diminution of the importance of rules by making them a sort of afterthought in the process of grammar construction. After all, given two levels of structure in advance, it is a trivial enterprise to construct rules linking them. As a consequence, in the fully developed generative semantics of the late 1960s and early 1970s, the third step was rarely taken, much less the fourth.[6]

Interestingly, the Katz-Postal book differs from the works that formed the principal inspirations of the other three periods in that few, if any, contemporary researchers explicitly recognized it as having played that role. The major foundational statement of generative semantics, G. Lakoff (1971a), mentions Katz and Postal only to dismiss it with the opinion that as a result of it, "a precedent had been set for the use of arbitrary markers, though that precedent was never justified" (1971a: 288).

By 1972, there were a number of signs that the hegemony of generative semantics was drawing to a close; by 1975 or 1976, the community of practitioners of that framework had collapsed utterly. Increasingly, the principles propounded by this framework proved to have serious empirical deficiencies (for extensive discussion, see Newmeyer 1986: 126–38), leading many linguists to question its theoretical foundations and to look elsewhere for a model in which to work.

For our purposes here, the interest lies in how the leading generative semanticists chose to deal with the empirical problems. For the most part, their general reaction was not to deny that they existed. Instead, it was to conclude that they would admit to a solution only if the type of data relevant for syntactic theory were expanded. So for example, difficulties with the Katz-Postal Hypothesis led generative semanticists to propose global derivational constraints (G. Lakoff 1970), which allowed transformations to have access to derivationally remote grammatical structures, in particular to semantic structures. Since there was no obstacle to encoding presuppositional information in the semantic representation of the sentence (G. Lakoff 1971b), it was an easy step to take to allow individual rules access to such information. Thus, the presuppositions of a sentence had now become data of relevance to syntax.

To give another example, by around 1970 it was clear that the principle that every anaphoric expression must have a structural antecedent in the sentence was untenable, if one were to accept the rather "shallow" conception of structure that had predominated to that time. The solution proposed by generative semanticists like Ross (1970) and Sadock (1974) was not to reject the principle, but to conclude that it could be saved if the nature of speech act represented by the sentence is encoded in the syntactic structure. As a consequence, information about speech acts had become syntactic data as well.

This broadening of the data base for syntactic theory had disastrous consequences. By 1972, the conclusion had been reached that virtually everything affecting a speaker's judgment about a sentence is a matter for syntactic analysis (for an explicit statement to this effect, see G. Lakoff 1974: 159–61). There was now so much data to be accounted for, and of such diverse types, that there was no way that it could be assimilated, much less integrated into a formal theory. Papers in late generative semantics as a consequence were often no more than lists of unanalyzed sentences that a theory might have to deal with, or were fascinating observations about language in use that were felt to bear in some way on the operation of a grammatical principle. Even important papers by leading practitioners of that framework had become little more than lists of sentences differing slighly from each other in their acceptability (G. Lakoff 1973) or a series of anecdotes about discourse conventions governing such matters as politeness (R. Lakoff 1973).

In short, by 1972 or 1973, generative semantics, which was born in the rejection of the turn toward descriptivism that was more and more characterizing work in early transformational grammar, had itself come to abandon theory-construction for a purely descriptively-oriented approach to linguistic phenomena.

Where would generative syntacticians now turn? At the time, essentially two options were offered. One was relational grammar. It is hardly an exaggeration to claim that this framework was born out of the wreckage of generative semantics. Its two leading figures, Paul Postal and David Perlmutter, were generative semanticists who had never abandoned the commitment to search for abstract principles of UG – the kind of commitment that had driven early work in that framework.[7] A number of other former generative semanticists flirted for a time with relational grammar in the mid and late 1970s.[8]

This is not the place to discuss the difficulties that relational grammar had in winning a substantial body of adherents, whether they had been generative semanticists or not (the matter is taken up in Newmeyer 1986: 218). However, suffice it to say that it was the other option that formed the basis for the next turn in generative syntax. For the remainder of the 1970s, the model for syntactic research was the paper "Remarks on nominalization" (henceforth "Remarks"), written by Chomsky in 1967 and published in 1970. This paper, and to a lesser extent Chomsky's 1971 paper "Deep Structure, Surface Structure, and Semantic Interpretation (henceforth "DSSSSI"), were to usher in the second rule-oriented period in generative syntax.

4   THE SECOND RULE-ORIENTED PERIOD: LEXICALISM

By the mid-1970s, mainstream work in generative syntax had again become rule-oriented. That is, the majority of papers were devoted to motivating or demotivating the existence of some particular rule in some language, or to arguing at what level a particular rule should apply. Most linguists carrying out such a program explicitly saw themselves carrying out the "lexicalist" program initiated in the "Remarks" paper and/or the "interpretivist" program of "DSSSSI."[9]

Reading these two papers, it is not immediately obvious why the orientation resulting from them should have turned out to be directed towards rules rather than principles. "Remarks" and "DSSSSI," like all period-initiating work, were skillful blends of arguments for general principles of UG in the context of careful attention to specific grammatical processes. The former paper contributed the idea of a richly structured lexicon, along with the first proposal of X-bar theory within generative grammar. The latter argued that superficial levels of syntactic structure are relevant for semantic interpretation. In fact, a moral of both papers was that there is more of theoretical interest "close" to the surface structure than had previously been considered to be the case.

The question, then, is why they should have initiated a rule-oriented period rather than principle-oriented one. The answer owes as much to the tactical needs of the minority within the field that agreed with these papers as to purely intellectual factors. Chomsky undoubtedly felt that the most effective way to fight the then predominant generative semantics framework was to bring syntax down to earth, so to speak, by subjecting one particular process to detailed examination. Despite the major theoretical innovations of "Remarks," the bulk of this long, intricate paper is devoted to arguing that *one* grammatical phenomenon, namely nominalization, is to be handled in the lexicon rather than via a transformational rule. The idea was that success in demolishing a nominalization transformation would challenge generative semantics as a whole, just as a card house can be toppled by removing one supporting card. The fact that Chomsky did not achieve instant success with this paper, i.e. that few generative semanticists were convinced to abandon their ideas as a result of it, led Chomsky's supporters to pick *other* rules and attempt the same sort of demolition. Hence, "Remarks" had a profound influence in shifting attention back toward language-particular rules. Once this process was set in motion, it continued even after generative semantics had fallen by the wayside.

"DSSSSI" had the same effect for a somewhat different reason. The possibility that semantic rules might apply to more than one level of syntactic structure raised the question for each particular semantic rule where it would apply. Hence it engendered a detailed look at individual rules of this sort to determine their point of application. Thus "DSSSSI" presents an interesting contrast with Katz and Postal's book. Both are concerned with the question of the level at which semantic interpretation takes place. But the conclusions of the latter drew linguistics' attention *away* from language-particular rules; if one accepts that semantic rules all apply at a single level and that syntactic rules have no effect on meaning, then that provides one less reason to be concerned with individual rules, whether semantic or syntactic. But if neither the semantic consequences of a syntactic rule nor the syntactic level at which a semantic rule applies are an automatic consequence of the theory, it becomes an essential task to study each one individually.

Two other factors steered this period in a rule-oriented direction. The first is the concern aroused by the results of Stanley Peters and Robert Ritchie (1969, 1971, 1973), who proved that transformational grammars, as they were then conceived, had the weak generative capacity of an unrestricted rewriting system (Turing machine). What this was interpreted to mean was that the then-current conception of transformational rules was so unconstrained that transformational grammar made no claim at all about any human languages except that its sentences could be generated by some set of rules. Peters and Ritchie showed further that the situation was not alleviated by either the recoverability condition or the principle of cyclic application. Thus many linguists felt that there was little point in *constraining* transformational rules, i.e. in developing principles of UG to limit their power. They concluded instead that the best hope was to *eliminate* them entirely by replacing them with presumably less powerful lexical rules. Hence transformational rule after transformational rule was subject to microscopic examination, essentially in the hope that evidence might be thereby forthcoming for its nonexistence.[10]

Secondly, the mid-1970s saw a dramatic increase in interest in formal semantics among linguists, particularly semantics of the model-theoretic variety that had been pioneered by Richard Montague. Montague himself had no interest in searching for syntactic principles of UG; in fact, he wrote: "I fail to see any great interest in syntax except as a preliminary to semantics" (1970: 373). Many linguists in this period were attracted to this idea, albeit perhaps in not such strong terms. But the attitude of more than a few seemed to be to get syntax over with as rapidly as possible, to postulate some formal rules generating the syntactic constructions of the language and get on to the interesting work – the semantics. Thus, their work in syntax, such as it was, was entirely rule-oriented.

Whatever the virtues of the two Chomsky papers, they did little at first to dislodge generative semantics from its position of hegemony. Aside from winning over the students at MIT to his position – never a difficult task for Chomsky! – they had little immediate effect in engendering significant movement among syntacticians as a whole to adopt the new approach to syntax.

To many syntacticians this work seemed like a vain attempt to prolong the life of descriptively-oriented early transformational grammar at a time when generative semantics was putting forward challenging principles of UG. Since in the common view of the time, the more distant a structure was from the surface, the closer it was to (universal) semantic representation, the generative semanticists were able to take full rhetorical advantage of the fact that their framework grounded syntax in meaning, contrasting it favorably with the rival Chomskyan school, whose attention to close-to-the-surface syntax seemed guaranteed to emphasize language-particularity at the expense of universality.

For a time, the majority of syntacticians agreed with George Lakoff's charge that Chomskyan work was not worth considering, given that "the elements used in [its] grammatical descriptions [were] arbitrary" (1972b: 76), as opposed to those of generative semantics which had a "natural (i.e. semantic) basis." And indeed a superficial examination of the "Remarks" paper, for example – which was certainly all that many generative semanticists bothered to grant to it – does convey a feeling of plodding detail, rather than that of the excitement of discovery that we find in many papers in the generative semantic framework.

But as the principles of generative semantics came increasingly to be regarded as untenable, the lexicalist work of the preceding years began to attract the attention that had been denied to it when it had first appeared. It did not take long for this work to fill the vacuum left by the collapse of generative semantics. And for the reasons discussed above, the new period that this work ushered in would be a rule-oriented one.

It was as true for the third period of generative syntactic research as it was for the first two that much of the most outstanding work produced was in the early days of the period. Actually, what are probably the two most impressive pieces of scholarship in the lexicalist framework were written while generative semantics was still in its heyday: MIT dissertations by Ray Jackendoff in 1969 and Joseph Emonds in 1970. While they were published later (in 1972 and 1976 respectively) under different titles, their original titles reveal their fundamentally rule-oriented nature: *Some Rules of Semantic Interpretation for English* and *Root and Structure Preserving Transformations*. Both are painstaking works devoted to detailed examination of particular rules in the context of defending the lexicalist alternative to the then-predominant generative semantics. The former discusses the general nature of rules of semantic interpretation along with their precise formulation and point of application; the latter argues that the structural effects of transformational rules are to a large extent predictable on the basis of their structural descriptions.

As the lexicalist period progressed, however, publications whose central theme was devoted to some general principle became increasingly rare, while those that focused on a language-particular rule or rules became increasingly common. In keeping with a principal theme of the "Remarks" paper, it became standard practice for several years to write papers demonstrating that a particular process should not be handled by means of a transformational rule or, usually equivalently, to argue that the deep and surface structures of some construction are coincident.

A look at some of the MIT Ph.D. dissertations written from 1972 on confirms both the rule-oriented nature of the period and the zeal with which the existence of once uncontroversial transformations was called into question. A five-year period saw a series of dissertations devoted to arguing that particular transformations should be greatly restricted in their scope or eliminated entirely: consider Wasow's work on Pronominalization (1972); Bresnan's on Complementizer Placement (1972); Lasnik's on Negative Placement (1972); Jenkins's on *There*-Insertion (1972); Bowers's on a variety of transformations (1973); Higgins's on a transformational account of pseudo-clefts (1973), and Oehrle's on Dative Movement (1976). In general, the prior transformational account was replaced by one involving base generation accompanied by a lexical rule relating the constructions or by a surface structure rule of semantic interpretation.

In short order, the contemporary spirit of demolishing long-accepted transformational rules extended beyond MIT. At the 1977 annual meeting of the Linguistic Society of America, over half of the generative syntax papers presented were devoted to showing that some grammatical process in some language should not be captured by means of a transformational rule.

The most common strategy used in this period to demonstrate that a process was to be handled lexically rather than transformationally appealed to the principle outlined in Chomsky (1965) that the lexicon is the repository of irregularity in language. That meant that many papers provided sets of examples showing that the process in question is not fully regular. So, for example, Oehrle (1976) appealed to the many apparent exceptions to the one-time well accepted transformational rule of Dative Movement, some of which are illustrated in the examples below, to argue that the process should be handled lexically:

(5)a I'll get a ticket for you / I'll get you a ticket
   b I'll obtain a ticket for you / *I'll obtain you a ticket

(6)a You should give back the package to the owner / You should give the owner back the package
   b You should return the package to the owner / *You should return the owner the package

Now it needs to be stressed that there is nothing more intrinsically "principled" or "explanatory" about a transformational analysis of a phenomenon than a lexical one. Nevertheless, the advocacy of a lexical solution to syntactic problems in this period tended to lead syntactic research into a new phase of emphasizing description over explanation, a phase that was accompanied by the same marked decline in standards of argumentation that was witnessed by the first two periods. This came about for two closely-related reasons: first, because it led linguists to be more concerned with surface irregularity in language than with abstract generalizations; and, second, because it tended to downplay the search for independent but interacting principles to handle complex data.

The concern with irregularity – the demonstration of which was considered to be the linchpin of the argumentation for a lexical treatment – became an obsession of the period. Many linguists of the time seemed to glory in it as, exaggerating a bit, linguistics for them had now become the search for irregularity in language. For example, Hust (1977), a paper arguing against a transformational account of the "unpassive" construction, is essentially a 35-page list of the irregularities and idiosyncrasies of the construction.

At the same time, once a process was attributed to the lexicon, the widespread conception of that component as being little more than an elaborate list provided little incentive for many linguists to probe further, to see if some deeper generalizations might be at work to account for at least some of the irregularities that had led to its being placed there. Thus having argued that a construction was not to be handled transformationally, many linguists were content simply to characterize it by means of item-specific subcategorization frames in the lexicon.

To make matters worse, as time went on, the *criteria* for transformation-hood were set so stringently that no process could hope to meet them. For example, Brame (1978) was even able to argue against a transformational rule of *Wh*-Movement on the basis of "irregularities" such as the following:

(7)a　What the hell did you see?
　b　*You saw something the hell.
　c　*You saw what the hell?

In other words, by the end of this period, "discovering" that a process was not transformational in nature had become no more than a logical consequence of the assumptions that guided the investigation.

The obsession with irregularity, and the descriptivist consequences that accompanied it, even affected work in this period which was not addressed to the question of the transformationality of a process. For example, a crucial argument for Pullum and Wilson's (1977) categorical reanalysis of the English auxiliaries depends on the irregular behavior of the marginal modals *dare*, *need*, and *ought*.

In other words, from the assumption that the lexicon is the repository of irregularity in language, many lexicalists seemed to derive the conclusion that language is one great trove of irregularity.

The bias towards lexical solutions was so great that there was rarely any attempt to show that the apparent irregularity threatening a transformational account was in reality a consequence of some independent principle. For example, to Freidin (1975), the absence of passives of the verbs *cost*, *resemble*, and *weigh*, illustrated in (8), was prima facie evidence against a transformational rule of Passive:

(8)a　*Ten dollars was cost by the book.
　b　*Mary is resembled by her sister.
　c　*A whole lot was weighed by the bag of groceries.

In his lexical analysis, these verbs were simply to be listed in the lexicon unsubcategorized for Passive. Yet an independent explanation for the ungrammaticality of sentences like (8)a–c had been put forward several years earlier. Jackendoff (1972), whom Freidin did not cite, attributed these ungrammatical passives to their violating the "Thematic Hierarchy Condition," which also accounted for unexpectedly bad reflexive and raising constructions, and at the same time explained many of Postal's (1971) "crossover" facts.[11]

To give another example of how lexical solutions went hand in hand with a lack of interest in the search for general principles, consider Brame's (1976) extended argument against verbs like *want* with surface VP complements (as in 9a) embedding full sentences, whether with lexical subjects (9b) or pronominal ones (9c):

(9)a   John wanted [_{VP} to leave]
  b   John wanted [_S John to leave]
  c   John wanted [_S PRO to leave]

Brame argued that (9)a is simply base generated, i.e. the verb *want* is subcategorized in the lexicon to take a VP complement. We need not dwell on Brame's arguments against (9)b, since by 1976 it had become well accepted that there is no rule of Equi-NP-Deletion deleting an embedded lexical subject under identity to a higher NP (for arguments to this effect, see Jackendoff 1972, chapter 5). But it is interesting to consider why he rejected (9)c. His most telling argument was that if *want* were to allow its complement to take a PRO (or dummy) embedded subject in deep structure, then nothing would prevent (10)a from being transformed by the rule of *There*-Insertion into ungrammatical (10)b:

(10)a   John wanted [_S PRO to be in class on time]
  b   *John wanted [_S there to be PRO in class on time]

Brame posed the issue clearly: the ungrammatically of (10)b could be attributed either to *want* being subcategorized for VP or to a principle that prevents PRO from occurring in nonsubject positions. It is clear that Brame took the former possibility to be the null hypothesis, since he made no attempt to formulate such a principle. Now he can hardly be faulted for not anticipating government theory (Chomsky 1980a, 1981), which would explain not only (10)b, but a host of other, seemingly disparate, phenomena. It is instructive, however, that, in keeping with the times, he chose the former alternative and opted for the most "visible" descriptive generalization, instead of searching for a broader principle at work.

Brame's solution to the problem of the complement structure of *want* illustrates the importance attributed to subcategorization features in the lexicalist period, at one and the same time the most descriptive and least explanatory way of handling any phenomenon. The message of the later lexicalist period seemed to be that since some grammatical phenomena have to be listed, rather than being attributed to some general principle, it is desirable that all should be listed.

It had become clear by the late 1970s that the nihilistic direction that lexicalist work had been heading could not last forever. If this rule-oriented period were to survive, positive proposals for rule-based systems that still maintained the lexicalists' principal results would have to be forthcoming. 1978 saw the publication of two such proposals: Bresnan's paper "A realistic transformational grammar" and Brame's book *Base-Generated Syntax*.

Both publications created a flurry of interest – particularly the former – but they probably had the effect of hastening the end of the second rule-oriented period. Bresnan's lexical entries paired subcategorization frames and functional structures in a manner that seemed to mimic directly the structural descriptions and structural changes of transformational rules. In fact, the mechanics of producing an interpretation in her theory seemed little different in content from that which would be produced by the application of intrinsically ordered transformational rules. Many linguists seemed to share Greg Carlson's "lukewarm" reaction and his feeling that the paper "did not contribute substantially to our understanding of language but instead showed that things done one way could be done another" (1983: 261).

Brame's book focussed on interpretive alternatives to long-distance transformational rules such as *Wh*-Movement and Topicalization, which he replaced by a process of "Operator-binding." But, as Kac (1980) pointed out, the notion "operator" was too obscure for it to be ascertained whether Brame presented a coherent alternative to a transformational account.

By the end of the 1970s, the rule-oriented lexicalist period had run its course.[12] At the same time, a second principle-oriented approach had arisen to replace it. This approach had its roots in Chomsky's 1973 paper "Conditions on transformations" (henceforth "Conditions").

5   THE SECOND PRINCIPLE-ORIENTED PERIOD: GOVERNMENT-BINDING

Chomsky's "Conditions" paper presented a marked contrast from the "Remarks" and "DSSSSI" papers that had preceded it by only a few years. The latter focused linguists' attention on lexical processes and close-to-the-surface generalizations in language. But the focus of "Conditions" was almost wholly on abstract principles governing the general form of grammars. The paper opens with Chomsky assuming the correctness of one principle, that of blind application of transformational rules. From that point, the reader is led inexorably to further ones, from the Tensed-S and Specified Subject Conditions, to Subjacency, to the principle that movement rules leave traces at their extraction sites, and to half a dozen more of lesser importance.

Chomsky had even less immediate success in winning over substantial sections of the population of syntacticians to the "Conditions" framework that he had had with the "Remarks" framework. Generative semanticists, most of whom by 1973 had ceased paying attention to anything that Chomsky produced, by and large ignored it. They were open to the idea of searching for general principles, it is true, but to them such principles had to be "natural" ones, i.e. ones grounded in semantics or perhaps in the processing of speech. Thus those who cared enough about Chomsky's ideas to read the "Conditions" paper at all dismissed it out of hand for its "unnatural," i.e. strictly syntactic, principles of UG.

Lexicalists, on the other hand, were appalled at the framework that seemed to grant centrality to transformational rules, even if its general thrust was to propose ways that such rules might be constrained. What is more, the abstractness of the principles in "Conditions" framework clashed head on with the increasingly concrete surface-oriented direction that lexicalists were taking.

Some lexicalists even saw in the "Conditions" framework a return to generative semantics (see Bach 1977: 140–1; Brame 1979; Gazdar 1982). Some of the analogies that were drawn between the two frameworks seem disingenuous, as, for example, identifying traces as similar in principle to the global rules of generative semantics. There is a vast difference between a theory that says that every movement rule must leave behind a trace and one that allows global rules to be constructed at will between any two random stages of a derivation. The former does not lead to a more powerful theory, only to a different theory; the latter, on the other hand, leads to a vastly more powerful theory (for more extensive discussion of the question of traces *vis-à-vis* global rules, see Chomsky 1975: 117–18).

But there is a real sense in which the "Conditions" framework, and the government-binding theory that it gave rise to, *are* like generative semantics. The frameworks share the commitment to prioritizing the postulation of a set of general explanatory principles governing UG. This has led both of them to look at the big picture first, to concentrate on the general form of grammars at the expense of constructing actual grammar fragments containing formalized rules. Both generative semanticists twenty years ago and GB practitioners today would willingly plead guilty to downplaying the language-particular, and would argue that doing so permits one to grasp more effectively the general principles of language organization.

In any event, throughout the 1970s, the "Conditions" framework was very much overshadowed by lexicalism. There were, to be sure, a handful of people developing it outside MIT, and almost from the beginning Chomsky was able to attract a following in Europe to his new approach to syntax. But numerically, the body of linguists following and developing "Conditions" was considerably smaller than that which the "Remarks" paper had engendered.

What then caused the turn to this framework around 1980? Two factors were responsible. First, as pointed out in the previous section, the lexicalist movement had sunk into a deep decline and had, for the most part, ceased to act as a major pole of attraction for students entering linguistics. But even more importantly, a qualitative change occurred in the rival Chomskyan framework.

The publication of the paper "On Binding" in 1980 and, much more importantly, the launching of GB in the following year by the publication of the book *Lectures on Government and Binding* (LGB), represented a quantum leap forward in the development of the "Conditions" framework. These works seemed to unify a great number of seemingly disparate grammatical phenomena in a conceptually simple and elegant overall framework of principles. In particular, the principles of *LGB* succeeded in subsuming many of the most troublesome and ad hoc features of the 1970s papers that followed "Conditions," in particular the bulk of the idiosyncratic filters that had been proposed.

The effect of *LGB* was explosive. It seemed as if overnight ten times as many people were working in GB as had been involved in its antecedent "Conditions" framework in the year before its publication; indeed, it seemed almost as if ten times as many people were doing generative syntax as had been before. And *LGB* had another result of interest: for the first time in over 15 years, the majority of people doing syntax were working in the framework currently being developed by Chomsky.

The fourth period of generative syntax followed the first three in the degree to which substantial progress was made in its initial years of predominance. Many early studies which were coincident with the advent of GB or which appeared soon afterwards have become classics: one thinks of Borer's (1980) showing that the set of permissible "landing sites" for movement rules follows from the theta-criterion; Rizzi's (1982) demonstration that the principle of subjacency can be maintained for Italian if it admits a slight degree of parameterization; and Huang's (1984) zero topic analysis of empty subjects in Chinese, Japanese, and other languages. In one 26-month period (July 1980 to September 1982) MIT dissertations appeared by Osvaldo Jaeggli, Hagit Borer, Luigi Burzio, Alec Marantz, Timothy Stowell, Joseph Aoun, Maria-Luisa Zubizaretta, Kenneth Safir, Denis Bouchard, and David Pesetsky. Each of them has left its mark on the shape of GB theory.

My characterization of the 1980s as a principle-oriented period might seem contradicted by the appearance of the frameworks of lexical-functional grammar (LFG) (see Bresnan 1982) and generalized phrase structure grammar (GPSG) (see Gazdar et al. 1985) almost simultaneously with GB. Both give the appearance of being lexicalist and rule-oriented; indeed, LFG appears to be a rule-oriented theory par excellence. The typical paper in this latter framework (Andrews 1982 could serve as an example) devotes most of its space to detailed examination of the linking, much of it language-particular, between grammatical relations, constituent structure, morphological markings, thematic roles, and functional structure.

Two points are in order. The first is that even if the characterization of both LFG and GPSG as rule-oriented is correct, given that so few people actually work in these frameworks, the fact is of little consequence. The body of linguists that works in LFG has barely transcended the circle around Joan Bresnan. A much larger number of linguists work in GPSG than in LFG, but even their number is relatively small. I compiled a list of what was published in 7 journals and presented at 4 conferences in 1986 and found 72 GB papers, but only 10 in GPSG and 2 in LFG (there were also 2 papers that attempted to unify GPSG and LFG).[13] There were actually more papers published and presented in relational grammar (8 in all) than in LFG, despite the popular wisdom that relational grammar was still-born in the 1970s.

The second point is that while LFG is clearly a rule-oriented theory, this characterization is less clearly true of GPSG. In its early stages, it is true that it essentially recapitulated the rule/construction homomorphism of early generative grammar: for the most part, each phrase structure rule or meta-rule served to characterize a particular construction in the language. But this is not true today; now a wide variety of interacting principles must be appealed to in the derivation of any single construction (see, for example, the discussion of the English "fronted auxiliary" construction in Gazdar et al. 1985: 60–5, in which four separate principles interact to yield the surface forms, only two of which are particular to the construction). Likewise, there are a number of cases in GPSG in which a single principle is involved in the generation of several constructions. For example, its foot feature principle is at work in the derivation of questions, relative clauses, reflexives, and reciprocals.

I have claimed that the first three periods, despite the solid advances that accompanied their coming into being, ultimately degenerated into little more than a form of descriptive linguistics with a generative veneer. Has this happened to the fourth period as well? I would answer this question in the negative, though it is clear that the potential is there for such a development. Ideally, GB should develop in the following manner: with each passing year the principles should broaden in scope, gradually subsuming what in previous work had to be stated in terms of a language-particular rule. At the same time, the degree to which each principle admits parameterization should come to be circumscribed within well-defined limits. In other words, in the ideal case, the deductive structure of the theory should become ever more profound.

It is easy to see what the alternative to this ideal case would be. In this worst-case scenario, the amount of parametric variation postulated among languages and the number of possible settings for each parameter would grow so large that the term "parameter" would end up being nothing but jargon for language-particular rule. In this scenario, as many different parameters and parameter-settings would needed as there are construction-types in language. Thus doing GB would become nothing more than listing a set of "parameters," each one a description of a recalcitrant fact in some language.

In fact, in a 1984 GLOW Newsletter, Bennis and Koster warned of this very possibility:

> Parametric syntax and phonology have quickly become very popular. Of necessity, this has led to some excesses: too often ill-understood differences among languages are simply attributed to some new ad hoc parameter. (Bennis and Koster 1984: 6)

One does feel uneasy at the language-specificity of some parameters that have been proposed within GB. Consider the papers from NELS-15 in 1985, six of which propose parameters of variation. Some of these in fact do seem fairly general, including one distinguishing nominative/accusative languages from ergative/absolutive languages; a parameter that states that in some languages, prepositions govern only elements in their subcategorization frames; and one that states that nominative case is assigned inherently in languages with no AGR. But others have the appearance of being uncomfortably language-particular, including one that states that Finnish is immune to the case filter; one which has *Wh*-Movement pass through INFL in Yoruba; and a parameter that states that a preposition must be properly governed in Dutch in order to be a proper governor itself.

It seems clear that the future success of GB – in particular, its success in avoiding the fate that befell the predominant frameworks in the three antecedent periods of generative syntax – will be determined in large part by its ability to constrain the language-particular parameterization of principles.

6   CONCLUSION

In this paper, I have suggested that we rethink the nature of the historical development of generative syntax. It is tempting to think that the history of this field can be interpreted as a straight-line development from *Syntactic Structures* to present-day theorizing, in which in gradual fashion principles of UG have allowed language-particular rules to be simplified and, ultimately, eliminated. But this tempting account is not a factual one. Instead, the field has seen alternating rule-oriented and principle-oriented periods, each of which has followed a remarkably similar course of development.

NOTES

I would like to thank David Gil, John Goldsmith, Randy Harris, Geoffrey Huck, and James McCawley for their helpful (albeit critical) comments on an early version of this paper.

1   Dingwall lists no fewer than 962 items in his bibliography. However, despite its title, *Transformational Generative Grammar: A Bibliography*, many of these works are in Zellig Harris's framework and others are in tagmemics. Additionally, a number deal with transformational generative grammar only to criticize it. Nevertheless, when all of the latter are factored out, well over 100 works remain that are written wholly within the *Syntactic Structures* framework.
2   Chomsky had proposed each of these in a series of lectures at the Linguistic Institute of the Linguistic Society of America, held at Indiana University in the summer of 1964. The lectures were later published as Chomsky (1966). The principle of cyclic application drew on work by Fillmore (1963).
3   Ross's dissertation was finally published in 1985 under the title *Infinite Syntax!*.
4   Generative semanticists joked in print about the hopelessness of writing formal rules. For example, Rogers (1972) stated that the derivation of constructions involving psychological predicates from the complex underlying structure he proposed "will probably have to be a modern miracle" (1972: 312).
5   Geoffrey Huck has suggested to me (personal communication) that *Aspects*, not Katz and Postal, should be regarded as the primary inspiration of generative semantics. As he points out, *Aspects* was the first work that thoroughly challenged the fundamental assumptions of *Syntactic Structures* on

the basis of problems that had surfaced in the execution of its research program. Some of the innovations of *Aspects*, such as the centrality of syntactic deep structure and the pairing of the Katz-Postal hypothesis with Fillmore's proposal for the cyclic application of transformational rules, were adopted unchallenged by generative semantics.

However, for the most part, what was new in *Aspects* was *reacted against* by generative semantics, in particular, the possibility of lexical rules, the approach advocated there for lexical insertion, and ultimately, the rationalist underpinnings of the theory. While it is true that the pairing of Katz-Postal with the cycle became architecturally central to generative semantics, after 1969 or so rules the rule orderings played such a small role in generative semantics that the cycle was never given more than lip service.

6   The common generative semantic practice of hinting at rules rather than stating them explicitly is presaged in Katz and Postal, as for example in the discussion on pages 141–2.

7   David Perlmutter's work prior to relational grammar was not for the most part "hard-core" generative semantics, since many of his most important contributions dealt with close-to-the-surface phenomena about which generative semantics had little to say (see, for example, Perlmutter 1970). However, he did take the essential generative semantic position that syntax and semantics are inseparable (Perlmutter 1969).

8   See, for example, Jacobson (1975), Frantz (1976), Cole and Sadock (1977), and Pullum (1977).

9   "Lexicalism," the position that derivational processes are lexical rather than transformational, and "interpretivism," the position that rules of semantic interpretation apply to superficial levels of syntactic structure, are logically independent. However, since in the 1970s it was extremely rare for a linguist to adopt one of these positions but not both, for purposes of exposition I will characterize them jointly as "lexicalism."

10 Chomsky (1980a, 1982) has argued that the Peters-Ritchie results have been "seriously misinterpreted" (1980a : 122), and that they became quite irrelevant as the conception of transformational grammar developed that sprung from the "Conditions on transformations" paper of 1973 (discussed below in section 5).

11 The Thematic Hierarchy Condition is criticized in Gee (1974) and Hust and Brame (1976). To be fair to Freidin, he explicitly considered the possibility that certain ungrammatical passives might result from some independent principle interacting with the passive rule (1975: 391).

12 Two of the descendents of 1970s lexicalism, lexical-functional grammar and generalized phrase structure grammar, will be discussed in the next section.

13 The journals are *Journal of Linguistics*, 22; *Language*, 62; *Linguistic Analysis*, 16, numbers 1–2; *Linguistic Inquiry*, 17 (articles only); *Linguistic Review*, 5, numbers 1 and 2; *Linguistics and Philosophy*, 9; and *Natural Language and Linguistic Theory*, 4. The conferences are annual meetings of the Chicago Linguistic Society, the Linguistic Society of America, the North Eastern Linguistic Society, and the West Coast Conference on Formal Linguistics.

REFERENCES

Akmajian, A. and Heny, F. 1975: *An Introduction to the Principles of Transformational Syntax*. Cambridge, Mass.: MIT Press.

Anderson, S. 1977: Comments on the paper by Wasow. In *Formal Syntax*, ed. by P. Culicover et al., 361–78. New York: Academic Press.

Andrews, A. 1982: The representation of case in modern Icelandic. In Bresnan (1982), 427–503.

Bach, E. 1962: The order of elements in a transformational grammar of German. *Language* 38: 263–9.

—— 1977: Comments on the paper by Chomsky. In *Formal Syntax* ed. by P. Culicover et al., 133–56. New York: Academic Press.

Baker, M. 1985: The mirror principle and morphosyntactic explanation. *Linguistic Inquiry* 16: 373–416.

Bennis, H. and Koster, J. 1984: GLOW Colloquium 1984, call for papers: parametric typology. *GLOW Newsletter* 12: 6–7.

Borer, H. 1980: Empty subjects in Modern Hebrew and constraints on thematic relations. *Proceedings of NELS* 10, pp. 25–38.

Borkin, A. 1972: *Where the Rules Fail: A Student's Guide. An unauthorized appendix to M. K. Burt's From Deep to Surface Structure*. Indiana University Linguistics Club Publication.

Bowers, J. 1973: Grammatical relations. Ph.D. dissertation, MIT.

Brame, M. 1976: *Conjectures and Refutations in Syntax and Semantics*. New York: North Holland.

—— 1978: *Base-Generated Syntax*. Seattle: Noit Amrofer.

—— 1979: *Essays toward Realistic Syntax*. Seattle: Noit Amrofer.

Bresnan, J. 1972: Theory of complementation in English syntax. Ph.D. dissertation, MIT.

—— 1978: A realistic transformational grammar. In *Linguistic Theory and Psychological Reality*, ed. by M. Halle et al., pp. 1–59. Cambridge, Mass.: MIT Press.

—— (Ed.) 1982: *The Mental Representation of Grammatical Relations*. Cambridge, Mass.: MIT Press.

Burt, M. K. 1971: *From Deep to Surface Structure*. New York: Harper and Row.

Carlson, G. 1983: Review of J. Bresnan, *The Mental Representation of Grammatical Relations. Natural Language and Linguistic Theory* 1: 261–80.

Chomsky, N. 1957: *Syntactic Structures*. The Hague: Mouton.

—— 1964: *Current Issues in Linguistic Theory*. The Hague: Mouton.

—— 1965: *Aspects of the Theory of Syntax*. Cambridge, Mass.: MIT Press.

—— 1966: *Topics in the Theory of Generative Grammar*. The Hague: Mouton.

—— 1970: Remarks on nominalization. In *Readings in English Transformational Grammar* ed. R. Jacobs and P. Rosenbaum, 184–221. Waltham: Ginn.

—— 1971: Deep structure, surface structure, and semantic interpretation. In *Semantics: An Interdisciplinary Reader*, ed. by D. Steinberg and L. Jakobovits, 183–216. Cambridge: Cambridge University Press.

—— 1973: Conditions on transformations. In *A Festschrift for Morris Halle* ed. S. Anderson and P. Kiparsky, 232–86. New York: Holt, Rinehart, and Winston.

—— 1975: *Reflections on Language*. New York: Pantheon.

—— 1980a: *Rules and Representations*. New York: Columbia University Press.

—— 1980b: On binding. *Linguistic Inquiry* 11: 1–46.

—— 1981: *Lectures on Government and Binding*. Dordrecht: Foris.

—— 1982: *On the Generative Enterprise*. Dordrecht: Foris.

—— 1986: *Knowledge of Language*. New York: Praeger.

Cole, P. and Sadock, J. eds. 1977: *Syntax and Semantics 8: Grammatical Relations*. New York: Academic Press.

Dingwall, W. O. 1965: *Transformational Generative Grammar: A Bibliography*. Washington: Center for Applied Linguistics.

Dowty, D. 1979: *Word Meaning and Montague Grammar*. Dordrecht: Reidel.

Emonds, J. 1970: Root and structure-preserving transformations. Ph.D. dissertation, MIT.

—— 1976: *A Transformational Approach to English Syntax*. New York: Academic Press.

Fillmore, C. 1963: The position of embedding transformations in a grammar. *Word* 19: 208–31.

Frantz, D. 1976: Equi-subject clause union. *Proceedings of BLS* 2, 179–87.

Freidin, R. 1975: The analysis of passives. *Language* 51: 384–405.

—— 1978: Cyclicity and the theory of grammar. *Linguistic Inquiry* 9: 519–50.

Gazdar, G. 1982: Review of M. Brame, *Base-Generated Syntax*. *Journal of Linguistics* 18: 464–73.

Gazdar, G., Klein, E., Pullum, G., and Sag, I. 1985: *Generalized Phrase Structure Grammar*. Cambridge, Mass.: Harvard University Press.

Gee, J. 1974: Jackendoff's thematic hierarchy condition and the passive construction. *Linguistic Inquiry* 5: 304–8.

Green, G. 1974: *Semantics and Syntactic Regularity*. Bloomington: Indiana University Press.

Higgins, F. R. 1973: The pseudo-cleft construction in English. Ph.D. dissertation, MIT.

Huang, J. 1984: On the distribution and reference of empty pronouns. *Linguistic Inquiry* 15: 531–74.

Hust, J. 1977: The syntax of the unpassive construction in English. *Linguistic Analysis* 3: 31–64.

Hust, J. and Brame, M. 1976: Jackendoff on interpretive semantics. *Linguistic Analysis* 2: 243–78.

Jackendoff, R. 1969: Some rules of semantic interpretation for English. Ph.D. dissertation, MIT.

—— 1972: *Semantic Interpretation in Generative Grammar*. Cambridge, Mass.: MIT Press.

—— 1983: *Semantics and Cognition*. Cambridge, Mass.: MIT Press.

Jacobson, P. 1975: Crossover and about-movement in a relational grammar. *Proceedings of BLS* 1, 233–45.

Jenkins, L. 1972: Modality in English syntax. Ph.D. dissertation, MIT.

Kac, M. 1980: Review of M. Brame, *Base-Generated Syntax Language* 56: 855–62.

Katz, J. and Postal. P. 1964: *An Integrated Theory of Linguistic Descriptions*. Cambridge, Mass.: MIT Press.

Lakoff, G. 1968a: *Deep and Surface Grammar*. Indiana University Linguistics Club Publication.

—— 1968b: Instrumental adverbs and the concept of deep structure. *Foundations of Language* 4: 4–29.

—— 1970: Global rules. *Language* 46: 627–39.

—— 1971a: On Generative Semantics. In *Semantics: An Interdisciplinary Reader*, ed. D. Steinberg and L. Jakobovits, 232–96. Cambridge: Cambridge University Press.

—— 1971b: Presupposition and relative well-formedness. In *Semantics: an Interdisciplinary Reader*, ed. D. Steinberg and L. Jakobovits, 329–40. Cambridge: Cambridge University Press.

—— 1972a: Foreword to A. Borkin, *Where the Rules Fail*, i–v. Indiana University Linguistics Club Publication.

—— 1972b: The arbitrary basis of transformational grammar. *Language* 48: 76–87.

—— 1973: Fuzzy grammar and the performance/competence terminology game. *Papers from the Ninth Regional Meeting of the Chicago Linguistic Society*, 271–91.

—— 1974: Interview. In *Discussing Language*, ed. by H. Parret, 151–78. The Hague: Mouton.

Lakoff, R. 1973: The logic of politeness; or minding your p's and q's. *Papers from the Ninth Regional Meeting of the Chicago Linguistic Society*, 292–305.

Lasnik, H. 1972: Analyses of negation in English. Ph.D. dissertation, MIT.

Lees, R. B. 1960: *The Grammar of English Nominalizations*. The Hague: Mouton.

May, R. 1977: The grammar of quantification. Ph.D. dissertation, MIT.

McCawley, J. 1967: Meaning and the description of languages. *Kotoba no uchu* 2, numbers 9–11.

—— 1968a: The role of semantics in a grammar. In *Universals in Linguistic Theory*, ed. by E. Bach and R. Harms, 125–70.

—— 1968b: Lexical insertion in a transformational grammar without deep structure. *Papers from the Fourth Regional Meeting of the Chicago Linguistic Society*, 71–80.

Montague, R. 1970: Universal grammar. *Theoria* 36: 373–98.

Newmeyer, F. J. 1974: The regularity of idiom behavior. *Lingua* 34: 327–42.

—— 1986: *Linguistic Theory in America* (Second edition). New York: Academic Press.

Oehrle, Richard 1976: The grammatical status of the English dative alternation. Ph.D. dissertation. MIT.

Perlmutter, D. 1969: On the separability of syntax and semantics. *Paper presented to the Forty-Fourth Meeting of the Linguistic Society of America*.

—— 1970: Surface structure constraints in syntax. *Linguistic Inquiry* 1: 187–256.

Peters, S. and Ritchie, R. 1969: A note on the universal base hypothesis. *Journal of Linguistics* 5: 150–2.

Peters, S. and Ritchie, R. 1971: On restricting the base component of transformational grammars. *Information and Control* 18: 483–501.

Peters, S. and Ritchie, R. 1973: On the generative power of transformational grammars. *Information Sciences* 6: 49–83.

Postal, P. 1970: On the surface verb "remind." *Linguistic Inquiry* 1: 37–120.

—— 1971: *Cross-over Phenomena*. New York: Holt, Rinehart, and Winston.

Pullum, G. 1977: Word order universals and grammatical relations. In Cole and Sadock (1977), 247–78.

Pullum, G. and Wilson, D. 1977: Autonomous syntax and the analysis of auxiliaries. *Language* 53: 741–88.

Riemsdijk, H. van and Williams, E. 1986: *Introduction to the Theory of Grammar*. Cambridge, Mass.: MIT Press.

Rizzi, L. 1982: Violations of the *wh*-island constraint and the subjacency condition. In *Issues in Italian Syntax*, ed. by L. Rizzi, 49–76. Dordrecht: Foris.

Rogers, A. 1972: Another look at flip perception verbs. *Papers from the Eighth Regional Meeting of the Chicago Linguistic Society*, 303–15.

Rosenbaum, P. 1967: *The Grammar of English Predicate Complement Constructions*. Cambridge, Mass.: MIT Press.

Ross, J. R. 1967: Constraints on variables in syntax. Ph.D. dissertation, MIT.

—— 1969: Auxiliaries as main verbs. In *Studies in Philosophical Linguistics* I, ed. by W. Todd 77–102. Evanston, IL.: Great Expectations Press.

—— 1970: On declarative sentences. In *Readings in English Transformational Grammar*, ed. R. Jacobs and P. Rosenbaum, 222–72. Waltham, Mass.: Ginn.

—— 1985: *Infinite syntax!* Norwood, NJ: Ablex.

Sadock, J. 1974: *Toward a Linguistic Theory of Speech Acts*. New York: Academic Press.

Selkirk, E. 1982: *The Syntax of Words*. Cambridge, Mass.: MIT Press.

Wasow, Thomas 1972: Anaphoric relations in English. Ph.D. dissertation, MIT.

Weinreich, Uriel 1966: Explorations in semantic theory. In *Current Trends in Linguistics*, 3, ed. by T. Sebeok, 395–478. The Hague: Mouton.

Williams, E. 1981: Argument structure and morhpology. *Linguistic Review* 1: 81–114.

10

Rules and Representations: Chomsky and Representational Realism

Zenon Pylyshyn

1   INTRODUCTION

Speaking as someone who has personally felt the influence of the "Chom-skyan Turn," I believe that one of Chomsky's most significant contribu-tions to psychology, or as it is now called, *Cognitive Science*, was to bring back scientific realism. This may strike you as a very odd claim, for one does not usually think of science as needing to be talked into scientific realism. Science is, after all, the study of reality by the most precise instruments of measurement and analysis that humans have developed.

Yet in the human sciences, realism about theoretical (and especially mental) entities had fallen out of fashion in the middle third of this century. Positivism, and in particular the doctrine of Operationalism, which in-flicted on psychology Bridgeman's misunderstanding of what goes on in Physics, was one reason. There were other reasons as well. Some of them may simply have been matters of fashion or of the sociology of the field: when physics was demonstrating its power over the physical world, psychology felt an urgent need to demonstrate its own scientific prowess by making predictions and by controlling behavior. Without many of the intellectual tools needed to formulate precise mentalistic theories, and without some way to understand, at least in principle, how behavior could ensue from mental structures, Cognitivism – which is, after all, very close to folk psychology – may have been left feeling old-fashioned and scientifically impotent. Whatever the reason, well-established common sense notions, such as knowledge, beliefs and desires, were banished from psychology as merely an imprecise way of speaking.

2   SOME BACKGROUND HISTORY

It seems to me that there were two things that made the difference in bringing mentalism, or perhaps I should say cognitivism, back into cognitive science. One was the work that began with Hilbert and was developed by Turing and Church and Markov and others who formulated the abstract notions of mechanism and of what we now call "information processing." This is the lineage that led to Cybernetics and later to Artificial Intelligence, though a very large proportion of the field would now probably dissociate itself from that "logicist" part of the family tree, just as earlier Logicists like Frege dissociated themselves from psychological pursuits.

The other development that brought mentalism back was the discovery that it was possible to treat some aspects of the human capacity for language in a way that made it at least appear to be compatible with mechanism. These developments encouraged many people to hope that one day we might have an explanatory theory of some of the mechanisms of linguistic competence, not just a taxonomic description of a corpus of linguistic utterances. This was, of course, the beginning of what people here have dubbed the "Chomskyan Turn." The specific results achieved in transformational grammar, coupled with the generative or procedural aspect of the theoretical mechanisms (which, after all, wore the formal garb of Post Production systems and of Markov Algorithms) gave us hope that we were on the track of a theory of language understanding and language production.

Well, we were wrong about a lot of things, and especially about how a theory of grammar might be incorporated into a theory of comprehension/production (recall, for example, the decisive failure of the "derivational theory of complexity"). Many of the early ideas of psycholinguistics were later abandoned. What remained, however, was the basic belief that *rules*, which included "rules of grammar," would play a central role in the theory not only of comprehension, but also of cognition more generally. Moreover, ever since those developments in the late fifties and early sixties, talk about rules no longer meant we were describing a corpus of behavior; rather when we spoke of rules we were referring to an internal property of some system or mind. We sometimes even spoke of the rules as being "internally represented."

However, what was meant by the phrase "internally represented" was far from clear – even to those of us who spoke that way. And it did not get any clearer if one adopted Chomsky's way of putting it when, for example, he said that a theory of the speaker/hearer "involves rules," or that the theory postulates a certain rule R "as a constituent element of [the speaker's] initial state" or "attributes to . . . [the speaker] a mental structure . . . that includes the rule R and explains his behavior in terms of this attribution" (Chomsky 1986a: 243); or when he says that a speaker is "equipped with a grammar" or "internalizes a system of rules." Yet, despite the uncertainties, none of us doubted that what was at stake in all such claims was nothing less than an empirical hypothesis about *how things really were inside the head of a human cognizer.* We knew that we were not speaking metaphorically; nor were we in some abstract way describing the form of the data.

With the passage of time, and with an understanding of computing as a concrete instance of a physical system that truly "represents," we refined and concretized our idea about what it might mean for something to be a "representation" and also what it might mean for something to "internalize a rule" – a refinement that for most Cognitive Scientists raised none of the problems that had perplexed Wittgenstein. For some of us this was the beginning of a new realism about the ontology of such mental constructs as rules and representations, as well as of such homely notions as knowledge and belief and goals. That's not to say that we all understood these notions in exactly the same way. Indeed I shall later discuss several ways in which some of us differ on these matters. But we all took it for granted that such mentalistic notions had precisely the same status in Cognitive Science as atoms and molecules have in physics. In both cases they constitute empirical hypotheses about the natural world, although of course the empirical status of the cognitive constructs is far more tentative at this time.

Chomsky was insistent on this realism from the start. He took the position that if one's best theory of some cognitive phenomena involved postulating, say, a representation X, then we have no more reason to doubt the existence of X on any a priori grounds, such as that we find it impossible to visualize how X could occur in the brain, than a physicist with comparably supportive evidence would have to doubt some particular physical hypothesis. Nor could we, in either domain, take the possibility that the phenomena *might* be compatible with some other, yet unformulated, hypothesis as an argument for some sort of inherent indeterminacy. Yet both of these avenues of resistance against realism have appeared – and are still counselled – in some quarters of Cognitive Science.

What I plan to do in this essay is to elaborate the idea of rules and representations along the lines of some of my own work, where I distinguished between "explicit representations" and what might be characterized as "implicit representations" (though in my own work I confine the term "representation" to the former case only). In the case of rules, this leads to distinguishing between rules that are "explicitly represented" or "explicitly encoded" and ones that merely describe constraints and regularities to which the system conforms, without doing so in virtue of explicitly encoded rules in the system. Since this is not a distinction that Chomsky has endorsed, I will attempt to defend this realism, perhaps even more radical than his, against some of his recently published views.

I will introduce these questions by first discussing the issue of "indeterminism" which both Chomsky and I have attacked in somewhat different but related ways. This will lead to a discussion of a notion of "strong equivalence" among cognitive models, that will in turn serve to introduce several additional points regarding the interpretation of the notion of an explicitly encoded representation and of the conditions under which such representations need to be postulated.

3   INDETERMINISM AND STRONG EQUIVALENCE

Chomsky devotes considerable attention in several of his papers (e.g. Chomsky 1984, 1986a) to various indeterminism theses – from those which say that it is impossible to decide among extensionally equivalent grammars (e.g. Quine, Lewis, Dummett, and others), to those (which Chomsky calls "Wittgensteinian") that maintain that it is never possible to decide which rules a system is following – or, indeed, whether it is following rules at all. Chomsky quite rightly admonishes these critics for their lack of imagination in considering how one might go about empirically settling such questions. In the course of these debates the distinction that remains central is between the question of what an empirical claim *is*, or what its truth conditions are, and how one might in practice go about testing it. Even if at any point in time you have no idea how some claim could be tested (e.g. the appropriate experimental methods or tools have not yet been invented), this does not make the claim either vacuous or indeterminate. So long as there is something that is being claimed – so long as the claim itself is well-defined and has truth conditions for its being true, it remains a perfectly sound scientific proposition.

I have also devoted considerable attention to pointing out the flaws in arguments put forward for various indeterminism theses by psychologists like John Anderson (Anderson 1978; Pylyshyn 1979). Now one might well wonder why anyone bothers to argue about such things: indeterminism claims are inherently boring (with the possible exception of ones that can be embedded within a theory as well developed as quantum mechanics – and even there they are only of marginal interest, in the view of many). After all, who pays any attention to the crank who says that you can't tell whether the earth is round or flat?

The reason one bothers, I think, is that the difference between a view of cognition that leads naturally to an indeterminism thesis and one that does not goes quite deep, and exposing it reveals something important about alternative ways of understanding the phenomenon of mind. Apart from issues of parsimony and generality, we do not argue about which of two equally predictive formulations of classical mechanics provides the correct explanation of planetary motion (say one which expresses the invariance principles in the form of the Hamiltonian, or directly in the form of Newtonian axioms), nor do we conclude that the issue is indeterminate. The question simply does not arise because in mechanics no ontological claims are made about the notation in which the equations are cast. To put it another way, in mechanics the empirical consequence of the equations lie in their extension, not their form or their intension.[1]

The same would hold of cognitive science if that field were about predicting overt behavior, as the behaviorists insisted.[2] Of course, there is a sense in which all we have is behavior – i.e. empirical observations – but nothing follows from this fact alone since we have to interpret the behavior we observe before it becomes relevant to the task of deciding among theories. For example, if we interpret a certain "response" as a judgment (of, say, the grammaticality of a sentence, or of whether a sentence correctly describes the contents of a picture), this piece of behavior no longer qualifies as *mere* behavior since it has a truth value – it is taken to mean something. Similarly, if we interpret reaction time as an index of computational complexity it too ceases to be mere behavior, to be accounted for in the same way as any other recorded response.

No psychologist would accept two theories of some process as equivalent just because they generated the same set of behavioral records,[3] say a list of pairs, the first of which was the predicted response of a subject and the second of which was a number representing the time at which the response occured. Suppose, for example, that two theories described behaviorally equivalent mechanisms, in that both correctly predicted the temporal pattern of a series of behavioral (i.e. input-output) events. If in one theory the time-of-occurrence was merely calculated in some way (say, using an equation) while in the other theory the time corresponded to the number of operations performed, or some other natural function of the internal processing, it is clear that the second theory would be preferred. There is nothing unusual about this case: one would get pretty general agreement about which of two behaviorally equivalent process theories is to be preferred. Psychologists are fairly reasonable people when they refrain from offering philosophical opinions about the nature of their work.

Some notion of *strong equivalence* is implicit in Cognitive Science practice. In cognitive science there is a tacitly accepted notion (perhaps not very well understood at present) of *how* some behavior is arrived at; not just how it is neurophysiologically realized, but by what cognitive mechanisms it is carried out, what cognitive states it goes through, and what rules determine the sequence of cognitive states it undergoes. Elsewhere (Pylyshyn 1984) I have tried to tease out the intuitions that the best practitioners in the field appear to share tacitly, and to attempt to sharpen and justify them. This analysis leads to a sharp distinction between what I call "the functional architecture of the cognitive system," and the "rules and representations" it uses. This distinction will be important in later considerations of the notion of strong equivalence and will, I hope, serve to sharpen the question of what it is to postulate a strong sense of "rule governed" or "representation governed" process.

4 A STRONG AND WEAK SENSE OF "FOLLOWING A RULE"

This brings us back to the central idea I want to discuss, namely the idea of behavioral regularities being based on rules and representations. When people appeal to the existence of rules in order to explain generalizations in actual and potential behavior, they may have one of a number of ideas in mind. In particular, they might justifiably claim that their theory "involves rules" or that a person has "internalized a system of rules" while making quite different assumptions about which aspects of the rule-system are empirically significant, or about *how* the system of rules enters into the causation of behavior.

There are many ways in which scientists might differ in the assumptions which they associate with a theory that contains a system of rules. These differ chiefly in terms of the intended grain of comparison between the theory, expressed in a certain standard form, and the empirical facts. For example, in the weakest case, it may be that the only empirical import of the set of hypothesized rules is their extension: *as a group* they account for regularities in behavior, for the structural relationships among behavioral elements, for judgments, and so on. The system of rules might meet what Chomsky has called "descriptive adequacy." In the the next more detailed case, the set of rules may decompose into subsets, with empirically relevant relations among the subsets. In this case, for example, there may be tie-breaking principles, ordering relations, and other conditions that hold over the subset-types, thus reifying the types themselves. This is clearly the case for the distinction among, for example, phonological and morphological rules. In that case morphological rules provide the elements and structures over which phonological rules apply.

Going down to an even finer level of comparison, the theory may reify individual rules by claiming that each rule corresponds to some individual internal object or property. In this case, for example, the fact that there are 30, as opposed to 40 rules would be empirically significant, so that if the set of 40 rules were to be reduced to an extensionally equivalent set of 30 rules the resulting system would be empirically different – they would correspond to different physical systems. Evidence for this level of ontology may, for example, come from observing that individual rules may be systematically added or deleted. That's the sort of evidence one might cite in the case of rules of etiquette or traffic rules. The reason for individuating rules may also rest on more subtle considerations, such as the fact that by individuating rules in a certain way we can show the operation of independent principles. (I shall later suggest that there is some reason to believe that this is the case of linguistic rules).

A further refinement would occur if we claimed that the individual terms and symbols in the canonical expression of each rule, as well as the structural relations among the symbols, correspond to distinct properties of the system, so that the *structure* of the expressions was empirically significant. This latter grain of comparison is precisely what I have in mind when I speak of rules, or other constructs, as being "explicitly" represented or encoded. In this case certain aspects of the actual notation used to describe what is represented in the mind, or what is "internalized," are assumed to map onto the empirical world.

Clearly it matters which of these senses of "involving rules" we intended. The motion of planets can also be described in terms of rules, but we don't want to ascribe any ontological status to the individual rules as expressed in some particular formulation of the theory, much less to the form that these rules take in some canonical notation. We don't intend the strongest of the above types of correspondence (the one I call "explicit encoding of rules"). That's why we would not say that planets behave the way they do because they *access* and *use* a representation of the rules. This is not a subtle point about how we should talk about our theories. It is a fundamental point about how we claim that some particular rule-governed system functions.

Perhaps the case of planets does not provide the best example because the "rules" in that case do not apply to representations, but to physical properties. A better example is provided by recent work on the computational processes in vision, where we see a clear distinction between implicit and explicit representations. Consider first the case of what is referred to as "early vision" (Marr 1982). The visual system is able to solve the following problem: given a 2-D image of a 3-D scene, recover the 3-D layout that gave rise to that image. This "inverse mapping" problem is underconstrained; there are an indefinite number of physically possible 3-D configurations that could have led to any given 2-D image. Yet the visual system usually produces a unique interpretation, and moreover it is generally veridical. The resolution of this puzzle consists in recognizing that the visual system behaves as though it were making certain assumptions about the nature of the physical world – assumptions which are often, though not always, satisfied in our sort of world. The "assumptions," called "natural constraints," include such things as that most of an image consists of light reflected from surfaces, that the distance of the surfaces from the perceiver varies gradually in most of the image, that certain kinds of discontinuous visual features in the image usually arise from physical discontinuities on the surface of smooth rigid 3-D objects, that contour discontinuities usually arise from occluding edges, that the light illuminating the object usually comes from above, and so on. The visual system acts in a manner that is consistent with its having made assumptions such as those sketched above about the world it is perceiving. One might wish to say that it has "internalized" knowledge of certain constraints that hold in the physical world. However, nobody actually believes that the visual system "uses" an explicit representation of these constraints. The constraints are *implicit* in the structure of the perceptual system in the sense that only interpretations compatible with the constraints are attempted.

Matters are quite different when it comes to more interpretive stages of perception. Here the process is more like that carried out by Sherlock Holmes in his examination of clues at the scene of a crime. Each piece of information is weighed in relation to Holmes' beliefs about the crime and his understanding of what goes on in the criminal mind. Holmes explicitly "uses" his beliefs and assumptions in interpreting the scene, in a way that the visual system does not "use" its assumptions about natural constraints in the early stages of vision. The two cases can be separated empirically; for example, in Holmes's case the process is what I call "cognitively penetrable." What Holmes will think next can be rationally and predictably altered with changes in his ancillary beliefs, whereas the "assumptions" in the early vision case act in a fixed manner, enter into no processes other than early vision, and are immune from changes that are attributable to differences in ancillary beliefs about the scene being perceived. The important point here is that the two distinct cases are quite different and a theory that addresses the process must specify which one is being claimed when terms like 'internalized' are invoked.

Whether it is true or not, a theory which claims that representations are "explicitly encoded" is making a much stronger claim that one which simply claims that the system has "internalized" the rules or representations. Similarly, a theory may make stronger or weaker claims about the *way* in which these representations generate behavior. Consider, for example, a theory that claims that under specified conditions the physical properties that instantiate the structures of symbolic codes cause the behavior in question (the conditions might, for example, specify that the physical codes must be in a certain relation to the system, e.g. located in a certain register or being in contact with a "read head," as in the Turing machine). Such a theory makes a much stronger claim than one which merely says that the behavior "involves" rules or representations. The difference between the weak and the strong versions of these theoretical claims is extremely important in cognitive science. Indeed, there is good reason to think that the distinction between the weak and the strong claims marks one of the unique ways in which cognizing systems are organized, in contrast with other complex systems in nature.

Note that there is no issue here with respect to the correctness of the rule-system as a description. It is not even a question of whether or not one is a realist about one's theoretical constructs. It is a question of the exact way in which the theory maps onto the world – of which aspects of the theoretical system are claimed to have ontological status. It is, to put it in terms more familiar to some people, a question of the truth conditions of the claim that a system "contains rules."

The claim that a system of rules is explicitly encoded in a certain form carries with it certain truth conditions. The rules are explicitly encoded if and only if there exists some mapping from the rules as inscribed in some canonical notation and the physical states of the system. We need not be committed to any particular form of this mapping, except insofar as we wish to claim that certain formal properties of the expression of the rules are empirically significant. If, for example, we claim that the structure of the rule (its individual parts and their relations to one another, for example their tree-structure) is empirically significant, then this structure must itself be preserved by the mapping.

The above ideas can be made mathematically precise. For example, the claim that the *form* of a symbolically encoded rule, or any other symbolic expression, is physically instantiated entails the existence of a mapping from the symbol structure to some physical properties of the machine (/brain), or to physical-state types, which is *structure preserving*. The formulation of such a mapping assumes the existence of a function from tokens of atomic symbols to distinct physical properties of the system. Then the mapping for complex elements which have a particular structural form is defined recursively in terms of this atomic-element mapping, together with the structure of the complex element. Thus the definition of the 'physical instantiation mapping' F for complex expressions would be given recursively in terms of F, assumed to be defined for *atomic* symbols, together with the *form* of the complex expression. The relevant mapping, for example, might state that for any expressions P and Q,

$$F[P\&Q] = \beta\{F[P],F[Q]\}$$

where β is some physical relation that holds between physical properties $F[P]$ and $F[Q]$ and which thereby instantiates the '&' relation among the symbolic expressions. In this schema, P and Q are replaced by whatever symbol structure occur in the specified position of the original expression. For example, in establishing the mapping from an expression such as "(A&B)&C," P and Q correspond to 'A&B' and 'C' respectively, so that the above mapping rule would have to be applied a second time to pick the relevant physical structures.

Of course, not *all* aspects of the way the expressions are written are supposed to map onto the world. For example, the particular fonts used or even the left-right order of the expressions may not matter. On the other hand, they *might*: the theory that accompanies the notation must tell us which aspects are intended to be empirically significant. This interdependence between theory and notation does not diminish the importance of the distinction between systems in which nothing about the notation is significant and ones in which the structure of certain expressions matters because the expressions are assumed to be instantiated in the system in a manner that preserves their structure.

Notice also that this particular level of correspondence, which I have referred to as "strong equivalence," does not just mean a more precise or a more detailed theory. It is a type of correspondence that has no precise parallel in physical theories,[4] because it claims that *tokens* of symbols in an expression (in this case the expression of a particular rule) map onto some distinct properties of the system in such a way as to preserve (a) the *symbol types* and (b) the *structure* of the expressions. The formula displayed above illustrates how these conditions might be met in a particular case. Meeting these conditions is functionally equivalent to "writing down" the symbols in some physical form in the system (or the brain).[5]

Explanations that appeal to such "stored symbolic expressions" are not just theories that posit a more detailed microstructure. They are theories that posit a particular kind of microstructure; a *representational* microstructure. The terms of the theory not only designate properties of the system; they designate properties of the system that have representational content – that have semantic properties.[6] The complex expression has a constituent structure that reflects the semantic structure of what it represents.

Although Chomsky has been one of the most vigorous exponents of a strong equivalence view, has spoken of linguistic processes as "computations," and has even emphasized the importance of the *form* in which rules are expressed, his writings have not acknowledged the distinction between the rules in a system being *explicitly encoded*, and a system merely implicitly *conforming to* rules – i.e. behaving as if it were following rules even though the behavior may arise from unspecified causes. Of course Chomsky is correct when he says that all we can hope to do is find the theory that best accounts for all the evidence, and that if such a theory postulates rules, then we assume that the system does indeed "contain rules." That's not the issue: everyone agrees about that. The question is, Exactly what do we take the claim of "containing rules" or "having internalized rules" to be? what are the truth conditions of such a claim? What does the claim say about the structure of the system and what does it commit us to (other than the obvious fact that by positing rules we can account for a certain range of phenomena). Some senses of "containing rules" entail consequences that other senses (equally compatible with the informal use of the phrase) do not.

I don't see how Chomsky can be noncommittal on this question, or how he can simply equate it with the question of whether the "best theory" posits rules. Before one can determine whether the best theory is justified in claiming that a system has internalized a rule we need to understand what such a claim means. As we have seen, there is a sense in which it can mean that the system conforms to the set of rules, taken as a whole. But there is also a clear sense in which it can mean that the rule is explicitly encoded. This is the strongest sense of having "internalized the rule" for it claims the strongest degree of correspondence between the rules as formulated in the theory and the structure of the system. One can't be agnostic about this issue while being a realist about strong equivalence. As in the various debates in which Chomsky has so vigorously opposed the indeterminacy thesis, one must distinguish between *what* a theory claims (what the truth conditions of the theory are), and what the evidence for the theory is. It is common to have two theories that coincide on all available evidence, yet have different truth conditions – i.e. make *different claims*.[7]

5   METHODOLOGICAL CONSIDERATIONS

Having made a distinction between several ways that a system can have "internalized" a representation (including one strong sense that is of particular interest), the question immediately arises: How do we know whether some particular sense of internalization (say the "explicit encoding" sense) is warranted in a particular case? Putting aside the purely philosophical concerns (raised below in footnote 7), it may be of interest to inquire whether there are interesting cases in which it is reasonable to conclude that explicit representations are involved. As usual, we can't specify in advance precisely what evidence will be critical for such cases. However, the way that evidence bears on specific claims depends a great deal on our understanding of the claim. One way to try to get some insight into what the strong claim implies is to examine some kinds of evidence that have in the past led us to postulate "explicitly encoded" representations or rules, at least in certain clear cases.

In what follows I will consider several kinds of evidence that have been used in Cognitive Science to try to sort out the distinction raised above. In this discussion I do not distinguish between "rules" and other forms of representations.[8] In fact, the question will be whether certain states of the system must take the form of explicit symbol structures.

The first type of evidence I will consider is concerned with so-called "higher cognitive processes". The type of evidence that can be cited in this case is quite different from that to which we typically appeal in the case of language. In the case of higher cognitive processes there are strong general reasons for holding that requirements of expressive power, as well as the productivity and systematicity of representational capacities involved in reasoning, demand symbol systems, and in particular that they require explicit structured representations. In addition, the plasticity and rationality of mental processes provides evidence for the ubiquity of explicit representation in reasoning generally. I will discuss examples drawn from the study of the "cognitive penetrability" of such processes as those involved in the use of mental imagery. Following this I will briefly raise the question of the status of linguistic representations, such as grammatical rules and the various representations of sentence structure that these rules define.

6   COGNITIVE CAPACITY AND COGNITIVE PENETRABILITY

In Cognitive Science, as in folk explanations, there appear to be two distinct kinds of explanatory principles; one that appeals to intrinsic functional properties or mechanisms, and one that appeals to the content of representations, such as knowledge, beliefs, goals and the like. This is pretty generally accepted in practice, if not in philosophical discussions. Thus nobody would think of trying to provide an explanation of why I am here and what I am doing at this moment which did not appeal to such facts as that I was invited to come here, that I was attempting to persuade you of certain propositions, and so on. This is not just a matter of convenience: the underlying empirical hypothesis is that there are certain regularities that can only be captured by the use of such a vocabulary. By contrast, nobody these days would think of giving an explanation for, say, the laws of perceived color mixing by appeal to such things as beliefs, goals, intentions, utilities, and so on.

What is the difference between the two cases just mentioned (explaining why I am here and explaining the laws of color mixing)? Let me just suggest one difference: whether perceived red and perceived yellow mix to form perceived orange is independent of what I believe I am looking at or what I believe about the psychophysics of color mixing. It is a cognitively robust psychophysical regularity. By contrast, whether I will appear at a conference at some exotic location and carry on a discourse on representation *is* dependent on all sorts of other collateral beliefs, even though it may still be quite a robust regularity (judging by my recent travel itinerary). It is, in fact, a regularity that can be readily disrupted in a way that is both systematic and rational. For example, I would not have made the trip here if someone had called me up and persuaded me that the conference had been canceled, whether or not it actually was. In other words, the invitation-accepting regularity is cognitively penetrable, whereas the color-mixing regularity is not. That's not the only criterion distinguishing the two cases, but it is one of the most important from my perspective, and I will return to it presently.

There is another way to look at this distinction that may be more revealing; namely, in terms of the distinction between cognitive capacity and representation-governed regularities. The reason that psychology cannot be viewed as concerned with predicting behavior or "accounting for variance" is that it matters a great deal *why* some particular regularity is manifested – whether it is because it is the only one possible, given the circumstances, or whether it is for some much more ephemeral reason – such as that the subject wishes to oblige, or understands it to be his task, or believes that it will serve his best interests, or just doesn't care enough to do anything more than free-associate or guess. Whenever we are concerned with *explaining* some regularity, as opposed to merely describing it, it is essential that we view the regularity against a background of what *might* have occurred given different circumstances.[9]

I would like to dwell on this point a bit since it connects my ideas on strong equivalence with the requirements for explanatory adequacy that Chomsky has so forcefully articulated over the past 25 years. I said that explaining some regularity requires that we be concerned not only with the occurrence of instances of the regularity, but also with the range of circumstances under which the regularity will remain fixed and the range under which it will vary, and in particular, with the *way* the regularity might be modulated by differences in circumstances. This is crucial: much depends on how the counterfactuals turn out. If in circumstances that differ only in terms of what a person believes or in terms of what the person's utilities are, we find quite different regularities, where the difference bears some logical relation to the difference in beliefs or goals, then we know that the regularities in question are not attributable to the person's cognitive capacity. Cognitive capacity may change, but not in ways that can be explained as rational responses to what the person believes: in other words, cognitive capacities are not cognitively penetrable.[10]

Strong equivalence of processes, as I have interpreted it, is closely tied to this distinction. In order for two processes to be strongly equivalent they must not only exhibit the same behavior (that would be extensional or weak equivalence), but they must generate the behaviors by the same cognitive mechanisms. In other words, they must have the same capacities.

The analogy here with computer algorithms is very close. In order for two computer systems to be strongly equivalent they must not only exhibit the same input-output behavior, but they must do so by means of the same algorithm and data structure – which is to say they must also have the same functional architecture, since identity of algorithm implies an identical set of basic operations.[11]

The notion of capacity I have tried to sketch above is closely tied to the distinction between the two senses of representation for which I have been arguing. If some particular cognitive regularity is part of the capacity of the system – if the system could behave in no other way over a certain range of counterfactual circumstances – then it is at least possible, barring other sorts of evidence to the contrary (some of which are sketched below), that we might get away without positing that the rules in question are actually represented. A perfectly acceptable interpretation *might be* (though it needn't be) that the system only behaves *in accordance with* rules or behaves *as if* it had certain beliefs – i.e. in a way that is consistently described in terms of the rules or beliefs. On the other hand, if the regularity was only one of many that were compatible with the system's capacity, *and* if it followed the other ones when it was rational for it to do so given the information at hand, then we need some account of how mere differences in beliefs or utilities could make that difference.

The problem to be explained is how systematic changes can occur that are attributable to differences in beliefs and utilities. More generally, it is to show how reasoning, leading to semantically characterizable plasticity, can occur in a physical system. Fodor and I have discussed this problem at length in connection with our analysis of the inadequacy of Connectionist models in accounting for reasoning (Fodor and Pylyshyn 1988). The basic argument is not unlike that given by Chomsky many years ago for the need for a generative grammar. The argument appeals to the fact that the capacity for reasoning, and for representing beliefs and other propositional attitudes in general, is both productive and systematic: in an intelligent system, the capacity to represent certain states of affairs almost never occurs in isolation from the capacity to represent systematically related and novel states of affairs, and the capacity to draw certain kinds of inferences always occurs together with the capacity to draw other kinds of inferences. This pattern of capacities is natural and involves no additional assumptions in systems that encode beliefs using a combinatorial system of codes, much as occurs in natural language. In systems that do not encode beliefs in this way, this kind of systematicity need not hold, so the pattern of capacities remains a mystery.

Thus in any system that represents beliefs by encoding them (or "writing them") in a system of symbolic codes with a combinatorial syntax and semantics (i.e. in a "language of thought"), it must be the case that if the system is capable of representing the situation P&Q it will also be capable of representing the situation P and the situation Q. Just as with natural language (which presumably encodes thoughts) if a member of a linguistic community is able to assert, say, that it is warm and sunny, he will in general also be able to assert that it is warm and he will be able to assert that it is sunny. The exceptions would be noteworthy. These include novel phrases memorized from a phrase book or idiomatic expressions that do not derive their meaning in the usual way from the meaning of their constituents.

Similarly, reasoning typically involves the application of rule schemas. Because of this we do not in general find that people are able to infer P from P&Q&R, but are unable to infer P from P&Q (e.g. are able to infer that John went to the store from knowing that John and Mary and Fred went to the store together, but are unable to infer that John went to the store from knowing that John and Mary went to the store together). A natural explanation for this regularity in the inferencing capacity is that classes of inference, such as those in the example, involve the application of a common rule schema. However, such a rule schema can only work if there are articulated symbolic expressions to which it can apply – if the beliefs in question are explicitly encoded as symbol structures. Furthermore, the rule itself – whether or not it is itself explicitly encoded in its entirety – must at least provide variables that can be bound to constituent parts of particular belief encodings. This sort of systematicity has been used by Fodor and Pylyshyn (1988) to argue that in general beliefs must be encoded by systems of symbols which have a constituent structure that mirrors the constituent structure of the situation being represented.

There is another way of viewing the need for drawing a distinction between regularities that arise from explicitly encoded representations and that arise from the intrinsic capacity of a system (or properties of its functional architecture). As every psychologist knows, when you are interested in explanatory power the first thing you have to do is minimize the number of free empirical parameters at your disposal. In higher cognitive processes, rules and representations function rather like free empirical parameters, inasmuch as they can vary from situation to situation with few independent constraints. By contrast, cognitive capacities remain more or less fixed, except for certain specified variations directly attributable to biological causes. Variations in capacity are conditioned by laws of growth, neural arborization, laws of chemistry and endocrinology, and the like. On the other hand, variations in rule-governed behavior, at least in the case of central cognitive processes, are approximately as broad as the set of computable functions. Therefore one must endeavor to attribute as much as possible to the *capacity* of the system or, in my terms, to properties of the *functional architecture*. Put another way, one must find the least powerful functional architecture compatible with the range of variation observed (or observable under some relevant condition). This is exactly the goal Chomsky declared many years ago for linguistics: find the least powerful formalism for expressing the range of human languages and you will have a formalism that you can view as intensionally (as opposed to merely extensionally) significant.

7   SOME PROPOSED CAPACITIES

Let me turn now to the question of whether certain particular cognitive phenomena can be ascribed to the intrinsic capacity of the cognitive system (i.e. its functional architecture) or whether they should be viewed as governed by representations.

Very little is known about the capacity of the central cognitive system. There is every reason to believe that it imposes strong constraints, as Chomsky has always claimed. Surely not every logically possible thought can be thought by humans. In addition, it is even more apparent that not all cognitive processes are equally complex – by whatever measure of complexity one might wish to use. Differences in complexity very likely reflect properties of the functional architecture. Indeed, measuring processing complexity using such techniques as reaction times has been used with considerable success in validating – in the sense of strong equivalence – computational models of small scale cognitive processes. Thus they provide one methodological route into the nature of cognitive capacity. Nonetheless, virtually every proposal for functions attributable to the cognitive capacity of the central cognitive system, or to its functional architecture, fails to stand up under scrutiny. Thus, for example, the laws of classical and operant conditioning appear to be cognitively penetrable (see the review by Brewer 1974) – i.e. they can be altered in a rational way by providing the subject with information (e.g. showing him how the apparatus is wired up, or explaining the reinforcement contingencies). Similarly various proposals for memory storage and retrieval mechanisms, such as holograms or quality spaces, are also inadequate because the processes being modeled are demonstrably penetrable by beliefs (e.g. the confusability profile of a set of stimuli is sensitive to what the stimuli are perceived as being, which in turn depends upon goals and beliefs). Gibson's direct perception thesis also falters on (inter alia) the facts of cognitive penetrability of much of the later stages of perception (what we see things *as*).

One of my favorite targets has been the various regularities observed in experiments in which subjects use mental imagery. Examples include the increase in time required to report a feature in a mental image when that image is made smaller, or as the location of the feature is made further away from the point on the image where one is currently focused (for other such examples, see Kosslyn 1980). Such regularities all appear to be cognitively penetrable – i.e. they can be changed in a rational way by changing what a subject takes the task to be, or what he believes would happen in the imagined situation. For example (cf. Pylyshyn 1984), if a subject is instructed to imagine a situation that he believes would involve an instantaneous switch of attention from one point of an image to another, the linear increase in reaction time with distance can be made to disappear. The conclusion in each of these cases is that the regularities obtain because the subject understands the task to be to reproduce what he believes would have happened had he been observing a real situation – and this he does very nicely because he often knows what would have happened, or can deduce it from general principles.

There have been a few interesting proposals for properties attributable to the central functional architecture. For example, there are proposals for the structure that can exist among attainable concepts – e.g. proposals by Osherson (1978) and by Keil (1979). There are even a few proposals for mechanisms involved in reasoning and problem solving, such as Newell's proposal for the primacy of the recognize-act cycle or some proposals for memory retrieval or property inheritance mechanisms. There are also proposals for resource-limited bottlenecks caused by the architecture, such as limits on working memory or on the number of internal referencing tokens available (cf. Pylyshyn, 1989). On the whole, however, nothing comparable to Universal Grammar has been proposed for the central processing system. Whether this is because we are missing a critical idea or methodology, or because our search for mechanisms has been conditioned too much by current computers, or because, as Chomsky suggests, the problem really is beyond our capacity to solve, I can't say. I can say, however, that the enterprise of taking strong equivalence seriously in Cognitive Science – which, in my view, is tantamount to the assumption that there exists something that deserves to be called Cognitive Science – is very much dependent on finding such properties; of discovering cognitively impenetrable basic capacities.

8   RULES AND REPRESENTATION IN COGNITIVELY IMPENETRABLE MODULES

Representation of beliefs, goals and other propositional attitudes is only one of two areas where explicit symbolic encodings have been postulated. The other area is in the study of such modular processes as those involved in language processing. In this case much of the process appears to be cognitively impenetrable, and therefore one of the principal reasons for inferring that they involve reasoning is not available. However, as I said earlier, cognitive penetrability, because it entails reasoning processes, is a necessary but not a sufficient reason for inferring that a process involves the manipulation of explicit representations. There are other kinds of representation-governed processes besides reasoning; and for these we require other sources of evidence.

The outstanding example of an impenetrable (or "encapsulated") process is the stage of language processing known as parsing – i.e. the stage at which only grammatical rules are brought to bear to extract the thematic structure (or the "logical form") of a sentence. At this stage the process involves operations that analyze a sentence in accordance with the structures given by a grammar. Some grammars describe the structures in terms of rules (such as phrase structure rules) whereas other describe them in terms of constraints and conditions. In either case, the question remains:

need we claim that the rules or principles are represented, in the sense of being explicitly encoded and accessed in the course of parsing?

The answer is far from obvious. There are some reasons for thinking that the rules are at least individuated, if not explicitly encoded. This is the argument made by Pinker and Prince (1988), in their critical analysis of a Connectionist model for the acquisition of past test morphemes, a model which quite deliberately eschews individual rules. As Pinker and Prince (1988) put it,

> rules are generally invoked in linguistic explanations in order to *factor* a complex phenomenon into simpler components that feed representations into one another . . . Rules are individuated not only because they compete and mandate different transformations of the same input structures (such as *break – breaked/broke*), but because they apply to different *kinds* of structures, and thus impose a factoring of a phenomenon into distinct components. Such factoring allows orthogonal generalizations to be extracted out separately, so that observed complexity can arise through the interaction and feeding of independent rules and processes. (p. 84)

The need to individuate rules has also been defended on a number of other grounds. For example, it has been based on the need to explain why there is a rough synchrony in the cross-over from the acquisition of rules in comprehension to their use in production; based on the convergence of rules inferred from judgments and those that appear to be needed for parsing or production – or (as suggested by Fodor, Bever and Garrett 1974) based on the observation that people can sometimes fail to follow some particular rules; based on the fact that certain universals appear to be stateable only over rules of a certain form; or that the parameters which specify particular languges are specific to certain formulations of grammar.

To my knowledge, however, there have been no arguments that the rules of language (i.e. rules of phonology, morphology, or syntax) are explicitly encoded. Indeed, the recent trend in linguistics has been to play down the role of rules in favor of general principles. As I have suggested, individuating rules or even principles is a different matter from claiming that they are explicitly encoded. The latter assumes that the symbolic expression of the rule or principle in some canonical notation is empirically significant – e.g. that the expression itself is mapped onto the physical system in a way that preserves its structure.[12]

Although there may be some doubt as to whether grammatical rules are explicitly encoded, there appears to be good evidence that both the output of the analysis (i.e. LF) and certain intermediate states in the parsing *are* so encoded. These have to do with the fact that certain universal properties of the language faculty appear to be stateable only in terms of certain properties of the parse tree. For example, the various constraints on movement are stated in relation to certain properties of the analysis of the sentence, and thus imply that such an analysis is actually available to the system in the course of parsing and/or generation. Attempts to design parsing systems have also suggested that not only the logical form itself, but also various intermediate stages of the grammatical analysis may be explicitly encoded. In other words it is likely that parts of the analyzed structure of the sentence appears as a symbolic code, although the rules themselves may not appear in such a form. In computer jargon, although the rules may simply be compiled into the functional architecture of the system and not accessed in interpreted mode, the data structures to which these rules apply are explicitly represented and their form is empirically significant.

9   CONCLUSION: "KNOWLEDGE" OF RULES

Finally, I want to comment on the use of the term "knowledge," especially in connection with Chomsky's use of the phrase "knowledge of the rules of grammar." Nobody has a proprietary right to the term. In fact it is widely used in a variety of ways. For example, it is frequently used as synonymous with "belief." Some people in Artificial Intelligence (e.g. Fahlman 1981) even speak of "implicit knowledge" in referring to properties of the functional architecture. This would be harmless if we still had a way of distinguishing between the strong and the weak sense of rule-governed or representation-governed processes. If when we say that someone *knows rule R* we do not imply that he has an encoded representation of R (i.e. the strong sense of rule following) we will have to invent a term meaning "has an encoded representation of R and uses it to generate instances of the behavioral regularity in question." My sense is that this is what the term means in the vernacular and I would make a plea to confine its use to this strong sense. Thus I would prefer not to speak of "knowledge of the rules of grammar," or "knowledge of the principals of UG," though I *would* speak of "knowledge of what a person meant (in uttering a particular sentence or sentence fragment)," or the knowledge that certain coreferential relations hold between parts of a sentence.

It seems to me that when I say that someone *knows P* or *believes P*, I intend you to understand that the same person, with exactly the same cognitive capacity, might not have known P, but might have believed something else, say Q, which might even entail not-P, and furthermore that it is even possible that he might yet come to believe Q under the right set of circumstances (i.e. given the right data). Of course we all know that people's beliefs cannot be changed willy-nilly, but it is part of our understanding of human nature and of rationality that under real information conditions people like you and I could come to believe pretty near the same things that I and you believe, respectively. Hope in the human race, you see, springs eternal in each of us.

NOTES

1   Chomsky (1986a) has quite rightly played down the notion of extensional
    equivalence of theories by pointing out that what we really have in mind when

we speak of "extensional equivalence" is not that two theories make all the same predictions, but that they coincide on some subset of the evidence. While this is both true and important to keep in mind, there is nonetheless a useful sense in which we can speak of two theories being extensionally equivalent; namely in cases where they are theories of a mechanism or a process. In that case it is useful to distinguish the input-output behavior of the process from the evidence that points to the detailed steps by which the process generates this input-output behavior. In cognitive science practice, the distinction between the two types of evidence usually is quite clear (although some people occasionally lose sight of it; e.g. Anderson 1978). When two theories specify different mechanisms which produce the same input-output behavior I refer to them as "extensionally equivalent" or "weakly equivalent."

2   Chomsky was fond of pointing out to the behaviorists that the parallel in physics would have been to insist that physics was the science of meter readings!

3   Psychologists, like most practicing scientists, are quite sensible people when they are engaged in doing science. This does not appear to be true, however, when they depart from this work in order to offer philosophical opinions about science. It is a strange fact about the field of psychology, that whenever psychologists do meta-science they appear inevitably to revert to behaviorism. This is true of the recent discussions about the significance of Connectionism (see the discussion of this in Fodor and Pylyshyn 1988).

4   Whether or not this makes representation-governed systems fundamentally different from other complex natural systems depends on what one takes to be fundamental. Certainly a science that deals with these systems is unlike physics, inasmuch as it is a science of a special part of the universe (it is what Fodor (1976) calls a "Special Science"). Like the systems studied by other "Special Sciences" (such as biology or economics), representation-governed systems are natural systems that function according to the basic laws of nature (i.e. the laws of physics). But equally clearly, they involve other levels of organization; not just as approximations, but as genuine levels over which explanatory generalizations can be expressed.

5   There is nothing mysterious about this notion: it's exactly what can happen in a computer when the computer is correctly described as following a rule (in the strong sense). In the case where the rule is being executed "interpretively" – when the formulation of the rule constitutes some "executable code" – there really is an explicit physical encoding of the rule that meets the conditions I have been discussing, and therefore that functionally corresponds to the rule being "written down" in the system and "read" in the course of processing.

6   To claim that such symbol structures have semantic properties is not to claim that they must represent the content of thoughts. Some of the symbols may represent things that we would not want to count as actual *thought contents*. These include various kinds of "features", aspects of the control structure or markers which keep track of where the process has reached, and so on. They may also include aspects of grammatical rules. We may not want to call these "thought contents" simply because they only have a role within some narrow and highly encapsulated system, because they do not enter into general reasoning, because the semantics of the symbols in question does not lie in the domain of the thoughts that are taking place at the time, and so on. They may be what Dennett calls "subpersonal" contents. Nonetheless, these symbols do have a semantic content: they are not just the names of physical states that

encode them (e.g. NP refers to the class of noun phrases, VP refers to verb phrases, and so on).

7   One might ask, What if two theories coincide on *all possible evidence*? Could they still be distinct theories? The answer is far from clear. In the debates over indeterminism, Chomsky has quite rightly denounced the very notion of "all possible evidence" by pointing out that this is not a well-defined class. There is no possible observation which can in principle be excluded in advance as irrelevant to some particular scientific hypothesis. That's what makes the problem of induction such a deep problem.

8   Indeed, in computer science the distinction between a rule and any other expression lies solely in what consequences following from accessing it on specific occasions. In contemporary programming languages, such as *Prolog*, the distinction between a rule and an assertion does not even exist. (Although one could perhaps think of "rules" as those assertions that have variables which may get bound differently on different occasions. But this would be a rather unusual way to view the distinction between a rule and an assertion).

9   The importance of considering a set of behaviors against a background of possibilities is important for other reasons as well. For example, it is only when a particular piece of behavior – e.g. the particular behavior I am emitting at this very moment – is viewed as a member of a certain equivalence class, that it becomes possible to explain it. Thus, if my present behavior is viewed as a member of a class of bodily movements, it calls for a different explanation than if it is viewed as a member of a class of utterances. Chomsky (1986a) has made a similar point against Wittgenstein's argument that since it is meaningless to ascribe rules to a person considered in isolation, then rule-following must be a conventional description used to predict the behaviors of members of a certain social community. Chomsky correctly pointed out that if a person is viewed as an individual whose behavior is completely unique, no scientific claims at all can be made. Theories, quite generally, apply to behaviors taken under a certain description, which means that they are viewed as non-unique both with respect to occasions and with respect to individuals.

10 Note, by the way, that this is not a deep point. It simply affirms that if you want to explain some phenomenon by appealing to the way certain mechanisms are used to process information, you can't then turn around and claim that the phenomenon is caused by the way the mechanisms themselves change. If that were true it would be a different explanation from the one you claimed you were giving. Capacities are supposed to be just those mechanisms whose behavior need not be explained in terms of rules and representations.

11 Of course it's always possible for one of the systems to explicitly emulate the functional architecture of the other and then execute the algorithm using the primitive operations provided by the emulated architecture. In that case, however, strong equivalence would only hold for the emulated system, not the original one. For more on the technical notion of strong equivalence, see Pylyshyn (1984).

12 Note that the question of whether the rules and/or principles are explicitly encoded is an empirical one, not one of principle. There is no problem in imagining a system which explicitly encodes, say the principles of GB theory, and carries out the parsing by referring to this encoding. indeed, my colleague Ed Stabler has designed a system that runs on a computer and does exactly that for Chomsky's (1986a) syntactic theory (Stabler, in press).

REFERENCES

Anderson, J. R. 1978: Arguments concerning representations for mental imagery. *Psychological Review* 85, 249–77.

Brewer, W. F. 1974: There is no convincing evidence for operant or classical conditioning in adult humans. In W. B. Weimer and D. S. Palermo, eds. *Cognition and the Symbolic Processes*. Hillsdale, NJ: Erlbaum.

Chomsky, N. 1986a: *Knowledge of Language: Its Nature, Origin, and Use*. New York: Praeger.

—— 1986b: *Barriers*. Cambridge, Mass.: MIT Press.

—— 1984: Changing perspectives on knowledge and use of language. Ms.

Fahlman, S. E. 1981: Representing implicit knowledge. In G. E. Hinton and J. A. Anderson (eds), *Parallel Models of Associated Memory*. Hillsdale, NJ: Erlbaum.

Fodor, J. A., Bever, T., and Garrett, M. 1974: *The Psychology of Language*. New York: McGraw-Hill.

Fodor, J. A. 1976: *The Language of Thought*. Sussex: Harvester Press.

Fodor, J. A. and Pylyshyn, Z. W. 1988: Connectionism and cognitive architecture: A critical analysis. *Cognition*, 28, 3–71.

Keil, F. 1979: *Semantic and Conceptual Development: An Ontological Perspective*. Cambridge, Mass.: Harvard University Press.

Kosslyn, S. 1980: *Language and Mind*. Cambridge, Mass.: Harvard University Press.

Osherson, D. 1978: Three conditions on conceptual naturalness. *Cognition*, 6, 263–89.

Pylyshyn, Z. W. 1979: Validating computational models: A critique of Anderson's indeterminism of representation claim. *Psychological Review*, 86, 383–94.

—— 1984: *Computation and Cognition: Toward a Foundation for Cognitive Science*. Cambridge, Mass.: MIT Press (Bradford Books).

—— (1989): The role of location-indexes in spatial perception. *Cognition*, 32, 65–97.

Stabler, E. (in press): *The Logical Approach to Syntax*. Cambridge, Mass.: MIT Press (Bradford Books).

11

On the Argument from the Poverty of the Stimulus

Ken Wexler

1 THE STATUS IN PSYCHOLOGY OF THE ARGUMENT FROM THE POVERTY OF THE STIMULUS

My theme is the relation of Chomsky's work to psychology. I take it that, in essence, this is the question of the relation of generative grammar to psychology. This is a large subject, and I will be able to mention only a few highlights, as I see them. It goes without saying that all the ideas I have considered on this topic owe a great debt to Chomsky. Without the example of his work, the ideas which I report here would have been impossible.

I have taken as my title, "On the Argument from the Poverty of the Stimulus" because, in my opinion, this is a central argument associated with generative grammar, possibly the argument most uniquely associated with generative grammar within current-day psychology. To see this, I'd like to review some of the psychological properties associated with the theory of generative grammar. Most important, presumably, is the reaction to Behaviorism. However, different properties result depending on what we take Behaviorism to be.

Behaviorism can be taken to be a methodological dictum which forbids theories which posit internal states. In this regard, the entire post World War II development of Cognitive Science is a reaction to the negation of Behaviorism. The positing of rules, internal mechanisms and representations is central to current day Cognitive Psychology. (I'll return to the issue of Connectionism.) Of course, generative grammar is a theory in which such representations play a central role. However, it seems to me that generative grammar is one of a number of streams of scholarship which played a role in this regard. Artificial Intelligence, Information Processing Psychology, biological approaches, all sorts of particular approaches within psychology, have come to postulate internal, cognitive representations.

Certainly generative grammar was one of the earliest, best-worked out and influential streams in this regard. However, this psychological property of generative grammar is now endemic.

Yet, from a psychological point of view, generative grammar is quite different from certain dominant streams within psychology. So there must be other properties, other reactions to Behaviorism which distinguish the approaches. The need for cognitive representations of abstract entities is really a need demonstrable at the level of description of linguistic phenomena. Constructs defined solely in terms of stimuli and responses simply can't begin to capture the nature of language or of other cognitive systems. Thus, Chomsky's early demonstration of the need for syntactic transformations was the demonstration of the existence of a particular kind of mental linguistic entity, one not definable in terms of stimuli and responses.

However, in a major way, Chomsky went beyond this and asked the question of explanation: How does the child construct her grammar? In other words, why is the adult output grammar the one that it is? Chomsky's answer notes that the attained grammar goes orders of magnitude beyond the information provided by the input data and concludes that much linguistic knowledge must therefore be innate. As Chomsky pointed out, this is an application of the classic rationalist argument from the poverty of the stimulus (we will call this the APS).

The APS is a reaction to another feature of Behaviorism – not a methodological claim, but a substantive claim, having to do with the theory of learning. Behaviorism had associated with it an empiricist theory of learning. Namely, the child is born with, in Locke's terms, a mind which is like a "blank slate." It is this feature of generative grammar, and of Chomsky's work, which is, for the most part, rejected by the mainstream approach in psychology. Namely, the usual assumption is that the child is born with no linguistic knowledge. Perhaps some general purpose learning mechanisms are innate, but no particular linguistic principles are present at birth. These have to be learned. Chomsky, on the contrary, has claimed that particular linguistic principles, of a highly detailed kind, must be innately given. The route to this conclusion is the APS.

I will concentrate in this paper on the APS and how it has come to be used in psychology. In so doing I will be passing over some other psychological properties which seem to be very much associated with generative grammar and Chomsky's work. First is the question of linguistic theory as a science of knowledge. Chomsky concludes that linguistic theory studies knowledge, not processing. Linguistic representations are representations of what a person knows. Most psychologists do not believe they are studying knowledge in the mind, but rather that they are studying processes which are taking place in time. And they believe that, in general, this is what is to be studied in the science of language. The second property that we will have to quickly pass over is Chomsky's insistence on the real nature of the entities that linguistic theory discovers. This is related to Chomsky's often repeated point that the only sense to be made out of the

notion of "psychologically real" is the notion of "true explanation."
Again, this is a point not generally accepted in psychology, even in
cognitive psychology. The mainstream assumption is that processing is real
and that "knowledge" is not something to which the property of reality is
to be attributed. However, all of these points are related to and reflected in
the APS.

APS, unlike the existence of cognitive representations, has not become
central to mainstream psychology. Psychology, for the century of its
existence as a separate field, has usually been characterized at a given time
by a central theoretical tendency, e.g. in this century, Introspectionism,
Functionalism, Behaviorism, and for the last 25 years or so, Information
Processing Psychology – a statement of mechanism. (It might turn out that
Connectionism will come to replace Information Processing Psychology –
to my mind a retrogression.) But alongside these so-called central theoretical concerns there have often existed sub-fields which continue to develop
in their own terms – physiological studies and perception provide good
examples. Linguistics and linguistic-influenced psycholinguistics are further examples. In all these fields, or at least sub-parts of them, the innatist
view, the APS, has come to be seen as natural. However, the central
theoretical tendency has not come to terms with the APS, it seems to me,
which thus remains radical from the standpoint of mainstream psychology.
In the next section I will give some examples of arguments in psychology
which have rejected (or ignored) the APS. In section 3, I will give some
examples of applications of the APS in the theory of language learning and
the study of language development.

2   PSYCHOLOGICAL ARGUMENTS AGAINST THE ARGUMENT
FROM THE POVERTY OF THE STIMULUS

There have been numerous attempts to show that the APS is mistaken and
that complex abilities can be learned without significant innate knowledge.
Among the most sophisticated of these attempts was that of Suppes (1969),
who attempted to show that a stimulus-response based learning theory
could "learn" to become any finite automaton. Now, a finite automaton is
far too simple a model for natural language, but still, it contains internal
states, which aren't directly related to responses. How could a stimulus-
response model learn to become any finite automaton? Also, all sorts of
results in learnability theory, which is an application of the APS, show that
the class of finite automata is not learnable, under input conditions which
seemed at first glance to be similar to Suppes's model. Looking into the
mathematics, the answer becomes clear. The trainer, or reinforcer, in the
model is assumed to have access to the internal state of the learner. Thus
something like mind-reading is necessary for the model to work. (For
demonstrations in different terms, see Arbib 1969, Nelson 1975, Kieras
1976, Batchelder and Wexler 1979.) Suppes's work is valuable work, in my
opinion, because it shows the empirically impossible conditions which

would be necessary in order even for the most sophisticated stimulus-response model to learn to become a finite automaton.

Or consider the recent proliferation of the Connectionist point of view. Radical Connectionism argues that symbolic representational levels don't exist. In this sense, Connectionism is a retrogression from the until-now dominant cognitive psychology, which at least assumed the necessary existence of mental representations for the purposes of descriptive adequacy. Why does Connectionism want to do away with the existence of very useful mental representations? In my view, it seems to me that a major motivation might be that the Connectionists don't want to accept the APS; one of the main claims of the APS is that there are highly specific formal aspects of grammar, unrelated in an obvious way to the information available to the learner. So Connectionism says that if the achieved abilities don't relate in an obvious way to the information available, this is because there is a highly complex, statistical kind of relation between input and output. And the output is not an abstract representation. Connectionism is a belief in a particular variety of general-purpose learning mechanism (one which might be far weaker, depending on exact definitions, than a hypothesis-formation general learning mechanism). Connectionist models in the cognitive sphere are essentially learning models which attempt to get around the APS by saying the achieved outputs aren't so complex after all. Although there are attempts to claim that the connectionist models can learn complex abilities, I know of no attempt to produce work like that of Suppes, that is, an attempt to show that connectionist models in principle can learn what appear to be complex representational systems.

Large numbers of arguments can be made against Connectionist models of language. The main thing, however, is that they don't work. There are no results. No significant piece of linguistic competence, say, can be modeled within a Connectionist system. There are very few papers about language. One of the most well-known, by Rumelhart and McClelland (1986) is concerned with an extremely trivial piece of linguistic competence, learning the particular form of the past tense of English verbs. Even on this trivial task, there are large numbers of arguments against the model (see the recent issue of *Cognition* (Pinker and Mehler, 1988) which contains reviews of this question).

Here let me just briefly mention the one other project about language learning in the Connectionist framework that I know of. Senjowski has developed a system called NETTALK that (I quote from a paper by Churchland and Sejnowski (1989: p. 25) "learns to convert English text to speech sounds." The authors say that NETTALK is "perhaps the most complex network model yet constructed," so that we should be getting a feel for the current outer achievements of Connectionism. The paper is presented in a rather confusing way, so it takes a good deal of work to figure out what is going on. The first thing to note is that the connectionist network they present does *not* convert English text to speech sounds. Rather it converts text to a sequence of "phonemes." This is somewhat surprising to many people since they have heard talks about this program in which a tape recording is presented of the "output," after some of the thousands of iterations of the Connectionist model. To my ear, the recording at first sounds like noise, as it is supposed to, and after thousands of iterations it sounds like not terribly awful synthetic speech. If a connectionist model actually learned to do this in a reasonable way, it would indeed be impressive. But how are the sounds made, since all the Connectionist model does is to learn to translate one kind of symbol (a letter) into another kind of symbol (a phoneme symbol)? Easy: the output symbols are run through DECTALK, a good piece of engineering developed by Klatt (1988) and others, which takes symbolic entities and produces physical entities. DECTALK contains thousands of rules, and is highly representational. So the real work of this output is done by a highly representational system.

So what does NETTALK do? That is, how can we state what NET-TALK's accomplishments actually are, at a level equivalent with Churchland and Senjowski's statement that it "learns to convert English text to speech sounds." Essentially, NETTALK memorizes a list of ordered pairs, which it is directly presented with. That is, the system is presented with a stream of English words and simultaneously, paired up with it, a stream of phonemes. Basically, the system learns that when the letter "b" is presented, paired with the phoneme /b/, it should memorize that this pair go together. Of course, certain letters have different phoneme correspondences depending on left and right context, for example "oo" is different depending on whether it's surrounded by a "b" and "t" in "boot," or a "b" and "k" in "book." So the program memorizes the association of a letter and a symbolic representation of a phoneme given a text of size three on each side of the target letter. That's all it does. Multiplying out a finite list of pairings by a finite number of contexts gives a finite list to memorize. Now it would be an utterly trivial matter to program the computer to perform this memorization. But this is a Connectionist model, so this learning takes place far less efficiently. At any rate, note that the reduction of the learning task to the problem of the memorization of a finite list means that the results, whatever they are, simply do not bear on the APS or on the question of the kind of complex learning mechanism that is required for language.

I want to repeat. The Connectionist model has only learned to memorize a finite list. It has not done the work to get to synthetic speech. And this for the most complex network model yet developed, perhaps. The very necessity of adding on a representational model to be able to achieve a result (the production of speech) should be ample evidence that Connectionist models haven't gotten anyplace. But note that the motivation here again seems to be the attempt to construct a general purpose learning model, to argue that there are no symbolic internal representations and that therefore learning can be general purpose.

3 PSYCHOLOGICAL APPLICATIONS OF THE APS

I want to turn in the rest of this paper to a few examples of the application of the APS, which has been central in the development of our understanding of language acquisition.

3.1 Learnability and Strong Nativism

I will discuss briefly some results in learnability theory, in order to see what is possible. Osherson, Stob and Weinstein (1986) derived a property of "strong nativism" on learnability grounds. Strong nativism is the claim that there are only a finite number of languages. (I will have to skip over the important distinctions to be made between languages and grammars.) OSW showed that, under certain assumptions, languages could be learned only if there were a finite number of them. This was interesting, because current models of generative grammar imply that there are only a finite number of grammars (this follows from the principles and parameters theory). Therefore there are only a finite number of languages, at least up to the lexicon, which itself might be finite in principle. However, the OSW assumptions seem far too strong, from an empirical point of view. Without going into details let me point out that their assumptions imply the following: no matter how much input the learner has had for language L, it is always possible for there to be a sequence S of input data from another language L' such that on that sequence S, the learner will unlearn her language and move to the new language L', that is, completely forget L. Obviously, this is far from true empirically. A reason OSW make such strong assumptions is that they want learning procedures to be very robust under ungrammatical input, but it does seem fundamentally wrong to assume that any person who had completely learned Chinese would forget it and learn English, if English input comes in. What often happens, of course, is separation into two languages, which implies that a small amount of data is enough to fix a language and then incompatible data is either ignored, or, if systematic enough, used to fix a second, different language. But because OSW rely so heavily on these assumptions in deriving strong nativism, their system is unlikely to give insight into the conditions underlying the finiteness of the number of languages.

Note, however, that there existed another derivation of strong nativism, though not called such. In "On Extensional Learnability" (Wexler 1982), I showed that the finiteness of number of languages follows from Boundedness, the assumption that all languages can be fixed on input of data which are of complexity less than a fixed complexity measure B. All that has to be assumed is that for any complexity C, there are only a finite number of input data of complexity C. This is true of all familiar measures such as sentence length (say, in terms of number of words) or derivational complexity, under the usual assumptions. The most well-worked out example is degree of sentence-embedding, as in the degree-2 theory

(Wexler and Culicover 1980). In that work it was shown that any transformational grammar of (a restricted version of) the standard theory variety could be fixed on input of complexity (degree of embedding) less than or equal to 2. Thus, by the result I mentioned, there could only be a finite number of languages. Further properties of that theory, in fact, imply that there are only a finite number of possible grammars. A more careful discussion would go into the issue of grammar vs. language and, in Chomsky's terms, extensional language vs. intensional language.

Note that both the OSW theory and my theory assume that all possible languages are learnable. This is not a necessary assumption, as Chomsky points out. Chomsky has said that it would be surprising if all possible languages were learnable. In Wexler and Culicover we allowed for this possibility by distinguishing between the possible and the attainable languages where "possible L" means Language allowed by UG and "attainable L" means a possible language which actually can be learned. Then results on finiteness etc. would only apply to the class of attainable languages, a class which might or might not have a particular elegant characterization. (It would be determined by the interaction of UG with a number of other factors.)

What is fascinating, however, is that contemporary research in linguistic theory seems to have vindicated the assumption that all possible grammars are learnable, that is, the identification of the class of possible and learnable grammars. If particular grammars are determined by the fixing of a finite number of parameters, each with only a small number of possible values, then it becomes quite plausible that all possible grammars can be learned.

And, in fact, to my knowledge, there has been no suggestion that any possible grammar within the domain of current linguistic theory can't be learned. The goal of the current principles and parameters approach is to reduce the parameters to a minimum, attaining maximum explanatory value in predicting related phenomena. And linguists are suspicious of parametric systems which have combinations of values which are not exhibited, in fact, by any existing language. The tendency, if these parametric values are found, is to say they represent an accidental gap, to explain the gap on functional grounds, or even to change the parametric theory and/or the underlying linguistic theory.

For example, consider the parametric theory of binding and its acquisition, presented by Manzini and Wexler (1987) and Wexler and Manzini (1987). Summarizing the variation literature, we presented evidence for two parameters in binding theory. The first is the "governing category parameter" (which I will discuss briefly soon). It says, very roughly, that some anaphors must have an antecedent quite locally (say, in the same clause as the anaphor) whereas other anaphors (in other languages, perhaps) may have an antecedent much further away. Call these latter "long-distance" anaphors. The second parameter, the "proper antecedent" parameter says that some anaphors can have any noun phrase (NP) as antecedent (subject to other conditions), whereas other anaphors may only have grammatical subjects as antecedents. Now, everything else being equal (and considering only "longest distance" anaphors, such as in Japanese or Chinese), there are 4 possible languages (obtained by crossing long-distance versus short-distance with subject only versus any NP antecedent). However, it has often been pointed out, as a criticism of the Manzini and Wexler theory, that it appears as if there are no long-distance anaphors with an "any NP" value for the proper antecedent parameter. That is, all long-distance anaphors demand that the antecedent be a subject. In fact, Manzini and Wexler noted this fact and provided a functional explanation for it. In general, however, linguists prefer that all values of parameters be instantiated and take it as a criticism of a theory if this is not so. (There are a number of theories which attempt to explain variation in binding possibilities while predicting the "subject only" value for proper antecedents. These theories involve movement of reflexives at LF. For the application of a theory of the latter type to language acquisition, see Wexler (1989).)

So we can conclude that linguistic theory assumes that all grammars are learnable. Note, in contrast, how different the situation is with respect to performance or processing theory. Here it is well-known that lots of grammatical sentences are not parsable. The most famous example is center-embedded sentences of more than minimal complexity, but there are many examples. For the most part, linguists do not attempt to change grammatical theory so as to characterize the class of parsable sentences.

So we have a very different situation in acquisition and in parsing, with results solid enough to suggest that the problems are fundamentally different. The question remains: why are all possible grammars learnable? The answer isn't known, but neither is the answer to a perhaps just as fundamental question – the opposite question – why is there more than one grammar?

Chomsky has suggested that it is surprising that all possible grammars are learnable. What this statement assumes, I think, is a model where the class of possible grammars is given by a module which is quite distinct from whatever accounts for learning in the human. However, if we analogize the grammar module to a biological organ, as Chomsky does, and as seems reasonable, then the growth of the grammar module should be analogized to the growth of a biological organ. And here, we don't have a major distinction between the organ itself and the processes guiding its growth, such that only some of the set of "possible" organs are grown. Really, on the strongest analogy, we would expect only one possible grammar, which, in fact, linguistic theory provides us with, up to parameters and a lexicon.

In fact, even parameters can probably be limited. For example, Borer (1984) proposed that parameters are restricted to certain properties of morphological or lexical items. In a related vein, Manzini and Wexler (1987) invoked the "lexical parameterization" hypothesis and, relating the issue to language acquisition, Wexler and Chien (1985) stated the "Lexical Learning Hypothesis." Fakui (in press) has made an even stronger hypothesis – that parameterization relates only to "functional" as opposed to lexical categories. Whatever the fate of these proposals, it seems clear that much of the direction of linguistic thinking is to state that most of the possible variation in grammars is in the lexicon.

The question remains, why is there any variation at all, or any systematic variation, that relates to "learning?" After all, there is not this kind of variation with respect to learning in the case of biological organs. Consider the strongest possibility with respect to variation that exists now. Suppose that variation is in a sub-part of the lexicon. If this is true then we should ask: why is there parametric variation with respect to the lexicon?

The lexicon is that module of linguistic theory which provides the interface between the formal system of syntax and the conceptual system. Suppose that linguistic variation exists, in evolutionary terms, because a certain (doubtless limited) amount of conceptual variation was useful, allowing for different possibilities of conceptual representation. (Or perhaps it was an evolutionary accident – there is no strong argument here.) Then it may be that the conceptual variation somehow necessitated what appears to be syntactic variation, located in the lexicon.

These suggestions are, of course, speculative. But I think it is important to make clear that it is at least as reasonable to ask the question, why is there more than one grammar, as it is to ask, why are all possible grammars learnable? I see no reason to believe that it is an accident that all grammars are learnable. Of course, it didn't have to be, but neither did it have to be that there is more than one grammar.

3.2   The Subset Problem

The APS is central to much other work in language acquisition. Consider, for example, the so-called Subset Problem. We assume that there is no negative evidence, that is, evidence which tells the child that certain sentences are ungrammatical. What empirical evidence exists, starting with Brown and Hanlon (1970), supports this assumption. Suppose a learner sets a parameter at value 0 and this yields a language which is a subset of the language obtained when the parameter is set at value 1. That is $L(0) \subseteq L(1)$. If the child ever selects value 1 as the parameter's value, in the absence of negative evidence, there will be no way for her to select value 0, which is a smaller, subset, language. The solution to this problem, as suggested by many people, is the Subset Principle, named by Berwick (1985) and extensively investigated by Manzini and Wexler (1987) and Wexler and Manzini (1987). Namely, the child will select the value of the parameter which yields the smallest language, consistent with the data she has heard. Such a learning procedure will yield the correct language in these cases.

I don't intend to discuss the many instances of the application of the Subset Principle in any detail – rather to point out how it is an instance of the APS. Namely, there is limited input data, no negative evidence, together with various possible attained structures. The solution to the problem is the usual one for the APS. Namely, assume additional knowledge on the part of the child – either knowledge of the Subset Principle together with an algorithm which makes relevant subset comparisons between 2 different parametric values or a genetically determined markedness hierarchy that is consistent with the Subset Principle. Either will do, given current empirical knowledge.

There are some interesting things to say, however. Manzini and I applied the Subset Principle to the case of variation in Binding Theory. Consider just the simplest case. Compare English and Japanese. In English, a reflexive must be bound quite locally, that is, it must have a c-commanding antecedent in a fairly local domain, as in (1).

(1)a Mary washed herself
   b *Mary said that John washed herself.

This is Chomsky's Principle A of the Binding Theory. In Japanese, both these sentences are all right with the Japanese reflexive *zebun* replacing *herself*. In other words, *zebun* can take a c-commanding antecedent arbitrarily far in the sentence. Since with respect to this (governing category) parameter *herself* yields a language which is a subset of that yielded by *zebun*, the Subset Principle implies that a local governing category is unmarked with respect to a distant governing category.

But Manzini and I note that there is also parametric variation in governing categories for pronouns, with possibly the same range of values as for reflexives, though there is less evidence for pronoun variation than for reflexives. Pronouns, however, are subject to Chomsky's Principle B. They must be free in their governing category, i.e. they can't have a c-commanding antecedent in their governing category. This can be seen in (2).

(2)a *John likes him (John = him)
   b John thinks Mary likes him (John = him)

But a moment's thought will show that Principle B and the Subset Principle imply that the larger governing category will yield a smaller language. If a pronoun had to be free everywhere in a sentence, then that language would provide a smaller language than English. Thus the markedness hierarchy for pronouns is the opposite hierarchy than the one for anaphors like reflexives.

Of course, UG could simply state two different markedness hierarchies, one for anaphors, one for pronouns, consistent with the Subset Principle. Alternatively, it might be more elegant and correct to have UG not state the hierarchies at all, but only the potential variation, and to allow the genetically determined Subset Principle to make the calculations.

Sometimes it is said that the calculations are too complex for the child. But I see no reason for this. Note, the child will not work with the language itself. After all, the language is an infinite object. There is no notion of a finite device directly computing an infinite object. Rather the child will have an algorithm for, probably fairly efficiently making the calculation on the basis of the grammars of the language. But I see no question of principle here.

It is sometimes said that the Subset Principle, because it appears to relate to a property of *languages* and not *grammars*, is an "extensional" and not "intensional" principle and therefore can't be right because, as Chomsky has argued, linguistics can sensibly study the "I-Language" but it is not clear that the "E-language" can be studied very coherently. However, I see nothing particularly "extensional" about the Subset Principle. After all, one way of instantiating the Principle in a learning device is to simply state the markedness hierarchy over the values of parameters, and that is clearly an intensional statement, part of the I-language. Even if the child calculates the subset values, as I pointed out in the last paragraph, the child does this with an (intensional) algorithm.

Furthermore, as shown in Wexler and Manzini (1987), even for the binding theory case, it can be seen that the sets of representations that go into the subset calculations are *indexed* representations. These representations are clearly part of the I-language.

The point is this: in every idea for "learning" that has been considered in linguistic-theory related acquisition, as long as data (input) are involved, these data provide a relationship to experience. That is what "learning" means. Although we have attempted to reduce learning to the minimum amount possible, nobody has succeeded in doing away with it from a coherent theory. (In Chomsky's formulations, the input is usually called the "primary data.") However, the Subset Principle is not particularly extensional, since it relates the learning to properties of the I-language.

It might be worth mentioning in passing that there *is* a suggested extensional learning theory, namely that of Chomsky (1975), where an extensional theory (called such) is quite tentatively proposed. The idea is that the grammar at any stage of development is a function of the new input data and the *language* of the preceding stage. (In more usual formulations, e.g. Wexler and Culicover (1980), it is the *grammar* of the last stage that is relevant.) As pointed out in Wexler and Culicover (1980), this theory really has to be intensional because there is no direct way for the child to compute the "language" of a grammar. One can straightforwardly formulate Chomsky's idea in an intensional theory, that is, as a specialization of the intensional theory. When formulated in this way, the idea relates learning to the I-language, although in my opinion it is far too strong a condition, not allowing the grammar a strong enough role in whatever learning has to take place. (See Wexler and Culicover (1980) for discussion of these points.) However, the discussion of these ideas took place without consideration of the possibility of maturation, which might in fact change the analysis. I will leave the matter here.

Returning to the Subset Principle, it is interesting that Lee and Wexler (1987) have found evidence that there is a stage in Korean in which the child will bind the reflexive (which is long-distance like Japanese) only locally. This is true until fairly late – age six at least. This is in accordance with a possibility allowed for by the Subset Principle. A problem remains, however; namely, why it should take so long for the child to learn the correct, long-distance value. (This is an instance of the Triggering Problem, to be discussed in the next section.) For a possible (maturational) solution, based on a theory which involves movement of the reflexive at Logical Form, see Wexler (1989).

3.3 The Triggering Problem and Maturation

I now want to mention an extension of the APS. Consider the maturational theories proposed by Borer and Wexler (1987, 1988, 1989). We note that many phenomena in language development precede other phenomena. Also, there is often a stage lasting for several months (or more) in which the child continues on with non-adult forms. Why should this be? Traditional accounts, even within modern linguistic-based research, assume that the move from the first to the second stage is based on learning. Evidence, called triggers, leads the child to the second stage.

But Borer and I have pointed to the existence of a problem here, the triggering problem. Why should it take several months for the triggering to take place? Why weren't the triggering data available earlier? We know from a number of empirical studies, including Newport, Gleitman and Gleitman (1977) that there is no teaching language, that adults don't systematically withhold the crucial data from the younger child. (See Wexler and Culicover 1980 for a review of this evidence.) So why is triggering not effective earlier? Furthermore, why is the first stage the way it is? What determines it? Why should certain stages be determined by UG as unmarked, where the markedness seems to play no role in linguistic theory itself, but is only used as a predictor of language acquisition ordering?

To take an example, consider Hyams's (1987) important work, in which she convincingly shows that at the earliest stage an English-speaking child has a null-subject language, one in which subjects can be silent, which is a characterization of such adult null-subject languages as Italian and Spanish, but not French or English. (For evidence that French is also null-subject at an early stage, see Pierce 1989 and Weissenborn 1988; for an argument that the null-subject stage cannot be attributed to processing effects, see Hyams and Wexler 1989.)

Hyams relates her analysis to the null-subject parameter, which is an important parameter in contemporary syntactic research. Her explanation of the generalizations she has found is twofold.

First, Hyams assumes that the null-subject setting is the unmarked setting of the parameter. Second, Hyams gives a learning, triggering, explanation of how English-speaking kids eventually determine that their language is not null-subject. As Hyams notes, a Subset Principle explanation doesn't work, since null-subject languages aren't subsets of non-null-subject languages. If anything, the opposite seems at first sight to be the case (since null-subject languages allow both null and non-null subjects). However, Hyams assumes a theory in which null-subject languages don't have expletive subjects, like "there." Thus hearing such expletive subjects will provide the triggering data for adult English. In other words, the two kinds of languages *don't* provide subsets of each other.

There is a Triggering problem, however, as Hyams agrees. Namely, why aren't these data effective earlier? Why are the kids in the null-subject stage until around two and a half?

Borer and I propose as a general answer to these questions the Maturation Hypothesis: that certain specific linguistic properties mature. They are not learned, that is, the underlying capacities don't require evidence to develop; they simply mature, like other biological capacities.

Before I give an example, to illustrate specific research in this regard, I want to point out how the argument that leads to the Maturation Hypothesis is really an extension of the APS. The APS says: the adult state A is of such and such a form – the information is of such and such a limited form. There is no way for the learner to get to the adult form without assuming specific innate aspects of UG.

The Maturation Hypothesis argument simply adds to the range of phenomena the time course of development. The logic is the same as the APS. We say that grammar G1 precedes grammar G2 and there is no way that the stimulus provides the relevant information for this order. Thus there must be an innately determined order.

Borer and Wexler (1987) state that Maturation is an extra hypothesis, so that everything else being equal, one would assume continuity, the assumption of unchanging abilities. Williams (1987) has replied that this makes continuity the unmarked, preferred hypothesis, the one that linguists will continue with as a working hypothesis.

But everything else is not equal. In my view, the facts demand the Maturation Hypothesis. As a comparison, consider the Innateness Hypothesis, as determined by the APS. Now, everything else being equal, the Innateness Hypothesis wouldn't be accepted, since it is more complicated than a hypothesis which says the mind is empty at birth, a hypothesis which assumes nothing. But again, everything else is not equal. As soon as we admit the simplest empirical considerations, one is driven to the Inateness Hypothesis. The same is true of the Maturation Hypothesis, though, clearly, much less has been worked out about it. Notice, by the way, how APS takes precedence in Chomsky's thinking over the somewhat vague conception of simplicity of scientific theories. There was even a time in the history of generative grammar when it looked as if the theory being developed wasn't particularly elegant. Nevertheless, based on the APS, Chomsky argued for this theory and wrote that on evolutionary considerations one wouldn't necessarily expect a simple and elegant grammar to have developed in the mind. If indeed, the current elegant theories are on the right track, we should consider ourselves lucky, but it wasn't foreordained. (This then becomes another puzzle: why is UG as elegant as it appears to be?)

I want to give an example of the Maturation Hypothesis that Borer and Wexler (1989) developed. First, consider past participle agreement in Italian. For simplicity, and to make the structure of the argument as transparent as possible in a short space, I will give all examples only in English. The past participle of an unaccusative verb – one which takes *essere*, "be" as auxiliary – agrees with the subject, as in (3).

(3)   They are gone ("gone" and "they" agree). (=They went)

In the intransitive there is no agreement, as in (4).

(4)   They have swum (no agreement between "they" and "swum")
      (=They swam)

Again there is no agreement with transitive verbs which have lexical direct objects, as in (5).

(5)   They have hit the balls (no agreement between "hit" and "the balls")
      (=They hit the balls)

But, interestingly, with a clitic object, there is agreement, as in (6).

(6)   She them has seen ("them" and "seen" agree) (=She has seen them)

There have been no satisfactory traditional explanations of these phenomena. Borer and Wexler slightly modify an analysis of Kayne's (1985), which explains the agreement patterns. Basically, the idea is that agreement is an instance of Spec-Head agreement. This fits with an assumption that is being widely investigated in grammatical theory, that basically, agreement *is* Specifier-Head agreement. Why agreement in the clitic case? Assume that the clitic is base generated where it is and has to govern the empty position associated with it, that is, the direct object position. Then considerations of government (minimality), basically a kind of locality condition, block government of the direct object position. The clitic is too far away from the object position. However, we assume, as has become accepted for Italian, that the structure of the VP is such that it contains an aux head, which has as sister a smaller VP headed by the participle.

This smaller VP has a Spec position. If an empty element (known as *pro*) is generated in this object position, it can freely move to the Spec position. Here it will be governed by the clitic and the sentence becomes acceptable, no longer violating conditions on government. However, Spec-Head coindexing and transitivity of indexing will yield agreement between the clitic and the participle.

I mention this analysis because of the following remarkable fact.

Antonucci and Miller (1975) (A&M) have shown that Italian children up to age two and a half show participle agreement with the lexical direct object. All seven children studied by A&M passed through this stage and, according to A&M, there were no exceptional sentences – they always showed the wrong agreement in all possible transitive verb, lexical object cases.

What's going on? I can only give the sketchiest suggestion of our research on these phenomena, but Borer and I have suggested that the child analyzes the transitive sentences in such a way that the adult verb phrase (i.e. the verb and direct object) is an adjective phrase, with the head verb an adjective, and the adult "object" is the specifier or subject of the AP. Assuming the child also views agreement as an instance of Spec-Head agreement, this will yield the proper agreement facts.

Now, why does the child go out of her way to come up with the wrong analysis? We assume that for the child, UEAPP, the Unique External Argument Proto-Principle, holds. (An external argument is a subject.) UEAPP says: each predicative element (i.e. each verbal element) has its own external argument (i.e. one not shared by any other predicative element).

So, in a transitive sentence there are two predicative elements (verbs), the auxiliary *have* and the participle. Each demands its own external argument. Since there is only one external argument in the adult analysis, this analysis can't satisfy the demand.

Therefore, the child creates the adjectival analysis I have indicated. (I'll skip considerations of morphology and what we know of young children's morphology that make this a plausible analysis.) We take UEAPP to be a maturationally-determined Proto-Principle. At some point – around two and a half – UEAPP simply matures away, and no longer holds. Rather, it develops into a full-blown principle, with somewhat different properties.

At that point, the child sees that she is making mistakes – by having the participle agree with the object – and reanalyzes, yielding the adult analysis. Before this, UEAPP made such an analysis impossible.

It appears as if UEAPP makes a terribly strong prediction that must be wrong. Consider intransitive sentences, like (7).

(7)   John has run

There are two predicative elements here and only one external argument. So there is no way, given UEAPP, that the child can give an analysis to a past tense intransitive sentence. Amazingly enough, data in A&M show that children at this age did not use intransitive sentences in the past tense, though they used plenty of intransitives in the present. They used unaccusatives and transitives in both present and past. Given that from a commonsensical point of view, transitives (and probably unaccusatives) are more complex than intransitives, this result yields a strong confirmation of our theory.

A&M attempt a conceptual explanation, suggesting the Defective Tense Hypothesis, namely, that children at this age don't know tense, but only aspect. Besides being implausible on the surface, child data on Polish obtained by Weist et al. (1984) explicitly disconfirm that theory and support the UEAPP analysis, although for reasons of space I won't go into it.

Let us turn to one last application that Borer and I have pursued. Consider null subjects again. Following Hyams' theory, based on Zagona's (1982) analysis, suppose that null-subject languages have a +N Infl and non-null-subject languages have a +V Infl. I won't go into the justifying details. Now, suppose the child attempts to set Infl = +V. But then, in an intransitive sentence in the present tense, there are two Vs, Infl and the verb, but only one external argument, the subject *e.g. John swims*. Thus, given UEAPP, there is no analysis even for the simple intransitive in the present tense – the first tense the child learns. However, if Infl = +N, there is no problem from UEAPP. Therefore the child, given UEAPP, will select Infl = +N. However, this implies that the language is null-subject. So English will be a null-subject language for the UEAPP child. When UEAPP is lost, the child can use the triggering evidence that Hyams notes to reanalyze English as a non-null-subject language.

The remarkable fact, again, is that, to the limits of what we can tell with current tools, the age at which an English-speaking child no longer drops subjects – about two and a half – is the same age at which the Italian-speaking child stops showing object agreement with the participle. Thus a number of facts of development which appear different on the surface all follow from a particular maturational assumption.

It is worth noting how far we have come in language acquisition, though we are really just beginning to develop explanatory theories. Maturational theory is such that it becomes crucially important not only what the attained adult grammar is, but what the order of development is, and furthermore, the age of development. If maturational development of a specific piece of linguistic competence takes place at a particular age, then the analysis of all sorts of different constructions should change at that age. The grain of the analysis has become finer.

Once again, this maturational theory is an example of an extension of the APS. One point is worth noting. In all our maturational work, Borer and I have found that every stage of the child's developing grammar is constrained by UG. Call this UG-Constrained Maturation (UGM). UGM is not necessary, given the APS. It is conceivable that the child could have a very different UG, which matures into adult UG. The child would then follow Gleitman's (1981) tadpole to frog analogy. (Gleitman doesn't propose this as a hypothesis; she simply notes that theories which posit that the earliest stages of child language are "semantic" would have to follow this line of development.) In our work, so far, however, the child's maturation displays increasing underlying abilities – e.g. the child matures to not demand a unique subject for each predicate. Similarly, Borer and Wexler (1987) propose another piece of maturational growth – that the child matures at a later age to be able to assign thematic roles out of canonical position – in technical terms, to be able to construct argument chains. (Note that a general theory of development begins to take shape – development away from particular kinds of biunique relations, and towards less restricted biuniqueness relations.)

This notion is different from the kind of maturational theory proposed by Felix (1984), in which principles mature. In Felix's conception there will be stages of the child's development in which particular principles don't govern the child's grammars. So far we have been able to maintain the more restrictive UGM. Thus we can maintain a growth theory of linguistic abilities. But I should point out again that this is not necessary, though perhaps it is natural.

If UGM is true, it joins a number of other strong properties which appear to be true, but which aren't explained by APS, ones which I have already mentioned – namely that all possible grammars are learnable, that there are a finite number of grammars and that Universal Grammar appears to constitute an elegant system. These properties (which represent puzzles) appear to form an interrelated complex that should tell us something about the fundamental nature of grammar, though precise understanding of them remains somewhat obscure.

4 CONCLUSION

In this paper I have proposed that the Argument from the Poverty of the Stimulus is Chomsky's most unique argument. It is a powerful argument at the foundation of linguistic theory and one which mainstream cognitive psychology has either ignored or rejected. I have attempted to give some examples of how the APS has been extended into related areas in the psychology of language development. Although the APS is the most powerful theoretical tool that we have available to us, there appear to be major properties of UG and its acquisition which are not explained by it. These properties constitute puzzles which for the moment, at least, remain.

REFERENCES

Antonucci, F. and Miller, R. (1975): How children talk about what happened. *Journal of Child Language* 3, 167–89.

Arbib, M. A. (1969): Memory limitations of stimulus-response models. *Psychological Review* 75, 507–10.

Batchelder, W. H. and Wexler, K. (1979): Suppes' work in the foundations of psychology. In *Patrick Suppes*, ed. by R. J. Bogdan. Reidel: Dordrecht.

Berwick, R. (1985): *The acquisition of syntactic knowledge*. MIT Press: Cambridge, Mass.

Borer, H. (1984): *Parametric syntax*. Foris Publications: Dordrecht.

Borer, H. and Wexler, K. (1987): The maturation of syntax. In *Parameter Setting*, ed. by T. Roeper and E. Williams. Reidel: Dordrecht.

Borer, H. and Wexler, K. (1988): On the acquisition of agreement. Paper presented at the 11th Generative Linguistics of the Old World Colloquium, Hungary, March 28–30.

Borer, H. and Wexler, K. (1989): The maturation of grammatical principles. Unpublished manuscript, University of California-Irvine, and MIT.

Brown, R. and Hanlon, C. (1970): Derivational complexity and the order of acquisition of child speed. In *Cognition and the development of language*, ed. by J. R. Hayes. Wiley: New York.

Chomsky, N. (1975): *Reflections on language*. Pantheon Books: New York.

Churchland, P. S. and Sejnowski, T. J. (1989): Neural Representations and Neural Computations. In *Neural connections, mental computation*, ed. by L. Nadel, I. Cooper, P. Culicover and R. M. Harnish. MIT Press: Cambridge, Mass.

Felix, S. (1984): Maturational aspects of universal grammar. In *Interlanguage*, ed. by C. Cripper, A. Davies and A. P. R. Howatt. Edinburgh University Press: Edinburgh.

Fukui, N. (in press): Deriving the differences between English and Japanese: a case study in parametric syntax. *English Linguistics*.

Gleitman, L. (1981): Maturational determinants of language growth. In *Cognition* 10, 103–14.

Hyams, N. (1987): The theory of parameters and syntactic development. In *Parameter setting*, ed. by T. Roeper and E. Williams.

Hyams, N. and Wexler, K. (1989): Pro-drop: Some alternative accounts. Paper presented at the 14th Annual Boston University Conference on Language Development, Boston, Mass.

Kayne, R. (1985): L'accord du participe passé en Français et en Italien. *Modèles Linguistiques* 7 (1).

Kieras, D. E. (1976): Finite automata and S–R models. *Journal of Mathematical Psychology* 13, 127–47.

Klatt, D. H. (1988): Review of selected models of speech perception. In *Lexical representation and process*, ed. by W. D. Marslen. MIT Press: Cambridge, Mass.

Lee, H. and Wexler, K. (1987): The acquisition of reflexives and pronouns in Korean. Paper delivered at the 12th Annual Boston University Conference on Language Development, Boston, Mass.

Manzini, R. and Wexler, K. (1987): Parameters, binding theory, and learnability. *Linguistic Inquiry* 18 (3), 413–44.

—— (1987): *Vol. 2: Psychological and biological models*, pp. 216–71. MIT Press: Cambridge, Mass.

Nelson, R. J. (1975): Behaviorism, finite automata and stimulus-response theory. *Theory and Decision* 6, 249–68.

Newport, E., Gleitman, H. and Gleitman, K. (1977): Mother, I'd rather do it myself. Some effects and non-effects of maternal speech style. In *Talking to children*, ed. by C. E. Snow and C. A. Ferguson.

Osherson, D., Stob, M. and Weinstein, S. (1986): *Systems that learn*. MIT Press: Cambridge, Mass.

Pierce, A. (1989): *On the emergence of syntax: A crosslinguistic study*. Doctoral dissertation: Department of Brain and Cognitive Science, MIT, Mass.

Pinker, S. and Prince, A. (1988): On language and connectionism. In *Connectionism and symbol systems*, ed. S. Pinker and J. Mehler, MIT Press: Cambridge, Mass. and London, 73–193.

—— Special Issue, *Cognition* 28, vol. 1, 2, pp. 1–332.

Rumelhart, D. and McClelland, J. (1986): On learning the past tenses of English verbs. In *Parallel distributed processing: Explorations in the microstructure of cognition*, ed. by J. McClelland and D. Rumelhart.

Suppes, P. (1969): Stimulus-response theory of finite automata. *Journal of Mathematical Psychology* 6, 327–55.

Weissenborn, J. (1988): Null subjects in early grammars: Implications for parameter-setting theories. Paper presented at the Thirteenth Annual Boston University Conference on Language Development.

Weist, R. M., Wysocka, H., Witkowska-Stadnik, K., Buczowska, E., Konieczna, E. (1984): The defective tense hypothesis: On the emergence of tense and aspect in child Polish. *Journal of Child Language* 11, 347–74.

Wexler, K. (1982): On Extensional learnability. *Cognition* 11, 89–95.

—— (1989): Some issues in the growth of control. Paper presented at the Workshop on Control, MIT.

Wexler, K. and Chien, Y. C. (1985): The development of lexical anaphors and pronouns. In *Papers and reports on child language development*, ed. by E. Clark and S. Levey. Department of Linguistics, Stanford University: Stanford, California.

Wexler, K. and Culicover, P. (1980): *Formal principles of language acquisition*. MIT Press: Cambridge, Mass.

Wexler, K. and Manzini, R. (1987): Parameters and learnability in binding theory. In *Parameter setting*, ed. by T. Roeper and E. Williams. Reidel: Dordrecht.

Williams, E. (1987): Introduction. In *Parameter setting*, ed. by T. Roeper and E. Williams. Reidel: Dordrecht.

Zagona, K. (1982): Government and proper government of verbal projections. Doctoral dissertation: University of Washington-Seattle.

Part III

12

On the Status of Referential Indices

Luigi Rizzi

INTRODUCTION

Sometimes, an old idea in a new context can provide the right insight. The history of the field offers various examples of concepts or techniques which, abandoned or radically revised at some point, were fruitfully resurrected within later frames of assumptions, and acquired new explanatory force and heuristic value. In this sense, the study of the history of the field can sometimes directly inspire the elaboration of the theory. Years ago, in an introductory course, Noam Chomsky forcefully argued for this unconventional view on the role of historical considerations, and stressed the importance of giving beginning students some exposure to the history of the discipline as a potential source of new insight.

The one non-technical goal that the present paper tries to achieve is to give a partial illustration of Chomsky's point through the study of a concrete case: it will be shown that a simple reflection on the historical motivation of a widely used technical device, the referential index, can allow us to improve the analysis of a significant empirical domain, at the core of the current theoretical debate on the role and properties of null elements. The asymmetric behavior of arguments and adjuncts with respect to various kinds of extraction processes will be amenable to a natural analysis, involving a simplified version of the Empty Category Principle and other minimal assumptions on the well-formedness conditions of empty categories. The presentation of the analysis will inevitably require the introduction of a certain amount of technical concepts and formal machinery used in contemporary syntactic theory. But let us start with some straightforward, non-technical considerations on the historical background.

1   THE ORIGINS OF REFERENTIAL INDICES

Referential indices were introduced by Chomsky in *Aspects of the Theory of Syntax*. The context was the discussion of the theory of reflexivization elaborated in the mid-sixties on the basis of Lees and Klima's (1963) classic article. According to this theory an NP could be deleted and replaced by a reflexive under identity with another NP in the same local environment, as in (1). Incorrect derivations like (2) would be excluded as violations of a general principle, recoverability of deletion: the information lost with the deletion of the object NP could not be locally recovered, a state of affairs excluded by the recoverability principle:

(1)a   John kicked John. $\longrightarrow$
   b   John kicked himself.

(2)a   John kicked Bill. $\xrightarrow{\times}$
   b   John kicked himself.

It soon became apparent that a version of the recoverability principle based on the simple formal identity was not sufficiently restrictive. Formally identical NPs can refer to different individuals, and in this case the reflexivization rule must be blocked: a state of affairs such that John Brown kicked John White can be properly described by (1)a, not by (1)b. The solution that Chomsky proposed was to keep a purely formal version of the recoverability principle, and to introduce the referential index as a device to encode sameness or difference of reference into the form:

> Suppose that certain lexical items are designated as "referential" and that by a general convention, each occurrence of a referential item is assigned a marker, say, an integer, as a feature [fn. omitted]. The reflexivization rule can be formulated as an erasure operation that uses one Noun Phrase to delete another ... By the recoverability condition on deletion, the reflexivization rule ... will apply only when the integers assigned to the two items are the same. The semantic component will then interpret two referential items as having the same reference just in case they are strictly identical – in particular, in case they have been assigned the same integer in the deep structure. (Chomsky 1965: 145–6)

Referentially distinct NPs would then bear different indices, a difference in interpretation would then always be reflected by a difference in form, and an optimally simple version of the recoverability principle would exclude incorrect derivations such as the following:

(3)a   John$_b$ kicked John$_w$. $\xrightarrow{\times}$
   b   John kicked himself.

In the course of the last twenty years or so the use of referential indices has evolved considerably, in part as a consequence of important theoretical developments such as the assimilation of the locality conditions on bound anaphora and movement, and the shift of focus from derivations to representations. Referential indices are often used in the recent literature to express membership of the same chain, agreement, predication, theta marking and other relations which are very different conceptually from the original use, the expression of referential dependencies between different arguments. The main proposal of this paper will be to take the name "referential index" seriously, go back to the original motivation of this device and restrict its use to cases in which a referential index is made legitimate by certain referential properties of the element bearing it. In order to evaluate the consequences of this shift, it is now necessary to come back to contemporary syntactic theory, and to the theory of empty categories.

2 ECP AND THETA-GOVERNMENT

The Empty Category Principle (ECP) is the component of syntactic theory which categorizes the distribution of traces, the empty categories which are created when syntactic positions are vacated by movement rules. The following paradigms illustrate some of the basic effects of the principle. The first example of each triple is a case of subject extraction, the second illustrates object extraction, and the third adjunct extraction, extraction of an adverbial element. The first paradigm concerns extraction from an indirect question, the second concerns extraction from an embedded declarative introduced by an overt complementizer. The third and fourth paradigms illustrate the corresponding cases in a language like Italian, which allows phonetically null pronominal subjects in tensed clauses (a null subject language):

(4)a *which student do you wonder [how [t could solve the problem t]]
   b ?which problem do you wonder [how [PRO to solve t t]]
   c *how do you wonder [which problem [PRO to solve t t]]

(5)a *which student do you think [t that [t could solve the problem]]
   b which problem do you think [t that [Bill could solve t]]
   c how do you think [t that [Bill could solve the problem t]]

(6)a ?che studente non sai [come [potrà risolvere il problema t t]]
        "which student don't you know how he could solve the problem"
   b ?che problema non sai [come [potremo risolvere t t]]
        "which problem don't you know how we could solve"
   c *come non sai [che problema [potremo risolvere t t]]
        "how don't you know which problem we could solve"

(7)a   che studente credi [t che [potrà risolvere il problema t]]
        "which student do you think that could solve the problem"
  b   che problema credi [t che [potremo risolvere t]]
        "which problem do you think that we could solve"
  c   come credi [t che [potremo risolvere il problema t]]
        "how do you think that we could solve the problem"

Let us comment on the different paradigms analytically. (4)a–b is a classical subject-object asymmetry: a subject cannot be extracted from an indirect question (*wh*-island), whereas object extraction is marginally acceptable.[1] All the versions of the Empty Category Principle (ECP) proposed since Chomsky's Pisa lectures ten years ago have tried to capture this sort of asymmetry in the following way: (4)a violates the ECP, a strong principle, (4)b does not, and its mild deviance is attributed to the violation of a weaker principle, Subjacency. A few years ago, James Huang noticed that extraction of an adjunct, as in (4)c gives rise to a violation as severe as subject extraction. Huang (1982) made the influential proposal that the two cases should be treated on a par, as ECP violations. Various formulations of the ECP proposed around the mid-eighties have tried to capture the symmetry between subjects and adjuncts.

Still, there are reasons to believe that this analogy is misleading, to some extent. A simple inspection of the other paradigms suggests a different, more complex picture. First of all, in cases of extraction from declaratives with an overt complementizer, adjunct extraction is possible, as are patterns with object extraction, as opposed to subject extraction (cf. (5)). Secondly, in cases of extraction from *wh*-islands in a null subject language like Italian, subject extraction is possible on a par with object extraction (the marginality of (6)b–c disappears if the extracted element is a relative pronoun, cf. Rizzi 1982, ch. II; the postverbal position of the subject trace is discussed later on), while adjunct extraction remains impossible (cf. (6)c). Paradigm (7) illustrates the different types of extraction from a *that* clause in a null subject language: here all three cases are possible. Particularly significant in the present context are (5)–(6), in that they manifest a double dissociation between subject and adjunct extraction. This casts serious doubts on the validity of the generalization suggested by (4). Moreover, a single theoretical statement does not seem to suffice to properly capture this articulated picture: there are too many distinctions to be drawn.

The theoretical path that I will provisionally follow (and later revise) is the one initiated by Jaeggli (1982), and recently developed by many linguists (Jaeggli 1985; Stowell 1985; Torrego 1985; Koopman and Sportiche 1986; Chomsky 1986b; Contreras 1986; Aoun, Hornstein, Lightfoot and Weinberg 1987; Rizzi 1987; etc.) according to which ECP consists of two clauses which must be simultaneously fulfilled. To phrase the idea within a proper theoretical context, we can think of the theory of each type of null element as consisting of two comonents: a principle of formal licensing, which characterizes the local environment in which the null element can be found; and a principle of identification, which recovers some contentive property of the null element on the basis of the phonetically realized environment (see Rizzi 1986 for more detailed discussion in the context of the theory of null pronominals). For the moment, I will adopt the following version of the ECP module (which is in essence the approach of Stowell 1985; see also Rizzi 1987 for detailed motivation of this particular way of phrasing the principle):

(8) ECP:
    Formal licensing: a trace must be canonically head-governed;
    Identification: a trace must be theta-governed, or antecedent-governed.

Government is the fundamental structural relation holding in a local environment such that no barrier intervenes between the governer and the governee (Chomsky 1986b). Canonical head-government is government by a head in the fundamental direction that the language chooses (left to right in VO languages, right to left in OV languages: see Kayne 1984). Theta-government is government by a theta assigner (e.g. government of the object by a theta-assigning verb), and antecedent-government is government by an antecedent, an element which governs and binds the governee (but see below for a more general formulation).

We can now see how this system properly accounts for the paradigms in (4)–(7). In (4)a the subject trace is not canonically head-governed. It is head-governed by Infl, but from right to left, hence non-canonically in English, a VO language. The formal licensing component of the ECP is thus violated. The identification component is also violated: the governor of the subject trace, Infl, is not a theta assigner, hence the subject trace is not theta-governed; it is not antecedent-governed either because its antecedent, the *wh* phrase *which student*, is too far away to govern it.[2]

The structure is then ruled out as a (double) violation of the ECP module. On the other hand, (4)b is ruled in, as far as ECP is concerned. Here we have to take into account two traces. Consider first the object trace: it is canonically head-governed by the verb, moreover it is theta-governed by the verb, hence both parts of the ECP are met. As for the trace of *how*, the latter being a VP adverbial, it is canonically head-governed by the verb (see Rizzi 1987 for relevant evidence and for a discussion of VP-external adverbials), and the formal licensing part is thus fulfilled. The adjunct trace is not theta-governed, but it is antecedent-governed by *how* in the local Comp, so that both components of the ECP are met. The mild deviance of the example is attributed to a Subjacency violation, given an appropriate counting of Subjacency barriers (Chomsky 1986b).[3]

Consider now (4)c. The object trace passes the ECP test, but the adjunct trace does not. It meets the canonical head-government requirement but not the identification requirement. The adjunct trace is not theta-governed, nor is it antecedent-governed, its antecedent *how* being too far away. The structure is thus ruled out by the ECP module. Within this account, the ill-formedness of (4)a and (4)c still receive a uniform account through the ECP, but the parallelism is partial: (4)a violates both clauses of the ECP, while (4)c violates only the identification requirement.

Consider now (5). In (5)a the subject trace meets the identification requirement, being antecedent-governed by the trace in Comp (at least in the system of Relativized Minimality), but it fails to meet the formal licensing requirement: it is head-governed by Infl, but non-canonically.[4]

In (5)b both the formal licensing and the identification requirement on the object trace are met by the verb, which canonically head-governs and theta-governs it. Moreover there is no subjacency violation, and the structure is fully acceptable. In (5)c the adjunct variable is canonically head-governed by the verb; moreover, it is antecedent-governed by the trace in Comp; in turn, the trace in Comp is canonically head-governed by the main verb and antecedent-governed by the operator in the main Comp. The two requirements of the ECP are thus met separately in this case.

Why is it that subject extraction is systematically possible from *wh*-islands and across overt complementizers in languages like Italian? It is well known that in these languages the subject can be placed in VP-final position, i.e. alongside (9)a we have (9)b, where the preverbal subject position is filled by the phonetically null expletive pronominal *pro*:

(9)a [un mio studente] [ha] [risolto il problema]
      "a student of mine has solved the problem"
   b *pro* [ha] [risolto il problema] [un mio studente]
      "has solved the problem a student of mine"

It is then natural to analyze such cases as (6)a, (7)a as involving movement of the subject of postverbal position (see Rizzi 1982, ch. IV, and, for important confirming evidence, Brandi and Cordin 1981). The subject trace therefore is canonically head-governed by Infl here, and the first requirement of the ECP is met. How is the identification requirement fulfilled? We can provisionally assume that the subject trace right-adjacent to the VP is theta governed by the VP (we will come back to this point later on). The analysis of (6)b–c, (7)b–c is the same as in the corresponding cases in English.

3 AGAINST THETA-GOVERNMENT

The approach to the ECP presented in the preceding section achieves a remarkable descriptive and explanatory success. It treats in a natural and

minimal way the various argument-adjunct asymmetries, making unnecessary a number of auxiliary assumptions required by other approaches, in
particular the assumption that ECP applies at distinct levels for arguments
and adjuncts (as in the influential trend initiated by Lasnik and Saito 1984).
Moreover, it successfully deals with the major cross-linguistic variation
attested in this domain.

Still, there are good reasons to doubt of the overall correctness of this
approach. There are, first of all, fairly obvious conceptual arguments
against the form of the ECP given in (8). Theta-government is in most
cases (perhaps in all cases, depending on the analysis of (6)a, a kind of
head-government, so that both clauses of the ECP require some sort of
head-government. One should wonder why. There appears to be a
disturbing conceptual redundancy in the system. A second problematic
property has to do with the disjunctive formulation of the second clause of
the ECP. Disjunctive statements are intrinsically unsatisfactory. Admitting
a disjunctive formulation amounts to admitting that the nature of a
generalization is not understood: if I write a principle as saying that either
property A or property B must be fulfilled, I am implicitly admitting that I
don't know the nature of the formal or functional equivalence holding of A
and B. Of course a disjunctive formulation can turn out to be extremely
productive, and even illuminating at certain stages of the understanding of
an issue (the whole history of the ECP is a good case in point), but the
desideratum of avoiding disjunctions is an important one, even in the face
of significant descriptive success.

Theta-government is at the intersection of the two conceptual problems.
It is then reasonable to single this notion out for further scrutiny. One
possible approach would be to keep the principle essentially as it is, and try
to do away with the explicit reference to theta-government by formally
unifying it with antecedent-government, as in Stowell (1981). We would
like to develop a different approach, departing more radically from
familiar formulations of the principle. Let us first of all take into account
some empirical arguments against theta-government.

Consider first lexically selected adverbials. A verb like *se comporter* (to
behave) in French obligatorily selects a manner adverbial and optionally an
argumental comitative complement[5]:

(10)   Jean se comporte *(bien) avec les amis
        "Jean behaves (well) with friends"

If we take seriously (the spirit of) the program of reducing categorical
selection to semantic selection (Grimshaw 1979; Pesetsky 1982; Chomsky
1986a), and we make the minimal assumption that semantic selection is
expressed by the thematic (theta) grid in Stowell's (1981) sense, the
inescapable conclusion is that the adverbial is mentioned in the theta grid
of the verb: there is no other way to express lexical selection within this
restrictive program. But then, if the adverbial is theta-marked, it is also

theta-governed by the verb; therefore, a theory of the ECP like the one described in section 2 would predict it to behave on a par with arguments with respect to extraction, in particular to be freely extractable from *wh*-islands. This prediction is incorrect: lexically selected adverbials behave on a par with non-selected adverbials like (4)c. In the case in point, there is a sharp contrast between extraction of the argumental and of the adverbial complement of *se comporter* from a *wh*-island:

(11)a ?avec qui ne sais-tu pas [comment [PRO te comporter t t]]
      "with whom don't you know how to behave"
  b *comment ne sais-tu pas [avec qui [PRO te comporter t t]]
      "how don't you know with whom to behave"

This is not expected given the theory of section 2, under reasonably restrictive assumptions on the nature of lexical selection (things are somewhat blurred in English by the idiomatic absolute use of *behave* meaning *behave well*; if proper abstraction is made from this case, the argument can be immediately reproduced).

The same kind of argument is provided by the behavior of lexically selected measure phrases. The case can be illustrated by ambiguous verbs like *weigh*. There is an agentive *weigh*, taking a direct object, and a stative *weigh*, selecting a measure phrase:

(12)a John weighed apples.
  b John weighed 200 lbs.

Both types of complements can be questioned, at a colloquial level, through the *wh* element *what*: the following question remains ambiguous:

(13) What did John weigh t?

But if *what* is extracted from a *wh*-island, only the agentive reading survives. The following marginal question

(14) ? What did John wonder how to weigh t?

can be properly answered "apples," not "200 lbs.," even in contexts that would make the stative interpretation pragmatically plausible (observation and example due to David Feldman; this argument is also discussed in Koopman and Sportiche 1988). In general, lexically selected measure phrases pattern on a par with unselected measure phrases, in that they cannot be extracted from *wh*-islands. This is not expected under the version of the ECP presented in section 2, given the adopted theory of lexical representations. According to this theory, the two verbs *weigh* presumably only differ in their theta grids, as follows:

(15)a   <agent, patient>
   b   <theme, measure>

Both kinds of complements are theta-marked, hence theta-governed, therefore they should be equally extractable from *wh*-islands: which is contrary to the facts.

A similar but independent argument is provided by the behavior of certain idiomatic expressions. It is well known that the nominal parts of some idioms can be *wh*-moved, on a par with the compositional material:

(16)a   what headway do you think [t [you can make t on this project]]?
   b   what project do you think [t [you can make headway on t]]?

But extraction from a *wh*-island is significantly more deviant if the element involved is the idiom chunk:

(17)   a   *what headway don't you know [how [PRO to make t on this project]]?
       b   ?what project don't you know [how [PRO to make headway on t]]

Since this effect has not been described so far (but see Cingue's (1984) discussion on the non-extractability of idiom chunks from stronger islands), it is worthwhile to mention some more cases. The nominal part of the Italian idiom *trarre partito da X* (take advantege from X) can be relitavized, but cannot be extracted from an indirect question, in clear contrast with the compositional PP:

(18)a   Il partito che penso di trarre dalla situazione è il seguente.
        "The advantage that I intend to take of the situation is the following."
   b   *Il partito che non so come trarre talla situazione è il seguente.
        "The advantage that I don't know how to take from the situation is the following."
   c   La situazione da cui non so come trarre partito è la seguente.
        "The situation of which I don't know how to take advantage is the following."

The same effect is shown by the minimal contrast, in Italian, between the compositional expression *prestare i soldi* (to lend money) and the idiomatic expression *prestare attenzione* (to lend attention = to pay attention). In both cases the nominal part can be relativized, but only in the first case is extraction from a *wh*-island possible:

(19)a   i soldi che ho deciso di prestare a Gianni sono molti.
        "The money that I decided to lend to Gianni is a lot."
   b   l'attenzione che ho deciso di prestare a Gianni è poca.
        "The attention that I decided to lend to Gianni is a little."
   c   i soldi che non ho ancora deciso a chi prestare sono molti.
        "The money that I haven't decided yet to whom to lend is a lot."
   d   *l'attenzione che non ho ancora deciso a chi prestare è poca.
        "The attention that I haven't decided yet to whom to lend is a little."

Another minimal pair is provided in Italian by *dare X a Y* (to give X to Y) and *dare credito a Y* (to give credit to Y = to put credit/trust in Y)[6]:

(20)a   che libro pensi di poter dare a Gianni?
        "What book do you think you can give to Gianni?"
   b   che credito pensi di poter dare a Gianni?
        "What trust do you think you can put in Gianni?"
   c   ?che libro non sai a chi dare?
        "What book do you not know to whom to give?"
   d   *che credito non sai a chi dare?
        "What credit don't you know in whom to put?"

According to the restrictive version of the Projection Principle argued for in Chomsky (1981: 37), nominal parts of idioms must receive a special, quasi-argumental theta role from the verb. Therefore, they are theta-governed, hence the version of the ECP referring to theta-government incorrectly predicts extractability from *wh*-islands for nominal idiom chunks.

In conclusion, lexically selected adverbials and measure phrases, as well as nominal parts of idioms, are theta-marked and theta-governed, under reasonable restrictive assumptions on the nature of lexical representations and on the Projection Principle. A theory of the ECP based on the notion of theta-government would then predict that such elements should pattern with other lexically selected arguments in the relevant respects. The prediction is incorrect. These elements strongly disallow extraction from *wh*-islands, on a par with non-lexically-selected adverbials and other adjuncts.

4   THE STATUS OF SUBJECT EXTRACTION

A different kind of empirical evidence against a formulation of the ECP in terms of theta-government is provided by long distance subject extraction. Concerning extraction of subjects in non Null Subject Languages, the approach presented in section 2 makes a clear prediction: no matter what the depth of the extraction site is, extraction from a *wh*-island should be on a par for subjects and adjuncts: both kinds of traces are not theta-governed, they should be antecedent-governed, but if extraction takes place from a *wh*-island a required antecedent-government relation necessarily fails to exist, so that an ECP violation should arise. The parallelism seems indeed to exist in simple cases of extraction like (4) or (21), as we have seen. The problem for the theta-government approach is that the subject/adjunct parallelism tends to disappear if we take into account more complex structures, obtained by adding one level of embedding. Consider a structure like (22), in which a declarative is embedded within an indirect question, and compare the three kinds of extraction:

(21)a   *who do you wonder whether t can help us?
   b   (?)?who do you wonder whether we can help t?
   c   *how do you wonder whether we can help Bill t?

(22)a   ?*who do you wonder whether we believe t can help us?
   b   ??who do you wonder whether we believe we can help t?
   c   *how do you wonder whether we believe we can help Bill t?

Speakers who try to process and evaluate sentences of this sort often find structures like (22)a worse than (22)b, but the contrast does not seem to be as sharp as typical contrasts induced by the ECP. This is what Pesetsky (1984) calls a "surprising subject-object asymmetry"; we agree with him that ECP is not responsible for this kind of contrast. On the other hand, adding one level of embedding does not improve things for adjunct extraction: (21)c and (22)c are generally judged on a par, and it appears fully legitimate to give a common explanation to both cases through the ECP. What is unexpected under the theory of section 2 is the subtle but systematic lack of parallelism between subjects and adjuncts.[7]

Let us have a closer look at the relevant cases: more accurate representations for (22)a–c are the following:

(23)a   Who do you wonder [whether [we believe [(t') [t can help us]]]]
   b   Who do you wonder [whether [we believe [(t') [we can help t]]]]
   c   How do you wonder [whether [we believe [(t') [we can help Bill t]]]]

I will assume, following Pesetsky (1982), that leaving a trace when movement takes place is not obligatory per se (even though independent principles may enforce the presence of a trace). This optionality is reflected by the fact that the trace in Comp (t') is parenthesized in the preceding structures. Let us see how the approach of section 2 deals with the different cases, and where it fails. Consider (23)c. If t' is not present, t violates the identification clause of the ECP: it is not theta-governed, nor is it antecedent-governed. On the other hand, if t' is present in (23)c, t is well formed: it is canonically head-governed by the verb and antecedent-governed by t'; so, the offending trace must be t': in fact, it is canonically head-governed by the higher verb, but it is not theta-governed nor antecedent-governed, whence the violation. In conclusion, no well formed representation is associated to the ungrammatical (22)c, a correct result. As for (23)b, t is canonically head-governed and theta-governed by the verb, therefore the ECP is satisfied; if t' is not present, the structure is well formed as far as the ECP is concerned. The other a priori possible representation of (22)b, the one in which t' is present, violates the ECP as in the preceding case; but the crucial fact is that in this system one well-formed representation (*modulo* Subjacency) can be associated to (22)b, again a correct result.

Consider now (23)a. If t' is not present, t would violate the identification requirement of the ECP, being neither theta-governed nor antecedent-governed (moreover, it would also violate the formal licensing requirement). If t' is present, t is antecedent-governed by it (moreover, formal licensing for t is presumably fulfilled through whatever technique makes short movement of the subject possible: cf. note 4). But then t' violates the identification clause of the ECP, and no well formed representation is assigned to (22)a; the case is thus treated by the approach of section 2 exactly on a par with (23)c as opposed to (23)b. We have seen that this assimilation is not justified by the pattern emerging from the judgements of relative acceptability, which tend to assign a special status to long distance subject extraction, intermediate between object and adjunct extraction, and systematically more acceptable than the latter. Again, the source of the problem seems to reside in the fully uniform status assigned by the theta-government approach to subjects and adjuncts.

This argument against theta-government is reinforced by the essentially parallel behavior of subjects and objects as opposed to adjuncts in the environment of negative operators. Ross (1983) noticed that negative elements induce object/adjunct asymmetries of the familiar type:

(24)a   who do you think we can help t?
    b   why do you think we can help him t?

(25)a   who don't you think we can help t?
    b   *why don't you think [t' [we can help t]]?

We argued elsewhere that the impossibility of (25)b in the intended reading (with lower construal of *why*) is excluded by the ECP; in essence, the intervening negative element blocks the required antecedent-government relation for t'. The approach presented in section 2 correctly predicts that no problem arises when a direct object is extracted from the scope of negation, as in (25)a: it is theta-governed, hence the identification requirement is locally fulfilled, and the representation of (25)a, in which no trace is left in Comp, is well formed. But this approach incorrectly predicts subject extraction to be on a par with adjunct extraction. A relevant case would be:

(26)   (?) who don't you think [(t') [t can help us]]

If t' is not present, t should violate the ECP in the usual manner; if t' is present, it should violate the identification requirement of the ECP because of the blocking effect of negation on antecedent-government. The subject case would then be predicted to be exactly on a par with the adjunct case. But this clearly is incorrect: speakers find at most a very slight degradation with respect to object extraction (this is what the parenthesized question mark is meant to suggest), and generally agree that the main dividing line is to be drawn between (25)b and (26)–(25)a. An approach based on theta-government seems to be intrinsically unable to deal with these cases of argument/adjunct asymmetries in which subjects and objects tend to pattern together, if compared to adjunct extraction. (Cf. note 14 for a conjecture on the weaker "surprising" asymmetry between subject and object extraction.)

5   A-CHAINS

A different kind of evidence against theta-government, already discussed in the literature, is provided by the locality conditions on A-chains (passive and raising). Here I will simply reproduce the argument given by Chomsky (1986b) and Baker (1988). While distant control from a non-adjacent clause is possible (SuperEqui), long-distance Raising (SuperRaising) is not:

(27)   John thinks [that it is difficult [PRO to shave himself in public]]

(28)   *John seems [that it is likely [t to shave himself in public]]

(were the second acceptable, it would have the perfectly sensible interpretation of "It seems that it is likely that John will shave himself in public"). Subjacency and the theory of binding do not seem to properly characterize the strong deviance of (28). Chomsky (1986b) observes that it appears to have the status of an ECP violation. In fact the version of ECP given in section 2 would seem to achieve the desired result: the subject trace is not theta-governed, it should be antecedent-governed, but the antecedent is too far away in (28); an ECP violation is thus produced. The problem is that this approach cannot capture the fact that passive at a distance is as impossible as distant raising: passivization of (29)a must be local as in b, and cannot skip the closest subject as in c (examples adapted from Baker 1988):

(29)a   It seems that someone told Bill that . . .
    b   It seems that Bill was told t that . . .
    c   *Bill seems that it was told t that . . .

in (29)c the trace in object position is theta-governed by the verb, so that the version of the ECP defined in terms of this notion cannot enforce antecedent-government here. This approach is then unable to give a uniform account of the impossibility of SuperRaising and SuperPassive under the ECP.

A parallel argument can be constructed on the basis of Kayne's (1987) analysis of cliticization in Romance. Kayne argues that the clause-boundedness of cliticization is best accounted for by the ECP: the clitic trace is antecedent-governed in a but not in b, whence the ill-formedness of the latter:

(30)a   Jean essaie [de le faire t]
        "Jean tries to do it"
    b   *Jean l'essaie [de faire t]
        "Jean tries to do it"

Again, this analysis requires that theta-government is not an independent way to fulfill the identification requirement of the ECP. If it was, antecedent-government could not be enforced for clitic traces, which in the general case are theta-marked by the governing verb.

In conclusion, various considerations have lead us to single out theta-government as the source of important conceptual and empirical inadequacies of the ECP, in the version adopted so far. The remainder of this paper will be devoted to a revision of our current assumptions which will take these problems into account. In order to do that, it is necessary to go back to the many asymmetries noticed so far in extraction processes, and try to adequately state the fundamental generalization that emerges.

6   ON RESTRICTING THE USE OF REFERENTIAL INDICES

Among the many proposals that can be found in the recent literature, the concise characterization of the fundamental generalization that fits the facts discussed best is the one put forth, for very different reasons and in different terms, by Joseph Aoun and Guglielmo Cinque: referential elements are (marginally) extractable from islands, non-referential elements are not.[8]

At a preliminary scrutiny, this informal characterization looks sufficiently promising to invite us to inquire further. Consider the asymmetries discussed in section 3: whatever precise definition of "referential" we will end up adopting, it is intuitively plausible that compositional complements should turn out to be referential in a sense in which nominal parts of idioms (*headway*, *credito*, etc.) are not; similarly, it makes intuitive sense to say that the direct object of agentive *weigh* and the comitative complement of *behave* are referential, while the measure phrase selected by stative *weigh* and the manner adverbial selected by *behave* are not, etc.

Our proposal is that the required notion of "referentiality" should be made precise in terms of thematic theory; this is so in part for empirical reasons to be discussed below, in part because thematic theory already possesses the necessary concepts, and no further elaboration is to be introduced. So, if the proposal to be developed eliminates theta-government from the ECP module, it still assumes that Theta Theory plays a crucial role in determining the possible occurrence of traces.

The first thing we need is a distinction between two types of theta roles. We continue to assume that all selected elements are theta-marked. Even so, there is a clear conceptual distinction to be drawn: some selected elements refer to participants in the event described by the verb (John, apples, books, etc.); other selected elements do not refer to participants: they rather qualify the event, compositionally (measure, manner, etc.) or idiosyncratically (idiom chunks). This split corresponds, in essence, to Chomsky's (1981: 325) distinction between *arguments*, referential expressions potentially referring to participants in the event, and *quasi-arguments*, expressions which receive a theta role but do not refer to a participant, such as the subjects of atmospheric predicates and the nominal parts of idioms. We can thus distinguish argumental or referential theta roles (agent, theme, patient, experiencer, goal, etc.) and quasi-argumental, non-referential theta roles (manner, measure, atomspheric role, idiosyncratic role in idioms, etc.).

Let us then restate the Aoun-Cinque generalization in terms of Chomsky's split: only elements assigned a referential theta role can be extracted from a (*wh*) island; everything else (non theta-marked elements and elements receiving a non-referential theta role) cannot.[9] What is the theoretical status of this generalization? Cinque's system is specifically designed to deal with stronger islands, adverbial islands and complex NPs, so that it is not directly applicable to our *wh*-island cases; moreover our system of assumptions is technically incompatible with Aoun's Generalized Binding approach (even though close to it in various respects). I would like to propose a different, quite straightforward approach, capitalizing on the remarks made at the outset of this paper on the original motivations for referential indices. In the spirit of that discussion, I would like to restrict the use of referential indices to cases made legitimate by the following principle:

(31)   A referential index must be licensed by a referential theta role

That is to say, a referential index is legitimate on a given linguistic representation only if it is associated to a referential theta role. For concreteness, we can mechanically interpret (31) precisely along the lines of the *Aspects* quote given at the outset: suppose that every position receiving a referential theta role is assigned a referential index at D-structure, under (31). The content of this position, if moved, can carry its index along. No other position can carry a referential index, under (31). We continue to assume that the binding relation is defined in terms of the notion referential index:

(32)   X binds Y iff
    (i)   X c-commands Y, and
    (ii)   X and Y have the same referential index

The net effect of (31), then, is to restrict binding relations to elements associated to referential theta roles, much in the spirit of the original approach. We claim that this restriction subsumes the essential effect of the identification clause of the ECP and properly captures the fundamental argument/adjunct asymmetries. We can thus simplify the ECP by reducing it to the former formal licensing requirement:

(33)   ECP: A trace must be canonically head-governed

We now are ready to show how the system works, for a first approximation. Principle (31) determines a split within A' dependencies which is visualized in the following structures:

(34)a Who_k did you see t_k?
   b   How did you behave t?

In (34)a the operator is connected to its variable through binding, as usual. The index k is licensed by the referential theta role that *see* assigns to its object, and can be legitimately used to express the A' dependency. On the contrary, no indexation is legitimate in the case of (34)b under (31), as no referential theta role is involved. So, the A' dependency cannot be expressed through binding. Still, for the structure to be interpretable the operator must be somehow connected to its variable. The system must then resort to some other connecting device. Now, if we look through the modular structure of the theory searching for devices apt to establish interactive connections between positions, we only find two major candidates; their theoretical prominence is so obvious that they are often used to refer to the whole framework: binding, used by Binding Theory and Control Theory, and government, used by Case Theory, Binding Theory, and the licensing modules of the various types of null elements. Binding being unavailable in (34)b, the system must resort to government to connect operator and variable.[10]

Of course, a fundamental difference between the two devices is that binding can hold at an arbitrary distance, while government is intrinsically local. There is then an essential asymmetry between the two modes of connection. I would like to claim that this is the source of the observed asymmetries. Let us reconsider the basic paradigms (4) and (6), repeated here for ease of reference:

(35)a *which student$_i$ do you wonder [how [t$_i$ could solve the problem t]]
   b ?which problem$_j$ do you wonder [how [PRO to solve t$_j$ t]]
   c *how do you wonder [which problem$_j$ [PRO to solve t$_j$ t]]

(36)a ?che studente$_i$ non sai [come [potrà risolvere il problema t t$_i$]]
       "which student don't you know how could solve the problem"
   b ?che problema$_j$ non sai [come [potremo risolvere t$_j$ t]]
       "which problem don't you know how we could solve"
   c *come non sai [che problema$_j$ [potremo risolvere t$_j$ t]]
       "how don't you know which problem we could solve"

(35)a violates the ECP, now reduced to (33), because the subject trace is not canonically governed. In (35)b there are two connections to take into account. The object trace can bear an index under (32), so that it can be connected to its operator long distance through binding; the adjunct trace cannot bear an index, but its operator is close enough for government to hold; both connections are thus properly established, and the sentence only gives rise to a mild subjacency violation. On the other hand, (35)c is ill-formed: the object trace does not raise any problem, but the adjunct trace does: it cannot be connected to its operator through binding because indexation is not legitimate in this case, nor through government because the operator is too far away. The connection cannot be established, hence the sentence is ruled out as uninterpretable. All the basic contrasts discussed in section 3 ((11)a–b, the two interpretations of (14), (17)a–b, (18), etc.) can be analyzed in a similar manner.

(36)b–c are dealt with on a par with (35)b–c. On the other hand, (36)a is well-formed because the subject is extracted from a position which is canonically governed by Infl; the ECP (34) is thus fulfilled; moreover, the subject trace is associated to a referential theta role; as such, it can be indexed under (32), hence connected long distance to its operator via binding. The status of (36)a is then accounted for, and it is not necessary to assume that a postverbal subject position is theta-governed.[11]

One may wonder at this point why the crucial distinction introduced by principle (32) should be stated through the mediation of Theta Theory. An alternative which comes to mind is to state it directly in terms of some naive theory of reference, or, more plausibly, in terms of the organization of what Chomsky (1981) calls "Domain D," the universe of discourse, the cognitive domain which contains representations of what we talk about. It could be that reasons, manners, quantities, etc. are not represented as individuals in this domain. If indices are restricted to designate individuals, the effect of (32) would be achieved, perhaps in a more straightforward way.

Still, it seems to be the case that a distinction in terms of general ontology is too crude. Some linguistic mediation is necessary. The nature of the entities involved is not the only relevant factor: also the particular linguistic conceptualization of the event seems to matter. Consider the following two sentences:

(37)a non so se potremo dire che Gianni è stato licenziato per questa ragione.
       "I don't know if we could say that Gianni was fired for this reason."
   b   non so se potremo dare questa ragione per il licenziamento di Gianni.
       "I don't know if we could give this reason for Gianni's firing."

These two sentences are semantically quite close, in that in both cases a reason is associated to a certain event. The difference is that the reason is expressed as a lexically-selected complement in (37)b and as an adjunct in (37)a. Extraction from a *wh*-island gives a notably different result in the two cases:

(38)a *per che ragione non sai se possiamo dire che Gianni è stato licenziato?
       "For what reason don't you know if we can say that Gianni was fired?"
   b   ?che ragione non sai se possiamo dare per il licenziamento di Gianni?
       "What reason don't you know if we can give for Gianni's firing?"

Since the entities involved are reasons in both cases, the distinction does not seems to be directly expressible in ontological terms. What seems to count is the specific linguistic structure chosen to express the relation between a reason and an event. This is done by making the reason a verbal argument in (38)b, but not in (38)a. In our terms, indexation and binding are available in (38)b but not in (38)a, which is then ruled out in the relevant interpretation. It thus seems to be necessary to mediate the licensing of indices through the particular linguistic conceptualization of events which is expressed by Theta Theory.[12]

7 REFINEMENTS

One crucial refinement is immediately suggested by the acceptability of long-distance extraction of an adjunct from a declarative:

(39)   how do you think [t' that [we can solve the problem t]]?

This shows that a non-indexed trace does not have to be directly governed by the operator: a sequence of government relations (here between t' and t between *how* and t') suffices to establish the connection. The theory already possesses a formal object consisting of a sequence of antecedent government relations, the chain. Following Chomsky (1986b) I will assume that a chain is partially defined as follows:

(40) $(a_1, \ldots, a_n)$ is a chain only if, for $1 < i < n$, a_i antecedent governs a_{i+1}.

We now need a definition of antecedent-government which does not make crucial reference to co-indexation, so that it will be equally applicable to indexed and non-indexed material. We can tentatively replace the co-indexation requirement of the usual definition with a global non-distinctness requirement (non-distinctness of indices if the elements are indexed, of category, feature, content, etc.) in order to rule out the possibility of forming crazy chains (e.g. of an adjunct trace with a verb or a direct object, and the like)[13]:

(41)   X antecedent governs Y iff
   (i)   X governs Y, and
   (ii) X and Y are non-distinct.

As for government, we don't have to enter into the technicalities of a particular complete definition. For the current purposes it is sufficient to assume that government holds between two elements when no barrier intervenes, in the sense of Chomsky (1986b).

On the basis of this refinement, our proposal now looks as follows: there are two (non-exclusive) ways to connect an operator and its variable: binding and a chain of government relations.[14] Binding requires co-indexation, a formal property now restricted by principle (31); when co-indexation and binding are not available, the chain of government relations is the only connecting device. But government relations are intrinsically local, hence if a link of the government chain fails, the connection between operator and variable cannot be established, and the structure is ruled out. The chain as such can cover an unbounded distance, but each link is local; this is the crucial difference between the two connecting devices.

As the reader can easily check, the system now deals with all the fundamental asymmetries discussed in this paper, with one important exception: the NP and clitic dependencies discussed in section 4. The relevant cases are the following:

(42)a   it seems that someone told Bill that . . .
   b   it seems that Bill was told t that . . .
   c   *Bill seems that it was told t that . . .

(43)a   Jean essaie [de le faire t]
       "Jean tries to do it"
   b   *Jean l'essaie [de faire t]
       "Jean tries to do it"

In (42)c, (43)b the object trace receives a referential theta role, an index is licit, hence the connection with the antecedent can be established long-distance via binding, and the ill-formedness of these examples does not seem to be amenable to a unitary treatment with the familiar asymmetries in our system. In fact, this case looks different irrespective of the particular analysis that one adopts for the extractions from *wh*-islands. It just seems to be the case that in A-type antecedent-trace dependencies (which include clitic dependencies, we assume) the argument/adjunct distinction which pervasively characterizes A′ dependencies is wiped out, and all A dependencies obey the strong locality conditions which are restricted to adjuncts in A′ dependencies. Why should it be so? The natural thing to do is to try to relate this strong asymmetry to some independent difference between the two types of dependencies. The most conspicuous difference concerns Theta Theory: antecedent-trace dependencies of the A-type typically relate an argument to a thematic position, hence some sort of transmission of theta role must be involved. A frequently adopted, straightforward way to properly state this kind of theta role inheritance without implying an actual transmission is to formulate the theta criterion directly in terms of the notion chain, along the following lines:

(44)   Theta Criterion:
     (i)   each theta position belongs to a chain containing exactly one argument;
    (ii) each argument belongs to a chain containing exactly one theta position.

Following a suggestion due to Norbert Hornstein (cf. also Aoun, Hornstein, Lightfoot, Weinberg 1987 note 24), and developing in a different way an intuition also underlying Williams's (1987) approach, we can then claim that (42)c, (43)b are not ill-formed owing to a generic failure to connect antecedent and trace, but owing to the failure of the specific connection required by Theta Theory: if the Theta Criterion is defined in terms of chain, and chain is defined in terms of antecedent-government, as in (40), then in (42)c, (43)b the object theta role cannot be assigned to the appropriate formal object, a chain containing the arguments *Bill* and *le*, respectively, hence these structures violate the Theta Criterion. No such effect arises for A' dependencies, which do not involve any sort of theta role inheritance, and in fact are not affected by Theta Theory at all.

In short, the strong locality conditions holding in A' dependencies with adjuncts and in all A dependencies can be unified and traced back to a common source, the antecedent government condition on chains. But chain formation is enforced for different reasons in the two cases. In the first case, it is the only connecting device available; in the second case, it is the specific connecting device required by Theta Theory. The fundamental difference between the two cases, the fact that the argument/adjunct distinction is obliterated in A dependencies, is then related to an independent asymmetry between the two types of dependency, their different status with respect to Theta Theory: with A dependencies a chain connection is required in all cases for theta-theoretic reasons.[15]

One final comment is demanded by paradigm (23), repeated here for convenience, which can now receive a different, more adequate analysis:

(45)a   ?*who$_i$ do you wonder [whether [we believe [t'$_i$ [t$_i$ can help us]]]]

  b   ??who$_j$ do you wonder [whether [we believe [(t'$_j$) [we can help t$_j$]]]]

  c   * how do you wonder [whether [we believe [(t') [we can help Bill t]]]]

In (45)c the variable t should be connected to its operator *how*. Binding being unavailable, a chain of antecedent-government relations is the only option. t' antecedent-governs t, but *how* is too far away to antecedent-govern t'. The connection thus fails, and the structure is not interpretable (whether or not t' is actually present). In (45)b indexing is licensed under (31), hence the connection between *who* and t can be established via binding. Under the current account, the presence of t' has no influence: a trace in Comp is not necessary to establish the required connections, and its presence does not give rise to an ECP violation *per se* (as it did under the theory of section 2), since it is canonically head-governed by the higher verb. So, its presence is optional (but see the following footnote). Consider now (45)a. Indexing is licit, hence (45)a can be connected to its variable t through binding, as in the preceding case. But in this case the presence of t' is necessary to induce C° agreement, which allows satisfaction of the canonical head-government requirement for t, under the proposal of footnote 4. ECP can thus be satisfied, the proper operator-variable connection can be established through binding, and the example is treated differently from (45)c, as its status seems to justify.[16]

8 CONCLUSIONS

Referential indices were introduced in syntactic theory to encode referential dependencies between arguments. In the spirit of the original proposal, we have argued that their use should be restricted to elements associated to referential theta roles. This move has the effect of significantly limiting the availability of binding as a book-keeping device to express relations of various sorts. In the domain of A' relations, binding can now only express the dependencies involving referential variables, in the sense made precise through Theta Theory. Variables which are non-referential in this sense (adverbs lexically selected or not, measure phrases, idiom chunks . . .) cannot be connected to their operators via binding, and must exploit the other connecting device offered by the system, government. So, this second kind of A' dependency can only be expressed via a chain of government relations. Binding can take place at an unbounded distance, provided that its two components (co-indexation and c-command) are met. Government, on the other hand, is intrinsically local. A chain of government relations can cover an unbounded distance only if each link meets the usual locality restrictions. We have argued that this fundamental difference is the source of the familiar argument/adjunct asymmetries with respect to island sensitivity. An adjunct variable can never be connected to its operator via binding, because of its non-referential nature; and it cannot be connected via government across an island because one of the necessary government relations inevitably fails. No connection can be established, and such structures are ruled out as uninterpretable. On the contrary, a referential variable can always be connected to its operator via binding, a relation which is unaffected by island barriers. The island sensitivity thus gives rise to less dramatic effects in this case, and is only manifested by the marginality arising from a violation of Subjacency.

NOTES

Preliminary versions of this paper were presented at the *Séminaire de recherche linguistique* (University of Geneva, November 1987), at the annual meeting of the *Rivista di grammatica generativa* (Florence, February 1988), and at the LAGB Meeting (Durham, March 1988). The approach presented here is developed in fuller detail in the revised version of Rizzi (1987). I wish to thank Ian Roberts for helpful comments and suggestions.

1 As is usual in current syntactic research, what is relevant is not the absolute acceptability of an example, but its status relative to another example. The

different diacritics are thus simply meant to clearly express a relational judgment rather than an absolute status.

2   In Chomsky's (1986b) system at least one barrier, CP, intervenes. If the relativized version of minimality is adopted (Rizzi 1987), the intervention of a potential antecedent governor, the embedded spec of CP, blocks a government relation between the subject trace and the main Spec of CP.

3   In the system of Chomsky (1986b) there must be an additional trace adjoined to VP mediating the relation between the adjunct operator and its variable. This refinement is not relevant for our purposes and will be omitted here.

4   If the complementizer is dropped, (5)a becomes acceptable. We have argued elsewhere that C° can be realized as an abstract agreement morpheme (overt agreement is possible in this position in some languages), in complementary distribution with *that* in standard English (but not in the dialects which allow (5)a). We thus have a representation like the following:

(i)   which student do you think [t' Agr [t can solve the problem]]

Agr in C°, agrees with its specifier t', as usual, and canonically governs t. See Rizzi (1987) for detailed discussion of this approach to *that*-trace effects.

5   According to the usual notational convention, a structure marked ". . .*(X) . . ." is ill-formed if the option X is not taken.

6   Notice that (20)d is possible in the non-idiomatic interpretation of *credito* = financial credit. The same facts hold in French:

(i)   ?Quel privilège ne sais-tu pas à qui accorder?
(ii)   *Quel crédit ne sais-tu pas à qui accorder?

the second example is excluded in the relevant idiomatic interpretation.

7   In the same vein, Lasnik and Saito (1984: 268) notice the relatively mild ill-formedness of cases of subject extraction from a declarative embedded in a *wh*-island: (their numbers and diacritics)

(124)a   ?*Who do you wonder whether John said t came?

They also notice that extraction of a subject deeply embedded within an island (in this case a Complex NP) tends to pattern with object extraction, not with adjunct extraction (actually, their choice of diacritics suggests fully parallel status for subjects and objects):

(120)a   *Why do you believe the claim that John left t?
      b   ?*What do you believe the claim that John bought t?

(121)a   *Who do you believe the claim that John said t came?

They conclude that no ECP violation is involved in cases such as (121)a, (124)a.

Similarly, Browning (1987: 296) gives examples of the following sort (her diacritics and numbers):

(91)b   ??which student did John wonder whether to believe t understood the problem
     b'   ?which problem did John wonder whether to believe Bill understood t

and concludes that the mild aggravation that the first example manifests cannot be an ECP effect.

8   According to Aoun (1986), the non-referential nature of adjunct traces has the property of not triggering the peculiar interplay of Principle A and Principle C which allows long distance binding of ordinary referential variables in his

system. According to Cinque's (1984, forthcoming) proposal, a non-referential element cannot be the antecedent of a (resumptive) pronoun, hence the use of a null resumptive pronoun, which underlies apparent island violations in his system, is not available with non-referential adjuncts.

9   In addition to non-lexically-selected adverbials, other cases of non theta-marked elements which are not extractable from *wh*-islands are predicated (see Roberts 1988 for detailed discussion) and quantifictional specifiers of NPs and APs in languages that allow short specifier extraction (*combien* extraction from NP in French, etc.; cf. Rizzi 1987 and references cited there).

10   C-command and m-command (and *a fortiori* the elementary relations of precedence and dominance) can be looked at as the formal building blocks of the substantive relations of government and binding. Sisterhood, the fundamental structural relation exploited by Theta Theory, is too local to be used as a proper connecting device, in the relevant sense.

11   This is a welcome result. According to Chomsky's (1986b) Bounding Theory, a subjacency barrier is a maximal projection not theta-governed. If postverbal subjects were theta-governed, one would expect extraction from a postverbal subject to be fully grammatical. In fact, this kind of extraction is slightly deviant (iii), and patterns by and large with extraction from a preverbal subject (ii), as opposed to the fully grammatical extraction from an object (i):

   (i)   il libro di cui ho letto [il primo capitolo t]
           "the book of which I read the first chapter"
   (ii)   ?il libro di cui [il primo capitolo t] mi ha convinto
           "the book of which the first chapter convinced me"
   (iii)   ?il libro di cui mi ha convinto [il primo capitolo t]
           "the book of which convinced me the first chapter"

See Belletti and Rizzi (1988) for more fine-grained distinctions. It seems appropriate to analyze (iii) as involving the crossing of at least one barrier, as is the case if the postverbal subject is not theta-governed, under the *Barriers* approach.

12   Concerning examples like (28), some speakers find extraction of an adjunct PP more acceptable than extraction of *why* (P. Coopmans, p.c.). So, for some speakers, in the relevant interpretation, (ii) is less deviant than (i):

   (i)   why do you wonder whether he was fired t?
   (ii) for what reason do you wonder whether he was fired t?

Given our analysis, in principle the two traces could not be indexed, and the two examples should be equally deviant. This indeed is the judgment that certain speakers give. But since other speakers detect a significant distinction here, we should ask how it can arise. We can notice that the two examples differ in that theta-marking still takes place within the adjunct *wh*-phrase in (ii), but not in (i) (no assigner and assignee can be distinguished within the one-word *wh* element). We can then suppose that (ii) allows for the marked possibility (not exploited by all speakers) of percolating the index of the NP up to the PP node (of which the NP is the "semantic head," in the sense of Abney 1987). This can marginally allow a binding connection to be established. No such marginal procedure can be available in the case of (i), there being no adjunct-internal theta-marking process. (i) is then more uniformly rejected.

13   Alternatively, we could allow non-referential elements to bear a different kind of index, say superscripts, which would not enter into binding relations, restricted to referential indices, but could be used in the definition of antecedent-government.

14   The two devices are not exclusive because in the following structure

    (i)   who$_j$ do you think [t'$_j$ [t$_j$ came]]

the variable is connected to its operator both via binding (because an index is licensed under (31)) and via government (because the chain (*who*, t', t) is well-formed). There are empirical reasons suggesting that a government connection is possible in cases like (i). Longobardi (1984) showed that certain instances of scope reconstruction involving "argumental" operator and variable are possible only in environments which would allow adjunct extraction (e.g., scope reconstruction is blocked across a *wh*-island). The natural interpretation would be to restrict scope reconstruction to cases in which the operator can be connected to its variable through a government chain, hence not across a *wh*-island, etc. A binding connection *per se* does not seem to suffice to allow scope reconstruction.

15   An A dependency connects an argument to a theta position in the typical case, but not always: in some structures the A dependency connects an expletive to an argument in a theta position:

    (i)   there seems t to be a horse in the garden

This sort of dependency also is strictly local, and disallows SuperRaising:

    (ii)   *there seems that it is likely t to be a horse in the garden

The account can be the same if we assume that (structural) case is a necessary ingredient for a chain to be visible at LF in the relevant sense (cf. Chomsky 1981, ch. 6, and, for some refinements, Belletti 1987). In (ii) the argument *a horse* should then form a chain with an element (necessarily a non-argument) bearing (structural) case. *It* does not qualify, as it is not the appropriate expletive for nominal chains in English. *There* would qualify, but it is too far away to antecedent-govern t in (ii), and the required chain (*there*, t, *a horse*) cannot be formed.

16   It remains to be determined why subject extraction is somewhat worse than object extraction in this environment. Under our analysis, one notable difference between the two cases is that the intermediate trace t' is necessarily present in the embedded Comp in the first but not in the second case. One could tentatively exploit this difference in the following way. Suppose that in the spirit of Chomsky's least effort guidelines (ch. 2, this volume) an element can be legitimately specified at LF only if it plays a role on that level; for the A' system, this would mean that each element must be an operator, or a variable, or an intermediate link of a chain connecting an operator and a variable. t' in (45)a is neither: in particular, it is not the intermediate link of a chain connecting *who* and t because it is too far away from *who* to be antecedent-governed by it. The connection can be successfully established anyhow because binding is available, but t' (necessary to allow Agr in Comp to occur) fails to meet this natural optimality condition on LF. The problem does not arise for the object case (45)b, because here there is always the option of not leaving the trace when movement applies. Whence the different status of the two cases. The plausibility of this approach to Pesetsky's surprising asymmetries depends in part on the complex question of whether the asymmetries tend to persist or to disappear with Exceptional Case Marking structures (the suggested approach would predict the latter). We will not discuss here the intricate facts that bear on this question. For different views on the general trends of acceptability judgements see Browning (1987), and Koopman and

Sportiche (1988). We also leave aside here, among other relevant facts, the surprising asymmetries which arise in different constructions involving null operators, on which see Stowell (1986), the detailed analysis in Browning (1987) and references cited there.

REFERENCES

Abney, S. 1987: *The English Noun Phrase in its Sentential Aspect*. Ph.D. Dissertation, MIT.

Aoun, J. 1985: *Generalized Binding*. Foris Publications, Dordrecht.

Aoun, J., Hornstein, N., Lightfoot, D., and Weinberg, A. 1987: "Two Types of Locality." *Linguistic Inquiry*, 18, 537–77.

Baker, M. 1988: *Incorporation*. University of Chicago Press.

Belletti, A. 1987: "The case of unaccusatives." *Linguistic Inquiry*, 19, 1–34.

Brandi, L. and Cordin, P. 1981: "Dialetti e italiano: un confronto sul parametro del soggetto nullo." *Rivista di grammatica generativa*, 6, 33–87.

Browning, M. 1987: *Null Operator Constructions*. Ph.D. Dissertation, MIT.

Chomsky, N. 1965: *Aspects of the Theory of Syntax*. MIT Press, Cambridge, Mass.

—— 1981: *Lectures on Government and Binding*. Foris, Dordrecht.

—— 1986a: *Knowledge of Language*. Praeger, New York.

—— 1986b: *Barriers*. MIT Press, Cambridge, Mass.

Cinque, G. 1984: "A-bar bound *pro* vs. variable." Manuscript, University of Venice.

—— (Forthcoming): *Types of A' Dependencies*. Manuscript, University of Venice.

Contreras, H. 1986: *Chain Theory, Parasitic Gaps, and the ECP*. Manuscript, University of Washington, Seattle.

Grimshaw, J. 1979: "Complement selection and the lexicon." *Linguistic Inquiry*, 10, 279–326.

Huang, J. 1982: *Logical Relations in Chinese and the Theory of Grammar*. Ph.D. Dissertation, MIT.

Jaeggli, O. 1982: *Topics in Romance Syntax*. Foris, Dordrecht.

—— 1985: "On certain ECP effects in Spanish." Manuscript, USC.

Kayne, R. 1984: *Connectedness and Binary Branching*. Foris, Dordrecht.

—— 1987: "Null subjects and clitic climbing." To appear in O. Jaeggli and K. Safir (eds), *The Null Subject Parameter*, Kluwer, Dordrecht.

Koopman, H. and Sportiche, D. 1986: "A note on long extraction in Vata and the ECP." *Natural Language and Linguistic Theory*, 4, 367–74.

—— 1988: "Subjects." Manuscript, UCLA.

Lasnik, H. and Saito, M. 1984: "On the nature of proper government." *Linguistic Inquiry*, 15, 235–89.

Lees, R. and Klima, E. 1963: "Rules for English pronominalization." *Language*, 39, 17–28.

Longobardi, G. 1984: "L'estrazione dalle 'isole' e lo *scope* dei sintagmi quantificati." Manuscript, Scuola Normale Superiore Pisa.

Pesetsky, D. 1982: *Paths and Categories*. Ph.D. Dissertation, MIT.

—— 1984: "Extraction domains and a surprising subject/object asymmetry." *GLOW Newsletter*, 12, 58–60.

Rizzi, L. 1982: *Issues in Italian Syntax*. Foris, Dordrecht.

—— 1986: "Null objects in Italian and the theory of *pro*." *Linguistic Inquiry*, 17, 501–57.

—— 1987: "Relativized minimality." Manuscript, Université de Genève.

Roberts, I. 1988: *Thematic Interveners*. Manuscript, Universitè de Genève.

Ross, J. R. 1983: "Inner Islands." Manuscript, MIT.
Stowell, T. 1981: *Origins of Phrase Structure*. Ph.D. Dissertation, MIT.
—— 1985: "Null operators and the theory of Proper Government." Manuscript, UCLA.
—— 1986: "Null antecedents and Proper Government." *NELS*, 16, 476–92.
Torrego, E. 1985: "On Empty Categories in Nominals." Manuscript, University of Massachusetts, Boston.
Williams, E. 1987: "NP Trace in theta theory." *Linguistics and Philosophy*, 10, 433–47.

13
Concepts of Logical Form in Linguistics and Philosophy

Shalom Lappin

The term "logical form" has come to occupy a central place both in analytic philosophy and in contemporary linguistic theory. It has also been the focus of considerable misunderstanding between philosophers and linguists. Many philosophers tend to associate the idea of the logical form of a sentence with a structure that reveals its ultimate meaning. With the entry of the term "logical form" into generative grammar in the late 1960s, some philosophers harbored expectations that research in formal syntactic theory would clarify such a level of meaning. These hopes were disappointed when it became apparent that linguists are working with an entirely different, theory-internal notion of logical form than the one philosophers are generally interested in. Matters have been further confused by the fact that the philosophical usage of the expression "logical form" has itself enjoyed a varied career, with the term being used to denote different concepts within the analytic tradition.

It is possible to distinguish at least three central notions of logical form within the philosophical literature. These may be characterized as (i) an inferential, (ii) an epistemic, and (iii) an ontological concept of logical form, respectively. They are not mutually incompatible, and at least some philosophers seem to sustain two, or all three of them simultaneously.

In section 1, I will briefly characterize these concepts of logical form. I will argue that they share an important property which distinguishes them from the concept of logical form current in contemporary linguistic theory. My purpose here is to identify a specifically philosophical view of logical form in order to set it aside and focus on the linguistic notion of logical form.

In section 2, I will outline the view of logical form (LF) which has been developed within Chomsky's (1981), (1982), (1986a), and (1986b) Government Binding (GB) model, and I will consider several of the main arguments which have been advanced for the existence of LF. The most recent and detailed elaboration of this view is presented in May (1985), and most of my remarks will center on this work.

In section 3, I will propose an alternative approach to the theory of grammar, according to which LF does not constitute a distinct level of syntactic representation, and rules of model theoretic semantic interpretation apply directly to S-structure.

In section 4, I will consider how the arguments for LF sketched in section 2 can be dealt with within the framework of this alternative view of grammar.

1 PHILOSOPHICAL THEORIES OF LOGICAL FORM

1.1 The Inferential View

In one prominent trend in analytic philosophy, the logical form of a sentence is identified with an expression whose structural features explicitly represent the logical properties and entailment relations of the sentence.[1] This expression is generally the translation of the sentence into a formal language with a well-defined syntax and semantics, or a paraphrase of the sentence in a quasi-formalized subpart of a natural language.

Frege's (1897) *Begriffschrift* offers a particularly clear instance of this idea of logical form. It is a first order language (in fact, the prototype of first order logic) in which entailment relations among sentences are structurally represented in an unambiguous way. Referring to grammatical features of sentences in natural languages, such as word order and grammatical roles, Frege says "In my formalized language there is nothing that corresponds; only that part of judgements which affects *possible inferences* is taken into consideration. Whatever is needed for a valid inference is fully expressed . . ." (p. 3, emphasis in the original). Sentences with the same grammatical form but different entailment properties receive distinct structural representations in the formal language. for example, (1) and (2) both have NP VP grammatical form, but they differ in their entailments. (2) implies (3), while (1) does not.

(1) John is amusing
(2) Every clown is amusing.
(3) If Bill is a clown, then he is amusing.

(1)–(3) correspond to (1′)–(3′), respectively.

(1′) A_j
(2′) $\forall x(Cx \supset Ax)$
(3′) $Cb \supset Ab$

Given the interpretation of logical constants and the association of the types of expressions in this first order language with kinds of semantic values, (2') implies (3') regardless of what interpretation is assigned to the non-logical constants of the sentences (i.e. by virtue of their structures alone), but (1') does not imply (3').

Similarly, sentences with different grammatical forms and identical entailments generally correspond to the same structure in the formalized language. Consider (4) and (5).

(4)   John is either amusing or not amusing.
(5)   Either John is amusing or John is not amusing.

Both (4) and (5) will translate into the tautologous structure

(6) $A_j \vee \sim A_j$

Russell's (1905) analysis of definite descriptions also invokes the inferential notion of logical form.[2] One of the primary motivations he offers for this analysis is that it permits us to deny both (7) and (8) while retaining the law of excluded middle.

(7)   The present King of France is bald.
(8)   The present King of France is not bald.

One possible translation of (8) is

(9) $(\exists x)(Kx \,\&\, \forall y(Ky \equiv x = y) \,\&\, \sim Bx)$

As (9) is not the negation of (7), taking both (7) and (8) to be false does not entail that (10) is also false.

(10)   Either the present King of France is bald or it is not the case that the present King of France is bald.

On the inferential view, then, the entailment relations of a sentence are exhibited through the structural properties of its logical form.

1.2   The Epistemic View

A second notion of logical form which has been influential among analytic philosophers identifies the logical form of a sentence with an explicit representation of its epistemic content. One of the most systematic presentations of this approach is Carnap's (1928) program for developing a constructional system.[3] Such a system seeks to construct the entire edifice of a unified (ideal) scientific theory on the basis of a set of sentences whose elementary non-logical constituents denote epistemically primary entities.

In Carnap's model, the constructional system is formulated in an extensional first order language augmented by the expressions of elementary set theory. The domain of basic entities which serve as the values of the variables for this language are individual sense perceptions. The basic predicates of the language denote sets of sense experiences, or sets of ordered n-tuples of such experiences. All predicates of higher order entities, such as physical objects, cultural events, or other minds, are defined as logical constructions built up from the elementary sentences of the system. Carnap claims that when a sentence about the world is appropriately translated into the formal language of the constructional system, its epistemic content is rendered transparent by virtue of the fact that the sentence is displayed as logically derived from epistemically basic sentences whose truth-values can be determined directly by observation.

The idea that the logical form of a sentence is given by its translation into an extensional first order language, in which every sentence is a truth-function or a quantification of elementary observational sentences, is perhaps the central component of the logical empiricist account of meaning.

1.3   The Ontological View

Finally, a third approach regards the logical form of a sentence as the structure which expresses its ontological import, or its connection with objects in the world.

The account which Wittgenstein (1922) gives of the way in which propositions represent states of affairs is one version of an ontological view of logical form. Contrary to Frege, as well as the logical empiricists, Wittgenstein does not identify the logical form of a sentence with its translation into a formal language, but with a level of structure which it shares with the possible state of affairs that it represents. At this abstract level of form there is a one-to-one correspondence between the basic objects of the possible state of affairs and the elementary constituents of the propositions which the sentence expresses. A sentence represents a possible state of affairs by virtue of a structural isomorphism between the organization of the elementary constituents of the proposition which it expresses and the configuration of objects which defines the state of affairs. It is this structure which Wittgenstein regards as the logical form of both the proposition and the state of affairs it represents.

He summarizes this idea as follows. "Propositions can represent the whole of reality, but they cannot represent what they have in common with reality in order to be able to represent it – logical form" (Wittgenstein 1922: 4. 12, p. 51).

Wittgenstein's account implies that logical form is a structural relation which must exist, at some level, between the sentences of any language which are capable of depicting possible states of affairs in the world and the situations they represent.

Quine's (1960) notion of canonical notation provides an alternative version of the ontological view of logical form.[4] Quine maintains that it is only when the sentences of a language are paraphrased as quantified formulas in an extensional first order language that it is possible to clearly determine the ontology which they imply. According to his criterion of ontological commitment, the objects which the speakers of a language assume to exist are the individuals which they are prepared to posit as the values of the bound variables of the quantified paraphrases of their sentences.

Quine also regards a canonical first order language as the most appropriate framework for formulating the statements of a unified scientific theory comprising the totality of our beliefs about the world. The formalized version of this theory displays the relative proximity of each of its statements to experience.[5] Moreover, it renders explicit the relations of logical entailment which hold among the statements of the theory by virtue of the fact that these relations are represented as features of sentence structure.

Therefore, Quine's notion of canonical notation also seems to embody the epistemic and inferential views of logical form.

1.4   The Common Basis of the Philosophical Concepts of Logical Form

The three views of logical form considered here constitute distinct notions of an abstract formal structure to which the sentences of a natural language correspond. However, they share an essential property. Each of these approaches regards the logical form of a sentence as a formal object or level of representation in which the relation of the sentence to something external to it is directly expressed through structural properties of the representation. On the inferential view, this external content is the network of logical entailment relations in which the sentence stands relative to other sentences in the language. In the case of the epistemic view, the relevant external entity is a perceptual experience. On the ontological view it is objects (or configurations of objects) in the world.

Therefore, on the philosophical account, logical form is exocentric and relational in that its properties are determined by the connection between sentences and entities external to them. It is also frequently a normative concept. This is particularly evident in the case of translational theories (such as those of Frege, Carnap, and Quine) which treat the logical form of a sentence not as a structure implicit in the sentence itself, but as a canonical form into which it must be cast to reveal its relation to extra-sentential phenomena.

2 THE ROLE OF LF IN GB

The Government Binding model of grammar postulates three principal levels of syntactic representation. D-structure is the abstract underlying form of a sentence which is projected from the argument structure schema specified in the lexical representations of the heads of the phrases that the sentence contains, in accordance with X'-theory. S-structure is derived from D-structure by the (optional) application of the rule Move-α, which inserts a constituent into the position of an empty category, or adjoins it to another constituent. Move-α as a rule schema that maps D-structures into S-structures is instantiated primarily by the operations of NP movement, which shifts an NP from an argument position into an empty argument position, and *wh*-movement, which moves a *wh*-phrase from an argument position into a non-argument (operator) position. Finally, logical form (LF) is obtained from S-structure by further application of Move-α to quantified NPs (QR) or in situ *wh*-phrases (*wh*-raising). In mapping S-structure into LF, Move-α always moves a constituent into operator position.

QR and *wh*-raising are characterized as "interpretive rules" which yield a structure that is the input to additional rules of semantic (and cognitive) interpretation. These latter rules define a mapping between linguistic structure and extra-linguistic entities.

Each level of representation is constrained by a variety of well-formedness conditions belonging to distinct modules of the grammar. If a well-formed S-structure is derived to which neither QR nor *wh*-raising can apply, then it is identified directly with the LF of the sentence. Therefore, LF is a distinct level of representation to the extent that its derivation involves one or more applications of QR or *wh*-raising.

May (1985) stipulates that quantified NPs and *wh*-phrases are not referential arguments which can receive theta roles, while variables (traces and pronouns locally bound by operators) are. This stipulation has the effect of making the application of QR and *wh*-raising obligatory. If a quantified NP or in situ *wh*-phrase is not moved into operator (A')-position at LF, the structure violates the theta criterion, which requires a one-to-one correspondence between arguments and theta roles at LF.

May also adopts a constraint on LF which specifies that only one operator can be adjoined to any given level of X' projection.[6] He allows LF movement to adjoin expressions to VP and NP. Given these assumptions, the LF representations of (11) and (12) are (13) and (14), respectively.[7]

(11) Somebody from every city despises it.
(12) Who saw what?
(13) $[_{IP'}[_{NP1}[_{NP2}$ every city$]$ $[_{NP1}$ somebody from $t_2]]$ $[_{IP}t_1$ despises $t_2]]$
(14) $[_{CP}[_{SPEC}$ $[$what$_2$ who$_1]$ $[_{IP}t_1$ saw $t_2]]]$.

(13) is obtained from (11) by adjoining the subject NP "somebody in every city" to the sentence (IP), and then adjoining the embedded NP "every city" to the NP (NP$_1$) adjoined to IP. (14) is derived from (12) by adjoining the object NP "what" to the NP node dominating "who" in the SPEC of CP position. Thus LF provides a structural representation of the scope of quantified NPs and in situ *wh*-phrases.

LF is an abstract level of syntactic structure which mediates between S-structure and those rules of semantic interpretation that define the truth-conditions (or appropriate analogue) of a sentence. Its properties are determined by precisely the same sort of empirical and theoretical considerations which are involved in motivating and characterizing other levels of grammatical representation, such as D and S-structure. It is clear, then, that, in contrast to philosophical notions of logical form, LF is endocentric and non-relational in nature. It is an element in a sequence of representations, each of which captures certain grammatical properties of a sentence. The LF of a sentence is not projected as the structural expression of its relation to an extra-sentential content, but as a formal object of the theory of sentence grammar. It is derived by the same sorts of operations and subject to the same kinds of constraints postulated for other levels within this theory. The existence of LF as a distinct level of representation and its specific properties are empirical questions internal to linguistic theory.

In what follows, I will briefly review five representative arguments for the existence of LF.[8]

2.1   *Wh*-Raising in Complement Structures

May follows Huang (1982) in basing an argument for LF on the distinct complement selection properties of "wonder," "believe," and "know." As (15)–(17) illustrate, "wonder" requires an indirect question complement, "believe" takes a non-interrogative propositional argument, and "know" allows either type of complement.

(15)a   John wonders who his mother saw.
   b   *Who does John wonder (that) his mother saw?
(16)a   *John believes who his mother saw.
   b   Who does John believe his mother saw?
(17)a   John knows who his mother saw.
   b   Who does John know his mother saw?

Huang observes that the Chinese counterparts of (15)–(17), in which the *wh*-phrase remains in situ, receive parallel interpretations.

(18)   Zhangsan xiang-zhido ta muqin kanjian shei.
       Zhangsan wonder his mother see who.
       Zhangsan wonders who his mother saw.

(19)   Zhangsan xiangin ta muqin kanjian shei.
        Zhangsan believe his mother see who
        Who did Zhangsan believe his mother saw?
(20)   Zhangsan zhidao ta muqin kanjian shei.
    a   Who does Zhangsan know his mother saw?
    b   Zhangsan knows who his mother saw.

May and Huang explain this correspondence of readings between the English and Chinese cases by assuming that the Chinese counterparts of the English verbs in (15)–(17) have the same complement selection properties, and maintaining that the in situ *wh*-phrases in (18)–(20) are moved into appropriate operator positions in LF. They claim that Chinese differs from English in that *wh*-movement is realized at LF in the former and at S-structure in the latter (where possible). Hence, by postulating a level of structure defined by *wh*-raising, they are able to account for the identity of interpretations which holds between sentences in a language with *wh*-movement at S-structure and sentences in a language that allows *wh*-phrases to occupy only argument positions at S-structure.

2.2   Antecedent-Contained Deletions

Consider the empty VP in the relative clause of the object NP in

(21)   Dulles suspected everyone who Angleton did.

As May observes, if we attempt to interpret this VP by copying the VP of the entire sentence into the empty VP position at S-structure, we will generate an interpretive regress. This is due to the fact that the matrix VP contains the empty VP as a constituent.

The LF which results from applying QR to (21) is

(22) $[_{IP'}[_{NP1}$ everyone who$_1$ Angleton did] $[_{IP}$ Dulles suspected $t_1]]$

If the VP of the IP in (22) is assigned to the empty VP of the adjoined NP, (23) is obtained, which represents the desired interpretation of (21).

(23) $[_{IP'}$ $[_{NP1}$ everyone who Angleton suspected $t_1]$ $[_{IP}$ Dulles suspected $t_1]]$

May concludes that antecedent-contained deletions can only be interpreted by a VP copying rule which applies at LF.

2.3   LF and the ECP

The case for LF depends, to no small extent, upon the argument that the Empty Category Principle (ECP) applies to the variables created by LF movement. The ECP requires that empty categories be properly governed.[9] It applies at S-structure to distinguish, for example, (24)a from (24)b–c.

(24)a   *who does John believe [$_{CP}$t' that [$_{IP}$t kissed Mary]]
   b   who does John believe [$_{CP}$t' [$_{IP}$t kissed Mary]]
   c   who does John believe [$_{CP}$t' that [$_{IP}$ Mary kissed t]]

(24)a is ruled out by the ECP by virtue of the fact that the complementizer "that" blocks proper government of the subject trace of "who" by the trace in SPEC of the complement CP. The subject trace of the complement is properly governed in (24)b, as nothing intervenes between "t'" and "t." In (24)c, the object trace is properly governed by the verb "kissed."[10]

If it can be shown that the ECP also applies at LF, this provides a strong argument for LF movement and the level of representation which it defines. Three phenomena have been cited in support of the claim that LF movement is sensitive to the ECP.

2.3.1   Subject-Object Asymmetries Involving Quantified NPs

Kayne (1981) and Chomsky (1981) use the ECP to explain the contrast between the following French sentences, each of which contains the negatively quantified NP "personne."

(25)a   Je n'ai exigé qui'ils arrêtent personne.
   b   *Je n'ai exigé que personne soit arrêté.

They assign (25)a–b the LF representations (26)a–b, respectively.

(26)a   [$_{IP'}$ personne$_1$ [$_{IP}$Je n'ai exigé qu'ils arrêtent t$_1$]]
   b   [$_{IP'}$ personne$_1$ [$_{IP}$Je n'ai exigé que t$_1$ soit arrêté]]

The trace of QR is properly governed in (26)a, but not in (26)b.

2.3.2   Subject-Object Asymmetries Involving Wh-Phrases: Superiority Effects

Aoun, Hornstein, and Sportiche (1981) and Chomsky (1981) suggest that applying the ECP to the results of wh-raising makes it possible to account for the difference in acceptability between (27)a and (27)b.

(27)a   who t saw what
   b   *what did who see t

If we assume that the in situ *wh*-phrase in (27)a–b is adjoined to the *wh*-phrase in SPEC of CP, the LF structures assigned to these sentences are

(28)a $[_{CP}$what$_2$ who$_1$ $[_{IP}$t$_1$ saw t$_2]]$
   b $[_{CP}$who$_1$ what$_2$ $[_{IP}$t$_1$ saw t$_2]]$

The subject trace is properly governed in (28)a, but not in (28)b.[11]

2.3.3 Subject-Object Asymmetries Involving Wh-*Phrases and Quantified NPs*

May observes that while (29)a is ambiguous between two scope readings, (29)b is not.

(29)a   What did everyone buy for Max?
   b   Who bought everything for Max?

(29)a can be interpreted with "everyone" within the scope of "what," or as having scope over it. The former reading yields a question which presupposes that everyone bought the same thing for Max. The latter produces a multiple-answer question which can be answered by supplying a different purchase for each person. (29)b, on the other hand, allows only a narrow scope reading of "everything" on which it is presupposed that a single person (or group of people) bought everything for Max.

The relevant LF for (29)a is (30). Assuming the possibility of VP adjunction, the possible LFs for (29)b are (31)a–b.

(30) $[_{CP}$ what$_2$ $[_{IP'}$ everyone$_1$ $[_{IP}$ [t$_1$ buy t$_2$ for Max]]]]$
(31)a $[_{CP}$ who$_1$ $[_{IP'}$ everything$_2$ $[_{IP}$ t$_1$ bought t$_2$ for Max]]]$
   b $[_{CP}$ who$_1$ $[_{IP}$ t$_1$ $[_{VP'}$ everything$_2$ $[_{VP}$ bought t$_2$ for Max]]]]$

Both the trace of *wh*-movement and the trace of QR are properly governed in (30). As IP is not a barrier to government, "what" and "everyone" govern each other. Therefore, each may have wide scope relative to the other, and (30) represents both possible readings of (29)a.

In (31)a, "everything" prevents proper government of the subject trace, and so the structure is ruled out by the ECP. (34)b satisfies the ECP, as both the subject and object traces are properly governed. According to May, the fact that the quantified NP adjoined to the VP is dominated (although not exhaustively dominated) by a maximal projection which does not dominate "who" in SPEC of CP position prevents either operator from governing the other. The *wh*-phrase c-commands "everything" asymmetrically, and so the sentence admits only the interpretation on which "who" has wide scope relative to the quantified NP.

The five arguments summarized in 2.1–2.3 are by no means the only arguments which have been advanced for LF, but they are certainly among the most central. In the next section I will suggest an alternative view of the relation between syntax and semantics which dispenses with LF.

3   SEMANTIC INTERPRETATION WITHOUT LF

In Lappin (1982), (1984), (1985), and (1988–9) I propose that rules of model theoretic interpretation apply directly to the S-structure of a sentence in order to yield its semantic interpretation. Williams (1986) also suggests that LF be reduced to S-structure. On this approach, S-structure is the input to semantic rules which define the truth conditions (or appropriate analogue) of a sentence, and there is no additional level of representation defined by QR (and *wh*-raising) which stands between S-structure and the application of these rules. I will refer to this view as "S-structure Interpretivism."

3.1   Interpretation of Quantified NPs in Situ

An important feature of S-structure Interpretivism is the claim that in at least some cases, quantified NPs are interpreted in situ, i.e. in the argument positions which they occupy at S-structure.

I will assume the treatment of NPs given in Montague grammar and generalized quantifier theory, according to which an NP denotes a set of sets.[12] A proper name like "John," for example, denotes the set of all sets containing John (the set of John's properties). "Every man" is assigned the set of all sets containing all men, "five students" is interpreted as the set of all sets containing at least five students, etc. The S-structure of a sentence is interpreted compositionally, with each syntactic constituent corresponding either to a semantic function or an argument of a function. Subject NPs are interpreted as functions from the sets denoted by their VPs to truth-values. For example, let E be the domain of individuals, S the set of students, and R the set of radicals. "Five students are radicals" is true iff

(32) $R \in \{X \subseteq E: |X \cap S| \geq 5\}$

When NPs occur in non-subject argument positions, their denotations are arguments of the functions denoted by the verbs and prepositions which subcategorize them.[13]

There are at least two reasons for holding that it must be possible to assign quantified NPs denotations in situ at S-structure. First, as has been frequently pointed out, intensional verbs like "seek" give rise to ambiguities.[14]

(33) Mary seeks a unicorn.

On the intensional (*de dicto*) reading, Mary seeks an entity whose existence we are not committed to, while on the extensional (*de re*) reading, there is a unicorn which Mary seeks. Given May's assumptions concerning QR, the LF assigned to (33) is (34), which represents only the extensional reading.

(34) $[_{IP'} [_{NP1}$ a unicorn$] [_{IP}$ Mary seeks $t_1]]$

May attempts to avoid this difficulty by partitioning the objects of the domain into existent and non-existent entities, and allowing intensional verbs to categorize for NPs which denote either variety of object. Thus "t_1" is interpreted as a variable which can take actual or non-actual objects as values.

This suggestion does not solve the problem posed by (33). The intensional-extensional ambiguity also arises in cases where the relevant NP is not an argument of the intensional verb, as in

(35) John believes that a girl loves him.

(35) also admits of two readings. On one, "a girl" has narrow scope relative to "believes," and on the other it has wide scope.

It would seem that in order to provide a unified analysis of (33) and (35), it is necessary to treat both sentences as involving ambiguity in the scope relation between an NP and an intensional verb. The intensional reading results when the NP is interpreted in situ and the function denoted by the verb applies to the intension of the NP, or to the intension of the sentence which contains it. The extensional reading requires that the NP be assigned an interpretation in a position outside of the scope of the verb.

The second reason for permitting in situ interpretation of quantified NPs is provided by VP adverbs like "simultaneously," "consecutively," "at once," and "in turn."[15] On May's analysis, (36)a is assigned (36)b and (36)c as possible LF representations.

(36)a John saw every student
$$\left\{ \begin{array}{l} \text{simultaneously} \\ \text{consecutively} \\ \text{at once} \\ \text{in turn} \end{array} \right\}$$

b $[_{IP'} [_{NP1}$ every student$] [_{IP}$ John saw t_1
$$\left\{ \begin{array}{l} \text{simultaneously} \\ \text{consecutively} \\ \text{at once} \\ \text{in turn} \end{array} \right\}]]$$

c $[_{IP}$ John $[_{VP'}$ $[_{NP1}$ every student] $[_{VP}$ saw t_1 $\left\{\begin{array}{l}\text{simultaneously}\\\text{consecutively}\\\text{at once}\\\text{in turn}\end{array}\right\}$]]]

"every student" has the entire IP as its scope in both (36)b and (36)c. As the trace which it binds is interpreted as a variable ranging over individuals, these structures yield an inappropriate interpretation for the sentence. On the required reading, the quantified NP is within the scope of the VP adverb.

If "every student" is interpreted in object position, an appropriate interpretation can be assigned to (36)a. Let NP′ be an NP denotation. Following Cooper (1983), I will take "saw" to denote

(37) $\{<a,NP'>: \{b: a \text{ saw } b\} \in NP'\}$

Applying this interpretation of "saw" to the denotation of "every student" yields (38) as the interpretation of the VP "saw every student."

(38) $\{a: \{b: <a,b> \in \{<x,y,>: x \text{ saw } y\}\} \in \{X \subseteq E: \{\text{students}\} \subseteq X\}\}$
  $= \{a: \{\text{students}\} \subseteq \{b: a \text{ saw } b\}\}$

VP adverbs denote functions from VP sets to VP sets. When the function denoted by "simultaneously" is applied to the set defined in (38), it will yield an appropriate subset of this set as value. This subset can be characterized as follows. Let t_i be a point in time.

(39) $\|$saw every student simultaneously$\|$ =
  $\{a: \{\text{students}\} \subseteq \{b: a \text{ saw } b \text{ at } t_i\}\}$

Therefore,

(40) $\|$John saw every student simultaneously$\|$ = true iff
  $\{a: \{\text{students}\} \subseteq \{b: a \text{ saw } b \text{ at } t_i\}\} \in \{X \subseteq E: j \in X\}$
  $\equiv \{\text{students}\} \subseteq \{b: j \text{ saw } b \text{ at } t_i\}$

(40) provides the correct truth conditions for (36)a, with "simultaneously" or "at once" taken as the VP adverb.

"Consecutively" can be taken to denote a function which maps the VP set defined in (38) into the VP set specified in (41). Let s_i be a temporal segment consisting of a sequence of consecutive points in time, and let s_i ... s_k be a sequence of consecutive over-lapping temporal segments.

(41) $\|$saw every student consecutively$\| =$
$\{a: \{students\} \subseteq \{b: b \in C\ (C = b_i \ldots b_k\ (1<k)$ & for every b_i, s_i, a
saw b_i in s_i & for every $j \neq i$, a did not see b_i in $s_j)\}\}$

C in (41) is a sequence of objects which were seen in succession.

May's requirement that, quantified NPs can only be interpreted in operator position at LF must be discarded, given that it is possible, and in some cases necessary to interpret these NPs in situ at S-structure.

3.2 Wide Scope Readings and NP Storage

While quantified NPs can be interpreted in their argument positions at S-structure, there are sentences whose preferred (or possible) interpretations require the assignment of scope to a quantified NP which is wider than the S-structure c-command domain of the NP. The most natural reading of (11) is one on which "every city" has wide scope relative to "somebody."

(11) Somebody from every city despises it.

Moreover, the extensional readings of (33) and (35) are obtained by giving "a unicorn" and "a girl" scope over "seeks" and "believes," respectively. How, then, can such wide scope interpretations of quantified Np's be represented within the framework of S-Structure Interpretivism?

Cooper (1983) proposes a rule of NP storage which assigns an NP in argument position a sequence consisting of a bound pronoun (variable) denotation and the stored denotation of the NP. This sequence remains a constituent in the interpretation of each successive expression containing the NP, until the NP denotation is retrieved from storage and applied to the set which is the denotation of the expression at the point of retrieval. Consider (33), for example.

(33) Mary seeks a unicorn.

If NP storage is applied to "a unicorn," then the denotation of the object NP is the sequence $<\{X \subseteq E: x_i \in X\}, \|a\ unicorn\|>$. The interpretation of "seeks" applies to the first element of this sequence to yield $<\|seeks\|$ $((\{X \subseteq E: x_i \in X\})^w)$, $\|a\ unicorn\|>$, and $\|Mary\|$ applies to the first element of the second sequence, giving $<\|Mary\|\ (\|seeks\|\ ((\{X \subseteq E: x_i \in X\})^w))$, $\|a$ unicorn$\|>$. The first element of this sequence is the interpretation of an open sentence which characterizes the set $\{a: Mary\ seeks\ ((\{X \subseteq E: a \in X\})^w)\}$. $\|a\ unicorn\|$ is released from storage at this point in the derivation of the interpretation of the sentence, and applied to this set. The resulting interpretation is

(42) $\{a:$ Mary seeks $((\{X \subseteq E: a \in X\})^w)\} \in \{X \subseteq E: X \cap$ unicorn $\neq \emptyset\}$
   $\equiv$ $\|unicorns\| \cap \{a:$ Mary seeks $((\{X \subseteq E: a \in X\})^w)\} \neq \emptyset$

(42) correctly represents the extensional reading of (33).

In the application of storage to an in situ *wh*-phrase, the stored *wh*-phrase interpretation corresponds to a lambda operator. When this operator is retrieved and applied to the denotation of an open sentence, it yields a set in terms of which the interpretation of a *wh*-relative clause or *wh*-question is defined. In situ *wh*-phrases will only be assigned sequences with stored *wh*-operators as their interpretations, and so storage is obligatory for these expressions.

There are at least two basic differences between QR (and *wh*-raising) and storage. First, while QR applies only to quantified NPs (and *wh*-raising to in situ *wh*-phrases), storage applies to NPs in general.[16]

Second QR (and *wh*-raising) is a movement rule that maps syntactic structures into phrase markers of the same kind. Storage, on the other hand, is a semantic rule which operates at the level at which the denotations of expressions are represented.

The fact that storage applies to non-quantified NPs permits us to capture intensional-extensional ambiguities which arise with proper names.

(43)a   Mary seeks Pegasus.
   b   John believes that Pegasus can fly.

At LF, only the intensional readings of (43)a–b are represented.

Independent motivation for incorporating a rule of storage into the semantic component of the grammar is provided by the interaction of VP deletion and wide scope readings of quantified NPs within the VP.[17] Hirschbuler (1982) observes that on the preferred reading of

(44)   A Canadian flag was hanging in front of many windows and an American flag was too.

"many windows" receives wide scope separately in each conjunct relative to both "a Canadian flag" and "an American flag." On this reading, the set of many windows in front of which an American flag was hanging need not be identical to the set of many windows in front of which a Canadian flag was hanging. The two possible LFs for the first conjunct of (43) are

(45)a $[_{IP'}$ $[_{NP1}$ $[_{NP2}$ many windows $]$ $[_{NP1}$ a Canadian flag$]]$ $[_{IP}t_1$ $[_{VP}$ was hanging in front of $t_2]]]$
   b $[_{IP'}$ $[_{NP1}$ a Canadian flag$]$ $[_{IP}t_1$ was $[_{VP'}$ $[_{NP2}$ many windows$]$ $[_{VP}$ hanging in front of $t_2]]]]$

The wide scope reading of (43) can only be obtained from (45)a. Following Williams (1977), I will assume that VP anaphora involves copying a representation of the antecedent VP into the empty VP which depends upon it. If the VP of (45)b is used, then "many windows" receives a narrow scope reading in both conjuncts. If the VP of (45)a is copied, the second conjunct will contain an unbound trace, t_2, and so the LF of (44) will be uninterpretable.

One might suggest copying the S-structure VP of the first conjunct of (43) into the empty VP, and then applying QR to "many windows" in both conjuncts. However, this derivation of the LF of (43) violates the autonomy of syntax, as it permits a discourse rule of VP copying to apply prior to QR, which is a rule of sentence grammar.[18]

If we assume that VP copying operates on denotations (or intensions) of VPs, we can avoid this difficulty. NP storage can be applied to "many windows" in the first conjunct of (44), and the VP denotation of this conjunct can be copied into the second conjunct at a point at which ‖many windows‖ is still in storage. ‖many windows‖ will then be retrieved in each conjunct, and applied separately to appropriate sets, giving the required localized wide scope reading. As storage is an interpretive rule which operates on (model theoretic) semantic representations, it need not be constrained by the condition that it apply prior to all discourse rules.

It is also worth noting that May's formulation of QR would appear to require that a semantic rule analogous to storage apply to certain LF structures. May stipulates that when a quantified NP is adjoined to VP, or to an NP adjoined to IP at LF, it has scope over the entire sentence in which it is contained. However, if we assume that LF is the input to model theoretic rules of semantic interpretation, it is not possible to assign an NP adjoined to VP or NP an appropriate interpretation in this position by means of compositional rules. It is necessary to apply an interpretive procedure that moves the denotation of the NP to a point in the function-argument structure of the sentence at which it can apply to the denotation of the (open) sentence, rather than to the denotation of the VP or NP to which it is adjoined.

Storage permits us to represent wide scope readings and to assign interpretations to in situ *wh*-phrases. Given that it is independently motivated, the question is whether we also require a rule of QR and the level of representation which it defines. The arguments presented in 2.1–2.3 provide putative empirical support for QR. In the following section, I will argue that the phenomena which these arguments invoke do not motivate QR.

4   QR REVISITED

4.1   In Situ *Wh*-Phrases and Complement Selection

The version of S-structure Interpretivism proposed here allows for a straightforward and natural explanation of the fact that Huang's examples

(18)–(20) receive the same readings as their English counterparts.

(18)   Zhangsan xiang-zhidao ta muqin.
       Zhangsan wonder his mother see who
       Zhangsan wondered who his mother saw.
(19)   Zhangsan xiangxin ta muqin kanjian shei.
       Zhangsan believe his mother see who
       Who does Zhangsian believe that his mother saw?
(20)   Zhangsan zhidao ta muqin kanjian shei.
       Zhangsan know his mother see who
   a   Who does Zhangsan know his mother saw?
   b   Zhangsan knows who his mother saw.

If we assume that "xiang-zhidao," like wonder, subcategorizes for an indirect question, then it denotes a function from a question denotation (or intension) to a VP extension. Hence, in order for the denotation (or intension) of the complement of (18) to constitute an appropriate argument for the function denoted by "xiang-zhido," the in situ *wh*-phrase "shei" must be retrieved from storage and applied to the open sentence denoted by the complement to yield the interpretation of an indirect question. Similarly, "xiangxin" denotes a function from sentence denotations to VP extensions. Consequently, the stored denotation of the in situ *wh*-phrase can be retrieved and applied only to the denotation of the matrix IP. "zhidao" is ambiguous in that it can denote either a function from question denotations to VP extensions, or a function from sentence denotations to VP extensions. The point at which the stored *wh*-phrase is retrieved in (20) is determined by which function is assigned to "zhidao." In general, the function denoted by the matrix verb in these examples will define the semantic type of the complement, and the point at which the *wh*-phrase is retrieved from storage is determined by the complement's type.

4.2   Antecedent-Contained Deletions

As Haïk (1987) observes, the *wh*-phrase in the relative clause of an antecedent-contained deletion structure like (21) is constrained by Subjacency.

(21)   Dulles suspected everyone who Angleton did.
(46)a   John read everything which Bill believes he did.
   b   *John read everything which Bill believes the claim that he did.

This poses difficulties for May's analysis. On this account, the VP of the relative clause in (21) and (46)a–b is empty at S-structure, and the *wh*-phrase binds a trace only after VP copying has applied to the LF produced by the movement of the object NP. But it is unclear why, on May's analysis, the A'-chain consisting of the *wh*-phrase and the object trace which it binds should obey Subjacency, given that this chain is defined at LF rather than S-structure. In particular, it will contain no intermediate traces in the SPECs of embedded CPs. The fact that antecedent-contained deletion observes Subjacency provides motivation for positing a trace bound by a *wh*-phrase (or empty operator) in the empty VP of the relative clause in sentences like (21) and (46)a.

There is an additional argument for postulating such traces at S-structure. Consider the contrast between (47)a–b and (47)c.

(47)a   I know which book John read and Mary didn't.
   b   I know which book John read and which book Mary didn't read.
   c   ?I know which book John read and which book Mary didn't.

While (47)c is not completely unacceptable, it does seem significantly worse than either (47a) or (47b). We can explain this contrast as follows. In (47)a, "which book" binds a trace in the first conjunct of the indirect question, but not in the second. In (47)b, each occurrence of "which book" binds a trace. Thus "which book" is not a vacuous operator in either of these sentences. However, in (47)c, the second occurrence of "which book" does not bind a variable at S-structure. If we assume that the prohibition against vacuous operators applies at all levels of representation (as Haïk 1987 suggests), then (47)c is ruled out. We can explain the fact that the sentence is marginal rather than completely unacceptable by assuming that it is in some sense repaired by VP copying, which provides a variable for the *wh*-phrase in the second conjunct. Antecedent-contained deletions are not marginal. In contrast to (47)c, (21) and (46)a are fully acceptable. Therefore, it is reasonable to assume that the *wh*-phrase in the relative clauses of these sentences binds a trace at S-structure.

Haïk proposes that the operator in the relative clause of an antecedent-contained deletion structure binds the empty VP as a variable. On this view, the S-structure of (21) is

(48)   Dulles suspected [$_{NP}$ everyone [$_{CP}$ who$_1$ [$_{IP}$ Angleton did [$_{VP1}$e]]]]

Haïk stipulates that Subjacency applies to A'-chains at S-structures, even when they do not arise through movement. She also requires that QR adjoin the object NP in (48) to the matrix IP, and assumes that a VP copying rule assigns the matrix VP to the empty VP at LF.

Haïk further stipulates that the operator of the relative clause is re-indexed so that it binds the object NP trace of QR in the copied VP. Thus (21) receives the post-LF structure (23), as it does on May's analysis.

(23)   [$_{IP'}$ [$_{NP1}$ everyone who Angleton suspected t$_1$] [$_{IP}$ Dulles suspected t$_1$]]

While Haïk's proposal captures the fact that antecedent contained deletion is sensitive to Subjacency, it does so at considerable cost. Specifically, it requires that an A'-chain in which an operator binds a VP variable at S-structure be redefined as a chain in which the same operator binds an NP variable at (post-) LF through re-indexing of the operator. This would seem to be an ad hoc and awkward device. Moreover, Haïk must assume that a binding relation between an operator and a VP variable which does not arise through movement conforms to Subjacency, although intermediate operators do not appear in the SPECs of embedded CPs separating the highest operator from the variable. There does not seem to be any independent motivation for this assumption.

However, more significant than either of these difficulties is the fact that Haïk's account (like May's analysis) does not extend to antecedent-contained deletion in adverbial structures. It has frequently been noted that comparative deletion obeys Subjacency ((49)a–c).[19]

(49)a   John succeeded more frequently than Mary did.
  b   John succeeded more frequently than Mary believes he did.
  c   *John succeeded more frequently than Mary wonders how he did.

Therefore, on Haïk's approach, it must be assumed that an operator-bound VP variable is present at S-structure in the comparative clauses of these AdvPs. But QR will not move adverbial phrases, as it applies only to quantified NPs and in situ *wh*-phrases. Therefore, an interpretive regress will arise when we attempt to assign the matrix VP to the empty VP of the comparative clause.

Alternatively, we could adopt Larson's (1987) proposal that QR does apply to comparative adverbial phrases (on the grounds that the interpretation of comparative terms like "more" involves quantification). Larson claims that elliptical PPs like "before Bill did" in (52)a are also subject to QR. The evidence he provides for this claim is that such PPs display scope ambiguities in intensional contexts, as in "John believes that Bill arrived before he did." However, this fact does not motivate Larson's claim. As noted in section 3.2, examples like (43)a–b indicate that proper names also permit both narrow and wide scope readings relative to intensional verbs, and, presumably, Larson does not want QR to apply to proper names. But even if one allows QR to adjoin comparative adverbs to the matrix IP, they will incorrectly be assigned sentential scope.

A comparative adverb is, in fact, a VP adverb which denotes a function from VP interpretations to VP interpretations. To see this, consider

(50)   Someone succeeded more frequently than Mary did.

The only reading available for (50) is that there is someone who has the property of having succeeded more frequently than Mary succeeded. It cannot mean, for example, that it was more frequently the case that there was someone (other than Mary) who succeeded than it was the case that Mary succeeded. But taking "more frequently than Mary did" as a sentential adverb requires an interpretation of the latter sort.

Allowing QR to adjoin the adverbial phrase in (49)a–b and (50) to the matrix VP will not solve the problem. Although the adverb will receive narrow scope with respect to the subject NP at LF, it will still, on May's account, be a sentential operator, given that quantified NPs which are adjoined to VP at LF are sentential operators. As in the case of adjunction to IP, it is not clear how an appropriate interpretation could be assigned to such an LF.

Finally, we might take the view that the comparative adverb is already adjoined to a core VP at D-structure. The S-structure of (49)a would then be (51).

(51)   John [$_{VP'}$ [$_{VP}$ succeeded] [$_{AdvP}$ more frequently [$_{CP}$ than Mary did [$_{VP}$]]]]

The core VP could then be assigned to the empty VP of the adjoined adverbial phrase without giving rise to an interpretive regress.

It is unclear how either May or Haïk can make use of this analysis. If May's analysis is extended to adverbs, then presumably there will be an empty operator in the SPEC of the comparative CP at S-structure, but no AdvP variable for this operator to bind (by analogy with his treatment of (21)). After the core VP is copied into the empty VP, the operator will remain vacuous. On Haïk's view, the empty operator binds the empty VP at S-structure. VP copying will cause the variable to disappear, and so the operator will also be vacuous on this analysis.

The same difficulty arises with antecedent-contained deletion in non-comparative adverbs. As (52)a–c illustrate, these structures also exhibit Subjacency effects.

(52)a   John arrived before Bill did.
  b   John arrived before Mary believed Bill did.
  c   *John arrived before Mary believed the claim that Bill did.

It seems, then, that neither May's analysis nor Haïk's provides an adequate account of antecedent-contained deletion in adverbial clauses.

Baltin (1987) proposes a treatment of antecedent-contained deletion which does not employ QR. He suggests that the relative clause of the object NP in (53)a is extraposed and adjoined to the matrix VP at S-structure, giving (53)b (he assumes that extraposition of a relative clause does not leave a trace). As the empty VP is not contained in its antecedent in (53)b, VP copying can apply without generating a regress, thus yielding (53)c.

(53)a   Bill hit the man who asked him to.
   b   Bill [$_{VP'}$ [$_{VP}$ hit [$_{NP}$ the man]] [$_{CP}$ who t asked him [$_{IP}$ PRO to [$_{VP}$
        ]]]]
   c   Bill [$_{VP'}$ [$_{VP}$ hit [$_{NP}$ the man]] [$_{CP}$ who t asked him [$_{IP}$ PRO to [$_{VP}$ hit
        the man]]]]

There are at least three serious problems with Baltin's analysis. First, it does not account for the fact that antecedent-contained deletion is sensitive to Subjacency, as it does not posit a variable in the S-structure of the empty VP.

Second, it is not clear how the analysis can handle (21), in which the N′ containing the relative clause has a quantified determiner, and the *wh*-phrase corresponds to an argument of the empty VP. After extraposition of the relative clause, the S-structure of (21) is (54)a. If the core VP is copied into the empty VP, the result if (54)b, which does not represent the desired interpretation.

(54)a   Dulles [$_{VP'}$ [$_{VP}$ suspected [everyone]] [$_{CP}$ who Angleton did [$_{VP}$]]]
   b   Dulles [$_{VP'}$ [$_{VP}$ suspected [everyone]] [$_{CP}$ who Angleton [$_{VP}$ sus-
        pected [everyone]]]]

If one assumes that comparative adverbs occur within VP, a similar problem arises when one attempts to extend Baltin's account to these adverbs by allowing extraposition of the comparative clause. The result of such extraposition in the case of (49)a is (55)a. VP copying yields (55)b, which is not an appropriate representation of the intended interpretation.

(55)   a   John [$_{VP'}$ [$_{VP}$ succeeded [$_{AdvP}$ more frequently]] [$_{CP}$ than Mary
            did [$_{VP}$]]]
       b   John [$_{VP'}$ [$_{VP}$ succeeded [$_{AdvP}$ more frequently]] [$_{CP}$ than Mary
            succeeded more frequently]]]

Finally, as May points out (p.c.), Baltin's analysis predicts that antecedent-contained deletion should not be possible in relative clauses within NPs that are not VP final. Extraposition and adjunction to the matrix VP can only occur from VP final position. However, as (56) illustrates, this prediction is incorrect.

(56)   John considers everyone who Mary does funny.

In (56), an antecedent-contained empty VP occurs within the subject NP of the small clause complement of "considers."

It is possible to account for the various properties of antecedent-contained deletion noted here if we assume that the empty VP of the relative or comparative clause is structured, and contains a trace of an appropriate category bound by a *wh*-phrase or empty operator at S-structure. A variant of this proposal was advanced in Wasow (1972), and adopted by Williams (1977). On the version of the structured empty VP analysis which I am proposing, (21) and (49)a have the S-structures (57)a and (57)b, respectively.

(57)a Dulles suspected [$_{NP}$ [$_{N'}$ everyone [$_{CP}$ who$_1$ Angleton did [$_{VP}$ [$_V$] [$_{NP}$t$_1$]]]]]

   b John succeeded [$_{AdvP}$ more frequently [$_{CP}$ O$_1$ than Mary did [$_{VP}$ [$_V$] [$_{AdvP}$t$_1$]]]]

The correct reading of each sentence is obtained by assigning the interpretation of "suspected" to the empty verb in the relative clause of (57)a, and that of "succeeded" to the empty verb in the comparative clause of (57)b, which yields (58)a–b.

(58)a Dulles suspected [$_{NP}$ [$_{N'}$ everyone [$_{CP}$ who$_1$ Angleton [$_{VP}$ [$_V$ suspected] [$_{NP}$t$_1$]]]]]

   b John succeeded [$_{AdvP}$ more frequently [$_{CP}$ O$_1$ than Mary [$_{VP}$ [$_V$ succeeded] [$_{AdvP}$t$_1$]]]]

This analysis explains the fact that antecedent-contained deletion structures conform to Subjacency straightforwardly. It assumes that an element of the empty VP has actually moved from the VP into SPEC of CP position at S-structure. Therefore, when embedded CPs intervene between the operator and the trace in argument position which it binds, intermediate traces will appear in the SPECs of these CPs.

An interpretive regress is avoided in both relative clause and adverbial cases, because copying assigns only selected constituents of the matrix VP to empty components of the embedded VP. This account characterizes antecedent-contained deletion as a relation of anaphoric dependence of certain constituents within an embedded empty VP upon their counterparts in the matrix VP, rather than as an instance of global VP anaphora.[20]

Haïk objects to (57)a as an S-structure representation of (21) on the following grounds. If *wh*-movement is involved in the derivation of the relative clause in (21), then it should be possible to relativize the object of a preposition in an empty VP and leave the preposition stranded. However, this is not the case.

(59)a Mary talked about everyone who Peter did.
   b *Mary talked about everyone who Peter did about.

This objection is not decisive. I will refer to the verbal head of a VP, its arguments, and its adjuncts as "major VP constituents." There appears to be a constraint on constituent anaphora which prohibits the appearance of non-major constituents as the only lexically realized elements of a partially empty VP. Thus, as Haïk herself notes, a preposition cannot be omitted in a gapping structure like (60), or in a comparative deletion structure like (61).

(60)   John wrote to Bill and Mary *(to) Sam.

(61)   John talks about politics more than he does *(about) linguistics.

Whatever the precise formulation of this constraint, it is sufficient to rule out (59)b. Therefore, the fact that prepositions cannot be stranded in isolation within antecedent-contained VPs is compatible with the view that these structures are derived by *wh*-(empty operator) movement.

The following examples of comparative deletion provide additional motivation for treating antecedent-contained deletion as constituent anaphora.

(62)a   John writes more books than Bill does articles.
   b   The University gives more money to the library for books than the city does to the orchestra for instruments.
   c   The University gives more money to the library for periodicals than it does for books.
   d   John wrote more for the journal about politics than he did about linguistics.

In (62)a, the verb of the comparative clause is empty, and the direct object is realized. In (62)b–d, the verb and the object or various adjuncts (or both) are empty, while other adjuncts are present.

Partially empty VPs of this kind are also possible in relative clauses and non-comparative AdvPs.

(63)a   John showed everything to Mary which he did to Bill.
   b   Mary argues about politics with everyone who she does about linguistics.
(64)a   Mary arrived in London before Sam did in New York.
   b   John reviewed the play for the *New York Times* shortly after Bill did for the *Washington Post*.

In all of these cases, the interpretation of the partially empty VP is obtained by a copying rule which operates on constituents of VPs.

Interestingly, this sort of constituent anaphora is generally not possible

in intersentential VP anaphora structures, where the anaphorically dependent VP is not contained within its antecedent.

(65)a John showed everything to Mary and Bill did too.
   b *John showed everything to Mary and Bill did to Sam.
   c John reviewed the play and Bill did too.
   d *John reviewed the play and Mary did the book.

It seems, then, that a global relation of VP anaphora holds only between
an entire empty VP and its antecedent in another clause.

Unlike the proposals of May, Haïk, and Baltin, the analysis given here
provides a unified account of antecedent-contained deletion in relative
clauses and adverbial phrases. It explains the fact that antecedent-
contained deletion obeys Subjacency, and it accounts for the appearance of
partially empty VPs in these structures. This analysis assumes that the rule
of constituent copying which interprets antecedent-contained (partially)
empty VPs applies at S-structure.

4.3   ECP Effects

4.3.1   Wide Scope Readings of Quantified NPs   Van Reimsdijk and
Williams (1981) and Williams (1986) suggest an alternative explanation of
the contrast between (25)a and (25)b.

(25)a Je n'ai exigé qu'ils arrêtent personne.
   b *Je n'ai exigé que personne soit arrêté.

They propose that "ne" is generated in a position adjacent to "personne"
in D-structure and cliticized at S-structure, leaving a trace in its original
position. This trace is properly governed in (25)a, but not in (25)b. This
analysis rules out (25)b as an ECP violation at S-structure.

Williams (1986) also observes that in (66)a, "not a single novel" can take
either narrow or wide scope relative to "want," while in (66)b, it receives
only a narrow scope reading.

(66)a John wants to read not a single novel.
   b John wants not a single novel to be read.

There is no barrier to the proper government of the trace of "not a single
novel" in (66)b (either by "wants," or through antecedent-government by
a trace of QR adjoined to the matrix VP). Therefore the wide scope
reading of this NP should be possible, even if the ECP applies at LF. As
Williams notes, the distinction between (66)a, and (66)b indicates that the

subject-object asymmetry with respect to the availability of wide scope readings of the quantified NPs in complement sentences is independent of the ECP.

It should also be pointed out that this asymmetry is by no means absolute or uniform. Consider

(67)   Some boy believes that each girl in the class is attractive.

It is possible to assign (67) an interpretation on which "each girl" receives wide scope relative to both "believes" and "some boy." The LF required for this reading violates both the ECP and the generalization that quantified NP subjects of complement sentences receive only narrow scope readings. It seems, then, that this generalization expresses a tendency of interpretation rather than a condition to be captured by a grammatical constraint. In any case, facts like (66)a–b and (67) clearly suggest that the subject-object asymmetry in wide scope readings of quantified NPs is not an ECP effect.

4.3.2 Superiority Effects   Kayne (1983) proposes the Connectedness Condition (CC) as an alternative to the ECP. He formulates the CC in terms of the notion of a g-projection.

(68)   Y is a g-projection of X iff
        (a)   Y is a projection of X or of a g-projection of X

        or

        (b)   X is a structural governor and Y immediately dominates W and
        Z, where Z is a maximal projection of a g-projection of X, and W
        and Z are in a canonical government configuration.

Kayne stipulates that the g-projection set G_β of β includes β and every g-projection of β. He states the CC as follows.

(69)   CC: Let $\beta_1 \ldots \beta_j, \beta_{j+1} \ldots \beta_n$ be a maximal set of categories in a
        tree such that $\forall \alpha$, $\exists_j$, β_j is uniformly bound by α. Then
        $\{\alpha\} \cup (\cup_{1 \leqslant j} G_{n \leqslant \beta j})$ must constitute a subtree of T.

The CC requires the g-projection sets of all expressions uniformly bound by an antecedent α, taken together with α, to form a subtree of the tree in which these expressions are contained. α uniformly binds β and δ if β and δ are both bound (in some extended sense) by α, and they are expressions of the same kind (e.g. both β and δ are empty categories).

The CC predicts the contrast between (27)a and (27)b.

(27)a   who t saw what
   b   *what did who see t

Assume that the *wh*-phrase in the SPEC of CP in both these sentences binds (in an extended sense) both its trace and the *wh*-phrase in argument position. The g-projection set of "what" in (27)a includes CP, and the union of "who" with this g-projection set constitutes a subtree of the tree for (27)a. IP is not a barrier to government, and so "who" governs its trace in (27)a. Hence the g-projection set of the subject trace includes CP, and the union of "who" and this set is also a subtree of the entire tree. Therefore, (27)a satisfies the CC. In (27)b, the g-projection set of "who" does not extend beyond the subject NP (its maximal projection) This is due to the fact that "who" is ungoverned, and, as "what" does not uniformly bind its trace and "who," the g-projection set of "who" does not connect with that of the governed trace. As a result, the union of the g-projection set of "who" and "what" does not form a subtree, and (27)b violates the CC.

It must be emphasized that the CC applies at S-structure rather than LF. If it were to apply to the output of *wh*-raising at LF, then the distinction between the *wh*-phrase in argument position and the *wh*-trace would be lost in (27)a–b. This distinction is necessary in order to prevent the g-projection set of "who" in (27)b from connecting with that of the object trace through uniform binding.

May replaces the ECP as a condition on LF with Pesetsky's PCC.[21] This condition specifies that for any set of A'-binding paths in a tree, if any of the paths intersect (have at least two successive nodes in common), then one path must contain the others. A path is a set of successive nodes each of which immediately dominates its successor. The initial element of a path dominates a binding element α, and its final element dominates a constituent which α binds. The LF of (27)b violates the PCC, while the LF of (27)a satisfies this condition.

(70)a

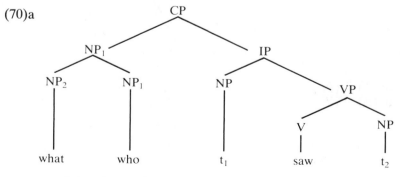

path (t_1) = {IP, CP}
path (t_2) = {VP, IP, CP, NP$_1$}

(70)b

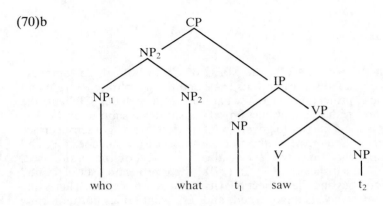

path (t_1) = {IP, CP, NP$_2$}
path (t_2) = {VP, IP, CP}

Consider the following examples.

(71)a   ?who did John talk to t about whom
   b   ?who did John talk to whom about t

While these sentences are somewhat marginal, they are significantly better than (27)b. The PCC rules out the LF representations of (71)a–b.

(72)a

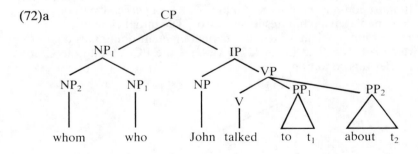

path (t_1) = {PP$_1$, VP, IP, CP}
path (t_2) = {PP$_2$, VP, IP, CP, NP$_1$}

(72)b

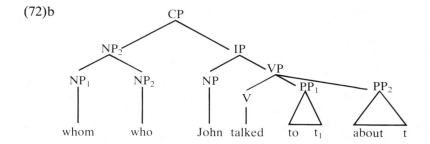

$$\text{path } (t_1) = \{PP_1, VP, IP, Cp, NP_2\}$$
$$\text{path } (t_2) = \{PP_2, VP, IP, CP\}$$

However, (71)a–b satisfy the CC at S-structure. Both the trace and the in situ *wh*-phrase are (properly) governed in each sentence, and their g-projection sets extend through the VP and IP to CP. Hence, the union of each g-projection set with the *wh*-phrase in SPEC of CP position constitutes a subtree.

(71)a–b provide motivation for preferring the CC account of superiority effects to the PCC analysis. It seems, then, that these effects can be adequately handled at S-structure.

4.3.3 Wh-*Phrase-Quantified NP Scope Interactions*

May's examples (29)a–b suggest that a quantified NP cannot take scope over a *wh*-phrase which binds a trace that c-commands it at S-structure.

(29)a   What did everyone buy for Max?
   b   Who bought everything for Max?

As in the case of the claim that quantified NPs in the subject position of a complement clause receive only narrow scope readings, this generalization expresses a tendency rather than an absolute condition. Consider the following examples in which the quantified NPs contain the quantifier "each," which tends to take wide scope.

(73)a   Who recommended each article?
   b   Who wants to date each girl?
   c   Who believes each film to be worth seeing?

The quantified NPs in (73)a–c can be given scope over the *wh*-phrases, yielding a multiple question reading in each case.

On May's account, these readings are expressed by an LF in which the quantified NP is adjoined to the matrix IP, which violates the ECP for the same reason that the LF required for the wide scope reading of (29)b ((31)a) does.

May also invokes the PCC to rule out (31)a. The PCC will also incorrectly exclude the LFs associated with the wide scope readings of (73)a–c.[22]

The interpretive tendency which (29)a–b illustrate can be captured by requiring that, in most cases, a quantified NP must be retrived from storage prior to the point in S-structure at which a *wh*-phrase trace or in situ *wh*-phrase appears. However, this constraint will not apply to NPs in which "each" appears as determiner. (73)a–b clearly indicate that the subject-object asymmetry in scope interaction between *wh*-phrases and quantified NPs is not the consequence of a grammatical condition.

5   CONCLUSION

In this paper I have identified three different concepts of logical form which appear in the philosophical literature. I have argued that, while they are distinct from each other, they share a common view of logical form as the canonical structure in terms of which the relationship between a sentence and an extra-sentential content of some sort is expressed. My purpose in discussing these concepts was to exhibit the differences between the philosophical and linguistic approaches to logical form.

Unlike the philosophical notion of logical form, LF is postulated as a level of representation in the derivation of a sentence provided by the rules of sentence grammar. It is obtained by the same sorts of operations which yield other levels of syntactic structure, and it is subject to many of the well-formedness conditions that apply to these representations. Therefore, the assumption of LF depends upon empirical and theoretical considerations of the same sort which are used to motivate other levels of structure posited within the grammar. I have briefly reviewed five of the major arguments which have been advanced for the existence of LF.

I have proposed an alternative view of the interface between syntactic structure and semantic interpretation, according to which model theoretic semantic rules apply to S-structure. With respect to each of the five arguments considered, the S-structure Interpretivist view provides an explanation of the relevant phenomena which is at least as adequate, and in some cases preferable to the analysis that posits LF. I conclude that it is not necessary to assume a distinct level of LF, and logical form, taken as the input to rules of semantic interpretation, can be identified directly with S-structure.

NOTES

I am grateful to Edit Doron, Robert May, Mori Rimon, Tanya Reinhart, and Ur Shlonsky for helpful discussion of several of the ideas discussed in this paper.

1   For criticisms of the inferential view of logical form see Etchemendy (1983).
2   Russell also claims that NPs that do not denote entities with which we have direct sensory "acquaintance" must be treated as descriptions and analyzed accordingly. Therefore, only constants which denote immediately accessible sensory entities and individual variables are logical arguments. It seems, then, that Russell's theory of descriptions also rests, in part, on the epistemic notion of logical form discussed in 1.2.
3   See in particular Part III, chapters B, C, and E.
4   See chapters V and VII in particular.
5   Quine, in contrast to Carnap, maintains that our beliefs about the world cannot be observationally evaluated in isolation from each other, but form constituents of a network of statements which stands against experience as an integrated whole.
6   May (1977) does not employ this condition, but allows multiple adjunction of quantified NPs to S by QR. Thus, for example, in May (1977) the two readings of

(i)   Every man loves some woman.

are represented by the LFs (ii) and (iii), respectively.

(ii) $[_s [_{NP1}$ every man] $[_s [_{NP2}$ some woman] $[s\ t_1$ loves $t_2]]]$
(iii) $[_s [_{NP2}$ some woman] $[_s [_{NP1}$ every man] $[_s\ t_1$ loves $t_2]]]$

As Ladusaw (1983) points out, LF representations like (ii) and (iii) correspond to the analysis trees in Montague's (1974) PTQ, which provide disambiguated syntactic representations of scope relations for sentences containing several quantified NPs. In May (1985), the LF assigned to (i) is

(iv) $[_s [_{NP1} [_{NP2}$ some woman] $[_{NP1}$ every man]] $[_s\ t_1$ loves $t_2]]$

As both NP_1 and NP_2 c-command each other in (iv), this structure expresses both scope readings. Therefore, in May (1985), LF does not necessarily provide a unique structural representation of the relative scope of the quantified NPs in a sentence. May (1989) provides a detailed discussion of the way in which LF structures containing mutually c-commanding quantified NPs allow multiple scope interpretations.

7   I follow Chomsky's (1986b) version of X' theory here, and I adopt his analysis of *wh*-movement as involving movement to the SPEC of CP.
8   In the original version of this paper prepared for the conference, I dealt with additional arguments for LF based on scope islands, weak crossover, and donkey pronouns. Constraints on space have forced me to omit these sections in the present version. My account of weak crossover is contained in Lappin (1985), and my proposed analysis of donkey pronouns appears in Lappin (1988–89).
9   According to Chomsky (1981), α properly governs β iff (i) α governs β and (ii) α is an element of a lexical category. Chomsky (1986b) reduces proper government to antecedent government in a chain. The difference between these definitions of proper government are not directly relevant to the present discussion of the ECP.

10 On the version of proper government proposed in Chomsky (1986b), the
    object trace in (24)c is antecedent-governed by the trace of "who" which is
    adjoined to the VP of the complement. "Who" is adjoined to VP prior to
    movement into the SPEC of the complement and matrix CP.
11 May invokes Pesetsky's (1982) Path Containment Condition (PCC) to provide
    an alternative explanation for the superiority effects illustrated in (27), as well
    as the *wh*-phrase-quantifier scope facts summarized in 2.3.3. I will discuss the
    application of the PCC to these phenomena in sections 2.4.
12 For an introduction to Montague grammar see Dowty, Wall, and Peters
    (1981). See Barwise and Cooper (1981) for a discussion of generalized
    quantifier theory.

    It is tempting to regard the LFs derived by QR as quasi-first order formulas
    in which a restricted quantifier binds a variable in the open sentence within its
    scope. In fact, the adjoined NPs in these structures must be assigned the same
    sort of interpretations which NPs in generalized quantifier theory receive.
    They must also be taken to denote functions from sets (corresponding to the
    denotations of lambda abstractions on the open sentences in their scope) to
    truth values. This is due to the fact that, as Barwise and Cooper point out,
    some quantificational determiners in natural language, like "most" and
    "many," cannot be interpreted by first order quantifiers. Thus, a plausible
    interpretation of "most," for example, is (i), where n is at least 51.

    (i) $\|most\ (A)\| = \{X \subseteq E: |X \cap A| \geq n\% |A|\}$

    This interpretation cannot be assigned to a first order variable binding
    operator.
13 See Cooper (1983) for an analysis of NPs in object position within an extended
    Montague grammar.
14 See, for example, Montague (1974) for the representation of the two readings
    of (33).
15 These are discussed in Lappin (1982) and (1984).
16 In fact, it may be necessary to extend storage to PPs. See Lappin (1984) on this
    point.
17 See Lappin (1984) for a detailed version of this argument for storage.
18 Williams' (1977) condition of "strict utterance" requires that all rules of
    sentence grammar apply prior to rules of discourse interpretation. This
    condition would seem to follow directly from the principle of the autonomy of
    syntax.
19 For the classical discussion of comparative deletion see Bresnan (1975) and
    Chomsky (1977). Grimshaw (1987) has recently presented additional argu-
    ments in support of Chomsky's claim that while comparative deletion struc-
    tures like (65)a–b involve movement, "subdeletion" cases like (i)a–b do not.

    (i)a   John writes more books than Bill writes articles.
      b   ??John writes more books than Mary believes Bill writes articles.

    At the end of this section I discuss a class of antecedent-contained deletion
    structures in which certain constituents of the contained VP are realized.
    Embedding of the partially empty VP seems somewhat better in these
    structures than in subdeletion cases like (i)b.

    (ii)a   John has more positions than he does applicants.
      b   ?John has more positions than Mary thinks he does applicants.

Partially empty VPs of this kind are also possible in relative clauses. Here embedding of the VP is relatively unproblematic.

(iii)   John argues about politics with everyone who Mary thinks he does about linguistics.

I will leave open the question of whether comparative subdeletion involves empty operator movement. However, (iii) does suggest that *wh*-movement is involved in the derivation of relative clauses with partially empty VPs.

20   This analysis of VP ellipses is implemented as an algorithm of VP anaphora resolution, which is presented in Lappin and McCord (1990).

21   May points out that the ECP fails to distinguish between (i)a and (i)b.

(i)a   ?Whom did you tell that Harry saw who?
   b   *Whom did you tell whom that Harry saw?

Both the S-structure and LF traces of *wh*-movement are properly governed in the LF representations of (i)a and (i)b. The PCC distinguishes between the LFs of these sentences in the required manner.

22   May (1985) and (1988) claims that "each," as opposed to "every," is inherently focused. On May's account, focused NPs are adjoined to CP rather than IP. Given this analysis, the quantified NP and *wh*-phrase in (73)a–c mutually c-command each other at LF without giving rise to an ECP violation. In fact, even if one accepts May's analysis of focus, his solution to the problem posed by (73)a–c will not go through. Consider

(i)a   Who interviewed each candidate for ABC?
   b   Who bought John each present he received?
(ii)a   Ted Koppel interviewed Dukakis and Peter Jennings interviewed Bush.
   b   Bill bought him a tie and Mary bought him a copy of *Barriers*.

As (ii)a–b indicate, "each candidate" and "each present" can be given wide scope in (i)a–b, respectively. If we assume that primary stress on an NP marks it as the focus of the sentence, then "each candidate" and "each present" receive wide scope in their respective questions despite the fact that neither is the focus.

Moreover, a possible reading of

(iii)   John claims to know who was elected mayor of every city in Ontario.

is that John claims to know for every city in Ontario, who was elected mayor of that city. This reading involves assigning wide scope to "every city in Ontario" relative to "who" in the most deeply embedded clause. Given May's assumption that NPs with the determiner "every" are not inherently focused, this reading requires the adjunction of the quantified NP to the lowest IP node, which gives rise to an ECP violation. Therefore, May's analysis incorrectly predicts that this reading of (iii) should not be available.

REFERENCES

Aoun, J., Hornstein, N. and Sportiche, D. 1980: "Some aspects of wide scope quantification." *Journal of Linguistic Research*, 1, 69–95.

Baltin, M. 1987: "Do antecedent contained deletions exist?" *Linguistic Inquiry*, 18, 579–95.

Barwise, J. and Cooper, R. 1981: "Generalized quantifiers and natural language." *Linguistics and Philosophy*, 4, 159–215.

Bresnan, J. 1975: "Comparative deletion and constraints on transformation." *Linguistic Analysis*, 1, 25–74.

Carnap, R. 1928: *The Logical Structure of the World*. Published in English translation, Routledge & Kegan Paul, London, 1967.

Chomsky, N. 1976: "Conditions on rules of grammar." *Linguistic Analysis*, 2, 303–51.

—— 1977: "On *Wh*-movement." In P. Culicover, T. Wasow, and A. Akmajian (eds), *Formal Syntax*, Academic Press, New York.

—— 1981: *Lectures on Government and Binding*. Foris, Dordrecht.

—— 1982: *Some Concepts and Consequences of the Theory of Government and Binding*. MIT Press, Cambridge, Mass.

—— 1986a: *Knowledge of Language: Its Nature, Use, and Limits*. Praeger, New York.

—— 1986b: *Barriers*. MIT Press, Cambridge, Mass.

Cooper, R. 1983: *Quantification and Syntactic Theory*. Reidel, Dordrecht.

Dowty, D., Wall, R. and Peters, S. 1981: *Introduction to Montague Semantics*, Reidel, Dordrecht.

Echemendy, J. 1983: "The doctrine of logic as form." *Linguistics and Philosophy*, 6, 319–34.

Frege, G. 1897: *Begriffschrift*. English translation of chapter 1 in P. Geach and M. Black (eds), *Translations from the Philosophical Writings of Gottlob Frege*. Blackwell, Oxford, 1970, 1–20.

Grimshaw, J. 1987: "Subdeletion." *Linguistic Inquiry*, 18, 659–69.

Haïk, I. 1987: "Bound VPs that need to be." *Linguistics and Philosophy*, 10, 503–30.

Hirschbuler, P. 1982: "VP deletion and across-the-board quantifier scope." In J. Pustejovsky and P. Sells (eds), *Papers from NELS*, 12, University of Massachusetts, Amherst, Mass., 132–9.

Huang, C.-T. J. 1982: *Logical Relations in Chinese and the Theory of Grammar*. Doctoral dissertation, MIT, Cambridge, Mass.

Kayne, R. 1981: "ECP extensions." *Linguistic Inquiry*, 12, 93–133.

—— 1983: "Connectedness." *Linguistic Inquiry*, 14, 223–49.

Lappin, S. 1982: "Quantified Noun Phrases and Pronouns in Logical Form." *Linguistic Analysis*, 10, 131–59.

—— 1984: "VP anaphora, quantifier scope, and logical form." *Linguistic Analysis*, 13, 273–315.

—— 1985: "Pronominal Binding and coreference." *Theoretical Linguistics*, 12, 241–63.

—— 1988–89: "Donkey Pronouns Unbound." *Theoretical Linguistics*, 15, 263–85.

—— and McCord, M. 1990: "Anaphora resolution in slot grammar." *Computational Linguistics*, 16, in press.

Larson, R. 1987: "Scope and comparatives." *Linguistics and Philosophy*, 11, 1–26.

Ladusaw, W. 1983: "Logical form and conditions on grammaticality." *Linguistics and Philosophy*, 6, 373–92.

May, R. 1977: *The Grammar of Quantification*. Doctoral dissertation, MIT, Cambridge, Mass.

—— 1985: *Logical Form: Its Structure and Derivation*. MIT Press, Cambridge, Mass.

—— 1988: "Ambiguities of quantification and *Wh*: a reply to Williams." *Linguistic Inquiry*, 19, 118–35.

—— 1989: "Interpreting Logical Form." *Linguistics and Philosophy*, 12, 387–435.

Pesetsky, D. 1982: *Paths and Categories*. Doctoral dissertation, MIT, Cambridge, Mass.

Quine, W. V. 1960: *Word and Object*. MIT Press, Cambridge, Mass.

van Riemsdijk, H. and Williams, E. 1981: "NP-structure." *Linguistic Review*, 1, 171–218.

Russell, B. 1905: "On Denoting." Reprinted in R. Marsh (ed.), *Logic and Knowledge*, George Allen & Unwin, London, 1956, 41–56.

Wasow, T. 1972: *Anaphora in Generative Grammar*, Ph.D. Dissertation, MIT, published by E. "Story"-Scientia, Ghent, 1979.

Williams, E. 1977: "Discourse and Logical Form." *Linguistic Inquiry*, 8, 107–39.

—— 1986: "A reassignment of the functions of LF." *Linguistic Inquiry*, 17, 265–99.

Wittgenstein, L. 1922: *Tractatus Logico-Philosophicus*. Published in English translation, Routledge & Kegan Paul, London, 1961.

14

Syntax, Semantics, and Logical Form

Robert May

In this paper I want to address two questions. The first is: What is it for a natural language to have a *logical form*? The second is dependent upon a clarification of the first: How does the grammar of a natural language *represent* this logical form? Clearly these questions are of central interest in semantics, as the answers we give to these questions will, by and large, frame just how we understand the relationship of the syntactic and logical structures of natural languages. The answer I will give to the first question – what is logical form? – is that logical form is the representation of the *form of the logical terms* of a language. Thus the study of logical form is, in this sense, the study of the formal, or *syntactic*, nature of a certain class of elements of language, the logical terms. The answer I will give to the second question – how in particular is this form represented? – is that the grammars of natural languages have, as one of their components, a level of LF, which represents the form of the logical terms. The study of LF, in this sense, is the study of the constraints on this level, and how they fix its structural properties. It is via the constraints that LF is individuated as a level of linguistic representation, and its properties determined.

To explicate the form of the logical terms, it is necessary to begin by specifying just what is meant by a "logical term," and what are its formal aspects. Intuitively, logical terms are expressions of the language which have, in some sense, *invariant* meanings, so that they are often referred to as the logical constants. Their fixed meanings arise from their being interpreted by general semantic rules. These rules are distinguished in that they form part of the recursive specification of the truth-definition for the language. Thus the logical terms are picked out through the role they play in the interpretation of the language. What then is the character of these semantic rules? To illustrate, consider an example from the broadest and most interesting class of elements to which they apply: the quantifier words. The rules for these expressions are their satisfaction clauses. So for instance, the rule which interprets occurrences of the quantifier *everyone* can be given by the following clause, where g is an assignment of values to variables:

(1) g satisfies "everyone$_i\phi_i$" iff every assignment g' satisfies ϕ_i, where g' differs from g in at most the values assigned to the ith-place.

(ϕ_i stands for an open sentence containing just x_i free.) While clauses such as (1) surely do not do full justice to the complexity of quantifiers in natural language, they do, however, display certain features which are essential, and hence are to be found in more precise formulations. These features are essential because they are the properties of the quantifier rules which determine their *application*. They specify that such rules apply only if certain *structural* properties can be recognized in the representation of a sentence being interpreted. Thus, to properly apply a clause like (1), it is necessary to be able to distinguish a *sentence* from a *sentential function*. This, in turn, requires that *free* occurrences be distinguishable from *bound* occurrences of variables; that is, they require a notion of *binding*. And binding requires a notion of *scope*, that is, of the domain of binding. A *logical form*, then, is a representation of such properties; that is, of those formal properties which are required to insure the proper application of the semantic rules. LF – a level of linguistic representation – will be a logical form, then, only if it manifests these properties.

In the case of the quantifiers, it is well-known that on now-standard assumptions regarding its characteristics, LF does have the relevant properties. This is achieved by deriving representations at this level transformationally, by QR, which has S-structure representations as its input (May 1977, 1985). At LF, the representation of quantification meets the criteria of a logical form, as can be garnered by inspection of a simple derivation via QR, as in (2):

(2) $[_S$ Philby suspected everyone$]$ $\Rightarrow$ $[_S{}^0$ everyone$_i$ $[_S{}^1$ Philby suspected $e_i]]$

Such LF-structures are completely transparent in representing the formal requirements for the satisfaction clause in (1); its logical structure can be just read off its structural properties. We equate e_i – the trace of QR – with the ith variable, and the scope of *everyone$_i$* with its c-command domain. This variable occurs free in S^1, a sentential function, and bound within S^0, a sentence, where the relevant notions of binding are made precise by the Binding Theory, in the sense of Chomsky (1982, 1986a). It is thus apparent that on this view the syntax of natural language does have a logical form, in that at LF it *represents the structure required for the application of semantic rules for logical terms.*[1]

Central to the notion of LF we are exploring, then, is that it represents what is formally necessary for a theory of truth for natural language. Quantifier and other logical terms are distinguished in that they place formal requirements for truth. Other, non-logical expressions place no such formal requirements, and in fact cannot, as they are not directly implicated in the recursive clauses of the truth-definition. The meaning specified by the semantics for these lexical items consists rather in their reference, so that their contribution to the truth-definition is indirect, only arising relative to the categorical composition of the syntactic structure of the language. Thus while expressions such as proper names or simple predicates have whatever reference they have as their meanings, they only play a role in determining truth through the various ways in which the grammar allows them to combine with one another to form sentences, for which truth is defined. Thus in projecting a theory of truth onto LF, its structure must be articulated so that both logical structure – that needed to explicate the direct role of the syncategoremic logical terms – and compositional structure – that needed to explicate the indirect role of the categoremic non-logical terms – is represented. If one of our goals is to show how meaning depends on structure, then at least this much seems necessary.

The constraints on the form of LF imposed by considerations such as these are in a sense *extrinsic* constraints, arising from requirements placed by the *semantic interpretation* of the syntax. These are to be contrasted with *intrinsic* constraints on LF, grammatical constraints within the syntax proper which determine the form of representations at this level. These range from derivational constraints, which determine the transformational properties of QR, to structural constraints such as ECP or the Binding Theory, which fix the well-formedness of LF-representations. Which sort of constraint – extrinsic or intrinsic – we focus on empirically will reflect, therefore, somewhat different aspects of LF. Primary attention to the intrinsic constraints will reflect the intuitively "syntactic" side of LF, while consideration of the external constraints will show off its "semantic" side. Where things become most empirically interesting, however, is when we consider phenomena in which the intrinsic and extrinsic constraints overlap in their structural demands. Thus, the study of quantification (and related issues of anaphora) in natural language has proven to be of enduring interest, since this is a central case where the intrinsic and extrinsic constraints on linguistic form intersect, most markedly on the notion of *binding*. On the one hand, the interpretive rules require that binding be structurally present for their application; on the other, binding theory determines the class of representations in which the appropriate form of binding is, in fact, present.

Considerations such as these indicate the need to clearly distinguish LF, the linguistic level, from logical form, which is a property of this level. It would be improper, therefore, to strictly *identify* LF with the logical form of natural language, although this is a possibility. Rather, it would be more proper to speak of LF as *embedding* a logical form, so as to allow for it to have purely syntactic aspects of its structure, for which there is no extrinsic motivation. Grammars will be most highly valued, however, to the extent that their intrinsic constraints articulate structure which satisfies the extrinsic conditions. Making us aware of this basic insight has been, in many ways, Noam Chomsky's central contribution to our understanding of the general relation of the syntax and semantics of natural language, dating back to his earliest writings. In *Syntactic Structures*, Chomsky writes that:

> ... we should like the syntactic framework of the language that is isolated
> and exhibited by the grammar to be able to support semantic description, and
> we shall naturally rate more highly a theory of formal structure that leads to
> grammars that meet this requirement more fully. (p. 102)

He reiterates this in the following comments:

> The appeal to meaning must be clearly distinguished from the study of
> meaning. The latter enterprise is unquestionably central to the general
> theory of language, and a major goal of the [*Syntactic Structures-Logical
> Structure of Linguistic Theory*] approach is to advance it by showing how a
> sufficiently rich theory of linguistic form can provide structural descriptions
> that provide the basis for the fruitful investigation of semantic questions.
> (Chomsky 1975a: 21)

These latter remarks, reflecting on his early work, were written during the
period in which Chomsky's contemporary views were crystallizing with his
first discussions of LF, nearly a decade and a half ago, in his papers
"Questions of Form and Interpretation" (1975b) and "Conditions on
Rules of Grammar" (1976).[2] Especially in the latter paper, which contains
his well-known discussion of weak crossover phenomena, Chomsky was
concerned to place LF within the system of linguistic rule and constraint, as
this is understood from such writings as "Conditions on Transformations,"
"On *Wh*-Movement," *Lectures on Government and Binding* and much
subsequent work. What Chomsky's continuing discussions of LF have
taught us to bear in mind is that logical aspects of natural language arise, so
to speak, *fortuitously*, in the sense that the devices needed for their
characterization are employed independently in the grammar. The *semantic* significance of LF, therefore, resides in that notions needed to define
semantically necessary concepts are syntactically grounded and are *independently required* for syntactic description. Thus, the syntactic nomenclature needed to describe the syntax of a simple *wh*-construction such as (3):

(3) $[_{S'}$ who$_i$ $[_S$ did Philby suspect $e_i]]$,

provides a sufficient vocabulary to characterize the logical structure of
LF-representations like (2). Given the notions of movement, trace and
binding central to describing the syntax of the construction (3) exemplifies,
we can define the notions of scope and binding needed to describe the
logical syntax of (2) (and (3) as well). Chomsky has emphasized that in
formulating a level of LF, one is not going about designing the syntax just
to meet certain semantic ends; there is no "appeal to meaning" in the sense
that some device is added to the grammar justified solely by its service to
semantic description.[3] However, to the extent that the grammar goes
about characterizing the logical structure of LF in the manner described

above, the theory of syntax will articulate the study of meaning, in that it independently contains the means to represent logical form, and hence can serve as the basis of a truth-definition for natural language.

Within the framework we are considering, it is thus an empirical hypothesis that there is a linguistic level which corresponds to philosophically and logically grounded ideas of logical form. In turn it counts as an empirical discovery that the intrinsic syntactic conditions allow of structure with extrinsic significance. Things could have been different. It could have been the case, for instance, that representing the form of the logical terms would require the introduction of representational devices which, while perhaps natural in the logical context, would be foreign to the description of natural language. If so, the syntax would have no extrinsic significance beyond representing compositional structure: it would have no logical form. This is very much the view expressed by Partee (1979), and endorsed by Cooper (1983). Their perspective flows from a belief that structurally representing *binding* would fundamentally distort the syntax of natural language, and would commit us to extensions of linguistic theory not otherwise empirically or conceptually justified. Consequently, Partee and Cooper want to proscribe grammars which represent binding syntactically, an effect achieved by Partee's "Well-Formedness Condition." The notion of binding needed to characterize the logical terms will now have to be worked out in some way which is strictly internal to the semantics. This is the intent of the "storage" systems developed by Cooper, and Partee and Bach (1984). The effect of Partee's condition on the syntax is to reduce it effectively to an immediate-constituent description, which is viewed as somehow "simpler," and hence "less costly" and more highly valued in linguistic theory. But, one might ask, if we are to weigh costs and benefits, why should "semantic" rules such as stores, and their constraints, be less costly or come at no cost to linguistic theory, as opposed to syntactic rules? Assuredly, any such speculation as this is idle – virtually by definition, the *right* theory is the simplest theory. But then, given an empirical stance, it becomes puzzling why we would want to ban logical form from the grammar, especially when one considers what an impoverished view of syntax we are left with, and what considerable descriptive burden must be shouldered by the semantics. The semantic notion of binding must suffice not only for quantification, but also for whatever phenomena which are otherwise described syntactically by binding – e.g. constraints on anaphora, *wh*-movement, raising, clitics, inversion, etc. It is far from clear what the scope of the impending empirical project would be – it certainly has yet to be undertaken except in barest outline – or that it could be carried out without a trip down the slippery road of recapitulating so much syntactic structure within the semantics that in the end some variant LF-like level is imported, now relabeled as residing in the "semantics," rather than in the "syntax." While we assuredly eschew any "appeal to meaning" – the introduction of structure solely to allow some term to be included in the truth-clause if that structure is not otherwise intrinsically determined – we also do not want to make an "appeal to form" solely to exclude structure which is extrinsically motivated. The goal, rather, is to attempt to discover empirically the proper tension between the two sources of constraint, and hence reveal the logical content of syntax. It may be null, but that is empirical, not a priori.[4]

In contrast to Partee and Cooper's approach, the grammatical notion of "binding" is of central importance to in the theory of LF, and to the characterization of the logical syntax of this level. The standard definition of this term breaks down into two parts. One is the notion of proper binding – that binding requires c-command. The other is provided by the Binding Theory, which builds on the prior notion of proper binding. Given the centrality of binding to our very conception of LF, we would expect that these defining conditions, and in particular the Binding Theory, would be applicable at this level, as it ought to be at any level at which (proper) binding is observed. Indeed, if the Binding Theory could be shown to require the particular articulation of structure found just at LF for its full application, this would constitute a sort of "existence proof" for LF, and the devices employed in deriving it. It would be nugatory to postulate the existence of an independent level if its sole duty was to represent logical structure, as it would, in some sense, no longer be a *syntactic* level. For a theory of LF to have content along the lines sketched, it ought not to be the case that all syntactically governed constraints hold of other syntactic levels, viz. of D-structure or S-structure, and are not applicable to LF.

The question to be broached, then, is whether in fact the Binding Theory applies at LF. The answer, it appears, is that it does.[5] It is possible to see this clearly in the context of verb phrase ellipsis, of which sentence (4) is an elementary instance:

(4)   Dulles suspected Philby, and Angleton did too.

As a point of departure, we simply assume that the antecedent VP is "copied" into the ellipsis site, under an appropriate identity condition. Sag (1976) and Williams (1977) observe, however, that regardless of how the notion of "copy" is made precise, that a problem arises with "antecedent-contained deletion," an example of which is displayed in (5):

(5)   Dulles suspected everyone that Angleton did.

The problem here is that the copying of the antecedent verb phrase into the elided position leads directly to a reconstructive regress. Let us suppose that the ellipsis site is represented as an empty VP. Then the S-structure of (5) will be (6):

(6)   Dulles [$_{VP}$ suspected everyone that Angleton did [$_{VP}$ e]]

The antecedent VP is that headed by *suspected*. Copying in that phrase derives (7); which in turn contains an instance of the empty VP.

(7)   Dulles [$_{VP}$ suspected everyone that Angleton [$_{VP}$ suspected everyone that Angleton did [$_{VP}$ e]]]

Clearly this will proceed *ad infinitum*, so that we could not possibly derive any definite representation for (5). But this sentence is grammatical, and hence must be assigned a well-formed structure by the grammar.

The problem here, it turns out, is that we have copied with respect to S-structure, and have ignored the fact that (5) contains a quantified phrase, and thus undergoes QR, as shown in May (1985). The result is (8):

(8)   [everyone that Angleton did [$_{VP}$ e]$_i$ [Dulles [$_{VP}$ suspected e_i]]]

The difference between this structure and (6) is that now, post-QR, the antecedent verb phrase contains just the trace of QR as its object. Copying in this phrase gives (9):

(9)   [everyone that Angleton [$_{VP}$ suspected e_i]$_i$ [Dulles [$_{VP}$ suspected e_i]]]

This structure, at LF, is perfectly well-formed; it will be true just in case everyone that Angleton suspected, Dulles suspected as well. Notice that under the copying two salutary effects were gained: not only was the elided VP reconstructed, but also a trace to serve as the variable bound by the quantifier/*wh*-phrase in the relative. Initially, then, antecedent-contained deletion provides a powerful argument for LF, as only there is the structure right for reconstruction.[6]

Fiengo and May (1989) make a series of observations building on this conclusion, which brings the situation of the Binding Theory at LF clearly into focus. They consider sentence (10), under an anaphoric interpretation of the pronoun.

(10)   Dulles suspected everyone that he did.

This sentence is grammatical, although semantically, it is analytic. From the point of view of the Binding Theory, it is perfectly permissible for the NP *Dulles* to be the pronoun's antecedent, since, after all, the pronoun is free within its governing category, which is the relative clause. The same comments carry over to (11), in which unsurprisingly *Mary* can stand as the antecedent, and which also has the same analytic flavor:

(11)   Mary introduced John to everyone that she did.

What comes as a real surprise, then, is what results when a masculine pronoun is substituted for the feminine one in (11):

(12)   *Mary introduced John to everyone that he did.

This sentence, strikingly, displays a disjoint reference effect: *John* and *he* must denote distinct individuals, they cannot be coreferential. Relative to the Binding Theory, this is completely surprising, since the pronoun in (12) is just as much in a transparent position as that in (11). In either case Principle B is satisfied. Things return to "normal," however, in the following example, where again the possibility of an anaphoric connection is unsurprising:

(13)   Mary introduced John to everyone that his mother did.

In this case *John* can serve as the antecedent of the pronoun, but here, note, without giving rise to an analytic interpretation.

We find the same sort of contrast between "normal" and "weird" interpretations in the contrast in (14):

(14)a Mary introduced his mother to everyone that John did.
   b   *Mary introduced John's mother to everyone that he did.

By all odds, both of these examples should allow of an anaphoric interpretation, since in neither case is there any c-command relation between the two NPs in question. But coreference is only possible in the (a) example, not in the (b).

The problem we are facing with these cases arises from once again considering matters in the context of S-structure constituency. Matters come clearly into focus when we consider the syntactic properties of these cases at LF. (15) is the LF-representation of (10), post reconstruction:

(15)   [everyone that he$_j$ [$_{VP}$ suspected e_i]$_i$ [Dulles$_j$ [$_{VP}$ suspected e_i]]]

In this structure, nothing has changed from the Binding Theory perspective – the pronoun remains appropriately free, and hence may take the NP *Dulles* as its antecedent. Again, the remarks carry over for the LF of (11):

(16)   [everyone that she$_j$ [$_{VP}$ introduced John to e_i]$_i$ [Mary$_j$ [$_{VP}$ introduced John to e_i]]]

Different remarks apply to the LF of (12), however. It is derived first by application of QR, giving (17):

(17)   [everyone that he$_j$ did [$_{VP}$ e]$_i$ [Mary introduced John$_j$ to e$_i$]]]

And then by copying in the VP antecedent:

(18)   [everyone that he$_j$ [$_{VP}$ introduced John$_j$ to e$_i$]]$_i$ [Mary introduced John$_j$ to e$_i$]

And here we are at the heart of the analysis: at LF, (18) stands in violation of Principle C of the Binding Theory, as post-QR/post-reconstruction the pronoun c-commands its antecedent.

   A Principle C violation is not similarly induced under reconstruction in the LF of (13), however:

(19)   [everyone that his$_j$ mother [$_{VP}$ introduced John$_j$ to e$_i$]]$_i$ [Mary introduced John$_j$ to e$_i$]

Here the pronoun is syntactically free of both occurrences of *John*, and hence they can be understood coreferentially. Precisely the same remarks carry over to the contrast in (14). Only for (14b) does QR/reconstruction feed Principle C, in contrast to the pronoun in the LF-representation of (14a), which is properly free in its governing category:

(20)a   [everyone that John$_j$ [$_{VP}$ introduced his$_j$ mother to e$_i$]]$_i$ [Mary introduced his$_j$ mother to e$_i$]
   b   [everyone that he$_j$ [$_{VP}$ introduced John$_j$'s mother to e$_i$]]$_i$ [Mary introduced John$_j$'s mother to e$_i$]

   These patterns of anaphora in the LF representations of antecedent-contained deletion are just those that we find independently in the sentences in (21):

(21)a   *After he introduced John to everyone, Mary introduced John to everyone.
   b   After she introduced John to everyone, Mary introduced John to everyone.
   c   After his mother introduced John to everyone, Mary introduced John to everyone.
   d   After John introduced his mother to everyone, Mary introduced his mother to everyone.
   e   *After he introduced John's mother to everyone, Mary introduced John's mother to everyone.

The difference is that these latter examples illustrate these patterns in base-generated structures, the antecedent-contained deletion examples show it in derived structure. Crucially, it is the derived structure that occurs at LF.

Further examples show directly that the full generality of Binding Theory holds of LF. Thus consider sentence (22) relative to Principle A:

(22)   The men introduced each other to everyone that the women did.

This sentence has a reading, perhaps the most natural, under which a reciprocal relation applies both to *the men* and to *the women*.[7] That is, it can mean that for each person the women introduced each other to, the men introduced each other to that person as well. This construal ought to be impossible, however, given the S-structure of (22), since *the women* is c-commanded by *each other*, and is thus precluded from binding the reciprocal by Principle A. At LF, however, where we have the structure in (23), matters are again unproblematic:

(23)   [everyone that the women [$_{VP}$ introduced each other to e_i]]$_i$ [the men introduced each other to e_i]

In this structure, after QR and reconstruction, both *the women* and *the men* locally c-command an occurrence of *each other*. Thus here Principle A is satisfied in a structure which gives rise to the desired interpretation.

Effects of Principle B can be observed by consideration of the contrast in (24):

(24)a   John introduced her to everyone that Mary wanted him to.
    b   *John introduced her to everyone that he wanted Mary to.

This is once again a very surprising contrast; we would expect (24)a to be just as much a disjoint reference case as (24)b, since in both structures the pronoun c-commands its antecedent, and hence both are blatant Principle C violations. But counter to expectation, (24)a does allow for coreference. The structures (24) at LF are given in (25), post-reconstruction.

(25)a   [everyone that Mary$_j$ [$_{VP}$ wanted him to introduce her$_j$ to e_i]]$_i$ [John introduced her$_j$ to e_i]
    b   [everyone that he [$_{VP}$ wanted Mary$_j$ to introduce her$_j$ to e_i]]$_i$ [John introduced her$_j$ to e_i]

These structures conform to the Binding Theory as expected. In (25)a both occurrences of *her* are locally free of the antecedent NP *Mary*, and hence may be coreferential with it. In (25)b, on the other hand, the reconstructed occurrence of the pronoun is *not* locally free; *Mary* is the subject of its clause. Thus, while QR *bleeds* Principle C in both of these cases, reconstruction *feeds* Principle B, resulting in (25)b being a violation of the Binding Theory, as opposed, correctly, to (25)a.

These examples, (24)a/(25)a in particular, show conclusively that Binding Theory must apply *after* LF-movement. This is because if it were to apply only prior, then Principle C would inescapably apply, and (24)a ought to show a disjointness effect just as much as (25)a. It is the LF-movement which breaks up the c-command relation. Notice that this will be so even if the elision site is fully endowed with categorical structure at S-structure, as suggested for instance by Lappin (1991). Lappin proposes this as an alternative to an LF/reconstruction account of antecedent-contained deletion, but his treatment does not appear to be tenable. He proposes a number of arguments for his conclusion. The first is based on an observation of Haïk (1987) that there are island effects in ellipsis, as shown in (26).

(26)   *Dulles suspected everyone that Angleton wondered why Philby did.

The argument here is that since Subjacency governs the locality of a binding relation, for it to apply both the binder and the bindee must be structurally present. Subjacency is a condition on S-structure, so that "reconstruction" must be prior to LF.

The weak link in Lappin's argument is the presumption that Subjacency is an S-structure condition. There has been considerable recent research showing that Subjacency (or its ancestral principles) applies at LF; see Longobardi (1991), May (1977), Nishiguachi (1986), Pesetsky (1987), Reinhart (1991) and Wahba (1991), among other references, and Chomsky (1986b), and Fiengo, Huang, Lasnik and Reinhart (1988) in the context of the Barriers framework. Indeed, Haïk's observation can be taken as a further argument to this conclusion. Note that if Subjacency applies at LF, and hence post-reconstruction, we can continue to assume that the elided VP is unstructured, i.e. $[_{VP} e]$ at other levels. This in turn implies that the *wh*-phrase in antecedent-contained deletion constructions, as well as any of its traces not in the ellipsis site, can be base-generated, so that we would expect to find the full range of *wh* extraction properties, as in fact we do.

In contrast to antecedent-contained deletion, Lappin assumes that standard ellipsis does contain an empty VP at S-structure. He argues for this on the basis of the examples in (27): [= Lappin (1991), exs. (47)a/(47)c]

(27)a   I know which book John read and Mary didn't.
   b   I know which book John read and which book Mary didn't.

Lappin adjudges (27)b to be marginal relative to (27)a. The reason he gives is that at S-structure the second *wh* is vacuous: Since the VP is structurally empty, there is no trace for the *wh*-phrase to bind at this level. Thus, contained and non-contained ellipsis are fundamentally different in their S-structure.

Lappin, however, agrees that (27)b is at best marginal, a difficulty, as vacuity normally gives rise to strong ungrammaticality. He thus proposes that such ellipsis structures, though ruled out at one level, can be "repaired" by copying at another level, presumably LF. It is very unclear how to make sense of this *prima facie* rather implausible suggestion. In fact, it is rather unclear that (27)b is ill-formed at all; see May (1988a). The difference between (27)a and (27)b seems to be that they just mean different things: (27)a only requires knowledge of one book, which John read and Mary didn't, while (27)b requires knowledge of two books, one of which John read and the other of which Mary didn't. Given this, the more obvious analysis is that both contained and non-contained ellipsis are non-distinct, in that at S-structure the VP is structurally empty, while at LF, post reconstruction, it is structurally realized. The peculiar properties of antecedent-contained deletion then arise from it having to undergo LF-movement in the course of its derivation.

Lappin presents a further argument, claiming that an LF analysis of antecedent-contained deletion leads to representations of wrong interpretations in certain cases. The type of case which concerns him is where the ellipsis site is within an adverbial phrase:

(28)   John succeeded more frequently than Mary did.

Lappin initially assumes that QR does not apply to such examples. This is incorrect, however, as Larson (1987) shows, so that it is assigned a representation as in (29):

(29)   more frequently than Mary did $\overline{\left[_{\text{VP}} e\right]}_i$ [John succeeded e_i]

After reconstruction, this gives just the right construal, to the effect that John's rate of success is greater than Mary's, as Larson points out. The trouble arises, according to Lappin, with the following example, in which an existential phrase has been substituted (= Lappin (1991), ex. 50):

(30)   Someone succeeded more frequently than Mary did.

Lappin observes that this sentence has a "specific" interpretation, so that it means that Mary has a rate of success that is less than that of some other particular person. He claims, however, that it lacks a "non-specific" interpretation, to the effect that, for any given event, it is more frequent that Mary fails, and that some other person, who may be different for each event, succeeds. (Note that this construal world would still be compatible with Mary having the highest overall frequently of success.) Lappin then claims that the LF-representation of (30), comparable to (29) with movement of the entire adverbial phrase, only expresses this latter reading, so that *ergo* the LF approach is flawed.

Lappin's argument is problematic, however, because he does not make explicit why the LF-representation of (30) has only the latter, and not the former, reading. He asserts that the incorrect reading represented at LF arises from taking *frequently* as a sentence adverb, while the correct reading must be given by taking it as a VP-adverb, (i.e. a function from VP-meaning to VP-meanings). But Lappin provides no analysis, syntactic or, more germanely, semantic, to support this contention, giving no way to determine whether taking *frequently* as a VP-adverb does or does not give the right interpretation, (or, for that matter, whether taking it as an S-adverb does either). But even granting the intuitive force of Lappin's remarks, it is by no means apparent that he is heading in the right direction, as it is unclear that the non-specific reading is absent in sentences of the form of (30). Thus, consider (31), which appears to display an ambiguity of just the sort described above:

(31)   In this game, someone else (usually) succeeds more frequently than Mary does.

Indeed, if anything, (31) seems to favor the non-specific interpretation which Lappin claims ought to be impossible.

The upshot of all this is that examples of the sort under consideration are ambiguous, in a way that is reflected as a matter of scope of quantification – if the existential has broader scope than the *more*-phrase, we obtain the specific reading, if it has narrower scope, the non-specific. We continue, therefore, to follow the analysis of Larson (1987) in assuming that the entire adverbial phrase is subject to LF-movement, which resolves the antecedent-contained effect. LF-movement of the existential phrase then gives rise to the possibility of ambiguity. In this regard, the treatment proposed for (30) is parallel to that of the equally scopally ambiguous (32).[8]

(32)   Someone suspected everyone that Angleton did.

To summarize, antecedent-contained deletion phenomena are extremely clear indications that Binding Theory constrains LF. Thus, we apparently have, as noted, what amounts to an existence proof for this level since it is only at this level that the proper articulation of syntactic structure is found for the proper application of the clauses of the Binding Theory.[9]

In placing extrinsic constraints on the structure of LF, the quantifier rules fix the interpretation of these expressions to applying only relative to certain structural configurations. The properties of these rules which determine the extrinsic constraints are universal; we would not expect the rules involved in determining the meanings of the quantifier words or the connectives to vary from language to language. Consequently, any grammar falling under UG must project the structure required, so that the child acquiring a grammar will bootstrap LF in conformity with these requirements. This makes the quantifiers the "engine" for the development of LF, and presumably for the properties of grammatical binding more generally. Since the extrinsic contraints could not be satisfied unless there was syntactic mechanism given which could derive the necessary structure, it follows that QR is universal. This result is corroborated by a simple learnability argument. Suppose that languages could vary in whether QR applies or not. What evidence could there be whether a child was learning a QR language or a non-QR language? Clearly, none, since in neither case could there be any evidence that QR had applied – in general, surface strings are not indicative of LF-structure. Since experience of a QR language and a non-QR language would be exactly the same, QR is unlearnable, and hence universal. But while there are universal constraints on bootstrapping LF, this must also occur within the limits on syntactic structure placed by the intrinsic constraints of particular grammars. Such syntactic constraints are known to admit of a certain variability among languages, along open parameters in Universal Grammar. Thus, a structural type well-formed in one language may not be in another, and finding out why this is so is the business of comparative syntax. In the case of LF, since it is conceived as a syntactic level, we might expect that the variability permitted in the syntax would extend to it, and indeed languages are known to vary in the properties of quantification (including *wh*) and binding which they display. But if QR is universal, how can this be? What has been observed, in way of resolution, is that while it follows that *the rule* QR is universal, it does not follow that its input will be universal. In fact, its input will vary just with respect to the range of learnable variation allowable for S-structure by UG. Consequently, while every language will represent quantification in the same way, they may associate distinct ranges of interpretation to a given construction. Such differences, however, would have to be traced back to differences in the syntactic constituency assigned to that construction. In this regard, our conception of LF makes possible a comparative semantics, as a branch of comparative syntax.[10]

Modulo these considerations, we understand LF-movement to be universal and general in its application, consistent with properly understanding QR as just concrete instances of the general transformational schema – move-α; see May (1985). Once this rule is in place, however, there is no reason to think that it is reserved for the exclusive use of quantificational expressions. Other types of expressions may make use of it, provided that the derived structure in which they occur is syntactically permissible and that they are otherwise semantically interpretable in that position. Reinhart (1991) documents an instance of the circumstance just described, based on properties of certain ellipsis constructions. She argues that the proper account of "exception-ellipsis," shown in (33):

(33)   No agent suspected Philby except Angleton,

involves deriving the complex quantified expression *no agent except Angleton*, whose interpretation will be identical to the base expression of that form. This is effected, Reinhart argues, not by syntactic extraposition or ellipsis, but rather by LF-movement, where QR attaches the subject NP to the "remnant" phrase:

(34) $[[e_1$ suspected Philby] no agent except Angleton$_1]$

In this structure, the derived phrase binds the subject variable, consistent with the definition of c-command (m-command) given in May (1985). Reinhart reinforces this result by showing that exception-ellipsis has just the syntax of QR, e.g. in being contrained by subjacency, but being possible from positions which permit of inversely-linked quantification, etc. Other "ellipsis" constructions, Reinhart points out, also show this paradigmatic behavior, such as bare-argument deletion:

(35)   Dulles suspected Philby, and Angleton, too.

Here, the resulting LF-structure is (36):

(36) $[[e_1$ suspected Philby] Dulles and Angleton$_1]$

In this structure, the trace is bound by a derived conjunction. Note that equally well the object NP could have been moved, so that (35) is ambiguous, as opposed to (33). This is because there is no interpretation otherwise available for *Philby except Angleton*. Also, note that while bare-argument deletion allows of ambiguity, it does not allow for a "split" interpretation, so that (37) cannot mean that Dulles and Blunt suspected Philby and Burgess:

(37)   Dulles suspected Philby, and Blunt and Burgess too.

This is because to derive this construal, the subject and object NPs would have to attach to the NPs in the remnant phrase. That is, they would have to attach *inside* the conjoining NP, positions from which they cannot c-command their traces. On the other hand, LF-movement of just one of the NPs, which attaches to the conjoined NP itself, would leave it in a position from which it does c-command its trace. In this regard, bare-argument deletion contrasts with gapping, of which the split construal is so characteristic:

(38)   Dulles suspected Philby, and Angleton Burgess.

This is because gapping is a true case of ellipsis, containing an empty verb, subject to reconstruction, and in this respect cousin to antecedent-contained deletion. Very similar bare-argument cases are simply ill-formed:

(39)   *Dulles suspected Philby, and Angleton Burgess too.

This is because the LF derived expression *Philby and Angleton Burgess* has no independently available construal.

Central to Reinhart's analysis of these constructions is that QR, the rule, can apply to both quantified and non-quantified expressions. The correctness of this assumption is indicated by the overlap of the syntax of bare-argument deletion and that of QR. This is, of course, consistent with our understanding of QR as move-α. But while movement is of a non-quantifier, the resulting structure is one of quantification. Plural expressions are ambiguous between their "collective" and "distributive" construals, a distinction which is based on whether the plural directly refers, or is under the scope of a distributor. The distributor turns the plural into a universal expression, so that on this construal *the men* has effectively the interpretation of *the men each*; see Heim, Lasnik and May (1990), as well as Roberts (1986) and Link (1987). Conjoined NPs are plurals, and are to be found occurring in contexts which require the distributed construal:

(40)   Philby and Angleton suspected each other.

Given that plurals can be quantificational, this predicts that bare-argument deletion will not be possible in collective contexts which preclude a distributive reading. Thus, we find that (41) is ill-formed, even though the subject will be bound by a plural NP at LF:

(41)   *Philby met in Cambridge, and Burgess too.

This contrasts with *Philby and Burgess met in Cambridge*, construed collectively. What this shows, then, is that while QR can apply to any phrase whatsoever, the resulting *interpretation* of that phrase must be quantificational, binding a singular variable. With exception-ellipsis, only movement of a quantifier can result in a quantificational interpretation, but for bare-argument deletion, a non-quantifier can be moved, but only so as to derive a quantificational expression, viz. a distributed plural.

Reinhart's observations, and the extensions just noted, are of great interest, therefore, in that they show the independence of QR, *qua* syntactic rule, from the quantificational interpretation of the derived representation. Because of its generality, NPs of all types can make use of QR. A further question which arises is whether all types of NPs can also make use of the *structure* QR derives, a rather more speculative matter. Thus, observe that just because a syntactic configuration represents the proper structure for quantification, it does not mean that this very same structure cannot be construed as another type of configuration, supporting a different sort of interpretation. Now, the non-logical expressions, in not being interpreted by rules of the sort which apply to the logical terms, are not constrained extrinsically. These are expressions whose meanings, in not being implicated in the truth-definition, are not determined by their structural position: their reference is their reference, and this can be expressed in any syntactic position. Whether this reference can be combined with others to form truth-bearing expressions is a function of the possibilities of categorical combination and argument structure of the language. In principle, there is no reason why these latter positions cannot include those otherwise reserved at LF for logical terms. Thus we can certainly imagine a situation in which syntactic Ā-binding serves either as the configuration of quantification or the configuration of predication, the latter perhaps comparable to what we find in clefts, topicalization or appositive relatives. The possibility of this type of structure doing double-duty, however, will be strongly limited by the conditions on well-formedness placed by internal syntactic constraints, and we might expect languages to vary in making it available. So, while if a phrase is to be interpreted quantificationally, it must occur in an Ā-binding structure – this much is universal, a linguistic reflection of the universality of quantification itself – whether a language also satisfies the stronger biconditional – an expression occurs in an Ā-binding structure if and only if it is interpreted quantificationally – is a function of its particular syntax. But notice that even in a language for which the biconditional fails – one which would allow expressions to receive non-quantificational construals in their moved positions – it would still be possible to distinguish the two types of terms. This is because predication, by definition, is an operation whereby an argument is combined with a predicate to form an expression to which truth is assigned – in Fregean terms, it alters an open expression into a closed one. It is fundamentally not iterative. Thus, for NPs such as proper names, only one application of QR is possible, as predication is the taking of a single argument. By contrast, quantification is iterative, so that for the quantifiers we have a notion of scope, and scope ambiguity, syntactically dependent upon multiple applications of QR.

From this dependency on multiple applications of syntactic LF-movement, it does not follow, however, that we can attribute the *cause* of scope ambiguities directly to the syntax. Attributing the source of ambiguity requires rather a finer anslysis of the interaction of syntactic and semantic rules. In May (1977) I argued that in LF-representations such as (42), derived by iterated applications of QR, the two quantified phrases *asymmetrically* c-command one another.

(42) $[_S \text{ someone}_i [_S \text{ everyone}_j [_S e_j \text{ admires } e_i]]]$

As such, (42) represents a single, univocal interpretation of *Everyone admires someone*, under which the existential phrase has scope broader than the universal. Another LF-representation, in which the quantified phrases are adjoined in the opposite order, was also derivable, and that represents the interpretation under which the universal has broader scope. On this analysis the classical ambiguities of multiple quantification are explained, in the context of the theory of transformations, as arising from syntactic causes. The role of the semantics (and the pragmatics, for that matter) was to complete the description of the phenomena; explanation, on this view, rested in the syntax. In contrast, in May (1985, 1989a), I argued that the syntactic construal of (42) is not as a structure of asymmetrical c-command, but as one of *symmetrical* c-command. This result was derived by replacing the definition of c-command deriving from work of Reinhart (1976) with one due to Aoun and Sportiche (1983), augmented by the theory of adjunction presented in May (1985). Since this is a structure of symmetrical c-command, it is, by hypothesis, compatible with any scopal interpretation of the sequence of quantifiers it contains, so that this single syntactic structure is itself ambiguous. The ambiguity of (42) thus arises rather from whether the universal clause applies prior to the existential, or vice versa. The explanation of this ambiguity of multiple generalization is therefore shifted to the semantics, being a function of the possibilities of iterative application of the semantic quantifier clauses.[11] Ambiguity in natural language can originate within any of the three components of the grammar – the syntax, the semantics or the pragmatics – and it is an issue which component provides an explanation for any perceived ambiguity, and which serve only to complete the description. How we make these attributions of explanation and description will be a function of the fine structure of the overall theory of language, as we have just seen in the case of quantification, where variation in the interpretation of syntactic structure at LF quite markedly changes our understanding of the source of the ambiguity at hand.[12]

As we have proceeded, we have individuated the logical terms through an intuitive notion of invariance attaching to them, seeking to make it more precise in the context of our discussions. What we have determined is that they are expressions whose meanings are fixed by rules of certain formal character arising from their role in the truth theory, a character which places precise extrinsic constraints on the structure of LF. The rules for the categoremic expressions place no such formal constraints. This, however, still begs an important question: By what criteria do we sort the expressions interpreted by one kind of rule from the otner, so to distinguish the logical from the non-logical expressions? With respect to our particular concerns, this amounts to asking whether it is possible to independently delimit the class of quantifiers in natural language in some well-motivated and well-defined fashion. There has been a considerable amount of thinking on this issue, deriving from Mostowski's seminal paper, "On a Definition of Quantifiers," dating from 1955. The central concern emanating from this line of research has been to formally characterize a notion of *logicality*, which attaches to just the elements which are intuitively logical terms. As mentioned above, what marks off the logical terms is that they must satisfy a certain invariance principle. For quantifiers, following Mostowski, this has taken the form of requiring that they care only about the *size of the sets* to which they apply – that is, to how many members it has – and not on the identity of those members, with regard to which they are invariant. Formally, this follows by defining a family of functions from subsets of the domain D onto truth-values, where for all automorphisms m, one-one mappings from D onto D:

$$f(X) = f(m(X))$$

That is, the truth-value assigned to a set of individuals X by a quantificational function f must be constant under arbitrary permutations of the domain. Quantifiers which satisfy this condition are logical.[13]

The intuitive content of the logicality constraint can be easily seen. Suppose that we have a domain of four individuals. Then the sentence *Three people left* will be true regardless of whether the extension of the predicate *left* is the set $\{a, b, c\}$ or the set $\{b, c, d\}$. It will be true so long as just three people left; it matters not just who these individuals are. If we think of the individuals of the domain as each assigned a unique ordinal number, then the logicality property can be summed up in the following slogan: Quantifiers respect only cardinality, not ordinality.

The question which arises at this point is whether there is some way to show the boundaries of the class of quantifiers which satisfy the logicality constraint. It turns out that there is a general method for doing this, as indicated by Mostowski. What can be proven is that there is a one-one mapping from quantifiers which respect automorphisms of their domains onto "cardinality" quantifiers, defined as follows. For some $X \subset D$, let a cardinal number $\alpha = |D|$, and let $\beta + \gamma = \alpha$, where $\beta = |X|$ and $\gamma = |\bar{X}|$, where $\bar{X} = D\text{-}X$, intuitively the number of things which are and are not members of X. Then a *cardinality quantifier* is a function $q_\alpha(\beta,\gamma) \mapsto 2$; that is, a function from cardinal numbers onto truth. To take some simplified examples, we can define *every*, *some* and *most* as the following cardinality functions:

$$every_\alpha(\beta,\gamma) = 1 \text{ iff } \gamma = 0 \qquad some_\alpha(\beta,\gamma) = 1 \text{ iff } \beta \neq 0$$
$$most_\alpha(\beta,\gamma) = 1 \text{ iff } \beta > \gamma$$

The fundamental theorem, which fixes the class of quantifiers as the class of such cardinality quantifiers is as follows:

Theorem: Let F be the set of logical quantifiers (i.e. those which respect automorphisms of their domain) and let C be the set of cardinality quantifiers. Then there is a function $\mu\colon F\to C$ which is well-defined, one-to-one and onto.

This theorem connects quantifiers, which apply to individuals, to cardinal measures of quantity, and hence establishes the intuitive result mentioned above, that quantifiers exclusively respect the size of sets. The class of measures of quantity, and hence the quantifiers of natural language, will then be closed under arithmetic operations on cardinal numbers.[14] For the primary case of interest for natural language quantification, where we are interested in *restricted* quantifiers – those which apply to pairs of sets – the theorem is proven by Higginbotham and May (1981).[15] Sher (1989), in important work, extends this way of characterizing the class of logical quantifiers to the full class of cases applicable to natural language by extending the results beyond quantifiers of single variables to quantifiers of many variables. This includes the absorbed quantifiers introduced by Higginbotham and May to account for crossed binding Bach-Peters sentences,[16] and the resumptive quantifiers of May (1989), involved in the analysis of certain cases of so-called branching quantification. As discussed in the latter reference, while absorbed and resumptive quantifiers have in common that they are both syntactically derived and apply to relations, they differ in that the former are composite quantifiers which encode scope, while the latter are simplex quantifiers, which are scopally independent (and first-order).[17]

The relation of LF to logical form is the relation of a formal level of grammatical representation to one of its properties. That property is that LF represents the form of the logical terms, doing so in a way which conforms to intrinsic syntactic constraints on well-formedness of representations and extrinsic constraints on the interpretation of representations. In distinguishing the logical elements in the way that we have, we are making a cleavage between lexical items whose meanings are formally, and presumably exhaustively, determined by UG – the logical terms – and those whose meanings are underdetermined by UG – the non-logical, or content, words. This makes sense, for to specify the meaning of quantifiers, all that is needed, formally, is pure arithmetic calculation on cardinalities, and there is no reason to think that such mathematical properties are not universal. For other expressions, learning their lexical meanings is determined causally, and will be affected by experience, perception, knowledge, common-sense, etc. But none of these factors is relevant to the meaning of quantifiers. The child has to learn the content of the lexical entries for the non-logical terms, but this is not necessary for the entries for the logical terms, for they are given innately.

To conclude. The nature of LF, and the theory of logical form more generally, have become over the past decade central topics of discussion in theoretical linguistics. In this paper, I have addressed an approach to these

matters which while speculative captures I believe many of the central
notions common to much of the thinking in this area.[18] The literature
reflects, however, any number of variations of assumptions, both central
and peripheral, in approaching LF, and how precisely to conceive of the
interface between syntax and semantics. This just reflects, in my opinion,
the empirical nature of the inquiry; given the situation of LF and logical
form within linguistic theory, we would expect our views to fluctuate and
develop in league with our fluctuating and developing views of grammatical
theory generally. The overall growth of our understanding over the past
fifteen years, however, has given us a level of insight into the relation of the
syntax and semantics of natural language which was unthinkable at the
dawn of Noam Chomsky's contributions to linguistics. Heightening our
awareness of the very important issues involved, in addition to his
particular empirical insights, will undoubtedly be counted among those
many contributions.

NOTES

I would like to take this opportunity to thank Robert Fiengo, Richard Larson and
Tanya Reinhart, who have been of great influence on me in reflecting on the
matters discussed herein. I was particularly pleased to have been able to present
this paper in honor of Noam Chomsky, who initially sparked my interest in these
topics, and has continually fueled them. His influence on the study of logical form
has been instrumental, as it has been in so many other areas. To say that his
personal influence on me has been instrumental as well as inspirational would be to
grossly understate. This paper is dedicated to him, with my deepest gratitude. I
hope that it lives up to the standards of inquiry he has set for our field.

1   Similar comments can be made for the seemingly simpler case of the logical
    connectives. But see Larson (1985) for a discussion of the scope of disjunction
    in the context of LF, and the complications which arise therein.
2   The former paper dates from a Golden Anniversary Lecture presented at the
    1974 Summer LSA Linguistics Institute at The University of Massachusetts,
    Amherst. The latter dates from class presentations at MIT in the Fall of 1975.
3   This is in distinction to proposals of Williams (1986). Williams suggests a novel
    indexing scheme to represent quantificational binding, which coindexes an S
    node and the (S-structure) position of a quantifier it dominates. Note that this
    coindexing is *not* binding, since c-command fails – no category c-commands
    any category it contains. Limitations of this approach are discussed in May
    (1988a). While Williams (1988) expresses agreement with the criticisms
    presented in May (1988a), he does bring up some quite subtle cases which on
    his view create difficulties for the approach of May (1985). Insofar as these
    cases are relevant, however, they pertain only to the proper formulation of
    constraints (ECP), and not to any putative issues of LF-movement.
4   Lappin (1991) adopts a variant of the view above, dropping the Well-
    Formedness Condition, while still adopting the Cooper-storage approach. But
    this hybrid view-binding in both the syntax and semantics – seems to weaken
    even more the rationale behind why the grammar should not express logical
    structure. This is because it allows to stand, as otherwise available for syntactic
    description, the formal nomenclature utilized to express logical structure,

nomenclature whose existence Lappin does not dispute, and in fact, otherwise makes use of. For further discussion of the Cooper/Partee approach to quantification and binding, see May (1986, 1988b), Higginbotham (1987) and Reinhart (1991).

5 Aoun (1985) marshals a wide range of data in support of the view that Generalized Binding, from which the Binding Theory can be derived, holds of LF. Hornstein and Weinberg (1988) provide further arguments for this perspective, under somewhat variant assumptions regarding LF-movement. On their approach, under which only a quantifier word is moved, rather than the NP of which it is the specifier, difficulties arise in treating antecedent contained deletion, which requires movement of the entire NP; see below. Similar difficulties with deletion plague the approach of Williams (1986); see May (1988a). Kitagawa (1989) provides further evidence from deletion phenomena that Binding Theory applies at LF. This result is also implied by Belletti and Rizzi's (1988) assumption that Binding Theory is applicable at any level, developed in the context of their analysis of psychological predicates. Heim, Lasnik and May (1990) urge the same conclusion in the context of reciprocal constructions.

6 The observation that the key to antecedent-contained deletion resides in observing its link to quantification is due to Sag (1976); Williams (1977, fn. 3) notes the problem, but offers no analysis. The analysis is placed in the context of LF in May (1985); also see Haïk (1987) and Larson (1987) for further discussion of interest. Baltin (1987) argues against the involvement of QR in antecedent-contained deletion, but his arguments are incorrect; see Larson and May (1990) for reasons why.

7 In contrast to this "sloppy" reading, this sentence has another "strict" reading of a type noted independently by Fiengo and May (1990) and Kitagawa (1989). On this construal, the women, rather than introducing women, introduced the men, so that every man was introduced by (at least) a man and a woman. There are a number of very interesting issues which arise in the description of this observation; see the references cited.

8 Lappin mentions one other putative argument, involving temporal adjuncts. He neglects to bring into consideration that such constructions involve movement of a null-operator, as Larson (1987) argues. Once this is taken into account, such examples become uniform with the others under consideration.

9 For a full development of the observations here and their implications for the Binding Theory, and on our precise conception of reconstruction and ellipsis, see Fiengo and May (1990).

10 There has emerged a wealthy comparative literature based on this premise. For just a sample, see Huang (1982), whose work has been seminal in this area, and Aoun and Li (1989) on Chinese, Hoji (1985, 1986) and Nishigauchi (1986) on Japanese, and the papers in Huang and May (1990) which examine these issues in a broad range of languages. Recent discussion by Aoun and Li (1989) indicates that overt syntactic movement may "free-up" the possibilities of scope, although based on observations of Kiss (1990) regarding Hungarian, it appears that this effect is limited to A-movement, since overt Ā quantifier movement in this language freezes scope possibilities. (Unmoved quantifiers in S-structure are free in their scope possibilities in Hungarian.) If this is so, then languages may differ in the patterns of scope they exhibit as a function of the chain-structures they manifest in S-structure. This is an interesting point, in need of further research.

11 Or of the formation of polyadic quantifiers, so that (42) is directly construed as

an absorption structure; see May (1989), and discussion below.

12　Heim, Lasnik and May (1991) make a similar point in the context of anaphoric relations in reciprocal constructions. They point out that assumptions about fine structure of binding can attune our understanding of both the cause of ambiguity, and of the distribution of types of anaphoric binding.

13　For recent research on characterizing logicality, see Higginbotham and May (1981), van Benthem (1983), de Mey (1987) and Sher (1989).

14　Thus natural languages are at least as expressively rich as arithmetic; this allows of some rather exotic expressions of quantity. See Sher (1989) for discussion of a range of examples.

15　Notice that these quantifiers, sometimes referred to a relational quantifiers, exclude proper names, as we cannot take them as operators relating sets (unless we treat them as disguised descriptions or general terms). This contrasts with the approach adopted by Barwise and Cooper (1981), who treat all noun *phrases* as generalized quantifiers. Thus, they take quantified express-ions to be categoremic terms, eschewing the logicality notion, which disting-uishes the logical from the non-logical, in favor of the notion of living on a set, which does not generate any such distinction.

16　For recent discussion of Bach–Peters sentences and absorption, see Clark and Keenan (1986) and May (1990). Epstein (1989) believes he has found an inconsistency in the absorption approach in the treatment of crossed and uncrossed binding. But Epstein is mistaken here. The matter he notes was already discussed in Higginbotham and May (1981, fn. 16), and can be shown to fall under basic constraints on absorption; see May (1990).

17　For further discussion of polyadic quantifiers, see Van Benthem (1989), Keenan (1987), May (1989, 1990) and Sher (1989).

18　For other general statements on the properties of LF, and its relation to meaning, see Higginbotham (1985, 1989), who additionally focuses concern on the semantics of non-logical lexical structure, and Hornstein (1984). While I am not in agreement with Hornstein's views on the relation of semantics and pragmatics, his book does contain many useful insights, some of which originate with May (1977).

REFERENCES

Aoun, J. 1985: *A Grammar of Anaphora*. MIT Press, Cambridge, Mass.
Aoun, J. and Li, T.-H. A. 1989: "Scope and Constituency." *Linguistic Inquiry*, 20, 141–72.
Aoun, J. and Sportiche, D. 1983: "On the Formal Theory of Government." *The Linguistic Review*, 2, 211–36.
Baltin, M. 1987: "Do Antecedent-Contained Deletions Exist?" *Linguistic Inquiry*, 18, 579–95.
Barwise, J. and Cooper, R. 1981: "Generalized Quantifiers and Natural Lan-guage." *Linguistics and Philosophy*, 4, 159–219.
Belletti, A. and Rizzi, L. 1988: "Psych-Verbs and θ-Theory." *Natural Language and Linguistic Theory*, 6, 291–352.
Benthem, J. van 1983: "Determiners and Logic." *Linguistics and Philosophy*, 6, 447–78.
—— 1989: "Polyadic Quantifiers." *Linguistics and Philosophy*, 12, 437–64.
Chomsky, N. 1957: *Syntactic Structures*. Mouton, The Hague.
—— 1975a: "Introduction" to N. Chomsky, *The Logical Structure of Linguistic Theory*. Plenum Press, New York.

—— 1975b: "Questions of Form and Interpretation." In R. Austerlitz (ed.), *The Scope of American Linguistics*, The Peter de Ridder Press, Lisse, Belgium. Also appears in *Linguistic Analysis*, 1, 75–109 and in N. Chomsky, *Essays on Form and Interpretation*, North-Holland, New York, 1977.

—— 1976: "Conditions on Rules of Grammar." *Linguistic Analysis*, 2, 303–51. Also appears in N. Chomsky, *Essays on Form and Interpretation*. North-Holland, New York, 1977.

—— 1982: *Some Concepts and Consequences of the Theory of Government and Binding*. MIT Press, Cambridge, Mass.

—— 1986a: *Knowledge of Language: Its Nature, Origin and Use*. Praeger Publishers, New York.

—— 1986b: *Barriers*. MIT Press, Cambridge, Mass.

Clark, R. and Keenan, E. 1986: "The Absorption Operator and Universal Grammar." *The Linguistic Review*, 5, 113–36.

Cooper, R. 1983: *Quantification and Syntactic Theory*. Reidel, Dordrecht.

Epstein, S. D. 1989: "Adjunction and Pronominal Variable Binding." *Linguistic Inquiry*, 20, 307–19.

Fiengo, R., Huang, C.-T. J., Lasnik, H. and Reinhart, T. 1988: "The Syntax of *Wh*-in-Situ." In H. Borer (ed.), *Proceedings of the Seventh West Coast Conference on Formal Linguistics*. Stanford Linguistics Association, Stanford, California.

Fiengo, R. and May, R. 1991: *Indices and Identity*. MS., The Graduate Center, City University of New York and University of California, Irvine.

Haïk, I. 1987: "Bound VPs that Need to Be." *Linguistics and Philosophy*, 10, 503–30.

Heim, I., Lasnik, H. and May, R. 1990: "Reciprocity and Plurality." *Linguistic Inquiry* 22, in press.

Higginbotham, J. 1985: "On Semantics." *Linguistic Inquiry*, 16, 547–94.

—— 1987: "The Autonomy of Syntax and Semantics." In J. Garfield (ed.), *Modularity in Knowledge Representation and Natural-Language Understanding*, Bradford Books, MIT Press, Cambridge, Mass.

—— 1989: "Elucidations of Meaning." *Linguistics and Philosophy*, 12, 465–517.

Higginbotham, J. and May, R. 1981: "Questions, Quantifiers and Crossing." *The Linguistic Review*, 1, 41–79.

Hoji, H. 1985: *Logical Form Constraints and Configurational Structures in Japanese*. Doctoral dissertation, University of Washington, Seattle, Washington.

—— 1986: "Scope Interpretation in Japanese and Its Theoretical Implications." In M. Dalrymple, J. Goldberg, K. Hanson, M. Inman, C. Piñon and S. Wechsler (eds), *Proceedings of the West Coast Conference on Formal Linguistics*, 5, Stanford Linguistics Association, Stanford, California.

Hornstein, N. 1984: *Logic as Grammar*. MIT Press, Cambridge, Mass.

Hornstein, N. and Weinberg, A. 1988: "The Necessity of LF.' MS., University of Maryland.

Huang, C.-T. J. 1982: *Logical Relations in Chinese and the Theory of Grammar*. Doctoral dissertation, MIT, Cambridge, Mass.

Huang, C.-T. J. and May, R. (eds) 1991: *Linguistic Structure and Logical Structure*. Kluwer Publishing Co., Dordrecht.

Keenan, E. 1987: "Unreducible n-ary Quantifiers in Natural Language." In P.Gärdenfors (ed.), *Generalized Quantifiers: Linguistic and Logical Approaches*, Reidel, Dordrecht.

Kiss, K. 1991: "Logical Structure in Syntactic Structure: The Case of Hungarian." In C.-T. J. Huang and R. May, (eds). *Logical Structure and Linguistic Structure*, Kluwer Publishing Co., Dordrecht.

Kitagawa, Y. 1989: "Copying Identity." MS., University of Rochester.

Lappin, S. 1991: "Concepts of Logical Form in Linguistics and Philosophy." In this volume.

Larson, R. 1985: "On the Syntax of Disjunction Scope." *Natural Language and Linguistic Theory*, 3, 217–64.

—— 1987: "'Missing Prepositions' and the Analysis of English Free Relative Clauses." *Linguistic Inquiry*, 18, 239–66.

Larson, R. and May, R. 1990: "Antecedent-Containment or Vacuous Movement: Reply to Baltin." *Linguistic Inquiry*, 21, 103–22.

Link, G. 1987: "Generalized Quantifiers and Plurals." In P. Gärdenfors (ed.), *Generalized Quantifiers: Linguistic and Logical Approaches*, D. Reidel Publishing Co., Dordrecht, The Netherlands.

Longobardi, G. 1991: "In Defense of the Correspondence Hypothesis." In C.-T. J. Huang and R. May (eds), *Logical Structure and Linguistic Structure*, Kluwer Publishing Co., Dordrecht.

May, R. 1977: *The Grammar of Quantification*. Doctoral dissertation, MIT, Cambridge, Mass.

—— 1985: *Logical Form: Its Structure and Derivation*. MIT Press, Cambridge, Mass.

—— 1986: "Review of R. Cooper *Quantification and Syntactic Theory*." *Language*, 62, 902–8.

—— 1988a: "Ambiguities of Quantification and *Wh*: A Reply to Williams." *Linguistic Inquiry*, 19, 118–35.

—— 1988b: "Bound Variable Anaphora." In R. Kempson (ed.), *Mental Representations: The Interface between Language and Reality*, Cambridge University Press, Cambridge, England.

—— 1989: "Interpreting Logical Form." *Linguistics and Philosophy*, 12, 387–435.

—— 1990: "A Note on Quantifier Absorption." *The Linguistic Review*, 7, 121–7.

Mey, S. de 1987: "Transitive Sentences and the Property of Logicality." In I. Rusza and A. Szabolcsi (eds), *Proceedings of the 1987 Debrecen Symposium on Logic and Language*, Akadémiai Kiadó, Budapest.

Mostowski, A. 1957: "On a Generalization of Quantifiers." *Fundamenta Mathematicae*, 44, 12–36.

Nishigauchi, T. 1986: *Quantification in Syntax*. Doctoral dissertation, University of Massachusetts, Amherst, Mass.

Partee, B. 1979: "Montague Grammar and the Well-Formedness Constraint." In F. Heny and H. Schnelle (eds), *Selections from the Third Groningen Round Table, Syntax and Semantics, 10*. Academic Press, New York.

Partee, B. and Bach, E. 1984: "Quantification, Pronouns and VP Anaphora." In J. Groenendijk, T. M. V. Janssen and M. Stokhof (eds), *Truth, Interpretation and Information*, Foris Publications, Dordrecht.

Pesetsky, D. 1987: "*Wh*-in-situ: Movement and Selective Binding." In E. Reuland and A. ter Meulen (eds), *The Representation of (In)definiteness*, MIT Press, Cambridge, Mass.

Reinhart, T. 1976: *The Syntactic Domain of Anaphora*. Doctoral dissertation, MIT, Cambridge, Mass.

—— 1991: "Elliptic conjunctions – Non-quantificational LF." In this volume.

Roberts, C. 1986: *Model Subordination, Anaphora and Distributivity*. Doctoral dissertation, University of Massachusetts., Amherst, Mass.

Sag, I. 1976: *Deletion and Logical Form*. Doctoral dissertation, MIT, Cambridge, Mass.

Sher, G. 1989: *Generalized Logic*. Doctoral dissertation, Columbia University, New York, New York.

Wahba, W. 1991: "LF-Movement in Iraqi Arabic." In C.-T. J. Huang and R. May (eds), *Logical Structure and Linguistic Structure*, Kluwer Publishing Co., Dordrecht.

Williams, E. 1977: "Discourse and Logical Form." *Linguistic Inquiry*, 8, 101–39.

—— 1986: "A Reassignment of the Functions of LF." *Linguistic Inquiry*, 17, 265–99.

—— 1988: "Is LF Distinct From S-Structure: A Reply To May." *Linguistic Inquiry*, 19, 135–46.

15

Elliptic Conjunctions –
Non-Quantificational LF

Tanya Reinhart

1

Since its introduction into linguistic theory, in Chomsky (1976) and May (1977), the level of LF has been a center of extensive debate. Much of this debate has conflated two questions which are, in fact, independent. The one is whether Surface-Structures (SS) can always be interpreted directly, or intermediate syntactic structures, which are invisible to phonetics, are needed. The other concerns the interpretation of quantification in natural language, and the question whether the distinction between referential and quantified NPs (QNP) should be captured in the grammar.

I believe that the real insights of LF theory lie within the first issue above. There is, by now, hardly any disagreement on the fact that standard compositional procedures applying at SS cannot yield the full range of possible interpretations in all cases, though opinions are divided on the mechanism needed to capture this full range (an issue I turn to in section 2.2.2). In this paper I will point out further evidence that a rule like QR (illustrated in (1)c) is needed in the grammar. The peculiar property of the structures I will consider is that QR must be used to form one constituent out of discontinuous units of SS. The syntax of QR in these structures provides, furthermore, strong support to current assumptions on syntactic and LF movement.

The issue of QR, however, is independent of the issue of the interpretation of quantification. In fact the structures under consideration here show that QR cannot distinguish quantified from referential NPs. Historically, LF was viewed as a level of quantification, and a major motivation for introducing it was that it provided the structures needed to translate sentences with quantified NPs (QNP) into formulae of classical logic. Assuming that (1)b must be translated as (1)d, where the QNP is a predicate rather than an argument, QR creates the structure (1)c in which the QNP is no longer in argument position, and a variable is available in its original position.

(1)a   Lucie smiled.
  b   every linguist smiled.
  c $[_{IP}[_{NP}$ every linguist$]$ $[_{IP}$ e_1 smiled$]]$
  d   every x (linguist (x)) (x smiled)

In (1)a, where the subject is referential, no translation operations are assumed to be needed, and the subject is interpreted as an argument. Crucially, then, QR applies to all and only quantified NPs, and the underlying view is that a syntactic level (LF) is needed to capture semantic differences between NPs, which are not reflected in their "visible" (SS) syntax.

It is an interesting historical development that the semantic school, following Montague, has taken a syntactic approach to the same problem: since syntactically there is no difference between the two types of NPs, there should be no syntactic level distinguishing them, and they should be treated uniformly, up to the stage of the actual assignment of denotation. This, however, entails that all NPs alike are semantically treated as functions, and that classical first-order logic is not sufficient to interpret natural language sentences. The last conclusion is supported, on this view, by the existence of non-logical quantifiers, like *most*, which cannot be treated within classical logic (see, for instance, Barwise and Cooper 1981).

Apart from meta-theoretic issues, such as a preference for first order logic, the view that QNP should be distinguished from referential NPs at some syntactic level was supported in Chomsky (1976) by what was, at the time, a decisive empirical evidence, namely that there exist syntactic contexts distinguishing them in the case of anaphora (known as "weak-crossover" contexts). However, given the later development of the binding theory, already at the transit to the GB stage, these cases no longer have the same implications. In fact, the same anaphora contexts show that quantified and referential NPs behave precisely the same way in all syntactic respects. (This is shown in detail in Reinhart 1983, 1986.) Since no other syntactic context has ever been established as distinguishing precisely these two types of NPs, the debate concerning this issue is, at this stage, purely meta-theoretical. Further progress on this issue depends, furthermore, on whether some answer will be offered to the question how non-logical quantifiers can be treated within first order logic.

We should also note that the question whether QR exists is not precisely identical to the question whether LF is a syntactic level. My claim below is only that QR must apply to capture non-compositional scope. In all other cases, whether quantified NPs are interpretable in situ is strictly theory-dependent. For convenience, however, I will use the term "LF" to refer to the outputs of QR.

2   ELLIPTIC-CONJUNCTIONS – EVIDENCE FOR QR

2.1   The Problem with "Exception" Ellipsis

The structures I will focus on are those in (2). Although they have not been discussed in the linguistic literature, they turn out to have syntactic distribution identical to that of more familiar structures which have been viewed as cases of ellipsis, such as the Bare-Argument Ellipsis in (3) (which is a subcase of gapping) or the Comparative Ellipsis in (4). I will refer to all three types as "Elliptic Conjunctions" (EC).

(2)   *Exception Conjunctions*
   a   *no-one* kisses his mother, except (for) *Felix*.
   b   Max was upset with *every woman* after the meeting, except *Lucie*.
   c   *no-one will* show up, but *Max*.
   d   you should invite *no journalist* to the party, but *Felix*.

(3)   *Bare-Argument (BA) Conjunctions*
   a   *the critics* liked your book and *the public* – too.
   b   the critics praised *your book* yesterday but not *your poem*.
   c   either *Lucie* will show up, or *Max*.
   d   *Lucie* will go, instead of *him*.

(4)   *Comparative Ellipsis*
   a   more people love *Bach* than *Mozart*.
   b   I spoke *with Lucie* longer than *with Lili*.
   c   she loves me more than *Max*.

(5)   Lucie will assist you $\left\{ \begin{array}{l} \text{despite Max.} \\ \text{because of him.} \end{array} \right\}$

Using ellipsis terminology we may refer to the italicized expression in the second conjunct as the "remnant" (of ellipsis) and to that in the first as its "correlate." Typically in such structures any NP in the first conjunct can serve as a correlate (subject to restrictions we return to). For instance in (2)a, c the correlate is the subject, in (2)d the object, and in (2)b the P-complement.

   The exception-cases, like the EC structures in (3)–(4), have semantic properties associated generally with ellipsis. Compare, for instance, (2)c and (3)c to (5). While in the first, the interpretation involves construing the property of future showing-up attributed to the correlate, *no-one* or *Lucie*, in the first conjunct and to *Max* in the second, no such construal is needed in the non-elliptic (5), and the sentence implies nothing concerning whether Max will show up or not. In (2)a the construed property of kissing one's own mother (λx (x kissed x's mother)) involves a bound variable whose value in the second conjunct will be *Felix*, an interpretation typical of ellipsis structures (Sag 1975; Williams 1977). Nevertheless, these structures also differ substantially from the better known ellipsis types, and, as we will see, they cannot, in fact, be viewed as actual ellipsis. All structures in (2)–(4) pose serious syntactic problems to an ellipsis analysis, to which I return in section 2.2.3, but in the case of exception-sentences, an ellipsis approach is infeasible also semantically.

In standard ellipsis structures, such as (6), the interpretation involves forming a predicate (at LF), as in (6)b, which is copied into the empty constituent, yielding (6)c. The interpretation is, then, identical to the parallel non-elliptic sentence (6)d, (Sag 1976; Williams 1977).

(6)a   everyone smiled. even Lucie did.
   b   everyone (λx (x smiled)) . . .
   c   even Lucie did (λx (x smiled))
   d   everyone smiled. even Lucie smiled.

Applying the same procedure to exception-structures yields dramatically wrong interpretive results. If, in (7)a, we copy a predicate from the first conjunct into the second, the result will be (the interpretation of) (7)b, which is clearly not the correct interpretation – while (7)b is a contradiction, (7)a is not. (7)a entails that Lucie is a linguist and that she smiled. So the second conjunct of (7)b must be true. But, then it must be false that no linguist smiled. The same is true of (8).

(7)a   no linguist smiled except/but Lucie.
   b   no linguist smiled, but Lucie smiled. (Lucie a linguist)

(8)a   I read every book already except "War and Peace."
   b   I read every book already except (that) I didn't read "War and Peace."

More generally, in the exception-cases, there is no equivalent non-elliptical form, using two full sentences. Rather, their interpretation is identical to (9), where the remnant and the correlate form one conjoined NP.

(9)a   no linguist except Lucie smiled.
   b   I read every book except "War and Peace" already.

Another indication that the except-phrase in the apparent ellipsis structures must be interpreted in conjunction with its correlate is the fact that there are restrictions on the relations of the sets in the two NPs. (10) is ill-formed (assuming that Lucie is not a man), just as its counterpart in (11).

(10)   no man smiled, except Lucie.
(11)   no man except Lucie smiled.

Keenan and Stavi (1986) argue that the *except* constituent in the exception-NPs of (9) are analyzed as part of a complex one-place determiner, e.g. *no except Lucie* taking *linguist*, in (9)a. Without entering the full details of their (rather unexplored) semantics, the truth conditions of the specific examples in (9) are given in (12).

(12)a   B ε ‖no A except Lucie‖ iff A ∩ B = {Lucie}
    b   B ε ‖every A except W&P‖ iff A ∩ B′ = {W&P}

That is, (9)a is true iff the intersection set of smiling linguists is the singleton set containing Lucie, and (9)b is true iff the intersection of books and the things I have not read contains only "War and Peace." A sentence like (11) can never be true, therefore, since Lucie is not a member of the A set (of men), hence it cannot be in any of its intersections.

In determining the denotation of exception-NPs, then, it is impossible to compute separately the denotation of the correlate and of the remnant and apply each separately to the same predicate, which is the standard procedure in ellipsis interpretation. Therefore, when they occur in the apparent ellipsis form, the only way to interpret the structure is to reconstruct, at some level, the relevant single NP at which both parts of the complex determiner are available.

At first glance, this fact may suggest that the structures under consideration are, indeed, not cases of ellipsis, but rather that (7)a and (8)a are derived from the deep structure of (9) by some syntactic rule. An obvious candidate is the transformation of extraposition which is believed to derive, e.g. (b), in (13) and (14), from (a):

(13)a   many reviews about this book appeared already.
    b   many reviews appeared already about this book.

(14)a   a man who went to school with me walked in.
    b   a man walked in who went to school with me.

But it turns out that exception-structures obey rather different syntactic restrictions than extraposition. While extraposition is known to be clause-bound, as witnessed by the inappropriateness of (15), exception-structures are not, as in (16). Another syntactic environment which allows exception-structures but not extraposition is illustrated in (20)–(21) below.

(15) *the editor agreed to publish many reviews [e]$_1$, when we pressed him, [about this book]$_1$

(16) the editor did not agree to publish anything, when we pressed him, except one short review.

Furthermore, extraposition is known to be highly sensitive to semantic considerations: the determiner must be weak (like "many" in (13)). Strong determiners, as in (17)a do not allow extraposition. The set of predicates allowing extraposition is, more or less, that which can occur in "there" sentences, as illustrated by a comparison of (13) and (17)b.

(17)a *most reviews/every review appeared already about this book.
   b *many reviews disappeared (from the library) about this book.

(18) everyone disappeared, except Felix.

Neither restriction holds for exception-structures, as can be checked in (18).

However, since extraposition is such a peculiar transformation, a reasonable move is to assume that it does not exist at all, but rather, that its "results" are base-generated, subject to interpretive conditions discussed, for instance, in Reinhart (1987). The question is, then, whether exception-structures can be an instance of a more straightforward rightward movement, subject to the standard constraints on syntactic movement. Although, as we shall see, exception-structures are sensitive to subjacency in the standard cases, their distribution is nevertheless not identical to that of syntactic movement. For instance, extraction from subjects is strictly prohibited at SS, as in (19). If (20)a is derived by syntactic extraction of *except Felix*, the derivation (given in (20)b) should be equally ruled out, which is not the case. Note that extraposition too is impossible from this position, as in the parallel (21).

(19) *who$_1$ were [jokes about e$_1$] told?

(20)a jokes about everyone were told except Felix.
   b *[jokes about everyone e$_1$] were told [except Felix]$_1$

(21) *jokes [about a woman e$_1$] were told [who went to school with me]$_1$

Such examples are sufficient to show that the correlate and the remnant cannot form a DS constituent. The option we are left with, then, is that the relevant constituent is formed at LF, and it is the correlate which is raised to join the remnant, rather than conversely. In section 2.3, we will see that under current syntactic theory, differences are predicted between the options of syntactic and LF movement in certain environments. It is precisely in these environments, one of which is (20), that exception-structures pattern with LF, rather than syntactic, movement.

2.2   Analysis

Let us turn to the mechanism forming the relevant constituent at LF. The analysis is based on that proposed in Reinhart and Rooth (forthcoming) for the other types of elliptic-conjunctions, surveyed in 2.2.3.

2.2.1   The remnant is base-generated adjoined (or conjoined) to IP, with no empty nodes, as in (22). I assume that in the exception-cases the remnant is an NP. The connectives in this case are obligatory case-assigners, hence they can only occur with an (accusative) NP.

(22)

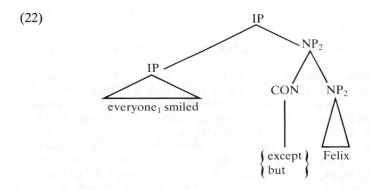

This structure appears unstandard: *except* NPs, such as NP_2, can normally form a constituent only with an NP and are uninterpretable as sentential modifiers. More generally, conjunctions require categorical identity of the conjoined constituents. At SS (or DS), therefore, such structures are uninterpretable, and they can be saved only if another structure is available, at which the relevant constituent is formed. This structure can be formed by QR, raising the correlate (*everyone*) and adjoining it to the remnant, yielding (23)a. (This is similar to the movement assumed, following Huang 1982, in the case of *wh*-in-situ).

(23)a

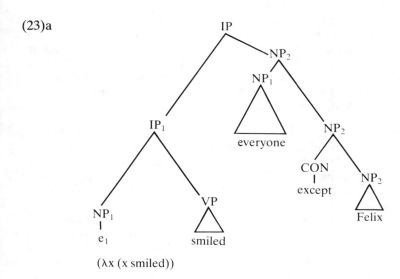

$(\lambda x \ (x \ \text{smiled}))$

b [Everyone except Felix] $(\lambda x \ (x \ \text{smiled}))$
c Everyone except Felix smiled

    In the current view of LF and syntactic movement, (23)a violates neither Subjacency nor the ECP, since no barriers are crossed, and the position the correlate is moved to c-commands (i.e. m-commands) its trace, given the segment definitions of domination and c-command in May (1985), and Chomsky (1986).[1] It has, at times, been argued (e.g. Huang 1982) that adjunction of this type should block antecedent government of the trace e_1, which would account for superiority-violations in *wh*-movement. However, alternative analyses of the superiority effects in terms of path-containment (Pesetsky 1982; May 1985) make such stipulations superfluous.[2] (In any case, see note 3 for an alternative analysis of the LF of (22) which does not require this specific form of adjunction.)
    Next, a λ-predicate is formed in the IP, which takes the whole new NP_2 as argument. Since the quantifier in the correlate is not the semantic binder of the trace, the mismatch of the trace index (e_1) and the argument index (NP_2) is irrelevant. Technically the binding of the trace can be obtained by coindexing it with the dominating IP, as assumed, for syntactic *wh*-movement, in Williams (1986). The result of these operations, then, is (23)b, which is equivalent, of course, to (23)c, where the full exception NP is base-generated. The interpretive procedure may proceed, then, in precisely the same way that it would in (23)c.
    As we saw, in defining the denotation of exception NPs, a complex determiner is formed (*every except Felix*). Syntactically, in neither (23)a nor (23)c does *every* form a constituent with the *except* constituent. At the

present, however, it does not seem necessary to apply further operations altering the internal structure of the NP. Rather, this can be done directly by the semantic rules determining their denotation. (For a discussion of a related issue of mismatch between syntactic and semantic NP-structure in the case of comparatives with two-place determiners, see Keenan 1987). In any case, the analysis proposed here for exception ellipsis is independent of the details of the treatment of exception NPs. The crucial point is only that such an NP is formed, to interpret these structures.[3]

2.2.2 This is the place to note that the question of how to capture seemingly non-compositional interpretations is subject to a debate concerning the mechanism that should be assumed for this process. Some alternatives competing with QR are semantic storage (Cooper 1983; Lappin 1984; and this volume) and SS indexing (Haïk 1984; Williams 1986). Since the latter do not specify the details of the semantics intended for the indexing, I assume that it is essentially that of semantic storage. Generally the storage analysis is known to be empirically equivalent to a QR analysis, but it is interesting to note that it is not yet obvious that the same is true for the structures under consideration here.

The difference between the QR and the storage approach is that while the first raises (or stores) uninterpreted syntactic units, in the second it is the denotation of the NP (a function) which is stored, and then applied to the predicate at the final stage, i.e. the stored unit is a semantic rather than a syntactic object. If exception-conjunctions were interpretable as elliptic structures, the storage approach would, obviously, be equivalent here too to the QR approach: first the correlate's denotation is stored, and then, both the correlate and the remnant functions are applied to the same predicate. However, as we saw in the discussion of (7)–(12) above, this is precisely what we cannot do in these cases.

Whether a reasonable solution is possible within the storage approach largely depends on whether the semantic analysis of exception NPs in Keenan and Stavi (1986) is correct. If the *except* constituent must, indeed, combine with the first determiner to form a complex determiner function applying to one N set, this cannot be done in the storage framework when these NPs occur in the elliptic-conjunction form (in a reasonable way – see note 4). What gets stored must be the denotation of the correlate, i.e. the full NP function (*everyone*) in (22), where the determiner function has already applied. When the remnant (*except Felix*) is encountered, the determiner *every* is no longer available for the remnant to form a complex determiner with. The crucial reason why this issue is not a problem for the QR approach is, precisely, that QR stores a syntactic constituent, and its denotation is computed in its new position. At this stage the correlate and the remnant form one syntactic unit and both *every* and *except Felix* are available.[4]

2.2.3 The procedure forming a constituent at LF was motivated so far only on semantic grounds and for somewhat esoteric quantificational structures. In fact, there is also substantial syntactic evidence that such a procedure is needed for these structures, independently of their semantics, and, furthermore, that it applies to a much larger set of cases than exception NPs. Reinhart and Rooth (forthcoming) argue that all the presumed ellipsis structures in (3)–(4), some of which are repeated below, are instances of the same phenomenon (as well as some other structures I will not discuss here).[5]

(24)   *Bare-Argument (BA) ellipsis*
   a   you can talk *about politics* as much as you want, but not *about linguistics*.
   b   the critics praised your book yesterday and your cooking too.
   c   neither Lucie can assist you, nor Max.
   d   Lucie Seemed *tired* after the meeting, but not *defeated*.

(25)   *Comparative Ellipsis*
   a   more people love Bach than Mozart.
   b   I spoke with Lucie longer than with Lili.
   c   she loves me more than Max.

The remnant in these structures can be any XP (e.g. a PP, in (24)a and (25)b, and an AP in (25)d). To generate them, we assume, therefore, that (22) is just a specific instance of the more general structural scheme in (26).

(26)

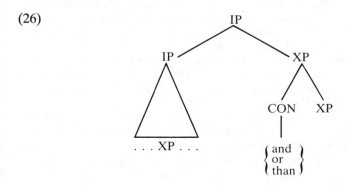

Under the standard conditions of conjunctions, a structure like (26) is, again, interpretable only if an XP matching in category and case is available, and it will be provided here too by QR, which adjoins the matching XP correlate (italicized in (24) and (25)) to the base-generated remnant. Unlike the *except* connectives, those in (24) and (25) are not case-assigners (except one type of *than*, known as "prepositional-than"). In case the remnant is NP, it is assigned arbitrary case at SS, but the structure is interpretable only if the raised correlate matches in case. In the case of comparatives, a further raising of a degree operator is involved.

The operators allowing elliptic conjunctions are the Boolean ones (*and*, *or*, *not*, and some derivatives such as *in addition to* for *and* and *instead of* for *not*) and the comparative operators. In these cases it is extremely difficult to decide between the competing analyses on semantic grounds, since in the standard cases, an ellipsis interpretation is indistinguishable from an interpretation based on forming one constituent. For instance, the interpretation of the (b) sentences, in (27) and (28) below is the one that an ellipsis analysis will assign to the (a) structures, and the interpretation of (c) is the one that a constituent analysis will assign them. In both cases (b) and (c) are equivalent paraphrases of (a).

(27)a the critics praised *your book* yesterday and your cooking too.
    b the critic praised your book yesterday and the critics praised your cooking yesterday too.
    c the critics praised your book and your cooking yesterday.

(28)a more men love Bach than women.
    b more men love Bach than women love Bach.
    c more men than women love Bach.

This is so, because in the standard (and extensional) cases, a proposition formed with a constituent conjoined by this operator does entail the conjunction of two propositions with the same operator, unlike the case of exception-conjunctions. Where this result is less clear, the judgments are very subtle. (See Heim 1986 for a discussion of the two competing interpretations in the case of comparatives.)

I believe that it is for this reason that an ellipsis analysis has appeared possible for BA and comparative structures. The crucial point, however, is that such analysis is syntactically infeasible. We may turn now to the syntactic motivation for the proposed analysis.

In the standard cases of ellipsis, which may be labeled constituent ellipsis, the elliptic, or "missing" material corresponds to a constituent. Hence, the remnant constituent can be generated as a clause containing an empty projection. This can be (among others) a V projection, as in the VP-ellipsis case of (29), or an I projection, as in the "sluicing" case of (30), where the empty constituent is IP.

(29) Lucie ate an apple and Max did [$_{VP}$ e] too

(30) I wanted to say something but I forgot [$_{CP}$ what [$_{IP}$ e]]

In such cases, a constituent corresponding to the empty projection is available, or formed at LF, in the antecedent clause and this constituent (more precisely, the LF predicate it forms) is copied into the empty node at the interpretation stage.

In the elliptic conjunctions, by contrast, there is no base-generated projection corresponding to the elliptic material. This is obvious when the remnant correlates with the object, as in (24)b (*The critics praised your book yesterday, and your cooking too*), where the nodes "missing" in the second clause should be the non-constituent sequence of the subject NP, I, V, and ADV.[6]

A way to get around this problem was proposed by Pesetsky (1982) for gapping. In essence, he gives gapping the same structural analysis as the sluicing cases of (30), arguing that the remnants are base-generated in the SPEC of CP, followed by an empty IP. Applying this analysis to Bare-Argument conjunctions, (32) will be generated the same way as its sluicing analogue in (31).

(31) I'd like to get one of these books soon. But [$_{CP}$ which one [$_{IP}$ e]]?

(32) I'd like to get one of these books soon but not [$_{CP}$ the one by Tom Wolfe [$_{IP}$ e]]

(33)a one of these books [$_{IP1}$ I'd like to get e$_1$ soon]
    b but which one [$_{IP2}$ e]?
    c but not the one by Tom Wolfe [$_{IP_2}$ e]

To interpret these structures, QR adjoins the correlate in the first conjunct, to IP, as in (33)a. The resulting LF predicate IP$_1$ (or rather the corresponding LF predicate: λx (I'd like to get x soon) can now be copied into IP$_2$ in both (33)b and (33)c.

The problem with this line of analysis is that despite the apparent similarity of (31) and (32), the structures under consideration have much more restricted distribution than that of constituent-ellipsis. They can occur only in conjoined structures, while no such restriction holds for constituent ellipsis. For instance, neither BA nor exception conjunctions can occur when the remnant is subordinate as in (35), compared to the standard sluicing case (34). (The same problem shows up also with gapping, as acknowledged by Pesetsky.)

(34) the police have interrogated some politician, but they didn't say which one [$_{IP}$ e]

(35)a *the police have interrogated the education minister, but they didn't say (that) the defense minister.
    b *the police interrogated all politicians but they say (that) except the defense minister.
    c *Felix sneezed since Max (too).

More precisely, the restriction on elliptic conjunctions is that the "antecedent-clause," i.e. the clause that will be interpreted as the predicate which takes the remnant as argument, must be a sister of the remnant's constituent at SS (as e.g. in (32)). For this reason (37) and (38) are ill-formed, unlike their sluicing counterpart in (36).

(36)   the fact that [$_{IP}$ some politician has resigned] got much publicity, but (I forgot) which one [$_{IP}$ e]

(37)   *the fact that [$_{IP1}$ some politician has resigned] got much publicity but not the defense minister [$_{IP_2}$ e]

(38)   *the fact that [all politicians have resigned] got much publicity except the defense minister [$_{IP_2}$ e]

(39)   *more rumors that [$_{IP_1}$ the education minister resigned] were spread than the defense minister [$_{IP_2}$ e]

(40)a   the fact that [$_{IP}$ some politician [$_{IP}$ e$_1$ has resigned]] got much publicity,
   b   but (I forgot) which one [$_{IP_2}$ e]
   c   *but not the defense minister [$_{IP_2}$ e]

To interpret (36) the correlate *some politician* is adjoined to its IP (as in (40)a. The IP$_1$ predicate (λx (x has resigned)) can now be copied into the empty IP$_2$, repeated in (40)b. If the BA case (37) has the same structures as (36), namely it has an empty IP node available for copying, it is hard to see what could prevent the procedure from copying the same IP$_1$ in (40)a into the IP$_2$ position in (40)c as well. The same holds, of course, for the exception-conjunction in (38) and the comparative in (39). In all three cases the antecedent IP$_1$ is not a sister of the remnant (and no predicate can be formed of the sister matrix-IP, since Subjacency prohibits raising the correlate all the way up into that IP).

More generally, it is well-known for all types of constituent ellipsis (Sag 1976; Williams 1977), that the procedure of copying a (well-formed) LF predicate into an empty projection is essentially unrestricted by the grammar – the two can lie as far apart as considerations of discourse coherence permit, and relating them is certainly not sensitive to subjacency or adjacency requirements. If elliptic conjunctions are generated as standard ellipsis structures, there is no way to derive from anything known about ellipsis an explanation for why they are so severely restricted.[7] More details on why this is so, as well as problems with imaginable lines of answers, can be found in Reinhart and Rooth (forthcoming).

Given the analysis proposed here, the difference between the two types of seemingly elliptic structures follows from the fact that the elliptic conjunctions do not involve a copy procedure, but the formation of a conjoined argument which takes one predicate, e.g., the structure of (37)–(39) is illustrated in (41) (for (37)).

(41)

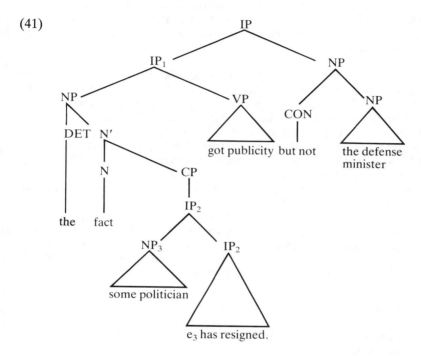

For this structure to be interpreted, the correlate (*some politician*) must be adjoined to the remnant (otherwise we are left with an uninterpretable conjunction of an IP and an NP). But it can only be raised here up to its own IP$_2$, as illustrated, since Subjacency prohibits further extraction from the subject NP (an issue I return to directly). As we saw, adjoining the correlate to its own IP$_2$ was sufficient for interpreting the sluicing case in (40)a, since it creates a predicate that can be copied into the empty node. But this predicate is irrelevant here, since the matrix conjunction remains uninterpretable.

The subordination cases of (35) are ruled out, under the present analysis, on several grounds. Assuming that their DS can be generated, to begin with, the correlate cannot be adjoined to the remnant (a lowering movement, crossing, furthermore, at least one barrier – the rightmost conjoined CP), and if it could, the result would have still been uninterpretable, since there is no predicate that this new argument could take.

2.3 Syntax of QR

If the analysis proposed here for elliptic conjunctions is correct, the structures allowed should be those in which the conditions on syntactic movement allow the extraction of the correlate. As we will see now, QR in these cases, obeys, indeed, the syntactic restrictions typical of *wh*-movement. Still, in view of other differences in the operations allowed at LF but not at SS, there are predictable areas of difference in the range of allowed extractions.

2.3.1   One of the earliest arguments for QR (May 1977) was that scope of quantified NPs is restricted by the same constraints that regulate *wh*-movement, which is what one expects if scope is determined by movement. It was later noted, however, that the actual scope assignment of QNP is much more restricted, and it appears to be clause-bound in many cases.[8] This is probably due to additional factors effecting the interpretation of quantifiers. It is also known that quantifiers vary in their ease at taking wide non-compositional scope, where *each*, for instance, is much easier than *every* in many contexts (May 1985) and, specifically, does not show clause-bound effects (May 1977). In the case of elliptic conjunctions, where such considerations are not involved, QR does behave as expected, as we saw already in (16). While scoping of the correlate from embedded clauses requires perhaps more contextual accommodations than from the matrix, it is clearly allowed, as in (43), where the embedded italicized correlates behave precisely as their *wh*-equivalent in (42).

(42)   what will Lucie admit that she stole e?

(43)a   Lucie will admit that she stole *the diamonds* if you press her, but not the car.
   b   Lucie did not admit that she stole *anything*, when we pressed her, except the little red book.
   c   more people said they will vote *for Bush*, in the last poll, than for Dukakis.

One advantage of checking the restrictions on QR with elliptic conjunctions, rather than with quantification, is that while in the later, the judgements of scope are semantic, in the first, they are syntactic. If QR cannot apply here, it is not just that the sentence lacks a certain interpretation out of several candidates – it lacks any interpretation, i.e. it is ungrammatical. Thus, the contrast between (43) and the cases below, where the scoping of the correlate violates subjacency, is as clear-cut as in the case of *wh*-movement.

(44)a   *what did you interrogate the burglar who stole e?
   b   *we have interrogated the burglar who stole *the car* already, but not the diamonds.
   c   *more people who loved *Bach* arrived than Mozart.
   d   *the people who loved *every composer* arrived except Mozart.

The scoping of the correlate is sensitive also to finer distinctions restricting *wh*-movement. In the Barriers framework, extraction is permitted in (45)a where the PP is L-marked and therefore not a barrier, but not in (46)a, where it is not-marked (the NP itself is not an inherent barrier here). Correspondingly, (45)b, c are interpretable, since the correlate can be raised, but (46)b, c are not.

(45)a   which of these topics did he mention [any books [about e]]?
   b   he mentioned books about *every topic* yesterday, except astrology.
   c   more people mentioned books about *astrology* in their talk, than linguistics.

(46)a   *?which of these shelves did he recognize [the books [$_{PP}$ on e?]]
   b   *?He recognized the books on *every shelf* yesterday except the second.
   c   *more people recognize books on *the first shelf* than the second.

These results appear to be in conflict with another instance of QR, in the case of *wh*-in-situ. Huang (1982) noted contrasts such as (47):

(47)a   who e stole the book you gave whom
   b   *who e stole the book you got how

Assuming that QR adjoins the *wh*-in-situ to the *wh* in COMP, the fact that (47)a is well formed suggests that it is not sensitive to subjacency. In (47)b, on the other hand, the derivation violates also the ECP, and it is ruled out. It has, consequently, been assumed at times that QR obeys the ECP, but not Subjacency. (See also Chomsky 1986.) However, an alternative account for (47)a was proposed by Nishigauchi (1986). He argues that rather than *whom* alone, the whole relative NP containing it is raised into COMP by QR. Hence there is no need to assume that QR can ever violate Subjacency. An alternative analysis of LF piped-piping, with the same conclusion, is proposed in Fiengo, Huang, Lasnik and Reinhart (1988).

We may conclude, then, that the scoping of the correlate, like all other instances of QR, is restricted by the standard restrictions on movement. (The aspects of ECP relevant to elliptic conjunctions are only those related to the "that-trace" effects, which are usually very weak at LF. Examples will be mentioned in section 3.1.)

2.3.2   As I mentioned in section 2.1, a crucial point in observing that elliptic conjunctions cannot be derived by syntactic movement is that, under current syntactic theory, certain differences are predicted between the options of syntactic and LF movement, even if QR is restricted by subjacency just like *wh*-movement. In these cases EC structures follow the LF rather than SS pattern.

One area of difference is in the case of *wh*-islands, illustrated in (48), where the movement of "by whom" from the lower to the higher VP crosses the CP (a barrier by inheritance from IP). In the case of QR, the movement is via adjunction to IP. Once a constituent is adjoined to the lower IP, this IP is no longer a BC (since it does not dominate the moved constituent), and hence the CP is not a barrier, and no barrier is crossed. We should therefore expect no *wh*-island effects in LF movement. As illustrated in (49), the scoping of the correlate is indeed possible in such structures. This movement is illustrated for (49)b in (50).

(48)   *by whom$_1$ do people remember what$_2$ e$_2$ was said e$_1$

(49)a   more people remember what was said *by Bush* than by Dukakis.
    b   people remembered what was said by Bush, in the last poll, but not by Dukakis.
    c   I'll tell you what I think about *everyone*, if you insist, except my boss.

(50)   [$_{IP}$ [$_{NP}$ by Bush but not by Dukakis] [$_{IP}$ people [$_{VP}$ t remember [$_{CP}$ what [$_{IP}$ t [$_{IP}$ e was said t]]]]]]

A more interesting prediction is in the area of extraction from subjects. Note, first, the different behavior of the *wh*-case and the EC cases in (51).

(51)a   *who do [jokes about e] amuse you?
    b   ?[jokes about *everyone*] amuse me except Felix
    c   ?[the letter to Max] got lost, but not (to) Felix
    d   ?more jokes about *Max* were told in the party than (about) Felix.

(52)a   *[Lucie's jokes about *every woman*]$_1$ amuse me, except Lili
    b   *[the man [$_{PP}$ near *every woman*]]$_1$ amuses me, except Lili

Though the EC cases are not equally good for all speakers, they are clearly better than their *wh*-equivalent. Furthermore, they contrast with the EC cases in (52), which do behave as predicted for *wh*-movement. To see what this difference could follow from, let's look first at the way QR applies to the first conjunct of (51)b, given the analysis of May (1985).

(53)a

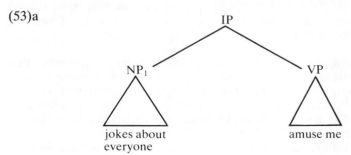

⇒ (53)b QR:

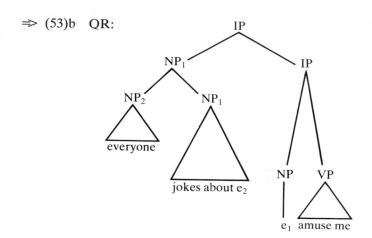

(53)c $[_{IP} [_{IP} [_{NP} (t_2)] [_{NP}$ jokes about $t_2]] [_{IP} t_1$ amuse me]] $[_{NP}$ everyone$_2$ except Felix]

(53)d everyone except Felix (λx (jokes about x (λy (y amuse me)))))

(54) jokes about everyone amuse someone.

In the Barriers framework it is assumed that adjunction to IP and NP is not permitted at SS, but it is permitted at LF. (Though there exist several proposals to derive the same results in a less stipulative way, they need not concern us here.) Hence, NP$_1$ of (53)a can adjoin to IP, and then (since NP$_1$ is no longer in argument position) NP$_2$ can adjoin to NP$_1$, as in (53)b. These operations have been assumed independently of our problem, to account for the fact that *everyone* in such structures can have a sentential scope. For instance, it can have scope over *someone* in (54). May argued that to capture this reading, the derivation in (53)b is sufficient, since *everyone* c-commands the VP. Note, however, that nothing in the current syntactic framework blocks further extraction of NP$_2$. Though in the SS (53)a, the top NP is a barrier for *everyone* (hence, a *wh*-equivalent cannot be extracted at SS), once the structure (53)b is construed, the same NP is no longer a barrier (since only a segment of this NP dominates "everyone"). Hence *everyone* can be extracted and adjoined to the remnant, as in (53)c. The relevant LF predicate for the interpretation of (51)b can, then, be formed, as in (53)d.

In the sentences of (52), the full NP$_1$ can be adjoined to the IP, but the second application of QR, which should adjoin "every woman" to this NP$_1$ is impossible, since there is an additional NP internal barrier blocking this move: In (52)b it is the non L-marked PP, and in (52)a it is whatever accounts for the specificity effects.

It is interesting to observe that precisely the same pattern is found in other instances of LF movement, as the pied-piping cases below.

(55)a   ?this is the man [jokes about whom] amuse me.
   b   *this is the man [Lucie's jokes about whom] amuse me.
   c   *this is the woman [the man near whom] amuses me.

The constraints on permissible pied-piping are a well-known mystery. (See for a survey Ishihara 1984.) However, under the assumptions above, (55) is explained in terms of LF movement: the pied-piped NP is, first, adjoined to IP. The *wh*-NP must then be further extracted into the spec of CP. In (55)a this is possible precisely as in (53). (IP is not a barrier since NP is not a BC for the *wh*, and since, in any case, IP does not dominate this NP.) In (55)b, c, just as in (52), an additional barrier prevents extraction out of the pied-piped NP, hence the structures are uninterpretable.

I should note that my point here is not crucially dependent on the specific details assumed here to account for why extraction from subjects is possible at LF, which are rather theory-dependent. An alternative account is proposed in Fiengo et al. (1988).

3   CONSEQUENCES: NON-QUANTIFICATIONAL QR

3.1   While the elliptic conjunctions I examined provide a strong evidence that a rule like QR is needed, since it forms constituents that are crucial for the interpretation and cannot be formed at any other level, the view of this rule assumed here is not consistent with the standard assumptions of LF theory. As we saw, in this framework, a distinction is drawn between referential and quantified NPs, and QR is restricted to (i.e. interpretable only with) quantified NPs. Arguments of the form "this XP is referential, hence it does not undergo QR" are quite standard in the LF literature. The exception-conjunctions pose no problem to this view, since the correlate here is always a quantified NP, hence "raisable" by QR. The point, however, is that these cases are just a specific instance of a much larger phenomenon. In the case of the Bare Argument (BA) conjunctions, for instance, there is no restriction on the correlate and QR must apply to referential NPs as well.

The only way to allow QR to apply here, within this framework, is to argue that the raised constituents are foci, since (following Chomsky 1976) the scope of focus constituents is believed to be determined by QR. This, indeed is the line taken by Sag (1976) and Pesetsky (1982) in their analysis of gapping. Although I believe that the LF focus analysis has not been substantially motivated to begin with, and focus assignment need not (in fact, cannot) depend on QR (see also Rooth 1985),[9] let us see briefly why BA conjunctions cannot be reduced to focus phenomena.

The crucial question here is whether the correlate and not the remnant must be a focus, since it is the correlate that must undergo QR. If this is restricted to focus, we should not be able to get BA conjunctions when the correlate is not a focus. But we clearly can, as in (56).

(56)a A: where is the ice-cream?
   B: I ATE it, and the cake too.

   b A: what happened to Felix?
   B: I don't know. We lost track of him on our way back, and of Lucie too.

The correlates here are unstressed pronouns with a previous discourse mention, so no formulation of focus can allow QR to raise them if it is restricted to foci.

We may note further, that the scope of the correlates in BA ellipsis is not, in fact, identical to that of foci. As we just saw, the BA scope is severely restricted by island constraints. It has often been observed (starting with Anderson 1972) that foci are not restricted in the same way (which is a problem for a QR analysis of focus). For instance the stressed NPs in (57) can serve as a focus of the whole matrix IP_1 even though they are contained in a strong (ungoverned) island. BA conjunction is impossible in the parallel (58).

(57)a [$_{IP}$ [$_{CP}$ that Linda argued with THE CHAIRMAN] is surprising.]
   b [$_{IP}$ [$_{NP}$ even the paper that LUCIE submitted to our journal] was weak]

(58) *even the paper which LUCIE submitted was weak, but not Linda/and even Linda.

(59) the doorman won't even tell you where THE MANAGER lives, if you don't bribe him.

(60) *the doorman will tell you where the manager lives if you bribe him, and the landlady too (i.e. and where the landlady lives).

That focus interpretation violates also the ECP was noted in Jaeggli (1980) and Chomsky (1981: 238). Even if their specific examples can be explained, in the case of (59) the association with the matrix *even* indicates that the scope of the embedded subject focus must be the matrix clause, though its LF movement into that clause would violate the ECP. The BA case, by contrast, behaves here too as predicted by a QR analysis, and the parallel (60) is much worse, though, as typical with LF movement, it is not as bad as syntactic extractions from this position.

Such facts indicate that while it is indeed unclear whether focus interpretation has anything to do with QR, the scope of the correlate in BA conjunctions is directly reducible to standard LF movement.

3.2 The view of QR as a rule specific to quantification stems from the assumption discussed in section 1, that scope is essentially a semantic problem, dependent on the semantic properties of NPs, and since (focus aside) only quantified NPs have scope, the LF level was designed, historically (Chomsky 1976, and May 1977), primarily for capturing their scope interpretation. What elliptic conjunctions can teach us is that scope is, as it should be (in analogy to classical logic), a purely syntactic issue. The potential (non-compositional) scope of all constituents alike is determined by syntactic considerations. In a framework assuming LF, this scope is uniformly the LF predicate of which a given constituent is an argument (or the constituent containing the argument's trace). What interpretative properties depend upon this scope assignment may vary, of course, with the semantics of NPs, and with non-quantified NPs, scope is often manifested only by the size of the LF predicates they can take in EC or in ellipsis structures. Once scope is viewed as a syntactic notion, QR can be generalized.

Let us assume that QR is an optional rule which, as proposed in May (1985) and Chomsky (1986), adjoins any constituent to any constituent. A similar assumption is explicit (in the case of NPs) in Heim's (1982) formulation of the LF rules. This much is implicit, anyway in current LF theory, if one takes seriously the claim that QR is just a syntactic instance of "move-α," hence that it cannot be sensitive itself to semantic properties of the moved constituents. The analysis here differs from the mainstream of LF theory only in assuming also that the results of QR are interpretable regardless of whether the raised constituent is quantified.

The next questions are, first, how one interprets the results of QR, and after that, what is the status of this rule. A further LF rule is required, to provide the operator binding the variables (traces) left by QR. This rule is independent of QR, and it is needed for binding *wh*-traces as well. The exact formulation of this rule is theory-dependent. One option is to bind all traces with the same λ-operator, regardless of the semantic properties of the raised constituent, as would be done in the generalized-quantifier framework. In this approach all QR does is capture non-compositional scope or other discourse phenomena, but it is not required for the interpretation of quantification (see for instance Keenan and Faltz 1978). To interpret a sentence like *Every woman smiled* it is not necessary to apply QR at all. Similarly, in *Every teacher likes some student*, QR will be used only to obtain wide scope for *some student*, but not in the unmarked case of *every teacher* with wide scope.

Although I have taken the position above, it should be noted that it is possible to maintain the view of QR proposed here and still treat quantifiers as classical-logic operators, as in the standard LF framework (to the same extent that it has been possible before). To do that, the relevant operator should be determined by the type of NP in the raised constituent. If the NP is quantified (including *wh*-NPs), the quantifier-determiner is further extracted from its raised constituent, after QR (an operation made explicit in Heim 1982), and then it is translated as the operator binding all coindexed variables. In all other cases, a λ-operator (or any equivalent, if desired) is introduced to bind the variables. Furthermore, it would be assumed, within this approach, that a quantified NP is uninterpretable, unless raised by QR, while the raising of referential NPs is required only for specific purposes, like the conjunction structures discussed here.

The crucial point, however, is that apart from one's beliefs about the nature of quantification in natural language, there is no other reason to ever distinguish quantified and referential NPs for issues of scope, or to treat them differently on any syntactic level, such as LF.

NOTES

Many ideas in my analysis of elliptic conjunctions were formed during work together with Irene Heim and Mats Rooth. For further discussion and comments I would like to thank Johan van Benthem, Gennaro Chierchia, Shalom Lappin, Richard Larson and Remko Scha.

1   The definitions are:

(i)   A *dominates* B iff every segment of A dominates B.
(ii)   A *m-command* B iff every maximal projection dominating A dominates B.

In the case of adjunction, which creates identical nodes, each occurrence of these nodes is viewed as a segment. I am using throughout the term c-command, for m-command.

2   It is assumed, following Huang (1982) that the *wh*-in-situ in (i)a and (ii)a below are adjoined, at LF to the *wh*-constituent in Comp, as in (b).

(i)a   I know who$_2$ e$_2$ bought what$_1$
   b   ... [what$_1$ [who$_2$]]$_2$ [e$_2$ bought e$_1$].

(ii)a   *I know what$_2$ who$_2$ bought e$_1$
   b   ... [what$_1$ [who$_1$]]$_1$ [e$_2$ bought e$_1$]

Huang argues, further, that (ii), known as "superiority violation" is ruled out since, unlike the well-formed (i), its trace needs antecedent-government, which is blocked in this type of adjunction. (In his formulation it was because who$_2$ was viewed as not c-commanding its trace.) Under the path-containment account, the derivation in (ii)b is independently blocked because the traces intersect. In the case of (23) there can be no intersection, since there is only one trace.

3   We may also note that, under the assumption of the "Barriers" model, it is not absolutely necessary to assume that the correlate is actually adjoined to the remnant. In fact, we may assume the more familiar application of QR, as in (i). Given the segment definition of domination, and c (or m)-command, NP$_1$ and NP$_2$ c-command each other, since the first IP above NP$_1$ is just a segment of the IP projection, and there is no projection of all whose segments dominate NP$_1$, but not NP$_1$. Independently of the segment definition, an underlying assump-

(i)

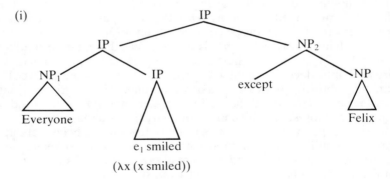

$(\lambda x\ (x\ smiled))$

tion of the use of c-command has been that compositionality is determined in terms of mutual c-command, rather than sisterhood. (See, for instance, Reinhart 1983, ch. 9.) For all interpretive purposes, NP_1 and NP_2 in (i) (as well as IP) count, therefore, as sisters. This means that the rule forming one NP out of them need not be a syntactic rule, but the same semantic rule applying to interpret the conjoined NP_1 and NP_2 in (23)b, c can apply directly to the structure (i).

4 Chierchia (p.c.) suggests that the problem can be handled, within the storage approach, if (put roughly) determiners like *every* and *no* are viewed as containing an extra "exception" slot. If an except-NP is not found the null set will be selected. While technically this line is possible, it involves deriving basic determiners of a language from its complex ones, e.g. viewing *every except NP* as a basic determiner from which *every* is derived. I do not consider such line a reasonable solution for the problem, when more reasonable alternatives are available. (Admittedly, though, this is not a sufficient argument against it.) An alternative line was proposed by Lappin (p.c.). He argues that Keenan and Stavi's analysis is not the only one conceivable, and the except-constituent can be analyzed as a function from NP denotation to NP denotation. If this can be worked out, when the remnant-function is encountered, it can, perhaps, apply to the stored correlate-denotation prior to further application to the predicate.

5 Non-elliptic base generation, though under different analyses, has been proposed before for comparatives by Napoli (1982) and Heim (1986), and for gapping, by Oehrle (1987). See also Chao (1988) and Haïk (1985).

6 When the remnant corresponds to the subject, it may appear to be possible to generate the sentence with an empty I' projection. This was proposed by Larson (1987) for the subject cases of temporal comparatives, as (i) (construed with Max as the correlate).

(i)   Max [$_{VP}$ saw Lucie [$_{PP}$ before [$_{IP}$ LiLi [$_{I'}$ e]]]]

However, as Larson notes, this is possible only in cases like (i), where the subject gets its case from *before*, as witnessed, e.g., by the dative in (ii). This is not the case with the other structures under consideration, such as (iii).

(ii)a   He arrived before her.
   b   *He arrived before she.

(iii)a   *He arrived and her too.
    b   He arrived and she too.

If the subject cannot get its case from P, it will not have a way to get case in structures with I' ellipsis, since the I node is empty.

7 The same is true for an alternative line of generating the remnant adjoined to an empty IP, which can be viewed as an extension of Sag's (1976) analysis of gapping.

8 See Aoun and Hornstein (1985).

9 The major basis for this focus analysis was anaphora facts, assuming that focus anaphora behaves like QNP anaphora. We should note, however, that at the time this was stated (in Chomsky 1976), the restriction on variable binding was assumed to be linear. (The pronoun cannot precede the antecedent at LF.) To the extent that the judgments on focus anaphora are correct at all, they really hold only as a restriction preventing backward anaphora, while the general restriction on variable binding is known, now, to be in terms of c-command, independently of linear order. Compare, for instance, (i)a, b.

(i)a a party without MAX_1 is inconceivable to his_1 mother
   b *a party without $everyone_1$ is inconceivable to his_1 mother

I believe that this linear effect is typical of pragmatic constraints on coreference, which have nothing to do with variable-binding. In Reinhart (1986) I suggest, briefly, that backward co-reference is possible only if the antecedent is the sentence topic, as witnessed by the difference between (ii)a, b.

(ii) a when he_1 entered the room Max_1 was ATTACKED by Lucie
      b ??when she_1 entered the room Max was ATTACKED by $Lucie_1$

Since focus is, usually, non-topic (unless it is a contrastive topic), the prohibition on backward co-reference will follow.

REFERENCES

Anderson, S. 1972: "How to get *even.*" *Language*, 48, 893–906.

Aoun, J. and Hornstein, N. 1985: "Quantifier types." *Linguistic Inquiry*, 16, 623–37.

Barwise, J. and Cooper, R. 1981: "Generalized quantifiers and natural language." *Linguistics and Philosophy*, 4, 159–219.

Chao, W. 1988: *On Ellipsis.* New York: Garland.

Chomsky, N. 1976: "Conditions on rules of grammar." *Linguistic Analysis*, 2, 303–51.

—— 1981: *Lectures on Government and Binding.* Dordrecht: Foris.

—— 1986: *Barriers.* Cambridge: MIT Press.

Cooper, R. 1983: *Quantification and Syntactic Theory.* Dordrecht: Reidel.

Fiengo, R., Huang, H., Lasnik, H. and Reinhart, T. 1988: "The syntax of *wh*-in-situ." In H. Borer (ed.), *Proceedings of the Seventh West-Coast Conference on Formal Linguistics.* Stanford: Stanford Linguistics Association.

Haïk, I. 1984: "Indirect binding." *Linguistic Inquiry*, 15, 185–224.

—— 1985: *The Syntax of Operators.* Ph.D. Dissertation, MIT.

Heim, I. 1982: *The semantics of definite and indefinite Noun Phrases.* Ph.D. dissertation, University of Massachusetts, Amherst.

—— 1986: "Notes on comparatives and related matters." Unpublished MS., University of Texas.

Huang, C. T. J. 1982: *Logical relations in Chinsese and the theory of grammar.* Ph.D. dissertation, MIT, Cambridge, Mass.

Ishihara, R. 1984: "Clausal pied piping: a problem for GB." *Natural Language and Linguistic Theory*, 4, 397–418.

Jaeggli, O. 1980: *On some phonologically-null elements in syntax*. Ph.D. dissertation, MIT, Cambridge, Mass.

Keenan, E. L. 1987: "Multiply-headed Noun Phrases." *Linguistic Inquiry*, 18, 481–90.

Keenan, E. L. and Faltz, L. 1978: *Logical types for Natural Language*. UCLA Occasional Papers in Syntax 3. UCLA, Los Angeles, CA.

Keenan, E. L. and Stavi, Y. 1986: "A semantic characterization of natural language determiners." *Linguistics and Philosophy*, 9, 253–326.

Lappin, S. 1984: "VP anaphora, Quantifier scope, and Logical Form." *Linguistic Analysis*, 13, 273–315.

—— 1990: "Concepts of Logical Form in linguistics and philosophy." In this volume.

Larson, R. 1987: "'Missing prepositions' and the analysis of English free relative clauses." *Linguistic Inquiry*, 18, 239–66.

May, R. 1977: *The Grammar of Quantification*. Ph.D. dissertation, MIT, Cambridge, Mass.

—— 1985: *Logical Form: Its Structure and Derivation*. Cambridge, Mass.: MIT Press.

Napoli, D. J. 1983: "Comparative ellipsis: a Phrase Structure analysis." *Linguistic Inquiry*, 14, 675–94.

Nishigauchi, T. 1986: "Japanese LF: in defense of subjacency." MS. Shoin College, Kobe.

Oehrle, R. 1987: "Boolean properties in the analysis of gapping." In Geoffrey Huck and Almerindo Ojedo (eds), *Syntax and Semantics*, vol. 20, *Discontinuous Constituency*. New York: Academic Press.

Pesetsky, D. 1982: *Paths and Categories*. Ph.D. dissertation, MIT, Cambridge, Mass.

Rooth, M. 1985: *Association with Focus*, Ph.D. dissertation, University of Massachusetts, Amherst.

Reinhart, T. 1983: *Anaphora and Semantic Interpretation*. London: Croom Helm, and Chicago: University of Chicago Press.

—— 1986: "Center and periphery in the grammar of anaphora." In B. Lust (ed.), *Studies in the Acquisition of Anaphora*, vol. I, Dordrecht: Reidel.

—— 1987: "Specifiers and operator-binding." In E. Reuland and A. ter Meulen (eds), *The Representation of (In)definiteness*. Cambridge, Mass.: MIT Press.

Reinhart, T. and Rooth, M. (forthcoming): "Bare-argument ellipsis."

Sag, I. 1976: *Deletion and Logical Form*, Ph.D. dissertation, MIT, Cambridge, Mass.

Williams, E. 1977: "Discourse and Logical Form." *Linguistic Inquiry*, 8, 107–39.

—— 1986: "Reassignment of the function of LF." *Linguistic Inquiry*, 17, 265–99.

16

LF and the Structure of the Grammar: Comments

Susan D. Rothstein

In their discussions about Logical Form (LF), May, Lappin and Reinhart, in this volume, all agree on a fundamental point: there are syntactic constraints on what semantic representations are available. Their debate over LF centres on how (some of) these syntactic constraints are to be represented. There are some constraints on semantic interpretation, in particular co-reference and pronominal binding, which can be stated over S-structure and do not involve LF. Thus, the Binding Theory consists of a series of syntactic constraints which hold at S-structure and which indicate where an anaphor must and a pronominal must not be bound, and the disjoint reference principle states the conditions under which two NPs cannot be coindexed. In this way we give the syntactic constraints on available interpretations: by stating that in (1),

(1)   he saw John

syntactic constraints prevent *He* and *John* from being co-indexed, we effectively state that there is no available interpretation for (1) where the two NPs are interpreted by the same individual.

Another area of semantic interpretation which is constrained by the syntactic structure of sentences is the assignment of scope to quantifiers.

The debate about whether there is a syntactic level of LF is essentially a debate about how to represent these syntactic constraints. One approach is to see them as a set of constraints on how a semantic interpretation is to be built up from S-structure, and this is the approach taken by Lappin in this volume, and by others such as Cooper (1983) with his theory of quantifier storage. Another approach is that developed by May, originally in his 1977 dissertation, and then in his 1985 book. He argues that there is a level of syntactic representation where the syntactic constraints on quantifier scope are made explicit. This is done by moving the quantifiers and adjoining them to the syntactic constituents over which they have scope. It is the level at which this movement is represented – LF – to which rules of semantic interpretation apply.

The arguments for and against LF have been vigorously debated over the last ten years, and here I want to address some of the issues which are at stake. I shall look at two topics: in section 1, the nature of the arguments for and against LF and in section 2 the consequences for the structure of the grammar of introducing such a level.

I

The arguments in favor of LF are what Pesetsky (1987) calls "the normal arguments for a level of representation," namely, there is a level of representation which is related to another level of syntactic representation by a movement rule, and which can be characterized by a cluster of syntactic properties. The movement rule is the rule of quantifier raising, which adjoins quantified NPs to the syntactic category over which they may have scope. Thus the LF representation of (2)a is (2)b:

(2)a $[_s$everyone suspected Philby]
   b $[_s$everyone$_1$ $[_s$ e$_1$ suspected Philby]]

May (1985) shows that these LF representations are subject to syntactic constraints on acceptability, in particular the Empty Category Principle (ECP)[1]; thus in the same way that *wh*-movement leaves a trace which must be properly governed, quantifier raising (QR) also leaves a trace which must be properly govenrned.[2] Thus (2)b is an acceptable representation, as the trace which fills the empty subject position (e$_1$) of the S is properly governed by the moved quantifier which is its antecedent. QR also raises and adjoins to Comp those *wh*-expressions which appear "in situ" at S-structure, thus (3)a will have the LF representation (3)b:

(3)a $[_{COMP}$ who$_1$ $[_s$ e$_1$ admires what]]
   b $[_{COMP}$ what$_2$ who$_1$ $[_s$ e$_1$ admires e$_2$]]

However, as May points out, the ECP fails to make all the necessary distinctions, and he suggests therefore that it be replaced by the Path Containment Condition (PCC). The PCC rules out everything excluded by the ECP as well as some additional problem sentences, including those judged ungrammatical because of superiority effects. It thus guarantees that when more than one element has been moved – either by *wh*-movement at S-structure or by QR at LF – the chains formed by movement may not overlap, but must be nested.

In Heim, Lasnik and May (1990) it is shown that another result of quantifier raising may be to allow multiple ways of co-indexing, and thus interpretational ambiguities which cannot be represented by co-indexing at S-structure may be represented by co-indexing at LF. They show that the raising of *each* in sentences like (4),

(4)   John and Mary convinced each other that they should leave

results in a structure whose NPs can be co-indexed in three different ways, thus representing the three way ambiguity of (4). In his paper in this volume May presents a further argument for LF, viz. that grammatical sentences which fail to meet syntactic constraints at S-structure do in fact meet them after quantifier raising. The classic example comes from VP ellipsis sentences such as (5):

(5)   Dulles suspected everyone that Angleton did.

The usual condition on VP ellipsis is that neither the missing verb nor its antecedent may c-command each other, but this condition is not met in (5), where the ellided VP is contained within its antecedent, and *suspect* c-commands *did*. May shows that after quantifier raising this syntactic condition is met. Further arguments for LF are presented at length in May (1985).

For those who would argue against there being a syntactic level of LF, the first task is to show that all those data which can be explained by LF can also be explained by an account which directly interprets the syntax. Lappin sets out to do this in his paper, taking a variety of problems which are representative of those which a theory of LF is supposed to solve, and showing that there exist alternative solutions. He makes use of Cooper's (1983) account of NP storage, a model-theoretic device which it is claimed allows the direct interpretation of S-structure. He calls this approach "S-structure Interpretivism." At this stage of the argument the burden of proof is on the proponents of S-structure Interpretivism to show the equivalence of the two approaches – hence the strength of May's claim in his review of Cooper (1983) that the discussion of constraints on *wh*-phenomena remain at the schematic stage, so that "it remains to be seen whether Cooper's theory can stand against more explicitly detailed syntactic theories, in particular those in which LF plays a crucial role in accounting for *wh*-phenomena." (May 1986: 906). However, the second part of an argument in favor of S-structure Interpretivism would be to show that a rule of QR does not generate the syntactic representations which will produce all and only the possible semantic interpretations. This may be for one of two reasons: first, that by raising quantifiers, we predict the availability of interpretations which in fact are not available, and secondly, that by obligatorily raising all and only quantifiers we fail to make available possible interpretations. The conjunction of these two approaches is what opponents of LF should be arguing for, and proponents of LF defending themselves against, for both these parts of the arguments would together show that a theory of semantic interpretation involving LF is not just an unnecessarily complex account which is extensionally equivalent to S-structure Interpretivism, but an account which makes incorrect predictions about the way in which syntax constrains the semantic interpretation of sentences.

The following are some of the issues which it seems to me should be central in the second part of the argument:

1   Independent and dependent quantifiers: May (1985) proposes that quantifiers are adjoined to S successively, and that a sequence of such adjoined quantifiers are free to take on any type of relative scope relation (this is called the *Scope Principle*). As a consequence, a sequence of quantifiers may either be interpreted as dependent on each other, or with each quantifier interpretively independent. This makes a prediction that for any LF representation, there will never be a sequence which can be interpreted only with the quantifiers independent of each other. Hintikka's sentences (see Hintikka 1974) of which the classic example is (6), thus seem to pose a serious problem for the theory, for he has claimed that there is no linear first-order representation for them, while an LF account will predict that there should be:

(6)   some relative of each villager and some relative of each townsman hate each other.

May, in his discussion of these sentences, cites Barwise (1979) as arguing that there is a weaker interpretation of (6) where the quantifiers are dependent on each other, but this appears to be an intuition on which there is not a clear consensus (see, for example, Fauconnier 1975, and Boolos 1984). Boolos (1984) discusses a variety of sentences which have been argued not to have linear first order representations, and which thus present similar problems for an LF account. These include the Geach-Kaplan sentence

(7)   some critics admire only one another

and Boolos's own examples (8)a and (8)b:

(8)a   for every A there is a B.
  b   there are some gunslingers each of whom has shot the right foot of at least one of the others.

Boolos discusses these examples and others, showing why they cannot be symbolized in first order logic, and thus prima facie they seem to cause problems for an account of quantifier raising which applies to all quantified NPs in the same way. (However, see Fauconnier (1975) for counter-arguments.)

2 The algorithmic nature of QR in relation to quantified NPs: The theory of LF proposes that the rule of quantifier raising applies obligatorily and mechanically to all quantified NPs. The first issue here is how a syntactic rule of quantifier raising can distinguish between NPs which are quantified and those which are not, for in most syntactic theories they are syntactically indistinguishable NPs at S-structure. The second issue is whether all quantified NPs do raise in a uniform manner. Discussions such as Pesetsky (1987) raise doubts. Thus, as May points out in (1985), where the rule is not taken to apply obligatorily, subjects of raising predicates may be either lowered or raised, to represent the ambiguity of (9):

(9)   a unicorn is likely to be apprehended today.

His explanation for this is essentially that movement from a non-thematic subject position does not leave a trace requiring an antecedent. But, whichever way this is phrased, it casts doubt on the purely mechanical nature of LF movement. The data in Pesetsky (1987) also does this. Pesetsky shows that superiority effects do not occur in *which N* phrases in situ, and suggests that this is because they, unlike other *wh*-phrases, are not moved by QR but are assigned scope via co-indexing. He further suggests that this is because of a semantic phenomenon: *which N* phrases are "discourse linked," and quantify over a presupposed set of individuals. He argues that if *which N* is not discourse linked, superiority effects occur, and conversely, when *who* or *what* are discourse linked, superiority effects do not occur, indicating that they too are not moved by QR. If Pesetsky's analysis is right, then serious questions are raised about the syntactic nature of quantifier-raising.

3 The distinction between quantified and non-quantified NPs: In (2) we asked whether QR applies to all quantified NPs, and here we ask whether it applies to only quantified NPs. If it turns out that non-quantified NPs are also assigned scope over constituents which they do not c-command at S-structure, then QR should not be restricted to quantified NPs. This is especially the case if scope assignment to non-quantified NPs also respects syntactic island constraints. The question of NP scope arises with respect to intensional contexts: the well-known ambiguity of (10)a in contrast to (10)b,

(10)a   Mary seeks a unicorn
    b   Mary met a unicorn

can be explained by allowing the quantified NP to be interpreted either in place (the intensional reading), or as having scope over the whole sentence (the extensional reading). But, as Lappin points out, this ambiguity extends to sentences where the object NP is not quantified, as in (11), and even more clearly in (12):

(11)   Mary seeks Pegasus.
(12)   they are looking for God.

If the intensional-extensional ambiguity is related to scope assignment, then we have here an indication that non-quantified NPs may also enter into scopal ambiguities. This issue thus poses a double problem for LF: first, in (10) QR seems to be optional, and second, in (11)–(12) non-quantified NPs enter into the same ambiguities. May (1985) therefore proposes to deal with the ambiguity by the ontological device of partitioning the world into existent and non-existent objects, with *seeks* selecting for either, while *meet* selects only for an existent object. There are many problems with such an "ontological" solution, one of them being how to deal with sentences such as (13):

(13)   John is looking for a Swedish wife.

Given that verbal selection for existent and non-existent objects does not solve the problem of intensional contexts, the default explanation is in terms of scope.[3] Thus doubts are raised about the fundamental property of QR, that it applies to all and only quantified NPs and thus distinguishes between quantified NPs and non-quantified NPs.

Reinhart's paper in this volume focuses on this issue. She claims that non-quantified NPs may be assigned scope outside their S-structure c-command domains, and shows that this occurs in "Bare Argument" ellipsis constructions. Her analysis of these constructions makes use of a rule of raising, and gives clear evidence that the rule is subject to typical syntactic island constraints.

"Bare Argument" ellipsis occurs in sentences like (15):

(15)   Lucie kissed Rosa and Lilli too.

Lilli can be interpreted either as the subject of the predicate *kissed Rosa* or as the object of *Lucie kissed*. Reinhart proposes that these interpretations are reached in the following way (the details are in her paper): an NP is raised out of the antecedent sentence at LF, leaving a sentence with a variable position to which is attached a λ-operator. This logical predicate is copied into the second sentence. Thus the LF representation of (15) is either (16)a or (16)b, depending on which NP in the antecedent was raised:

(16)a   Lucie (λx (x kissed Rosa)) & Lilli (λx (x kissed Rosa))
   b   Rosa (λx (Lucie kissed x)) & Lilli (λx (Lucie kissed x))

Syntactic island constraints block the derivation of an LF representation when the antecedent clause is contained in an island, and therefore (17) is ungrammatical:

(17)   *the fact that Felix was late is upsetting, but at least not Max.

Reinhart's analysis, as she points out, is extremely pertinent to the debate about LF. On the one hand, she shows that NPs may be assigned scope over constituents which they do not c-command at S-structure, and that if they are raised and adjoined to the constituents over which they have scope, then standard syntactic island constraints limit this raising. On the other hand, she shows that the assignment of scope (semantically) and the raising of constituents to indicate their scopal possibilities (a syntactic phenomenon) has nothing to do with the distinction between quantified NPs and non-quantified NPs. A consequence of this is that a level of syntactic representation where quantified and non-quantified NPs are distinguished is not motivated. Furthermore, as the raising of NPs is not mechanical (not all, and maybe not any, NPs are raised in a given structure), it is clear that a syntactic movement rule cannot be a formal algorithm for deriving LF from S-structure. She suggests that it is more insightful not to look at QR as a rule which creates a linguistic level or as an obligatory step in the process of assigning semantic interpretations, but rather to identify it as a procedure available for "deriving marked interpretations."

The fundamental issues to be addressed in a discussion of LF are then not only whether such a linguistic level is necessary, but also whether the notion of this level as it has been defined is coherent. Does it generate representations all of which define interpretations? Is the linguistic rule of quantifier raising which derives LF algorithmic? Is the basic distinction which it makes between quantified and non-quantified NPs valid?

II

The second issue that I want to address is the properties of the grammar which we are committed to if we introduce the syntactic level of LF. More specifically, I want to look at the implications of introducing this level for the debate on whether the relation between levels of syntax is derivational or representational.

A "derivational" approach to syntax views S-structure as derived from D-structure via applications of move-α; S-structure chains thus represent the derivational history of a moved category, and the head of a chain has all those properties which it has accumulated in the course of the derivation. On this view, each of the two syntactic levels has an independent "reality." However, it is also possible to view D-structure as a "transparent" representation of what Chomsky (1981) called GFθ, and not as a stage in a derivation. In this approach, which Rizzi (1986) calls "representational," chains are formed algorithmically at S-structure, and D-structure is deduced formally from S-structure information. D-structure does not need to have any psychological, or even syntactic reality: constraints on D-structure can be rephrased as constraints on S-structure chains. This is possible because all the information needed to deduce the form of the chains, and thus the D-structure representation, is available at S-structure. Furthermore, and crucially, the fact that certain constituents are "displaced" is syntactically self-evident and thus we need no stipulation that movement is involved. Thus, unsatisfied subcategorization requirements of heads will result in a sentence being ungrammatical unless a chain can be built between the empty position and an argument *wh*-phrase in Comp, and the ECP acts as a constraint on the chain building. Adjunct *wh*-phrases are adverbial expressions, and must be predicated of an event argument (or, on a different approach, must modify VPs or other appropriate constituents) and they must therefore be connected by a chain to a position where this can legitimately occur. A string will be judged ungrammatical at S-structure if no chain can be built without violating the relevant conditions. Thus, (18a) violates the theta criterion, because the NP chain headed by *who* is not assigned a theta role:

(18)a   *who did he see John?
    b   *who did he like the fact that John saw e?

and (18)b is ungrammatical because the chain which must be built between *who* and *e* violates the ECP.

On an "Occam's razor" argument, the representational approach is preferable. There are, in addition, three pieces of syntactic evidence in favor of it. The first is Rizzi's (1986) work on chain formation. He argues that chain formation at S-structure need not be equivalent to derivational chain formation, and that the former best explains the facts about cliticization in Romance syntax. He shows that sentences containing passive verbs and reflexive-reciprocal clitics (and thus two instances of move-α), which should be acceptable on a derivational theory of chain formation, are systematically ungrammatical in French and Italian, and he argues that an algorithmic account of chain formation at S-structure can explain the interaction of the properties of passive and cliticization so as to account for the ungrammaticality.

The second piece of evidence is the examples of pseudoclefts, cited and discussed in Williams (1986):

(19)a   what John is is [certain t to leave]
    b   what John might do is [appear t to leave]

Here it is unclear what the "derivational history" ought to be, though an account in terms of chain formation is straightforward.

The third piece of evidence comes from the discussion of V-raising in Chomsky (1986), where V can be raised over VP, a blocking category and thus in principle a barrier, because *after* raising, it can L-mark VP. That "constraints on movement" *must* be expressed as constraints on S-structure chains is further evidence for a representational approach.

The relation between S-structure and LF is very different; it must be a derivational relation and thus LF chains must represent the derivational history of a quantifier. There is no grammatical information present in an S-structure which indicates that quantifier raising must take place. The evidence for LF is not, as it was for D-structure, that without the building of chains certain conditions on grammaticality, such as subcategorization requirements, will not be met. Thus, we cannot *deduce* that movement constrained by grammatical conditions relates two levels, and then build the relevant chain algorithmically, as we can do when relating S-structure to D-structure. Instead, when deriving LF we must *stipulate* that movement takes place, move the relevant constituents, and then use the ECP as a condition on the output. Note that if LF movement was not stipulated but was fully predictable it could not in principle be optional.

There are two important implications of this discussion. One concerns the argument that LF must be a syntactic level because its relation to S-structure parallels the relation between S-structure and D-structure. As we have seen, there are important distinctions between movement and chain formation at each level which call into question the extent of the parallelism. The second implication concerns the general issue of the nature of the relation between levels of syntactic representation. The introduction of a level of LF which must be derivationally related to S-structure means that either the relation between syntactic levels is consistently derivational – which conflicts with the evidence that we have about D-structure and S-structure – or that while the relation between D- and S-structure is not derivational, the relation between S-structure and LF is. This, however, undermines the claim that LF is a truly syntactic level because its relation to S-structure so closely parallels the latter's relation to D-structure, and it also raises doubts about the unified nature of the grammar as a whole.

There are thus serious doubts about whether LF and a syntactic rule of quantifier raising can capture all the semantic aspects of scope which are dependent on syntactic structure. There are also serious doubts as to whether there is a mechanical rule of quantifier which shares the syntactic properties of the move-α rule relating to D-structure and S-structure. Under these circumstances, it may be that LF should not be identified as part of syntax. Syntactic constraints on semantic interpretation will either be expressed in a Cooper-style system of interpreting S-structure as Lappin suggests, or, as is implied by Reinhart's paper, LF will be seen not as a third syntactic level, but as a semantic level, where a variety of syntactically sensitive semantic phenomenon, including scope assignment, are represented. We then need not be concerned either by the non-algorithmic nature of QR, nor by the fact that what validates the derivation of LF formulae is not, ultimately, syntactic constraints, but the semantic constraint of whether the particular interpretation that a formula represents is in fact available.

NOTES

This paper is an extended version of comments on Lappin's, May's and Reinhart's papers, read in *The Chomskyan Turn* conference. It was prepared with the financial help of a grant from the Israeli Ministry of Absorption.

1   It is important to note, as a methodological point, that the ECP (and PCC) hold at LF, because of the decisions which have been made as to how much information about the semantic representation LF is to contain. Thus in May (1977) QR is supposed to disambiguate sentences such as (i):

(i)   everyone loves someone

by providing them with two LF representations corresponding to the two readings where *everyone* and *someone* have wide scope respectively, as in (ii) and (iii):

(ii) $[_s$ everyone$_2$ $[_s$ someone$_1$ $[_s$ e$_2$ loves e$_1]]]$
(iii) $[_s$ someone$_1$ $[_s$ everyone$_2$ $[_s$ e$_2$ loves e$_1]]]$

depending on whether *everyone* or *someone* was first moved by QR. In May (1985) it is pointed out that the ECP will allow only (iii) because in (ii) *everyone* is prevented from properly governing its trace by the intervening presence of *someone*. Therefore, May (1985) suggests that LF does not disambiguate sentences like (i) but indicates the possible scope of quantifiers relative to sentential constituents and not relative to (all) other quantifiers.

2   *Proper government* is defined in Chomsky (1981, 1986).

3   Hornstein (1984) suggests that this ambiguity is not the concern of linguistic competence at all, but is essentially a matter for pragmatics.

REFERENCES

Barwise, J. 1979: "On Branching Quantifiers in English." *Journal of Philosophic Logic* 8/1, 47–80.
Boolos, G. 1984: "To Be Is To Be The Value Of A Variable." *Journal of Philosophy* 81, 430–49.
Chomsky, N. 1981: *Lectures on Government and Binding*. Foris, Dordrecht.
—— 1986: *Barriers*. MIT Press, Cambridge, Mass.
Cooper, R. 1983: *Quantification and Syntactic Theory*. Reidel, Dordrecht.
Fauconnier, G. 1975: "Do Quantifiers Branch?" *Linguistic Inquiry* 6, 555–78.
Heim, I., Lasnik, H., and May, R. 1990: "Reciprocity and Plurality." *Linguistic Inquiry*, 22, in press.
Hintikka, J. 1974: "Quantifiers vs. Quantification Theory." *Linguistic Inquiry* 5/2, 153–77.
Hornstein, N. 1984: *Logic as Grammar*. MIT Press, Cambridge, Mass.
May, R. 1985: *Logical Form: Its Structure and Derivation*. MIT Press, Cambridge, Mass.

—— 1986: Review of *Quantification and Syntactic Theory* by R. Cooper. *Language* 62/4, 902–8.

Pesetsky, D. 1987: "*Wh*-in-situ: Movement and Unselective Binding." In E. Reuland and A. ter Meulen (eds) *The Representation of (In)definiteness*. MIT Press, Cambridge, Mass.

Rizzi, L. 1986: "On Chain Formation." In H. Borer (ed.) *The Syntax of Pronominal Clitics*, Syntax and Semantics 19. Academic Press, New York.

Williams, E. 1986: "A Reassignment of the Functions of LF." *Linguistic Inquiry* 17/2, 265–301.

Subject Index

Name Index